Environmental Remediation Estimating Methods

Second Edition

Environmental Remediation Estimating Methods

Second Edition

 Reed Construction Data

Copyright © 2003
Construction Publishers & Consultants
63 Smiths Lane
Kingston, MA 02364-0800
781-422-5000

The editors for this book were Danielle Georges and Andrea St. Ours. The managing editor was
Mary Greene. The production manager was Michael Kokernak. The production coordinator was
Marion Schofield. The electronic publishing specialist was Sheryl Rose. The proofreader was
Robin Richardson. The book and cover were designed by Norman R. Forgit.

Printed in the United States of America

10 9 8 7 6 5 4 3 2 1

Library of Congress Cataloging in Publication Data

ISBN 0-87629-615-0

Table of Contents

Foreword

In 1980, the United States Congress passed the Comprehensive Environmental Response, Compensation, and Liability Act (CERCLA), also known as the Superfund law, in response to hazardous waste disasters like Love Canal. Since then, hazardous waste site owners, potentially responsible parties (PRPs), brownfield redevelopers, insurance companies, and government agencies have spent billions of dollars trying to control or reduce their environmental liability. From 1980 to the mid-1990s, site owners were at the mercy of regulators, lawyers, and environmental practitioners who have determined owners' financial liability by establishing cleanup standards and remediation approaches with minimal material input from owners and other parties who were paying the bills. Studies by the U.S. government, universities, and private institutions consistently show that too much money has been spent to accomplish too little cleanup, and owners still face huge financial liabilities. Clearly, the old system has not worked well.

Beginning in the late 1990s a new trend developed. Owners of hazardous waste sites began taking direct control of remediation costs through better planning and cost management. Environmental consultants and remedial action contractors also began to be proactive on behalf of their clients in cost management issues, and were also forced to show better cost management to survive in the increasingly competitive hazardous waste market. Thus, owners and regulators are now taking a co-leadership role and detailed hands-on positions in establishing regulatory goals, managing site remediation activities, and settling disputes.

An important part of this change has been the introduction of sophisticated cost management methods, tools, and cost estimating systems to the environmental remediation marketplace. These tools have allowed owners and regulators to understand the cost implication of the decisions they make *before* they make them, thus allowing better cost management. This, in turn, has led to documented savings of up to 75% of the total cost of remediation.

Effective cost management of remediation projects requires an understanding by the cost engineer of how much remediation activities will cost, and use of this knowledge to control project requirements and activities. A key, then, is to estimate costs accurately and in enough detail to be of practical use. More importantly, the cost estimate must be available before the project is under way; otherwise, there is really nothing to manage. While this may seem elementary, in the past most owners and environmental practitioners resigned themselves to not being able to accurately estimate project costs until the project was fully designed and all project requirements were known.

There are two types of cost estimates commonly used for remediation projects: parametric cost estimates used during project planning and design-and-detailed-takeoff estimates used during project execution. While this book is useful for both types, it is particularly valuable for preparing parametric estimates before design details are known. The cost estimating and cost management activities discussed in this book are based on having estimates available early enough to plan and manage costs. Parametric estimates are used for these functions.

Acknowledgments

This book, which is the second edition, was a collaborative effort. The technical information has been compiled from many sources, including government publications, manufacturers' literature, discussion with remedial action contractors, and review of completed and ongoing remedial action contracts. The cost estimating information is derived largely from the technical information that is used by the RACER® remedial action cost estimating system, which is owned by Earth Tech, Inc. RACER®, a patented cost estimating process, was originally developed for the U.S. Air Force beginning in 1990. The development effort and system were owned and managed by Talisman Partners, Ltd., working with the U.S. Air Force Civil Engineer Support Agency, the U.S. Army Corps of Engineers, the Department of Energy, and numerous private industry site owners. Talisman Partners became part of Earth Tech, Inc. in 2001. I had the pleasure of developing the RACER design concept and managing an excellent development team from 1990, when the system was originally developed and fielded, through 1997. My wife, Jacqueline Rast, P.E., who is co-author on this second edition, had direct charge of the development team beginning in 1998 at Talisman Partners and continuing through 2001 when Talisman was purchased by Earth Tech, Inc. RACER has been tested on thousands of projects throughout North America and to a lesser extent in Europe and Asia. We have learned that accurate cost estimates can be developed during planning and design. The lessons learned through that experience form the technical basis of this book.

Special thanks go to Kevin Klink, Scott Beckman, Kristen O'Gallagher, Hope Wallace, Scotty Martin, John Claypool, Steve Ferries, and Kent James who helped assemble and update much of the background technical information contained in this book.

Richard R. Rast, President
Azimuth Group, Ltd.
Castle Rock, Colorado

Jacqueline C. Rast, P.E., Sr. Vice President
Earth Tech, Inc.
Englewood, Colorado

Richard R. Rast

Richard Rast is the President of Azimuth Group, Ltd. in Castle Rock, Colorado. For the past 25 years, he has specialized in construction project management, development economics, and cost containment methods for environmental and construction projects in North America, southern Europe and the Middle East. Mr. Rast has supervised cost and time management services for over $5 billion (construction value) of environmental restoration and civil construction projects in the last ten years. He led the initial design and development team for the development of RACER, a patented environmental remediation cost estimating system. He is also the senior editor of the *Echos Environmental Remediation* Cost Books, published jointly with RSMeans, a product line of Reed Construction Data. These books are the only commercially available, complete cost data base for hazardous, toxic, and radiological waste (HTRW) cleanup.

Mr. Rast has lectured in construction management, environmental remediation project management, and cost engineering at the University of Colorado, Georgia Institute of Technology (Georgia Tech), the University of Maryland, the Air Force Institute of Technology, and has presented more than 100 individual training classes and seminars for government and industrial clients. He was the course director for conceptual estimating for the Design-Build Institute of America and has authored numerous technical papers and several books on construction management, cost estimating, development economics, and privatization. He is a graduate of Georgia Tech in Building Construction.

Jacqueline Rast, P.E.

Jacque Rast is an environmental engineer and registered professional engineer. Over the past 20 years she has managed environmental cleanup, compliance, and pollution prevention projects throughout the U.S. and internationally in positions as a Vice President of CH2M Hill, a Senior Vice President of Earth Tech, and as CEO of Talisman Partners, Ltd. She specializes in environmental cost management and assists organizations in preparing cost estimates and establishing cost management procedures and cost/performance benchmarks.

Ms. Rast has overseen the preparation of more than 1,000 cost estimates for environmental projects and has trained more than 500 environmental practitioners in government, private industry, and A/E/C firms on environmental cost management procedures. She was the project manager for the development of the CORA (Cost of Remedial Action) conceptual cost estimating system for the EPA in the mid-1980s and then led the development team for the patented RACER parametric cost estimating system at Talisman Partners from 1997–2001. Ms. Rast is a recipient of the American Council of Engineering Companies (ACEC) Grand Award for Excellence in Consulting and Engineering. She is a graduate of Penn State University in Civil/Environmental Engineering.

How to Use This Book

The purpose of this book, and the companion cost data included in the *ECHOS Environmental Restoration Assembly* and *Unit Cost* books, is to provide information that allows cost engineers to develop accurate estimates for remediation projects. The *ECHOS* books provide detailed cost information for all types of remediation work, as well as estimating forms and instructions that can be used to prepare estimates. This book provides background information about the environmental processes and insight on estimating methods for each process. The ECHOS cost data books and this book are designed to be used together.

Chapters 1–7 of this book provide general information relevant to most types of remediation projects. This information includes coverage of regulations that govern remediation projects, a step-by-step overview of the remediation estimating process, how to use remedial action treatment trains to address complete remediation approaches, and special conditions that affect remediation project costs.

Chapters 8–59 cover specific estimating approaches for 51 remediation technologies, from air sparging to underground storage tank closure. Chapters 60 and 61 address operations and maintenance costs and work break-down structures. These chapters are organized into major topic areas to deal with different classes of remediation, including ex situ approaches, containment approaches, in situ approaches, discharge technologies, and new sections on radioactive waste and ordnance removal. Each chapter provides a description of the technology; design options; information needed to develop an estimate; and site work items and other costs.

Chapters 62-64 address estimating methods for contractors' general conditions, overhead, and profit. These costs can be relatively high for remediation projects when compared to traditional construction, and should be carefully considered as part of any estimate.

All of the remedial technologies, site work, overhead, general conditions, and profit items discussed in this book can be found in the *ECHOS Environmental Remediation Assembly* and *Unit Cost* books. These cost data sources are updated annually and are published and distributed by Azimuth Group, Ltd. and RSMeans, a product line of Reed Construction Data.

Part I

The Remediation Process

Chapter 1

Overview of Cost Engineering for Remediation Projects

This book provides information that is useful in preparing cost estimates for environmental remediation projects. There are other publications and reference books available that deal with cost estimating for certain types of remediation and construction projects. For example, some references address the design, construction, and cost of hazardous waste landfills and landfill covers, while others cover groundwater extraction systems and certain remedial technologies. This book is different from those more specialized texts in that we have compiled cost estimating guidance for most of the common types of remedial action technologies that are in use in the United States today.

The purpose of the book is to provide a comprehensive reference that can be used by site owners, environmental consultants, engineers, construction managers, and other interested parties to:

- Prepare preliminary budget estimates,
- Develop more detailed engineering estimates,
- Compare the cost of different remedial action alternatives to select the most cost-effective solutions,
- Estimate the financial liability associated with remedial action requirements on a site or group of sites,
- Support competitive proposals to obtain Brownfields Cleanup Revolving Loan Fund loans from the Environmental Protection Agency,
- Review estimates prepared by others (e.g., an owner may want to evaluate costs in an estimate provided by a contractor prior to negotiation of the contract),
- Negotiate reasonable settlements in insurance cost recovery cases,
- Consult as a resource for other related applications.

The types of projects discussed in this book are primarily those covered under the Comprehensive Environmental Response Compensation and Liability Act (CERCLA)—also known as the Superfund Law, and the Brownfields Revitalization Act These three laws, and their implementing regulations and amendments, deal with remediation of hazardous substances in groundwater, soils, surface water, debris, soil gas, and contaminated facilities.

The remediation process occurs in 4 basic stages for both RCRA and CERCLA. For brownfields sites, some stages may be expedited to promote more rapid redevelopment. The stages are:

Stage	Step
PA/SI (Identification)	Discovery and Notification (D & N) Preliminary Assessment (PA) Site Inspection (SI)
RI/FS (Investigation)	Remedial Investigation/Feasibility Study (RI/FS)(Scoping) Site Characterization Development of Alternatives Screening of Alternatives Treatability Investigations Analysis of Remedial Alternatives Remedy Selection
RD/RA (Cleanup)	Remedial Design (RD) Remedial Action (RA) Long-Term Operations/Long Term Maintenance
SC (Closeout)	Site Closeout (SC)

Note: The RD/RA phase of the CERCLA process is analogous to the RCRA Corrective Measure Implementation (CMI) phase, which follows the RCRA Facility Investigation/Corrective Measures Study (RFI/CMS) phase. Although the CERCLA terminology is used, cost estimates apply to both CERCLA- and RCRA-designated sites.

This book provides cost estimating guidance that can be used to help in all project stages, but it is focused on estimates of project costs primarily in the RI/FS and RD/RA and Site Closeout (SC) phases of remediation. Additional guidance is available via Web site reference to determine applicable treatment trains for various media and containment combinations (see Chapter 4.)

Examples of Remediation Cost Management Activities

Most cost management attention is placed on the execution phase for activities such as contract negotiation, change order management, and claims negotiation. While this phase is very important, most project costs are determined during the planning phases. This is because the decisions made during planning set the requirements for the overall project, which in turn determine its costs. Historically, owners and engineers did not manage costs during planning very effectively, because they did not have the tools and expertise to do so. However, this has changed as parametric estimating tools and data have provided the capability to estimate and manage costs from the very beginning of the project. Following are some examples of cost management applications.

Planning Remediation Efforts
Remediation projects include many activities, but can generally be described in three phases:

1. Site characterization and remedy selection
2. Remediation
3. Long-term operations and monitoring

Planning is required before each of these phases is begun. Budget estimates are developed during the planning phase to establish funding requirements and to compare different approaches to completing the work.

Selecting Site Investigation Methods

Site investigation is expensive. For some remediation projects, the site characterization and remedy selection process can cost more than the actual cleanup. There are many different ways to characterize a site, with radically differing costs. In the early days of the Superfund programs, site characterization requirements were determined by regulators who wanted to know everything, combined with environmental firms who had a vested interest in doing more than is absolutely necessary to increase fees and reduce risk.

Cost management and early estimating allow the owner to determine the costs and requirements for site investigation and compare the relative costs and benefits of different approaches. This process reduces costs without reducing effectiveness. Working with owners over the last ten years on dozens of projects, we have seen an overall cost reduction of approximately 30% in site characterization efforts when owners take an active role in negotiating with contractors and regulators about site characterization requirements.

Selecting Remediation Technologies

Most types of contamination can be remedied in more than one way. Containment, ex situ treatment, in situ treatment, and natural attenuation, are among the common remediation strategies. In addition, risk-based cleanups—where the remediation goal is based on the re-use plan for the property—have provided a whole new spectrum of remediation alternatives and costs.

The myriad alternatives complicate the decision process for remediation technology selection. At the same time, however, having a choice offers significant opportunity for cost reduction. The owner needs to be able to accurately estimate the cost of different cleanup approaches before making a selection, and then compare the alternatives to determine the best choice. Parametric estimating data such as that found in the ECHOS cost books, and parametric estimating systems such as Earth Tech's RACER system, allow this to be done early in the site investigation process. This capability has resulted in tremendous savings.

Negotiating with Regulators

In the early days of environmental remediation, many owners and environmental practitioners took the position that regulators were unreasonable, and that they had no concern for cost-effectiveness. While this may have been true of some regulators in the past, the reality is that a well-educated and well-prepared owner can reach a reasonable settlement on site investigation and remediation approaches that save money. By bringing cost information to the table, owners can show regulators the cost implications of marginal regulatory decisions and negotiate lower cost alternatives in most cases, as long as the true technical requirements of the project are met. Detailed early cost estimates provide much of this data.

Conclusion   The areas described in this chapter are some examples of the types of cost management activities owners can pursue to save money on remediation projects. The remainder of this book provides information to assist in the preparation of cost estimates in support of these cost management activities.

Chapter 2

Environmental Remediation Laws and Regulations

Environmental remediation is controlled by numerous federal, state, and local laws and regulations. Although these regulations are in a constant state of review and change, basic remediation processes are governed primarily by two federal laws: the *Comprehensive Environmental Response, Compensation, and Liability Act* (also known as *CERCLA* and/or the *Superfund Law*), and the *Resource Conservation and Recovery Act (RCRA)*. These two laws guide most remediation processes performed in the United States. This book is not intended to provide detailed analyses of these laws; instead, it provides background information for estimating environmental remediation projects. This section is an overview of CERCLA and RCRA.

Comprehensive Environmental Response, Compensation, and Liability Act (CERCLA)

CERCLA, also known as "Superfund," is the basis for a national program for responding to releases of hazardous substances to the environment. CERCLA created a national emergency response program, provided for cleanup of abandoned sites and active facilities that are not regulated under the RCRA corrective action program, established a trust fund to pay for cleanup of abandoned sites, and created a National Priority List (NPL) of the nation's most contaminated sites. CERCLA establishes the procedures for identifying and cleaning up contaminated sites (see Figure 2.1). CERCLA was amended in 1986 by the *Superfund Amendments Reauthorization Act (SARA)*. SARA reauthorized the trust fund to fund government response actions, extended CERCLA, and added new provisions. References made to CERCLA in this book should be interpreted as meaning, "CERCLA as amended by SARA."

The Environmental Protection Agency (EPA) is the federal government agency with the lead responsibility for implementing CERCLA. The EPA's response powers include cleanup of not only hazardous substances, but also pollutants and contaminants that may present an imminent and substantial danger to public health or welfare. The government's response authority includes short-term "removal" actions to mitigate immediate threat to public health, and longer-term "remedial" actions that are consistent with a permanent remedy. The circumstances under which removal or remedial actions are appropriate are identified in the National Contingency Plan (NCP) and summarized on the following pages.

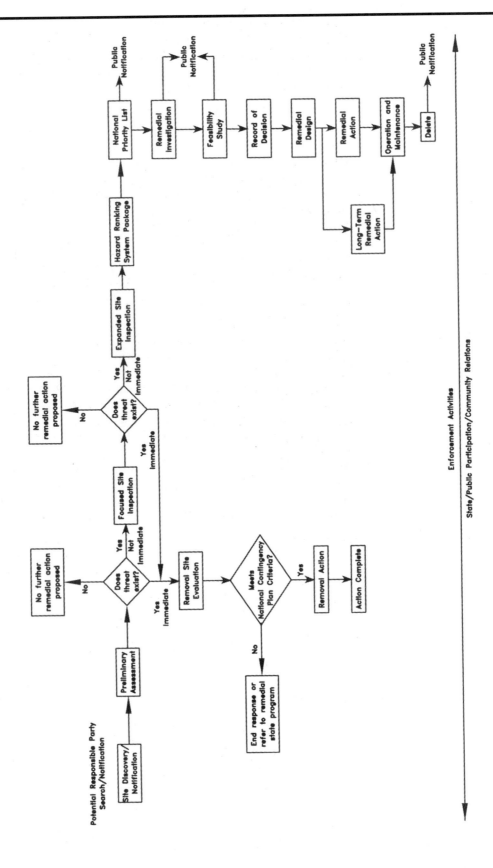

Figure 2.1 The Superfund Process

National Contingency Plan

The National Contingency Plan (NCP) is the regulatory blueprint for implementing the statutory requirements of CERCLA. It is the EPA's primary tool for issuing its interpretations of policy and guidance to meet the requirements of Superfund.

The NCP is in Title 40 of the Code of Federal Regulations (40 CFR), Part 300. The methods and criteria for determining the extent of hazardous substance response actions are in 40 CFR 300, Subpart E. The NCP also covers issues such as hazardous substance and extremely hazardous substance release reporting requirements, establishment of national and regional response teams, development of contingency plans to respond to releases, and response phases for cleanup of oil discharges in violation of the Clean Water Act. This section addresses only the hazardous substance response actions.

CERCLA provides two major response authorities—*removal actions* and *remedial actions*—to respond to releases of hazardous substances and pollutants or contaminants. The NCP specifies a different set of requirements for removal and remedial actions, as discussed in the following paragraphs.

Removal Actions

Removal actions are short-term actions in response to a release of hazardous substance(s) that may present an imminent and substantial danger to human health and welfare or the environment. The EPA's removal actions are limited to 12 months or $2 million to ensure proper use of the removal action process. Under CERCLA Section 104 and Executive Order 12580, the U.S. government is authorized to conduct removal actions when the release is on or from a government installation. The 12 months or $2 million limits do not apply to removal actions conducted by the U.S. government. Figure 2.2 illustrates the removal action process.

The decision to perform a removal action can be made any time during or prior to implementation of the remedial action process, even when the site is not included on the National Priorities List (NPL). The regulations governing removal actions are in 40 CFR 300.415.

A removal action is appropriate when:

- A release of hazardous substances creates an actual threat to human health and welfare or for the environment.
- A release of hazardous substances has the potential for direct contact with humans, animals, or sensitive environments.
- A known hazardous substance has the potential to migrate to humans, animals, or sensitive environments.
- A fire or explosion hazard is present.
- A release may occur as the result of the integrity of hazardous waste storage or bulk storage containers.
- The release or migration of hazardous substances may be caused or hastened by weather conditions.
- Other appropriate federal or state response mechanisms are unavailable to respond to a release of hazardous substances.
- Other factors may pose a threat to public health and welfare or the environment.

In simplest terms, whenever there is an actual or potential threat of a hazardous substance migrating to, or directly contacting, human or other biological receptors, a removal action is taken to separate or maintain a separation between the receptor and the hazardous substances.

A removal action is not always a permanent solution. A removal action may simply eliminate the immediate problem so the more time-consuming remedial action process may properly characterize and more effectively remediate the contaminated site. Therefore, a removal action should always be consistent with any anticipated future remedial actions.

There are 2 basic types of removal actions:

- **Emergency removal:** Used when site cleanup or mitigating procedures must be implemented within 6 months after determining that a removal action is appropriate.
- **Removal with a 6-month planning period:** Used when the planning period for site cleanup or mitigating procedures may exceed 6 months after determining that a removal action is appropriate.

The following is a list of some examples of potential removal actions. The list does not include every possible option.

- Sealing and removing drums that pose a fire and explosion hazard.
- Installing security fencing and warning signs to prevent direct contact with humans and animals.
- Removing debris or other materials that might attract people to enter the site.
- Evacuating an area and containing the spilled or released material.
- Discontinuing use of contaminated groundwater and supplying an alternate source of drinking water.
- Excavating, consolidating, and removing highly contaminated soils.
- Draining lagoons and providing cover to prevent run-on or run-off.
- Capping a disposal area to minimize infiltration of precipitation.
- Constructing drainage controls to prevent (divert) run-on and minimizing or capturing run-off from a highly contaminated area before the rainy season.
- Applying absorptive or damping materials to minimize the spread of contamination.
- Stabilizing and maintaining the integrity of existing structures.

Remedial Actions

Remedial actions (RA) are permanent remedies taken instead of, or in addition to, a removal action in response to a release or threatened release of hazardous substances. The objective is to ensure that the hazardous substances do not migrate, causing substantial danger to present or future public health and welfare or the environment.

The RA process begins once it is established that a removal action is not warranted or has been completed (see Figure 2.3). The lead agency performs a remedial site evaluation (40 CFR 300.420), which includes conducting a remedial *preliminary assessment (PA)* and a *remedial site inspection (SI)*. The goal of these pre-remedial activities is to gain a better understanding of the nature of the threat. For sites that do pose a threat, the goal is to collect the necessary data to score the site using the *Hazard Ranking System (HRS)* and to identify sites that require immediate response. The HRS provides a numerical ranking that estimates the risk posed by the site. The PA/SI determines whether a site has ever handled hazardous substances and whether it has released, or has the potential to release, hazardous substances to the environment.

The detailed site investigation and cleanup alternative selection process is referred to as the *Remedial Investigation/Feasibility Study (RI/FS)* process (40 CFR 300.430(a)(2)). An RI/FS includes activities such as project scoping, data collection, risk assessment, treatability studies, analysis of alternatives, and remedy selection. The RI covers site assessment activities to determine site conditions and the nature and extent of contamination. The FS develops and evaluates the cleanup options on which a remedy is based. The goal of the remedy selection process is to select remedies that protect human health and the environment, that maintain protection over time, and that minimize untreated waste. The detailed analysis of alternatives for selecting a remedy involves assessing individual alternatives against nine evaluation criteria listed in 40 CFR 300.430(e)(9)(iii).

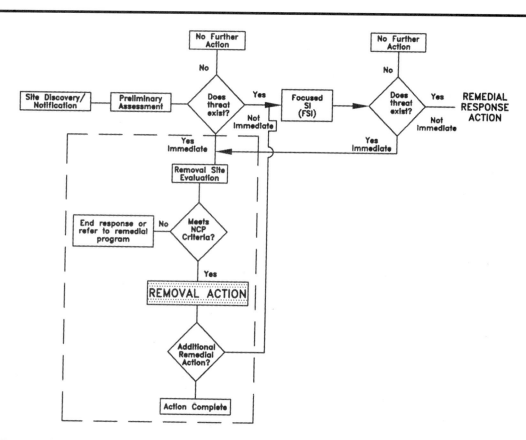

Figure 2.2 Removal Action Process

The selected remedy is documented in a *Record of Decision (ROD)*, along with supporting documentation. The ROD is signed by the site owner, other responsible parties, the EPA, and other regulators and affected agencies. The regulations governing remedial actions are given in 40 CFR 300.420 through 300.435.

State "Superfund" Laws

Superfund does not preempt states from enacting their own mini-Superfund laws and imposing additional requirements with respect to cleanup of hazardous substance releases. Many states now have such laws. CERCLA Section 120(a)(4) provides that state laws regarding removal and remedial action are applicable to federal facilities not on the NPL. (RAs taken at NPL sites must comply with the substantive portions of state environmental and facility siting laws, provided the laws are applicable or relevant and appropriate.)

Resource Conservation and Recovery Act (RCRA)

The Resource Conservation and Recovery Act of 1976 (RCRA) established a federal program regulating solid and hazardous waste management. RCRA actually amends earlier legislation (the Solid Waste Disposal Act of 1965), but the amendments were so comprehensive that the Act is commonly called RCRA rather than its official title.

The Act defines solid and hazardous waste, authorizes the EPA to set standards for facilities that generate or manage hazardous waste, and establishes a permit program for hazardous treatment, storage, and facilities.

Hazardous Waste Regulation

Subtitle C of RCRA concerns the hazardous waste management program. A waste is hazardous if it is ignitable, corrosive, reactive, or toxic, or appears on a list of about 100 industrial process waste streams and more than 500 discarded commercial products and chemicals. The 1976 law expanded the definition of solid waste—of which hazardous waste is a subset—to include sludge and other discarded material, including solid, liquid, semi-solid, or contained gaseous material. The broadened definition is particularly important with respect to hazardous wastes, at least 95% of which are liquids or sludges. Some wastes are specifically excluded, however, including irrigation return flows, industrial point source discharges (regulated under the Clean Water Act), and nuclear material covered by the Atomic Energy Act.

Under RCRA, hazardous waste generators must comply with regulations concerning record keeping and reporting; the labeling of wastes; the use of appropriate containers; the provision of information on the wastes' general chemical composition to transporters, treaters, and disposers; and the use of a manifest system. Facilities generating less than 100 kilograms of waste per month are exempt from the regulations.

Transporters of hazardous waste must also meet certain standards. These regulations were coordinated by the EPA with existing Department of Transportation regulations. A manifest system, effective since 1980, is used to track wastes from their point of generation, along their transportation routes, to the place of final treatment, storage, or disposal.

Treatment, storage, and disposal (TSD) facilities are required to have permits, to comply with operating standards, to meet financial requirements that show the capability to perform emergency actions in case of accidents, and to close their facilities in accordance with EPA regulations. Bulk or noncontainerized hazardous liquid wastes cannot be disposed in any landfill, and severe restrictions are placed on the disposal of containerized hazardous liquids as well as on the disposal of nonhazardous liquids in hazardous waste landfills. The land disposal of specified highly hazardous wastes was phased out over the period from 1986 to 1990. The EPA was directed to review all wastes defined as hazardous and to make a determination as to the appropriateness of land disposal for those wastes. Minimum technological standards were established for new landfills and surface impoundments requiring, in general, double liners, a leachate collection system, and groundwater monitoring.

States are encouraged and financially assisted to assume the EPA's hazardous waste program. Virtually all states are assisting the EPA in implementing RCRA under agreements called *Cooperative Arrangements*. The Cooperative Arrangements enable the states to participate in the program (e.g., assist in evaluating permits or

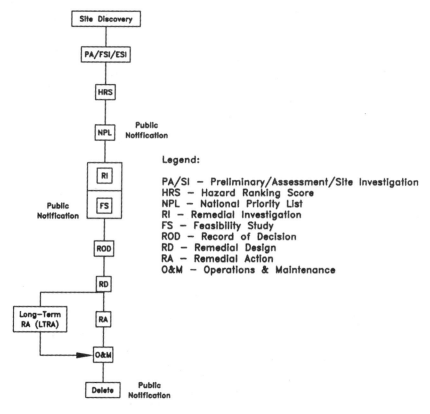

Figure 2.3 Remedial Response Action Process

operating the manifest system) and gain experience, as well as to receive assistance in developing their programs while working toward full authorization.

Solid Waste Provisions

The major solid waste provision in RCRA is the prohibition of open dumps. This prohibition is implemented by the states, using EPA criteria to determine which facilities qualify as sanitary landfills and may remain open. The EPA's criteria were originally promulgated in 1979; open dumps were to close or be upgraded by September 13, 1984.

In the 1984 amendments to RCRA, the EPA was required to revise the sanitary landfill criteria for facilities that receive small quantity generator hazardous waste or hazardous household waste. Using this authority, the EPA promulgated revised regulations applicable to municipal solid waste landfills in October 1991, with an effective date of October 9, 1993 for most provisions. In general, the new criteria require liners, leachate collection, groundwater monitoring, and corrective action at municipal landfills.

Underground Storage Tanks

To address a nationwide problem of leaking underground storage tanks (USTs), Congress established a prevention, detection, and cleanup program through the 1984 RCRA amendments and the 1986 Superfund Amendments and Reauthorization Act (SARA).

The 1984 RCRA amendments created a federal program to regulate USTs containing petroleum and hazardous chemicals to limit corrosion and structural defects, and thus minimize future tank leaks. The law directed the EPA to set technical standards for tank design and operation, leak detection, reporting, corrective action, and tank closure. The UST program (new RCRA Subtitle I) is administered primarily by states and requires registration of most USTs, bans the installation of unprotected tanks, sets federal technical standards for all tanks, coordinates federal and state regulatory efforts, and provides for federal inspection and enforcement.

In 1986, Congress created a petroleum UST response program by amending Subtitle I of RCRA through SARA (P.L. 99-499). Before SARA, the EPA lacked explicit authority to require cleanup of contamination from leaking petroleum USTs, as Congress had officially excluded petroleum products (although not petrochemicals) from the Superfund law. The new provisions authorized the federal government to respond to petroleum spills and leaks, and created a Leaking Underground Storage Tank Trust Fund to clean up leaks from petroleum USTs. The money in the fund is derived primarily from a 0.1 cent-per-gallon federal tax on motor fuels and several other petroleum products.

The 1986 amendments directed the EPA to establish financial responsibility requirements for UST owners and operators to cover costs of taking corrective action and to compensate third parties for injury and property damage caused by leaking tanks. The law required the EPA to issue regulations requiring tank owners and operators selling petroleum products to demonstrate financial responsibility insurance coverage of $1 million.

Amendments to RCRA

RCRA has been amended 8 times. The 3 most significant sets of amendments occurred in 1980, 1984, and 1992.

1980 Amendments

The Solid Waste Disposal Act Amendments of 1980 provided tougher enforcement powers to the EPA to deal with illegal dumpers of hazardous waste; restricted the EPA's authority to regulate certain high-volume, low-hazard wastes; authorized funds to conduct an inventory of hazardous waste sites; and extended RCRA authorizations for appropriations. Amending language contained in Superfund, P.L 96-510, established an Assistant Administrator for Solid Waste and Emergency Response.

Hazardous and Solid Waste Amendments of 1984

The most significant set of amendments, the Hazardous and Solid Waste Amendments of 1984, is a complex law with many detailed technical requirements. In addition to restrictions on land disposal and the inclusion of small-quantity hazardous waste generators (those producing between 100–1,000 kg of waste per month) in the hazardous waste regulatory scheme summarized above, the law also created the new regulatory program for USTs (also described above). The EPA was directed to issue regulations governing those who produce, distribute, and use fuels produced from hazardous waste, including used oil. Under HSWA, hazardous waste facilities owned or operated by federal, state, or local government agencies must be inspected annually, and privately owned facilities must be inspected at least every 2 years. Each federal agency was to submit to the EPA an inventory of any hazardous waste facilities ever owned by the agency.

The 1984 law also imposed on the EPA a timetable for issuing or denying permits for treatment, storage, and disposal facilities; required permits to be for fixed terms not exceeding 10 years; terminated in 1985 the "interim status" of land disposal facilities that existed prior to RCRA's enactment, unless they met certain requirements; required permit applications to be accompanied by information regarding the potential for public exposure to hazardous substances in connection with the facility; and authorized the EPA to issue experimental permits for facilities demonstrating new technologies. The EPA's enforcement powers were increased, the list of prohibited actions constituting crimes was expanded, penalties were increased, and the citizen suit provisions were expanded. Other provisions prohibited the export of hazardous waste unless the government of the receiving country formally consented to accepting it; created an ombudsman's office in the EPA to deal with RCRA-associated complaints, grievances, and requests for information; and reauthorized RCRA through FY88 at a level of about $250 million per year.

Federal Facility Compliance Act of 1992

The third major set of amendments was the Federal Facility Compliance Act of 1992. This Act resolves the legal question of whether federal facilities are subject to enforcement actions under RCRA, unequivocally waiving the government's sovereign immunity from prosecution. As a result, states, the EPA, and the Department of Justice can enforce the provisions of RCRA against federal facilities, and federal departments and agencies can be subjected to injunctions, administrative orders, and/or penalties for noncompliance. Furthermore, federal employees may be subject to criminal sanctions, including both fines and imprisonment under any federal or state solid or hazardous waste law. The Act also contains provisions applicable to mixtures of radioactive and hazardous waste at Department of Energy facilities and to munitions, military ships, and military sewage treatment facilities handling hazardous wastes.

RCRA Corrective Action Process

RCRA Corrective Actions are the means by which the EPA and states remediate contaminated sites that are regulated under RCRA. The key terms used in describing RCRA corrective actions are:

Solid Waste Management Unit (SWMU): Waste management unit from which hazardous wastes or constituents may migrate, even if the unit is not intended for management of hazardous waste. Also, any area that becomes contaminated as a result of routine and systematic release of waste (e.g., spill area).

- **Regulated Unit:** A subset of the SWMU. A regulated unit is any surface impoundment, waste pile, land treatment unit, or landfill that received waste after July 26, 1982.
- **Hazardous Constituent:** Any substance listed in 40 CFR Part 261 Appendix VIII.

Under RCRA, the EPA or the states can require permitted facilities that release hazardous materials from regulated units to take corrective action only on those releases to the uppermost aquifer, or clean up any other contaminated media.

The corrective action process has 4 main components. Each component is made up of a number of steps. The number of steps and level of complexity of the process vary from site to site depending on the severity of the problem. The 4 major components of the process are described in the following paragraphs.

RCRA Facility Assessment

The RCRA Facility Assessment (RFA) includes records review, physical inspection, and sampling to determine the extent of releases of hazardous materials into different environmental media (e.g., soil, groundwater, air, surface water, subsurface gas). The outcome of this step will be one or more of the following actions:

- No Further Action (NFA) required under the RCRA corrective action program at this time.
- An RCRA Facility Investigation (RFI) by the facility owner or operator is required as a result of RFA findings.
- Interim corrective measures are required because the regulatory agency believes that expedited actions are necessary to protect human health and the environment.

RCRA Facility Investigation

The RCRA Facility Investigation (RFI) is required when the RFA determines that further investigation is needed to determine the extent of contamination in the environmental media. Generally, the investigation will begin with confirmation of the suspected release and, when confirmation exists, further characterization of the waste. The RFI also includes the regulatory agency's interpretation of release characterization data against established health and environmental criteria to determine whether a Corrective Measures Study (CMS) is needed. Identifying and implementing interim corrective measures may also be part of the RFI process. If the RFI identifies a condition that indicates that adverse exposure to hazardous materials is occurring or is imminent, an interim corrective measure may be used to mitigate the situation.

Corrective Measures Study

If the RFI indicates the need for corrective measures, the owner or operator is required to perform a Corrective Measures Study (CMS). This involves identifying and recommending steps to correct the release.

Corrective Measures Implementation

The Corrective Measures Implementation (CMI) process includes designing, constructing, operating, maintaining, and monitoring the selected remedy.

Conclusion

Laws and regulations affecting hazardous waste are complicated and, in some cases, contradictory. The interpretation and implementation of these laws and regulations can be a major cost driver in remediation projects. While it is not reasonable to expect a cost engineer to become a regulatory specialist, it is important for the cost engineer to maintain a basic understanding of these requirements and how they affect the project.

Chapter 3

Remedial Action Cost Estimating Process

Creating a cost estimate for an environmental remedial action (RA) project is a multi-stage process that includes seven basic steps:

1. Develop the project description.
2. Classify project sites.
3. Identify the technologies and treatment trains to be used.
4. Estimate the quantity of work and direct cost of each technology.
5. Estimate sampling and analysis and professional labor costs required to support the project.
6. Identify miscellaneous direct costs required to complete the project.
7. Estimate indirect costs, general conditions, overhead and profit.

This chapter provides an overview of each of these steps.

Step 1: Develop the Project Description

The project description includes general information about the project: project identification, location, preparer's name, and date of estimate. Provide a general description of the project, including prior and current use. Finally, identify the "sites" that comprise the project. Also include a sketch plan of the project and each project site as a reference.

Step 2: Classify Project Sites

Smaller projects such as underground storage tank (UST) removals may involve only one site, but more complex projects are often divided into multiple sites, zones, or operating units for management and reporting purposes. The definition of sites within a project is somewhat arbitrary, but site definitions should be developed in a way that corresponds to the actual project activities and helps to organize the project for estimating and reporting purposes. For example, many large environmental remediation sites are divided into operable units or zones. These zones may be based on types of contaminants, physical locations on site, remediation approaches, or environmental media such as groundwater, surface impoundments, or soil.

In addition to physical sites, the cost estimate may include a "project activity site" that is used to estimate costs for project support activities that support the entire site. Examples include site health and safety functions, decontamination facilities, storage facilities, sampling and analysis, professional labor, and general conditions items. By separating these items from site-specific activities, the estimator can ensure that they are not left out or "double counted" in the estimate.

Site-specific information should include details of structures on site, location of suspected contamination in relation to these structures, information about the site surroundings, and indications of whether the site is level or sloping and whether there is surface water at the site. Provide information about the soil and groundwater conditions at the site. If a typical boring log is available for the site, include it for reference.

Provide information about the contamination on the site, including estimates of whether soil, soil gas, or water are contaminated, the quantity and extent of contamination, and an estimate of the concentrations of the 5 most prevalent contaminants on the site. If actual results of site investigation activities are available showing contamination concentrations, then an estimate of the concentrations is not necessary.

Also provide additional information related to the site, including precipitation, population distribution, and distances to nearest water bodies. This information is important for assessing the hazard at the site.

Step 3: Identify the Technology/Treatment Train

The RA process is generally performed by implementing a collection of independent remedial technologies into a "treatment train." The preparation of the direct cost portion of an RA cost estimate is actually a compilation of cost estimates for each of the remedial technologies that make up the project. This step is used to identify and describe those technologies by referring to engineering design information, discussing the technology with the project engineering team, or selecting presumptive remedies based on the project and site information described above. Regardless of the source of information, the description of remedial technologies within the treatment train and the interaction of these technologies should be determined as fully as possible before the estimate is prepared. Chapter 4, "Types of Treatments and Treatment Trains," describes technologies and treatment trains in more detail. Chapter 5, "Treatment Technology Functional Groupings" provides guidance on compiling technologies into treatment trains.

Step 4: Estimate the Quantity of Work and Direct Cost of Each Technology

Direct cost estimates are prepared using estimates for each of the technologies included in the treatment train(s) for the sites in the project. Chapters 8–56 of this book provide specific information on estimating costs for various remedial technologies. Each section contains general information about the technology, where it is applicable, typical design features, required information for estimating, and additional technical information that may be used to help define the project. Chapter 60 provides guidance on operations and maintenance costs for remediation approaches.

Required Information
The cost engineer/estimator should review these chapters for each technology to ensure that the information needed to prepare the estimate is available. An example of the required information for air stripping (covered in Chapter 10) is:

- System configuration
- Influent flow rate
- Volatility of contaminants
- Operating period
- Safety level

Detailed Design Information

In addition to the required information for each technology, additional design information can make the estimate more precise and accurate. The cost engineer should review this material and gather the information before preparing the estimate. An example of this secondary information for air stripping is:

- Tower diameter and quantity
- Packing height
- Sump tank quantity/size
- Sump pump quantity/size
- Chemical feeder
- Piping material and length

Quantity Development

Once the information listed above is developed, the next step is to compute the actual quantities of work that make up the project. This quantity development can be based on assumed values as discussed in the technology descriptions in Chapters 8 through 56, or based on actual takeoff from engineering design information (if available).

To continue with the air stripping example, assume that the influent flow rate is 30 GPM through a single tower with a moderate contaminant volatility (required parameters). Based on the information discussed in Chapter 9, the cost engineer could select one 1.5′ diameter tower with a 27′ packing height as the design solution, along with 100 L.F. of PVC piping for the influent and 100 L.F. of PVC piping for the effluent. The estimate would also include one 550-gallon plastic sump tank, one 75 GPM sump pump, and a 5-gallon, 175 PSIG biofouling prevention chemical feeder. These quantities are calculated based on generic design information described in this book and can be adjusted as necessary to reflect actual design requirements.

Direct Costs

Once the quantities are developed, direct costs can be estimated. The *ECHOS Environmental Remediation Cost Data-Assemblies* and ECHOS *Environmental Remediation Cost Data-Unit Price* books provide a complete reference for cost information for the technologies discussed in this book. The basic assembly costs in the *ECHOS Assemblies Cost* book include the costs of labor, equipment, and materials and are the sum of the unit cost line items from the *ECHOS Unit Cost Book*. These costs are based on a U.S. national average price base and should be adjusted to reflect pricing at the specified site by applying the location cost factors, which can be determined based on information provided in each book.

Step 5: Estimate Monitoring and Professional Labor Costs Required to Support the Project

Monitoring and RA phase professional labor management are estimated after all other RA technologies are estimated. This is because these two activities are used to support the installation and operation of the remedial technologies; the specific requirement for monitoring and professional labor cannot be fully established until other project requirements are known and estimated.

Monitoring is performed during RA for the purposes of: reporting progress to regulators, testing results of specific activities, providing guidelines for site worker health and safety, and providing reporting and public information. Monitoring activities are generally associated with each RA technology being implemented on the site. Chapter 57, "Monitoring" and provides guidelines for estimating sampling and analysis costs.

RA phase professional labor includes activities that evaluate the performance of remedial actions. These activities generally occur during the construction, startup/shakedown, and operation and maintenance (O&M) phase of the remediation process. Typical professional support activities associated with RA construction include oversight of site-specific construction activities, permit acquisition, and "as built" drawings. Typical site-specific professional support activities associated with RA operations and maintenance include evaluation of sampling and analysis data, comparison of results with project goals, coordination of field activities, and documentation and reporting of all efforts. Chapter 46, "Remedial Action Phase Professional Labor," provides guidelines for estimating RA phase professional labor.

Step 6: Identify Miscellaneous Direct Costs Required to Complete the Project

The bulk of this book is focused on estimating costs for environmental remediation technologies. However, nearly all RA projects include other direct costs. For example, most RA technologies require some level of site preparation, utilities, and other supporting facilities and site work. These requirements are highly site specific. Other direct costs may include community relations activities, legal fees, permits, and other related items. These costs may be significant cost and must be considered and included in the estimate. The cost engineer should carefully review the requirements of the entire project; and discuss the requirements with the engineering team, owner, regulatory officials, and other parties who may affect the project to ensure that important cost items are not omitted from the estimate.

Step 7: Estimate Indirect Costs, General Conditions, Overhead and Profit

The final step is to estimate indirect costs, general conditions, overhead and profit, including the following:

- Contractor general conditions
- Contractor overhead and profit
- Escalation
- Contingencies

These costs support the entire project. Part III, Chapters 62, 63, and 64, provides guidance.

Escalation is used to adjust prices from the current date (or the effective date of the cost data) to the date on which the work will be performed. Estimated escalation rates are published by a number of government agencies, such as the Office of Management and Budget, and technical trade references, such as *Engineering News Record (ENR)*.

Contingencies are used in an estimate to cover costs for unknown or unforeseen conditions that may increase costs during the execution of the project. This is particularly important for environmental projects, since unforeseen conditions are likely. The development and use of contingency funds is often a management decision that affects how the project funds will be controlled. The amount of the contingency to be applied at each stage of the project is a function of the quality of the information used to prepare the estimate. The cost engineer should work with the management team for the project to determine how contingencies will be used, then develop a strategy that takes into account uncertainty about scope, pricing, and unknown risks.

Conclusion

There are many ways to develop cost estimates. The exact steps to be performed will vary from project to project, depending on the nature of the project, reporting requirements, and the personal preference of the estimator. The seven steps described in this section will result in a thorough estimate if performed properly. However, the estimator should make adjustments to these steps, as appropriate, to meet the individual needs of the project.

Chapter 4

Types of Treatment and Treatment Trains

Environmental remediation projects generally involve some combination of three primary strategies:

- Containment or immobilization of the contaminants.
- Destruction or alteration of contaminants to reduce or eliminate the risk.
- Removal or separation of contaminants from the media.

Technologies commonly used for containment or immobilization of contaminants include stabilization, solidification, and containment. Examples include construction of secure landfills, capping, slurry walls, and in situ solidification. These technologies are effective, but only temporarily, so long-term monitoring and maintenance are generally required.

Destruction technologies usually involve a biological, thermal, or chemical process that converts the hazardous or toxic material into a non-hazardous condition. Examples include biodegradation, incineration, and low-temperature thermal desorption. These technologies are effective because they eliminate the waste from the environment, thus reducing or preventing the need for long-term operations and monitoring.

Removal and separation technologies are used to remove the waste from the current media prior to further treatment or disposal. Common processes include groundwater treatment by carbon adsorption, air stripping, ion exchange, phase separation, or some combination of these; and soil treatment by soil washing, solvent extraction, soil vapor extraction, or thermal desorption. Typically, these processes are used in combination with other removal/separation technologies and follow-up treatment or disposal options.

Treatment Trains

In most cases, multiple technologies are required to remediate an entire site. Several treatment processes are combined to meet the varying requirements of the contaminants affecting the site. This combination is known as a *treatment train*.

Treatment trains are developed on a case-by-case basis to meet the specific needs of the project. However, a number of common treatment applications use similar treatment trains repetitively. For example, pump and treat systems have been used for years to treat groundwater contaminated with volatile organic compounds (VOCs) such as fuel. The treatment train for these systems typically includes extraction wells, air strippers, carbon adsorption/gas, carbon adsorption/liquid, and a water discharge system (e.g., discharge to POTW or injection wells). Other technologies may be added to this treatment train to deal with site-specific situations or to enhance its operation. Figure 4.1 is an example of a treatment train for a groundwater and soil vapor fuel extraction system.

Treatment trains can be categorized based on the primary function to be performed, the contaminated media, and the type of contaminants. Most active treatment processes will be used to deal with one of the media groups shown in Figure 4.2. Common contaminants are shown in Figure 4.3.

Once the media and the contaminant group are known, common remedial technologies can be considered as part of an overall treatment process. The following website reference contains a spreadsheet summary of treatment trains. This reference is available exclusively to purchasers of this book, and is located at **http://www.rsmeans.com/ supplement/environ.html** The downloadable spreadsheet is first divided into the following tables for media:

- Free product
- Groundwater
- Sediment/Sludge
- Soil
- Solids
- Surface water

On each tab, there are numerous combinations of primary and secondary contaminants (see Figure 4.3), approach (in situ or ex situ), and up to seven different treatment trains. Each treatment train is made up of several different technologies, which are specifically designed to meet the site conditions.

Treatment trains are the basis for defining the requirements for construction and operation of a remedial action (RA) project. The final step in defining the treatment train, once technologies are determined, is to ascertain the "linkage" between the different technologies. This in turn will determine the need for items such as piping, electrical power supply, excavation of trenches, and so on. The cost engineer should work closely with the design team to define the treatment train and the links between the technologies. If no design is available, it is a good idea to prepare a sketch of the site plan to make sure it will all fit together, and that items are not missed or double-counted in the estimate.

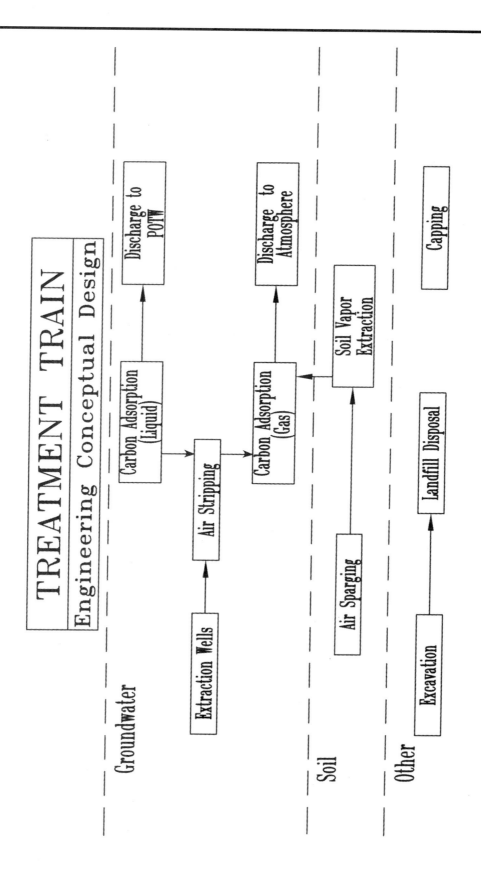

Figure 4.1 Treatment Train

Media Treatment Groups
Free Product (Ex Situ, In Situ)
Groundwater (Ex Situ, In Situ)
Sediment/Sludge (Ex Situ, In Situ)
Soil (Ex Situ, In Situ)
Solids (Ex Situ, In Situ)
Surface Water (Ex Situ, In Situ)
Air (Ex Situ)

Figure 4.2 Media Treatment Groups

Common Contaminant Categories
Acids/Caustics
Asbestos
Fuels
High-Level Radioactive
Low-Level Radioactive
Metals
Ordnance
Ordnance-Environmental Constituents
PCBs
Pesticides
Semivolatile Organic Compounds
Volatile Organic Compounds

Figure 4.3 Common Contaminant Categories

Chapter 5

Treatment Technology Functional Groupings

Many of the remediation technologies discussed in this book can be used for more than one of the strategies discussed in Chapter 4. For example, extraction wells can be used as part of a removal/separation scheme where groundwater will be pumped to an ex situ treatment system. Or wells may be part of a containment system where they are placed at the leading edge of a groundwater contamination plume and are used to prevent plume migration by pumping contaminated water out of the aquifer before it can migrate.

When considering the application of different treatment technologies, the design engineering team will first consider the goals of remediation (e.g., removal, separation, containment, or destruction). Once the goals are established, the team will consider technologies or groups of technologies to meet these goals. There are many sub-classifications of the three strategies discussed in Chapter 4, "Types of Treatments and Treatment Trains," but one of the most useful ways to classify technologies is to group them according to media and strategy. Under this classification, the remediation technologies discussed in this book can be grouped into the following categories:

- Ex Situ Treatments
- In Situ Treatments
- Soil Treatments
- Air Treatments
- Groundwater Treatments
- Disposal Methods
- Removal Technologies
- Ordnance Technologies
- Radioactive Waste Technologies
- Transfer Technologies
- Destruction Technologies
- Separation/Reduction Technologies
- Isolation/Containment Technologies
- Remediation Evaluation Support
- Site Work and Supporting Utilities
- Contractor Costs

These categories are not mutually exclusive. In fact, many technologies will fall into 2 or more of these categories. This list simply serves as a functional guide to help in the selection of technologies for a particular remediation project. Figure 5.1 lists the technologies, by category, that are discussed later in this book.

Remediation—Ex Situ Treatments
Advanced Oxidation Process
Air Stripping
Carbon Adsorption (Gas)
Carbon Adsorption (Liquid)
Coagulation/Flocculation
Dewatering (Sludge)
Ex Situ Bioreactors
Ex Situ Land Farming
Ex Situ Solidification/Stabilization
On Site Low-temperature Thermal Desorption
Media Filtration
Metals Precipitation
Neutralization
Off Site Transportation and Thermal Treatment
On Site Low-temperature Thermal Desorption
Soil Washing
Solvent Extraction
Thermal & Catalytic Oxidation

Remediation—In Situ Treatments
Air Sparging
Bioventing
Heat-enhanced Vapor Extraction
In Situ Biodegradation (Saturated Zone)
In Situ Land Farming
In Situ Solidification
In Situ Vitrification
Passive Water Treatment Phytoremediation
Soil Flushing
Soil Vapor Extraction

Figure 5.1 Remediation Treatments and Technologies

Remediation—Soil Treatments
Bioventing
Dewatering (Sludge)
Ex Situ Bioreactors
Ex Situ Land Farming
Ex Situ Solidification/Stabilization
Heat-enhanced Vapor Extraction
In Situ Land Farming
In Situ Solidification
In Situ Vitrification
Off Site Transportation and Thermal Treatment
On Site Low-temperature Thermal Desorption
Phytoremediation
Soil Flushing
Soil Vapor Extraction
Soil Washing
Solvent Extraction

Remediation—Air Treatments
Carbon Adsorption (Gas)
Thermal & Catalytic Oxidation

Remediation—Groundwater Treatments
Advanced Oxidation Processes
Air Sparging
Air Stripping
Carbon Adsorption (Liquid)
Coagulation/Flocculation
Free Product Removal (French Drain)
In Situ Biodegradation (Saturated Zone)
Media Filtration
Metals Precipitation Neutralization Permeable Barriers
Slurry Wall

Remediation—Disposal Methods
Discharge To POTW
Infiltration Gallery
Injection Wells
Off site Transportation and Waste Disposal

Remediation Removal Technologies
Asbestos Removal
Contaminated Building Materials Dismantling
Excavation
French Drain
Groundwater Extraction Wells
Surface Decontamination
Transportation
UST Closure/Removal

Figure 5.1 Remediation Treatments and Technologies (cont.)

Remediation—Ordnance Technologies
Excavation
Offsite Transportation and Landfill Disposal
Ordnance and Explosives Removal Action
UXO Active Target Clearance

Remediation—Radioactive Waste Technologies
Contaminated Building Materials Dismantling
D&D Sampling and Analysis
In Situ Vitrification
Surface Decontamination

Remediation—Isolation/Containment Technologies
Capping
Ex Situ Solidification/Stabilization
Extraction Wells
In Situ Biodegradation (Saturated Zone)
In Situ Vitrification
Passive Water Treatment Permeable Barriers
Slurry Wall

Remediation—Remediation Evaluation/Support
D&D Sampling and Analysis
Groundwater Monitoring Wells
Monitoring
Professional Labor-Management
Residual Waste Management

Figure 5.1 Remediation Treatments and Technologies (cont.)

Cost Data for Site Work
Access Roads
Arterial Roads/Divided Highways
Bridges
Cleanup and Landscaping
Clear and Grub
Communications
Demolition—Buildings
Demolition—Catch Basins/Manholes
Demolition—Curbs
Demolition—Fencing
Demolition—Pavements
Demolition—Pipes
Demolition—Sidewalks
Excavation, Cut & Fill
Excavation, Trench/Chanel
Fencing
Gas Distribution
Heating/Cooling Distribution System
Lighting—Interstate, Roadway, Parking
Load and Haul
Materials Plan
Overhead Electrical Distribution
Parking Lots
Railroad Tracks and Crossings
Restriping Roadways/Parking Lots
Resurfacing Roadways/Parking Lots
Retaining Walls, C.I.P Concrete
Sanitary Sewer
Structures—Culverts
Treatment Plants/Lift Stations
Underground Electrical Distribution
Water Distribution
Water Storage Tanks

Contractor Costs
Contractor General Conditions
Contractor Overhead & Profit
Risk Contingency

Figure 5.1 Remediation Treatments and Technologies (cont.)

Chapter 6

Site Work and Utilities

Site work and utilities work items are a necessary part of most remediation projects, but are not considered environmental tasks. In many cases, site work and utilities can be a significant cost. Estimates are required for these items as part of the overall project cost. The types of site work and utilities items often found in environmental remediation projects include the following:

- Access roads
- Arterial roads/divided highways
- Bridges
- Cleanup and landscaping
- Clear and grub
- Communications
- Demolition—buildings
- Demolition—catch basins/manholes
- Demolition—curbs
- Demolition—fencing
- Demolition—pavements
- Demolition—pipe
- Demolition—sidewalks
- Excavation, cut and fill
- Excavation, trench/channel
- Fencing
- Gas distribution
- Heating/cooling distribution system
- Lighting, roadway or parking
- Load and haul
- Materials plant
- Overhead electrical distribution
- Parking lots
- Railroad tracks and crossings
- Restriping roadways/parking lots
- Resurfacing roadways/parking lots
- Retaining walls
- Sanitary sewer
- Sidewalks

- Sprinkler system
- Storm sewer
- Structures—culverts
- Treatment plants—lift stations
- Underground electrical distribution
- Water distribution
- Water storage tanks

Site work and utilities requirements for an environmental remediation project are determined based on the support features required by the particular technologies (e.g., electricity, concrete pads, piping, access roads) and the availability of these features at the site. For example, an air stripper requires an electric power supply and an access road for installation and operation. If these requirements are not available at the site, they will need to be provided. The estimator should be careful to identify these requirements and include them in the estimate. Often, site work and utilities are among the last details of the design process and are, therefore, likely to be left out of early estimates.

Chapters 8–56 describe the estimating process for environmental remediation technologies. Each chapter includes a list of site work and utilities items that may be required to support the technology. These lists serve as a starting place for identifying potential project requirements, but the cost engineer should work with the design team to determine requirements and then verify that these items are not available at the site before completing the estimate.

Chapter 7

Safety Levels

Worker safety level has a significant impact on labor and equipment productivity. Cost estimates must be adjusted to account for the reduced level of productivity associated with increased safety level requirements. Safety levels A, B, C, and D are based on the Occupational Safety and Health Administration (OSHA) regulations in 29 CFR Part 1910. Safety Level E corresponds to the EPA "No Hazard" designation.

The productivity factors shown in Figure 7.1 are based on information in EPA/600/2-87/087, "Compendium of Costs of Remedial Technologies at Hazardous Waste Facilities." These values provide reasonable estimates of the labor productivity that can be expected on a "typical" project, but the estimator should carefully consider the site conditions and make adjustments as appropriate. For example, in very hot conditions, worker productivity in Safety Levels A and B can decline further because the amount of time a field worker can remain in full coverage is limited by the heat.

Definitions of the 5 safety levels referred to throughout this book are as follows.

Safety Level A: Level A personal protection should be worn when the highest level of respiratory, skin, and eye protection is needed. Level A consists of a fully encapsulating suit with a self-contained breathing apparatus.

Safety Level B: Level B personal protection should be worn when the highest level of respiratory protection is needed, but a lower level of skin protection is required. Level A respiratory and eye protection is required, but the maximum skin protection of a fully encapsulating suit is not required.

Safety Level C: Level C personal protection should be worn when air-purifying respirators are required. Level C personal protection includes a full face air-purifying respirator and chemical-resistant clothing.

Safety Level D: Level D personal protection should be worn only as a basic work uniform and not on any site with respiratory or skin hazards. Level D provides minimal protection against respiratory hazards. Coveralls, a hard hat, leather or chemical-resistant boots/shoes, and safety glasses or chemical splash goggles are required. Personal dosimeters are also included for level D radioactive sites.

Safety Level E: Level E implies that no personal protection equipment is required, such as in an office environment or a normal construction environment. This safety level corresponds to the EPA "No Hazard" designation.

Safety Level	Level Of Productivity	
	Labor	Equipment
A	37%	50%
B	48%	60%
C	55%	75%
D	82%	100%
E	100%	100%

Figure 7.1 Level of Productivity

Part II

Cost Estimating for Remediation —Treatment Technologies

Chapter 8

Advanced Oxidation Processes

Advanced oxidation processes (AOPs) are used to remediate and purify aqueous and gaseous waste streams. Oxidation is popular because it is a destructive technology that can be used on site. Waste generators are required by state and federal law to reduce levels of pollutants in discharged waste streams and to eliminate potential hazards associated with the handling and transport of hazardous wastes. These requirements enhance the desirability of treatment technologies that result in partial or complete destruction of pollutants on site.

The oxidation process uses an oxidation and reduction mechanism for hazardous waste degradation. A number of different vendors have developed individual oxidation processes. Processes that generate hydroxyl radicals, which include ultraviolet (UV) photolyzed oxidation are generally categorized as *Advanced Oxidation Processes* (AOPs). AOP applications are the most common form of oxidation used for environmental remediation. This chapter guides the preparation of cost estimates for the AOP groups that use UV light to enhance generation of hydroxyl radicals.

AOPs destroy contaminants by chemical reaction with hydroxyl radicals. Hydroxyl radicals are formed through the various combinations of ozone and hydrogen peroxide, both with and without UV light. The AOP systems currently in use include O_3/high pH, H_2O_2+O_3, O_3/UV light, H_2O_2/ O_3/UV light. These variations can be used with or without a cavitation chamber. During the oxidation process, chemical bonds are broken, and new compounds are formed. The technology has the potential to oxidize various organic compounds to carbon dioxide, water, and salts.

Applications and Limitations

Applications

- Removes organics such as petroleum hydrocarbons, halogenated solvents, phenol, pentachlorophenol, pesticides, dioxins, glycols, polychlorinated biphenyls, creosote, Freon 113, vinyl chloride, BTEX, methyl tertiary butyl ether, and cyanide.
- Removes explosives such as TNT, RDX, and HMX.
- Has also proven to be effective on ferricyanides.

Limitations

- The aqueous stream must provide adequate light transmission.
- Effectiveness limited when free radical scavengers, such as excessive dosages of chemical oxidizers, are present.
- Effectiveness can be limited by the presence of heavy metal ions and insoluble oil or grease.
- Influent streams containing suspended solids or iron, may require pretreatment to prevent ongoing maintenance of the system.
- If treating volatile organics, off-gas treatment may be required to remove the volatilized contaminants.

Process Configurations and Treatment Train Configurations

There are limiting factors that affect both the viability and operation of AOP as a remediation approach. Key factors include:

- Heavy metal ion concentrations of the influent stream should be limited to less than 10 mg/l to reduce the potential for fouling.
- Typical electrical loads for AOP are 65 watts for ozone systems, and 15–60kW for hydrogen systems.
- Oxidant dosing systems are typically designed with multiple dosing points to ensure sufficient potential for oxidation to occur.
- Handling and management of oxidizers may require special safety considerations.
- AOPs can be configured in batch or continuous operation.
- Bench-scale or pilot testing is usually required to determine necessary design parameters.

Typical System Design Components

There are 3 general mass transfer classifications for treatment technologies: dilution, concentration, and destruction. To understand the difference between these applications, consider the following example. Trichloroethylene (TCE), a chlorinated solvent, is a common groundwater contaminant. There are several different treatment alternatives that can be used to remove TCE from an aqueous solution. These include air stripping (dilution, through media transfer), carbon adsorption (concentration), and UV oxidation using AOPs (destruction). Both air stripping and carbon adsorption transfer the contaminant to a different phase (gas or solid, respectively), which may lead to further treatment and/or disposal. The AOP system causes the TCE to react, forming nontoxic byproducts that can be released directly to the environment. AOP processes can treat cyanides, carbonyls, many aromatic compounds, phosphorus and sulfur pesticides, and polychlorinated biphenyl and dioxins. AOPs are not used for heavy metals, fluorides, acids, and many aliphatic compounds.

AOPs destroy contaminants by a chemical reaction with hydroxyl radicals. Hydroxyl radicals are formed through the multiple combinations of ozone (O_3), hydrogen peroxide (H_2O_2), and UV light. AOP systems that are currently being used include the following, each of which is used both with and without a cavitation chamber:

- O_3/high pH
- $H_2O_2 + O_3$
- O_3/UV light
- H_2O_2/O_3/UV light

During the oxidation process, chemical bonds are broken, and new compounds are formed. This technology can oxidize organic compounds to carbon dioxide, water, and salts. One disadvantage is the possible formation of intermediate compounds that are more hazardous than the original contaminant and less reactive to UV oxidation.

There are 6 questions that should be considered by the design team to determine if AOCs are a competitive treatment alternative. These are:

- Is a destruction technology preferred?
- Are there any restrictions on air discharge?
- Is the principle contaminant a poor candidate for air stripping?
- Do any of the principal contaminants load poorly on activated carbon in the liquid phase (i.e., <50 mg/g carbon @ 1 ppm)?
- Does the background water chemistry consume large amounts of liquid phase activated carbon or interfere with carbon operation (e.g., high iron or high chemical oxygen demand)?
- Are there handling or disposal concerns associated with loading contaminants on to activated carbon (e.g., loading and concentrating explosive or carcinogenic compounds on the carbon bed)?

If the answer is "yes" to 3 or more of these questions, then one should consider AOCs. The graph in Figure 8.1 analyzes the comparisons for UV oxidation and carbon adsorption.

There are 3 distinct classifications of systems that use ultraviolet light to break down contaminated waste streams. UV oxidation is the most common type of system. UV oxidation uses UV light in conjunction with an oxidant or cavitation to produce free radicals. These free radicals oxidize the contaminant to produce a simpler molecule that is nonhazardous. In this case, the UV light energy (photon) is absorbed by the oxidant—hydrogen peroxide (H_2O_2), ozone (O_3), or both—to form a hydroxyl radical (OH^-). Some systems use a combination of these 2 oxidants to improve the stoichiometry of the chemical reaction.

The second type of system is UV photolysis, which uses UV light energy absorption of the contaminant to break molecular bonds. As the bonds break, the contaminants become less complex and typically less toxic. Each contaminant has specific energy requirements (absorption wave length), and waste stream characteristics limit the applicability of the UV photolysis process. Because of these limitations and high operational costs, UV photolysis is not commercially viable.

The third and newest system is the photocatalytic process, which exposes a catalyst to the UV light source. Water, in either the air or the aqueous stream, then reacts with the catalyst to produce the hydroxyl radical (OH^-), which reacts with the contaminant. The most commonly used catalyst is titanium oxide. The photocatalytic technology has been demonstrated in tests, but is not in widespread use at this time.

This chapter deals primarily with the UV oxidation system. Ozone generation, hydrogen peroxide, UV source types, and system reaction chambers are included in the technology. Each of these components is complex and contains multiple parts. Pretreatment—such as media filtration, coagulation/flocculation, and pH adjustment—may be required and is discussed in Chapters 14 and 24 of this book. Effluent handling and disposal costs are not discussed here, but should be

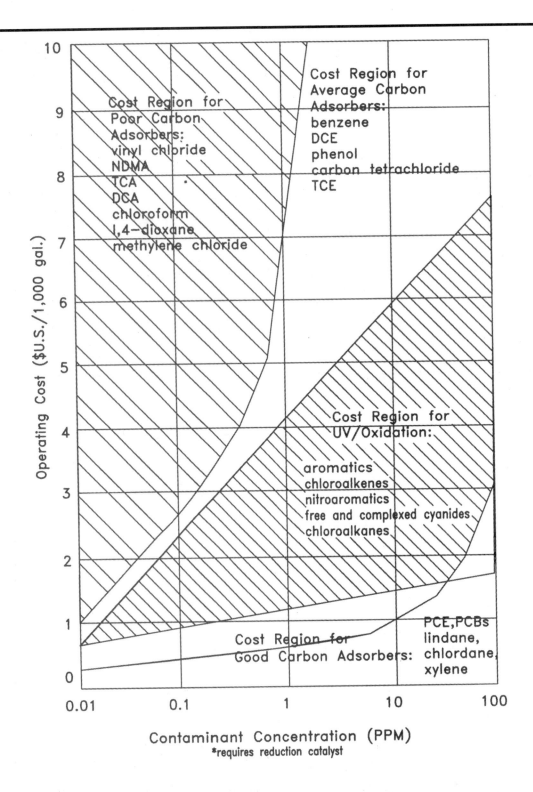

Figure 8.1 Cost Comparison Curves

evaluated and added to the estimate as required. Examples of disposal technologies include infiltration galleries, discharge to POTW, and injection wells. The equipment options discussed in this chapter treat aqueous waste streams exclusively.

Figures 8.2, 8.3, and 8.4 illustrate 3 of the most common system configurations for AOPs.

Basic Information Needed for Estimating

It is possible to create a reasonable cost estimate using a few required parameters. If more detailed information is known, one can create a more precise and site-specific estimate using a secondary set of parameters.

To estimate the cost of UV oxidation, certain information must be known. This information is discussed in the following paragraphs.

Contaminant Type

The type of contaminant is important to the UV oxidation process because it determines whether the technology is applicable. Figure 8.5

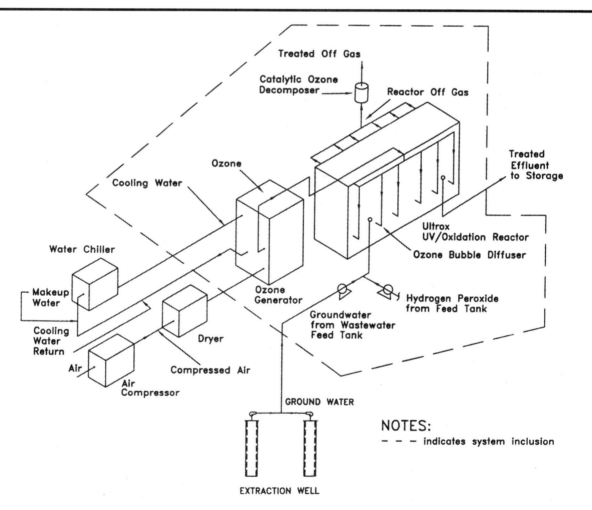

Figure 8.2 UV/Ozone Peroxide System

45

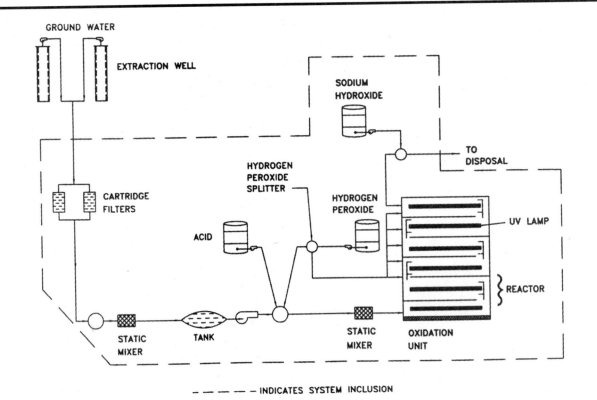

Figure 8.3 Peroxide System

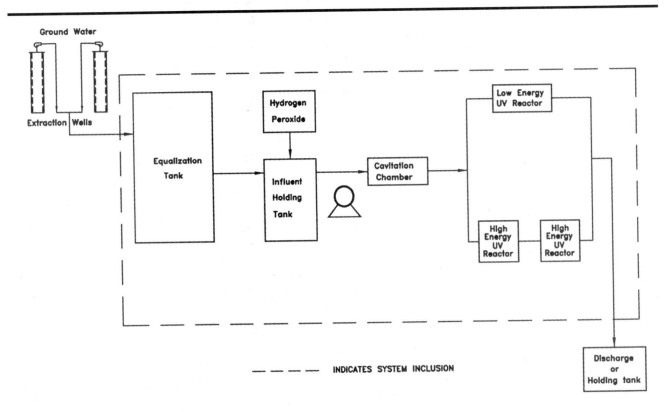

Figure 8.4 Cavitation/UV System

46

lists contaminants that have been treated using the three different UV oxidation system configurations. For a contaminant that is not listed, contact a vendor to determine if UV oxidation is appropriate.

Primary Contaminant

The primary contaminant is generally the contaminant with the highest concentration in the influent mixture. However, in some instances, the primary contaminant is established based on the complexity or difficulty of achieving destruction in the UV oxidation system. The primary contaminant is used to select the system configuration, as shown in Figure 8.5.

Secondary Contaminant

Based on the selection of the primary contaminant, a list of compatible secondary contaminants can be compiled. The secondary contaminant(s) availability is based on ability to be treated by the system design. The number of potential contaminants in the influent is limited only by the compatibility with the system design. See Figure 8.5 for compatibility of contaminants and systems.

Concentration

The concentration is used only for System Two configuration (see Figure 8.5). Concentration is measured in parts per million (ppm). Concentration can vary from 0.0001 ppm, or milligrams per liter (mg/l), to 10,000 ppm. The efficiency of the system and the process time varies with different concentration levels.

Influent Flow Rate

The flow rate determines the size of the treatment equipment. The most common reaction chamber is a stainless steel tank. A large system may require multiple reaction chambers. The valid range of flow rates depends on the system configuration and ranges from 0–10,000 gallons per minute (GPM). Figure 8.5 includes valid ranges for the three system configurations.

Treatment Period

The total treatment duration is divided into startup and operations and maintenance (O&M). The costs associated with the startup period (equipment acquisition, installation, and optimization) are considered capital costs, and the O&M costs are identified separately. Normally, 4–6 weeks are required for startup. The O&M period is generally measured in months. Most systems use a 24-hour operational day.

O&M costs are affected by the water characteristics, treatment process design, and operation. The variables related to water characteristics include the type and concentration of inorganic and organic contaminants, light transmittance of the water, and type and concentration of dissolved solids. UV and oxidant dosage are the variables directly related to treatment process design. Once the system design is fixed, the lamp maintenance and oxidant dosage costs are essentially fixed. These operating expenses are based on the waste stream characteristics. For example, if the turbidity of the influent increases, the efficiencies of the oxidant(s) and UV light are reduced, which increases the operating expenses to achieve the same treatment criteria.

Worker Safety Level

Safety level refers to the levels required by OSHA 29 CFR Part 1910. The four levels are designated as A, B, C, and D; where "A" is the most protective, and "D" is the least protective. A safety level of E is also included to simulate normal construction, "no hazard" conditions as prescribed by the EPA.

Applicable System Configurations By Contaminant			
Contaminant	**System Configuration[1]**		
	One	Two	Three
1,1 Dichloroethane	NA	D	A
1,2 Dichloroethane	D	NA	NA
1,1 Dichloroethylene	A	D	A
1,4 Diethylene dioxide	A	D	A
1,1,2,2 Tetrachloroethane	D	NA	NA
Bis (2-chloroethyl) ether	NA	NA	D
cis-1,2 Dichloroethylene	D	NA	NA
trans 1,2 Dichloroethylene	D	NA	NA
Acetone	D	NA	NA
Atrazine	NA	D	A
Benzene	A	D	A
Carbon Tetrachloride	D	NA	NA
Chlordane	D	NA	NA
Chlorobenzene	NA	D	A
Chloroform	NA	D	NA
Citric Acid	D	NA	NA
Cresols	D	NA	NA
Creosote	NA	NA	D
Cyanides	D	NA	A
DBCP	D	NA	NA
DNT	D	NA	NA
Dioxins	D	NA	A
Dioxanes	NA	NA	D
EDB	**D**	**NA**	**NA**
EDTA	D	NA	NA
Ethylbenzene	D	NA	NA
Freon	NA	D	A
Furans	D	NA	NA
HMX	D	NA	NA
Iron Cyanide	NA	D	NA
Lindane	D	NA	NA

Figure 8.5a Applicable System Configurations by Contaminant

NA = Not Applicable
D = Default
A = Applicable and Available

Applicable System Configurations By Contaminant			
Contaminant	**System Configuration**[1]		
	One	**Two**	**Three**
Methyl-Ethyl Ketone (MEK)	NA	NA	D
Methylisobutal Ketone	NA	NA	D
Methylene chloride	NA	NA	D
Nitrobenzene	D	NA	NA
Nitrophenol	D	NA	NA
Nitrosodimethylamine (NDMA)	NA	D	NA
PAHs	D	NA	A
PCB	D	NA	A
Perchloroethylene	A	D	NA
Pentachlorophenol	A	D	A
Phenol	A	D	NA
Phthalates	D	NA	NA
RDX	D	NA	NA
Tetrachloroethene	NA	NA	D
Tetrahydrofuran	NA	NA	D
Toluene	A	D	NA
Trichloroethane	NA	D	A
Trichloroethylene	A	D	A
Triglycol dichloride ether	NA	NA	D
Trinitrobenzene (TNB)	D	NA	NA
Trinitrotoluene (TNT)	A	D	NA
Xylene	A	D	NA
Vinyl Chloride	A	D	A
Valid Ranges			
Flow Rate	1 to 250	1 to 10,000	1 to 25
UV Radiation Source	LI	HI	Both, HI
Ozone Generation	D	NA	NA
Hydrogen Peroxide	A	D	A
Cavitation Chamber	NA	NA	D

[1]System Configurations:
Configuration One: U/V Ozone Peroxide System
Configuration Two: Peroxide System
Configuration Three: Cavitation - U/V System
Flow Rate in Gallons Per Minute (GPM)
LI = Low Intensity UV Radiation Source
HI = High Intensity UV Radiation Source
NA = Not Applicable
D = Default System Process
A = Applicable and Available

Figure 8.5b Applicable System Configurations by Contaminant

Design Information Needed for Detailed Estimates

Following are descriptions of the types of detailed information that, when available, can add detail and accuracy to estimates. Also included are design criteria and estimating rules of thumb that the estimator typically uses to determine values that are not known, or to check information provided by others.

Ultraviolet System Design

The components of the UV system design are the UV radiation source, ozone generation, hydrogen peroxide, and cavitation chamber. The default values are set based on the selection of the primary contaminant.

UV Radiation Source

The UV radiation source depends on the primary contaminant. Potential sources of radiation are high- and low-intensity UV lamps. The lamps play an important role in the formation of OH and in direct photolysis of some contaminants. The electrical requirements for most of the UV systems may impose limits based on electrical availability at the site; therefore, the electrical output of the lamps is a design consideration. The output of the lamp must be sufficient to facilitate the oxidation reaction, but not excessive. Electrical costs can be minimized by optimizing the energy requirement with the type of contaminant and concentration. Lamp selection is based on the selection of one of the three system configurations shown in Figure 8.5.

Ozone Generation

Ozone generation is not required for all systems. Ozone generation is a function of the type of treatment equipment selected to remediate the specific contaminants to the desired cleanup level. Costs for this aspect of the UV system are based on the equipment used to generate the ozone, the amount of ozone required, and the operation and maintenance of the handling and production equipment. Ozone systems typically sparge the ozone in the system using some type of bubble diffuser. Influent and effluent ozone concentrations can be monitored by UV spectrophotometry. Ozone generation is included in System One configuration and is not available for the other system configurations. This is based on the selection of the primary contaminant (see Figure 8.5).

Hydrogen Peroxide

Hydrogen peroxide is added through a traditional feed system comprised of a tank with secondary containment, one to two feed pumps, and distribution piping. Major cost considerations are the tank and the quantity of hydrogen peroxide used by the system. Most UV oxidation systems use hydrogen peroxide as a source of hydroxyl radicals; therefore, hydrogen peroxide is available for all three system configurations.

Cavitation Chamber

Cavitation chamber is another method used to create OH radicals. It may or may not be used in combination with hydrogen peroxide. Cavitation is a relatively new process that is limited to lower flow conditions. System Three includes cavitation system as the typical system configuration.

Pretreatment Equipment

The pretreatment equipment serves two functions: first, to equalize the influent flow rate and, second, to reduce the suspended solids content of the influent. Cartridge filters and equalization tanks are used as pretreatment equipment.

Cartridge Filters

Cartridge filters are used to reduce the amount of suspended solids entering the UV reactor. This increases the transmission of UV light to the contaminated matrix and decreases the amount of competition for oxidants. Filter selection is based on the flow rate; package systems handle flows of 0–100 GPM, and multiple 60 GPM filters handle flows that exceed 100 GPM. Filter size options include:

- 15 GPM CPVC
- 30 GPM CPVC
- 45 GPM CPVC
- 25 GPM PP
- 42 GPM PP
- 60 GPM PP
- 0–50 GPM Equipment
- 50–100 GPM Equipment

Equalization Tanks

Equalization tanks help to maintain a consistent influent waste stream. For example, if the system is treating groundwater from multiple extraction wells, the equalization tank provides a repository for the water to be mixed (i.e., consistent contaminant loading), allows suspended solids to settle out, and produces a consistent influent flow rate. Tank selection is based on the influent flow rate. Options typically available are shown in Figure 8.6.

Influent Piping

The influent piping diameter depends on the flow rate. The most common influent flow mechanism is force main. Typically, the piping would be PVC, placed above ground. Other options include:

- Carbon steel
- Stainless steel
- Polyethylene
- Double-walled (DW) PVC
- DW carbon steel
- DW stainless steel
- Cast iron

Effluent Piping

The effluent piping is usually the same type and size as the influent piping.

Other Related Costs

The following items are the other related costs for UV oxidation.

Building, Pad, Covered Area for Treatment Equipment

The system is assumed to be assembled on a concrete slab. Clearing and construction of a slab to support the system and associated workspace should be included in the estimate. Temporary or permanent buildings may need to be added, although the equipment can be operated outdoors.

Treatability Study and Pilot Plant

During the initial evaluation of the waste stream, a treatability study is performed at the vendor's facility using generator-supplied water samples. Following this study, a mobile pilot plant may be sent to the site to further refine the treatment requirements. These activities are used to identify operating parameters such as hydraulic retention time, ozone dose, hydrogen peroxide dose, UV lamp intensity, influent pH level, and gas/liquid (O_3/H_2O_2) flow rate ratio. Generally, the vendor charges the generator for these services.

System Maintenance

System maintenance requirements are highly variable and can represent a large portion of the total cost. Maintenance requirements can be segregated into the ozonation system, UV lamp assembly, ozone decomposer unit, and miscellaneous components.

Equalization Tanks	
55 gal.	Nalgene Horz. XLPE Tank w/o legs
110 gal.	Nalgene Horz. XLPE Tank w/o legs
200 gal.	Nalgene Horz. XLPE Tank w/o legs
300 gal.	Nalgene Horz. XLPE Tank w/o legs
500 gal.	Nalgene Horz. XLPE Tank w/o legs
1,000 gal.	Nalgene Horz. XLPE Tank w/o legs
1,650 gal.	Nalgene Horz. XLPE Tank w/o legs
2,500 gal.	Nalgene Horz. XLPE Tank w/o legs
60 gal.	Nalgene Horz. XLPE Tank w/ legs
125 gal.	Nalgene Horz. XLPE Tank w/ legs
225 gal.	Nalgene Horz. XLPE Tank w/ legs
300 gal.	Nalgene Horz. XLPE Tank w/ legs
500 gal.	Nalgene Horz. XLPE Tank w/ legs
1,575 gal.	Conical Bottom Vertical XLPE Tank
2,200 gal.	Conical Bottom Vertical XLPE Tank
2,600 gal.	Conical Bottom Vertical XLPE Tank
3,000 gal.	Conical Bottom Vertical XLPE Tank
4,200 gal.	Conical Bottom Vertical XLPE Tank
6,000 gal.	Conical Bottom Vertical XLPE Tank
8,000 gal.	Conical Bottom Vertical XLPE Tank
550 gal.	S.S. Abv. Grd. WW Holding Tank, rental
630 gal.	PE Abv. Grd. WW Holding Tank, rental
400 gal.	PE WW Tank, rental
4,000 gal.	PE WW Trailer Mounted Tank, rental
6,000 gal.	PE WW Abv. Grd. Tank, rental
21,000 gal.	Steel WW Holding Tank, rental
21,000 gal.	Steel WW hold tank open top rental

Figure 8.6 Equalization Tanks

Typically, the ozonation system can be divided into three operations: air preparation system, ozone generator, and ozone contacting equipment. The air preparation system requires a particulate filter, compressor, refrigeration line or cooling water source, and desiccant dryer. The ozone generator requires cleaning and maintenance of the dielectric tubes. Maintenance requirements for the contact equipment involve checking piping, valves, fittings, supports, brackets, and spargers for deterioration.

Lamp assembly maintenance consists of replacing bulbs and controlling scaling.

The ozone decomposer requires daily checks on the operating temperature and routine maintenance on the heating element and catalyst.

Other system maintenance issues include checking flow meters, valves, pumps, pipelines, and wastewater and chemical feed tanks.

Effluent Handling and Disposal

The system effluents are treated wastewater, treatment residuals, and gas emissions. The treated wastewater may be discharged to a POTW, to surface water, to land surface, or reinjected to groundwater, depending on the system treatment efficiency and regulatory discharge permit requirements. For UV systems, treatment residuals are any materials that precipitate during the treatment process. In most cases, the amount of residual is minimal. Gas emissions are considered in the system design, since the release of ozone and other system byproducts (chlorine, hydrochloric acid, carbon monoxide) are regulated under the Clean Air Act. In systems using ozone, the process should be designed to prevent the emission of ozone and stripped volatile organic compound emissions.

Sampling and Analysis

Monitoring programs are site- and contaminant-specific. Typical sampling and analysis includes pH, total suspended solids, total dissolved solids, cyanide, nitroaromatics, dioxins, PCB, total petroleum hydrocarbons, volatile organic compounds, and PAH analyses. The number of samples taken is based on one per day for the first week, weekly for the first month, and one per month thereafter. The influent liquid stream is tested for operating factors, and the effluent is tested for contaminant(s).

Site Work and Utilities

Site work and utilities that may be applicable for UV oxidation include:

- Access roads
- Clear and grub
- Excavation, cut and fill
- Fencing
- Load and haul
- Overhead electrical distribution
- Underground electrical distribution
- Water distribution

These must also be included in the estimate.

Conclusion   AOPs are a proven method of on-site contaminant destruction. These systems are becoming more common for a wide variety of site remediation problems. The primary cost drivers for these systems are the type and concentration of contaminant, the system type, the flow rate, and the operating period. Different system configurations can be used effectively on many of the same primary contaminants; the selection of the configuration may be largely driven by cost considerations. The estimator should work with the design team to evaluate different design alternatives and determine which configuration leads to the most cost-effective solution based on capital costs, operating periods, and project requirements.

Chapter 9

Air Sparging

Air sparging is an in situ process in which air is bubbled through a contaminated aquifer to remove volatile contaminants, such as volatile organic compounds (VOCs) and fuels, from groundwater. Injected air bubbles move vertically and horizontally through the soil, creating an underground air stripping process that removes contaminants through volatilization. Generally, the air bubbles carry the contaminants to a vapor extraction system. Vapor extraction is used with air sparging to remove the generated vapor phase contamination. Air sparging is also sometimes used in conjunction with groundwater extraction and treatment systems to enhance the overall performance and recovery rate of those systems.

The basic goal of air sparging is to maintain a high flow rate, which increases the contact between the groundwater and the soil. This process "strips" more volatile contaminants from the groundwater than would be possible with vapor extraction or groundwater extraction and treatment systems alone. The best operating flow for air sparging ranges from 10^{-2} cm/sec to 10^{-6} cm/sec. At higher permeability, other remediation methods may be more effective. At lower permeability, the systems are generally ineffective because it is harder to move air.

The most common air sparging process injects air into groundwater through injection wells. Typically, pressurized air is injected below the water table. The injected air bubbles move horizontally and vertically through the saturated soil zone. Volatile compounds that are exposed to this sparged air convert to gas phase and are carried by the air into the vadose zone.

From the vadose zone, the volatiles either migrate to the ground surface and are released to the atmosphere or are captured by a soil vapor extraction system. Vapor extraction can be added to the treatment train through the use of a soil vapor extraction (SVE) system (see Chapter 32). The sparged air contains a high dissolved oxygen content, which enhances natural biodegradation.

In low permeability (10^{-4} cm/sec) heterogeneous formations, sparging requires a groundwater recovery system so that mobilized dissolved hydrocarbons are not pushed downgradient. Groundwater recovery is typically performed with extraction wells (see Chapter 43) and some form of post-extraction treatment.

Applications and Limitations

Applications

- Removes volatile organic compounds (VOCs) and some fuels and semi-volatile organic compounds (SVOCs) from groundwater. These include less volatile and tightly sorbed contaminants that are not amenable to vapor extraction.
- Enhances natural biodegradation when oxygen is added to the groundwater.
- Enhances co-metabolism of chlorinated organics when methane is added to the groundwater.
- Most effective for sites with relatively permeable, homogenous soil conditions. This allows for sufficient contact between the sparged air and the media while enabling effective extraction.
- Air sparging is generally applicable for depths to groundwater greater than 5'.

Limitations

- Fine-grained, low permeability soils will limit effectiveness.
- Low permeability heterogeneous formations require a groundwater recovery system (extraction wells).
- Potential for uncontrolled flow of dangerous vapors as air-flow through saturated zone may not be uniform.
- Site geology and depth to contaminants must be known.
- May be ineffective if air flow does not reach contaminated zones due to soil heterogeneities.
- Should not be used at sites with free-floating product due to the potential for product migration from groundwater mounding.
- Need to use air compressor if above the maximum pressure range for blowers (typically above 15 psi).

Process Configurations and Treatment Train Considerations

- Soil vapor extraction (SVE) is often used in tandem with air sparging to collect vapors from the sparging process.
- When air sparging is used in conjunction with SVE, the location of the sparge well is important. SVE wells must be located to encompass the entire range of influence of the sparge wells so that volatilized contaminants are properly captured.
- Several commercially available, proprietary in-well technologies perform a combination of air sparging and soil vapor extraction in a single well.
- Extracted vapors may require treatment, although this may be avoided by adjustment of injection and extraction rates.

System design should consider the possibility of aquifer clogging from iron precipitation or biomass accumulation caused by increased oxygen in the aquifer.

Typical System Design Elements

The basic components of an air sparging system include:

- Air injection wells (sparge points)
- An air compressor
- A blower
- Air flow monitoring and control instruments
- Monitoring systems

Figure 9.1 is a schematic of a basic air sparging system. The soil vapor extraction component is illustrated as part of this system since it is frequently used in conjunction with air sparging. Air injection wells are screened below the depth of the dissolved contamination. Vapor-extraction wells are screened in the vadose zone and sometimes down to or into the water table. Nests of air injection and vapor extraction wells, installed in the same bore hole, are also used (see Figure 9.2).

Remediation progress is monitored by analyzing groundwater samples taken from the extraction wells, and by using groundwater monitoring wells. These analyses track the magnitude and extent of dissolved contamination. Monitoring wells are generally installed as part of the site study process that precedes the remediation phase, but additional wells are required in some instances. (See Chapter 57 for a discussion of remedial action phase monitoring.)

Sparge points are designed to provide overlapping influence and adequate site coverage. Design of the air sparging system requires pilot tests to determine the radius of influence of the air sparging points and the presence of any barriers that would significantly affect air flow. The pilot tests are generally completed during the remedial design phase, but additional pilot tests are sometimes required during the installation of the system.

Air sparging system designs vary. While some air sparging networks are installed along the downgradient edge of the dissolved plume, others are designed to encompass the entire plume. Networks may be composed in a variety of configurations such as: sparge points in the center of the plume and vapor extraction points along the perimeter, sparge and extraction points in nests, or an equal number of nests and sparge points.

Injected air may be at ambient temperature; it may be steam enhanced; or it may be heated. The use of heat and/or steam reduces the treatment time and increases the compounds that can be stripped. However, these systems cost significantly more to operate and maintain than ambient air systems, so cost/benefit should be carefully considered during the design stage.

Basic Information Needed for Estimating

It is possible to create a reasonable budget cost estimate for air sparging using a few required parameters. If more detailed information is known, one can create a more precise and site-specific estimate using a secondary set of parameters.

To estimate the cost of the system, certain basic information must be known. This information is discussed in the following paragraphs.

Soil Type
Air sparging network specifications depend on the soil type, area extent of contamination, and depth to ground water. General groupings of soil type are: coarse sand, silty sand, silt, or clay. The radius of influence of compressed air extends over a longer distance in soils with higher permeability.

Surface Area of Groundwater Contamination
Depth & Number of Air Sparge Points
This parameter is used in conjunction with the air sparge point spacing to calculate the number of air sparge points (ASPs). The technology

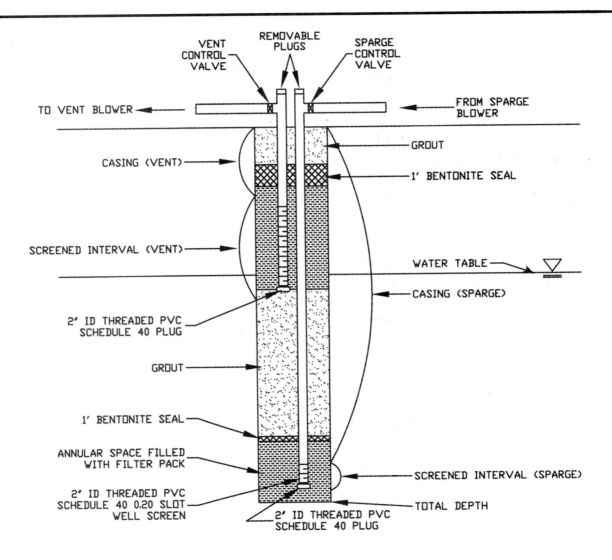

Figure 9.1 Typical Air Sparge/Vent Point Construction

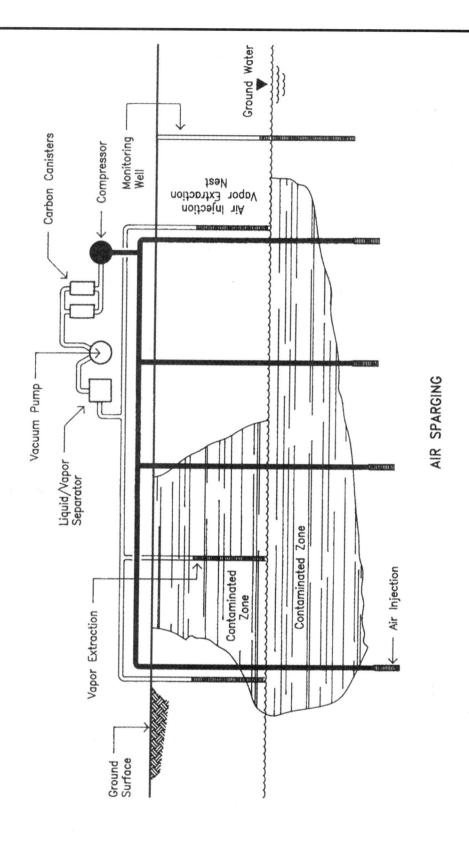

Figure 9.2 Closed Loop Air Sparging System

assumes that a network of sparge points will encompass the area with a grid installation pattern. The square foot value can be derived from site sampling data or calculations using historical contaminant release information and site subsurface characteristics. The valid range is 100–1,000,000 S.F.

Depth to Groundwater

This parameter must be less than the depth to the base of contamination. The difference between the depth to groundwater and the depth to base of contamination determines the water column height for air sparging. Typically, water column heights of up to 30' are within the pressure range of conventional blowers. Compressors are typically needed for sparging water column depths greater than 30'.

Depth to Base of Contamination

This parameter determines the depth of the air sparge points. Air injection must be below the contamination to volatilize the contaminants. The Depth to Base of contamination must be greater than the Depth to Groundwater. Air sparge points are generally placed at a depth 4' below the base of the contamination. The depth to the base of groundwater contamination minus the depth to groundwater cannot be greater than 65', or it will exceed the capacity of the systems. However, since air sparging applies to volatile contaminants, and volatiles are low-density compounds, dissolved contamination will typically be less than 30'.

Treatment Period

The total treatment duration can be divided into a startup period and an O&M period. The costs associated with the startup period (equipment acquisition, installation, and optimization) are considered capital costs; the O&M costs are identified separately. While not necessary, it may be helpful to divide the project into startup and O&M periods to allocate costs to different types of labor and often to different contractors.

Worker Safety Level

The contaminant(s) at the site affect the safety of workers. Safety level refers to the levels required by OSHA in 29 CFR Part 1910. The four levels are designated as A, B, C, and D, where "A" is the most protective, and "D" is the least protective. A complete description of safety levels and associated requirements is located in Chapter 7.

Design Information Needed for Detailed Estimates

Following are descriptions of the types of detailed information that, when available, can add detail and accuracy to estimates for air sparging systems. Also included are design criteria and estimating rules of thumb that the estimator typically uses to determine values that are not known, or to check information provided by others.

Air Sparge Points (ASPs) and Piping

The number and spacing of air sparge points (ASPs) are key cost drivers for air sparging systems. If the values are not known, the information provided in Figure 9.3 can provide an approximate number of air sparge points based on the soil type. The radius of influence depends on the soil type. The spacing—and ultimately the number of—air sparge points depends on the soil type.

The number of ASPs is calculated based on well spacing and the surface area of groundwater contamination using the following equation:

$$N = \frac{A}{(p \times L^2)/4}$$

Where:

N = the number of ASPs
A = the surface area of groundwater contamination
L = lateral well spacing

Drilling Method

The most common drilling method for wells with a total depth of less than 150' is a hollow stem auger. The mud rotary method is commonly used for drilling greater than 50'. Another option is air rotary drilling. Figure 9.4 indicates bore hole diameters for different drilling methods.

ASP Construction Material

ASPs and monitoring wells (MWs) are typically constructed of either PVC or stainless steel screen and casing. Primary selection considerations are cost and material compatibility with the contaminant. For example, for contaminants that are corrosive to PVC, stainless steel would be required. The most common ASP material is Schedule 40 PVC for the construction of wells less than 85' deep. When the depth of the wells is greater than or equal to 85', Schedule 80 PVC material is generally used for greater strength.

Where practical, all connection piping is generally installed above ground. The estimator should consider whether site conditions such as traffic, safety hazards, or other conditions require underground piping. In either case, the most common approach to connection piping is Schedule 40 PVC, 2" diameter pipe. For very long runs or larger manifold applications, larger pipe may be required. If design documents are not available, a reasonable rule of thumb for connection piping is the radius of influence times the number of ASPs, plus half again.

Depth of ASP

The depth of a sparge well depends on the depth of groundwater contamination. Typically, air sparge points are installed to the depth of

Air Sparge System Design Parameters	
Soil Type	Lateral Well Spacing (Feet)
Coarse Sand	40
Silty Sand	20
Silt	15
Clay	10

Figure 9.3 Air Sparge System Design Parameters

Note: Values are based on empirical data. The radius of influence is dissolved oxygen, which is more conservative than pressure influence. The air injection pressure is assumed to be 15 pounds per square inch.

contamination plus 4'. Short screen intervals are generally used in air sparging wells because the majority of the air exits through the top or the screened interval where pressure head is minimized. A typical application would be a screen interval of 2'.

Drill Cutting Containment

Drill cuttings are generally placed in 55-gallon drums and stored until disposal options have been evaluated for contamination levels and, if required, follow-on treatment and disposal.

Soil Sample Collection

Sample collection during bore hole advancement allows characterization of the geology beneath the site and definition of the magnitude and extent of contaminants in the vadose zone. Generally, regulations require that soil samples shall be collected every 5', or at each change in lithology, whichever is less. Drill cuttings can be collected as the bore hole is advanced for general geologic information. Discrete samples are collected in unconsolidated sediment using a variety of methods including split spoon, shelby tubes and the California brass ring. Samples are screened with an Organic Vapor Analyzer (OVA) for volatile organics and described for the lithologic log by the geologist supervising drilling.

If laboratory analysis is required, the estimator should determine how many soil samples and what type of analysis will be required, then add these soil analyses to the estimate.

Blower Specifications

Air injection pressures are governed by the static water head above the sparge point, the air entry pressure of the saturated soils, and the gas injection operating flow rate. The air injection pressure assumed when determining the radius of influence of the air sparge points is generally 15 pounds per square inch (psi). Overpressurizing the sparge system can cause increased downgradient contaminant migration as a result of turbulent air flow. Although 15 psi is used as a rule of thumb, the psi value should be slightly greater than the hydraulic head.

Formation Type	Average Well Depth	Drilling Method	Casing Diameter	Bore Hole Diameter	Well Material
Consolidated	0–100	Air Rotary	2	6	PVC SCH 40
Consolidated	101–300	Air Rotary	4	8	PVC SCH 80
Consolidated	301–500	Air Rotary	4	8	SS
Consolidated	>500	Air Rotary	4	8	SS
Unconsolidated	0–100	Hollow Stem Auger	2	8	PVC SCH 40
Unconsolidated	101–300	Air Rotary	4	8	PVC SCH 80
Unconsolidated	301–500	Air Rotary	4	8	SS
Unconsolidated	>500	Air Rotary	4	8	SS

Figure 9.4 Formation Type

The equation to calculate static water head is:

$$SWH = (D - DTW) \times 0.434$$

Where:

SWH = static water head (psi)
D = well depth (ft)
DTW = depth to water (ft)
0.434 = conversion factor (from ft of water to lbs/S.F.)

Blower Type

Air injection blowers are oil-less or oil-free reciprocation (piston-type) compressors or rotary lobe-type high-pressure blowers. Blower attachments include: particulate filter on inlet, pressure control valve on pressure side of sparge blower, overpressure relief valve, and noise silencers. A full range of blowers are on the market with varying combinations of SCFM, H.P., and psi. The blower chosen should be site-specific. Figure 9.5 provides a range of blowers and selection criteria.

Number of Blowers

The number of blowers required depends on the number of air sparge points in the system. Flow rates typically used in the field are between 3–10 CFM per sparge point.

The equation to calculate the required flow rate is:

$$Q = N \times 10 \text{ CFM}$$

Where:

Q = flow rate (CFM)
N = number of sparge points
10 CFM = the high end of the range typically applied

The quantity of blowers is then determined by the following equation:

$$B = Q/\text{CFM of the blower}$$

Where:

B = number of blowers
Q = flow rate (CFM)

Related Costs The previous sections describe the technology and the direct work elements required to install and operate an air sparging system. This chapter describes other cost elements that are typically required for implementation.

Figure 9.5 Blower Type Based On Water Column Height

Blower Type Based On Water Column Height	
Water Column Height (Ht.) (Feet)	Blower Type
Ht. = less than 11'	98 SCFM, 3.2 H.P., 5 psi
Ht. = 11' to 23'	170 SCFM, 10.3 H.P., 10 psi
Ht. = 23' to 35'	163 SCFM, 15 H.P., 15 psi
Ht. = 35' to 65'	426 SCFM, 84 H.P., 30 psi

Remedial Action Professional Labor

The number of staff hydrogeologist hours includes time spent supervising drillers, OVA screening, and collecting split spoon samples. The following rules of thumb may be used for hydrogeologist labor-hours related to well installation:

- If sample collection is required, then supervision for the ASP installation will be at a rate of 20' per hour plus 2 hours per point for ASP completion.
- If sample collection is not required, then supervision for the ASP installation will be at a rate of 40' per hour plus 2 hours per point for ASP completion.

Decontamination of Drilling Equipment

Decontamination procedures for the monitoring well screen, riser, and caps, as well as decontamination of drilling tools (e.g., hollow stem augers), will be conducted prior to and between each bore hole/well installation. Typical procedures consist of steam cleaning with a high-pressure steam-generating pressure washer and detergent.

Typical decontamination procedures for split spoon samplers, bailers, and hand augers consist of:

- Cleaning with tap water and detergent using a brush
- Rinsing thoroughly with tap water
- Rinsing with deionized water
- Rinsing twice with pesticide-grade isopropanol
- Rinsing with organic-free deionized water
- Allowing to air dry

Operations and Maintenance

Maintenance of the air sparge system includes adjusting the blower flow rate and valves, and general maintenance. A reasonable rule of thumb is for a maintenance/sample crew to be on site once a week for the first month and once a month thereafter. Sampling and analysis should also be added as appropriate.

Site Work and Utilities

Site work and utilities, if applicable, must be covered by the estimate. Possible items include:

- Overhead electrical distribution
- Fencing and signage
- Clear and grub

Conclusion

Air sparging is an active treatment process that is typically used with other technologies, such as soil vapor extraction or groundwater pump-and-treat systems. Key cost drivers for air sparging are the length of time the system will operate and the size of the sparge field. The estimator should work closely with the design engineer during the planning stages to optimize these elements.

Chapter 10

Air Stripping

Air stripping is a process that removes Volatile Organic Compounds (VOCs) from water. The process has been widely and successfully applied to groundwater remediation for a number of contaminants, including TCE, benzene, toluene, xylene, and methylene chloride. A number of different air stripping systems have been proven effective for groundwater remediation. These include single packed towers, multiple packed towers in series, parallel towers, low-profile tray systems, and others. Both packed-tower air strippers and low-profile tray stacks are used to treat extracted groundwater impacted by VOCs.

In an air stripper, contaminated water and induced air streams flow countercurrently through trays or packing. This allows mass transfer contact, which enables contaminants to volatilize into the air stream. Packed towers are typically cylindrical shells filled with plastic packing. Low-profile systems have highly efficient trays that can achieve similar levels of contaminant removal with significantly reduced overall equipment heights.

Applications and Limitations

Applications

- Removes VOCs from water. Also successfully used to remediate groundwater contaminated with TCE, BTEX (benzene, toluene, ethyl benzene, and xylene), chloroethane, DCE, PCE, and methylene chloride.
- Typical liquid loading rate for air stripping towers varies from 5–30 GPM/S.F.
- Air stripping at elevated temperatures will increase removal rates.

Limitations

- Will not remove inorganic compounds.
- Typically effective only for organic compounds with a Henry's Law Constant greater than 10 atmospheres/mole fraction.
- Effluent off-gas may require additional treatment before release.
- Local zoning laws may restrict tall towers.

- Contaminated water may require pretreatment or periodic column cleaning to prevent packed towers from fouling or plugging.
- Lowering the pH of the incoming stream in a holding tank or sump can mitigate iron fouling. Inorganic fouling may also occur as a result of manganese oxidation and carbonate deposition. As a rule of thumb, for Fe and Mg concentrations less than 2 mg/l, only routine maintenance is required.
- Chlorine treatment of the incoming stream can mitigate biofouling.
- Contaminated groundwater may require preheating for compounds with low volatility at ambient temperatures.
- Thermal Desorption and Catalytic Oxidation are typically used to treat high initial concentrations of VOCs in off-gas. For lower contaminant concentrations, Carbon Adsorption may be used. Carbon Adsorption usually requires preheating and relative humidity of the influent gas of less than 40%.
- If water influent flow fluctuates excessively, a holding tank or sump may be necessary to equalize flow.
- Additional treatment of water effluent may be necessary to reduce contaminants to target levels.
- Tower height is directly related to removal efficiency in conventionally designed towers. The taller the tower, the greater the efficiency.
- Air-to-water ratio ranges from 10:1 to 200:1 (volume equivalent basis) depending on the volatility of the target contaminants.

Typical System Design Elements

The principle air stripper components are as follows:

- Tower shell and internals, or low-profile unit
- Packing materials
- Blower
- Tower support system (a structural skid slab)
- Piping for raw contaminated water and processed water
- Instrumentation controls

See Figure 10.1 for an illustration of a packed tower system and Figure 10.2 for an illustration of a low profile tray system. Water enters the top of the tower and flows down the packing as air is forced up from the bottom of the tower. The volatile, soluble components in the water are transferred to the air mass and exhausted at the top of the column.

The mass transfer process from liquid to vapor phase (the starting point in the design process) is expressed by an equation that incorporates the required operating parameters. The key variables in the equation are Henry's Law Constant and the mass transfer coefficient. Henry's Law Constant is a measure of the "strippability" of the compound. The Constant has been determined for a number of VOCs, and the values are available in published tables. The mass transfer coefficient is a function of gas/liquid physical properties and packing surface area, and can be determined by applying appropriate physical laws and mathematical expressions.

There are 4 other treatment processes that maybe required, depending on site-specific and regulatory considerations. These processes are defined in the following paragraphs.

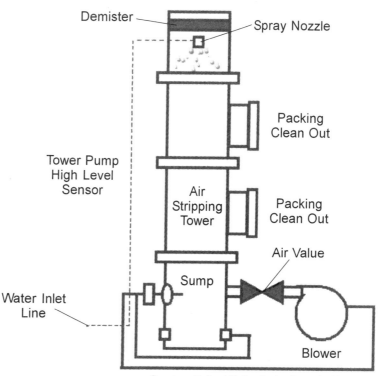

Figure 10.1 Packed-Tower Air
Stripper

Courtesy Federal Technologies Roundtable (www.frtr.gov)

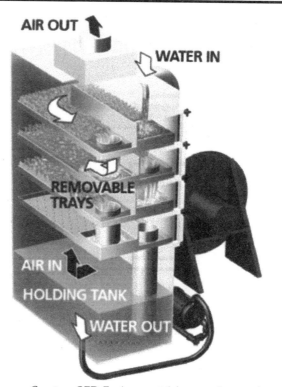

Figure 10.2 Low-Profile Tray
System

Courtesy QED Environmental (www.qedenv.com)

Air Emissions Treatment

Since all of the air-stripped contaminants are transferred to the exhausted air, local regulations may require air emissions treatment. Standard air treatments include activated carbon adsorption, catalytic oxidation, and thermal desorption. Activated carbon adsorption and thermal desorption are discussed in Chapters 12 and 28. Using an activated carbon adsorption system substantially increases operations and maintenance (O&M) costs, because the carbon canisters must be changed regularly during the operating life of the stripping unit.

Catalytic oxidation is generally applied during system startup when contaminant concentrations are high. Costs are limited to unit rental and electric power charges. Additional costs can be incurred when contaminant extraction causes the oxidation level to fall above and below the efficient operational range.

Thermal desorption is applied similarly to catalytic oxidation. The cost of thermal desorption is limited to unit rental and additional combustion agents, such as propane.

Influent Water Pretreatment

Influent water pretreatment reduces fouling, or the accumulation of precipitates on the packing. Iron fouling is most common and is mitigated by lowering the pH of the influent in a treatment tank prior to stripping. Biological fouling (for example, by bacteria) can sometimes be corrected through chlorination. Effluent Treatment Air stripping alone may not achieve the required effluent contaminant concentration reduction, particularly for semi-volatile contaminants, such as those contained in diesel fuel. For these cases, it may be necessary to treat the air stripping effluent. Activated carbon adsorption is the most common secondary treatment for removing additional organics. Carbon adsorption, both gas and liquid, is described in Chapters 12 and 13.

Flow Equalization

If the flow from the extraction system fluctuates excessively, or if a post-treatment system is required, a holding/sump tank may be required. A sump tank on the influent side of the air stripping tower provides a source for constant influent flow: water level switches activate a feed pump, controlling flow to the packed tower. Influent waters may also be pretreated within the holding tank. A sump tank on the effluent side of the air stripping tower provides a basin from which the tower effluent may be pumped, at a constant flow rate, through post-treatment system.

Basic Information Needed for Estimating

It is possible to create a reasonable cost estimate for an air stripping system using a few required parameters. If more detailed information is known, one can create a more precise and site-specific estimate using a secondary set of parameters. To estimate the cost of an air stripping system, certain basic information must be known. This information is discussed in the following paragraphs.

System Configuration

System configuration refers to the number of air stripping towers and their configuration relative to each other. Typical options for packed tower air stripping configurations are:

- Single tower
- 2 or 3 towers, in parallel or series
- 2 low-profile units, in parallel or series
- Single low-profile unit with trays (usually up to 6)

Total System Influent Flow Rate

Total system influent flow rate refers to the total flow rate of contaminated water to the system, which is typically measured in gallons per minute. The flow rate has a direct impact on the tower dimensions or sizing of a low-profile system for tower systems. If the selected system configuration is 2 or 3 parallel towers, the total influent flow rate is divided by the number of towers; the diameter of the towers is based on the portion of the total flow rate that is directed to each tower. If the selected system configuration is single tower, 2 towers in series, or 3 towers in series, the default tower diameter will depend on the total influent flow rate. Typical liquid loading rates for air stripping towers vary from 5–30 GPM/S.F. of tower diameter.

A good rule of thumb for determining tower diameter is a maximum liquid loading rate of 20 GPM/S.F. Example default tower diameters for each system configuration and range of flow rates are listed in Figure 10.2.

Volatility of Contaminants

Volatility of contaminants refers to the volatility of the contaminant(s) in the influent water. This relative value (very high, high, medium, or low) affects the height of the packing material of the air stripping tower. If two contaminants in the influent water are at equal concentrations and have the same effluent requirements, the contaminant with the lower volatility will require a greater packing height than the contaminant with the higher volatility, and thus will govern the design packing height for the tower. However, if 2 or more contaminants are not at equal concentrations, or they have different effluent requirements, the contaminant with the lowest volatility may not govern the design packing height for the tower. By considering the volatility of the contaminants and their relative concentrations, the estimator may determine which contaminant(s) is likely to control the design packing height.

Refer to Figure 10.4 for rules of thumb for packing heights. Figure 10.5 is a list of common contaminants, their relative volatility, and corresponding Henry's Law Constant ranges.

To estimate the design elements of a low-profile air stripper, it is often easiest to consult a vendor and provide basic project information. For manual calculation, the steps are as follows:

1. Determine the volume of water to be stripped, the minimum temperature of the water, and the maximum concentration of volatile organic compounds to be removed.
2. Determine the desired percent removal of VOCs (desired concentration in treated water).
3. Calculate the theoretical number of sieve trays needed to remove the VOCs to the desired concentration.
4. Estimate the tray efficiency and the number of trays needed.
5. Estimate the cross sectional area of the perforated plate section of each tray.
6. Estimate the pressure drop of the air stripper.
7. Estimate the size of the blower motor.

A detailed description of calculation methods is available in a design guide published by the U.S. Army Corps of Engineers titled, *Engineering and Design, Air Stripping, Design Guide 1110-1-3*, October 2001. Web site: **http://www.usace.army.mil/inet/usace-docs/design-guides/ dg1110-1-3/appc.pdf**

Default Tower Diameters	
System Configuration = Single Tower, 2 Towers In Series, Or 3 Towers In Series	
Total Influent Flow Rate	**Default Tower Diameter**
1–15 GPM	1.0 ft
16–35 GPM	1.5 ft
36–60 GPM	2.0 ft
61–140 GPM	3.0 ft
141–250 GPM	4.0 ft
251–400 GPM	5.0 ft
401–570 GPM	6.0 ft
571–1,000 GPM	8.0 ft
1,001–1,570 GPM	10.0 ft
1,571–2,250 GPM	12.0 ft

Figure 10.3 Default Towers Diameters

Default Packing Heights	
System Configuration = Single Tower, 2 Parallel Towers, Or 3 Parallel Towers	
Volatility Of Default Packing Contaminant(s)	**Height Per Tower**
Very High	10 ft
High	18 ft
Moderate	27 ft
Low	40 ft
System Configuration = 2 Towers In Series	
Volatility Of Default Packing Contaminant(s)	**Height Per Tower**
Very High	10 ft
High	14 ft
Moderate	19 ft
Low	25 ft
System Configuration = 3 Towers In Series	
Volatility Of Default Packing Contaminant(s)	**Height Per Tower**
Very High	10 ft
High	13 ft
Moderate	16 ft
Low	20 ft

Figure 10.4 Default Packing Heights

Treatment Period

The total treatment period is divided into two phases: startup and O&M. The startup costs are included with the capital costs; O&M costs are identified separately. These parameters may be used to either identify the startup period, as the name implies, or cover the entire treatment period.

Worker Safety Level

The safety of workers is affected by the contaminant(s) at the site. Safety level refers to the levels required by OSHA in 29 CFR Part 1910. The four levels are designated as A, B, C, and D, where "A" is the most protective, and "D" is the least protective. An additional safety level of E is sometimes used for normal construction, "no hazard" conditions as prescribed by the EPA.

| Volatilities For Common Contaminants ||
Relative Compound Name	Volatility
Carbon Tetrachloride	Very High
Tetrachlorethylene	Very High
1, 1-Dichloroethylene	High
Vinyl Chloride	High
1,1,1-Trichloroethane	High
Trichloroethylene	High
Chloromethane	Moderate
Ethylbenzene	Moderate
cis-1,2-Dichloroethylene	Moderate
Chloroethane	Moderate
trans-1,2-Dichloroethylene	Moderate
Toluene	Moderate
1,1-Dichloroethane	Moderate
Benzene	Moderate
Xylenes (total)	Moderate
Chlorobenzene	Moderate
Chloroform	Moderate
1,3-Dichlorobenzene	Moderate
1,2-Dichlorobenzene	Moderate
1,2-Dichloropropane	Moderate
Methylene Chloride	Moderate
Bromobenzene	Moderate
Naphthalene	Low
1,2-Dichloroethane	Low
1,1,2-Trichloroethane	Low
1,2-Dibromoethane	Low
1,1,2,2-Tetrachloroethane	Low
Ethylene Dibromide (EDB)	Low
Methyl Tert Butyl Ether	Low

Henry's Law Constant for relative volatility ratings in atm x m³/mole
- Very High >0.028   - Moderate 0.0012-0.144
- High 0.0145-0.027   - Low <0.0012

Figure 10.5 Volatilities for Common Contaminants

Applicable regulations will determine requirements regarding air emissions abatement and acceptable levels of contaminant in the air stripper effluent. The acceptable levels are prescribed in the *applicable or relevant and appropriate requirements* (ARARs). Local building codes may also affect construction costs for items such as tower foundation systems, electricity supply, and access road requirements.

Design Information Needed for Detailed Estimates

The primary installation and O&M costs for packed tower air strippers are determined by the type and size of towers, and the packing height. These costs can be estimated using the information provided above. The following discussion provides the types of detailed information that, when available, can add detail and accuracy to estimates for air stripping systems. Also included are design criteria and estimating rules of thumb that the estimator typically uses to determine values that are not known, or to check information provided by others.

The two main categories of items to be considered are accessories and piping.

Accessories

A sump tank may be required on the influent side or the effluent side of the air stripping tower, or on both sides. Transfer pumps may also be required to carry the water to or from the tower or sumps. Typical accessories include sump tanks, transfer pumps, and biofouling prevention chemical feeders.

Sump Tanks

The need for a sump tank depends on the influent flow rate. Sump tanks are available in a wide range of sizes in both plastic and steel. The tank size and construction material selected depend on the characteristics of the contaminant, the site, and operating conditions at the site. If this information is not known, a good rule of thumb is to include one plastic sump tank for each tower or group of towers connected in series or parallel operations.

Transfer Pumps

The need for a transfer pump depends on the influent flow rate and whether or not a sump is present. There is a wide range of sump pumps and centrifugal transfer pumps. If a sump system is anticipated, but the design information is not available, a good rule of thumb is to use one sump pump per sump tank.

Type and Size of Biofouling Prevention Chemical Feeder

The operation of air stripping towers can create biofouling in some areas. If it is not managed correctly, biofouling clogs the air stripping tower and reduces or even eliminates the effectiveness of the stripping process. To determine the need for biofouling prevention equipment, tests can be run during the design and startup phases of the air stripping process. Chemical feeders with pumping systems are used to pre-treat water when biofouling prevention is required.

Piping

Influent and effluent piping are required for the air stripping tower(s) to transfer the contaminated water from the pumping source of pre-treatment equipment and to transfer treated water to the discharge system or sewers. The piping parameters are influent material and length, and effluent material and length.

Influent Piping Material

Users can select from a wide range of influent piping materials. Generally, PVC pipe is used where it is acceptable because it is inexpensive and easy to assemble.

Influent Piping Length

The total influent piping run is determined by the distance from the air stripper to the extraction system or pre-treatment process. The total air stripping pipe lengths are a function of specific site conditions.

Effluent Piping Material

The user may choose from a wide range of effluent piping materials. Again, PVC pipe is generally used where it is acceptable because it is inexpensive and easy to assemble.

Effluent Piping Length

The effluent piping length is determined by the distance from the air stripper to the post-treatment or disposal system.

Related Costs

Costs for operating and maintaining the air stripper equipment during remedial action include packing reconditioning, electricity to run the blower, and total system maintenance. Sampling and analysis related to construction, treatment, monitoring, and disposal phases will generally be required.

The primary cost drivers for the items discussed in the following paragraphs are the startup and O&M periods and system performance.

Emergency Shutdown System

If the air stripping components malfunction, contaminant influent must be controlled so effluent quality is maintained. Specifically, blower malfunction, tower packing congestion, and/or discharge line blockage could result in restricted influent. Controllers are available to prevent passage of non-treated or partially treated liquid; these controllers have a substantial impact on system costs. A typical system would include pressure switching on the packed tower and on the air blower and a level control in the air stripping tower sump.

Packing Reconditioning

Generally, there are no repacking requirements during the first 6 months of operation. The packing material in the air stripper should be steam-cleaned as needed. The frequency and depth of cleaning is based on the level of fouling and volatility and the concentration level of contaminants. An allowance of 10 hours semi-annually for steam cleaning, which includes associated technicians' time and steam cleaner rental, is a good rule of thumb.

Electricity

The cost of electricity to operate the blower must be considered. The power requirement for pumps, blowers, and accessory equipment can be determined from the rated power consumption of each piece of equipment. Power charges should be checked with the local power provider.

Blower Motor Maintenance

If the air stripping process will continue for more than 18 months, the blower motor will need to be reworked. This includes checking and replacing the bearings, shaft, and gasket, if necessary.

Site Work and Utilities

Site work and utilities may include:

- Overhead electrical distribution
- Fencing
- Signage

If the site is remote, a temporary access road may also be required to deliver the stripping equipment and to access the site during the O&M periods. When applicable, site work and utilities must also be covered in the estimate.

Conclusion

Air stripping is a common process with applications to many groundwater problems. The main cost drivers are the size of the system and the length of the operating period. Another common issue that drives cost is carbon fouling caused by excessive non-volatile matter in the influent. Pre-treatment of the water can reduce these problems, but this adds additional operating and capital cost. The cost engineer should work closely with the design team during planning and field testing to optimize these issues.

Chapter 11

Bioventing

Bioventing is a biodegradation process that involves microbial transformation of organic contaminants, which affects cleanup of soils, groundwater, and/or other contaminated media. Biodegradation of organic compounds in soil/groundwater systems is a natural process in which native microorganisms obtain energy and/or carbon through the metabolism of organic contaminants. Several terms are commonly used to describe essentially the same remediation technology:

- In situ biodegradation
- In situ bioremediation
- In situ bioreclamation
- Enhanced bioreclamation
- Bioremediation or biodegradation

All refer to processes in which contaminants are degraded by in-place biological processes.

Bioventing, also called soil venting, is one means of performing in situ biodegradation. Bioventing can be particularly effective for removing volatile contaminants, which are highly susceptible to physical removal. Bioventing has been developed and applied by the petroleum industry to remediate fuel-contaminated sites. This discussion assumes that the contaminants of concern are petroleum hydrocarbons.

Applications and Limitations

Applications

- Removes POLs (petroleum, oils, and lubricants), volatile organic compounds (VOCs), semi-volatile organic compounds, nonvolatile organic compounds, nonchlorinated solvents, wood preservatives, and some pesticides.
- Can remove volatile contaminants near or under structures.
- Medium- to long-term technology. Cleanup ranges from a few months to several years.

Limitations

- Will not degrade inorganic contaminants.
- Effectiveness limited in low permeability soils, saturated soils, or if the water table is within several feet of the ground surface.

- Requires sufficient nutrients, soil moisture, active indigenous microbial population, and a relatively neutral pH (pH of 6–9) to degrade contaminants.
- Remediation process is relatively slow and can be further slowed by low soil temperatures.
- Dangerous vapors can accumulate in building basements within the radius of influence of air injection wells.
- Off-gas monitoring at ground surface may be necessary.

Typical System Design Elements

Figure 11.1 is an illustration of the in situ bioventing process described in this section. Bioventing is similar to soil vapor extraction (see Chapter 32), except that it intentionally stimulates in situ biodegradation. This process uses one or more vacuum extraction wells (screened outside the contaminated zone) which direct oxygen from the surface through the subsurface. Extracted air can be either pulled directly through soil pores from the atmosphere or supplied by one or more injection wells. This procedure physically removes volatile organic compounds (VOCs) in the soil gas and establishes a contaminant gradient between the solid/liquid and gas phases, allowing continuous removal as contaminants redistribute into the gas phase. Pulling air through the subsurface also provides oxygen that can be used as an

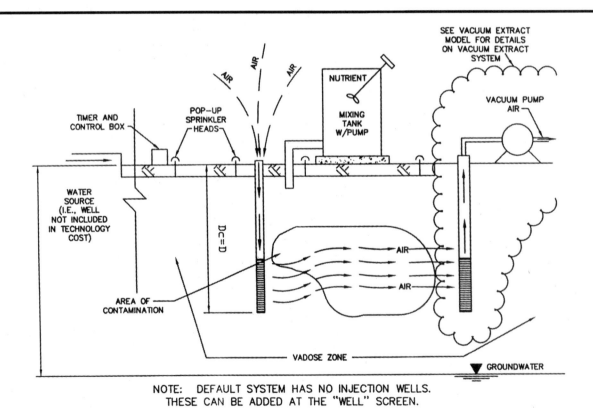

Figure 11.1 In Situ Bioventing Process

electron acceptor in aerobic biodegradation of organics. The oxygen combined with moisture, nutrients, and possibly microorganisms supplied by either sprinkler systems or infiltration trenches/galleries—stimulates in situ biodegradation of organic contaminants.

One of the main advantages of aerobic biodegradation of petroleum hydrocarbon contaminants is that the contaminants are completely destroyed, as the by products are primarily carbon dioxide, water, and biomass. Biodegradation avoids generating hazardous byproducts and additional waste streams.

Growth factors that affect the rate of microbial degradation include soil moisture, oxygen requirements, soil pH, soil nutrients, and soil temperature.

Soil Moisture

Moisture control may be achieved by supplementing water to the site (irrigation), removing of excess water (drainage, wellpoints), or other methods (e.g., soil additives). Adding vegetation to a site also helps retard the downward migration of water (e.g., leaching). When natural precipitation cannot maintain soil moisture sufficient for microbial activity, irrigation may be necessary. Water can be applied by standard irrigation methods (e.g., sub-irrigation, sprinkler irrigation) when shallow contamination does not exceed 10'. For deep soil contamination, injection wells may be installed for injection of water with or without nutrients and microbial culture. Moisture control depends moisture depends on how easily water is controlled at the site and on the availability of a suitable water source (considering factors such as transport distance, drilling of new wells, availability, and cost of energy for pumping). Controls to manage run-off at the site are necessary to prevent drainage and erosion problems.

Bioventing can be used in saturated soil columns if the groundwater table is lowered to expose more of the contaminated layer. Air injected into the subsurface is drawn through the contaminated zone to stimulate biodegradation and to physically strip volatile contaminants. Water and nutrients are provided via infiltration.

Oxygen Requirements

Aerobic degradation is the most desirable process for microbial transformation of petroleum hydrocarbon contaminants because it proceeds more rapidly than anaerobic processes and does not produce the noxious by products associated with anaerobic decomposition. For aerobic degradation of petroleum hydrocarbons, approximately 3.5 pounds of oxygen are required per pound of hydrocarbon. For bioventing, it is critical to ensure that the vacuum wells keep the subsurface aerated. Passive injection vents provide a path for air to be pulled through to the subsurface.

Soil pH

Depending on the nature of the hazardous waste components contaminating the soil, it may be advantageous to optimize the soil pH for a particular segment of the microbial community, because microbial structure and activity are both affected by the soil pH. Near-neutral pH values are most conducive to microbial functioning in general; the acceptable range is 7.0–8.5.

Soil Nutrients

To survive, indigenous microbial populations must have specific inorganic nutrients (e.g., nitrogen, phosphorus, potassium, calcium, magnesium) and a carbon and energy source. A pilot study should define the nutrients necessary to stimulate in situ biodegradation in the subsurface. Carbon, nitrogen, and phosphorus amendments to the soil can be added at variable rates depending on microorganism requirements. Standard agricultural methods are used to add nutrients to the soil. Sufficient nitrogen and phosphorus must be reapplied to ensure that they do not limit the microbial and metabolic activity.

Soil Temperature

Soil temperature is one of the most important factors that control microbiological activity and the rate of decomposition of organic contaminants. Temperature also influences the rate of volatilization of compounds from the soil. Optimal growth of the microbial populations that are responsible for biodegradation of petroleum products occurs between 20°–35 °C (68°–95°F).

Because plant cover has insulating properties, vegetation plays a significant role in soil temperature. Bare soil unprotected from the sun's direct rays becomes very warm during the hottest part of the year; it also loses heat rapidly during colder seasons. A well-vegetated soil does not become as warm as a bare soil during the summer, and is insulated against heat loss from the soil in the winter.

Basic Information Needed for Estimating

It is possible to create a reasonable cost estimate using a few required parameters. If more detailed information is known, one can create a more precise and site-specific estimate using a secondary set of parameters. To estimate the cost of the bioventing system, the following information must be known.

Type of Installation

The two installation options are vertical or horizontal vapor extraction points (VEPs). Vertical installations are most common and are generally considered to be most effective for depths greater than 5'. Horizontal trenches with horizontal screens are effective in areas with shallow water tables. Generally, a pervious layer is required to prevent short-circuiting of air from the surface. Each option is discussed in more depth later in this chapter.

Area of Contaminated Soil

Typically, sites with an area of contamination greater than 10 acres are remediated in stages, or divided into smaller areas and addressed as independent cells.

Soil Type

The soil properties greatly affect the design of the in situ bioremediation system. The primary controlling soil parameter is *permeability*. Permeability should be sufficient to permit adequate flow of air through the contaminated matrix. The radius of influence of applied vacuum at the VEP extends over a greater distance in soils with higher permeability.

Soil permeability relates directly to the soil particle size. For estimating purposes, soil types may be classified into four groups based on particle size. See Figure 11.2 for ranges of permeability for different soil types.

Average Depth to the Top of Screen

The average depth to the top of screen is used to estimate drilling (vertical installation) and construction materials. This measurement is the distance from the surface of the ground to the top of the screen area on the well casing.

Horizontal Trench Depth

Trench depth is used to estimate trenching (horizontal installation) and construction materials. Normally, horizontal trenching is not feasible for sites less than 3' deep or for sites deeper than 30'.

Screen Length

In the vertical bioventing system, the screen length is designed to span the vertical extent of soil contamination. The total depth of the vertical bioventing well is the sum of the depth to the top of the screen plus the screen length.

In the horizontal installation, the screen length is designed to effectively remediate the entire site. The screen length is based on the radius of influence of the vapor extraction well and the area of contaminated soil.

Treatment Period

The total treatment duration is divided into startup and operations and maintenance (O&M). The costs associated with the startup period (e.g., equipment acquisition, installation, optimization) are considered capital costs. The O&M costs are generally identified separately.

Worker Safety Level

Worker safety is affected by the contaminant(s) at the site. Safety level refers to the levels required by OSHA in 29 CFR Part 1910. The four levels are designated as A, B, C, and D, where "A," is the most protective and "D" is the least protective. A safety level of E is also included to simulate normal construction, "no hazard" conditions as prescribed by the EPA.

Soil Permeability	
Soil Type	Range Of Soil Permeability (cm/sec.)
Inorganic Silt, Silty Clay	1.0×10^{-6} to 1.0×10^{-3}
Sand-Silt or Sand-Clay Mixtures	1.0×10^{-4} to 1.0×10^{-1}
Sands, Gravelly Sands	1.0×10^{-2} to 1.0
Gravel, Gravelly Sands	1.10×10^{-1} to 10

Figure 11.2 Soil Permeability

Design Information Needed for Detailed Estimates

Following are descriptions of the types of information that, when available, can add detail and accuracy to estimates. Also included are design criteria and estimating rules of thumb that the estimator typically uses to determine values that are not known, or to check information provided by others. The design parameters are divided into the following groups: VEP design; vertical VEPs; horizontal VEPs; soil additives; and decontamination.

VEP Design

The following factors are considered in the design of bioventing extraction systems.

VEP Spacing

Vapor extraction system design depends primarily on the soil type. Since the radius of influence depends on the soil type, factors such as VEP spacing, number of VEPs, gas flow rate, and blower specifications also depend on the soil type. Figure 11.3 shows assumed values for VEP spacing and gas flow rate.

In bioventing, the purpose of vapor extraction is not to cause volatilization of organic compounds, but merely to provide sufficient vacuum to cause the infiltration of ambient air (resulting from the development of a pressure gradient) into the subsurface soils to promote biorespiration. Therefore, it is not advisable to apply high vacuum at the vapor extraction well—this would cause volatilization of organic compounds, thus creating a need for treatment of the extracted subsurface vapors.

Number of VEPs

The number of VEPs (N) is calculated based on well spacing using the following equations:

Bioventing System Design Parameters		
Soil Type	VEP Spacing (ft)	Gas Flow Rate (CFM/L.F.)*
Inorganic Silt, Silty Clay	15	0.6
Sand-Silt or Sand-Clay Mixtures	35	1.5
Sands, Gravelly Sands	50	3.55
Gravel, Gravel-Sand Mixtures	100	15.5

*CFM/L.F. = Cubic Feet per Minute/Linear Feet

Figure 11.3 Bioventing System Design Parameters

80

For vertical installation:

$$N = \frac{A}{[(p \times L^2)/4]} \quad \text{(Round up to the next whole number)}$$

For horizontal installation:

$$N = \frac{A}{(L \times SL)} \quad \begin{array}{l}\text{(Round up if the remainder is > 0.5.)}\\\text{(Round down if the remainder is < 0.5.)}\end{array}$$

Where:

A = Surface area of contaminated soil (S.F.)
L = Well spacing (ft)
SL = Screen length (ft)

Gas Flow Rate

The quantity of blowers is determined from the total flow rate (Q). Q is calculated from the following equation:

$$Q = SL \times (GFR) \times N$$

Where:

SL = Screen length (ft)
GFR = Gas flow rate (per foot of screen)
N = Number of VEPs

Blower Specification

Four blower sizes are most commonly used for applications of this technology. Figure 11.4 shows selection criteria for the type and quantity of blowers.

Vertical VEPs

Following are descriptions of parameters that influence installation requirements and costs for vertical VEPs.

Drilling

Vertical VEPs can be installed using a variety of vertical drilling techniques, depending on site hydrogeology and the desired depth of the bore hole. The three most common vertical drilling techniques are:

- Hollow stem auger
- Water/mud rotary
- Air rotary

The hollow stem auger method is typically used for depths less than 150' below ground surface (bgs). The water/mud rotary method is most commonly used for drilling depths greater than 150' bgs. Air rotary drilling is much less common. If the subsurface is a consolidated formation, then the user should use water/mud rotary or air rotary rather than hollow stem augers, even for depths less than 150' bgs. Figure 11.5 provides bore hole diameters for different drilling methods.

Diameter

The most common VEP installation uses 2" diameter vertical VEPs. However, 4" diameter vertical VEPs are also available when large air flows are required. The VEP diameter affects the diameter of the borehole and cost of construction material and drill cutting containment (drumming).

Construction Material

Vertical VEPs are typically constructed of either PVC (Schedule 40 or Schedule 80) or stainless steel screen and casing. The choice between materials is based primarily on cost and material compatibility with the contaminant.

For estimating purposes, assume Schedule 40 PVC for the construction of vertical VEPs less than 85' deep. When the vertical VEP exceeds 85', assume Schedule 80 PVC material. Stainless steel is used only when PVC is incompatible with the soil environment.

All connection piping is normally installed above ground. For estimating purposes, assume that the amount of connection piping is the radius of influence times the number of VEPs. The amount of manifold pipe can be assumed at half the length of the connection piping, and is the same material as the connection pipe. A pressure gauge and other piping appurtenances are also required.

Figure 11.4 Blower
Specifications Defaults

Blower Specification Defaults		
Flow Rate (Q) SCFM	Type Of Blower	Quantity Of Blowers
Q ≤ 98	98 SCFM, 1 H.P.	1
98 < Q ≤ 127	127 SCFM, 1.5 H.P.	1
127 < 0 ≤ 160	160 SCFM, 2 H.P.	1
Q > 160	280 SCFM, 5 H.P.	Q/280*

(Round to the next whole number)

Figure 11.5 Bore Hole
Diameters for Different Drilling
Methods

Borehole Diameters For Different Drilling Methods		
VEP Diameter (In.)	Drilling Method	Borehole Diameter (In.)
2	Hollow Stem Auger	8
	Mud Drilling	6
	Air Rotary	6
4	Hollow Stem Auger	10
	Mud Drilling	8
	Air Rotary	8

The connection and manifold pipe size selection criteria for vertical VEPs are shown in Figure 11.6.

Soil Sample Collection

Sample collection during bore hole advancement allows characterization of the geology beneath the site and definition of the magnitude and extent of contaminants in the vadose zone. For estimating purposes, assume that any required soil samples will be collected every 5' or at each change in lithology, whichever is less for lithologic description. Drill cuttings can be collected as the bore hole is advanced for general geologic information. Discrete samples are collected in unconsolidated sediment using a variety of methods, including split spoon, shelby tubes, and California brass ring.

Soil samples are typically collected with a split spoon sampler with standard penetration tests at 5' intervals during bore hole advancement. Samples are screened with an Organic Vapor Analyzer (OVA) for volatile organics and described for the lithologic log by the geologist supervising drilling.

Drill Cutting Containment

The drill cuttings are generally placed in 55-gallon drums and stored until disposal options have been evaluated.

Remedial Action Phase Professional Labor

The professional labor-hours spent in the field supervising the installation of vertical VEPs are generally included with VEP installation costs. For estimating purposes, assume the following guidelines for staff hydrogeologist hours related to vertical VEP installation:

- If sample collection is being performed during drilling, VEPs are drilled at a rate of 20' per hour, plus 2 hours per well for well completion. Total labor-hours are for drilling supervision by a staff hydrogeologist.
- If sample collection is not being performed during drilling, VEPs are drilled at a rate of 40' per hour, plus 2 hours per well for well completion. Total labor-hours are for drilling supervision by a staff hydrogeologist.

Figure 11.6 Piping Specifications Defaults for Vertical VEPs

Piping Specification Defaults For Vertical VEPs		
VEP Specifications	Connection Piping	Manifold Piping
2" Vertical PVC	2" Sch. 40 PVC	4" Sch. 40 PVC
2" Vertical Stainless Steel	2" Sch. 40 S.S.	4" Sch. 40 S.S.
4" Vertical PVC	4" Sch. 40 PVC	4" Sch. 40 PVC
4" Vertical Stainless Steel	4" Sch. 40 S.S.	4" Sch. 40 S.S.

Horizontal VEPs

Following are descriptions of parameters that influence installation requirements and costs for vertical VEP installation.

Trenching

Horizontal installation involves excavating a narrow trench and installing a screened or perforated pipe at a common elevation. The installation method depends on the depth of installation. A chain trencher is commonly used when the depth of installation is less than or equal to 4'. A crawler-mounted hydraulic excavator is used when the installation is deeper than 4', but less than or equal to 20'. The Horizontal Dewatering Systems, Inc. (HDSI) proprietary method is commonly used for installations between 21–30' deep. For bioventing applications greater than 10', additional controls—such as a trench box, well points, sheeting, or side sloping—may be required to prevent cave-ins resulting from soil conditions.

The HDSI proprietary method uses specialized equipment to drill a 14"- wide hole to set a vertical PVC blank pipe. After drilling, the machine digs in either a forward or backward direction to create a horizontal VEP. As it digs, a high-density polyethylene (HDPE) perforated pipe is laid horizontally. The pipe is simultaneously covered with a filter pack and connected to the vertical PVC pipe.

The trenching methods do not permit collection of discrete soil samples for laboratory analysis. Therefore, the soil sample collection option is not provided for horizontal VEP installation.

Construction Material

Material options for horizontal VEPs are the same as for vertical VEPs (discussed earlier in this section).

Diameter

Typically, 2" diameter horizontal VEPs are used for installation depths less than or equal to 20'. However, 4" diameter horizontal VEPs are also available. When the installation is deeper than 20', horizontal VEPs are typically installed by the HDSI proprietary method. For this construction method, either 4" or 6" diameter perforated HDPE horizontal pipe is used; 4" is the most common.

Containment of Trench Cutting

The trench cuttings can be placed in 55-gallon drums and stored until disposal options have been evaluated. Another alternative is to stockpile the waste soil at a location near the bioventing area. The amount of waste soil to be drummed using the HDSI proprietary method is less than that drummed using conventional excavating equipment. This is because the subsurface soil is only slightly disturbed when the HDSI method is used.

Remedial Action Phase Professional Labor

The professional labor-hours spent in the field supervising the installation of the horizontal VEPs are generally included with the VEP installation costs. For estimating purposes, assume the following guidelines for staff hydrogeologist hours related to vertical VEP installation:

- 45 minutes per VEP for vertical blank PVC pipe installed by a staff hydrogeologist.
- 1 minute per 2' of horizontal screen section installed by a staff hydrogeologist.
- 1.5 hours for loading, moving, and setting up on site.

Soil Additives

Soil additives are used to increase the efficiency of the process. The correct level and balance of moisture, nutrients, and microorganisms will enhance the natural biodegradation process and reduce the time required to eliminate contaminants from the soil.

Watering

Moisture and nutrients will generally be delivered to the soil by one of 3 methods: spray irrigation (sprinkler system), infiltration gallery, or injection wells. Sprinkling is the most common and least expensive method.

Nutrients

The most basic bioremediation processes involve the addition of oxygen and appropriate nutrients, typically nitrogen and phosphorus. The optimal nutrient mix must be determined by laboratory growth studies and geochemical evaluations of the site; however, a rough estimate of nutrients and quantities can be determined using a nitrogen/phosphorus/potassium (20:20:20) pulverized fertilizer at an application of 800 lbs/acre.

Microorganisms

When naturally occurring microorganisms are scarce or absent, or when rapid cleanup is desired, acclimated organic matter may be added to the soil to be treated. The acclimated organic matter supplies organisms that can initiate the degradation process. The application for the microorganisms, if chosen, will be 0.5 pounds of bioculture per gallon of water. The monthly application can be estimated at 25 pounds of bacteria per 1,000 C.Y. of waste. This corresponds to 200 gallons of water and bioculture per month per 1,000 C.Y. of contaminated soil.

Decontamination

Decontamination procedures for the VEP screen, riser, caps, and drilling tools (e.g., hollow stem augers) are conducted prior to and between each bore hole/well installation. Steam cleaning is done with a high-pressure, steam-generating pressure washer and detergent.

Decontamination procedures for split spoon samplers, bailers, and hand augers are as follows:

- Clean with tap water and detergent using a brush.
- Rinse thoroughly with tap water.
- Rinse with deionized water.
- Rinse twice with pesticide-grade isopropanol.
- Rinse with organic-free deionized water.
- Allow to air dry.

Monitoring wells (MWs) are usually installed on the periphery of the soil contaminant plume. MWs are not addressed in this section, but are discussed in the Sampling and Analysis chapter of this book.

Related Costs

Maintenance of the bioventing system includes adjusting the blower flow rate and valves, general maintenance, and collecting samples. Typically, a maintenance/sample crew of two field technicians will be on site once a week for the first month, and once a month thereafter, to perform sampling tasks. An air blower effluent air sample will be collected at each sampling event and analyzed for volatile organics. An organic vapor analyzer is used for each sampling event. Monitoring points at the VEPs will be monitored with an OVA during each sampling event to ensure that each well is extracting air from the subsurface and is operating properly. One soil sample per vapor extraction well for VOC analysis will be collected during installation.

Site Work and Utilities

Site work and utilities that may be applicable in bioventing, and should be covered in the estimate, are:

- Site preparation, fencing, and signage
- Clearing and grubbing
- Water distribution
- Overhead distribution
- Groundwater monitoring wells

Conclusion

Bioventing is an efficient and cost-effective method of treating hydrocarbon contamination in soil. Although it is similar to soil vapor extraction, bioventing has the advantage of being an on-site process that does not require follow-on treatment of the contaminants. In many cases, this means that bioventing is less expensive than other approaches of remediating petroleum-contaminated soils. The primary cost drivers are the number of vapor extraction wells; the number of injection wells, if any; the type and extent of soil additives required; and the operations period. In many cases, there are trade-offs between these cost elements. For example, fewer injection wells may lead to a longer operating period, thus requiring more soil additives, power, and operating labor. The cost engineer should work closely with the design team to optimize these variable design parameters.

Chapter 12

Carbon Adsorption—Gas

Gas-phase adsorption is a natural process in which molecules of a gas are physically attracted to and held at the surface of a solid. To treat waste streams by adsorption, contaminants (the adsorbate) are transferred and concentrated from one medium (gas) to another (the adsorbent). The most commonly used adsorbent is "granular activated carbon."

Gas-phase carbon adsorption is actually a secondary treatment that usually follows a primary treatment. Treatments that commonly precede gas-phase carbon adsorption include, but are not limited to, steam stripping, air stripping, and soil vapor extraction. Also, prior to gas-phase carbon adsorption, the relative humidity (RH) of the gas stream must be lowered so that the activated carbon can be used efficiently. To lower the RH, an air heater raises the temperature of the gas stream by 20–25°F above ambient. At high RH values, most of the pores are filled with water, thereby reducing the capacity of the GAC. As the temperature increases, the RH is reduced, drying more of the pores and increasing the capacity of the GAC. However, excessive drying also reduces the GAC capacity. At RH values between 40–50% with the temperature no greater than 100°F, the effects of RH and temperature balance out, and maximum adsorption to the carbon is possible.

Applications and Limitations

Applications

- A secondary treatment technology to clean gaseous effluent streams from other treatments like soil vapor extraction and air stripping.
- Removal of VOCs (volatile organic compounds) from contaminated air.

Limitations

- High relative humidity (greater than 50%) can reduce carbon capacity.
- Compounds with low molecular weight and high polarity are not recommended for carbon adsorption treatment.

- Pretreatment of air streams with high contaminant concentrations may be necessary.
- Elevated temperatures (greater than 100°F) inhibit adsorption capacity.
- Biological growth or large particulates on Granular-Activated Carbon (GAC) material can reduce air flow through bed.
- Spent GAC may require hazardous waste handling and transportation before being disposed.
- Adsorbed contaminants must be destroyed (usually by thermal treatment/incineration).

Process Configurations and Treatment Train Considerations

Considerations for carbon adsorption process configuration and treatment train are listed below:

- On-site regeneration systems should be considered where vapor phase carbon must be operated with high organics loading (e.g., exceeding 50 ppm).
- For efficient carbon usage, the vapor stream should be maintained at below 100°F and below 50% relative humidity.
- If the organic vapor content drops below the site-specific regulated limit, switching to direct discharge may be an option.
- Pilot testing is often required to determine optimal contact time in the Granular-Activated Carbon (GAC) unit.
- GAC adsorbers may be single- or multi-stage. Multi-stage systems make optimal use of carbon stock, but increase O&M costs.
- Various types of GAC are available, each having unique adsorptive qualities.
- High levels of organic material (1,000 mg/l or higher) in the influent may result in rapid exhaustion of carbon.
- Solids collected from backwashing may require management as hazardous waste.

Typical System Design Elements

In gas-phase carbon adsorption, the contaminated gas comes into contact with the carbon by passing through one or more adsorbers, which are usually the fixed-bed type. A fixed-bed adsorber is a stationary canister packed with GAC. The activated carbon selectively adsorbs organic molecules, which are held in the internal micropores of the carbon granules.

Once the micropore surfaces of the adsorbent (GAC) are saturated with organics, the adsorptive capacity of the carbon is exhausted, and the contaminant concentration increases in the effluent. This process is known as *breakthrough*. The time it takes for breakthrough to occur is the single most critical operating parameter. The carbon must then be removed, thermally regenerated or recycled, and replaced. Factors affecting the carbon replacement frequency include the quality of carbon used and the presence of fouling substances in the gas stream, such as entrained water. The fouling substances "compete" with organics for carbon pore spaces.

The adsorption characteristics of any particular combination of contaminants in a waste stream are unpredictable. A pilot test using a sample of the gas of interest in comparable conditions is often required to accurately determine the optimal contact time and carbon usage rate at a specific site. Once the efficiency of carbon has been established for a particular compound, a dynamic column test should be conducted. In this test, the gas is pumped through a series of carbon-filled canisters, and effluent samples are collected from each canister. Information gathered from this test will better define the design of the carbon adsorption system, including the optimum number of canisters. Pilot tests and dynamic column tests are normally incorporated in the remedial design phase of the project.

Adsorption efficiency depends on several factors:

- Strength of the molecular attraction between the adsorbent and adsorbate
- Molecular weight of the adsorbate
- Type and characteristic of the adsorbent
- Humidity and temperature of the gas stream
- Surface area of the adsorbent

Figures 12.1 and 12.2 illustrate typical carbon adsorption systems. GAC adsorbers may be operated as either single-stage or multi-stage. In multi-stage (series) use, the leading adsorber removes most of the contamination, while the next adsorber acts as a "polishing" step, removing any residual organics from the gas. In series operation, the entire adsorptive capacity of the carbon is used. The lead adsorber can be used past breakthrough because the second adsorber continues to remove the contaminants. After the spent carbon of the lead adsorber is replaced, the piping is reversed so the new carbon becomes the polishing bed. Multi-stage systems with 4 or more units are not uncommon. Although multi-stage operation makes optimal use of carbon, operations and maintenance costs are higher than single-stage and may not always be justified, especially where discharge limitations are not stringent. The design cost drivers to be considered include:

- System configuration
- Bulk regeneration or disposal
- Loading rate
- Type of contaminant
- Site location

GAC works best for low-solubility, high-molecular weight, nonpolar, branched compounds. Alcohols, ketones, and ethers are poor adsorbers, whereas most solvents and pesticides are excellent adsorbers. Therefore, in multi-contaminant situations, additional treatment may be required as GAC selectively adsorbs certain contaminants (e.g., organics).

Since GAC originates from several different materials (e.g., bituminous coal, coconut shells, lignite), different GAC products have different adsorptive capacities. This also holds true for regenerated (reactivated) versus virgin carbon. Reactivated carbon, which costs considerably less, is normally acceptable unless the type of contaminant removed makes the spent carbon a hazardous material, which in turn requires additional treatment and/or disposal.

Basic Information Needed for Estimating

It is possible to create a reasonable cost estimate for gas carbon adsorption using a few required parameters. If more detailed information is known, one can create a more precise and site-specific estimate using a secondary set of parameters.

To estimate the cost of a gas carbon adsorption system, certain basic information must be known. This information is discussed in the following paragraphs.

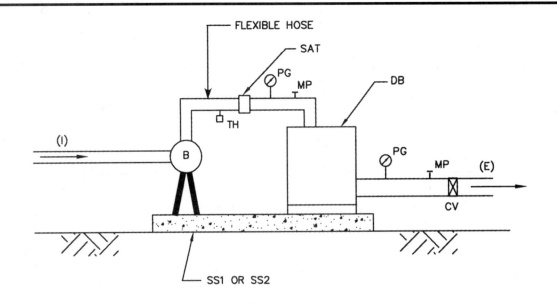

PROFILE

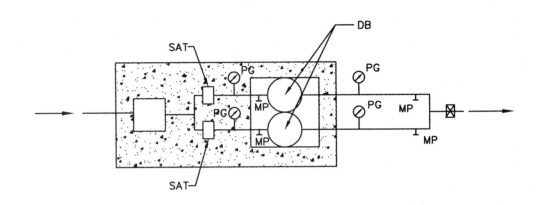

PLAN

VARIABLES

SAMPLE PORT	= MP	BLOWER	= B
CHECK VALVE	= CV	DUAL BED ADSORBER	= DB
PRESSURE GAUGE	= PG	8" STRUCTURAL SLAB	= SS1
THERMOSTAT	= TH	12" STRUCTURAL SLAB	= SS2
HUMIDITY CONTROL		25' X 6" FLEX S.S. HOSE	= FH
SATURATION INDICATOR	= SAT	INFLUENT PIPING	= I
		EFFLUENT PIPING	= E

Figure 12.1 Typical Variable Qualifications, Parallel Dual Bed Carbon Adsorbers

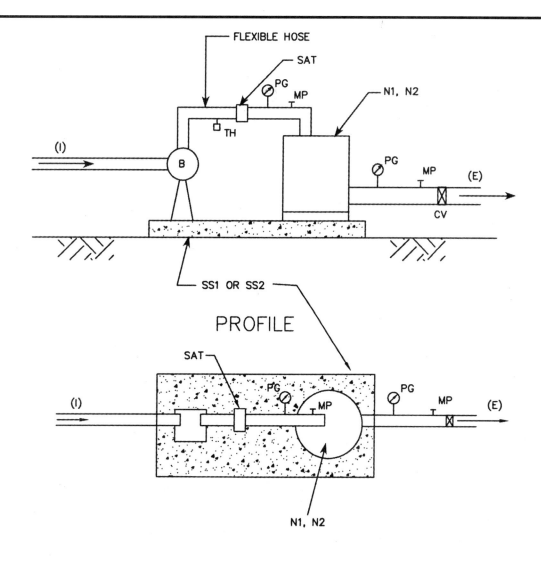

FLEXIBLE HOSE
SAT
PG
MP
TH
N1, N2
(I)
B
PG
MP
(E)
CV
SS1 OR SS2

PROFILE

SAT
PG
MP
PG
MP
(I)
(E)
N1, N2

PLAN

VARIABLES

SAMPLE PORT	= MP	BLOWER	= B
CHECK VALVE	= CV	MODULAR CARBON ADSORBER	= N1, N2
PRESSURE GAUGE	= PG	8" STRUCTURAL SLAB	= SS1
THERMOSTAT	= TH	12" STRUCTURAL SLAB	= SS2
HUMIDITY CONTROL		25' X 6" FLEX S.S. HOSE	= FH
SATURATION INDICATOR	= SAT	INFLUENT PIPING	= I
		EFFLUENT PIPING	= E

Figure 12.2 Typical Variable Qualifications, Modular Carbon Adsorption System

Flow Rate (CFM)

The influent flow rate will affect the selection of the canisters on dual-bed systems. The flow rate is generally a value between 1,000–8,000 cubic feet per minute (CFM). A flow rate greater than 8,000 CFM is extremely uncommon in cleanup operations. Generally, the flow rate will be dictated by the primary treatment technology, such as air stripping or soil vapor extraction.

Type of System

Three types of GAC systems are commonly used in environmental cleanup projects:

- The **dual bed system** is a packaged treatment system consisting of 2 carbon adsorbers, a pump, and associated piping, which can be configured in series or in parallel depending on facility requirements. Dual-bed systems are the most common for total flow rates of 1,000 CFM or more.
- The **modular permanent system** consists of 1 adsorber that can be emptied and reused on-site. Because a new canister is not necessary after breakthrough occurs, the modular permanent system is less expensive to operate.
- The **modular disposable system** consists of 1 adsorber, which is disposed and replaced after the carbon is spent (and breakthrough occurs).

The designer can add more dual-bed systems or canisters as needed. GAC adsorption can employ a single-stage adsorber (1 adsorber) or multi-stage adsorbers (dual-bed or multiple adsorbers), with multi-stage adsorbers being the optimal arrangement for efficiency; however, capital costs are higher for the multi-stage configuration. Down-time for maintenance and replacement is generally longer for permanent and dual-bed systems, but does not significantly impact the cost.

Treatment Period

The total treatment period may be divided into startup and O&M periods. The costs associated with the startup period are generally included with the capital costs, while O&M costs are identified separately.

Worker Safety Level

Worker safety is affected by the contaminant(s) at the site. Safety level refers to the levels required by OSHA in 29 CFR Part 1910. The 4 levels are designated as A, B, C, and D, where "A" is the most protective, and "D" is the least protective.

Design Information Needed for Detailed Estimates

The primary installation costs and cost drivers for O&M of gas carbon adsorption systems are described above. The following discussion provides the types of detailed information that, when available, can add detail and accuracy to estimates for gas-phase adsorption systems. Also included are design criteria and estimating "rules of thumb" that the estimator typically uses to determine values that are not known, or to check information provided by others.

Carbon Adsorption Units

The type of carbon adsorption unit selected depends on the type of contaminants, the operating period, flow rate required, and operator preference. A range of typical options for system size and type are shown in Figures 12.3 and 12.4. These tables show the selections available for packaged dual-bed units, modular disposable units, and modular permanent units.

Number of Carbon Adsorbers

The number of carbon adsorbers depends on the type of system. The normal number of adsorbers for common unit types are:

- Dual-bed—2 adsorbers per dual bed unit
- Modular disposable—1 adsorber
- Modular permanent—1 adsorber

Replacement Carbon

Replacement carbon is available in many different forms. Carbon types differ in terms of available pore space and affinity for particular organics. Costs can vary by more than 50% for different types. If the units will operate for an extended period of time, the selection of carbon type can become a significant cost driver. The estimator should determine the differences and applicability in their site-specific condition. Common carbon types include the following:

- Coal-based—Virgin carbon (permanent and dual-bed)
- Coconut-based—Virgin carbon
- Potassium Hydroxide (KOH) impregnated for H_2S, acid gas, or mercaptan
- Reactivated carbon
- Replacement with new disposable adsorbers (disposable)

The most common carbon type used for both permanent adsorbers and dual-bed adsorbers is coal based. Disposable adsorbers are normally replaced with new disposable adsorbers.

Figure 12.3 Packaged Dual-Bed Carbon Adsorption Units Selection Criteria Based on Air Flow Rates

Packaged Dual-Bed Carbon Adsorption Units Selection Criteria Based On Air Flow Rates		
Air Flow Rate (CFM)	**Qty.**	**Type And Size Of Unit**
1-1,000	1	Dual-Bed, 500 CFM Series, 1,000 CFM Parallel, 2,000 lb. Fill, Each, includes 10 H.P. Blower
1,001-2,000	1	Dual-Bed, 1,000 CFM Series, 2,000 CFM Parallel, 2,000 lb. Fill, Each, includes 10 H.P. Blower
2,001-4,000	2	Dual-Bed, 1,000 CFM Series, 2,000 CFM Parallel, 2,000 lb. Fill, Each, includes 10 H.P. Blower
4,001-6,000	3	Dual-Bed, 1,000 CFM Series, 2,000 CFM Parallel, 2,000 lb. Fill, Each, includes 10 H.P. Blower
6,001-8,000	4	Dual-Bed, 1,000 CFM Series, 2,000 CFM Parallel, 2,000 lb. Fill, Each, includes 10 H.P. Blower

Replacement Schedule

The replacement schedule for spent carbon adsorbers depends on the adsorption efficiency. If this value is not known or has not yet been determined based on pilot studies, a reasonable rule of thumb is to replace the spent carbon every 3 months. The total quantity of carbon required for replacements is based on the system type, the duration of carbon treatment, the carbon adsorber unit chosen, the number of adsorbers, and the replacement schedule.

As mentioned, disposable carbon adsorbers are generally replaced by new adsorbers. The spent carbon must then be regenerated at the supplier facility or disposed via commercial disposal. Disposal could be a significant cost and should be carefully considered, particularly if the spent carbon will be considered a hazardous waste (because of the nature of the adsorbed material).

Following is an example of the amount of carbon needed over the service life of the treatment:

Operating and Startup Period:	24 Months
System:	Modular Permanent
Carbon Adsorber Unit:	1–50 CFM, 110 lbs Fill, Closed Upflow Unit
Number of Adsorbers:	1
Replacement Schedule:	3 months
Calculation:	$110 \times (24/3-1) = 770$ lbs of Coal Based Replacement Carbon

An engineer and/or company technician must supervise the replacement of carbon in the system. Carbon replacement can take from 1–12 hours; the average time is 6 hours. This includes travel time to and from the site.

Blowers

In some cases, a blower may be required to transport gas through the canisters (e.g., following air stripping). If carbon adsorption follows soil vapor extraction, a blower may not be required. If a blower is used, selection of the proper blower size is based on the pressure and flow required for the chosen adsorber. Normally, 1 blower will be used for each adsorber. A dual-bed packaged unit is an exception; it already contains a blower within the system, so no external blower is required.

The blower size is related to the air flow rate, in cubic feet per minute, and the carbon adsorber specified. If 2 adsorbers are chosen, then 2 blowers will also be chosen. It is possible that one blower with a higher CFM rating and pressure rating could be used. Figure 12.5 shows typical blower selections.

Heaters

The temperature and the relative humidity (RH) of the air stream both affect the maximum adsorptive ability of the carbon. In cold climates, an air heater may be required to raise the temperature and dry out the air. The need for a heater is generally based on the results of the pilot test.

If a heater is required, selection is based on the carbon adsorption unit and the CFM required. Normally, air heaters used on carbon adsorbers are explosion-proof hazardous air location heaters. The heater will

Modular Carbon Adsorbers: Disposable And Permanent		
Air Flow Rate (CFM)	**Qty.**	**Unit**
1-50	1	50 CFM, 110 lb. Fill, Closed Upflow, 7″ Pressure Drop
0	0	50 CFM, 100 lb. Fill, Closed Upflow, 7″ Pressure Drop HDPE
0	0	100 CFM, 150 lb. Fill, Closed Upflow, 5″ Pressure Drop
51-100	1	100 CFM, 200 lb. Fill, Closed Upflow, 6.8″ Pressure Drop
0	0	100 CFM, 200 lb. Fill, Closed Upflow, 6.8″ Pressure Drop HDPE
101-150	1	150 CFM, 300 lb. Fill, Closed Upflow, 7.9″ Pressure Drop
0	0	250 CFM, 400 lb. Fill, Closed Upflow, 11.3″ Pressure Drop
151-250	1	250 CFM, 400 lb. Fill, Closed Upflow, 11.3″ Pressure Drop HDPE
251-500	1	500 CFM, 1,200 lb. Fill, Closed Upflow, 8.5″ Pressure Drop HDPE
0	0	500 CFM, 1,400 lb. Fill, Closed Upflow, 11.5″ Pressure Drop
0	0	500 CFM, 200 lb. Fill, Radial Flow, 4.8″ Pressure Drop
501-750	1	750 CFM, 3,200 lb. Fill, Closed Upflow, 11.5″ Pressure Drop
751-1,000	1	1,000 CFM, 400 lb. Fill, Radial Flow, 4.8″ Pressure Drop
1,001-1,500	1	1,500 CFM, 5,700 lb. Fill, Closed Upflow, 11.5″ Pressure Drop
0	0	1,500 CFM, 300 lb. Fill, Radial Flow, 4.8″ Pressure Drop
1,501-2,200	1	2,200 CFM, 3,000 lb. Fill, 6 x 6 Closed Traverse, 8″ Pressure Drop
2,201-3,000	1	3,000 CFM, 1,600 lb. Fill, Radial Flow, 4.8″ Pressure Drop
3,001-4,000	1	4,000 CFM, 5,300 lb. Fill, 8 x 8 Closed Traverse, 8″ Pressure Drop
4,001-5,000	1	5,000 CFM, 4,700 lb. Fill, Radial Flow
5,001-8,000	1	8,000 CFM, 6,300 lb. Fill, Radial Flow

Figure 12.4 Modular Carbon Adsorbers: Disposable and Permanent

Packaged High Pressure Blower Systems
50 CFM, 7″ Pressure, 3/4 H.P.
100 CFM, 5″ Pressure, 1/3 H.P.
150 CFM, 8″ Pressure, 3/4 H.P.
250 CFM, 12″ Pressure, 1-1/2 H.P.
500 CFM, 5″ Pressure, 1 H.P.
500 CFM, 9″ Pressure, 2 H.P.
500 CFM, 12″ Pressure, 5 H.P.
750 CFM, 12″ Pressure, 5 H.P.
1,000 CFM, 5″ Pressure, 1-1/2 H.P.
1,500 CFM, 12″ Pressure, 10 H.P.
1,500 CFM, 5″ Pressure, 3 H.P.
2,200 CFM, 8″ Pressure, 7-1/2 H.P.
3,000 CFM, 5″ Pressure, 7-1/2 H.P.
4,000 CFM, 8″ Pressure, 15 H.P.
5,000 CFM, 8″ Pressure, 20 H.P.
8,000 CFM, 8″ Pressure, 25 H.P.

Figure 12.5 Packaged High Pressure Blower Systems

Packaged Hazardous Air Heaters
7.5 KW, 25,600 BTU
10 KW, 34,150 BTU
15 KW, 51,200 BTU
20 KW, 68,300 BTU

Figure 12.6 Packaged Hazardous Air Heaters

generally be able to raise the ambient air temperature 20°F, with the exception of the 20 kW heater, which raises the temperature of the 8,000 CFM flow rate unit by only 8°F. Figure 12.6 is a list of typical heaters.

Related Costs

Other costs associated with gas-phase carbon adsorption include:

- Sampling and analysis of the influent and effluent stream
- The blower
- Heater and motor maintenance
- Electricity to operate the system

Sampling and analysis related to treatment, monitoring, or disposal during remedial action are addressed in Chapter 57. Treatment duration is the driving factor affecting the quantity and cost of sampling and analysis and blower maintenance. An estimating rule of thumb for sampling and analysis of the adsorber effluent gas is weekly for the first month, monthly for the first year, and quarterly for the duration of the treatment. Conservatively, assume that sampling of both influent and effluent is required. This may not always be the case. For example, carbon adsorption would be used following soil vapor extraction (SVE), where SVE requires influent and effluent sampling. The effluent for the SVE unit may also be the influent for the carbon adsorption unit(s).

Blower, heater, and motor maintenance includes inspecting and reworking the associated motors. A rule of thumb is to inspect and rework motors every 18 months during treatment. In severe or corrosive environments, the interval may be shorter.

The electrical cost to operate the blowers and heaters is based on the number of blowers and heaters and the corresponding horsepower rating for the selected equipment. The quantity of electric usage is based on the duration of the treatment technology.

Another related cost may be foundation support for the carbon adsorption unit, which is based on the adsorber unit size. Typical slab thickness is 8". The area of the slab is based on the canister size.

Site Work and Utilities

Site work and utilities that may be applicable include:

- Electrical distribution
- Access roads
- Fencing

When used, these must also be covered by the estimate.

Conclusion

Gas carbon adsorption systems are commonly used as a secondary treatment system for soil gas or groundwater extractions and treatment systems. The cost drivers are the size of the system, the frequency of carbon replacement, and the operating period. The cost engineer should work closely with the design team to determine whether off-gas treatment is required.

Chapter 13

Carbon Adsorption—Liquid

Liquid-phase carbon adsorption is basically the same process as gas-phase carbon adsorption, as discussed in Chapter 12, except that the media to be treated is liquid instead of gas. Liquid adsorption is a natural process in which molecules of a liquid are physically attracted to and held at the surface of a solid. To treat waste streams by adsorption, contaminants (the adsorbate) are transferred and concentrated from one medium (liquid) to another (the adsorbent).

The most common adsorbent is granular-activated carbon (GAC). Carbon adsorption often follows other treatment processes in a treatment train. Pretreatment for carbon adsorption may include sedimentation, filtration, metals removal, oil removal, air stripping, and pH adjustment. Pretreating the aqueous stream can substantially reduce the costs of carbon adsorption.

Applications and Limitations

Applications

- Target contaminants are hydrocarbons, SVOCs (semi-volatile organic compounds), and explosives.
- Best suited for removing organics with relatively high molecular weights, low water solubility, low polarity, and a low degree of ionization.
- Contaminant concentrations should be less than 10,000 ppm, with suspended solids less than 50 ppm, and dissolved inorganics, oil, and grease less than 10 ppm.
- Carbon type, pore size, quality, and operating temperature will affect process performance.
- Broad flow range systems are available from fractional GPM to thousands of GPM.

Limitations

- Limited effectiveness may be achieved on halogenated VOCs (Volatile Organic Compounds) and pesticides.
- High costs if used as primary treatment of fluids with high contaminant concentrations.
- Spent Granular-Activated Carbon (GAC) may require hazardous waste handling and transport before being disposed.

- Influent streams with high suspended solids (>50mg/l) or oil and grease may cause GAC fouling.
- Metals can foul GAC systems.
- GAC used to treat explosives or metals contaminated groundwater cannot be regenerated.

Process Configurations and Treatment Train Considerations

- Carbon Absorption Liquids are used to treat water discharges from other remedial activities as a polishing step to achieve regulatory compliance. Compatible technologies include sedimentation, filtration, metals removal, oil removal, air stripping, and pH adjustment.
- Effluent from gravity GAC adsorbers may require pumping.
- Adsorber may require backwashing if suspended solids are present.

Typical System Design Elements

In liquid-phase carbon adsorption, contaminated liquid comes in contact with the carbon by flowing through one or more packed bed adsorbers. A packed bed adsorber is simply a column packed with GAC. The activated carbon selectively adsorbs organic hazardous constituents that are attracted to and held in the internal micropores of the carbon granules.

Once the micropore surfaces of the adsorbent (GAC) are saturated with organics, the adsorptive capacity of the carbon is exhausted and the contaminant concentration in the effluent increases. This process is known as *breakthrough*. The time it takes for breakthrough to occur is the single most critical operating parameter for a GAC adsorber system. The carbon must then be removed, thermally regenerated or recycled, and replaced. Carbon longevity will significantly affect operating costs. The presence of fouling substances, such as iron or particulates, also affects carbon efficiency.

Most liquid-phase adsorption treatment applications use GAC adsorbers, which operate in a downflow series mode, either by gravity or under pressure. The downflow gravity adsorber operates as a filter, and flow is limited. The effluent from a gravity adsorber may require pumping if a pressure water system is used. The adsorber may require backwashing if suspended solids are present in the influent. A pressurized adsorber allows greater bed depth, which can be used for higher surface loading rates while maintaining the same contact time, resulting in a higher flow rate. The downflow fixed bed series mode is cost-effective and produces lower effluent concentrations than other carbon adsorber designs (e.g., downflow in parallel, moving bed, upflow-expanded). The adsorbers may be connected in parallel to provide increased hydraulic capacity.

The adsorption characteristics of combinations of contaminants in a waste stream are usually not predictable, except for certain common chemicals with which the design engineer has application experience. Even under these conditions, a pilot test using a sample of the water of interest in comparable conditions is often required to accurately determine the optimal contact time and carbon usage rate for a specific site.

To conduct an initial estimate of carbon column sizing, the following data must be established during pilot plant testing:

- Contact time (minutes)

- Flow capacity (GPM)
- Carbon usage (lbs/1,000 gallons)
- Collected volume of treated waste water at breakthrough (gallons)
- Carbon density (weight of carbon/C.F.)

Adsorption efficiency depends on several factors:

- Strength of the molecular attraction between the adsorbent and adsorbate
- Molecular weight of the adsorbate
- Type and characteristic of adsorbent
- Electrokinetic charge
- pH of the waste stream
- Surface area of the adsorbent

The effectiveness of carbon adsorption can be evaluated through an adsorption *isotherm*. The isotherm relates the amount of solute adsorbed per weight of adsorbent to the solute concentration remaining in the liquid at equilibrium. The isotherm is essentially a way to describe the capacity of carbon for a particular compound, or the efficiency of carbon to remove that compound. Isotherm data for some of the more common organic compounds are available through various publications.

Once the efficiency of carbon has been established for a particular compound, a dynamic column test should be conducted. In this test, the liquid is pumped through a series of carbon-filled canisters, and effluent samples are collected from each canister. Information gathered from this test will better define the design of the carbon adsorption system, including the optimum number of canisters.

Figures 13.1 and 13.2 illustrate typical carbon adsorption systems. GAC adsorbers may be operated as either single-stage or multi-stage. In multi-stage use, the leading adsorber removes most of the contamination, while the next adsorber acts as a "polishing" step, removing any residual organics from the water. In series operation, the entire adsorptive capacity of the carbon is used. The lead adsorber can be used past breakthrough because the second adsorber continues to remove the contaminants. After the spent carbon of the lead adsorber is replaced, the piping is reversed so that the new carbon becomes the polishing bed. Systems with parallel series of 4 or more units are not uncommon. Although multistage operation makes optimal use of carbon, the cost is higher than single-stage and may not always be justified, especially when discharge limitations are not stringent. Therefore, in multi-contaminant situations, additional treatment may be required since the physical properties of the organics result in preferential selection by GAC pore spaces.

GAC works best for low-solubility, high-molecular weight, nonpolar, branched compounds. Alcohols, ketones, and ethers are poor adsorbers, whereas most solvents and pesticides are excellent adsorbers. Contaminant concentrations should be less than 10,000 ppm, suspended solids less than 50 ppm, dissolved inorganics and oil and grease less than 10 ppm.

Since GAC originates from several different materials (e.g., bituminous coal, coconut shells, lignite), different GAC products have different adsorptive capacities. This also holds true for regenerated versus virgin

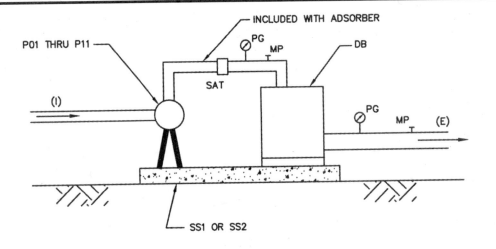

PROFILE

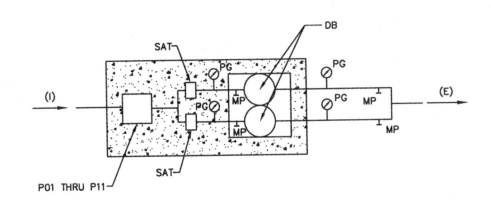

PLAN

VARIABLES

SAMPLE PORT	= MP	PUMP SIZE	= P01 THRU P11
CHECK VALVE	= CV	DUAL BED ADSORBER	= DB
PRESSURE GAUGE	= PG	8" STRUCTURAL SLAB	= SS1
THERMOSTAT	= TH	12" STRUCTURAL SLAB	= SS2
HUMIDITY CONTROL		25' X 6" FLEX S.S. HOSE	= FH
SATURATION INDICATOR	= SAT	INFLUENT PIPING	= I
		EFFLUENT PIPING	= E

Figure 13.1 Variable Qualifications, Typical Parallel Dual Bed Carbon Adsorption System

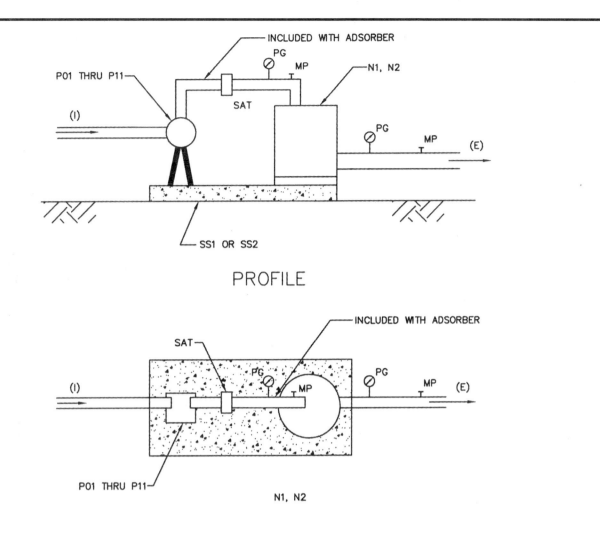

PROFILE

PLAN

VARIABLES

SAMPLE PORT	= MP	PUMP SIZE	= P01 THRU P11
CHECK VALVE	= CV	MODULAR CARBON ADSORBER	= N1, N2
PRESSURE GAUGE	= PG	8" STRUCTURAL SLAB	= SS1
THERMOSTAT	= TH	12" STRUCTURAL SLAB	= SS2
HUMIDITY CONTROL		25' X 6" FLEX S.S. HOSE	= FH
SATURATION INDICATOR	= SAT	INFLUENT PIPING	= I
		EFFLUENT PIPING	= E

Figure 13.2 Variable Qualifications, Typical Modular Carbon Adsorption System

carbon. When the effluent will be used for drinking purposes, virgin carbon must be used. Reactivated carbon, which costs considerably less, is normally acceptable when the effluent is discharged to surface or groundwater through land application, surface water (requires federal NPDES permit), POTW, or infiltration gallery.

Basic Information Needed for Estimating

It is possible to create a reasonable cost estimate for liquid-phase adsorption using a few required parameters. If more detailed information is known, one can create a more precise and site-specific estimate using a secondary set of parameters.

To estimate the cost of a water carbon adsorption system, certain basic information must be known. This information is discussed in the following paragraphs.

Flow Rate

The influent flow rate will affect the selection of the GAC canisters or dual bed system. Generally, the flow rate is dictated by the primary treatment technology, such as air stripping. Typically the flow rates are limited to around 750 GPM, but larger systems can be built using parallel strippers.

Type of System

The choices of carbon adsorption systems are as follows:

- The **dual bed system** is a packaged treatment system consisting of two carbon adsorbers that can be configured in series or in parallel, depending on the facility requirements. This is the most common type of system in current use.
- The **modular disposable system** consists of one adsorber, which is disposed or replaced after the carbon is spent (and breakthrough occurs).
- The **modular permanent system** consists of one adsorber that can be emptied and reused on-site. Because a new canister is not necessary after breakthrough occurs, the modular permanent canisters are less expensive to operate. The user can add more dual bed systems or canisters as needed.

As mentioned earlier, GAC adsorption can employ a single-stage adsorber (one adsorber) or multi-stage adsorbers (dual-bed or multiple adsorbers). Although multi-stage adsorbers are the optimal arrangement for efficiency, capital costs are higher for the multistage configuration. Down-time for maintenance and replacement is generally longer for permanent and dual-bed systems, but does not have a significant impact on cost.

Treatment Period

The total treatment period may be divided into startup and O&M periods. The costs associated with the startup period are generally included with the capital costs, and the O&M costs are identified separately.

Worker Safety Level

Worker safety is affected by the contaminant(s) at the site. Safety level refers to the levels required by OSHA in 29 CFR Part 1910. The 4 levels are designated as A, B, C, and D; where "A" is the most protective and "D" is the least protective.

Design Information Needed for Detailed Estimates

Following are descriptions of the types of detailed information that, when available, can add detail and accuracy to estimates for the systems. Also included are design criteria and estimating rules of thumb that estimators typically use to determine values that are not known or to check information provided by others.

Type of Carbon Adsorber(s)

The selection of the carbon adsorber unit depends on the type of contaminants, the operating period, flow rate required, and operator preference. A range of system options and configurations is shown in Figures 13.3, 13.4, and 13.5. These figures show typical selections available for packaged dual bed units, modular disposable units, and modular permanent units, respectively.

Number of Units

The number of carbon adsorber units depends on the flow rate and type of system being used. The system designer decides the number of units. In most cases, for flow rates of up to 150 GPM, the number of adsorbers for each system type is as follows:

- Dual bed—2 adsorbers
- Modular disposable—1 adsorber
- Modular permanent—1 adsorber

The user should consider the advantages of using combinations of the 50–150 GPM adsorbers when flow capacities are greater than 150 GPM. Larger or odd-sized units can significantly increase capital costs.

Replacement Carbon

The choice of replacement carbon is normally based on one of the following:

- Coal based—Virgin carbon (permanent and dual bed; not available for disposable adsorbers)
- Coconut based—Virgin carbon (not available for disposable adsorbers)
- Activated aluminus—Virgin carbon (not available for disposable adsorbers)
- Reactivated carbon (not available for disposable adsorbers)
- Replacement with new disposable adsorbers (disposable; only available for disposable adsorbers)

Both permanent adsorbers and dual bed adsorbers are most commonly replaced with coal based—virgin carbon. Disposable adsorbers are typically replaced with new disposable adsorbers.

Replacement Schedule

The schedule for replacing spent carbon adsorbers depends on the adsorption efficiency. The spent carbon is typically replaced every 3 months. A user who has knowledge of a particular contaminant and concentration may opt for a different replacement schedule.

Disposable carbon adsorbers are replaced by the same type of adsorbers. The spent carbon must then be regenerated at the supplier facility or disposed via commercial disposal. Any type of carbon process could include significant disposal costs. In most cases, the cost of disposal could be included in arrangements with carbon contractors.

Packaged Dual-Bed Carbon Adsorption Units		
Flow Rate (GPM)	**Qty.**	**Unit**
1-100	1	Dual-Bed, 50 GPM Series, 100 GPM Parallel, 1,760 lb. Fill, Each
101-130	1	Dual-Bed, 2–4′ Diameter, 65 GPM Series, 130 GPM Parallel, 2,000 lb. Fill, Each
131-150	1	Dual-Bed, 750 GPM Series, 150 GPM Parallel, 3,300 lb. Fill, Each
151-350	1	Dual-Bed, 2–7.5′ Diameter, 175 GPM Series, 350 GPM Parallel, 10,000 lb. Fill, Each
351-700	1	Dual-Bed, 2–10′ Diameter, 350 GPM Series, 700 GPM Parallel, 20,000 lb. Fill, Each

Figure 13.3 Packaged Dual-Bed Carbon Adsorption Units

Modular Carbon Adsorbers–Disposable		
Flow Rate (GPM)	**Qty.**	**Unit**
1-5	1	5 GPM, 85 lb. Fill, DOT 5B Drum
	(or) 1	5 GPM, 85 lb. Fill, HDPE DOT Spec 34
6-15	1	15 GPM, 165 lb. Fill, DOT 5B Drum
	(or) 1	15 GPM, 165 lb. Fill, HDPE DOT Spec 34
16-20	1	20 GPM, 250 lb. Fill
21-25	1	25 GPM, 330 lb. Fill
	(or) 1	25 GPM, 330 lb. Fill, HDPE
26-35	1	35 GPM, 1,050 lb. Fill
36-50	1	50 GPM, 1,650 lb. Fill
	(or) 1	50 GPM, 1,050 lb. Fill, HDPE
51-100	1	100 GPM, 3,000 lb. Fill
101-200	1	200 GPM, 6,000 lb. Fill
201-400	2	200 GPM, 6,000 lb. Fill
401-600	3	200 GPM, 6,000 lb. Fill
601-700	4	200 GPM, 6,000 lb. Fill

Figure 13.4 Modular Carbon Adsorbers-Disposable

The following is an example of the amount of carbon needed over the service life of the treatment:

Startup Period:	24 Months
System:	Modular Permanent
Carbon Adsorber Unit:	1–50 GPM, 880 lbs Fill, 316L Stainless Steel
Number of Adsorbers:	1
Replacement Schedule:	3 months
Default Algorithm:	$880 \times (24/3-1) = 6{,}160$ lbs of Coal Based Replacement Carbon

An engineer and/or company technician must supervise the replacement of carbon in the system. Depending on the facility, carbon replacement can take from 1–12 hours. The average time for carbon replacement is 6 hours, including travel time to and from the site.

Related Costs Other costs associated with liquid carbon adsorption include the sampling and analysis of the influent and effluent stream, pump and motor maintenance, and electricity to operate the system. The duration

Modular Carbon Adsorbers–Permanent		
Flow Rate (GPM)	Qty.	Unit
1-25	1	25 GPM, 330 lb. Fill, HDPE
	(or) 1	25 GPM, 330 lb. Fill, HDPE Lined Steel
	(or) 1	25 GPM, 330 lb. Fill, 316L Stainless Steel
26-35	1	35 GPM, 660 lb. Fill, HDPE Lined Steel
	(or) 1	35 GPM, 660 lb. Fill, 316L Stainless Steel
36-50	1	50 GPM, 1,050 lb. Fill, HDPE
	(or) 1	50 GPM, 880 lb. Fill, HDPE Lined Steel
	(or) 1	50 GPM, 880 lb. Fill, 316L Stainless Steel
51-75	1	75 GPM, 1,650 lb. Fill, HDPE Lined Steel
	(or) 1	75 GPM, 1,650 lb. Fill, 316L Stainless Steel
76-100	1	100 GPM, 3,000 lb. Fill, HDPE Lined Steel
	(or) 1	100 GPM, 3,000 lb. Fill, 316L Stainless Steel
101-200	1	200 GPM, 6,000 lb. Fill, HDPE Lined Steel
	(or) 1	200 GPM, 6,000 lb. Fill, 316L Stainless Steel
201-400	2	200 GPM, 6,000 lb. Fill, HDPE Lined Steel
401-600	3	200 GPM, 6,000 lb. Fill, HDPE Lined Steel
601-700	4	200 GPM, 6,000 lb. Fill, HDPE Lined Steel

Figure 13.5 Modular Carbon Adsorbers-Permanent

of the startup and O&M periods will be the driving factor affecting the quantity and cost of sampling and analysis and pump maintenance. Sampling and analysis of the adsorber influent and effluent are typically done weekly for the first month, monthly for the first year, and quarterly for the duration of the treatment. Both influent and effluent sampling may not always be required. For example, when carbon adsorption follows air stripping, air stripping requires influent and effluent sampling. The effluent for the air stripper may also be the influent for the carbon adsorption unit(s). In this case, the costs would be included twice.

Pump and motor maintenance includes inspecting and reworking the motor. Inspection and rework are typically done once every 18 months during treatment.

Other related costs include the cost of the pump and associated electrical costs. The default pump selection is based on the system used, the number of absorber units, and the type of carbon adsorber chosen. One pump will default for each permanent or disposable absorber. The dual bed adsorber comes complete with a compressed air mechanism to deliver the waste stream through the carbon; therefore no pumps need to be added to these systems. The pump size in gallons per minute will reflect the recommended adsorber flow rates.

The cost to operate the pumps is based on the number of pumps and the corresponding horsepower rating for the selected pumps. The quantity of electric usage is based on the duration of the treatment technology.

Finally, the cost of the foundation support for the carbon adsorption unit is based on adsorber unit size. The slab thickness is either 8" or 12", depending on the weight of the canister. A 12" slab is generally used for canisters with an operating weight of greater than or equal to 25 tons. The dimensions of the slab are based on the canister floor area required.

Site Work and Utilities

The estimate must account for any site work and utilities that may be applicable, such as:

- Overhead electrical distribution
- Fencing

Conclusion

Liquid carbon adsorption is a treatment process for removing organic compounds from water. This technology is commonly used as part of a treatment train that includes pretreatment. In some cases, carbon adsorption is used as a secondary treatment process to complete a process of contaminant removal that was partially performed using another process, such as air stripping.

The primary cost drivers are the capacity of the system, the operating period, and the frequency of required carbon replacement. These values are determined in concert with the other technologies in the treatment process. The cost engineer should carefully review the design of the entire process and work with the design team to determine the values of these cost drivers.

Chapter 14

Coagulation and Flocculation

Coagulation and flocculation are 2 processes used to remove extremely fine particles and/or colloids from water and waste water. During this process, colloids suspended in a liquid medium are made to agglomerate into larger particles to promote settling. Coagulation reduces the net electrical repulsive forces at the particle surface by electrolytes in the solution, while flocculation is aggregation by chemical bridging between particles.

The coagulation/flocculation combination is rarely a stand-alone technology. Instead, it is generally part of a treatment train that may include precipitation as a pretreatment, then coagulation/flocculation, followed by sedimentation and/or filtration. Three types of coagulants are used for environmental remediation projects: inorganic electrolytes, organic polymers, and synthetic polymers. Inorganic electrolytes are the most common and are the focus of this chapter. If the cost engineer is dealing with a different type of application, the basic principles of this chapter are still valid.

Applications and Limitations

Applications

- Removal of fine particle wastes and colloids from water and waste water.
- Removal of dissolved toxic metals and radionuclides from liquid waste.

Limitations

- The presence of multiple metal species may lead to removal difficulties because of the amphoteric nature of different compounds (i.e., optimization in removing one metal species may prevent removal of another).
- As discharge standards become more stringent, further treatment may be required.
- Reagent addition must be carefully controlled to preclude unacceptable concentrations in treatment effluent.
- Dissolved salts are added to the treated water as a result of pH adjustment.

Process Configurations and Treatment Train Considerations

- Treatment train may include precipitation as a pretreatment, then coagulation/flocculation, followed by sedimentation and/or filtration.
- Process may generate toxic sludge, which will require proper disposal.
- Three types of commonly used coagulants are inorganic electrolytes, organic polymers (polyelectrolytes), and synthetic polymers.
- Inorganic electrolytes include aluminum sulfate (alum), lime, and various iron salts, with alum being the most widely used.
- The dosage of alum used is typically 5–50 milligrams per liter (mg/l). An effective pH range for alum coagulation is 5.5–8.0.
- Metal hydroxide sludges must pass TCLP prior to land disposal.
- Coagulant aids may be added to the waste stream to improve coagulation efficiency by increasing or reducing the floc size. Weighting agents (e.g., bentonite clays), adsorbents (e.g., activated carbon), and oxidants (e.g., chlorine, ozone, and potassium permanganate) are commonly used.
- The process options for coagulation/flocculation include treatment in separate stages or treatment combined into one stage. The separated treatment may include precipitation, rapid mix, flocculation/coagulation, and sedimentation.
- Flocculation is affected by the overflow rate, the depth of the basin, the velocity gradients in the system, the concentration of particles, and the range of particle sizes.
- Treated water will often require pH adjustment.

Typical System Design Elements

Coagulation/flocculation involves 3 main steps:

1. Adding coagulants to the waste stream.
2. Mixing rapidly to disperse the coagulant.
3. Mixing slowly and gently to promote agglomeration of the colloids.

Other related technologies include:

Pretreatment

- Oxidation
- Neutralization
- Reduction

Polishing treatment for aqueous residuals

- Neutralization
- Sedimentation
- Filtration
- Ion exchange
- Carbon adsorption
- Membrane processes

Polishing treatment for solid residuals

- Sedimentation
- Solids dewatering
- Solidification/stabilization

A typical contact clarifier where coagulation/flocculation takes place is illustrated in Figure 14.1. The coagulation/flocculation process can take place in separate stages or in one combined stage. The separate stages may include precipitation, rapid mix, flocculation/coagulation, and sedimentation. The combined treatment includes all of the processes in a single contact clarifier. Figure 14.2 is a photo of a typical flocculation tank.

Basic Information Needed for Estimating

It is possible to create a reasonable cost estimate for the coagulation/flocculation process using a few required parameters. If more detailed information is known, one can create a more precise and site-specific estimate using a secondary set of parameters.

To estimate the cost of the system, certain basic information must be known. This information is discussed in the following paragraphs.

Flow Rate

Coagulation and flocculation systems for remediation are usually purchased or leased as package systems. The flow rate, measured in gallons per minute (GPM), determines the hydraulic sizing for a package coagulation/flocculation clarifier system. The clarifier system includes a clarifier tank and mechanism, a flocculation chamber and mixer, and a polymer feed system. Typical ranges are 1–2,000 GPM. Figure 14.3 shows standard flow rates and appropriate clarifier sizes.

Treatment Period

The treatment period determines how many consumables and utilities are required to run the system to completion and is a major cost driver. The total treatment period is generally divided into startup and O&M. The costs associated with the startup period are included with the capital costs, and O&M costs are identified separately.

Worker Safety Level

Worker safety is affected by the contaminant(s) at the site. Safety level refers to the levels required by OSHA in 29 CFR Part 1910. The 4 levels are designated as A, B, C, and D; where "A" is the most protective and "D" is the least protective.

Design Information Needed for Detailed Estimates

Following are descriptions of the types of information that, when available, can add detail and accuracy to estimates for the systems. Also included are design criteria and estimating rules of thumb that estimators use to determine values that are not known or to check information provided by others.

Coagulants

Determine the primary coagulant, the additive rate, secondary coagulants, if any, and their additive rate. The following section explains each coagulant.

Primary Coagulants

Several types of coagulants can be used. The most common coagulants used for water and wastewater treatment are aluminum and iron salts. Aluminum sulfate (alum) is a common metal salt, and is a good coagulant for water containing appreciable organic matter. Iron coagulants operate over a wider pH range and are usually more effective in removing color from water.

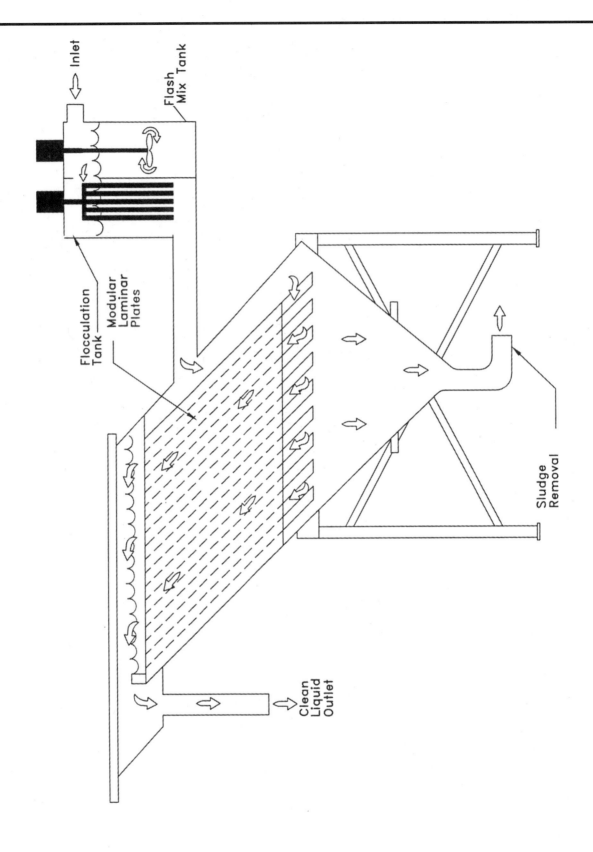

Figure 14.1 Typical Contact Clarifier Profile

112

Figure 14.2   Flocculation Tanks

Figure 14.3   Clarifier Selection Table

Clarifier Selection	
Flow Rate	**Clarifier Diameter**
1–25 GPM Waste Flow	9′
26–45 GPM Waste Flow	12′
46–70 GPM Waste Flow	15′
71–130 GPM Waste Flow	20′
131–208 GPM Waste Flow	25′
209–305 GPM Waste Flow	30′
306–546 GPM Waste Flow	40′
547–850 GPM Waste Flow	50′
851–1,194 GPM Waste Flow	60′
1,195–1,645 GPM Waste Flow	70′

Primary Coagulant (Additive Rate)

The primary coagulant rate refers to the application rate of the chemicals required for the proper operation of the clarifier. Alum dosage typically ranges from 5–50 mg/l. The conversion factor for conveying mg/l to lbs/1,000 gallons is 0.008345. A reasonable rule of thumb for alum dosage rate is 40 mg/l (0.334 lbs/1,000 gals). The O&M costs will vary depending on the primary coagulant application rate required for specific contaminants and concentrations.

Secondary Coagulants

Coagulant aids may be added to the waste stream to improve coagulation efficiency by increasing or reducing the floc size. As noted previously, weighted agents (e.g., bentonite clays), adsorbents (e.g., activated carbon), and oxidants (e.g., chlorine, ozone, and potassium permanganate) are commonly used. Typically, a secondary coagulant is not required, but it can increase efficiency. Options for secondary coagulants include the following:

- Soda ash, powdered
- Quicklime, 1/4" nominal granules
- Quicklime, 3/4" nominal granules
- Quicklime, 1/4" and 3/4" nominal granules
- Hydrated lime, powdered bulk
- Montmorillonite, bulk
- Sodium hectorite, bulk
- Dispersible sodium bentonite, bulk

Secondary Coagulant (Additive Rate)

The secondary coagulant rate is measured in the same units (lbs/1,000 gal) as the primary coagulant rate. The O&M costs will vary depending on the secondary coagulant application rate required for specific contaminants and concentrations.

Piping

Determine the piping requirements for the system using the following guidelines.

Influent Piping Length

The influent piping length is the length of the piping from the previous treatment train component to the coagulation/flocculation unit. In most cases, the piping is installed above ground.

Effluent Piping Length

The effluent piping length is the length of the piping from the coagulation/flocculation unit to the next treatment train component.

Piping Material

PVC is the most common and cost-effective piping material for coagulation/flocculation systems. Occasionally, project requirements dictate carbon or stainless steel piping.

Related Costs

Capital expenses for coagulation/flocculation include costs for the solid-contact clarifier, associated piping, and installation. Operational costs include electricity for running the clarifier pumps, periodic effluent testing, and maintenance. Sludge treatment, hauling, and disposal are normally required as well.

Site Work and Utilities

Site work and utilities that may be applicable for coagulation and flocculation include:

- Overhead electrical distribution
- Fencing and signage
- Clear and grub
- Grading and excavation

Conclusion

The primary cost drivers for coagulation/flocculation systems are the capacity of the system, the operating period, and the disposal costs for solids precipating from the system. When these systems are used as part of a larger treatment train process, the cost engineer must understand their cost implications.

Chapter 15

Dewatering (Sludge)

Dewatering is a physical process that reduces the moisture content of slurries or sludges. Reducing the moisture content enables handling and prepares the materials for final treatment and/or disposal. Selecting the appropriate method depends on factors such as the volume of the slurry, the solids content of the waste stream, the availability of land space, and the degree of dewatering required prior to treatment and/or disposal.

Applications and Limitations

Applications

- Appropriate for a wide variety of sludges, both hazardous and non-hazardous.
- Vacuum filtration units are available in various sizes, and they are generally used in larger facilities where space is limited or when dewatering is necessary for maximum volume reduction.
- Advantages of centrifugation include relatively limited space requirements and rapid startup and shutdown. Also, since centrifugation is essentially an enclosed process, emissions are minimal.

Limitations

- Dewatering is a physical separation process that does not eliminate contaminants.

Process Configurations and Treatment Train Considerations

- Filtration includes vacuum, pressure, and belt press filters and allows the filtrate to pass through the filtering medium while retaining a significant fraction of the solids on the medium's surface. The collected solids are then physically removed from the filtering medium.
- Dewatered sludge must be removed periodically from drying beds and lagoons by manual labor or mechanized equipment. Structural support requirements for the drying beds may depend on the method that will be used to remove sludge from the drying beds (e.g., spade, end loader, or other mechanical removal device).
- The effectiveness of centrifugation depends on the particle sizes and shapes, the solids concentration, and other factors.

- Dewatering is a well-developed and widely available technology. Skid-mounted dewatering and pilot equipment are readily available, and many vendors offer technical assistance.

Typical System Design Elements

Methods used to dewater solid waste streams include:

- Filtration
- Centrifugation
- Drying beds
- Drying lagoons

Filtration is the most common method of dewatering used for environmental applications in the United States. This section covers the estimated process for belt press filtration.

Belt press filtration units are available in various sizes, and they are generally provided as a packaged system including tanks, pumps, and mixers, in addition to the filter press. Typical filter press units are illustrated in Figures 15.1, 15.2, and 15.3.

Filtration can be used to dewater solids over a wide range of concentrations and particle sizes. A particular application's effectiveness depends on the type of filter used, and the particle size distribution and concentrations.

A filter press is a liquid-solid separation technology used to dewater sludge. A slurry is pumped into a series of chambers. Filtered liquid (filtrate) passes through filter cloths and a press, which physically separates the sludge solids from the liquid. The dewatered sludge that is left behind is called *filter cake*. When the press is opened, the cake is discharged by gravity as each plate is shifted.

Filter press units are usually available as package units either via permanent or mobile installation.

After the dewatering process, the dewatered cake is suitable for landfilling, heat drying, incineration, or land spreading. The moisture content of the final cake can have a significant impact on transportation and disposal costs. The additional mass of absorbed water is inexpensive to transport, and free liquids generally are not accepted by land disposal sites.

Other Dewatering Processes

Though not discussed in detail, the following are general descriptions of other dewatering methods.

Centrifugation separates solids and liquids using the centrifugal force developed by rapid rotation of a cylindrical drum or bowl. Centrifuges can be used to concentrate or dewater soils or sediments ranging in size from fine gravel to silt.

Drying beds use gravity or vacuum-aided percolation through fine sand beds to dewater sludges. Solar heat input increases evaporation, helping the drying process, but its usefulness depends on the local climate.

Dying lagoons use percolation and evaporation to remove water from thickened waste stream. Again, solar heat input can aid drying. Decanting clarified liquids from the surface is also widely practiced to help drying.

118

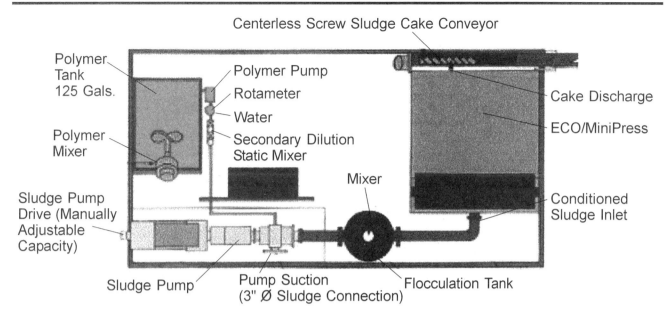

Figure 15.1 Typical Sludge Belt Filter Press Unit Including Tanks, Pumps & Filter Press
Courtesy The EcoPress™

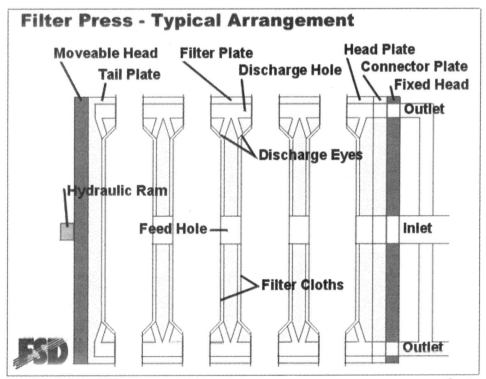

Courtesy of FSD

Figure 15.2 Sample Filter Press Schematic

Basic Information Needed for Estimating

It is possible to create a reasonable cost estimate using a few required parameters. If more detailed information is known, one can create a more precise and site-specific estimate using a secondary set of parameters.

To estimate a cost of a dewatering system, certain information must be known. This information is discussed below.

Dry Solids Flow Rate

The dry solids flow rate is the solids feed rate, in pounds per hour (pph), to the dewatering unit on a dry basis (solids only, no water). This value may be calculated as follows:

Dry Solids Flow Rate (pph) = Fluid Stream Flow × Fluid Density × Fraction of Solids in Fluid × Time Conversion

Where:
Fluid Stream Flow is in gallons per minute (GPM).
Fluid Density is in pounds per gallon.
Fraction of Solids in Fluid is in ppm.
Time Conversion is 60 minutes per hour.
A typical valid range for dry solids flow rate is 0.1–500 pounds per hour.

Wet Cake Density

The wet cake density is the weight of wet filter cake in pounds per cubic foot (PCF). A typical value is 20 PCF. Values usually range from 15–50 PCF.

Cycle Time

Cycle time is the total time that it takes for a complete cycle to load the filter press to capacity with solids, to remove the solids from the filter press, and to clean the filter press and bring it back online for dewatering processing. A typical cycle time is 4 hours. Practical ranges are 1–100 hours.

Treatment Period

The treatment period can be divided into startup and operations and maintenance (O&M). The startup period begins after initial installation of the system, when the system is monitored, adjusted, and regulated, until the desired performance is achieved. Typically, the startup period is several weeks to several months. This period will have a higher labor cost than the O&M period, so determining an appropriate startup period will affect the final cost estimate.

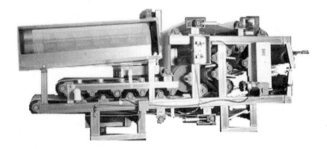

Figure 15.3 Typical Filter Press

The O&M period, typically measured in months, will depend on the total quantity of sludge to be dewatered. The hours of daily operation will affect the number of months of operation.

Worker Safety Level

Worker safety is affected by the contaminant(s) at the site. Safety level refers to the level required by OSHA in 29 CRF Part 1910. The 4 levels are designated as A, B, C, and D; "A" is the most protective and "D" is the least protective. A safety level of E is also included to simulate normal construction "no hazard" conditions as prescribed by the EPA.

Design Information Needed for Detailed Estimates

Following are descriptions of the types of detailed information that, when available, can add detail and accuracy to estimates. Also included are design criteria and estimating rules of thumb that the estimator typically uses to determine values that are not known, or to check information provided by others.

Dry Solids Flow Rate (Following Metals Precipitation)

When metals are present in contaminated water, metals precipitation technology is often used prior to sludge dewatering. When this occurs, the Dry Solids Flow Rate can be calculated as follows:

Dry Solids Flow Rate (Pounds per Hour) = 0.005 × Flow Rate × [(2.6 × Metals Concentration) + Influent Total Suspended Solids Concentration + (2 × Other Precipitating Anions and Cations Concentration)].

Where all Concentrations are in mg/l (milligrams per liter)

Influent and Effluent Piping Length

The influent piping length is the length of the piping from the previous treatment train component in the filtration unit. The effluent piping length is the length of the piping from the dewatering unit to the next treatment train component. Where possible, the most cost-effective piping is placed above ground. Buried piping, however, is sometimes required because of site access requirements or weather conditions.

Piping Material

The piping material can be different for influent and effluent flow. The most common and least expensive piping material is PVC. Other options include carbon steel, chemical-resistant flexible hose, polypropylene, and stainless steel.

Related Costs

Analysis of Influent/Effluent Concentrations

For the first month of operation, a weekly sample should be taken of the vacuum filtration unit effluent water and filter cake to ensure adequate sludge thickening and suspended solids removal. After the first month, a monthly sample should be taken throughout the life of the dewatering unit. Other analytical work may be required, depending on the Record of Decision (RoD) and associated restrictions.

Electricity

The cost of electricity to operate the pump motor must be considered. The estimator should contact the local power company to determine a location-specific energy charge, since energy rates vary from one power company to another. The pump size and operating hours per week will determine the actual power consumption.

Operation & Maintenance

Maintenance and upkeep of dewatering units is a time-consuming and expensive task. The O&M cost will vary depending on the size of the unit. Filter media replacement, pump, and motor maintenance, and other related maintenance costs as well as operation costs for labor, electric power, and facility maintenance are included in this section of the estimate.

Site Work and Utilities

Site work and utilities cost items that may be applicable for dewatering include:

- Overhead electrical distribution
- Chemical storage building

Conclusion

Dewatering is a volume reduction methodology that can be quite effective in reducing overall treatment costs for hazardous wastes. The primary cost drivers are the size of the system, the process options chosen, the length of the operating period, and the disposal costs for the solids and liquids generated by the process. The cost engineer should be able to obtain this information from the design team early in the design process, and should work with the designer to optimize the system size versus the operating period trade-off.

Chapter 16

Ex Situ Bioreactors

Ex Situ Bioreactors use micro-organisms to degrade contaminants in water. The chief agents of biological degradation are heterotrophic bacteria and fungi. These organisms can use organic substrates as sources of carbon for energy and for the biosynthesis of new cellular material. Biological treatment systems can be used for a wide range of organic contaminants, including polycyclic aromatic hydrocarbons (PAHs), phenols, gasoline, chlorinated solvents, diesel fuel, and chlorobenzene.

For a biological treatment process to effectively remove a compound from waste water, an organism capable of using the compound as substrate must exist and be able to proliferate in competition with other micro-organisms in the system. The culture of biomass that develops in the system will depend on the relative concentration of all the substrates in the waste water and on the characteristic of the seed material used to provide the initial biomass during startup. Some compounds may be metabolized by a variety of organisms; others require a specialized organism.

In the basic remediation process, an influent stream containing the contaminant enters a bioreactor, either aerobic or anaerobic. Once inside the bioreactor, the contaminant is biodegraded by the micro-organisms, then exits the bioreactor in the effluent stream.

Applications and Limitations

Applications

- Bioreactors treat SVOCs, fuel hydrocarbons, and any biodegradable organic material.
- Bioreactors with cometabolites are used to treat PCBs, halogenated VOCs, and SVOCs.
- The process may be less effective for some pesticides.
- Successful pilot-scale field studies have been conducted on some halogenated compounds, such as PCP and chlorobenzene and dichloro-benzene isomers.

Limitations

- Air pollution controls may be needed if there is volatilization from activated sludge processes.

123

- Residuals from sludge processes require treatment or disposal.
- Treated effluents may require special handling and disposal.
- Startup time can be slow if organisms need to be acclimated to the wastes.

Process Configurations and Treatment Train Considerations

- Treatment with bioreactors may take up to several years.
- Nutrient addition may be necessary to support microbial activity.
- Nuisance micro-organisms may reduce reactor effectiveness.
- Low ambient temperatures significantly decrease biodegradation rates, resulting in longer cleanup times or increased costs for heating.
- Very high contaminant concentrations may be toxic to micro-organisms and require special design approaches.
- Using cultures that have been previously adapted to specific hazardous wastes can decrease startup and detention times.

Typical System Design Elements

Bioreactors use two types of aerobic bioreactors: suspended growth and attached growth (fixed film). A third type of aqueous biological treatment involves anaerobic degradation, where contaminants are biodegraded in the absence of oxygen. The difference between aerobic and anaerobic bacteria is that the aerobic bacteria use molecular oxygen as their terminal electron acceptor, and anaerobic bacteria use some other compound as their terminal electron acceptor. There are specialized applications for anaerobic systems in groundwater contamination, such as landfills, explosives, and chlorinated solvents.

In a suspended-growth system, active biological solids are mixed with the waste water and held in suspension by aeration as the microbial bloc takes the organic matter out of the solution. The common name for this suspended-growth process is activated sludge.

The advantages of the activated sludge system are:

- The process produces lower effluent concentrations.
- The system can treat many organics at the same time.
- The same equipment can be used for a variety of influent conditions.

The main disadvantages are:

- Labor expense is needed to keep the system adjusted to the influent conditions.
- Oxygen transfer is more expensive than fixed-film systems.
- The bacteria must be kept in a growth stage in which the settling characteristics are at a maximum.

Attached growth systems use fixed-film biological processes (biofilm). Biofilms are aggregates of bacteria that adhere to a static support media. In this system, the contaminant must be brought to the biofilm by the aqueous stream. The contaminant is degraded as it contacts the biomass. However, the biofilm that grows on the submerged media surface can actually grow so thick that it causes excess growth to slough off. A clarifier may be required to remove suspended solids.

Figure 16.1 is a typical process flow diagram for a fixed-film biological process (biofilm). The process starts by pumping contaminated groundwater (or other waste water stream) into a mix tank, where pH may be adjusted. If necessary, the water is heated and then pumped into the bioreactor containing the biofilm. In aerobic bioremediation, oxygen and inorganic nutrients are supplied and the contaminants are biodegraded. Biodegradation that is completely mineralized consists primarily of end products of carbon dioxide, water, and bacteria cell material. Optimally, the treated water is reinfiltrated into the contaminated area to enhance in situ biodegradation. Contaminant or specific organic removal rates can be expected to range from 85–95%.

The main component of an aerobic biological fixed-film treatment system is a reactor in which the waste water and biomass are mixed together while maintaining favorable environmental conditions. Environmental conditions that affect the growth rate of micro-organisms include temperature, pH, nutrient availability, presence or absence of toxicants, and dissolved oxygen concentration.

Ex situ water bioremediation is generally used in conjunction with any of the following treatment technologies: extraction wells, oil/water separation, and/or liquid carbon adsorption. This process begins when a waste water stream enters a mix tank and ends when the treated water effluent exits the bioreactor. This process would generally be followed with a treated groundwater disposal model, such as infiltration gallery, injection wells, or discharge to POTW. These processes are described later in this book.

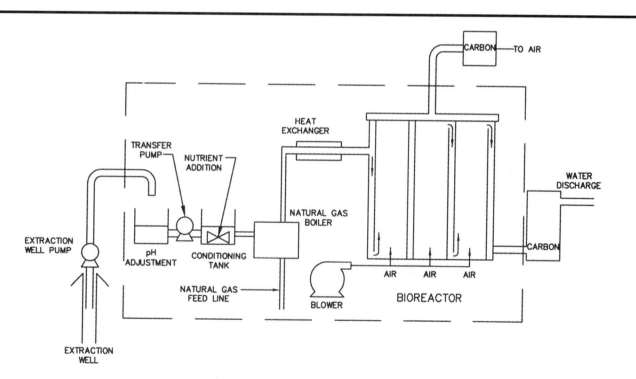

Figure 16.1 Typical Fixed Film Bioreactor System

Bioreactor system design can vary considerably from one site to another. In general, a typical design includes a reactor vessel, fixed-film packing, individual reactor cell cover, diffusers, blower system, header system, nutrient feed system, and control panel. System options include heating, pH adjustment, and nutrient addition. Generally, the estimator may assume that the existing microbial population will be sufficient to degrade the contaminant, since this is most commonly the case. However, microbes can be added if the user wishes to include them in an estimate.

The biological treatment process is almost always performed on-site. Usually, the bioreactor and associated components are set up on a concrete slab or other stable surface. The treatment system design is typically based on a pilot-scale or bench-scale study to fit site-specific conditions.

In most cases, a waste water stream contains indigenous micro-organisms capable of degrading hydrocarbon contaminants. Naturally occurring biodegradation can be enhanced by supplementing the feed stream with the deficient nutrients. The relative amounts of elements present in micro-organisms are listed in Figure 16.3. Nutrients must be maintained in sufficient proportion with respect to the available organic carbon to ensure that the contaminant is the limiting reactant.

Advantages and Disadvantages of the Fixed-Film System

There are two important advantages of the fixed-film system: the bacteria are maintained in a high concentration without the need of a clarifier, and oxygen can be supplied at a low cost. A third advantage is the general ease of operation, since a fixed-film system does not require the same operator attention needed for an activated-sludge system. This factor can dramatically reduce the O&M cost over the treatment duration.

Figure 16.2 Fixed Film Reaction
Source: *www.tmgates.com*

The disadvantage of a fixed-film reactor is that it is a plug flow system. In a plug flow system, water comes in one end of the reactor, passes by the bacterial film, and exits at the other end. Because of the high concentration of the contaminant in the influent stream, the system may be affected by the toxic levels of contaminants destroying the bacteria. The system may require an equalization basin or tank prior to entering the bioreactor. Recycling the effluent water can minimize this effect, but it also adds to the cost of the operation. In completely mixed reactors, the influent is immediately mixed with the contents of the tank.

Although biological treatment systems are widely used and can be very cost effective, they are subject to certain restrictions. The main restriction is that the bacteria require relatively constant temperature, oxygen, and nutrient conditions; therefore, the system must run 24 hours a day, 7 days a week. Another restriction is that the bacteria must be grown to a sufficient concentration to effectively remove the contaminants. This growth period can take 2–8 weeks, which may be an unacceptable delay on short-term projects.

Bioremediation also has contaminant limitations. Not all wastes are biodegradable, and occasionally the byproducts can be more toxic than the parent compound. These considerations make it difficult to predict removals of specific compounds without performing bench-scale or pilot-scale studies. Figure 16.4 provides a partial list of compounds affected by 3 types of biodegradation (i.e., oxidation, metabolism, and anaerobic digestion). The time required for biodegradation varies with each contaminant.

Measuring Bioreactor Performance

The performance of a bioreactor is usually measured in terms of either biochemical oxygen demand (BOD) or chemical oxygen demand (COD) removals. BOD is the quantity of oxygen used in the aerobic stabilization of waste water. COD is a measure of the oxygen equivalent of the organic matter susceptible to oxidation by a strong chemical oxidant. The relationship between BOD and COD concentrations must be defined for each individual waste water. Ideally, for a waste water composed of biodegradable organic substances, the COD concentration approximates the ultimate carbonaceous BOD value.

Before the bench-scale or pilot-scale study, a general organic analysis should be performed, including BOD, COD, and total organic carbon (TOC) tests. These tests will provide the engineer with information on the total amount of organics in the waste water (not just the specific compound)—data needed to design the treatment system. The ratio of the results from these tests also gives the design engineer some idea about the degradability of the organic compounds in the groundwater. The optimum test results would produce a range for BOD:COD:TOC. The acceptable lower end of the range is 1:2:1 and the upper end is 1:3:1. Low values for BOD may indicate there is nondegradable organic material present. Low values for the TOC may indicate the presence of inorganic oxygen demand.

Basic Information Needed for Estimating

It is possible to create a reasonable budget cost estimate using a few required parameters. If more detailed information is known, one can create a more precise and site-specific estimate using a secondary set of parameters.

To estimate the cost of a fixed film bioreactor system, certain basic information must be known. This information is discussed in the following paragraphs.

Flow Rate

The flow rate, in conjunction with the chemical oxygen demand parameter, will determine the bioreactor configuration. Typical unit capacities range from 1–100 gallons per minute.

Chemical Oxygen Demand

The chemical oxygen demand (COD) is a measure of the oxygen equivalent of the organic matter susceptible to oxidation by a strong chemical oxidant. A COD test should be run as part of the bench-scale or pilot-scale study. The practical range of COD is 50–1,000 ppm.

Relative Percentage Of Elements In Micro-organisms	
Element	**Percentage Of Total Weight**
Oxygen	65.0
Carbon	18.0
Hydrogen	10.0
Nitrogen	3.0
Phosphorous	1.0
Potassium	0.4
Sulfur	0.3

Figure 16.3 Relative Percentage of Elements in Micro-organisms

Partial List Of Environmental Pollutants Recognized As Biodegradable		
Acenaphthalene	Dichlorobenzene	Naphthalene
Acenaphthene	Dichloroethane	Nitroglycerine
Acetone	Dichloroethylene	Nonane
Acrylonitrile	Diesel Fuel	Octane
Anthracene	Dioxane	PCBs
Atrazine	Dioxin	Pentachlorophenol
Benzene	Dodecane	Phenanthrene
Benzoic Acid	Ethyl Benzene	Phenol
Benzo(a)anthracene	Ethylene Glycol	Phytane
Benzo(a)pyrene	Fluoranthene/Fluroene	Pristane
Benzo(g,h,i)perylene	Gasoline	Pyrene
Benzo(k)fluoranthene	Heptanehexane	Styrene
Butanol	Indeno(1,2,3)pyrene	Tetrachloroethylene
Butylcellosolve	Isopropyl Acetate	1,1,1–Trichloroethane
Chlordane	Jet Fuel	Trichloroethylene
Chloroform	Kerosene	Tridecene
Chrysene	Lindane	Trinitrotoluene
P–Cresol	2–Methyl Naphthalene	Vinyl Chloride
Crude Oil	Methylene Chloride	Xylenes
DDT	Methylethyl Ketone	
Dibenzo (a,h)–anthracene	Methylmethacrylate	

Figure 16.4 Partial List of Environmental Pollutants

Treatment Period

The total treatment duration is divided into startup and O&M. The costs associated with the startup period (equipment acquisition, installation, and optimization) are considered capital costs, and the O&M costs are identified separately. It normally takes 6–8 weeks of startup time for the bioreactor to reach full operating capacity.

The O&M period extends after the startup period until the remediation phase is completed. This can be several months or even several years, depending on the extent of contamination to be treated. Systems generally run 24 hours per day during this period.

Worker Safety Level

The safety level will be affected by the contaminants at the site. Safety level refers to the levels required by OSHA in 29 CFR Part 1910. The 4 levels are designated as A, B, C, and D; where "A" is the most protective and "D" is the least protective.

Design Information Needed for Detailed Estimates

The following discussion provides the types of detailed information that, when available, can add detail and accuracy to estimates for fixed-film bioreactor systems. Also included are design criteria and estimating rules of thumb that the estimator typically uses to determine values that are not known, or to check information provided by others.

Remember that several factors affect the growth of micro-organisms. The most important factors are the presence of contaminant (carbon source), oxygen supply, pH, temperature, and availability of nutrients. The contaminant-laden influent stream provides the carbon source, and oxygen supply is added to the system via blowers attached to the bioreactor. The last 3 items discussed here are optional, based on site-specific requirements.

pH Adjustment

The pH range for optimal biological growth is 6–9. The natural pH of waste water is usually within the acceptable range. If the pH is not within acceptable range, pH adjustment agents can be added to the influent waste stream. These would be either acidic or basic reagents, which are used to increase or decrease the pH, respectively. If pH adjustment is anticipated, the estimator must determine the amount of neutralization reagent required. If pH range information is not available, a reasonable rule of thumb for the neutralization reagent additive rate is 0.5 pounds of reagent per 1,000 gallons of water. The normal range is 0.01–10 pounds per 1,000 gallons of water.

Equipment required for pH adjustment includes an additional mixing tank and transfer pump. This equipment is added to the front end of the bioreactor.

Nutrients

For biological processes to take place, nutrients such as nitrogen and phosphorus must be available for micro-organisms. The quantities of nutrients required for degradation are generally expressed as a ratio of the carbon source to the nutrients. A common ratio used for carbon:nitrogen:phosphorous is 100:10:1. The optimum nutrient mix must be determined based on laboratory bench-scale tests; however, a default ratio of one 50-pound bag of nutrients per week is a reasonable rule of thumb for a 50 GPM system. The nutrients are mixed in a feed tank at a constant rate prior to introduction into the bioreactor.

Influent Water Temperature

Influent water temperatures lower than approximately 20 °C (68°F) may not sustain adequate microbial activity. In such cases, the influent should be heated to between 20–35 °C (68°–95°F) prior to entering the bioreactor. The influent water temperature, combined with the process water temperature, is used to determine the water boiler capacity. A reasonable default temperature of groundwater is 12.8 °C (55°F).

Process Water Temperature

Process water refers to the water that enters the bioreactor. The optimal growth of microbial populations responsible for biodegradation occurs between 20–35 °C (68°–95°F). Microbial degradation rates generally fluctuate with changes in the waste stream influent temperature. As the temperature decreases, the degradation rates generally decrease. The process water temperature, in conjunction with the influent water temperature, is used to determine the default water boiler capacity. A reasonable default process water temperature is 26.7 °C (188°F).

Boiler Capacity

Boiler capacity is expressed in million British Thermal Units per hour (MBH). The boiler selection is based on the required boiler output, calculated as shown in the equation below, assuming a heat exchanger efficiency of 75% and a water unit weight of 62.4 pounds per cubic foot or 8.342 pounds per gallon.

$$BO = (IT-PT) \times FR \times .667$$

Where:

BO = Boiler output in MBH
IT = Initial temperature measured in degrees Celsius (°C)
PT = Process temperature measured in degrees Celsius (°C)
FR = Flow rate measured in gallons per minute (GPM)

If the influent and process water temperatures are equal and are between 68°–95°F, then a boiler will not be required. Boiler selection criteria are shown in Figure 16.5.

Boiler Quantity

As demonstrated in Figure 16.6, a single boiler is usually sufficient except in situations where a very large boiler capacity is required, or if redundancy is needed for some operational reason.

Heat Exchanger Capacity

When the influent temperature is too slow to sustain adequate microbial activity, the influent is passed through a heat exchanger prior to entering the bioreactor. The heat exchanger is connected to a boiler by a closed piping loop. Heat exchangers are sized based on influent flow rate, as shown in Figure 16.5.

Related Costs

Operations costs for the bioreactor include electric utilities and natural gas for the boiler and equipment, nutrients and pH, adjusting the pH and nutrient systems, maintaining the boiler, periodically cleaning the fixed film if the growth becomes too great, and cleaning the clarifier, if one is used.

Site Work and Utilities

Site work and utilities that may be applicable for bioremediation must be accounted for in the estimate. These may include:

- Overhead electrical distribution
- Natural gas distribution (or bottled gas systems)
- Fencing and signage
- Clear and grub

Conclusion

Biological treatment of waste water has been used for many years and is a proven technology. The main cost drivers are the size and type of system, the operating period, and the cost to heat water (if required). The cost engineer should work closely with the design team to identify these elements in order to make the best estimate possible.

Default Heat Exchanger Selections	
Flow Rate (GPM)	Default Heat Exchanger
1–7	7 GPM
8–16	16 GPM
17–34	34 GPM
35–55	55 GPM
56–74	74 GPM
75–86	86 GPM
87–100	112 GPM

Figure 16.5 Default Heat Exchanger Selections

Boiler Output, MBH	Default Boiler, MBH	Default Quantity
1–200	200	1
201–275	275	1
276–360	360	1
361–520	520	1
521–600	600	1
601–720	720	1
721–960	960	1
961–1220	1220	1
1221–1440	1440	1
1441–1680	1680	1
1681–1920	1920	1
1921–2160	2160	1
2161–2400	2400	1
2401–2880	1440	2
2881–3360	1680	2

Figure 16.6 Default Boiler Selections

Chapter 17

Ex Situ Land Farming

Land farming is a process for treating contaminated soil that requires excavation and movement to a treatment cell. The contaminated soil is spread in a thin layer over an area to enhance volatilization, aeration, biodegradation, and photolysis. This section discusses cost estimates to construct and operate a lined treatment cell to enhance the biodegradation process. Also covered are options to stimulate growth of indigenous bacteria (biostimulation) or to cultivate and add bacteria to the site (bioaugmentation).

State and local regulations often affect the location, design, and operation of a land farming treatment cell. Normally, land farming is used when the cell is located on the same property as the contaminated soil and is enclosed by a berm and covered. The soil is typically tilled at least once a week.

Figure 17.1 depicts a typical bioremediation cell.

Applications and Limitations

Applications

- Biodegradation (including ex situ land farming) is readily applicable to petroleum products, aromatic compounds such as benzene and xylene, and to lesser extents, polynuclear aromatic hydrocarbons, polychlorinated biphenyls (PCBs), and the organic (H, C, N, and O) portions of pesticide compounds.

Limitations

- A large land area requirement.
- Inorganics will not be biodegraded.
- Compounds that produce free halides, fluorine, chlorine, bromine or iodine, when degraded, will kill bacteria.
- Run-off collection and monitoring facilities are required.
- Long remediation times are required due to uncontrollable factors that affect rate of biodegradation (e.g., rainfall and temperature).
- Pretreatment of volatile contaminants (e.g., solvents) is required to avoid potential air pollution.

133

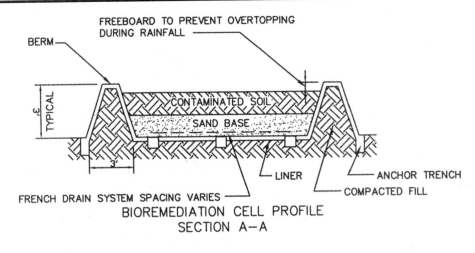

BIOREMEDIATION CELL PROFILE
SECTION A—A

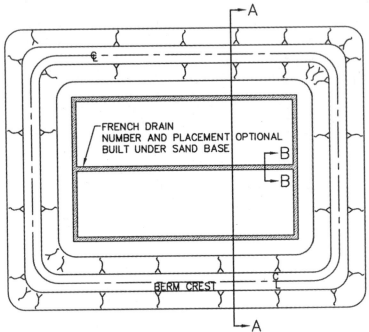

BIOREMEDIATION CELL PLAN VIEW

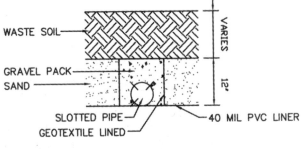

FRENCH DRAIN LINE DETAIL
SECTION B—B

Figure 17.1 Bioremediation Cell Plan View

Process Configurations and Treatment Train Considerations

- Feasibility studies and pilot tests are often appropriate prior to beginning cell construction to ensure the treatment approach is applicable to the site and to determine if existing microbial populations are adequate to degrade the contaminant.
- The pH level should be between 6.5–9.0 for optimum operation. Lime may be used to adjust the pH level.
- The best temperatures for microbial activity are between 90°–100° F.
- The moisture of the soil in the cell must be adjusted to between 30–80%, with the optimum between 50–75%.
- High clay soils take longer to remediate because of the porosity and binding properties of clay.
- Sandy soils require more frequent watering or addition of bulking agents such as wood chips or humus.

Conditions Affecting Biodegradation

The biodegradation process uses microorganisms to degrade contaminants. These organisms use organic substrates as sources of carbon for energy and for the biosynthesis of new cellular material. Biodegradation is readily applicable to petroleum products; aromatic compounds such as benzene and xylene; and, to lesser extents, polynuclear aromatic hydrocarbons, polychlorinated biphenyls (PCBs), and the organic (H, C, N, and O) portions of pesticide compounds. Naturally occurring microbes, when nourished, often work better than cultured microbes. Initially, cultured microbes may be detrimental to natural colonies and are counterproductive when colonies try to establish themselves and reach equilibrium. Therefore, naturally occurring microbes are used whenever possible.

Some bacteria will not grow in soil with a high iron or heavy metals content. Compounds that produce free halides, fluorine, chlorine, bromine, or iodine, when degraded, will kill bacteria. Feasibility studies and pilot tests are often done before beginning cell construction to ensure that the treatment approach is appropriate for the site and to determine whether existing microbial populations are adequate to degrade the contaminant. Costs for feasibility studies and pilot tests are usually included in the remedial design phase of a project, but the estimator should be sure that these costs are accounted for in some manner.

Conditions that affect the growth rate of microorganisms, and thus the rate of biodegradation, include the following.

Oxygen Concentration

Soil tilling introduces oxygen to the soil. Forced air injection is an alternative, but it is more expensive than tilling. The forced air cells typically include enhanced volatilization methods that are beyond the scope of this discussion. Aeration is achieved by using standard agricultural disks (plows) that limit the depth of soil in the cell to 18". The soil must be tilled regularly—normally at least once a week—to maintain a high concentration of oxygen. While the agricultural disk is designed to break up, mix, and aerate the soil, tilling also enhances volatilization and reduces the concentration of volatile contaminants.

In some cases, land farming is successfully implemented by tilling as infrequently as once every 3 months. If accelerated treatment is not required, frequent tilling may not be cost-effective. Tilling frequency should be adjusted as appropriate for the site conditions.

Nutrient Availability

Agricultural fertilizer generally provides the nutrient supply for the microbes. Fertilizer application rates vary depending on the nitrogen content of the treated soil.

Soil pH

The pH level of the soil should be between 6.5–9.0 for optimal operation. Lime may be used to adjust the pH level.

Soil Temperature

The best temperature range for microbial activity is between 90°–130°F. However, land farming has been used successfully at arctic sites where soil temperatures rise above 32°F only a few weeks during the year. Microbial activity approximately doubles with each 18°F rise in temperature up to 130°F, then tapers off until the temperature reaches 170°F, where the microbes begin to die. Normally, the ambient temperature at the site is sufficient to sustain microbial activity, so heating elements are not included.

Soil Moisture

Moisture is essential to biodegradation. Water can be added as needed, before or during the tilling process. The moisture of the soil in the cell must be adjusted to between 30–80%. The optimal range is between 50–75%; the higher the better.

Soil Type

The soil type affects the availability of nutrients and water to the microbes. Some soils will bind and absorb water and nutrients. High clay soils take longer to remediate because of the porosity and binding properties of clay. Sand requires more frequent watering or the addition of bulking agents such as wood chips or humus.

Typical System Design Elements

The project starts with the construction of the cell. Treatment cells are often placed on parking lots or other clear, level surfaces. If the site is not already cleared, site clearing and grubbing costs should be estimated for removing trees or underbrush. The area of the cell is based on the volume of contaminated soil. The treatment cell is typically lined with 40 mil PVC and is surrounded by a 3' tall earthen berm, as shown in Figure 17.1. Equipment entrance/exit ramps are installed at regular intervals along the berm. The liner is covered with 12" of sand to prevent the aerating plow from ripping the liner. The liner covers the berm and terminates in an anchor trench along the outer edge of the berm. Most projects require only a single liner.

A French drain, consisting of slotted PVC pipe and gravel, is installed along the inner perimeter of the berm. The berm is constructed with soil excavated from the French drain, and it is used along with clean borrow material. Water with leachate that collects in the French drain is pumped back onto the remediation soil pile to provide moisture and to ensure that the chemical degradation of any contaminants is completed. Normally, a sump pump is also installed as part of the French drain system.

To complete cell construction, contaminated soil is placed 6–18" deep over the sand base. The soil depth is limited by the effective depth of the aerating plow. Nutrients are added when the soil is put into the cell—either as solids tilled into the soil or as liquids sprinkled in with water. When all adjustments to the soil have been made to ensure optimal microbial activity, the cell is covered with a reinforced plastic sheet to keep rain water from saturating the cell or creating run-off containing hazardous products. The cover also helps to maintain a constant soil moisture content, including evaporation control in dry climates, and a higher ambient temperature in the waste pile.

The cell area is based on the volume of contaminated soil. When space limitations preclude constructing a treatment cell large enough to treat all contaminated soil at one time, the soil is typically divided into a series of smaller batches. If there is a large volume of soil to treat or the cell can support long-term cleanup, a concrete slab and curb may be a viable alternative to the treatment bed. On the other hand, if the volume of soil to be treated is relatively small or the treatment duration will be less than 6 months, a treatment cell could be constructed by placing the liner over hay bales.

Knowledge of existing site conditions is necessary to establish treatment specifications and frequencies and to develop a meaningful cost estimate. For example, land farming may include the following sequence of events:

- Preliminary soil analysis
- Clearing the land for the cell
- Hauling off debris
- Constructing the cell
- Excavating and moving soil
- Loading the cell
- Treating soil within the cell
- Monitoring progress
- Returning soil to the site
- Closing (demolishing) the cell

The costs for constructing the cell, loading the cell, treating soil within the cell, and closing (demolishing) the cell are discussed in this section. Costs for the remaining tasks may be estimated using guidance provided in other parts of this book. For example, after the soil has been treated and contaminants are reduced to target levels, the estimator should consider the requirements and cost for decontamination facilities over and above the limited decontamination of the tilling equipment and water truck provided for in this chapter.

Basic Information Needed for Estimating

It is possible to create a reasonable cost estimate using a few required parameters. If more detailed information is known, one can create a more precise and site-specific estimate using a secondary set of parameters.

To estimate the cost of the land farming system, certain information must be known. This information is discussed in the following paragraphs.

Total Volume of Soil Treated

The total ex situ volume of contaminated soil to be treated is measured in loose cubic yards. Bank or in situ soil swells to approximately

110–130 times its original volume when excavated. Assuming a swell factor of 1.3 (130%), a 1-acre area would be needed to land farm 2,500 loose C.Y. (1,900 bank C.Y.) of soil 18" deep. For this reason, it may be more desirable to treat larger volumes of soil in a series of successive batches rather than construct a treatment bed large enough to treat all of the soil at one time.

Volume of Soil per Batch

The ex situ volume of contaminated soil that will be treated at one time is measured in loose cubic yards. The volume of soil per batch determines the size of the treatment cell, setup parameters, amount of tilling, quantity of nutrients, and cell parameters applicable to the site. In most cases, the optimal volume of soil per batch is between 1,000–2,000 L.C.Y. Larger volumes would require excessively large treatment beds.

The primary cost driver in an ex situ land farming application is the construction of the treatment bed. Therefore, treating soil in a series of successive batches rather than treating all of the soil at one time will reduce the overall cost of treatment. In determining the optimal volume of soil per batch, the estimator may wish to prepare several different scenarios and observe the costs for each one.

Number and Size of Temporary Holding Areas

The scheduling and coordination of ex situ soil remediation projects often require the contaminated soil to be temporarily stockpiled adjacent to the treatment bed. Contaminated stockpiles should be placed in lined holding areas and covered with plastic. The number of temporary holding areas should correspond to the maximum number of stockpiles that will be present at any one time. The temporary holding area is typically lined with a 40 mil PVC liner and is surrounded by a 1.5' high berm to prevent surface water intrusion. Each holding area typically includes one pump and one holding tank for collection and containment of accumulated rainwater or leachate.

If more than one temporary holding area is needed, the size of each must be determined. A conservative estimate would be a stockpile height of 8' and a soil angle of repose of 34°.

Treatment Duration per Batch

The treatment duration is the total time that each batch will be in the bioremediation cell. Treatment time can be estimated from information obtained in the bench and pilot studies. The duration depends on the application rates of nutrients, moisture, pH, and microorganisms, as well as the specific contamination and concentration of the contaminant. Climate and soil type also influence treatment duration. Biodegradation progresses slowly in colder climates. Also, soils having high clay contents require longer treatment than sandy soils.

The estimator should consider the climate and the soil type when determining the treatment duration. The amount of nutrients, moisture, pH, and cultured bacteria are important but can be controlled.

Total treatment duration is determined by multiplying the treatment duration per batch by the number of batches. The duration for a single treatment is usually between 8–20 weeks; however, longer durations are not uncommon.

Worker Safety Level

Worker safety is affected by the contaminants at the site. Safety level refers to the levels required by OSHA in 29 CFR Part 1910. The 4 levels are designated as A, B, C, and D; where "A" is the most protective and "D" is the least protective. A safety level of E is also included to simulate normal construction, "no hazard" conditions as prescribed by the EPA.

Design Information Needed for Detailed Estimates

Following are descriptions of the types of detailed information that, when available, can add detail and accuracy to estimates. Also included are design criteria and estimating rules of thumb that the estimator typically uses to determine values that are not known, or to check information provided by others.

Cell Area

A square treatment cell is the most cost-efficient shape. The surface area of the remediation cell should be calculated based on 2 factors: the volume of soil to be treated and the depth of soil placed in the remediation cell. Be certain that soil volumes are based on ex situ or loose soil volume measurements. Quantity estimates based on bank (in situ) volumes must be converted to loose volume by multiplying the bank soil volume by the appropriate swell factor.

Depth of Contaminated Soil in the Cell

The depth of contaminated soil in the biodegradation cell is typically 1–18", depending on the capability of the aerating plow. The most common depth is 12". The depth of the soil affects the size of the containment cell, the equipment used, and possibly the duration of treatment.

Note: A minimum soil depth of 6" is recommended. An 18" depth, if soil conditions allow, minimizes the required treatment cell area, which will reduce costs.

Size of French Drain

A French drain is normally included for leachate collection. The leachate flows (via gravity) to a low end of the bermed area and is pumped from there. Leachate is pumped back onto the soil for continued remediation. Leachate holding tanks may sometimes be used to handle variations in soil moisture or to provide storage between tilling cycles. The typical French drain size is 18" × 18", but other sizes are available.

At sites with predominantly dry seasons, leachate collection systems may not be required, as evaporation and periodic covering of the land farm will control excess saturation.

Sump Pump Capacity

The typical sump pump has a capacity of 75 GPM. If electrical service is not available at the site, a portable gasoline-powered water pump may be used. For cost estimating purposes, the water truck used to sprinkle the soil can be used as a pumper truck to remove water to a treatment facility or holding tank.

Tilling Frequency

The tilling frequency affects the amount of aeration. Tilling is usually done once a week. A small dozer or farm tractor may be used for tilling.

For estimating purposes, assume that the tiller will remain on site for the entire project if the tilling frequency is greater than 2 days per week and the time required for each day of tilling is greater than 4 hours. Otherwise, assume that the tiller will be removed from the site at the conclusion of each day of tilling. The tiller is decontaminated before leaving the site.

Number of Passes per Day

Typically, the tiller will pass through the soil twice a day. If the tilling frequency (number of days per month of tilling) is decreased, then the number of passes should be increased. The number of passes per day directly affects the number of hours required for each day of tilling. The number of hours required for each day of tilling depends on the cell area, number of passes per day, and the productivity of the tiller.

Assume a minimum of 4 hours of dozer rental for each day of tilling. This rental time is assumed to include equipment mobilization.

Watering Frequency

The watering frequency specifies the number of times per month that water must be applied to the contaminated area to retain a consistent moisture content. Maintenance of soil moisture is vital during very dry periods, particularly in low-humidity areas. On the other hand, high humidity or excessive rainfall may reduce or eliminate the need for watering.

Assume that the moisture content of new soil put into the remediation cell is less than 80%. If the soil becomes too wet, additional plowing may be required to enhance evaporation. Also, in climates where rainfall exceeds the evaporation rate, excessive watering will result in increased leachate requiring treatment and disposal.

If the watering frequency is unknown, assume a frequency of once per week. Water trucks are commonly used for this purpose, but sprinkler systems can also be used.

Fertilizing Frequency

Nutrients can be added with the water. The addition of nutrients for the microorganisms, primarily in the form of nitrogen and phosphorus along with the oxygen from soil tilling, is critical to good growth. The nutrient mix will vary from site to site; the optimal mix is determined through pilot studies and geochemical evaluations of the site. If the fertilizing frequency is unknown, the estimator can assume 0.5 pounds of 20:20:20 fertilizer per cubic yard of contaminant, with a fertilizing frequency of once per month.

Microorganisms

Bacteria may be cultured and added to the contaminated soil. This is not as common in bioremediation as is enhancement of existing bacteria. If microorganisms are added, they are applied at 50 lbs per 1,000 C.Y. initially and 25 lbs per 1,000 C.Y. on a monthly basis thereafter.

Containment Cover

A containment cover is recommended and is required in some states. A cover forms a barrier over the cell area to limit moisture infiltration into and out of the contaminated soil. A typical cover is a 135-pound tear strength, fiberglass-reinforced plastic sheet.

Related Costs

Other costs related to this technology include the following.

Electrical Service

If electrical service is not available at or near the site, it may be economical to use a portable generator or gasoline-powered pumps.

Sampling and Analysis

Throughout operation, weekly monitoring will ensure that optimal conditions are being maintained in the treatment cell to allow for maximum degradation. Land treatment generally involves weekly sampling for pH, moisture content, phosphorus, nitrite/nitrate, ammonia nitrogen, and acidity/alkalinity. Samples are taken at intervals of one sample per 2,000 C.Y.

Closure sampling for site close-out includes obtaining 1 sample per analysis and analyzing for the following contaminants: TCLP, TAL metals, pesticides/PCBs, volatiles, and BNAs. Since this technology is used primarily for cleanup of hydrocarbon contamination, total petroleum hydrocarbon (TPH) analysis is the most common contaminant analysis.

Sampling is also required at site closure to confirm regulatory-agency target levels of contamination.

Monitoring the system may also be necessary to ensure that any hydraulic control requirements are being met to contain contaminant and nutrient migration.

The requirements for air monitoring depend on the contaminants as well as state and local regulations. Air monitoring may be required if hydrogen sulfide or other volatile organic compounds are present in the soil or are produced as reaction byproducts.

Equipment Mobilization and Decontamination

The number of times the tiller is decontaminated depends on the tilling frequency and the project duration. Assume that the tiller will remain on site for the entire project if the tilling frequency is greater than 2 days per week and the time required for each day of tilling is greater than 4 hours. Otherwise, assume that the tiller will be removed from the site at the conclusion of each day.

Site Work and Utilities

Site work and utilities that may apply to land farming include:

- Clear and grub
- Load and haul
- Access roads
- Overhead electrical distribution
- Underground electrical distribution
- Sprinkler system
- Excavation, cut and fill

When applicable, these items must be accounted for in the estimate.

Conclusion

Land farming is a cost-effective method of treating petroleum, aromatic compounds and other organic compounds. The primary cost driver is the volume of soil to be treated. Other cost drivers include the soil filling frequency, the distance from the excavation site to the treatment site, and the extent of nutrients required.

Often, there will be a design trade-off between the size of the treatment area and the total treatment time. When the total soil volume to be treated is large, it may be more efficient to treat the soil in multiple batches, thus reducing the size of the treatment system. The cost engineer should work with the design team to optimize these types of trade-offs during the project planning stages.

Chapter 18

Ex Situ Solidification/ Stabilization

Ex Situ Solidification/Stabilization (S/S) is a treatment technology in which chemical reagents are mixed with waste, creating complex chemical and physical reactions that improve physical properties and reduce contaminant solubility, toxicity, and/or mobility. S/S is a viable treatment for contaminated materials when the constituents cannot be treated, recovered, or destroyed by other methods because of technical or economical limitations.

Solidification is a physical treatment, in which a reagent is added to transform a sludge, sediment, or soil into a solid form. Solidification immobilizes the contaminants within the crystalline structure of the solidified material, thus reducing the contaminant leaching potential, although the effectiveness varies depending on waste, soil, and reagent characteristics. Stabilization is a chemical treatment, in which a reagent is added to transform the material so that the hazardous constituents are in their least mobile or toxic form. Compatibilities of common reagents with various waste components are shown in Figure 18.1.

Applications and Limitations

Applications

Used to solidify or immobilize inorganic compounds, volatile and non-volatile metals, PCBs (depending on concentration), asbestos, and radionuclides.

- Short- to medium-term technology.
- Generally most effective for inorganic compounds and radionuclides.

Limitations

- Some processes may increase total volume of contaminant.
- Organics are typically not immobilized.
- Long-term immobilization of contaminants may be affected by environmental conditions.

Process Configuration and Treatment Train Considerations

The decision to use S/S can be driven by several key factors. If S/S is selected as the treatment approach, additional factors need to be addressed. Key factors include:

- Wastes with high moisture content, organic content, or clays can create problems in mixing.
- If landfilling is used, then the technology must meet the requirements of the Land Disposal Restrictions (LDRs) under the Resource Conservation and Recovery Act (RCRA).
- If treated waste meets specified clean-up levels, it can be used on the site for backfill.
- Depending on the wastes and processes involved, hot gases and vapors may be produced that could require additional treatment and safety precautions.
- Chemical processes of adsorption, complexation, precipitation, and nucleation can interfere with S/S effectiveness.
- If the waste contains PCBs, then the waste disposal is regulated by the Toxic Substance Control Act (TSCA).
- EPA guidelines require a minimum unconfined compressive strength (UCS) of 50 pounds per square inch (psi) for land disposal.
- Handling of non-homogeneous materials (i.e., rock, debris) may mechanical sorting, crushing, or possibly hand-sorting.

Typical System Design Elements

A bench-scale laboratory program usually determines the type and amount of S/S reagents required to satisfy regulatory treatment objectives.

S/S is generally most effective for inorganic compounds and radionuclides. Specific contaminants or contaminant groups in which S/S is effective include volatile and non-volatile metals (with some exceptions, including anionic complexes of metals such as chromium, selenium, arsenic, cyanides, strong acids, oxidizing agents, and reducing agents); other inorganics (inorganic corrosives and inorganic cyanides); polychlorinated biphenyls (PCBs); asbestos; and radionuclides. S/S has been used to treat some semi-volatile

Reagent Compatibility			
Waste	**Cement Based**	**Pozzolan Based**	**Asphalt**
Organic Solvents	May impede setting	May impede setting	Organics may vaporize
Solid/organics, tars, etc.	Good	Good	Possible binding agent
Acid Wastes	Cement neutralizes acids	Compatible, will neutralize	Neutralize before incorporation
Oxidizers	Compatible	Compatible	May cause matrix breakdown
Sulfates	May retard set	Compatible	Dehydrate and rehydrate problems
Halides	Possible leaching	May retard set	Dehydrate and rehydrate problems
Heavy Metals	Compatible	Compatible	Compatible
Radioactive Materials	Compatible	Compatible	Compatible

Figure 18.1 Reagent Compatibility

compounds, but treatment of volatile organic compounds (VOCs) is currently the focus of research and debate.

S/S technology can be performed using a variety of methods, including open pit/trench/area mixing, in situ/in-drum mixing, and ex situ treatment in a mixing unit. The open pit/trench/area mixing method requires the reagent to be dumped on top of the waste and mixed with conventional earth-handling equipment.

The ex situ S/S process requires excavation, conveyance, or pumping of a contaminated medium into a mixing unit (pugmill), where a reagent is added. The treatment train includes excavation of the waste pile (see Chapter 41, "Excavation"), the S/S process, and transportation and disposal of the waste at a landfill once it is treated. This chapter discusses costs incurred once the waste has already been transported to a landfill, assuming an S/S batch plant is set up at the landfill to solidify the waste material. Any transportation of waste to or from the mixer must be included with the estimate. If drummed waste is to be treated, then the cost for moving drums from the staging area or waste pit to the S/S unit should be included in the estimate. If contaminated soil is excavated from a site, then the excavated area may need to be backfilled with clean soil or with the solidified soil from the process.

Disposal options should be evaluated before the technology is selected. If landfilling is chosen, then the S/S technology must meet the requirements of the Land Disposal Restrictions (LDRs) under the Resource Conservation and Recovery Act (RCRA). If the waste contains PCBs, then the waste disposal is regulated by the Toxic Substance Control Act (TSCA). EPA guidelines require a minimum unconfined compressive strength (UCS) of 50 pounds per square inch (psi) for land disposal.

Preparing non-homogeneous materials (rock, debris, etc.) for processing can be expensive. Handling these materials may include sorting, crushing, or possibly hand sorting.

Basic Information Needed for Estimating

It is possible to create a reasonable cost estimate using a few required parameters. If more detailed information is known, one can create a more precise and site-specific estimate using a secondary set of parameters.

To estimate the cost of the ex situ S/S system, certain information must be known. This information is discussed in the following paragraphs.

Type of Waste
The type of waste is typically described as one of the following:

- Solid
- Sludge
- Incinerator ash

The type of waste will affect the S/S mix design. Waste with high concentrations of organics (such as loam, peat, inorganic clays, fat clays, inorganic silts, and diatomaceous fine sandy or silty soils) are not generally suitable for this technology. Solid waste is assumed to have a maximum moisture content of 30%. Sludge, based on this criteria, would have a moisture content between 30–70%. It is assumed that the sludge is pumpable or capable of being dredged.

Density of Waste

The density of the waste is generally measured in pounds per cubic foot (P.C.F.). This measurement is used to calculate the mix design and volume expansion encountered after the solidified waste has cured. If the density is unknown, it can be estimated based on the values shown in Figure 18.2.

Total Volume of Waste

The volume of the waste directly affects the S/S cost. The volume should be converted to tons, because reagent-to-waste ratios using weight comparisons are most commonly used. The total volume of waste and the system size will provide the information needed to determine the process equipment cost. Sludges can be converted from gallons to cubic yards by dividing the number of gallons by 202.

Mobile Solidification/Stabilization System Size

Four system sizes are readily available. The system sizes are based on the EPA SITE (Superfund Innovative Technology Evaluation) Program Reports and conversation with vendors. The batch mix plants' capacities are 2, 5, 10, and 15 C.Y. mixers.

Batch Rate

For estimating purposes, the batch rate includes the following cycle times: loading (5 minutes), mixing (14 minutes), and unloading (1 minute). Thus the most common batch requires 20 minutes, and the average number of batches per hour is 3. Other assumptions include the following:

- There will be 22 8-hour working days per month.
- The volume of waste and system size will drive the duration of the project.
- Labor and equipment costs will be based on the project duration, which is a function of the mixer capacity.
- Batch times will vary from 10–120 minutes.

Worker Safety Level

Worker safety is affected by the contaminants at the site. Safety level refers to the levels required by OSHA in 29 CFR Part 1910. The 4 levels are designated as A, B, C, and D, where "A" is the most protective, and "D" is the least protective. A safety level of E is also included to simulate normal construction, "no hazard" conditions as prescribed by the EPA.

Waste Density	
Type Of Waste	**Default Density**
Solid	100 P.C.F
Sludge	80 P.C.F.
Incinerator Ash	52 P.C.F.

Figure 18.2 Waste Density

Design Information Needed for Detailed Estimates

Following are descriptions of the types of detailed information that, when available, can add detail and accuracy to estimates. Also included are design criteria and estimating rules of thumb that the estimator typically uses to determine values that are not known, or to check information provided by others.

Initial Moisture Content

The initial moisture content of the waste varies depending on the waste medium. The moisture content will help to determine the mix design for the waste and additives. Values for initial moisture content are shown in Figure 18.3. The mix design should be adjusted to consider moisture effects. Moisture content, along with chemical constituency, should be considered when changing the mix design constituents and ratios.

Minutes Per Batch

The time required to complete a batch ranges from 10–120 minutes. A typical batch requires 20 minutes, including loading, mixing, and unloading. Pilot tests will determine the actual number of batches achievable per hour.

Chemical Additive Ratios

Many chemical additives can be used effectively in the S/S process. However, additive ratios are highly waste-specific and should be determined by bench and/or pilot testing.

Additives include water, proprietary chemical binders, Portland cement, fly ash, cement kiln dust, hydrated lime, bitumen, and activated carbon. Other additives that are not used as often, but may still be suitable include polyolefins, urea formaldehyde, modified clay, blast furnace slag, polycrylates, and polyacrylamides. The most common additives are water (solid & ash only), chemical binder, and Portland cement. Specific example project data is provided in Figure 18.4.

Figure 18.5 provides additive-to-waste ratios based on weight. Figure 18.6 provides a summary of specific gravity and weight for both chemical additives and waste streams. These weights and specific gravities are used for material balances. Additional water is generally needed for the mix, although the cost may be negligible if the owner obtains water from an existing groundwater installation.

Figure 18.3 Initial Moisture Content

Initial Moisture Content	
Type Of Waste	**Default Moisture Content**
Solid	15%
Sludge	60%
Incinerator Ash	20%

Volume of Waste to be Disposed

The volume of waste that is left after treatment and curing must be disposed of in either a Subtitle "C" (hazardous) or Subtitle "D" (non-hazardous) landfill, depending on the outcome of the Toxicity Characteristic Leaching Procedure (TCLP) analytical results. If the waste is an EPA RCRA-listed waste, then it must be delisted prior to disposal in a non-hazardous waste landfill (see Chapter 3 for definition of listed wastes).

Other Related Costs

Other related costs for ex situ S/S are as follows.

Permitting

Permitting costs vary from state to state and should be included in the estimate.

Bench/Pilot Testing

Bench and pilot tests may help to determine the adequacy of the admixture application rates.

Since most waste treated by the S/S technology is inorganic, the waste analysis will include a scan for the 17 priority metals. Other tests that may be performed on the treated waste include pH, compaction, and permeability. Unconfined compressive strength (UCS) is required to ensure that the treated waste is capable of meeting landfill structural integrity. The number of samples collected will be equal to 5% of the waste batches. If the throughput rate is not known, assume that the throughput process is 40 batches per week, regardless of the mixer size.

Portland Cement[1] Application Summary Solidification/Stabilization			
Waste Material	**Water Content %**	**Contaminants Treated**	**Portland Cement Dose % Wet. Wt.**
Sludge	N.K.[2]	Arsenic	100
Arc Furnace Dust	N.K.	Heavy Metals	5
Wood Preserving Waste	N.K.	Heavy Metals	10
Cadmium Nitrate Sludge	N.K.	Cadmium	41
Wood Preserving Waste	N.K.	Heavy Metals	10 to 20
Hydroxide Sludge	N.K.	Lead	41 to 45
Hydroxide Sludge	70	Zn, Cr (VI)	28 to 45
Hydroxide Sludge	75	Heavy Metals	90
Oily Pond Sludge	42 to 62	Oil Sludge	3 to 15
Leachate	100	VOCs/Semi VOCs	10 to 40

These solidification doses are based on information obtained in the last eight references of this chapter.
[1] Data presented for S/S mixes using cement only, without proprietary reagents or pozzolanic reagents.
[2] N.K.=Not known; detailed review of the reference was not performed.

Figure 18.4 Portland Cement Application Summary

Mix Ratios By Weight Basis			
Valid Range†	**Additive Ratio‡**		
0.000 - 3.000[1]	*	:1	Cement:Waste
0.000 - 1.000[2]	0.400	:1	Water:Cement (Solids & Ash only)
0.000 - 5.000	0.010	:1	Proprietary Chemicals[3]:Waste
0.000 - 3.000	0.000	:1	Fly Ash:Waste
0.000 - 3.000	0.000	:1	Cement Kiln Dust:Waste
0.000 - 3.000	0.000	:1	Hydrated Lime:Waste
0.000 - 3.000[1]	0.000	:1	Bitumen:Waste
0.000 - 3.000	0.000	:1	Activated Carbon:Waste

†Range refers to the allowable input for additive ratios. A range of 0.000 to 3.000 delineates the minimum and maximum values that can be entered for that particular parameter.

‡Additive ratio refers to the total weight of the waste mix. For example, a ratio of 2.0 for cement would be 2 parts cement to 1 part waste or, on a weight basis, 2 pounds of cement per each pound of waste.

*Ash: 0.100
Solids: 0.150
Sludge: 0.400

[1]Either cement of bitumen must be added to the waste in order to provide the strength and binding characteristics required.

[2]In this case, the default is based on the water:cement ratio rather than the water:waste ratio. The water:cement ratio is similar to that for general concrete mix design.

[3]Urrichem Proprietary Additive - Solidtech Corp.
Chloranan Proprietary Additive - EM TECH Corp.
P4 and P27 Proprietary Additives - Silicate Technologies Corp.

Figure 18.5 Mix Ratios by Weight Basis

Default Specific Gravity And Weights For Material Balances		
Materials	**Specific Gravity**	**Density (P.C.F.)**
Chemical Additives		
Portland Cement	3.15	94.0
Proprietary Binders	2.90	100.0
Fly Ash[1]	2.45	65.0
Cement Kiln Dust	2.45	90.0
Hydrated Lime	2.65	94.0
Water	1.00	62.4
Bitumen	1.30	81.0
Activated Carbon	1.55	97.0
Waste Streams		
Waste Solid	1.60	100.0
Waste Ash	0.68	42.5
Waste Sludge	1.28	80.0

[1]Composite Average of 24 fly ash densities from 24 different coal-fired plants, *Air Pollution Engineering Manual,* Air and Waste Management Association, Van Nostrand Reinhold, 1992. Table 4, pg. 211

Figure 18.6 Default Specific Gravity & Weights

In this case, 2 treated waste samples will be collected per week. Typically, an additional 10% of all chemical analyses is sampled for control and assurance.

Site Work and Utilities

Site work and utilities that may apply to the S/S process include:

- Overhead electrical distribution
- Underground electrical distribution
- Clearing and grubbing
- Access roads
- Fencing and signage
- Water distribution
- Gas distribution
- Sanitary sewer
- Communications

These must also be included in the estimate.

Conclusion

Solidification/stabilization is part of a treatment and disposal process commonly used for inorganic hazardous wastes. The primary cost driver is the volume of waste to be treated. Other significant cost drivers include the type of waste, soil moisture content, the size of the system, and worker safety level. These factors depend on specific site conditions; the cost engineer must be certain that all of these factors are understood and factored into the estimate as appropriate. If the site conditions are not known, contingency estimates can be prepared by varying the assumed quantity of waste and other factors.

Chapter 19

Ex Situ Soil Vapor Extraction

Soil vapor extraction (SVE) removes volatile organic compounds (VOCs) from a soil matrix. There are two common SVE techniques: in situ SVE and ex situ SVE. This chapter discusses the ex situ approach. Chapter 32 covers the in situ approach.

Contaminant volatility is the physical basis for the successful application of soil vapor extraction. *Volatility* refers to the tendency of a substance to vaporize or "escape" from the liquid phase, or from the surface of a solid, to the vapor phase. Contaminants with higher volatilities are more easily removed by soil vapor extraction. Air drawn through the contaminated soil matrix by a vacuum pump removes contaminated soil gas and induces additional volatile compounds to vaporize. Vaporized contaminants are drawn out of the soil matrix with the exiting air stream, and uncontaminated air from beyond the treatment zone is drawn in to repeat the process.

Applications and Limitations

Applications

- Normally chosen in cases where reduced treatment times or immediate contaminant source removal are required.
- Suitable for treatment of contaminated spoil material resulting from construction projects, UST removals, or other remediation projects.
- Medium- to long-term remedial action duration.
- Removes volatile organic compounds (VOCs) like TCE, benzene, and toluene, and some fuels from contaminated soils.
- Typically applies only to volatile compounds with a dimension less Henry's Law Constant, greater than 0.01, or with a vapor pressure greater than 0.02"-Hg.

Limitations

- Capture and monitoring of off-gas emissions from soils may be necessary during excavation.
- Clay soils will tend to clump together, precluding adequate exposure of the contaminated particles to air.
- Large amount of space is required.
- Will not remove heavy oils, metals, PCBs, or dioxins.

Typical System Design Elements

In the ex situ application of SVE, contaminated soil is excavated from a site and placed in a soil vapor extraction bed. The treatment bed is usually underlain by an impermeable liner and surrounded by a berm to prevent intrusion of surface run–off. The liner is normally covered by a 6–12" thick layer of gravel to protect it from damage. A perforated pipe grid is placed on the gravel surface. The grid is attached to a common header pipe leading to a vacuum pump, which pulls air through the soil.

Ex situ soil vapor extraction is a batch process. Once the treatment bed is filled with contaminated soil, the vacuum pumps are started, and the soil is left in the bed until target contaminant levels are reached. Depending on the types and levels of contamination, extracted vapor is either vented to the atmosphere, flared, or passed to a catalytic oxidation or vapor phase carbon adsorption unit. Most regulatory agencies require that soil piles be covered with plastic to minimize volatile emissions, even though this may impair the performance of the vapor extraction system. A cover or roof may be built over the treatment bed to prevent rainwater intrusion. In cases where vapor emissions are a major concern, or in severe climates, the treatment bed may be fully enclosed.

There are several advantages to using ex situ SVE systems. Ex situ systems offer greater control over air flow through the soil matrix than in situ systems. Ex situ soils are more permeable than in situ soils, because the soil swells from excavation and handling. This allows for faster contaminant removal rates than can be obtained through in situ vapor extraction. Ex situ SVE is normally chosen when reduced treatment time or immediate contaminant source removal is required. Ex situ SVE is well suited to treating contaminated spoil material from construction projects, UST removals, or other remediation projects. In such cases, ex situ SVE could eliminate the need for long-term stockpiling of contaminated soils, as contaminated soils could be treated immediately after excavation.

The advantages of ex situ SVE must be weighed against the added expenses of excavation, transportation, and ultimate disposal of contaminated materials. Local regulatory agencies may require mitigation of volatile emissions during excavation and stockpiling, which can increase costs significantly. The cost of constructing the treatment bed must also be considered. Normally, the treatment bed is constructed on or immediately adjacent to the contaminated site unless space limitations dictate otherwise. Treating contaminated soil from several sites in a central treatment bed could result in inadvertent mixing of different contaminants and is generally not encouraged. Also, it is important to note that ex situ SVE is not effective on soil with a high clay content. Clay soils tend to clump together, so the contaminated particles are not adequately exposed to air. The clay particles may also clog the vapor extraction screens, preventing adequate air flow through the contaminated soil. Clay soils may be more effectively treated by in situ SVE.

Figure 19.1 illustrates the treatment bed design. The treatment bed length and width are calculated based on the volume of soil to be treated. The soil pile in the treatment bed is surrounded by a 10' wide alley on all 4 sides, which provides unrestricted access to the track

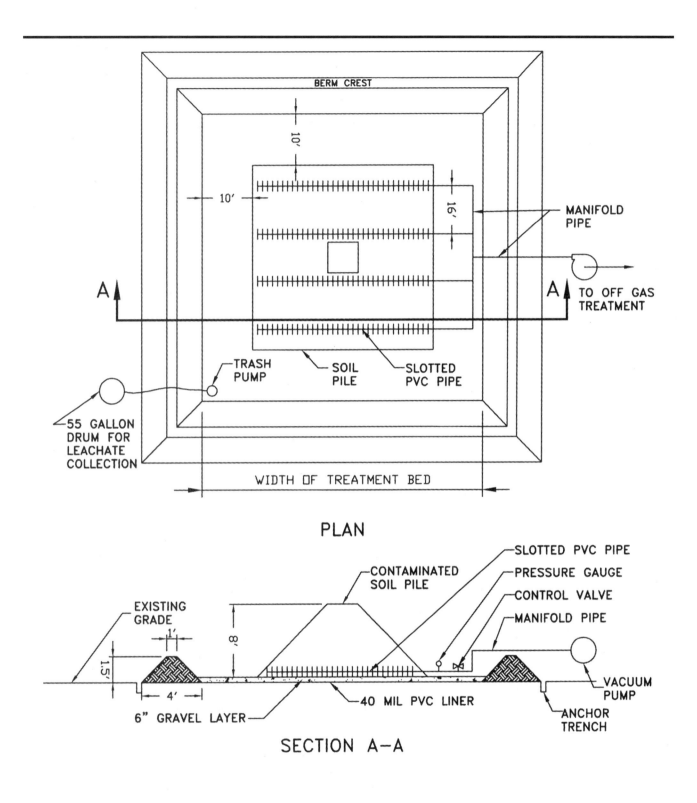

Figure 19.1 Plan and Cross-section of Ex Situ SVE Treatment Bed

loader used to build and dismantle the soil pile in the treatment bed. The treatment bed is lined with 40 mil PVC and is surrounded by a 1.5' high berm. The berm is constructed using clean borrow material. The liner is protected by a 6" cover of gravel.

Equipment entrance/exit ramps are assumed to be constructed at regular intervals along the berm. The PVC liner covers the berm and terminates in an anchor trench. Normally, the soil pile is covered with plastic to contain air emissions and limit rainwater intrusion. A pump located in one corner of the treatment bed is used to pump leachate to a holding tank. The estimator will need to determine the quantity of leachate generated and include costs for leachate treatment or disposal. (Information on disposal methods and costs can be found in the disposal chapters of this book, including Chapter 45, "Discharge to POTW," ex situ water treatment methods, and Chapter 15, "Dewatering (Sludge).") Fan-forced aeration is normally assumed, and the vacuum pump capacity and quantity are based on the volume of soil treated.

The estimating approach described in this chapter assumes that contaminated material has already been stockpiled adjacent to the treatment bed. At the end of this process, clean material is removed from the bed and stockpiled for final disposal. Costs for excavating soil from its original location and transporting it to and from the treatment bed are not included in this discussion. Chapter 41 addresses estimating excavation costs.

Basic Information Needed for Estimating

It is possible to create a reasonable cost estimate using a few required parameters. If more detailed information is known, one can create a more precise and site-specific estimate using a secondary set of parameters.

To estimate the cost of an ex situ SVE system, certain information must be known. This information is discussed in the following paragraphs.

Total Volume of Soil Treated
Depending on the volume of contaminated soil, it may be desirable to treat the soil in a series of successive batches rather than constructing a treatment bed large enough to treat all of the soil at one time.

Volume of Soil per Batch
If all the soil on a site will be treated at one time, this parameter should be equal to the total volume of contaminated soil. If soil will be treated in a series of successive batches, the largest volume of soil that will be treated at one time should be entered. The treatment bed dimensions and quantities for slotted pipe and vacuum pumps are based on the volume per batch. Therefore, the largest volume of soil to be treated at one time should be determined, and the system sized accordingly.

The optimal volume of soil per batch is between 500–10,000 loose cubic yards (L.C.Y.). Larger volumes may require excessively large treatment beds. For volumes smaller than approximately 500 L.C.Y., the treatment cost per cubic yard increases sharply because of the cost of constructing the treatment cell.

Generally, treating soil in a series of successive batches is less expensive than treating it all at once. Reducing the volume per batch decreases bed construction, and equipment costs but also increases total treatment time, resulting in increased operational labor and utilities costs. Consequently, as the volume per batch is reduced while all other required parameters are held constant, the total remediation cost decreases to a point and then starts to increase again. In determining the optimal volume of soil per batch, the user may wish to estimate several different scenarios and compare the costs for each scenario.

Number of Temporary Holding Areas

The scheduling and coordination of ex situ soil remediation projects often require the contaminated soil to be temporarily stockpiled adjacent to the treatment bed. Contaminated stockpiles should be placed in lined holding areas and covered with plastic. The number of temporary holding areas should correspond to the maximum number of stockpiles that will be present at any one time. The holding area is typically lined with a 40 mil PVC liner and surrounded by a 1.5' high berm to prevent surface water intrusion. For each holding area, one pump and one holding tank are normally included for collection and containment of accumulated rainwater or leachate.

Temporary Holding Area Size

Assuming a stockpile height of 8' and a soil angle of repose of 34° will yield a conservative estimate for the holding area size required for a given volume of contaminated soil.

Treatment Duration Per Batch

Treatment duration, measured in weeks, depends on the volume of soil and the initial and target contaminant levels, and is typically determined during the remedial design phase. The estimator can calculate the number of batches by dividing the total volume of soil by the volume of soil per batch. Total treatment duration is determined by multiplying the treatment duration per batch by the number of batches.

Worker Safety Level

Worker safety is affected by the contaminant(s) at the site. Safety level refers to the levels required by OSHA in 29 CFR Part 1910. The 4 levels are designated as A, B, C, and D; where "A" is the most protective and "D" is the least protective.

Design Information Needed for Detailed Estimates

Following are descriptions of the types of detailed information that, when available, can add detail and accuracy to estimates. Also included are design criteria and estimating rules of thumb that an estimator typically uses to determine values that are not known, or to check information provided by others.

Base Area of Soil Pile

The base area is calculated from the volume of soil to be treated and is used in determining the length and width for the treatment bed. For estimating purposes, soil piles are assumed to be rectangular. A reasonable estimating assumption is that the soil pile has a length-to-width ratio of 2 and a 34° angle of repose, as shown in Figure 19.1. Assume a height of 8' if the volume of soil per batch is 200 L.C.Y. or more, and a height of 6' if the volume of soil per batch is less than 200 L.C.Y. A single row of screens will be installed on the bed floor. Taller soil piles occupy less bed area, but may require additional rows of screens at various depths throughout the soil pile. The following equation gives a reasonable approximation for the base area of the soil pile.

$$\sqrt{\text{Base Area}} = \left[\sqrt{\frac{V \times 27}{H} - (H \times SS)^2} + 2 \times \frac{H}{2} \times SS \right]^2$$

Where:

V = Volume of Soil Treated (C.Y.)
H = Height of Soil Pile (ft):   If Vol per Batch > 200 lcy, H = 8
                                   If Vol per Batch < 200 lcy, H = 6
SS = Side Slope of Soil Pile:
        Assume 1.5 based on 34° angle of repose

Bed Width

The total bed width includes clearance between the soil pile and the inner edges of the containment berm. The width depends on the base area of soil pile. The assumed bed width is based on a soil pile twice as long as it is wide. Normally, designs allow for 10' of clearance between the soil pile and the inner edges of the berm, as shown in Figure 19.2. Thus for estimating purposes the width can be calculated as:

(base area of soil pile/2)$^{1/2}$ + 20'

Bed Length

The total length of the bed includes clearance between the soil pile and the inner edges of the containment berm. The assumed bed length is based on a soil pile twice as long as it is wide. Normally, designs allow

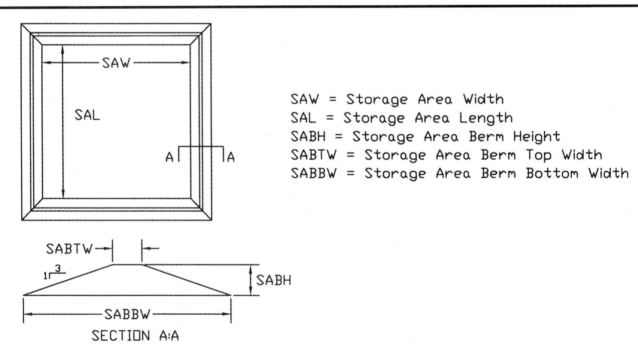

SAW = Storage Area Width
SAL = Storage Area Length
SABH = Storage Area Berm Height
SABTW = Storage Area Berm Top Width
SABBW = Storage Area Berm Bottom Width

SECTION A:A

Figure 19.2 Soil Bermed Storage Area

for 10' of clearance between the soil pile and the inner edges of the berm, as shown in Figure 19.2. Thus for estimating purposes the bed length is:

$$(\text{base area of soil pile} \times 2)^{1/2} + 20'$$

Extraction Screen Diameter

The most common extraction screen diameter is 4", which in most cases is large enough to minimize head losses caused by friction. In cases where higher volumes are needed, a 6" screen may be used.

Screen Length

Normally, the screens are installed parallel to the width of the bed, and the screens are set back 5' from the edges of the soil pile. Shorter screens set in the interior of the pile, away from the edges, equalize air flow path lengths and improve system performance. The optimum screen configuration is project-specific and is normally verified through a flow net analysis to ensure that air is drawn through the entire matrix of the soil pile. For estimating purposes, the screen length can be calculated as:

$$(\text{base area of soil pile}/2)^{1/2} - 10$$

Number of Vapor Extraction Screens

Typically, screens are located on the bed floor and are spaced 16' apart. Quantities for manifold piping and associated fittings are calculated based on the number of vapor extraction screens. Each screen has its own control valve, which provides greater control of the air flow through the soil pile. For estimating purposes, the number of screens can be calculated as:

$$(\text{base area of soil pile} \times 2)^{1/2}/16$$

Extraction screens are installed in passive and active aeration systems. In passive aeration systems, vacuum pumps are omitted.

Calculated Total Air Flow Rate

The total air flow rate determines the vacuum pump capacity. The required total air flow rate depends on the types of contaminants that are present, initial and target contaminant concentrations, and volume of soil. In determining the total air flow rate, a reasonable assumption would be an ex situ soil porosity of 40% (air voids comprise 40% of the total volume of the soil pile) and an air exchange rate of 50 pore air volumes per day. For example, 10,000 C.F. of soil at 40% porosity contains 4,000 C.F. of air. An air exchange rate of 50 pore air volumes per day would require 50 × 4,000 = 200,000 standard cubic feet of air per day, or 140 standard cubic feet per minute (SCFM). Normally, a more detailed analysis is required to determine the required flow rate and the appropriate blower size.

Vacuum Pump Capacity

Five different vacuum pump capacities are commonly available. The vacuum pump capacity depends on the calculated total air flow rate. Total treatment duration equals treatment duration per batch, times total volume, divided by volume per batch. If the total treatment duration is 10 months or more, it is generally more economical to purchase the vacuum pumps. Otherwise, vacuum pumps are usually rented on a monthly basis. The common sizes of vacuum pumps are:

- 5 H.P., 90 SCFM
- 7.5 H.P., 140 SCFM
- 10 H.P., 190 SCFM
- 15 H.P., 290 SCFM
- 30 H.P., 580 SCFM

Vacuum Pump Quantity

The number of vacuum pumps depends on the calculated total air flow rate. Normally, it is most economical to use one vacuum pump if the total air flow rate is less than 580 SCFM. For air flow rates greater than 580 SCFM, the default vacuum pump quantity is the calculated total air flow rate divided by 580 (rounded up).

Related Costs   Other costs associated with ex situ SVE include the following.

Bed Loading/Unloading

If the specific equipment for bed loading/unloading is not known, one can assume that a 2 C.Y. track loader will be used, with a loader productivity of 111 C.Y. per hour. Costs for bed loading/unloading include labor costs.

System Maintenance

Maintenance requirements for this system are minimal. Normally, a maintenance crew is on site once a week for the first month and once a month thereafter. The maintenance crew is responsible for adjusting the air flow rate and the control valves, and general system maintenance. The maintenance crew is also responsible for collecting air samples.

Sampling and Analysis

As mentioned above, the maintenance crew is responsible for collection of air samples, which will occur once a week for the first month and once a month thereafter. An air blower effluent sample will be collected during each sampling event and analyzed for principle organic hazardous constituents. Also, an organic vapor analyzer will be rented for each sampling event.

Monthly sampling of the soil pile is typical for monitoring system performance. Composite samples will be obtained based on the volume of soil treated, as shown in Figure 19.3. Composite samples are assumed to consist of grab samples taken from at least 4 separate locations and combined into 1 sample for analysis. All samples will be analyzed for total petroleum hydrocarbons (TPH) and benzene, toluene, ethylbenzene, and xylenes (BTEX).

Default Number Of Composite Samples	
Volume Of Soil Treated (C.Y.)	**Number Of Composite Samples**
Volume ≤ 100 C.Y.	1
100 < Volume ≤ 500 C.Y.	3
500 < Volume ≤ 1,000 C.Y.	5
Volume > 1,000 C.Y.	5+ (Volume–1,000)/500 (Round up)

Figure 19.3 Default Number of Composite Samples

Utilities

Utilities costs include the electrical cost for operating the vacuum pumps, which is directly related to the motor horsepower. Electrical cost is calculated assuming a motor efficiency of 75% and a conversion of 0.7457 kW/H.P. (kilowatts per horsepower).

Piping

The category of piping includes costs for both piping and associated fittings. For each screen, the fittings include one pressure gauge, one control valve, one tee, and 5' of connection piping. All screens are connected to a manifold pipe, which runs the full length of the soil pile. For connecting the vacuum pumps to the manifold piping, assume 25' of piping, one tee, and one 90° elbow for each vacuum pump. Normally, connection piping and manifold piping are the same. The piping and fitting quantities may be adjusted at the assembly level if necessary to fit site-specific conditions. All piping is normally PVC and is installed above ground.

Site Work and Utilities

If site work and utilities apply to the ex situ SVE system, they must be included in the estimate. Site work and utilities that may be applicable are:

- Overhead electrical distribution
- Fencing
- Clear and grub

Conclusion

Soil vapor extraction (SVE) has proven to be one of the most effective methods of removing volatile compounds from soils and reducing the need for groundwater remediation. The primary cost drivers for an SVE system are the size of the system, the number and depth of VEPs, and the operating period. Since SVE often reduces the need for active groundwater treatment, the cost engineer should be aware of the overall treatment process and work with the designer to optimize trade-offs between SVE and other processes.

Chapter 20

Heat-Enhanced Vapor Extraction

Heat-enhanced vapor extraction is an in situ process designed to remove volatile and semi-volatile organic compounds from vadose zone soils. The process is very similar to standard soil vapor extraction (SVE). Soil vapor extraction by itself is fairly effective in removing volatile organics, but it is less effective on semi-volatiles. Contaminant removal rates are limited by the volatilities of the contaminants present in the soil matrix. *Volatility* refers to the tendency of a substance to vaporize or "escape" from the liquid phase, or from the surface of a solid, to the vapor phase. The volatility of a contaminant is measured by its vapor pressure, which increases rapidly when temperature increases. Steam injection reduces the required treatment time by accelerating the vaporization of the most volatile contaminants. In addition, the resulting increase in soil temperature increases both the in situ vapor pressure and the vapor phase concentrations of less volatile compounds that might otherwise remain in the liquid phase.

Steam injection also causes a pressure gradient to form between the injection and extraction wells, which drives the flow of steam and vaporized contaminants toward the extraction wells. Vaporized contaminants are drawn out of the soil matrix with the exiting air stream. Because of the increased vapor phase contaminant concentrations caused by the increase in soil temperature, contaminants are removed from the soil in concentrated form. Most of the contamination in the exiting air stream is condensed to liquid in a condenser or heat exchanger. The condensate is typically drained to a holding tank to await ultimate disposal. Condensation of the air stream in this manner reduces the amount of waste requiring treatment or disposal and facilitates recycling of many compounds.

Applications and Limitations

Applications

- The system is designed to treat SVOCs, but will also treat VOCs.
- Thermally enhanced vapor extraction is also effective in treating some pesticides and fuels, depending on operating temperatures.
- As an ancillary benefit, vapor extraction prepares the subsurface for biodegradation of residual contaminants.

Limitations

- Debris or other large objects buried in the media can cause operating difficulties.
- Highly compacted soils or soils with high moisture content will reduce the efficiency of heat-enhanced vapor extraction.
- Soil with high organic content has a high sorption capacity of VOCs, which results in reduced removal rates.
- Hot air injection has limitations due to the low heat capacity of air.

Process Configurations and Treatment Train Considerations

- Steam injection is best suited for contaminated zones that lie between 10–150' below the surface.
- Performance in extracting certain contaminants varies depending on the maximum temperature achieved in the process selected.
- Carbon adsorption is commonly used to treat the off-gas stream from the vacuum extraction pump.
- Residual liquids and spent activated carbon may require further treatment.
- Soil with highly variable permeabilities may result in uneven delivery of gas flow to the contaminated regions.
- Air emissions are regulated, a process that could require treatment and permitting.
- Underground sewer and utility conduits can cause short-circuiting of air flow, allowing air to enter the soil through the utility conduits and/or sewer and reducing the airflow through the soil matrix. This would make the system either less effective or totally ineffective.

Typical System Design Elements

In heat-enhanced vapor extraction, steam is injected into the subsurface through a series of injection wells, and contaminants are removed through a series of extraction wells known as vapor extraction points, or VEPs. Figure 20.1 shows the equipment typically used in a heat-enhanced vapor extraction system.

The surface equipment for this system can be separated into 2 subsystems: the steam generation and distribution system, and the vacuum extraction system. The *steam generation and distribution* system consists of a trailer-mounted, gas-fired water tube boiler, including related feedwater treatment and preheating equipment, along with the related steam piping, flowmeters, and traps. The *vacuum extraction* system is similar to that of a traditional soil vapor extraction system, except for the addition of a condenser or heat exchanger to condense steam in the exiting air stream. Also included are condensate holding tanks. The discharge of the vacuum extraction pump is typically followed by off-gas treatment, such as gas phase carbon adsorption.

In some cases, soil vapor extraction may be enhanced through injection of hot air. However, the relatively inefficient transfer of heat from air to soil results in large flow rate and temperature requirements, which render hot air injection economically infeasible unless a source of waste heat (e.g., off-gas from a flaring system) is readily available. In addition, federal, state, and local regulations may limit or prohibit the reinjection of off-gas from a combustion unit. In the absence of a suitable on-site heat source, steam injection is often more economically desirable. Steam injection heats the soil more rapidly than hot air, and portable steam boilers are readily available in a wide range of capacities.

The equipment used limits the areal extent and depth of contamination for which this process is appropriate. As the area increases, the required steam injection rate increases, which necessitates an increase in either the number of boilers or the boiler capacity. Trailer-mounted steam boilers are typically available in capacities of up to 12,000 pounds of steam per hour. Also, the optimum injection pressure is directly proportional to the depth to the contaminated zone. The maximum injection pressure possible from most trailer-mounted steam generators is about 250 pounds per square inch gauge (PSIG). Larger-capacity boilers are considerably more expensive to rent, transport, and operate.

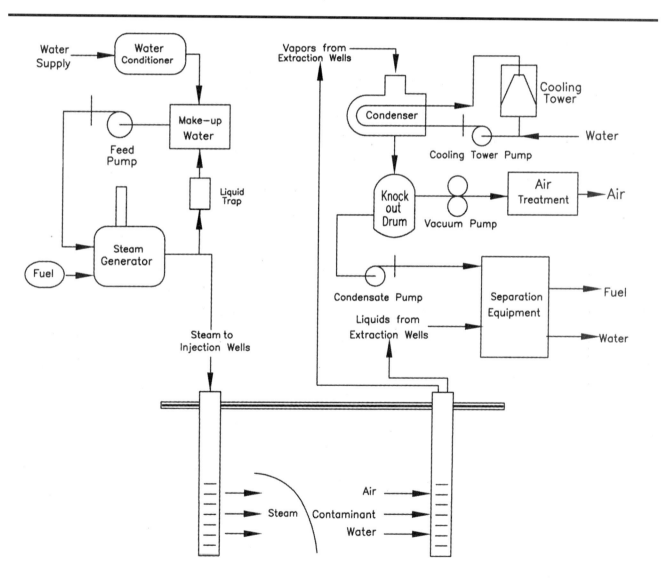

Figure 20.1 Schematic of Heat-Enhanced Vapor Extraction Process
Courtesy of Praxis Environmental Technologies, Inc.

Condensers and cooling towers used to condense the vapor stream are also sized according to the steam injection rate. Condensers suitable for this application are not readily available; they are usually purchased directly from a manufacturer. Although vapor condensers can be fabricated in any capacity, large custom-made condensers are very expensive, as are the cooling towers that accompany them. For these reasons, heat-enhanced vapor extraction is best suited for contaminated areas of one acre or less. Larger sites are best treated in a series of smaller sections to reduce the costs of steam generation and vacuum extraction equipment. In addition to the scope of the site, soil permeability affects the applicability and design of a heat-enhanced vapor extraction system.

The optimal soil permeability for heat-enhanced vapor extraction ranges from approximately 0.1–5 darcies. In lower-permeability soils, the steam will most likely flow along a preferred pathway instead of an even sweep across the full thickness of the contaminant plume. In a heat-enhanced vapor extraction system, VEP spacing is limited by the distance over which control of horizontal steam propagation can be maintained. An increase in soil permeability means an increase in the radius of influence of applied vacuum at the VEPs. However, higher permeability soils offer less resistance to buoyant forces that induce upward migration of the steam. Excessive upward migration of steam could leave large portions of the contaminated zone untreated. As a result, well spacing does not increase when soil permeability increases. Furthermore, as permeability increases, steam injection and vacuum extraction rates must increase to offset the increased effect of buoyancy. The applicability of heat-enhanced vapor extraction to a particular site also depends heavily on the types and levels of contamination, as well as the proximity of the contamination to the saturated zone.

Heat-enhanced vapor extraction is effective on many halogenated and non-halogenated volatiles and semi-volatiles, polynuclear aromatics, and some organic solvents. However, it also mobilizes dioxins. Steam injection sterilizes the area in which it is applied, killing off most or all indigenous microorganisms. Thus heat-enhanced vapor extraction may not be appropriate for sites where natural biodegradation would result in sufficient contaminant removal. (For example, for vadose zone contamination that is close to an uncontaminated aquifer.) This is because steam injection may mobilize contaminants into the saturated zone, especially in the case of DNAPL contamination. However, if contamination has already penetrated the saturated zone, steam injection into the saturated zone, coupled with dual phase extraction wells, may remove contamination from both the vadose and saturated zones.

The typical estimating process starts with well drilling and installation and includes all drilling, screen, and casing costs, as well as costs for steam distribution and vapor collection piping. Stainless steel is typically used for well and collection piping, and galvanized steel is used for steam distribution piping. Steam boilers, extraction blowers, and the associated utility costs are also included in the estimate. All injection wells and VEPs described in this chapter are assumed to be installed in the vadose zone; groundwater extraction is not included in this process. However, it is possible to develop a reasonable cost estimate for steam injection in the saturated zone by assuming well installation into the saturated zone and a groundwater extraction rate sufficient to dewater the contaminated zone.

Chapter 43, "Groundwater Extraction Wells," may be used to estimate costs for collection of contaminated groundwater. The chapter ends prior to off-gas and effluent treatment. Chapter 12, "Carbon Adsorption—Gas" may be used to estimate costs for off-gas treatment.

Basic Information Needed for Estimating

It is possible to create a reasonable budget cost estimate using a few required parameters. If more detailed information is known, one can create a more precise and site-specific estimate using a secondary set of parameters.

To estimate the cost of the heat-enhanced vapor extraction system, certain information must be known. This information is discussed in the following paragraphs.

Area of Contamination

The approximate areal extent of contamination drives the number of injection wells and vapor extraction points (VEPs). Heat-enhanced vapor extraction is typically used for contaminated areas of 1 acre or less. As the area of contamination increases, the size and cost of the steam generators and vapor condensers become prohibitive. For soil permeabilities up to 5 darcies, systems of up to 100,000 S.F. are efficient. For permeabilities greater than 5 darcies, the typical limit is 43,560 S.F. (one acre). Permeabilities greater than 5 darcies require considerably larger steam injection and vacuum extraction equipment, which can significantly increase cost. Sites with soil permeabilities greater than 5 darcies should be treated in smaller sections to offset the equipment costs.

Soil Type

The design of any SVE system is site-specific and heavily influenced by soil type. The soil properties influence the recovery pressure, air and steam flow rates, and ultimately, the required cleanup time. Based on the soil type, values for air flow rate, soil permeability, and soil density can be assumed, as shown in Figure 20.1.

Options for soil type are:

- Silty clay, clay
- Mixed sandy, silty, clayey soils
- Primarily sand
- Sand and gravel

Soil Permeability

Soil permeability is based on the user-specified soil type, as shown in Figure 20.2. If site-specific soil permeability data are available, the value should be adjusted to reflect such data, as permeability has a direct impact on the performance of the system. As soil permeability increases, the air flow rate and steam injection rate (mass flow rate of steam) increases, and the time required to heat the contaminated zone to steam temperature decreases. This results in the selection of larger boilers and vacuum extraction pumps, which can significantly increase costs.

Depth to Top of Contamination

The distance from ground surface to the top of the contaminated zone drives the injection well and VEP casing lengths. Steam injection is best suited for contaminated zones that lie 10–150' below the surface. The optimal injection pressure per well is directly proportional to the depth to top of contamination. At depths greater than 150', the injection pressure requirements exceed the capabilities of most portable steam generation equipment. Furthermore, field data has not been able to predict the performance of steam injection at depths greater than 150'.

Steam injection is also not feasible at depths less than approximately 6–10' unless an impermeable surface barrier, such as a low-permeability clay layer or man-made cap, is present. Otherwise, surface air will short-circuit and steam will escape to the surface, leaving large portions of the contaminated zone untreated.

Thickness of Contaminated Zone

The thickness of the contaminated zone affects the air flow and steam injection rates. This dimension also drives the default injection well and VEP screen lengths. Typically, VEP screens begin at the top of the contaminated zone, or at a specified distance below the top, and extend all the way to the bottom of the contaminated zone. However, steam injection screens that span the entire contaminated interval become less desirable when the thickness of the contaminated zone increases. This is because the steam flow rate is greatest at the top of the injection screen and decreases over the length of the screen.

Injection well screens longer than approximately 30' may distribute too much steam near the top of the contaminated zone and leave the lower extremes unswept by the steam. This problem is normally overcome by installing short injection screens at 2 or more different depths throughout the contaminated zone.

Soil Properties			
Soil Type	Air Flow Rate Per Linear Foot Of Screen (CFM/Ft.)	Soil Unit Weight (Lb./C.F.)*	Soil Permeability (darcies)**
Silty Clay, Clay	0.60	114	0.10
Mixed Sandy, Silty, Clayey Soils	1.50	125	1
Primarily Sand	3.55	127	5
Sand and Gravel	15.50	135	20

* Bank (In-situ) Unit Weight
** 1 darcy = 1.06 x 10E–11 S.F.

Figure 20.2 Soil Properties

In a steam injection system, each injection well can have only one screened interval, because injection wells with multiple screened intervals result in uneven distribution of steam. Consequently, one set of injection wells is required for each injection depth; a set being a series of wells with the same depth to top of screen and screen length. Contaminated zones thicker than 75' typically require steam injection at three or more discrete depths.

Injection Well Configuration

This parameter is based on the thickness of contaminated zone. If the thickness of contaminated zone is 30' or less, the *single set* configuration is recommended. In the single set configuration, all injection wells on the site are screened over the entire thickness of the contaminated zone.

If the thickness of the contaminated zone is greater than 30', the *double set* configuration is recommended. The double set configuration consists of 1 set of injection wells screened in the upper third of the contaminated zone and another set screened in the lower third. In the double set configuration, each set contains half of the total number of injection wells. A set is a series of wells with the same depth to top of screen and screen length. The actual contaminated zone thickness at which the double set configuration becomes more appropriate than a single set may vary depending on site-specific soil properties.

Treatment Period

The total treatment duration is divided into startup and operations and maintenance (O&M). The costs associated with the startup period (equipment acquisition, installation, and optimization) are considered capital costs, and the O&M costs are identified separately. Normally, the vapor extraction system will operate 24 hours a day.

Typical project duration for heat-enhanced vapor extraction ranges from 6 months to 1 year. Steam injection continues only until the entire contaminated zone has been heated to steam temperature and steam breakthrough has occurred at the extraction wells. After that, the flow of steam continues only intermittently while the vacuum extraction pumps continue to operate. The time required for steam breakthrough is based on the soil type and size of the contaminated zone. On most sites, steam breakthrough will occur within 60 days.

Worker Safety Level

Worker safety is affected by the contaminant(s) at the site. Safety level refers to the levels required by OSHA in 29 CFR Part 1910. The 4 levels are designated as A, B, C, and D; where "A" is the most protective and "D" is the least protective. A safety level of E is also included to simulate normal construction, "no hazard" conditions as prescribed by the EPA.

Design Information Needed for Detailed Estimates

Following are descriptions of the types of detailed information that, when available, can add detail and accuracy to estimates. Also included are design criteria and estimating rules of thumb that the estimator typically uses to determine values that are not known, or to check information provided by others. The design parameters are divided into 3 groups: well parameters, pumps/boilers, and well drilling.

Well Parameters

The well parameters address the design of the injection well and VEP networks and are as follows.

Depth to Top of Injection Well Screen

The distance from ground surface to the top of the injection well screen depends on the injection well configuration selected. The defaults for both the single set and double set configurations are shown in Figure 20.3 (refer also to Figures 20.4 and 20.5).

Injection Well Screen Length

The screen length depends on the injection well configuration. For the single set configuration, all injection wells are typically screened over the entire thickness of the contaminated zone. For the double set configuration, assume that one set of injection wells is screened over the top third of the contaminated zone, and the other set is screened over the bottom third, as shown in Figure 20.5.

Injection Well Diameter

Typical injection wells are 4" in diameter. Although the steam injection pressure is limited by the depth to the top of the contaminated zone, greater mass flow rates of steam are possible with larger diameter wells.

Depth to Top of VEP Screen

The distance from ground surface to the top of the vapor extraction screen is assumed to be the same for all VEPs, regardless of the thickness of the contaminated zone. Typically, VEP screened intervals begin at the top of the contaminated zone. However, if surface air short-circuiting is a concern, it may be necessary to set the VEP screens below the top of the contaminated zone. Deeper set screens often serve to lengthen air flow paths and reduce surface air short circuiting.

VEP Screen Length

Unlike steam injection wells, all VEP screens are assumed to span the entire thickness of the contaminated zone, regardless of the thickness of the contaminated zone.

VEP Diameter

The normal VEP diameter is 4", but 6" diameter tubes are also used.

Depth To Top Of Injection Well Screen Defaults	
Injection Well Configurarion	**Default Is Equal To:**
Single Set	Depth to Top of Contamination
Double Set	
1st Set	Depth of Contamination
2nd Set	Depth to Top of Contamination + (2/3 x Thickness of Contamination Zone) (Round to nearest whole number)

Figure 20.3 Depth to Top of Injection Well Screen Defaults

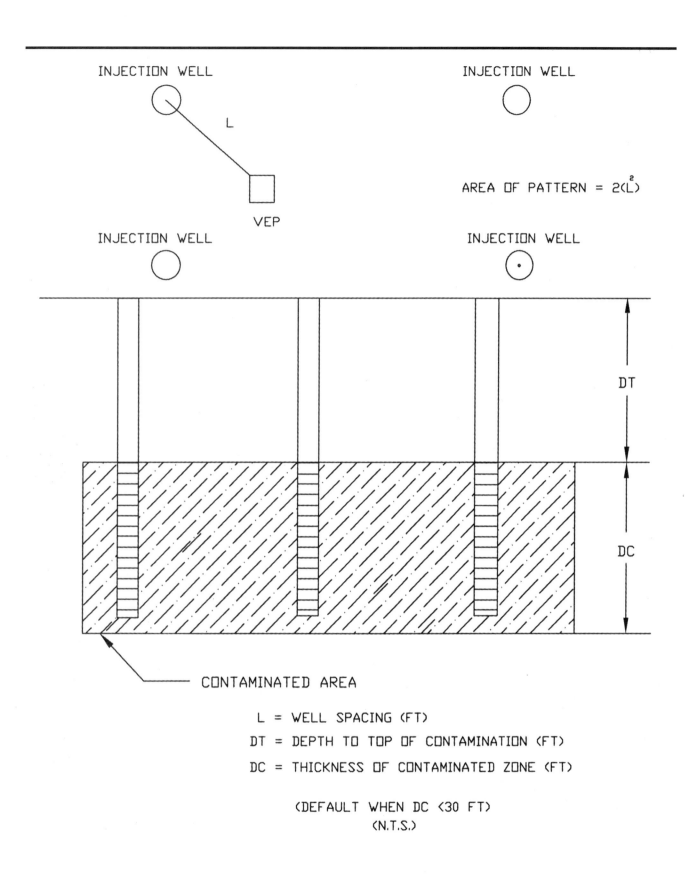

INJECTION WELL

INJECTION WELL

L

VEP

AREA OF PATTERN = $2(L^2)$

INJECTION WELL

INJECTION WELL

DT

DC

CONTAMINATED AREA

L = WELL SPACING (FT)

DT = DEPTH TO TOP OF CONTAMINATION (FT)

DC = THICKNESS OF CONTAMINATED ZONE (FT)

(DEFAULT WHEN DC <30 FT)
(N.T.S.)

Figure 20.4 Single-Set Injection Well Configuration

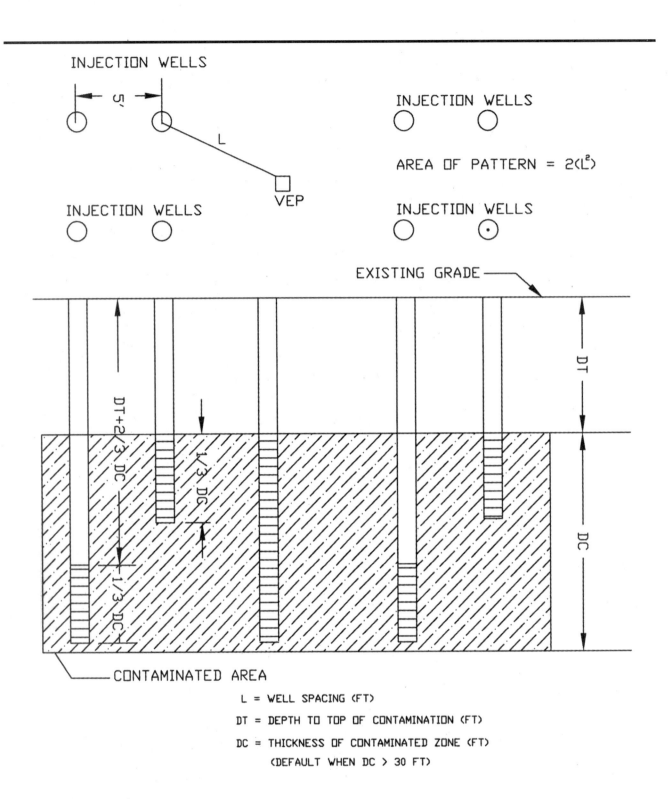

Figure 20.5 Double-Set Injection Well Configuration

Extraction Pressure per VEP

The extraction pressure per VEP depends mainly on soil permeability and air flow rate. As soil permeability increases, the flow rate of air that can be passed through the soil matrix increases, and the applied vacuum required to maintain the desired flow rate decreases:

$$(P_{vacuum} = P_{atmospheric} - P_{absolute})$$

The default extraction pressure is a function of soil type and is shown in Figure 20.6.

Steam Injection Pressure per Well

The maximum steam injection pressure per well is limited by the weight of the overburden, which depends only on soil density and depth to top of contamination. The default injection pressure, P_i, is calculated based on the depth to top of contamination and soil density, as shown in the equation below. Since injection pressure is limited by the weight of the soil overlaying the contaminated zone, the injection pressure is the same for *all* injection wells, even in a double set configuration. Trailer-mounted steam generators have a maximum operating pressure of 250 pounds per square inch gauge (PSIG):

$$(P_{absolute} = P_{atmospheric} + P_{gauge})$$

Depending on the injection pressure, state or local regulations may require that a licensed boiler technician be on site to operate the boilers, which may add to the cost of the project.

$$P_i = \left[\frac{\gamma_s D_t}{144}\right] + 14.7$$

Where:

γ_s = unit weight of soil (lb./ft^3) (from Figure 20.1)

D_t = depth to top of contaminated zone (ft)

Well Spacing

The typical well pattern is a 5-spot pattern, which consists of a central VEP surrounded by either 4 or 8 injection wells on a square, as shown in Figures 20.4 and 20.5, respectively.

Default Extraction Pressures	
Soil Type	Extraction Pressure P$_r$ (PSIA)[*]
Inorganic Silt, Silty Clay	10.76
Sand-Silt or Sand-Clay Mixtures	11.93
Sands, Gravelly Sands	13.16
Gravel, Gravel-Sand Mixtures	13.72

Figure 20.6 Default Extraction Pressures

[*]PSIA = Pounds per Square Inch at one Atmosphere

Additional 5-spot patterns are created by adding one more VEP and either 2 or 4 more injection wells to form an adjacent square. The well spacing is the diagonal distance from 1 of the corner injection wells to the central VEP. The maximum well spacing over which control of horizontal steam movement may be maintained is limited by the difference between the injection and extraction pressures and by the effect of buoyancy acting on the steam. As soil permeability increases, the radius of influence of applied vacuum at the VEPs increases. However, soils with higher permeability offer less resistance to buoyant forces that cause upward migration of the steam. This precludes increasing the well spacing with increasing soil permeability.

As shown in the equation below, the well spacing, L, is calculated by equating the hydraulic gradient of the condensate to the difference in the specified injection and extraction pressures. The areal extent of contamination is divided by the area per pattern to determine the required number of patterns, and consequently the required number of injection and extraction wells.

$$L = \frac{(P_i - P_r) \times 144}{\gamma_w}$$

Where:

P_i = steam injection pressure per well (PSIA)

P_r = extraction pressure per VEP (PSIA)

g_w = unit weight of water (lb/C.F.) : (assume 62.4 lb/C.F.)

Once well spacing is calculated, determine the number of five-spot patterns, NP, as shown below.

$$NP = \frac{AC}{2(L)^2} \quad \text{(Rounded to nearest whole number)}$$

Where:

AC = areal extent of contamination (S.F.)

Since well spacing depends on only injection and extraction pressures and not the areal extent of contamination, the estimator could calculate a well spacing that would cause the area per pattern to exceed the areal extent of contamination. In this case, the well spacing is limited by the areal extent of the contamination. One 5-spot pattern (NP = 1), with the injection wells near the "corners" of the contaminated area and one VEP in the center of the contaminated area, should be used. In this case, calculate the default well spacing based on the areal extent of contamination, as shown in the equation below.

$$L = \frac{1}{2} \times \sqrt{2 \times AC}$$

When the well spacing is calculated based on the areal extent of contamination rather than the injection and extraction pressures, the injection pressure is then back-calculated from the well spacing.

$$P_i = \frac{\gamma_w L}{144} + P_r$$

Number of Injection Wells

Steam injection wells are located in each corner of each 5-spot pattern. If the single set configuration is chosen, the typical application is 1 injection well in the corner of each pattern. For the double set configuration, the typical application is 2 injection wells in each corner of each pattern. This means that the double set configuration requires twice as many injection wells as the single set configuration. The number of wells is calculated as shown in the following equation. The minimum number of injection wells is 4 for the single set configuration and 8 for the double set configuration.

$$N_i = NS [2 + 2(NP)]$$

Where:

NP = Number of patterns
NS = Number of injection well sets
    If injection well configuration = single set, NS = 1
    If injection well configuration = double set, NS = 2

Number of VEPs

Normally, one VEP is installed per pattern, regardless of the thickness of the contaminated zone. VEPs are located in the center of each 5-spot pattern.

Pumps/Boilers

The pumps/boilers parameters address the quantities and sizes of the vacuum pumps, steam boilers, and condensers.

Calculated Total Air Flow Rate

The total air flow rate is based on the air flow rate per linear foot of screen (from Figure 20.2), the VEP screen length, and the number of VEPs. The total air flow rate determines the vacuum pump capacity.

Vacuum Pump Size/Capacity

The vacuum pump capacity depends on the calculated total air flow rate, as shown in Figure 20.7.

Figure 20.7 Default Vacuum Pump Capacities

Default Vacuum Pump Capacities	
Calculated Total Air Flow Rate QT (SCFM)*	Vacuum Pump Capacity
$1 < QT \leq 90$	5 H.P., 90 SCFM
$90 < QT \leq 140$	7.5 H.P., 140 SCFM
$140 < QT \leq 190$	10 H.P., 190 SCFM
$190 < QT \leq 290$	15 H.P., 290 SCFM
$QT > 290$	30 H.P., 580 SCFM

*SCFM = Standard Cubic Feet per Minute

Vacuum Pump Quantity

The vacuum pump quantity depends on the calculated total air flow rate. For calculated total air flow rates less than or equal to 580 SCFM, the typical application is one vacuum pump. For calculated total air flow rates higher than 580 SCFM, the number of vacuum pumps equals the calculated total air flow rate divided by 580 SCFM, rounded up.

Calculated Total Steam Injection Rate

The total steam injection rate determines the required boiler capacity. The steam injection rate depends on the well spacing, the injection and extraction pressures, injection well diameter and screen length, and soil permeability. The steam injection rate may be determined assuming a compressible, steady-state flow of steam. The following equation shows the calculation of the steam injection rate, m_s, in pounds of steam per hour.

$$C_r = \left[\frac{12L}{0.5BD_r} \right]^4 - 1 \quad C_i = \left[\frac{12L}{12L - 0.5BD_r} \right]^4 - 1$$

$$m_s = \frac{N_i}{NS} \left[\pi \frac{H_i + H_r}{2} \frac{1.06 \times 10^{-11k}}{\mu_v R_u T_v} \frac{(P_i \times 144)^2 - (P_r \times 144)^2}{1nC_r - 1nC_i} \right] \times 3600 \times g$$

Where:

H_i = Injection well screen length (ft)

H_r = VEP screen length (ft)

m_v = Viscosity of steam (lb sec/S.F.):
Model assumes 2.72×10^{-7} (lb sec/S.F.)

R_u = Universal gas constant (ft lb/slug° R):
Model assumes 2,761 ft lb/slug° R

T_v = Temperature of steam (°R): Model assumes 672° R

BD_r = Diameter of VEP borehole (in): Model assumes 11"

g = Gravitational constant, 32.2 ft/sec²

Steam Boiler Size/Capacity

The boiler size required depends on the calculated total steam injection rate. Since the steam boiler must be sized commensurate with the steam injection rate, boiler capacities are expressed in pounds of steam per hour (pph). Default boiler capacities are shown in Figure 20.8.

Although boilers can burn either natural gas or diesel fuel, regulatory constraints often limit or prohibit the use of diesel-fired equipment on remediation sites. Depending on the injection pressure, state or local regulations may require that a licensed boiler operator be on site to run the boilers. This will add an extra expense to the project.

Steam Boiler Quantity

Determine the quantity of boilers based on the guidelines in Figure 20.8. The 12,000 pound per hour boiler is used only for calculated total steam injection rates in excess of 20,000 pph. For lower steam injection rates, use of the appropriate quantity of 5,000 pph boilers will result in lower fuel consumption rates (e.g., for a steam injection rate of 14,000 pph, three 5,000 pph boilers would consume less fuel than two 12,000 pph boilers). For calculated total steam injection rates greater than

20,000 pph, divide the calculated total steam injection rate by 12,000 pph to determine the steam boiler quantity.

Steam Breakthrough Time

The time required, in days, to heat the contaminated zone to steam temperature affects the total duration of steam injection. Greater steam injection rates are possible with higher permeability soils, and the steam breakthrough time decreases when the steam injection rate increases. The time required to heat the contaminated zone to steam temperature is obtained by dividing the heat capacity of the volume of soil to be heated by the calculated total steam injection rate.

The following equation is a calculation for steam breakthrough time in days. The actual time required for steam breakthrough, and the temperature at which breakthrough occurs, depends partly on the initial temperature of the soil matrix and is normally verified through pilot studies. If this information is not known, for estimating purposes assume an initial soil temperature of 60°F and a final soil temperature at breakthrough of 212°F. On most sites, steam breakthrough will occur within 60 days.

$$t_b = \frac{\epsilon V \left[(1-\phi)\gamma_s c_{ps} + \phi S_w \gamma_w c_{pw} \right] \Delta T}{(24 \times m_s) \left[h_{fg} + c_{pw} \Delta T \right]}$$

Where:

e = Heat loss factor: Model assumes 1.33

V = Volume of contaminated zone (C.F.)

f = Soil porosity: Model assumes 0.3

c_{ps} = Heat capacity of soil (BTU/lb °F): Model assumes 0.2388 BTU/lb °F

S_w = Soil degree of saturation: Model assumes 0.3

c_{pw} = Heat capacity of water (BTU/lb °F): Model assumes 1.007 BTU/lb °F

DT = Temperature difference: Model assumes 212°F - 59°F = 153°F

h_{fg} = Latent heat of vaporization of water (BTU/lb): Model assumes 970.4 BTU/lb

Steam Injection Duration

Steam injection is rarely continued throughout the project. Once the entire contaminated zone is heated to steam temperature and steam breakthrough occurs at the extraction wells, the flow of steam continues only intermittently while the vacuum extraction pumps continue to operate. Vacuum extraction removes much of the remaining contamination. Typically, the boiler(s) run continuously until breakthrough occurs. After breakthrough, the boilers will be run 1 day (24 hours) a week for the remainder of the project.

The steam injection duration is used to determine the total quantity of natural gas consumed by the steam boiler(s); it does not affect the boiler rental costs if the boilers will remain on-site for the entire project duration.

Condenser Size/Capacity

Extracted vapor is passed through a condenser, and liquid from the condenser is drained to a holding tank to await ultimate disposal. Continual changes in the temperature and relative humidity of the extracted vapor stream complicate the selection of the appropriate condenser size. The condenser must be sized to handle a mixture of steam and air. It is possible to create a reasonable estimate for condenser size by assuming condensation of steam to near ambient temperature at *one-half the steam injection rate* because the condenser capacity depends on the calculated total steam injection rate (as shown in Figure 20.9). Condenser capacities are expressed in pounds per hour (pph). Cooling towers for the condensers are sized assuming vapor inlet and outlet temperatures of 212°F and 90°F, respectively, and cooling water inlet and outlet temperatures of 100°F and 70°F, respectively.

Default Steam Boiler Quantities And Capacities				
Total Steam Injection Rate m_s(pph)	Boiler Quantity	Boiler Capacity (pph)	Gas Consumption Rate (Ft.^{3}/Hr.)	Diesel Consumption Rate (Gal./Hr.)
$1 < m_s \leq 1,700$	1	1,700	2,095	12
$1,700 < m_s \leq 3,400$	1	3,400	4,190	31
$3,400 < m_s \leq 5,000$	1	5,000	6,100	45
$5,000 < m_s \leq 20,000$	$m_s/5,000$ (round up)	5,000	6,100 x Boiler Qty.	45 x Boiler Qty.
$m_s > 20,000$	$m_s/12,000$ (round up)	12,000	14,670 x Boiler Qty.	107 x Boiler Qty.

Figure 20.8 Default Steam Boiler Quantities and Capacities

Default Condenser Capacities And Quantities			
Calculated Total Steam Injection Rate (pph)	Condenser Capacity (pph)*	Condenser Quantity	Cooling Tower Capacity (tons)
$1 < m_s \leq 1,000$	500	1	40
$500 < m_s \leq 3,000$	1,500	1	100
$3,000 < m_s \leq 5,000$	2,500	1	200
$5,000 < m_s \leq 12,000$	6,000	1	400
$12,000 < m_s \leq 20,000$	10,000	1	700
$m_s > 20,000$	10,000	$(m_s 2)/10,000$ (Round up)	700

* Condenser capacity is based on one-half of the calculated total steam injection rate.

Figure 20.9 Default Condenser Capacities and Quantities

Condenser Quantity

The total number of condensers required is based on one-half the calculated total steam injection rate, as shown in Figure 20.9. Each condenser includes an appropriately sized cooling tower and circulating pump and an anti-fouling chemical feeder. Two hundred feet of 3" PVC piping is also assumed for each condenser-cooling tower combination. Cooling tower capacities are based on a cooling tower inlet temperature of 100°F and an outlet temperature of 70°F.

Ideally, the vapor extraction system would have one condenser for every blower, although steam injection rates and air flow rates often render this impractical. It is not imperative that there be 1 condenser for every blower. Depending on the arrangement of the manifold piping, 1 blower may be served by more than 1 condenser, and vice versa.

Well Drilling

Well drilling parameters address the drilling method and sample collection during drilling.

Drilling Method

The selection of a drilling method is a function of site-specific geologic conditions, well specifications, and degree of subsurface disturbance. All well installation is assumed to be in unconsolidated formations, since SVE is not effective in consolidated formations. The typical drilling methods are:

- Hollow stem auger (typical for well depths $\geq$ 150')
- Water/mud rotary (typical for well depths > 150')
- Air rotary

Sample Collection During Drilling

Sample collection during bore hole advancement allows characterization of the geology beneath the site and definition of the extent of contamination in the vadose zone. Split spoon sample collection, with standard penetration tests at 5' intervals, is typical.

Drum Drill Cuttings

During installation, soil cuttings from the drill bit and subsequent hole are often drummed and stored until disposal options have been evaluated. The conservative approach assumes that all drill cuttings will be drummed.

Related Costs

Other costs associated with this technology include the following.

Professional Labor

Professional labor costs are for supervision of drilling and well installation. Assume that a staff hydrogeologist will supervise well drilling and installation, OVA screening and collecting split spoon samples. The following assumptions provide reasonable guidelines for staff hydrogeologist hours related to injection well and VEP installation:

- If soil samples are collected during drilling, staff hydrogeologist hours are based on drilling at a rate of 20' per hour plus 2 hours per well for well completion.
- If soil samples are not collected during drilling, staff hydrogeologist hours are based on drilling at a rate of 40' per hour plus 2 hours per well for well completion.

Professional labor costs are discussed in Chapter 58, "Remedial Action Professional Labor Management."

System Maintenance

Maintenance requirements for this system are minimal. A maintenance crew will generally be on site once a week for the first month and once a month thereafter. The maintenance crew is responsible for adjusting the air and steam flow rates, adjusting control valves, and general system maintenance. The maintenance crew is also responsible for collecting air samples.

Sampling and Analysis

The maintenance crew will collect air samples once a week for the first month and once a month thereafter. An air blower effluent sample will be collected during each sampling event and analyzed for principle organic hazardous constituents. Also, an organic vapor analyzer will be used for each sampling event.

Utilities

Utilities costs include electricity for the vacuum pumps and fuel for the steam boilers. Electrical costs are related directly to the motor horsepower of the vacuum pumps. Electricity consumption is calculated assuming a motor efficiency of 75% and a conversion of 0.7457 kW/H.P.

The boilers are capable of burning either natural gas or diesel fuel, but natural gas is usually more efficient and easier to regulate. Costs for natural gas are directly related to the gas consumption rates of the boilers, which are shown in Figure 20.8. Assume a conversion of 1,000 BTU/C.F. of natural gas.

Piping and Fittings

The design of the system will dictate the quantity of piping and associated fittings based on the number and configuration of injection wells and VEPs. If the design is not known, include a pressure gauge, control valve, one 90° elbow, one tee, and a quantity of pipe equal to 1.5 times the well spacing for each injection well and VEP. In addition, thermocouples are assumed to be installed on each VEP at 5' intervals down the length of the VEP screens. Assume that manifold piping and connection piping are the same, and the quantity of piping assumed for each injection well and VEP accounts for both manifold piping and connection piping. All injection wells and VEPs are made of stainless steel to withstand the high operating temperatures. All collection piping is stainless steel, and all steam distribution piping is galvanized steel.

Site Work and Utilities

If site work and utilities such as the following are applicable, they must also be included in the estimate.

- Overhead electrical distribution
- Gas distribution
- Water distribution
- Fencing
- Clear and grub

Conclusion   Heat-enhanced vapor extraction can be an effective process, but it is expensive when compared to traditional soil vapor extraction. The primary cost drivers are the volume of soil to be remediated, volume of contaminants, contaminant volatility, soil permeability, operating period, and time required to reach steam breakthrough. Capital costs are marginally higher than for traditional SVE, but operating costs may be orders of magnitude higher, depending on the above parameters. The cost engineer should be knowledgeable of site conditions and offer alternatives by comparing costs with other soil vapor and groundwater treatment methods.

Chapter 21

In Situ Biodegradation Saturated Zone

In the environmental restoration process, *biodegradation* is the use of naturally occurring biological agents to degrade hazardous wastes to a non-hazardous state. The technology is used primarily for treating chemical spills and hazardous waste problems.

In situ biodegradation is used to recycle organics and inorganics in place, in the biosphere. Through a series of complex reactions, a pollutant can be biologically converted into innocuous chemicals. To drive the biochemical conversions, the bacterial population transforms a portion of the pollutant into carbon dioxide and water.

One advantage of biodegradation is that it is an ecologically sound, "natural" process. Existing microorganisms that perform the biodegradation process can increase in number when the proper proportions of nutrients are present. When nutrient proportions are insufficient, the microbial population declines. Biodegradation is a desirable option for several other reasons:

- The residues from the aerobic biological processes are usually harmless products, such as carbon dioxide, water, and fatty acids.
- Biodegradation offers a final solution to a waste site. The pollutant is not immobilized or vaporized to reappear later. When properly conducted, biodegradation eliminates pollutants from the environment.
- Biodegradation is less costly than other treatment technologies.

A potential disadvantage of biodegradation is treatment time. Biodegradation is a more time-intensive remediation option compared to other remediation alternatives, such as excavation and landfill disposal.

Organic compounds can be ranked according to their relative ease of biodegradation. For example, aromatic compounds are slower to biodegrade than aliphatic compounds. Any halogenation/chlorination of an organic compound makes it more resistant to biodegradation by microorganisms. The higher the degree of halogenation, the more resistant the compound is to degradation. Generally, the less soluble compounds are slower to break down.

Applications and Limitations

Applications

- An in situ treatment used to treat soils contaminated with petroleum hydrocarbons (diesel fuel, No. 2 and No. 6 fuel/oils, JP-5 jet fuel, oily sludge, PCP, creosote, and certain pesticides).
- Has also been successfully applied to phenols, cresols, acetone, and cellulosic wastes.

Figure 21.1 provides a partial list of the compounds affected by biodegradation processes.

Limitations

- Biodegradation will not degrade inorganics.
- Toxic levels of contaminants may significantly limit biodegradation.
- Geologic heterogeneities may interfere with the injection of electron acceptors and nutrients.
- Byproducts are occasionally more toxic than the parent compound.

Process Configurations and Treatment Train Considerations

- Site-specific studies are essential to determine the feasibility of microbial enhancements.
- Performance is influenced by bioavailability of the particular compounds at a given site.
- Microbial populations require a minimum threshold contaminant level for biodegradation to occur. This level may be above target contaminant remedial levels for the site.

Partial List Of Environmental Pollutants		
Recognized As Biodegradable		
atrazine	DDT	methylethyl ketone
acenaphthalene	dichlorobenzene	methylmethacrylate
acenaphthene	dichloroethane	naphthalene
acetone	dichloroethylene	nitroglycerine
acrylonitrile	diesel fuel	nonane
anthracene	dioxane	octane
benzene	dioxin	pentachlorophenol
benzo (a) anthracene	dodecane	phenanthrene
benzoic acid	ehtyl benzene	phenol
benzo (k) fluoranthene	ethyl glycol	phytane
benzo (a) pyrene	fluroanthenefluorene	PCBs
benzo (g,h,i) perylene	gasoline	pristane
butanol	heptanehexane	pyrene
butylcellosolve	indeno (1,2,3) pyrene	styrene
chlordance	jet fuel	tetrachloroethylene
chloroform	isopropyl acetate	1,1,1-trichloroethane
chrysene	kerosene	trichloroethylene
p-cresol	lindane	tridecene
crude oil	2-methyl naphthalene	trinitrotoluene
dibenzo (a,h)	methylene chloride	vinyl chlorode
anthracene xylenes		

Figure 21.1 Partial List of Environmental Pollutants

- Alternate electron acceptors, such as nitrate and sulfate, may be used in situations where it is difficult to deliver sufficient oxygen to the contaminated zone.
- The typical configuration, known as the Raymond Process, involves a combination of extraction, nutrient and electron acceptor addition, and re-injection.
- In most cases, native microorganisms are used for biodegradation. However, at some sites it may be necessary to use exogenous microorganisms to degrade the target contaminants.
- Injection wells may be subject to various state and local regulations.

Typical System Design Elements

In situ biodegradation of the saturated zone promotes and accelerates natural biodegradation by introducing oxygen and nutrients into the contaminated aquifer. Injection wells, infiltration galleries, and surface irrigation are all potential methods of distributing oxygen and nutrients to areas of fuel contamination. The most common process consists of installing injection wells in the contaminant plume area. The injection wells infiltrate the nutrients in the aquifer. Figure 21.2 shows a typical injection well.

The formulation of the nutrient solution is based on laboratory bench scale studies. The bench studies simulate field conditions to determine the nutrient proportions required to enhance naturally occurring biodegradation. The microbial population in the subsurface is analyzed for biodegradation feasibility. If the laboratory results indicate that the field microbial population is incapable of promoting biodegradation, it may be necessary to add cultured microbial population into the aquifer. The bioculture formulation depends on the contaminant type, contaminant concentration, extent of contamination, and site chemistry.

In most cases, the subsurface environment contains indigenous microorganisms that can degrade hydrocarbon contaminants. Naturally occurring biodegradation can be enhanced by supplementing deficient nutrients. Figure 21.3 lists the relative amount of elements present in microorganisms. The organic pollutants are used as a carbon source only if other elements are supplied in sufficient proportion. Nutrients must be maintained in sufficient proportion with respect to the available organic carbon to ensure that the contaminant is the limiting reactant.

The nutrient infiltration rate is determined based on site-specific conditions. As a precaution against microbial clogging ("biofouling") of the injection wells, the nutrient solution should be shut off on a periodic basis. Cycling the nutrient addition may also provide a rejuvenation of slow growing bioplumes because constant pumping creates equilibrium and possible channeling. Subsurface dynamics must be managed to produce optimal contaminant consumption.

Using a formulated (foreign) bioculture for in situ bioremediation poses a problem for the foreign bioculture. A foreign microbial population infiltrated into the groundwater will require time to acclimate to the environment. During this time period, a portion of the bioculture may die, and biodegradation may not occur effectively.

The nutrient infiltration into the aquifer causes a mounding effect, generating a steeper hydraulic gradient, which leads to a higher rate of

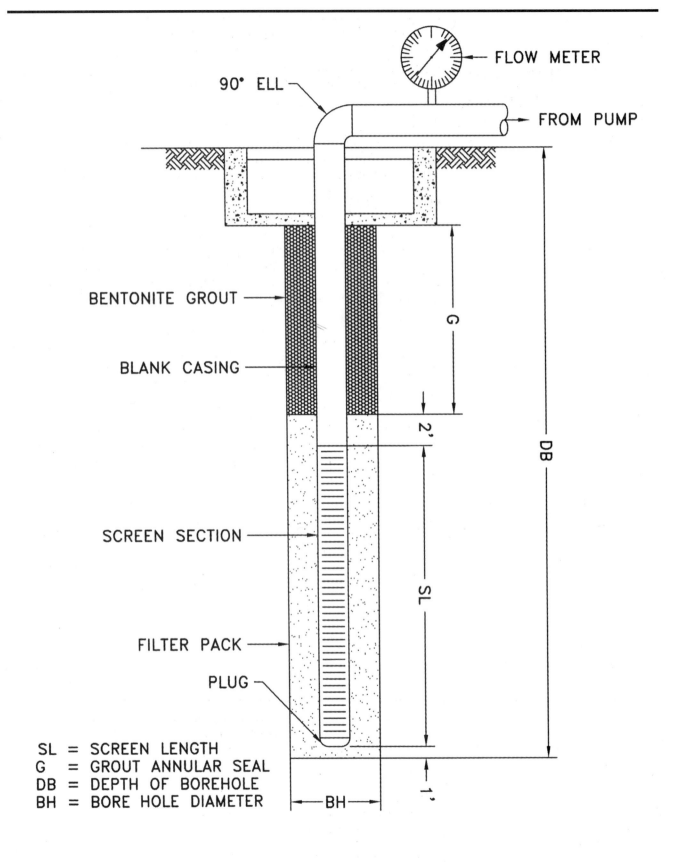

FLOW METER

90° ELL

FROM PUMP

BENTONITE GROUT

BLANK CASING

G

2'

DB

SCREEN SECTION

SL

FILTER PACK

PLUG

1'

BH

SL = SCREEN LENGTH
G = GROUT ANNULAR SEAL
DB = DEPTH OF BOREHOLE
BH = BORE HOLE DIAMETER

Figure 21.2 Schematic of Injection Well

184

contaminant migration. Therefore, monitoring wells may be installed to monitor the remedial action progress and possible contamination migration.

Basic Information Needed for Estimating

It is possible to create a reasonable cost estimate using a few required parameters. If more detailed information is known, one can create a more precise and site-specific estimate using a secondary set of parameters.

To estimate the cost of an in situ biodegradation system, certain information must be known. This information is discussed in the following paragraphs.

Depth to Top of Aquifer
The depth to the top of the aquifer is the depth to the top of the groundwater layer to receive the injection fluid to promote biodegradation. Typically, the fluid is injected through a single casing well. The sum of the depth to the top of the aquifer plus the aquifer thickness is used to calculate the drilling depth. In the case of multiple injection wells, this value may be considered an average drilling depth for all wells to be estimated.

Aquifer Thickness
The aquifer thickness is the distance from the top of the aquifer to the bottom of the aquifer. This value drives the screen length.

Injection Rate
The injection rate per well is typically measured in gallons per minute (GPM). The injection rate drives the quantities and cost of the transfer piping and pumps. High injection pressures tend to fracture subsurface strata. The following equation can be used to determine the approximate injection rate per well:

Confined Aquifer:

$$Q_r = \frac{Kb(h_w - H_o)}{528 Log_{10}(r_o/r_w)}$$

Relative Percentage Of Elements In Microorganisms	
Element	Percentage Of Total Weight
Oxygen	65
Carbon	18
Hydrogen	10
Nitrogen	3
Phosphorous	1
Potassium	0.4
Sulfur	0.3

Figure 21.3 Relative Percentage of Elements in Microorganisms

Unconfined Aquifer:

$$Q_r = \frac{K(h_w^2 - H_o^2)}{1055 \text{Log}_{10} (r_o/r_w)}$$

Where:

Q_r = Rate of injection (GPM)
K = Hydraulic conductivity (GPD/S.F.)
h_w = Head above the bottom of aquifer while recharging (ft)
H_o = Head above the bottom of aquifer when no pumping is taking place (ft)
r_o = Radius of influence (ft)
r_w = Radius of injection well (ft)
b = Aquifer thickness (ft)

Number of Injection Wells

The estimator should determine the number of wells for the entire project, or for series of projects.

Treatment Period

The total treatment duration is divided into startup and operations and maintenance (O&M). The costs associated with the startup period (equipment acquisition, installation, and optimization) are considered capital costs. The O&M costs are identified separately.

Worker Safety Level

Worker safety is affected by the contaminant(s) at the site. Safety level refers to the levels required by OSHA in 29 CFR Part 1910. The four levels are designated as A, B, C, and D; where "A" is the most protective, and "D" is the least protective. A safety level of E is also included to simulate normal construction, "no hazard" conditions as prescribed by the EPA.

Design Information Needed for Detailed Estimates

Following are descriptions of the types of information that, when available, can add detail and accuracy to estimates. Also included are design criteria and estimating rules of thumb that estimators use to determine values that are not known, or to check information provided by others.

Drilling Method

A hollow stem auger is generally used for injection well installation when the well depth is less than 150' below ground surface (bgs). The water/mud rotary method is used for drilling depths greater than 150' bgs. Air rotary drilling is also available. If the subsurface formation is consolidated, then water/mud rotary or air rotary methods are generally used rather than hollow stem augers, even for depths less than 150' bgs.

Injection Well Construction Material

Injection wells are typically constructed of either PVC (Schedule 40 or Schedule 80) or stainless steel screen and casing. The choice is based primarily on cost and material compatibility with the contaminant.

Injection Well Diameter

Injection wells are available in 2", 4", 6", and 8" diameters. Diameters can be estimated based on the injection rate. (See to Figure 21.4.)

Soil Sample Collection

Sample collection during bore-hole advancement allows characterization of the geology beneath the site and definition of the magnitude and extent of contaminants in the vadose zone. Normally, soil samples are collected every 5' or at each change in lithology, whichever is less for lithologic description. Drill cuttings can be collected as the bore hole is advanced for general geologic information. Discrete samples are collected in unconsolidated sediment using the split spoon method.

The most common method for the collection of soil samples is to use a split spoon sampler with standard penetration tests at 5' intervals during bore hole advancement. Samples are screened with an organic vapor analyzer (OVA) for volatile organics and described for the lithologic log by the geologist supervising drilling.

Drum Drill Cuttings

The drill cuttings are generally placed in 55-gallon drums and stored until disposal options have been evaluated.

Screen Length

The screen length is assumed to be the saturated aquifer thickness. If the aquifer is confined, then screen length may vary with the pump head and aquifer pressure.

Influent Pipe Material

The most common influent pipe material is 2" stainless steel. PVC Class 150 and 200 are also available.

Influent Pipe Length

All connection piping is normally assumed to be installed above ground. If the design is not known, the estimator can assume that the length of piping is 100' per well.

Influent Piping Diameter

The default influent piping diameter is based on the injection rate per well. Figure 21.5 displays typical values for influent piping.

Figure 21.4 Default Well Diameters

Default Well Diameters	
Injection Rate Range GPM	**Well Diameter (In.)**
$0.1 \leq Q < 50$	2
$50 \leq Q < 150$	4
$150 \leq Q < 300$	6
$300 \leq Q < 1,000$	8

Q = injection rate in gallons per minute

Types of Feed Tank

Feed tanks are used to store and supply the nutrient solutions. The following is a list of feed tank sizes and materials commonly used for this process:

- 550-gal. stainless steel aboveground holding tank
- 630-gal. polyethylene aboveground holding tank
- 4,000-gal. polyethylene holding tank
- 5,000-gal. steel holding tank
- 6,000-gal. polyethylene holding tank
- 10,000-gal. steel holding tank
- 20,000-gal. steel holding tank
- 35,000-gal. steel holding tank

Types of Mixing Tanks

Mixing tanks are used to mix the additives, particularly the electron acceptor compound. The projected system flow rate per day determines the default mixing tank. The default mixing tank is designed to have the capacity to hold one 24-hour supply of nutrient mixture. The following is a list of mixing tank sizes and materials commonly used in this process:

- 550-gal. steel, aboveground
- 1,500-gal. steel, aboveground
- 2,000-gal. steel, aboveground
- 5,000-gal. steel, aboveground
- 550-gal. plastic, aboveground
- 1,000-gal. plastic, aboveground
- 2,000-gal. plastic, aboveground
- 4,000-gal. plastic, aboveground
- 6,000-gal. plastic, aboveground
- 8,000-gal. plastic, aboveground
- 10,000-gal. plastic, aboveground
- 12,000-gal. plastic, aboveground
- 15,000-gal. plastic, aboveground
- 20,000-gal. plastic, aboveground
- 25,000-gal. plastic, aboveground
- 30,000-gal. plastic, aboveground
- 40,000-gal. plastic, aboveground

Figure 21.5 Typical Values for Influent Piping

Injection Rate per Well (GPM)	Typical Influent Piping Diameter
0–49	2" PVC Schedule 80
50–149	4" PVC Schedule 80
150–299	6" PVC Schedule 80
300–9,999	8" PVC Schedule 80

Number of Monitoring Wells

The monitoring wells are installed to support the injection of nutrients and/or microorganisms. The estimator should evaluate the number and placement of existing monitoring wells at the site to determine how many new wells will be required, if any.

Monitoring Well Drilling Depth

For estimating purposes, assume a well drilling depth equal to the injection well depth.

Monitoring Well Diameter

The monitoring well diameter is typically 2" or 4".

Monitoring Well Construction Material

For estimating purposes, assume the construction material for the monitoring wells is the same as that selected for the injection wells.

Soil Additives

Soil additives support the naturally occurring microbial population with required chemicals and/or supplemental microorganisms. The three secondary parameters related to soil additives are described in the following paragraphs.

Microorganisms

Under favorable conditions, soil microorganisms will degrade most fuel hydrocarbon compounds. Controlled laboratory studies have demonstrated that a variety of indigenous soil microbes can aerobically degrade the mixture of aliphatic and aromatic compounds found in distillate fuels. Microorganisms that can completely degrade fuel components into carbon dioxide and water show greatest productivity in the presence of sufficient oxygen and inorganic nutrients such as nitrogen and phosphorus, a near neutral pH, and warmer soil temperatures. The application rate of the microorganisms is highly-site specific and generally proprietary to the companies that develop the respective biocultures. The estimator should contact prospective vendors to determine applicable injection concentrations.

This cost is assumed to occur at the beginning of the project. However, nutrients and electron receptors are added continuously, so the cost for the microorganisms will be presented in the capital cost (startup period). If additional microorganisms are needed at a later date or periodically, these costs should be added to the estimate.

Nutrients

The most basic bioremediation process involves the addition of oxygen and appropriate nutrients; typically nitrogen, phosphorous, and potassium (N-P-K). The optimal nutrient mix must be determined based on laboratory bench scale studies. However, a reasonable estimate can be prepared by using bio-nutrients that consist of a 20:20:20 pulverized fertilizer. The solution is normally pumped through the injection wells on a continuous basis 24 hours per day, although some applications may allow for cycled nutrients (e.g., pumps turned on and off at certain intervals to stimulate growth of in-place microorganisms). The nutrients are mixed in a feed tank before they are introduced into the injection stream.

Electron Acceptor

The rate of pollutant biodegradation is limited by the availability of an electron acceptor. An electron acceptor is required for the chemical process of biodegradation. The organisms require a final sink for the electrons transferred during the metabolic processes. In aerobic digestion, the electron acceptor is oxygen. The quantity of oxygen required depends on the biochemical oxygen demand (BOD) and quantity of contaminated water. The typical electron acceptor of choice is hydrogen peroxide (H_2O_2), often provided as 500-pound drums of 50% solution hydrogen peroxide. It is reasonable to assume that the hydrogen peroxide/water mix will be introduced into the saturated soil at a concentration of 300 mg/l, 24 hours per day. A hydrogen peroxide feed tank will also be included.

Theoretically, it would take the following number of years to clean up a 1,000-gallon jet fuel site assuming that the contaminated area was 100' × 100' with an average induced gradient of 0.2 (20') of differential across the site, based on 4 different soil types:

Oxidant injection	300 mg/l hydrogen peroxide
Available oxygen	150 mg/l
Minimum volume of water required to remediate 1,000 gallons of fuel:	15,000,000 gal.
Theoretical minimum pumping time required to treat 1,000 gallons of fuel:	
Gravel	0.02 yrs.
(k = 10^4 gal/day/S.F.)	
Sand	2.0 yrs.
(k = 10^2 gal/day/S.F.)	
Silt	200 yrs.
(k = 1 gal/day/S.F.)	
Clay	200,000 yrs.
(k = 10^{-3} gal/day/S.F.)	

According to theoretical calculations and pilot tests on fuel sites, hydrogen peroxide tends to clean up sites more quickly than either air-entrained water or oxygen-saturated water.

Related Costs

The following assumptions can be used to estimate labor-hours related to well installation:

Wells are drilled at a rate of 20' per hour, plus 1 hour per 50' for well construction, and 2 hours per well for well completion. Total labor-hours are for drilling supervision by a staff hydrogeologist.

Decontamination procedures for the injection well screen, riser, caps, and drilling tools (e.g., hollow stem augers) are conducted prior to and between each bore hole/well installation. Procedures consist of steam-cleaning with a high-pressure steam-generating pressure washer and detergent.

Decontamination procedures for split spoon samplers and hand augers are as follows:

- Clean with tap water and detergent using a brush.
- Rinse thoroughly with tap water.
- Rinse with deionized water.
- Rinse twice with pesticide-grade isopropanol.
- Rinse with organic-free deionized water.
- Allow to air dry.

Maintenance of the injection well system includes adjusting the pumping rate and valves, general maintenance, and collecting injection water samples, if necessary. A maintenance crew of two field technicians is generally on site once a week for the first month and once a month thereafter for system inspection and maintenance.

Site Work and Utilities

The estimate may need to include site work and utilities items such as:

- Overhead electric distribution
- Clear and grub
- Access roads
- Roads

Conclusion

In situ biodegradation is an appealing approach to hazardous waste cleanup because it can be inexpensive, and the risk of new hazardous releases to the environment are minimal. However, the process can be lengthy, and there is a real potential for contaminants already in the soil and groundwater to migrate and cause other costly problems. These risks can be estimated and should be considered by the cost engineer and the design team during the planning stages.

The cost drivers for an in situ biodegradation project include the number and type of injection and monitoring wells, the sampling and analysis requirements, type and extent of nutrients, and the operating period. Bench scale tests are important for determining these parameters. The cost engineer should carefully review each of these elements and develop the estimate accordingly. Sensitivity analysis on the project duration can be used to estimate the potential for cost growth if the time required to remediate the site is not predicted accurately.

Chapter 22

In Situ Land Farming

Land farming, or solid-phase treatment, uses conventional soil management practices to stimulate biodegradation of organic comlbs in a layer of contaminated soil up to 24" (0.6 meters) thick. Biodegradation is stimulated by increasing aeration, maintaining moist conditions, providing nutrients, and, in some cases, adding microorganisms. Conventional agricultural equipment is used to break up, mix, and aerate the soil. To maintain aeration, the soil is tilled regularly during treatment. Moisture and nutrients are added as needed using irrigation equipment such as spray irrigators, overhead sprinklers, and watering attachments to farming equipment.

Land treatment has been applied for remediating soils contaminated with gasoline, diesel, and other fuels; benzene, toluene, ethylbenzene, and xylenes; creosote and polynuclear aromatic hydrocarbons (PAHs); pentachlorophenol; and certain pesticides.

Land treatment can be performed in situ; ex situ on a prepared bed; or in situ after the soil has been removed, amended, mixed, and replaced on-site for treatment. This section deals with in situ land treatment of soils. Ex situ land farming is discussed in Chapter 17.

Applications and Limitations

Applications

- Soils contaminated with gasoline, diesel, and other fuels; benzene, toluene, ethylbenzene, and xylenes; creosote and polynuclear aromatic hydrocarbons (PAHs); pentachlorophenol; and certain pesticides.
- Short-term process for most petroleum hydrocarbons.

Limitations

- Biodegradation will *not* degrade inorganics.
- Toxic levels of contaminants may significantly limit biodegradation.
- Land farming requires a large land area.
- Natural conditions affecting biological degradation (e.g., temperature, rainfall) may increase the length of time to complete remediation.
- Tilling and other material handling operations may result in dust releases.

- Topography, erosion, climate, soil stratigraphy, and permeability of the soil at the site must be evaluated to determine the optimum design.

Typical System Design Elements

A balanced fertilizer and enough water to provide 50% moisture content in the soil should be applied to the contaminated tilled area. Nitrogen levels in the soil should be maintained at 40 ppm. To reach this goal, 20:20:20 fertilizer should be applied at 500 lbs per 1,000 C.Y. Application rates of fertilizer and water will vary depending on the in situ nitrogen and moisture contents of the subject soil.

Bench and pilot tests may indicate that existing microbial populations are adequate to degrade the contaminant. In this case, no additional biocultures are necessary. Overall, bioaugmentation (addition of microbes) is relatively inexpensive.

If biocultures are to be added, the first dose should be applied within 24–48 hours after the initial fertilizer has been added. Dose the area with a bioculture of 1 lb of formulated culture per 2 gallons of water. This will allow an application rate of 50 lbs of bacteria per 1,000 C.Y. of contaminated soil. The soil should be tilled as often as possible to mix the bioculture, nutrients, and water. Tilling also aerates the soil, providing the microbes with the oxygen needed to reproduce. Tilling every day is the most effective means of introducing oxygen to all particles of the soil, but if it can not be done every day, it should be done at least once a week. On Day 15 of the project, the bacterial culture should be applied at a rate of 25 lbs per 1,000 C.Y., which is one-half the initial dosage. Biocultures of 25 lbs per 1,000 C.Y. should be applied every 30 days thereafter.

Moisture content, pH, temperature, and fertilizer concentrations should all be monitored to confirm that optimal limits are maintained.

Case studies have indicated that light petroleum hydrocarbons such as gasoline and diesel degrade at a rate of approximately 50% every 20 days. Heavy hydrocarbons such as oils degrade 20% every 30–60 days. Therefore, a gasoline (light petroleum) spill leaving 20,000 ppm in the surface soil would have 10,000 ppm remaining after 20 days of biotreatment. A calculation of the time required to meet permit target levels can be estimated from this correlation. In a hypothetical case, if the contaminated surface soil was initially at 20,000 ppm, and the permit target level was negotiated at 10 ppm benzene to remain in soil from a gasoline spill, then the estimated time required for bioremediation using in situ land treatment would be 220 days, or approximately 7.5 months.

The cost of land treatment can vary greatly depending on many factors. Once specifications on treatment applications and frequencies have been determined (or estimated), a reasonable estimate can be prepared. Local regulatory requirements involving permitting can also have a significant impact. Some states are very strict with the in situ treatment aspects, while others are more lenient. The estimator should investigate local regulations.

Growth factors that affect the rate of microbial degradation include the following.

Soil Moisture

When natural precipitation cannot maintain soil moisture within an optimal range for microbial activity, irrigation may be necessary. Water can be applied by standard irrigation methods (i.e., water trucks, subirrigation, or sprinkler system). Typically, water is applied to soil in the treatment cell using a water truck or attachment to a tractor or dozer. Irrigation should be applied frequently in relatively small amounts that do not exceed field capacity. Moisture control depends on the methods used at the site and on the availability of a suitable water source (considering transport distance, drilling of new wells, availability, and cost of energy for pumping).

Oxygen Requirements

Aerobic degradation is the most desirable microbial process for breaking down petroleum hydrocarbon contaminants because it proceeds at a more rapid rate and does not produce the noxious byproducts associated with anaerobic decomposition (e.g., methane, hydrogen sulfide). For petroleum hydrocarbons, approximately 3.5 lbs of oxygen are required per pound of hydrocarbon. For land treatment it is critical to ensure that the soil is tilled regularly.

Soil pH

Depending on the nature of the waste contaminating the soil, it may be advantageous to optimize the soil pH for a particular segment of the microbial community, because both microbial structure and activity are affected by the soil pH. Near-neutral pH values are most conducive to microbial functioning in general, but a range of 7.0–8.5 is acceptable. If the pH needs to be adjusted, agricultural lime may be used.

Soil Nutrients

As in the case of all living organisms, indigenous microbial populations require specific inorganic nutrients (e.g., nitrogen, phosphorus, potassium, calcium, magnesium) and a carbon and energy source. A pilot study can define the nutrients necessary to stimulate in situ biodegradation in the soil. Adding fertilizer will make carbon, nitrogen, and phosphorus available in the soil. Vendor specifications indicate that a balanced fertilizer (20:20:20) is best. Standard agricultural methods are used to add nutrients to the soil. Sufficient nitrogen and phosphorus must be reapplied to ensure that lack of these nutrients do not limit microbial and metabolic activity.

Soil Temperature

Soil temperature is one of the most important factors controlling microbiological activity and the rate of decomposition of organic contaminants. It also influences the rate of volatilization of compounds from the soil. Optimal growth of microbial populations responsible for biodegradation of petroleum products occurs between 20–35° C.

Basic Information Needed for Estimating

It is possible to create a reasonable cost estimate using a few required parameters. If more detailed information is known, one can create a more precise and site-specific estimate using a secondary set of parameters.

To estimate the cost of the land farming system, certain information must be known. This information is discussed in the following paragraphs.

Area of Contaminated Soil

The area of contaminated soil determines the required quantity of nutrients, moisture, and microorganisms, and the amount of tilling. The area of the site is determined during the remedial investigation and/or remedial design phases of site investigation. Although there is no theoretical limit to the area that can be remediated using land treatment, typical areas range from 1,000–1,000,000 S.F.

Depth of Contamination

In situ land treatment of soil can generally be performed to a depth of 1–18". The depth of contamination will affect the required quantity of nutrients, moisture, and microorganisms.

Treatment Duration

Bench and pilot studies can determine the duration of treatment. The duration depends on the application rates of nutrients, moisture, and microorganisms, as well as the specific contamination and concentration of the contaminant. Land farming can be a continuous operation at facilities such as oil refineries or chemical manufacturers. Land farming is most commonly performed as a remediation technique for less than 52 weeks.

Worker Safety Level

Worker safety is affected by the contaminant(s) at the site. Safety level refers to the levels required by OSHA in 29 CFR Part 1910. The 4 levels are designated as A, B, C, and D; where "A" is the most protective and "D" is the least protective. A safety level of E is also included to simulate normal construction, "no hazard" conditions as prescribed by the EPA.

Design Information Needed for Detailed Estimates

Following are descriptions of the types of detailed information that, when available, can add detail and accuracy to estimates. Also included are design criteria and estimating rules of thumb that the estimator typically uses to determine values that are not known, or to check information provided by others.

Tilling Frequency

The tilling frequency determines the number of days that a tiller will be required at the site. Tilling aids in aerating the soil, which provides oxygen to the microorganisms. The tilling frequency is the number of passes over an area multiplied by the days of operation per week. Typically, tilling frequencies range from 10–30 times per week.

Watering Frequency

The watering frequency determines the number of times that the watering truck should apply water to the contaminated area to retain a consistent moisture content. This frequency will vary considerably depending on the humidity level and rainfall at the site. If no value is available, a reasonable estimate is one watering per week. Sprinkler systems may be used, but are not recommended, since they are often damaged by plowing activity.

Fertilizing Frequency

The most basic bioremediation processes involve the addition of oxygen and appropriate nutrients, typically nitrogen and phosphorus. The optimal nutrient mix must be determined by pilot studies and geochemical evaluations of the site. However, a rough estimate of nutrients and quantities can be made by assuming a 20:20:20 fertilizer application at 800 lbs/acre, once per month. This is about 500 lbs/C.Y. over a 12" thick layer of soil.

Microorganisms

When naturally occurring microorganisms are scarce or absent, or when rapid cleanup is desired, acclimated organic matter may be added to the soil to supply organisms that are capable of initiating the degradation process. If used, application rates are based on those provided in the introduction of this chapter.

Related Costs

The operation should be monitored weekly to ensure that optimal conditions are being maintained in the treatment cell to allow for maximum degradation. Typically, the sampling protocol for land treatment is weekly sampling for pH, moisture content, phosphorus, nitrite/nitrate, ammonia nitrogen, and acidity/alkalinity. Samples are taken at intervals of one sample per 2,000 C.Y. The system may also need to be monitored to ensure that any hydraulic control requirements are being met to contain contaminant and nutrient migration.

A closure sampling for site close-out includes obtaining one sample per analysis and analyzing for the following contaminants: TCLP, TAL metals, pesticides/PCBs, volatiles, and BNAs. Since this technology is used primarily for cleanup of hydrocarbon contamination, total petroleum hydrocarbon (TPH) analysis is a common contaminant analysis.

At site closure, sampling must also confirm regulatory-agency target levels of contamination. Analyses include, but are not limited to, SW methods 8240, 8270, 8080, 1311, and TAL metals. Each analysis will be performed for each site.

If the plowing equipment stays on site for the duration of the project, the equipment is decontaminated at the end of the project. The quantity of equipment is based on the acres of area to be tilled divided by the equipment rate (acre/day). Assume that the equipment operates during four passes a day for tilling. The equipment (rented by the site owner) is idle for rest of the day.

Site Work and Utilities

Site work and utilities that may be applicable in land farming include:

- Fencing and signage
- Clear and grub
- Monitoring wells
- Decontamination facilities
- Storm sewer

These must also be covered in the estimate.

Conclusion

In situ land farming is an extremely cost-effective method of treating soil contaminated with petroleum and other organic contaminants. Typically this method can only be used for spills where the contaminants have not migrated deeper than 2–3' into the soil. The primary cost drivers are the depth and area of the contamination and the degradation lots of the contaminant, which in turn determine the treatment period. The cost engineer should work with the design team to define these elements.

Chapter 23

In Situ Solidifcation

In solidification, chemical reagents are mixed with waste to produce complex chemical and physical reactions that improve physical properties and reduce contaminant solubility, toxicity, and/or mobility. Solidification is a viable treatment for contaminated materials when the constituents cannot be treated, recovered, or destroyed by other methods because of technical or economical limitations.

Solidification is a physical treatment, that adds a reagent to transform a liquid, sludge, sediment, or soil into a solid form. Solidification immobilizes the contaminants within the crystalline structure of the solidified material, and reduces the contaminant leaching potential; which varies depending on waste, soil, and reagent characteristics.

Applications and Limitations

Applications

- Used to solidify or immobilize inorganic compounds, volatile and non-volatile metals, PCBs (depending on concentration), asbestos, and radionuclides.
- Short- to medium-term technology.

Limitations

- Process may be limited by depth of contaminant.
- Future use of solidified site may affect ability to maintain immobility of contaminant.
- Post-sampling to confirm contaminant immobility can be difficult.
- Solidification may have limited effectiveness against SVOCs and pesticides and no expected effectiveness against VOCs.
- Dewatering of contamination below the water table may be necessary.
- Solidification may increase resultant volume of immobilized contaminant.
- Treatability studies may be necessary to confirm that in situ solidification is compatible with waste to be solidified.

Typical System Design Elements

A variety of equipment can be used in solidification. Methods include open pit/trench/area mixing, in situ/in-drum mixing, and ex situ treatment in a mixing unit. In the *open pit/trench/area mixing method*, the reagent is dumped on top of the waste and mixed with conventional earth-moving and earth-handling equipment. The *in situ/in-drum method* requires a specialized or patented piece of equipment (usually a hollow stem auger or multiple auger rig) that injects and mixes a reagent into the waste in place and can be used at depths up to 120' below grade. The *ex situ treatment method* requires that the contaminated material be excavated, conveyed, or pumped into a mixing unit, where a reagent is added. Treatment is processed through a pugmill (mixing apparatus). The process described in this chapter is in situ using crane-mounted mixing augers. The ex situ process is described in Chapter 18 of this book.

Solidification is generally most effective for inorganic compounds and radionuclides. Solidification is especially appropriate for these contaminants or contaminant groups:

- Volatile and non-volatile metals (with some exceptions, anionic complexes of metals such as chromium, selenium, arsenic, cyanides, strong acids, oxidizing agents, and reducing agents)
- Other inorganics
- Polychlorinated Biphenyls (PCBs)
- Radionuclides

Solidification has been used to treat some semivolatile compounds, but treatment of volatile organic compounds (VOCs) is currently the focus of research and debate. A bench-scale laboratory program can usually determine the type and amount of solidification reagent required to satisfy regulatory treatment objectives. Figure 23.1 shows how different wastes will respond to the common reagents used for solidification.

Reagent Compatibility			
Waste Component	**Cement Based Reagent**	**Pozzolan Based Reagent**	**Asphalt Reagent**
Organic Solvents	May impede setting	May impede setting	Organics may vaporize
Solid/organics, Tars, etc.	Good	Good	Possible binding agent
Acid Wastes	Cement neutralizes acids	Compatible, will neutralize	Neutralize before incorporation
Oxidizers	Compatible	Compatible	May cause matrix breakdown
Sulfates	May retard set	Compatible	Dehydrate and rehydrate problems
Halides	Possible leaching	May retard set	Dehydrate and rehydrate problems
Heavy Metals	Compatible	Compatible	Compatible
Radioactive Materials	Compatible	Compatible	Compatible

Figure 23.1 Reagent Compability

The solidified material can usually be left in place and capped. However, local and state regulations should be reviewed to evaluate provisions for in-place disposal of solidified material. In situ solidification eliminates the higher costs and additional hazards associated with excavation, handling, and transport of hazardous materials associated with on-site treatment and/or off-site disposal. When the solidified material cannot be left in place, disposal options should be evaluated before the technology is selected.

If landfilling is the disposal option of choice, then the solidification process needs to anticipate the requirements of Land Disposal Restrictions (LDRs) under the Resource Conservation and Recovery Act (RCRA). If the waste contains PCBs, then disposal is regulated by the Toxic Substance Control Act (TSCA). EPA guidelines recommend a minimum unconfined compressive strength (UCS) of 50 pounds per square inch (psi) for treated waste that is disposed in a landfill with no free liquids phase. For in situ applications, UCS should be adequate to serve the anticipated future uses of the site.

The total cost for this remediation technology varies depending on the chemical and physical characteristics of the waste, the site characteristics, and the treatment requirements.

Basic Information Needed for Estimating

It is possible to create a reasonable cost estimate using a few required parameters. If more detailed information is known, one can create a more precise and site-specific estimate using a secondary set of parameters.

To estimate the cost of the in situ solidification system, certain information must be known. This information is discussed in the following paragraphs.

Type of Waste

The type of waste is generally either solid or sludge. Sludges are usually pumpable. The type of waste will affect the S/S mix design. Waste with high concentrations of organics and other miscellaneous materials (i.e., oil and grease, peat, highly plastic clays) may inhibit the effectiveness of solidification technology.

Soil Type (Solid Waste Only)

The type of soil affects the size of the boring equipment. The most common soil types are:

- Silty clay, clay
- Mixed sandy, silty, clay soils
- Primarily sand
- Sand and gravel

Worker Safety Level

Worker safety is affected by the contaminant(s) at the site. Safety level refers to the levels required by OSHA in 29 CFR Part 1910. The four levels are designated as A, B, C, and D; where "A" indicates the most protective and "D" indicates the least protective. A safety level of E is also included to simulate normal construction, "no hazard" conditions as prescribed by the EPA.

Total Volume of Waste

The volume of the waste is specified in cubic yards. The volume should be converted to weight because ratios using weight comparisons are most commonly used. Sludges can be converted from gallons to cubic yards by multiplying the number of gallons by 0.005. The volume of waste can be converted to weight by multiplying the density by the volume. See below for density of waste.

Depth of Material to be Treated

The depth of the contaminated waste to be solidified drives the size of the equipment used for treatment.

Treatment Surface Area

Treatment surface area is affected by the boring for the S/S process. The boring surface area drives the number of borings required.

Design Information Needed for Detailed Estimates

Following are descriptions of the types of detailed information that, when available, can add detail and accuracy to estimates. Also included are design criteria and estimating rules of thumb that the estimator typically uses to determine values that are not known, or to check information provided by others.

Initial Moisture Content

The initial moisture content varies depending on the waste medium. The moisture content will help to determine the mix design for the waste and additives.

If the initial moisture content is unknown, the estimator can use the following guidelines:

	Typical	Range
Solid	15%	0–30%
Sludge	60%	31–70%

Density of Waste

The density of waste is specific to the waste medium and is generally measured in pounds per cubic foot (P.C.F.). This figure provides information needed to calculate the mix design and volume expansion encountered after the solidified waste has cured. The unit weight can be adjusted to the field conditions of the waste.

If the density of waste is unknown, the estimator can use the following guidelines:

	Typical	Range
Solid	100 P.C.F.	60–200 P.C.F.
Sludge	80 P.C.F.	40–200 P.C.F.

Chemical Additive Ratios

Many chemical additives can be used effectively in the solidification process. However, additive ratios are highly waste-specific and should be determined by bench and pilot testing.

Additives include such materials as water, proprietary chemical binders, Portland cement, fly ash, cement kiln dust, hydrated lime, asphalt, bitumen, polyolefins, epoxy, urea formaldehyde, activated carbon, modified clay, pumice, blast furnace slag, polycrylates, and polyacrylamides.

If the specific additives are unknown, the estimator can use one or more of the following: water, proprietary chemical binder, fly ash, kiln dust, or Portland cement. The mix proportions will be weight-based and contingent on the initial moisture content and unit weight of the waste. Figure 23.2 provides a list of typical weights of additive to waste ratios. Figure 23.3 provides a summary of specific gravity and weight for both chemical additives and waste streams.

Estimated Mix Ratios By Weight Basis‡	
Valid Range†	**Additive Ratio**
0.000-3.000[1]	* :1 Cement:Waste
0.000-1.000[2]	0.400 :1 Water:Cement (Solids only)
0.000-5.000	0.010 :1 Proprietary Chemicals :[3] Waste
0.000-3.000	0.000 :1 Fly Ash:Waste
0.000-3.000	0.000 :1 Cement Kiln Dust:Waste
0.000-3.000	0.000 :1 Hydrated Lime:Waste
0.000-3.000[1]	0.000 :1 Bitumen:Waste
0.000-3.000	0.000 :1 Activated Carbon:Waste

† Range refers to the normal upper and lower boundary for additive ratios.

‡ Additive ratio refers to the total weight of the waste mix. For example, a ratio of 2.0 for cement would be 2 parts cement to 1 part waste or, on a weight basis, 2 pounds of cement per 1 pound of waste.

*Solids: 0.150
Sludge: 0.400

[1] Either cement or bitumen must be added to the waste to provide the required strength and binding characteristics.

[2] In this case, the default is based on the water:cement ratio rather than the water:waste ratio. The water:cement ratio is similar to that for general concrete mix design.

[3] Urrichem Proprietary Additive - Solidtech Corp.
Chloranan Proprietary Additive - EM Tech Corp.
P4 and P27 Proprietary Additives - Silicate Technologies Corp.

Figure 23.2 Estimated Mix Ratios by Weight Basis

Specific Gravity And Weights For Material Balances		
Materials	**Specific Gravity**	**Density (PCF)**
Chemical Additives		
Portland Cement	3.15	94.0
Proprietary Binders	2.90	100.0
Fly Ash	2.45	65.0
Cement Kiln Dust	2.45	90.0
Hydrated Lime	1.00	64.0
Water	1.00	62.4
Bitumen	1.30	81.0
Activated Carbon	1.55	97.0
Waste Streams		
Waste Solid	1.60	100.0
Waste Sludge	1.28	80.0

Figure 23.3 Specific Gravity and Weights for Material Balances

Volume of Treated Waste

In general, the volume of the treated waste will increase based on the amount of chemical additive that has been added in treatment. This increase in volume will raise the ground surface of the site above the limits of the untreated waste if the treated material is left in place. Depending on plans for future use, the site may require grading and capping.

If the treated material will be disposed of in a landfill, the total volume of the treated waste will indicate the amount that will be disposed either in a Subtitle "C" (hazardous) or Subtitle "D" (non-hazardous) landfill, depending on the outcome of the Toxicity Characteristic Leaching Procedure (TCLP) analytical results. Groundwater monitoring adjacent to the solidified material may be required and should be estimated.

Related Costs

If the site is not fully accessible by heavy equipment (e.g., 100-ton crane, large earth-moving equipment), site access roads may need to be included in the estimate. Other related costs for solidification are as follows.

Permitting

Permitting costs vary from state to state and should be considered in developing an estimate.

Bench/Pilot Testing

Bench/pilot tests may be helpful in determining the adequacy of the admixture application rates.

Site Work and Utilities

Site work and utilities that may be applicable for solidification are:

- Overhead electrical distribution
- Underground electrical distribution
- Clear and grub
- Access roads
- Fencing and signage
- Water distribution
- Gas distribution
- Sanitary sewer
- Communications

These must also be included in the estimate.

Conclusion

In situ solidification is an effective containment methodology for a wide variety of hazardous wastes in soil and sludges. The primary cost driver is the volume of waste to be treated. Other significant cost drivers include the type of waste, additive requirements, the depth of material to be treated, and the worker safety level. Many of these cost drivers are variable and can be affected by design decisions. The cost engineer should work with the design team to estimate different design scenarios to help optimize the project.

204

Chapter 24

Media Filtration

Media filtration is a physical process that removes suspended solids from an aqueous waste stream by forcing the fluid through a porous medium. The 2 most common types of filters are discussed in this chapter. These are granular media filters and cartridge filters. The type of filter media used depends on the solids loading rate and application.

Applications and Limitations

Applications

- Can remove heavy metals, organic compounds, total dissolved solids, oil emulsions, and suspended solids.
- Cartridge media applications include removal of precipitated solids after clarification; filtration of spray water recirculation streams, pump seal water, condensate, boiler feed water, and cooling tower water; also immediate pretreatment for reverse osmosis systems, ion exchange resins, catalyst beds, and in-line instruments.
- Granular media applications include: removal of solids after clarification following precipitation and coagulation reactions; removal of residual biological floc from secondary treatment; and pretreatment for protection of air strippers, ion exchange systems, and other treatment processes.
- Granular media filtration can be used to handle waste water containing less than approximately 200 mg/l suspended solids, depending on the desired effluent quality.

Limitations

- Membrane filters are prone to clogging and fouling. This can reduce their efficiency and increase cost.
- Cartridge filtration is not optimum or economical for clarifying liquid streams with a total suspended solids content greater than 10 mg/l.

Typical System Design Elements

Granular media filters remove suspended solids from waste water as the liquid is forced through a porous granular medium. The filter bed may be a single medium such as sand; dual media such as sand with an upper layer of anthracite (coal); or multimedia including garnet, sand, and anthracite, from bottom to top. The bed, contained within a basin, is supported by an underdrain system (typically perforated pipes)

205

that allows the filtered liquid to be drawn off while the filter media is retained in place. As the bed becomes loaded with solids, the filtration rate decreases as a result of the increased pressure drop across the bed. To prevent plugging, the filter is periodically backwashed with water at a high velocity to dislodge the particles.

Most filters operate in a batch mode and are taken out of service for backwashing. Filter systems are usually designed with extra capacity so that a filter can be taken off line for backwashing without disrupting flow through the overall system. Backwash cycles are often automated and require little or no operator attention.

Granular media filtration can be used to handle waste water that contains less than approximately 200 mg/l suspended solids, depending on the desired effluent quality. Greater suspended solids loading will reduce the removal efficiency, as frequent backwashing will be required. The suspended solids concentration of the effluent depends largely on particle size distribution, but granular media filters generally are capable of producing a filtered liquid with a suspended solids concentration ranging from as low as 1 mg/l to 10 mg/l.

Design considerations for granular media filters include filter configuration; types, size, gradation, and depths of filter media; backwash requirements; filtration rate; quantity and characteristics of the water applied; and desired effluent quality. Pilot-plant studies can determine the best design. Membrane porosities vary in size depending on the target contaminants.

Granular media filtration is the most widely used active filtering process for solids removal. Granular media filtration can be used to remove solids after clarification following precipitation and coagulation reactions; remove residual biological floc from secondary treatment; and pretreat for protection of air strippers, ion exchange systems, and other treatment processes.

Cartridge filters are comprised of one or more replaceable or renewable cartridges that contain the active element. The liquid is fed to the filter under pressure, and solid particles are trapped in the element as the liquid passes through. Because filter elements and housings can be constructed from many different materials, they can handle a variety of fluids. Cartridge filters can remove relatively small quantities of suspended solids because the cartridge has limited space for accumulated solids. When a cartridge filter becomes saturated with solids, it is usually replaced or cleaned by air scouring backwashing. Cartridge filtration is not economical for clarifying liquid streams that have a total suspended solids content greater than 10 mg/l. Cartridge filtration is typically used for removing precipitated solids after clarification; filtrating spray water recirculation streams, pump seal water, condensate, boiler feed water, and cooling tower water; and pretreating for reverse osmosis systems, ion exchange resins, catalyst beds, and in-line instruments.

Basic Information Needed for Estimating

It is possible to create a reasonable cost estimate using a few required parameters. If more detailed information is known, one can create a more precise and site-specific estimate using a secondary set of parameters.

To estimate the cost of the media filtration system, certain information must be known. This information is discussed in the following paragraphs.

Flow Rate

The flow rate determines the required size of the filter. The flow rate is measured in gallons per minute (GPM).

Treatment Period

The total treatment period is divided into startup and operations and maintenance (O&M). The costs associated with the startup period are included with the capital costs; the O&M costs are identified separately.

Worker Safety Level

Worker safety is affected by the contaminant(s) at the site. Safety level refers to the levels required by OSHA in 29 CFR Part 1910. The four levels are designated as A, B, C, and D, where "A" is the most protective, and "D" is the least protective. A safety level of E is also included to simulate normal construction, "no hazard" conditions as prescribed by the EPA.

Design Information Needed for Detailed Estimates

Following are descriptions of the types of detailed information that, when available, can add detail and accuracy to estimates. Also included are design criteria and estimating rules of thumb that the estimator typically uses to determine values that are not known, or to check information provided by others.

Filtration Rate

The filter area and diameter can be determined from the filtration rate and the flow rate (see Figure 24.1). The filtration rate is measured in gallons per minute per square foot (GPM/S.F.) If the filtration rate is unknown, the estimator can assume a rate of 5 GPM/S.F.

Number of Filtration Units

Tank diameter is determined from the area of filtration, which is the flow rate divided by the filtration rate. Normally, at least two filter units are used to provide flexibility of operation. This way, when one filter is out of commission for backwashing, the other comes on line.

Influent Piping Length

The influent piping length is the length of piping leading from one treatment process to another. For example, overflow from a settling pond might be directed via piping into the filtration unit for further solids removal.

Effluent Piping Length

The effluent piping length is the length of piping leading from one treatment process to another. For example, treated water might be transferred from the filtration unit to a cartridge filtration unit to further reduce the solids concentration.

Piping Material

Piping material options are PVC, carbon steel, and stainless steel. Normally, PVC is preferred over the other choices.

Other Related Costs

O&M for automatic media filtration units is relatively inexpensive. The system is self-sufficient in that inspection and on-site labor costs are also minimal. A field technician inspects and conducts maintenance on the filtration unit one day per week during the life of the project.

O&M costs vary depending on waste stream suspended solids concentration, which affects backwashing rates and the life of the filter sand. When selecting a packaged filtration unit, the estimator should contact the equipment manufacturer prior to or during the remedial design period so that the system meets the specific waste flow characteristics of the site.

Each filtration unit has the approximate equivalent of a 1 H.P. pump, which generally operates continuously 24 hours per day. Maintenance and electrical charges for the pumps need to be added to the estimate.

Filter sand should be replaced and disposed in a properly permitted disposal area once every five years.

Costs for sampling and analysis typically include one day of sampling influent and effluent streams for total suspended solids once a week for the first month, once a month for the first year, and quarterly thereafter.

The cost of treating backwash water is addressed in Chapter 27, Off-site Transportation and Thermal Treatment.

Site Work and Utilities

Site work and utilities that may apply to media filtration are:

- Fencing
- Water distribution
- Overhead electrical distribution

These must also be included in the estimate.

Filtration Rate (GPM/S.F.)	Flow Rate GPM				Filter Dia. (ft)	Filter Area (S.F.)
	GPM	3 GPM	4 GPM	5 GPM		
	14	21	28	35	3	7.1
	25	37	50	63	4	12.6
	39	58	78	98	5	19.6
	56	85	113	147	6	28.3
	77	116	154	192	7	38.5
	100	151	201	250	8	50.3

Figure 24.1 Filtration Rate

Conclusion

Media filtration is commonly used for removal of particles from a liquid waste stream. This technology can be used for waste volume reduction or as a pretreatment method to increase the efficiency of a primary treatment process such as air stripping. In nearly all cases, media filtration is a part of a larger treatment train. The primary cost drivers are the flow rate, the treatment rate, and the operating period. While media filtration is rarely the primary cost driver for a treatment train, the cost engineer should still work carefully with the design team to determine and estimate the requirements for the process.

Chapter 25

Metals Precipitation

Metals precipitation is typically used to treat aqueous waste streams that have high metals concentrations. Metals precipitation from contaminated water involves converting soluble heavy metal salts to insoluble salts that will precipitate. The precipitate can then be removed from the treated water by physical methods such as clarification (settling) and/or filtration. Chemical precipitation is generally used to remove heavy metals such as cadmium, chromium, copper, lead, mercury, nickel, and zinc. However, because the chemical precipitation process is not selective, the order of metals precipitation depends on each metal's equilibrium conditions. In addition to the metals of concern, most water contains some combination of calcium, iron, magnesium, manganese, aluminum, and barium. These metals will co-precipitate during the process. The process must have a proper chemical addition to ensure that all metal concentrations are reduced to a minimum.

For purposes of this discussion, the processes of chemical addition and sedimentation are described as chemical precipitation. Additional technologies that are often used in conjunction with chemical precipitation to precipitate metals include Groundwater Extraction Wells (Chapter 43), Media Filtration (Chapter 24), and Dewatering (Chapter 15). Depending on the required treatment standards, the water effluent stream may require polishing through ion exchange, reverse osmosis, or some other finishing method.

Applications and Limitations

Applications

- Precipitation is commonly used to remove heavy metals such as cadmium, chromium, copper, lead, mercury, nickel, and zinc.
- In addition to the metals of concern, most water contains some combination of calcium, iron, magnesium, manganese, aluminum, and barium. These metals will co-precipitate during the process.

Limitations

- Specific limitations are associated with various methods and reagents that are used for precipitation.

- Does not eliminate the metal contaminants; it only facilitates separation.

Process Configurations and Treatment Train Considerations

The decision to use precipitation can be driven by several key factors. If precipitation is selected as the treatment approach, additional factors need to be addressed. Key factors include:

- Precipitation is commonly used in conjunction with extraction wells, coagulation/flocculation, media filtration, and sludge dewatering.
- Depending on the required treatment standards, the water effluent stream may require polishing through ion exchange, reverse osmosis, or some other finishing method.
- Precipitation processes are defined by the type of reagent being used. Typical chemicals include metal hydroxide, lime or soda, metal sulfide, alum or ferric salt, and phosphate/carbonate ion addition.
- The pH of the influent stream has a dramatic effect on the precipitation process. For hydroxide precipitation the pH can range from 8–12, with an optimum around 9.5. Lime or soda softening pH is usually at or above a pH of 11 to remove calcium and magnesium.
- Secondary reagents may be required in special circumstances to induce floc formation.
- The effluent pH may require adjustment before discharge.

Typical System Design Elements

Metals precipitation is generally used in conjunction with other technologies to form a complete treatment and train. Key issues to consider when evaluating precipitation as a remediation option include:

1. Ensuring flow equalization (because the clarification process requires a constant flow rate)
2. Adding chemicals and forming precipitate
3. Beginning the clarification process as the precipitate begins to fall out of solution

The chemical mechanisms that govern chemical precipitation are:

- Reductions in solubility through the reduction or increase in pH
- Oxidation/reduction of the metals
- Formation of ionic salts
- Formation of molecules with covalent bonds

Five types of precipitation processes are identified by the type of chemical added to produce precipitation. They are:

- Metal hydroxide
- Lime or soda
- Metal sulfide
- Alum or ferric salt
- Phosphate/carbonate ion addition

The most common is lime or soda. The addition of these chemicals creates hydroxide ions for the precipitation process.

Figures 25.1 and 25.2 illustrate the most common chemical precipitation systems—a vertical plate clarifier and an incline slope circular clarifier. Vertical plate clarifiers are typically used for lower flow rates—up to approximately 30 gallons per minute (GPM). The incline

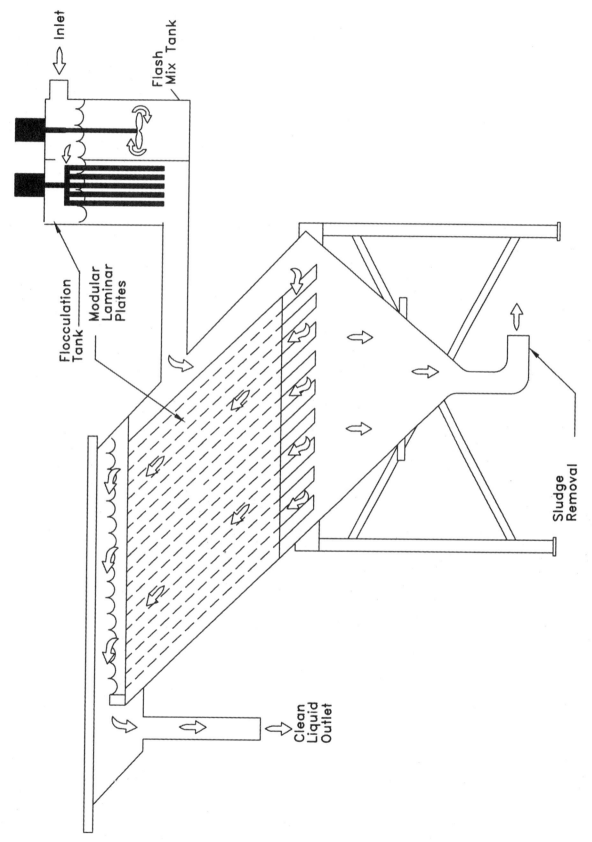

Figure 25.1 Vertical Plate Clarifier

slope circular clarifier is typically used for higher flow rates—ranging from 25 GPM to over 1,500 GPM, depending on the application. System components include piping, pumps, the clarifier units, holding tanks, foundation systems, instrumentation, and electrical power.

Basic Information Needed for Estimating

It is possible to create a reasonable cost estimate using a few required parameters. If more detailed information is known, one can create a more precise and site-specific estimate using a secondary set of parameters.

To estimate the cost of a chemical precipitation system, certain basic information must be known. This information is discussed in the following paragraphs.

Type of Metal and Concentration Level

System design and operation depend in part on the type of metal to be removed. The types of metals that are commonly removed using precipitation are shown in Figure 25.3. The chart also illustrates the concentration level and typical ranges that can be treated with precipitation.

If multiple metals are to be treated, determine the types and concentration levels of each. For aqueous solutions, milligrams/liter (mg/l) is equivalent to parts per million (PPM). Both the metal type and the concentration are used in calculating feed rate and sludge generation.

Typical toxic heavy metals include cadmium, chromium, copper, nickel, silver, and zinc. Metals are commonly cations (ions with a positive

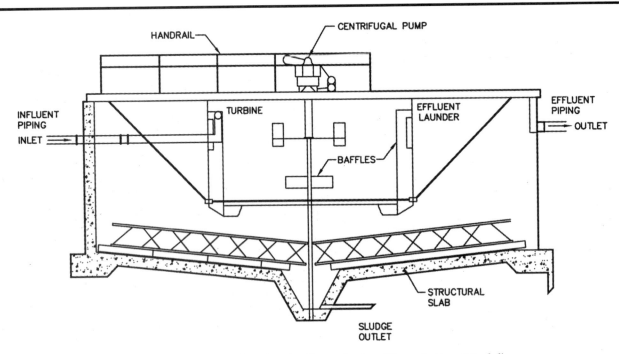

Figure 25.2 Incline Slope Circular Clarifier (in the Coagulation Flocculation Model)

214

charge) in certain charge states in acidic waste matrices. However, metals may be present in forms (such as certain anionic complexes) that cannot be removed by simple precipitation. For example, trivalent chromium will precipitate as a metal hydroxide, but hexavalent chromium must first be reduced to trivalent chromium before it will precipitate as a metal hydroxide. (Reducing trivalent chromium can be accomplished by first reducing the pH to 2–3 by adding acid, then adding an adequate chemical reducing agent.) The valid range is 0–1000 milligrams per liter (mg/l).

Flow Rate

The flow rate describes the volume per unit of time entering the system. This value is used to determine the size of the treatment system equipment, the rate of chemical feed, and the quantity of effluent streams. Typically, the flow rates for these systems range from 350–1,000 GPM for a process stream, and from 1–125 GPM for a groundwater remediation project. If media filtration and/or dewatering (sludge) technologies are used to complete the chemical precipitation process, the backwash water and the water generated by the dewatering process should be considered in the flow rate. A system will be selected based on the flow rate. Figure 25.4 details the default clarifier, pump and slab size based on flow rate. Skid–mounted vertical plate clarifiers are used for the low flow rate applications typical of groundwater remediation.

Influent pH

The pH of the influent stream has a dramatic effect on the precipitation process. For hydroxide precipitation, the pH can range from 8–12; the

Figure 25.3 Metals and Concentration Levels Typically Treated with Precipitation

Metals And Concentration Levels Typically Treated With Precipitation	
Metal	**Valid Range**
Aluminum	1 to 1000 mg/l
Arsenic	1 to 1000 mg/l
Barium	1 to 1000 mg/l
Cadmium	1 to 1000 mg/l
Calcium	1 to 1000 mg/l
Trivalent Chromium	1 to 1000 mg/l
Hexavalent Chromium	1 to 1000 mg/l
Copper	1 to 1000 mg/l
Iron	1 to 1000 mg/l
Lead	1 to 1000 mg/l
Magnesium	1 to 1000 mg/l
Manganese	1 to 1000 mg/l
Mercury	1 to 1000 mg/l
Nickel	1 to 1000 mg/l
Selenium	1 to 1000 mg/l
Zinc	1 to 1000 mg/l

optimum level is around 9.5. Lime or soda softening pH is usually at or above a pH of 11 to remove calcium and magnesium.

Figure 25.5 lists the approximate pH for minimum solubility for several metals for hydroxide and sulfide precipitation. (These levels do not account for co-precipitation, soluble metal complexes, or other solution impacts on metal solubility.) Designers use pH to calculate the chemical feed rate for lime or soda addition. If the pH has to be adjusted by more than 2 pH units, an additional Reaction Tank may be required. A reasonable estimating rule of thumb is to assume that one pH adjustment unit is always required and that the rapid mix tank that is included with the clarifier is used for secondary chemical additions. Multiple pH tanks may be needed for a combination of flow rate and metals concentrations.

Effluent pH

The effluent pH value is used to determine whether there is a requirement for adjustment before discharge. If the pH is in the range of 6–8, effluent pH adjustment is not normally required. If the effluent pH is out of this range, systems will normally be included to neutralize the pH for discharge.

Treatment Period

The total treatment period is divided into startup and operations and maintenance (O&M). Normally, the costs associated with the startup period are included with the capital costs, and the O&M costs are identified separately.

Clarifier, Pump, And Foundation Slab Requirements		
Clarifier Size	**Capacity of In-Line Pump**	**Slab Size (Ft²)**
2 GPM Vertical Plate	10 GPM, 1/2 H.P.	60
10 GPM Vertical Plate	10 GPM, 1/2 H.P.	60
15 GPM Vertical Plate	50 GPM, 3 H.P.	60
9 Ft. Diam., 25 GPM	50 GPM, 3 H.P.	64
30 GPM Vertical Plate	50 GPM, 3 H.P.	60
12 Ft. Diam., 45 GPM	50 GPM, 3 H.P.	113
15 Ft. Diam., 70 GPM	100 GPM, 5 H.P.	117
20 Ft. Diam., 130 GPM	200 GPM, 10 H.P.	315
25 Ft. Diam., 208 GPM	250 GPM, 10 H.P.	491
30 Ft. Diam., 305 GPM	500 GPM, 20 H.P.	707
40 Ft. Diam., 546 GPM	750 GPM, 30 H.P.	1,257
50 Ft. Diam., 850 GPM	1,050 GPM, 40 H.P.	1,964
60 Ft. Diam., 1,194 GPM	1,500 GPM, 60 H.P.	2,828
70 Ft. Diam., 1,645 GPM	2,000 GPM, 75 H.P.	3,849

Figure 25.4 Clarifier, Pump, and Foundation Slab Requirements

Worker Safety Level

Safety level refers to the levels required by OSHA 29 CFR Part 1910. The 4 levels are designated as A, B, C, and D; where "A" is the most protective, and "D" is the least protective. The safety level is a reflection of the level of productivity and affects all labor and equipment categories.

Design Information Needed for Detailed Estimates

Following are descriptions of the types of detailed information that, when available, can add detail and accuracy to estimates. Also included are design criteria and estimating rules of thumb that the estimator typically uses to determine values that are not known, or to check information provided by others.

System Design

The basic clarification system design normally includes pH adjustment, a rapid mix tank/flocculator unit, and a clarifier. A single pump is used with this setup. Additional system design factors that can affect the capital and operations and maintenance costs are described below.

Total Suspended Solids

The amount of total suspended solids is a common wastewater characteristic that influences the amount of sludge that will be generated by the system. A typical range is 50–1,000 ppm. If this value is not known, a reasonable estimating rule of thumb is 200 ppm.

Pump Efficiency

The efficiency of the pump depends on where on the system efficiency curve it is operating. Normally, pumps are designed to operate at an efficiency of 75%. The valid range for pump efficiency is 60–90%.

Figure 25.5 Approximate pH Values for Minimum Solubility

Approximate pH Values for Minimum Solubility		
Metal	**Compound**	**pH**
Chromium (trivalent)	Metal Hydroxide	7.5
Copper	Metal Hydroxide	9
Zinc	Metal Hydroxide	10
Lead	Metal Hydroxide	>10
Nickel	Metal Hydroxide	>10
Cadmium	Metal Hydroxide	>10
Silver	Metal Hydroxide	>12
Cobalt	Metal Sulfide	>11
Zinc	Metal Sulfide	>11
Cadmium	Metal Sulfide	>11
Lead	Metal Sulfide	>11
Silver	Metal Sulfide	>11

Hours of Operation per Day

The number of hours the system operates each day directly affects all of the process consumables (chemical additions, labor, electricity, etc.). Because of the nature of the process, the system normally runs 24 hours per day, except for maintenance down-time.

Holding Tanks

Holding tanks may be used to equalize flow and wastewater characteristics for the influent, effluent, or both. Although holding tanks are used for groundwater treatment projects, the "typical" system does not normally include tanks. If a holding tank is selected, the normal design would include one tank. In some cases, additional tanks may be required. Typical tank sizes range from 55 gallons to over 20,000 gallons, depending on the application.

Sludge Generation

The quantity of sludge generated has a direct impact on cost, provided that it is categorized as a hazardous waste. In addition, this information is used to determine the volume of sludge required for dewatering, if that technology is used as part of the treatment train.

Precipitation System Reagents

The two classes of reagents used for precipitation are *primary* and *secondary*. The secondary reagent enhances the agglomeration of metal salts formed during the precipitation process. The default configuration will change based on the metal(s) selected as a required parameter.

Primary Reagent

Typical reagents used for precipitation are lime or caustic. Lime is preferred for the majority of groundwater treatment systems. The quantity of sludge generated by lime is greater than that generated when using caustic; however, the cost difference between reagents is usually greater than the difference for sludge disposal.

Additive Rate

The additive rate is calculated using constants for the alkalinity or acidity, pH factors, metal factors, influent pH, and metal(s) concentrations. An estimating rule of thumb is 1.0 mg/l (0.00834 lb/ 1,000 gal.) of aqueous solution to be treated.

Secondary Reagent

The secondary reagent is selected based on the type of metal(s) to be precipitated. In most cases, no secondary reagent is required because lime and caustic will initiate precipitation and allow for formation of floc in most metals. However, special cases require additional chemicals and flocculation additives. Ferrous sulfate functions as a reducing agent for hexavalent chromium to form a less toxic trivalent chrome precipitate. Ferric chloride is used in the precipitation of arsenic by aiding in the formation of floc to agglomerate the fine arsenic particles. If both hexavalent chromium and arsenic are selected as required parameters, the ferric chloride will be selected as the secondary reagent.

Additive Rate

Figure 25.6 lists the default additive rates for secondary reagents for most probable conditions. The ratio additions are based on one part reagent to 3 or 8 parts hexavalent chromium and arsenic, respectively.

pH Adjustment

Many applications require the system to adjust both the influent and effluent pH. Influent pH adjustments are most commonly related to improving the precipitation process. Effluent pH adjustment is most commonly related to meeting discharge requirements.

Influent Reagent

The influent reagent is used to either increase or decrease the pH of the system. In most cases, none is required. However, if any combination of arsenic, hexavalent chromium, or iron is present, and the influent pH is greater than 4, then sulfuric acid may be required to adjust the pH.

Effluent Reagent

The effluent reagent is based on the effluent pH. If the effluent pH is between 6–8, then no reagent is normally required. If the effluent pH is less than 6, then sodium hydroxide solution is typically added to raise the pH. If the effluent pH is greater than 8, then sulfuric acid is typically added to lower the pH.

Additive Rate

The additive rate identifies how much reagent will be added to the influent and/or effluent to adjust the pH. A reasonable rule of thumb for the additive rate is 1.5 lb./1,000 gallons. The typical valid range is 0.1–100 lb/1,000 gallons.

Retention Time

The retention time and flow rate are used to determine the capacity of the pH adjustment unit(s). Because of the nature of the precipitation process, influent pH adjustment may require extended retention time. When an influent reagent is selected, a typical influent retention time is 5 minutes. If arsenic is one of the selected metals, the typical retention

Figure 25.6 Secondary Reagent Additive Rates

Secondary Reagent Additive Rates	
Condition	**Additive Rate**
No Secondary Reagent	0.0
Ferrous Sulfate Secondary Reagant	3:1
Ferric Chloride Secondary Reagent	8:1
Other Selected Secondary Reagent	0.334 lb./1000 gal.

time is 30 minutes. If hexavalent chromium or iron is one of the selected metals, the typical retention time is 20 minutes. A longer retention time is normally required when arsenic is combined with hexavalent chromium and/or iron. The normal effluent retention time is 5 minutes when an effluent reagent is selected.

Influent Piping

Influent piping connects the chemical precipitation treatment system to the source of the treatment water (e.g., an extraction well). The normal influent flow mechanism is via force main. For groundwater treatment systems, the piping is usually above ground, but buried applications may be required if traffic or risk of freezing is a factor. PVC is most commonly used for the piping, although carbon steel and stainless steel pipe are sometimes used. For highly acidic or basic solutions, PVC should be used.

Effluent Piping

Effluent piping connects the precipitation unit to a post-treatment technology or to a disposal point (e.g., a sewer connection). Normally, effluent piping is the same size and type as the influent piping.

Related Costs

Other items generally required are effluent handling and disposal, and sampling and analysis.

Effluent Handling and Disposal

The system effluents are treated wastewater, treatment residuals, and gas emissions. The treated wastewater may be discharged to a POTW, to surface water, to land surface, or re-injected to groundwater, depending on the system treatment efficiency and regulatory discharge permit requirements. Chemical precipitation systems generate a large quantity of treatment residuals, predominantly sludge. The classification of this sludge as hazardous depends on the type and quantity of the metals that are precipitating from the influent. In most cases, precipitated sludges are hazardous, and sludge treatment is required using technologies such as dewatering.

Sampling and Analysis

Monitoring programs are site- and contaminant-specific. Typical sampling and analysis includes pH, total suspended solids, total dissolved solids, and selected required parameter metals. The number of samples taken is usually 1 per week for startup and 1 per month for operations and maintenance periods for both the influent and effluent.

Site Work and Utilities

Site work and utilities that may be applicable in chemical precipitation are:

- Overhead electrical distribution
- Fencing and signage
- Clear and grub
- Grading and excavation

These must also be covered in the estimate.

Conclusion

Chemical precipitation is a common process that has been demonstrated on numerous projects over many years. The main cost drivers are the capacity of the system, the process option used, the operating period, and disposal costs. Incline slope circular clarifiers generally cost more to construct/install than vertical plate clarifiers. For large quantities of treatment with high flow rates, this cost increase is justified by lower long-term operating costs. However, the cost engineer should work with the design team to consider alternatives that would result in the lowest overall cost, while meeting the technical requirements for the project.

Chapter 26

Neutralization

One of the main requirements for chemical treatment is the *neutralization* of excess acidity or alkalinity in waste water, measured as pH. A pH between 0–6 is considered *acidic*, and a pH between 9–14 is considered *alkaline*. A pH between 6–9 is considered *neutral*. Neutralization renders acidic or alkaline wastes non-corrosive by adjusting the pH. The resulting residuals include insoluble salts, metal hydroxide sludge, and neutral effluent containing dissolved salts. The goal of neutralization is usually a final pH of 6–9.

Neutralization can be used to treat any waste water that requires pH control. This process often precedes biological treatment, since bacteria is sensitive to rapid changes in pH and to values outside a pH range of 6–9. Aquatic ecosystems are also pH-sensitive. Therefore, waste water must be neutralized before it is discharged to a receiving body of water. When waste water is hazardous if it is corrosive, waste water may need to be neutralized before it can be accepted for disposal. Neutralization is also used as a pretreatment for several chemical treatment technologies such as carbon adsorption, ion exchange, air stripping, wet-air oxidation, and chemical oxidation.

Applications and Limitations

Applications

- Used to treat any waste water that requires pH control.
- Serves as pretreatment for several chemical treatment technologies, such as carbon adsorption, ion exchange, air stripping, wet-air oxidation, and chemical oxidation.
- Used to neutralize discharges to meet pH discharge limits, thereby protecting aquatic life and human health.
- Used as a preliminary treatment to allow subsequent effective operation of biological treatment processes.
- Provides neutral pH water for recycling in process streams.
- Prevents metal corrosion and/or damage to other construction materials as part of a metals precipitation process.

Limitations

- Applicable only for aqueous waste streams.

Typical System Design Elements

The neutralization system defined in this section is part of an overall treatment train in an ex situ process. The most common neutralization application is a pre-treatment process in which aqueous wastes are neutralized (pH balanced) before they enter a further stage of treatment or disposal. The system generally consists of influent/effluent piping, one or more batch neutralizer tanks with one pump per tank, and the reagent chemicals.

Neutralization is a well-developed technology for treating aqueous waste streams and hazardous waste spills. Neutralization of an acidic or basic aqueous waste stream is necessary to achieve a desired pH in a variety of situations.

One of the primary steps in waste water neutralization is to determine the nature of the ions causing the acidity or alkalinity. This can be achieved by preparing titration curves in the laboratory. These curves show the quantity of alkaline material needed to adjust the pH of an acid waste water to a selected pH. They work similarly for alkaline waste water. Some waste water shows only a slight change in pH after a reagent is added, while others have a dramatic change. This is an important factor in designing a neutralization system if close control of pH is needed.

The most common way to neutralize acidic or basic waste water involves one, two, or three stages, using feedback, feedforward, or feedback-feedforward control. The type of control depends on a number of factors, including waste characteristics, hydraulic retention time of the reaction vessel, mixing, and reaction lags. Detention times for each stage of pH control are typically between 2–10 minutes. If limestone or some other relatively slow-reacting chemical is used for neutralization, the detention time could be considerably longer.

Common neutralizing chemicals for acid wastes include calcium or sodium carbonate, caustic soda (sodium hydroxide), lime, and limestone. Neutralizing chemicals for alkaline wastes include sulfuric acid, hydrochloric acid, and nitric acid. Sulfuric acid is often used because of its low cost. Factors that determine which chemical reagent will be used include cost, neutralization capacity, reaction rate, storage, and feeding requirements. Sodium hydroxide costs much more than the other materials, but is often used because it provides uniformity, ease of storage and feeding, rapid reaction rate, and soluble end products. The lime materials have a relatively low cost, but a longer reaction time, resulting in higher capital and operating costs.

Basic Information Needed for Estimating

It is possible to create a reasonable cost estimate using a few required parameters. If more detailed information is known, one can create a more precise and site-specific estimate using a secondary set of parameters.

To estimate the cost of the neutralization system, certain information must be known, as discussed in the following paragraphs.

Flow Rate

The flow rate of the waste directly affects the treatment cost. From the known flow rate, secondary information can be calculated, such as the size of the reaction tanks and the amount of reagent required. The unit of measure for flow rate is gallons per minute (GPM). Flow rates typically range from 1–300 GPM.

Category of Waste (Acid or Alkaline)

The type of waste determines the chemical reagent used for neutralization. The available chemical reagents are described later in this chapter. If the precise pH is unknown, the estimator could conservatively assume that the waste stream is either highly acidic (pH < 2) or highly alkaline (pH > 12).

Influent pH

The pH is assumed to be an average for the entire flow. The influent pH is used in conjunction with the effluent pH to determine neutralization chemical usage. The valid range is 2–12.

Effluent pH

If the precise target effluent pH is not known, a default effluent pH of 7 can be assumed. The effluent pH is used in conjunction with the influent pH in order to determine neutralization chemical usage. The valid range is 4–9.

Treatment Period

The total treatment period is divided into startup and operations and maintenance (O&M). The costs associated with the startup period are included with the capital costs, and the O&M costs are identified separately.

Worker Safety Level

Worker safety is affected by the contaminant(s) at the site. Safety level refers to the levels required by OSHA in 29 CFR Part 1910. The four levels are designated as A, B, C, and D, where "A" is the most protective, and "D" is the least protective. A safety level of E is also included to simulate normal construction, "no hazard" conditions as prescribed by the EPA.

Design Information Needed for Detailed Estimates

Following are descriptions of the types of detailed information that, when available, can add detail and accuracy to estimates. Also included are design criteria and estimating rules of thumb that estimators use to determine values that are not known, or to check information provided by others.

Batch Neutralizer Tank

The size of the batch neutralizer tank is based on the system flow rate and the retention time. Tank sizes for pre-packaged systems range from 10–200 gallons. The estimator should determine the size of the tank and allow for some excess capacity for surges in demand and system down-time for maintenance. For example, if the flow rate is 30 GPM, and the retention time is 5 minutes, the system capacity would need to be 150 gallons (30 GPM × 15 minutes), but the estimator should consider using a 200-gallon system to allow for contingency operations.

Reagent

The type of waste determines the type of reagent used. If the waste is alkaline, there will be a variety of applicable options. A similar variety will be available for acidic wastes. Also, the flow rate of waste determines the total amount of reagent required. Reagent options are shown in Figure 26.1.

Reagent Additive Rate

The reagent additive rate is the rate at which the reagent is added to the batch neutralizer to adjust the pH to a desired value. The reagent rates are listed in Figure 26.2. Reagent rates are quoted in pounds of reagent per thousand gallons of influent (lb/1,000 gal.).

Retention Time

The retention time is the number of minutes, that the influent must remain in the batch neutralizer to neutralize the pH. Retention times of less than 5 minutes are sufficient if only gross pH adjustment is required. The minimum recommended retention time for neutralization of aqueous waste streams to a specific pH is 15 minutes.

Reagents
Acidic Wastes
Sodium Hydroxide
Sodium Hydroxide Solution, Drummed Liquid
Sodium Hydroxide, Container, Beads
Sodium Hydroxide, Container, Flakes
Soda Ash
Soda Ash, Powdered
Lime
Quicklime, 1/4 Inch Nominal Granules, Bulk
Quicklime, 3/4 Inch Nominal Granules, Bulk
Quicklime, Combination 1/4 Inch and 3/4 Inch Granules, Bulk
Hydrated Lime, powdered
Alkaline Wastes
Sulfuric Acid Solution, Drummed Liquid

Figure 26.1 Reagents

Reagent Additive Rate	
Reagent	**Reagent Additive Rate (Lbs./1,000 Gal.)**
Sodium Hydroxide	1.5
Soda Ash	1.0
Lime	1.0
Sulfuric Acid	1.5

Figure 26.2 Reagents Additive Rate

Piping Material

The piping material is generally either polypropylene, stainless steel, or PVC. Polypropylene is the most common choice because the waste water may exhibit high acidity or alkalinity that would corrode PVC or stainless pipe. Where possible, piping is installed above ground to reduce costs and simplify maintenance.

Figure 26.3 provides guidance on available piping material alternatives. The flow values have been calculated using the Hazen-Williams pipe flow equation.

$$V = kCR_h^{0.63} S^{0.54} \text{ where } S = \frac{h_f}{L} \text{ \& } Q = VA \text{ \& } R_h = \frac{D}{4} \text{ for circular pipe.}$$

Piping Length

The piping length refers to both influent and effluent piping. The piping costs should assume above-ground piping supported on hangers and include fittings every 10' unless the specific site conditions require buried pipe.

Other Related Costs Capital costs for a neutralization system include chemical storage, chemical feeding, and mixing. A concrete structure slab is required for the batch neutralizer tank and pump system. Typically, an 8" structural slab is used.

The primary operating costs are the reagent costs. Other operating costs include electricity for running the pumps, mixers, etc., and costs for weekly influent and effluent testing.

Piping Material Options	
Flow Rate (GPM)	**Piping**
1-40	1-1/2" Polypropylene
41-95	2" Polypropylene
96-220	3" Polypropylene
221-375	4" Polypropylene
1-23	1" Stainless Steel
24-95	2" Stainless Steel
96-220	3" Stainless Steel
221-375	4" Stainless Steel
1-23	1-1/4" PVC
24-95	2" PVC
96-220	3" PVC
221-375	4" PVC

Figure 26.3 Piping Material Options

Sampling and analysis testing will take place once a week for the first month, monthly for the first year, and quarterly for the duration of the treatment.

Pump and motor maintenance will occur after 18 months of operation, and every 6 months per neutralizer thereafter.

Site Work and Utilities

Site work and utilities that may apply to neutralization include:

- Overhead electrical distribution
- Fencing and signage

These must also be included in the estimate.

Conclusion

Neutralization is almost always used as part of a larger treatment train process. The primary cost drivers are the flow rate, the additive rate, and the operating period. While neutralization is rarely a significant cost driver for a remediation process, overlooking its cost may be the most significant estimating risk. For this reason, the cost engineer should work closely with the design team to determine whether neutralization will be required and, if so, the extent of the requirement.

Chapter 27

Off-Site Transportation and Thermal Treatment

Disposal is the last link in the "cradle to grave" hazardous waste management system described in the Resource Conservation and Recovery Act (RCRA), Subtitle C program. RCRA defines *disposal* as the introduction of any constituent into the environment as a result of discharge, deposit, injection, dumping, spilling, leaking, or placing of any solid or hazardous waste into or on any land or water.

Off-site disposal may be accomplished through the use of commercial transportation and disposal services. By using an off-site disposal service, the generator may access the resources of a comprehensive waste manager who can assist with administrative responsibilities connected with hazardous waste generation. However, the generator of the waste is ultimately responsible for the proper handling of the hazardous waste until it has been eliminated. The three main types of commercial disposal are:

- Disposal to a landfill
- Off-site thermal treatment
- Deep well injection

This chapter addresses off-site thermal treatment. Injection wells are discussed in Chapter 47, and landfill disposal is covered in Chapter 48.

To determine the feasibility of off-site thermal treatment, one must be aware of RCRA regulations (40 CFR 260 to 268) and other state government regulations. The land disposal restrictions contained in 40 CFR Part 268 identify hazardous wastes that are restricted from land disposal and define the limited circumstances under which an otherwise prohibited waste may continue to be land-disposed. Land disposal of restricted wastes can continue with an approved petition showing there will be no migration of hazardous constituents from the disposal zone, that an extension was received to an effective date, that the waste meets relevant treatment standards; or, that the waste is placed in a surface impoundment and the requirements of 40 CFR 268.4 are being met. The land disposal restrictions in 40 CFR 268 also specify treatment standards and storage prohibitions.

Generators, storers, transporters, and disposers of regulated quantities of hazardous waste must comply with manifest requirements when handling waste removed, or to be removed, from the site at which it was generated. These and other requirements for hazardous waste handlers are found in 40 CFR 262 through 265. In addition, the generator must ensure that the facility receiving the waste has an acceptable compliance history with federal, state, and local regulatory agencies. Permitted RCRA facilities must notify the generator in writing that they will accept specific wastes from the generator and that they are permitted to do so. This is also true if hazardous waste is to be sent off site to be incinerated in a permitted boiler or industrial furnace. Permitting and performance standards are required for commercial facilities that burn hazardous wastes in these types of devices.

Applications and Limitations

Applications

- Off-site thermal treatment includes thermal desorption, incineration, and solid waste incineration.
- Low-temperature Thermal Desorption (LTTD) is applicable for removal of non-halogenated VOCs and petroleum hydrocarbons from contaminated soils.
- High-temperature Thermal Desorption (HTTD) is also used to remove SVOCs, PAHs, PCBs, pesticides, and volatile metals.
- Off-site incineration and solid waste incineration are used to remove all contaminant groups.

This technology is applicable for:

- Volume reduction
- Energy recovery
- Detoxification
- Materials recovery

Limitations

- High moisture content greatly increases required heat input (increasing fuel costs) and reduces the effectiveness.
- Not applicable to metal or other inorganic wastes or aqueous wastes.
- Dewatering may be necessary for soils with moisture contents greater than 20%.
- Off-gas of volatile heavy metals may require scrubbers for removal.
- Some highly aqueous wastes or noncombustible solids are not incinerable.
- Specific feed size and handling requirements directly impact cost.
- High organic content reduces efficiency.
- Transportation of hazardous material is costly, and proper disposal is the responsibility of the waste generator.
- Distance from the site to the treatment facility will directly affect the cost.

Configurations and Treatment Train Considerations

Several key factors affect the selection and viability of off-site transportation and thermal treatment when compared to other treatment approaches. Key factors include:

- Many incinerator types are available to suit technical requirements.
- Incineration requires comprehensive waste characterization to ensure compatibility with the chosen incinerator.

- Low-temperature Thermal Desorption (LTTD) becomes cost-competitive with other technologies with a minimum of 5,000 C.Y. of treatable material.
- Drum shredders are required to handle drummed waste in thermal treatment processes.
- High temperatures are required in thermal desorption processes to volatilize metals.
- With desorption processes, very high moisture content may result in low contaminant volatilization and a need to recycle the soil through the desorber.
- Total organic loading is limited to 10% in some systems.
- Polymers may foul or plug heat transfer surfaces in chambers.
- Thermal treatment may alter the physical properties of soil, making it susceptible to destabilizing forces, such as liquefaction.
- Requires excavation and screening of large objects (greater than 2" diameter).
- Volatiles in effluent gas streams may be burned, captured with carbon adsorption, or recovered via condensation equipment.
- Soils and sediments with water concentrations greater than 20–25% may require installation of a dryer to reduce energy costs.

Typical System Design Elements

Off-site thermal treatment normally includes the elements defined in the following paragraphs.

Preparation of Wastes

When drums or multiple impoundments are present, it is often cost-effective to consolidate compatible hazardous waste contents in a tank truck. Compatibility testing can ensure that consolidation will not result in toxic gases, vapors, fumes, or large volumes of waste that are unacceptable for off-site disposal. Compatibility testing refers to simple, rapid, and cost-effective testing procedures that are used to segregate wastes into broad categories. By identifying broad waste categories, compatible waste types can be safely bulked on-site without the additional risk of fire, explosion, or release of toxic gases, and disposal options can be determined without an exhaustive analysis of each waste type.

A detailed waste analysis is generally required before a waste is accepted by a treatment/disposal facility. Testing to determine gross halogen content is sometimes eliminated if all insoluble wastes will be incinerated at a facility that is capable of handling chlorinated organics. However, testing for PCBs is required regardless of the need for testing other halogenated compounds. Requirements vary considerably depending on the facility permits, state regulations, physical state of the wastes, and the final disposal method.

On-site pretreatment of wastes may be required to make them acceptable for off-site transport or to meet the requirements of an incineration or disposal facility. For incineration or land disposal facilities, pretreatment will likely be limited to the following:

- Acid-base neutralization (land disposal and incineration)
- Metal precipitation/solidification (land disposal)
- Hypochlorite oxidation of cyanide and sulfide (land disposal and incineration)
- Flash point reduction (land disposal)

- Removal of free liquids by addition of soils, lime, fly ash, polymers, or other materials which remove free water (land disposal)

Transportation

The transportation of hazardous waste is regulated by the Department of Transportation (DOT), the Environmental Protection Agency (EPA), the states, and, in some cases, local ordinances and codes. In addition, more stringent federal regulations govern the transportation and disposal of highly toxic and hazardous materials such as PCBs and radioactive wastes. Applicable DOT regulations include:

- Department of Transportation 49 CFR Parts 172–179
- Department of Transportation 49 CFR Part 1387 (46 FR 30974, 47073)
- Department of Transportation DOT-E 8876

The U.S. EPA regulations under RCRA (40 CFR 262 and 263) adopt DOT regulations pertaining to labeling, placarding, packaging, and spill reporting. These regulations also impose certain additional requirements for compliance with the manifest system and record keeping.

Vehicles for off-site transport of hazardous wastes must be DOT-approved and must display the proper DOT placard. Liquid wastes must be hauled in tanker trucks that meet certain requirements and specifications for the waste trailers or flat bed trucks. The trucks should be lined with plastic and/or absorbent materials. Before a vehicle is allowed to leave the site, it should be rinsed or scrubbed to remove contaminants. Both bulk liquid containers and box trailers should be checked for proper placarding, cleanliness, tractor-to-trailer hitch, and excess waste levels. Bulk liquid containers should also be checked for proper venting, closed valve positions, and secured hatches. Box trailers should be checked to ensure correct liner installation, secured cover tarps, and locked lift gates.

Before the waste is transported to a disposal/treatment facility, the waste stream will need to be analyzed to determine the breakdown of the constituents. The cost for initial waste stream evaluation for both PCB and non-PCB wastes should be included.

State taxes and other fees on hazardous wastes and substances can be major cost drivers. Taxes and fees vary greatly from state to state and are generally based on waste type (e.g., non-RCRA, RCRA, Extremely Hazardous, mine tailings). Landfill disposal sites often operate as treatment sites (incinerators) as well as storage areas. The main fee categories include:

- Post-closure fee
- TSDF (Treatment, Storage, and Disposal Facility) permit application fee
- TSDF licensing fee
- TSDF maintenance and inspection fee
- Generator fee
- Disposal fee

Direct disposal fees are direct costs incurred by a third party such as a contractor or generator. A detailed reference of disposal fees by state, published by the National Solid Wastes Management Association, is entitled "1990 Guide to State Taxes and Fees for Hazardous Waste Generation and Management."

Thermal Treatment

Off-site thermal treatment includes both incineration and thermal desorption (high-temperature and low-temperature) processes. Incineration processes are designed to oxidize and destroy contaminants at very high temperatures. Thermal desorption uses direct or indirect heat exchange to volatilize contaminants from soils, sediments, or sludges.

EPA regulations (under RCRA) for hazardous waste incineration require that particulate emissions be no more than 180 mg/m^3 and that hydrogen chloride removal efficiency from the exhaust gas be no less than 99%. Before a permit is issued, trial burns are conducted to determine the maximum ash and chlorine content that an incinerator can handle. Thus the facility is likely to have maximum limits for halogen content and ash. Incineration of PCBs requires special permits; there are only a limited number of facilities permitted to handle these wastes.

Basic Information Needed for Estimating

It is possible to create a reasonable cost estimate for incineration using a few required parameters. If more detailed information is known, one can create a more precise and site-specific estimate using a secondary set of parameters.

To estimate the cost of the system, certain basic information must be known. This information is discussed in the following paragraphs.

Waste Type

Commercial waste treatment costs, as well as transportation costs, can vary greatly depending on the nature (hazardous or non-hazardous) of the contaminant and the waste matrix. The incinerator permitting cost is significantly higher for hazardous waste compared to non-hazardous waste. The cost for waste analysis is also higher for hazardous waste.

For the purposes of this technology, the waste material should be classified as either hazardous or non-hazardous, depending on the waste characteristics. The EPA has developed two ways of determining whether a material is a hazardous waste. The first is based on the characteristics of the solid waste (as per RCRA definition). The four characteristics that identify a hazardous waste under RCRA in 40 CFR Part 261 are:

- Ignitability
- Corrosivity
- Reactivity
- Toxicity

There are three types of listed hazardous waste:

- Specific Source (40 CFR Part 261.31)
- Specific Source (40 CFR Part 261.32)
- Commercial Chemical Products (40 CFR Part 261.33)

Non-hazardous waste, for the purpose of this technology, is waste material that is contaminated, but does not exhibit the aforementioned characteristics. Miscellaneous residual waste (demolished cover, clean fill) is not applicable to this technology.

Waste Form

The incineration/treatment method varies depending on whether the waste is solid, liquid, or sludge. The physical characteristics help to determine the waste's compatibility with the proposed thermal treatment methodology. The input capabilities of thermal treatment unit depend on feed mechanism and furnace design.

For the purposes of this technology, there are two waste forms: solid and liquid/sludge. Bulk solid is assumed to be loaded by a wheel loader and have a moisture content of less than 30%. The technology assumes that bulk liquid is pumpable material with a moisture content greater than 70%. Bulk sludge is any material with a moisture content between 30–70%. This material is assumed to be pumped via tanker trucks.

Condition of Waste

The condition of waste prior to treatment, either bulk or in drums, will affect waste preparation tasks such as container costs, transferring waste into drums, and loading waste into a truck. The technology has assemblies based on bulk and drummed waste.

Options:

- Bulk to be Drummed
- Bulk to Remain as Bulk
- Non-Leaking Drums
- Leaking Drums

For purposes of this discussion, Leaking Drums or Non-Leaking Drums assumes that the waste is already packaged in drums. Therefore a cost is not typically added for purchasing drums. The estimator should assume that all leaking drums require overpacks, the cost of which should be included in the estimate.

Quantity of Waste

This parameter refers to the volume of waste to be transferred and treated. The volume of waste is used to determine the number of transport units and the number of drums required, if applicable. The quantity of waste value directly affects the cost of transportation and treatment.

Treatment Type

Thermal treatment is a term associated with the use of high temperatures as the principle means of destroying or detoxifying contaminants. Thermal treatment offers essentially complete destruction of the original organic waste. The destruction and removal efficiency (DRE) achieved for waste streams incinerated in properly operated thermal processes often exceeds the 99.99% requirement for hazardous wastes.

Options:

- **Incineration:** There are typically three types of incineration used to volatilize and combust halogenated and other refractory organics in hazardous waste as well as other bulk solid wastes:

  1. Circulating bed combustors (CBCs),
  2. Fluidized bed combustors (CFBs), and
  3. Rotary kilns.

All three incineration types are commonly used by off-site waste disposal service providers. An average incineration cost is provided by this technology.

- **Low-temperature Thermal Desorption:** Wastes are heated to between 200–600°F (90–320 °C). These low-temperature thermal desorption (LTTDs) units are typically used for VOCs and other petroleum hydrocarbon contamination in all soil types. LTTD units are commonly used by off-site service providers.
- **High-temperature Thermal Desorption:** A full-scale technology in which wastes are heated to between 600–1,000°F (320–560 °C). High-temperature thermal desorption (HTTDs) services are commonly available from off-site waste disposal facilities specializing in thermal treatment and are used to primarily treat SVOC contaminated soils.

Distance to Off-Site Facility (One Way)

Travel distance is the most important factor in the cost of transporting any material. Generally, transporters base their rates on either a *running mile* or *loaded mile*. A running mile rate includes all of the miles traveled by the transporter (i.e., the charges begin when the truck leaves the terminal and end when the truck is back at the terminal). The loaded mile rate includes the number of miles between the generator and the ultimate treatment location.

This chapter uses the loaded mile approach, but the estimator can adjust to the running mile method if that is the method used by the waste hauler. For short hauling distances, the costs will be based on either a loaded mile or a minimum charge, depending on the type of material. The calculated number of trips is based on the volume of waste divided by the mode of transportation capacity.

Treatment Fees

These are the costs per unit that the treatment facility will charge to accept (treat) the waste. The cost varies depending on the waste type, form, and condition prior to treatment.

For either solid or liquid/sludge, the estimator may assign an average treatment fee based on the waste type and form. Rates can be determined based on published price lists or by contacting the specific waste handling facility. Depending on waste characteristics, location of the site, or other cost driving factors, an "average" treatment might not be appropriate. In this case, the estimator should break down wastes into specific categories and price each category separately. Typical categories include:

- NHAZ = Non-Hazardous
- HAZ = Hazardous
- SW = Solid Waste
- LW = Liquid/Sludge Waste
- BTB = Bulk to Remain as Bulk
- BTD = Bulk to be Drummed
- LD = Leaking Drums
- NLD = Non-Leaking Drums

State Tax/Fee

Most states have taxes and/or fees for treatment and disposal of hazardous waste. These rates can vary significantly from one location to another. Typically, rates are based on a cost per cubic yard, gallon, or drum.

Safety Level

The safety level is driven by the potential human interaction with the contaminants in the loading, en route to the treatment facility, and at the site and treatment facility. Safety levels refer to those levels as defined by OSHA in 29 CFR Part 1910. The 4 levels are designated as A, B, C, and D, where A is the most protective, and D is the least protective. A safety level of E is also included to simulate normal construction ("no hazard") conditions as prescribed by the EPA.

The safety level is a reflection of the level of productivity and affects all labor categories in defaulted or selected assemblies. Safety level will not affect the productivity of the driver during transportation, since this would violate DOT and EPA regulations.

Design Information Needed for Detailed Estimates

Following are descriptions of the types of detailed information that, when available, can add detail and accuracy to estimates. Also included are design criteria and estimating rules of thumb that the estimator typically uses to determine values that are not known, or to check information provided by others.

Containment Berm

Once the contaminated soil/water/sludge has been removed, a containment berm may be required for temporary storage until the waste is transported to the disposal site. While containment berms are not required in most cases, the estimator should consider the need for a berm and add it to the project estimate where required. Typical inflatable berm sizes are shown in Figure 27.1.

Inflatable Containment Berms
10' x 10' x 17",   750 Gallon
13' x 13' x 17", 1,800 Gallon
18' x 18' x 17", 3,400 Gallon
24' x 24' x 17", 6,100 Gallon
32' x 32' x 17", 10,800 Gallon
32' x 32' x 34", 21,600 Gallon
74' x 34' x 34", 53,400 Gallon
45' x 15' x 17", 7,600 Gallon
65' x 16' x 17", 11,000 Gallon
50' x 22' x 17", 11,600 Gallon

Figure 27.1 Inflatable Containment Berms

Type of Drum

Depending on the type of contaminants in the waste and the waste form, appropriate containers for waste transport may vary. The default container is a 55-gallon, steel, closed-head drum. Alternate container selection will affect the material cost for the containers. The following types of containers are the most common for holding and transporting waste.

- 55-gal, steel, closed-head drum
- 55-gal, steel, open-head drum
- 55-gal, polyethylene, closed-head drum
- 55-gal, polyethylene, open-head drum

Storage containers with capacities ranging from 10–350 gallons are readily available, but because they are less often used, they are generally more expensive.

Fill Capacity Factor

This figure represents the average percent drums are filled. The fill capacity factor applies to non-leaking drums that will remain drummed, and for bulk waste that is to be drummed. The fill capacity factor is used to determine the actual volume of waste and/or the number of drums required. Because drums are generally not entirely full, a rule of thumb is 90%.

Quantity of Overpacks

The Quantity of Overpacks is assumed to be equal to the number of leaking drums. The estimator may want to add additional overpacks for reserves or damage during loading and/or transportation.

Type of Overpacks

The typical default overpack is an 85-gallon steel drum. In some cases the waste material is incompatible with the overpack material, and a different overpack material may be required. A common alternative is 85-gallon polyethylene. The estimator should perform a materials compatibility test prior to selecting an option.

Site Work and Utilities

If site work and utilities apply, they must also be covered in the estimate. Examples of site work and utilities that may apply to incineration include:

- Overhead electrical distribution
- Access roads
- Fencing and signage
- Clear and grub

Conclusion

Incineration is a proven technology that has significant potential as a final stage in the hazardous waste management process. However, incineration is also an emotional public policy issue, and its technical merits are often overshadowed by the political implications. For this reason, obtaining a permit may be expensive, and delays are common. This process drives the cost of incineration projects. The cost engineer should maintain a realistic awareness of both the technical and political issues surrounding an incineration project and factor in appropriate costs.

Chapter 28

On-Site Low-Temperature Thermal Desorption

Thermal desorption removes organic contaminants from soils, sludges, and other solid media. It is not an incineration or pyrolysis system. Thermal desorption does not encourage chemical oxidation and reactions, and does not form combustion by-products. The organic contaminants are removed as vapors or condensed liquids, characterized by a high British thermal unit (BTU) rating, which may then be destroyed in a permitted incinerator or used as a supplemental fuel. Because of low temperatures (100–400 °C) and gas flow rates, this process is less expensive than incineration.

Typical System Design Elements

The low-temperature thermal desorption unit uses a rotary kiln as a primary unit to volatilize water and organic contaminants into an inert carrier gas stream. The processed solids are then cooled with treated condensed water to eliminate dusting. The solids are placed and compacted in their original location.

The organic contaminants and water are transported out of the dryer by an inert nitrogen gas. The carrier gas flows through the duct to the gas treatment system, where organic vapors, water vapors, and dust particles are removed and recovered from the gas. Dust particles and 10–30% of the organic contaminants are removed by air emission control devices.

The organic air stream exiting from the air emission control devices is either oxidized in a secondary chamber at 1,400–1,600°F for 0.75–1.0 seconds and subsequently passed through a baghouse for final particulate removal, or passed through a series of condensers that produce liquid organics for final disposal to an off-site incinerator or an appropriate recycling facility.

Most of the carrier gas that passes through the gas treatment system is reheated and recycled to the dryer. Approximately 5–10% of the gas is cleaned by passing through the particulate filter and a carbon adsorption system before it is discharged to the atmosphere. The discharge helps maintain a small negative pressure within the system and prevents potentially contaminated gases from leaking. The discharge allows for makeup nitrogen to be added to the system, so oxygen concentrations will not exceed combustibility limits.

Thermal desorption may be used to remove volatile organic compounds from soils or similar solids. It is effective on a variety of soils, from sand to very cohesive clays. However, this process is not suitable for aqueous waste. High mercury levels in the waste are undesirable because the boiling point of mercury (356 °C) is close to the operating temperature of thermal desorption. For economic reasons, a single location should have a minimum 5,000 C.Y. (7,500 tons) of material for the technology to be cost competitive with other treatment technologies.

Applications and Limitations

Applications

- Applicable for removal of non-halogenated VOCs and petroleum hydrocarbons from contaminated soils.

Limitations

- High moisture content greatly increases required heat input (increasing fuel costs) and reduces the effectiveness of the LTTD process.
- Not applicable to metal or other inorganic wastes.
- Dewatering may be necessary for soils that have a moisture content greater than 20%.
- Soil screening may be necessary to remove large rocks and other abrasive feed.
- Clays, silts, and other soils with a high humic content act to bind contaminants and thus increase the reaction time of the LTTD process.

Process Configurations and Treatment Train Considerations

- Low-temperature Thermal Desorption (LTTD) becomes cost-competitive with other technologies with a minimum of 5,000 C.Y. of treatable material.
- Drum shredders will be required to handle drummed waste in thermal treatment processes.
- With desorption processes, very high moisture content may result in low contaminant volatilization and a need to recycle the soil through the desorber.
- Total organic loading is limited to 10% in some systems.
- Polymers may foul or plug heat transfer surfaces in chambers.
- Thermal treatment may alter the physical properties of soil, making it susceptible to destabilizing forces, such as liquefaction.
- Volatiles in effluent gas streams may be burned, captured with carbon adsorption, or recovered via condensation equipment.
- Soils and sediments with water concentrations greater than 20–25% may require installation of a dryer or belt filter press to reduce energy costs.

Basic Information Needed for Estimating

It is possible to create a reasonable budget cost estimate using a few required parameters. If more detailed information is known, one can create a more precise and site-specific estimate using a secondary set of parameters.

To estimate the cost of a low-temperature thermal desorption system, certain information must be known, as discussed in the following paragraphs.

Nature of the Waste

The nature of the waste (e.g., hazardous or non-hazardous) affects the cost of the project. In this chapter, waste refers to solid waste—not liquid or sludge. The initial waste stream analysis will cost significantly more for hazardous waste than for non-hazardous waste. However, the unit operating cost does not differ significantly. The low-temperature desorption units generally operate at 100–400 °C, which ensures volatilization of undesirable organics in the waste.

Volume of Bulk Waste

The volume of waste directly affects the cost of low-temperature thermal desorption. When conversion of cubic yards to tons is necessary, assume a conversion factor of 1.5 tons per cubic yard, unless more precise information is available. This conversion factor has been developed based on unit weight of soil as 110 pounds per cubic foot.

Distance from the Vendor

The distance from the vendor determines the mobilization and demobilization cost of the process unit. Most process unit vendors charge the client a fixed mobilization/demobilization cost for any distance less than or equal to 1,000 miles. An additional charge is imposed for every mile over 1,000 miles.

Firing System

The rotary kiln used in low-temperature thermal desorption could be fired directly by use of a flame burner or indirectly by thermal radiation. In either case, the organics in the soil are volatilized to be recovered or burned in an afterburner. The cost of indirect firing is 30% higher than direct firing. The actual operation cost will depend on the location of the project.

The direct firing system consists of convective heat transfer using heated air to make intimate contact with soil and desorb the organic contaminants. Rotary dryers are the most common direct firing systems, and are designed to effectively and safely treat organic concentrations up to 3% (see Figure 28.1). Direct firing is generally adopted for most petroleum-related organics and a wide range of contaminants, such as volatile organics and pesticides.

The indirect firing system relies on conductive heat transfer using a sealed rotary cylinder with the feed material tumbling inside and the heat source on the outside. The contaminated solids, coming in contact with the inner wall of the cylinder, are conductively heated and allow for desorption of organic contaminants up to 10% in most cases. The rotary calciner is an example of an indirect firing system. Indirect firing is used when the contaminant concentration is very high or when contaminants are less volatile in nature (semi-volatile organics such as chresols, chrysene, phenols, pyrenes, and ethers). Indirect firing is recommended for refinery-type waste, RCRA waste, and wastes that are regulated under the Toxic Substance Control Act (TSCA), such as PCBs.

Figure 28.2 shows the comparison between the direct and indirect firing systems.

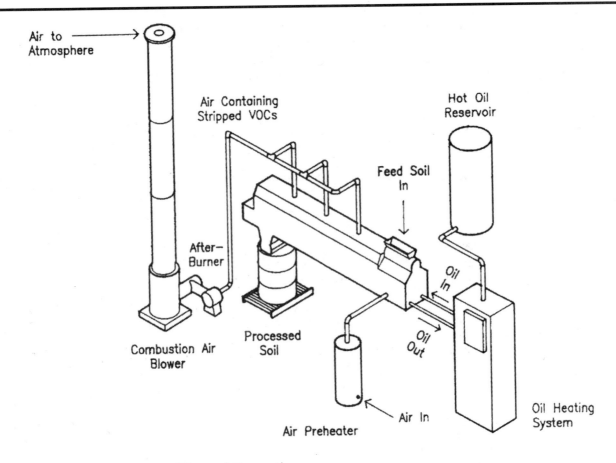

Figure 28.1 Low-temperature Thermal Desorption

Comparison of Features: Direct And Indirect Firing Systems		
System Feature	**Direct System**	**Indirect System**
Primary Unit	Rotary Dryer	Rotary Calciner
Primary Heat Transfer Method	Convection	Conduction
Soil Throughput (tons/hr.)	25-50	5-15
Maximum Soil Feed	2"	2"
Soil Residence Time (minutes)	7-30	30-70
Operating Temperature (°F)	400-900	600-900
Contaminant Vapor Treatment	Secondary Oxidizer	Condensed
"Best Fit" Applications		
Type of Contaminants	Petroleum/RCRA	RCRA/TSCA
Level Of Contamination	Light	Moderate
Size of Site (tons)	>5,000	>10,000

Figure 28.2 Comparison of Features: Direct and Indirect Firing Systems

Number of Drums

The feeding mechanisms of the process unit are not designed to accept waste in drummed form. If the waste at the site is drummed, drum shredders will be needed. The drum shredder has an in-feed opening to accept drums and a cutter that shreds the drums, separating the drum contents. The shredded drum is delivered in the form of plates, which can be recycled.

If drums are present, then a drum shredder and operation will be included in the estimate regardless of the choice for pretreatment. The number of drums at the site must be known in order to determine the operating cost of the shredder. If all the waste at the site is in bulk form, the number of drums will be zero, and a drum shredder will not be required. If the contents are not solid, then low-temperature thermal desorption will not work.

Moisture Level in the Waste

Wastes with a high moisture content can be treated by the low-temperature thermal desorption process. However, the moisture content influences the kiln volume design, waste material handling and feeding, and especially the off-gas treatment unit. The maximum permissible moisture level in the waste feed is 60%. If the moisture content of the solid waste is above 60%, the waste is pretreated using a belt filter. The belt filter consists of a perforated belt, where gravity drainage takes place. The thickened waste is pressed between a series of rollers to produce a dry cake, and moisture content is reduced to less than 1%.

Particle Size of the Waste

The particle size of the waste is restricted by the process unit's feeding mechanism. The maximum particle size the process unit will accept is 2". Larger waste particles are pretreated using a rotary shear electric shredder.

Worker Safety Level

Worker safety is affected by the contaminant(s) at the site. Safety level refers to the levels required by OSHA in 29 CFR Part 1910. The four levels are designated as A, B, C, and D, where "A" is the most protective, and "D" is the least protective. A safety level of E is also included to simulate normal construction, "no hazard" conditions as prescribed by the EPA.

Design Information Needed for Detailed Estimates

Following are descriptions of the types of detailed information that, when available, can add detail and accuracy to estimates. Also included are design criteria and estimating rules of thumb that the estimators use to determine values that are not known, or to check information provided by others.

Pretreatment Equipment

For waste pretreatment, the following additional equipment is available. Equipment selection is based on the nature of the waste.

Hopper

A hopper is typically required for feeding the waste material onto the conveyor system. The size of the hopper should be less than the width of the conveying belt, 24". The typical hopper is 18" in diameter and made of aluminized steel. Generally, a hopper is used for material handling at the site if pretreatment is required.

Primary Screens

The normal primary screen included with the system is a 5' × 10' double-deck screen consisting of wire cloth with a 0.5" wire diameter. This screen is capable of screening solid material at a rate of 50–75 tons per hour. The waste material fed into the hopper is conveyed to the primary screens. The screened finer material, less than 2" in diameter, is conveyed to the process unit, while the waste material held on the screen, which is greater than 2" in size, is conveyed to the material shredder prior to incineration. Primary screens are required if the average particle diameter is greater than 2".

Secondary Screens

Secondary screens are usually a 4' × 12' single-deck, consisting of wire cloth with 0.5" diameter. This screen is capable of screening solid material at a rate of 50–75 tons per hour. Secondary screens are generally required if the average particle diameter is greater than 2".

Conveyors

Conveyors are required if the average particle diameter is greater than 2". Three different types are used:

- Auto conveyor, 41.5' in length, 24" belt, 45' per minute, center drive, horizontal belt
- Auto conveyor, 61.5' in length, 24" belt, 45' per minute, center drive, horizontal belt
- Auto inclined conveyor, 25 degrees, 34' in length, with loader and end idler assembly

The quantity of each type of conveyor is based on the pretreatment equipment selections, described below, and the average particle diameter. If the design of the system is incomplete or unavailable, the following assumptions can be used for estimating purposes:

- Assume 20' of horizontal conveyor for each primary screen, secondary screen, and shredder. This is for the waste that passes through the shredder or screens and is ready for incineration. Also include one 41.5'–long horizontal conveyor for each primary and secondary screen. These are the feed conveyors for untreated waste.
- Assume two 61.5'–long horizontal conveyors, one at each end of the pretreatment unit.
- Assume one inclined conveyor for each primary screen, secondary screen, and shredder. There is also one at the end of the pretreatment unit to provide an end dump mechanism for the pretreated waste.

Electric Shredder Purchase

When the average particle size is greater than 2", an electric rotary shear material shredder will be required. These shredders are usually rented for brief projects. However, when the quantity of solid waste at the site is large (typically greater than 11,000 tons) or when multiple site remediation is proposed for a project, it would be economical to purchase a material shredder.

Slab for Pretreatment Equipment

To determine the cost of the concrete slab for the setup of the pretreatment equipment, the estimator should determine the proposed concrete slab area in square feet. Typically, an 8" thick structural slab is used. The construction cost of concrete slab for unit setup is included in the operation cost.

Site Work and Utilities

Site work and utilities that may apply to low-temperature thermal desorption include:

- Overhead electrical distribution
- Water distribution
- Storm sewer
- Access roads
- Parking lots
- Fencing
- Clear and grub

These must also be included in the estimate.

Conclusion

Thermal desorption is a proven technology that provides a cost-effective alternative to incineration for many types of contaminants, assuming the quantity of waste to be treated is large enough to offset the initial set-up costs of the system on site. The primary cost drivers are the nature and quantity of waste to be remediated. Pretreatment costs for waste (e.g., moisture reduction, shredding, drum removal) can also drive costs of operation. The cost engineer should review the design and actual site conditions to determine the specific requirements of the project. Cost comparisons with other technologies including incineration and landfill disposal should be performed when total waste volumes are less than 5,000 C.Y.

Chapter 29

Passive Water Treatment

Passive water treatment has applications in the remediation of storm water run-off containing organic constituents, metallic ions, and acidic mine drainage contaminated with heavy metals. Compared to active water treatment methods, such as chemical precipitation and neutralization, passive treatment methods generally have lower operations and maintenance (O&M) costs, but require more land area.

Applications and Limitations

Applications

- Used for remediating storm water run-off containing organic constituents, metallic ions, and acid mine drainage contaminated with heavy metals.
- Can be implemented in municipalities, subdivisions, industrial developments, airports, and sites needing surface water treatment.
- Constructed wetlands have historically been used in waste water treatment for controlling organic matter, nutrients, and suspended sediments.

Limitations

- Passive water treatment methods require varying amounts of land for implementation. Implementing the method using less than the suggested amount of land will reduce the treatment effectiveness.
- Passive water treatment methods must be adjusted to account for differences in geology, terrain, climate, and soils composition.
- Passive water treatment effectiveness can be difficult to control and monitor due to the open nature of the treatment system.
- Passive water treatment by detention pond usually requires the construction of several detention ponds to achieve cleanup goals.
- The effectiveness of passive water treatment by constructed wetlands is not well established. Wetland aging may be a problem, which may contribute to a decrease in contaminant removal rates over time.

Process Configurations and Treatment Train Considerations

- Passive water treatment is implemented following storm water run-off collection. Some methods of passive water treatment also require treated water discharge. Thus, a collection step and a discharge step should be added to the treatment train as necessary.
- Some scenarios may require implementation of more than one passive water treatment technology. For example, a settling pond and/or wetland can follow an anoxic limestone drain to allow removal of metal precipitates through oxidation and hydrolysis.
- Some passive water treatment methods may require byproduct management. For example, spent compost used for storm water filtration may be sent to a land-farming cell, where further bioremediation converts the material into a stable soil amendment.
- Passive water treatment technology implementation may include other costs not directly estimated as part of the passive water treatment system, such as:
  - Land acquisition
  - Airport storm drainage piping
  - Backup treatment
  - Sludge removal
  - Sludge hauling and disposal
  - Treatment of compost
  - Groundwater monitoring
  - Monitoring

Typical System Design Elements

Typical methods used to accomplish passive water treatment include storm water filtration, run-off detention ponds, anoxic limestone drains, and constructed wetlands (anaerobic compost wetlands and aerobic wetlands). Each method is described briefly below.

Storm Water Filtration

A patented technology has been developed to treat surface run-off when scarce or expensive land requirements exclude other Best Management Practices (BMP), such as ponds, swales, and infiltration galleries. This technology consists of filtering storm water run-off through a bed of compost media prepared from treated deciduous leaves. The compost is contained in an underground concrete vault, where the storm water enters, the kinetic energy is dissipated, the flow is spread out, filtration occurs, and the treated effluent leaves through an under-drain. The treated water can then be routed to a storm sewer or a receiving water body, such as a lake, stream, or river. The technology has been reported to remove suspended sediment, heavy metals, and organic constituents through a combination of filtration, ion exchange, and bioremediation occurring in the compost bed. The compost bed is removed and replaced on an annual basis, or when conditions dictate that contaminant saturation in the bed has occurred.

Run-off Detention Ponds

If more land is available (e.g., an airfield), an extended detention pond can be installed prior to the storm sewer or creek. Typically, these ponds are sized to store the mean volume from a precipitation event for a period of 24 hours to remove up to 90% of the particulate pollutants. Besides particulate removal, detention ponds lengthen the period of time over which the receiving body obtains run-off. Airport drainage in this model is handled by several (default value is three) detention ponds, each receiving its flow from a collection headwall. Generally, one headwall is used to drain each of the following three main paved areas of an airfield: runways, taxiways, and aprons.

Outflow in a detention pond exits through a riser pipe notched with slots or outfitted with a cutout section wrapped with wire mesh screen. The water rises in the pond to the height of the outlet. The riser pipe is fitted with a removable cap to permit semi-annual clean-outs of trash, leaves, and twigs. Depending on the infiltration and evaporation rates, a marshy area in the pond below the riser opening may develop to support some bioremediation of organic wastes, such as vehicular fluids, fertilizers, herbicides, and de-icing solutions. Maintenance of the ponds includes mowing and trash or sediment removal as needed.

Anoxic Limestone Drains

Anoxic limestone drains, or ALDs, consist of a buried bed (9' W x 4' D) of limestone, through which acidic mine drainage can be routed to add alkalinity to net acidic (acidity greater than alkalinity) water. ALDs use baseball-size limestone (typically no. 3 or 4) with a high $CaCO_3$ (80–95%) content. The limestone bed is kept sealed from the atmosphere with a vapor barrier of plastic and soil to prevent armoring of the limestone surface with ferric hydroxide precipitates. To this end, the influent water should have low concentrations of dissolved oxygen (DO), ferric iron (Fe^{+3}), and aluminum (Al). This makes an ALD an ideal means of treating acidic mine drainage that has had minimal exposure to the atmosphere. Organic material, such as spent mushroom compost (hay, manure, brewer's mash, etc.) can be added to the limestone to promote the growth of anaerobic sulfate-reducing bacteria, which results in the precipitation of metal sulfides.

Constructed Wetlands

If sufficient land is available, a constructed wetland can be installed to add alkalinity, remove metals, and bioremediate organics through microbial processes. Aerobic wetlands remove metals through a combination of oxidation and hydrolysis reactions and are best suited for net alkaline water containing sufficient DO content to support the aerobes. Anaerobic wetlands, better suited for more acidic water with low DO content, contain an organic substrate such as a 1.5' thick layer of spent mushroom compost. The compost promotes the growth of anaerobic sulfate-reducing bacterial colonies, which remove metals as sulfide precipitates and add alkalinity to the water. Both aerobic and anaerobic wetlands can be planted with emergent vegetation, such as cattails (Typha latifolia). Besides improving the aesthetics of the completed wetland cells, planting vegetation has the added benefits of anchoring the substrate through a root network, providing a carbon source for micro-organisms, and incorporating metals and organic constituents in the plant material through phytoremediation processes. The choice of vegetation should be based on considering native species that can tolerate and prosper in the location's climate. Figure 29.1 shows the passive water treatment process.

Basic Information Needed for Estimating

A reasonable cost estimate can be developed using a few required parameters. A more precise estimate will require more detailed, site-specific information in the form of a secondary set of parameters.

Developing an estimate for a passive water system is a hierarchical process. Information must be assembled in a certain order, as the

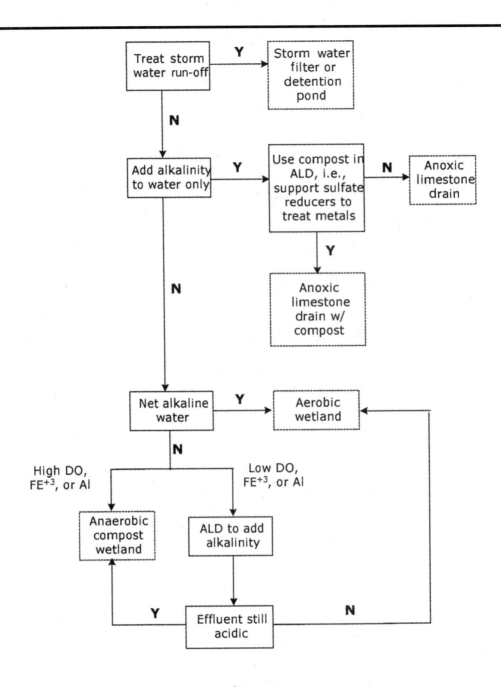

Figure 29.1 The Passive Water Treatment Process

design requirements are defined. The first items to determine are addressed in the following paragraphs.

Type of System

The common types of passive water systems are summarized below. The type of system will drive the area requirements of any wetland, settling pond, and anoxic limestone drains (ALDs) in the selected design.

Options:

- Storm water run-off filter
- Run-off detention pond
- Airport drainage
- Anoxic limestone drain without compost
- Anoxic limestone drain with compost
- Anaerobic wetland without ALD
- Anaerobic wetland with ALD
- Aerobic wetland without ALD
- Aerobic wetland with ALD

Flow Rate

To treat run-off using compost filters, determine the peak run-off flow expected to be routed into the filter during a precipitation event, in gallons per minute (GPM). The typical minimum and maximum flow rate range for run-off filters is 1–3,500 GPM. For all other applications, except for detention ponds and airport drainage, determine the average flow rate entering an ALD or wetland system in GPM. The typical minimum and maximum flow rate range is 1–250 GPM. Figure 29.2 shows the selection criteria for a passive water treatment system.

Drainage Area (Run-off Detention Pond Only)

The drainage area is the number of acres in a developed watershed from which run-off is routed to a detention pond. The drainage area includes channeled run-off from parking lots, roadways, homes, and businesses flowing into a common storm sewer or creek.

System Type	Treatment Objectives	Influent
Storm Water Filter	Parking Lots, Roadways, & Subdivisions	Storm Water Run-off
Detention Pond	Parking Lots, Roadways, & Subdivisions	Storm Water Run-off
Airport Drainage	Runways, Taxiways, Aprons, & Parking Pads	Storm Water Run-off
ALD without Compost	Acidity	Acidic; low DO, Fe^{+3}, & Al
ALD with Compost	Acidity & Metals	Acidic; low DO, Fe^{+3}, & Al
Anaerobic without ALD	Acidity, Metals, & Organics	Acidic; high DO, Fe^{+3}, or Al
Anaerobic with ALD	Acidity, Metals, & Organics	Acidic; low DO, Fe^{+3}, & Al
Aerobic without ALD	Metals & Organics	Alkaline; high DO, Fe^{+3}, or Al
Aerobic with ALD	Acidity, Metals, & Organics	Alkaline; low DO, Fe^{+3}, & Al

Figure 29.2 Selection Criteria for Passive Water Treatment Systems

Paved Airport Area (Airport Drainage Only)

The paved airport area is the combined area in acres of the runways, taxiways, aprons, special purpose parking pads (e.g., refueling, de-icing, or loading areas), and wash-racks that can be considered relatively impermeable to storm water infiltration. This developed area creates storm drainage that may have to be collected and detained during operation of an airfield.

Metal Concentration (Anaerobic or Aerobic Wetland Options Only)

Estimate the wetland area based on sizing criteria developed for iron (Fe) or manganese (Mn) removal. The estimator should select the primary metal of concern and its influent concentration in units of milligrams per liter (mg/l), 1 mg/l = 1 ppm. The two most common options are iron (Fe) and manganese (Mn).

Safety Level

The contaminant(s) at the site determine its safety level. Safety level refers to the 4 levels as required by OSHA in 29 CFR Part 1910, defined as A, B, C, and D; where level "A" is the most protective, and "D" is the least protective. A safety level of E (Modified Level D) is also included to simulate normal construction (no hazard) conditions as prescribed by the EPA.

Design Information Needed for Detailed Estimates

This section describes the kinds of detailed information that, when available, can add accuracy to estimates. Included are design criteria and estimating rules of thumb that estimators use to determine values that are not known, or to check information provided by others. Detailed information will vary depending on whether a passive water system is being used to treat storm run-off or mine drainage. Each scenario is addressed separately in the following discussion.

Detailed Estimates for Storm Run-off Systems

The following items should be considered when preparing detailed estimates for storm run-off passive water systems.

Compost Replacement

The recommended replacement of compost in the storm filters is a function of the flow rate for the system. Other external factors, such as the annual amount of precipitation, storm flow intensity (inches per rainfall), and the type and amount of pollutants washed into storm drains, should also be considered. For flow rates of less than 400 GPM, a closed-top filter design is typically used with a compost replacement frequency of approximately every 12 months. If the flow rate is 400 GPM or greater, an open-top design with a default compost replacement frequency of 48 months is more commonly used. The compost replacement frequency is longer in the open-top design because this design uses a lower loading factor (gallons per minute of flow per square foot of filter area) than the closed-top design, and the compost is tilled to extend its useful life.

Tilling Frequency

If an open-top filter design is used, it is recommended that the compost bed be raked of sediment and tilled annually to extend its useful life. A tilling frequency of every 12 months for open-top units is common and a good rule of thumb. The closed-top units are too confined for this activity, so the compost is never tilled.

Run-off Coefficient

This parameter applies to a detention pond. The run-off coefficient is a function of the degree of development, topography, and cover, but is mainly determined by the percentage of imperviousness in a watershed. A common rule of thumb for this parameter is a run-off coefficient of 0.65, which is representative of a multi-unit residential or light-industrial development. The valid range for this parameter is 0.01 (extremely permeable) to 1.00 (completely impervious). Figure 29.3 lists the typical run-off coefficients.

Mean Volume

Mean volume applies to the *detention pond* system. The mean volume is the amount of precipitation, measured in inches, received during a typical rainfall (annual rainfall total/annual no. of rainfall events). A more conservative approach can ensure adequate pond size by using the heaviest rainfall amount during a 1-, 2-, 5-, or 10-year storm event. The National Weather Service (NWS) or agriculture extension office provides location-specific information on precipitation amounts during a typical rainfall event.

Rainfall Intensity

Rainfall intensity applies to the *airport drainage* type of passive water system. The rainfall intensity is measured as the total rainfall, in inches, over a period of one hour during a 2-year storm event (the greatest amount of rainfall in one hour that occurred in a 2-year period). The National Weather Service (NWS) provides meteorological records of rainfall at an existing or proposed airfield location.

Headwall Points

Headwall points also apply to the *airport drainage* system. A headwall is the discharge point for the run of reinforced concrete pipe (RCP) stormwater drainage pipe that drains a portion of an airfield. This parameter determines the number of detention ponds required to temporarily store the drainage from an airfield. The number of headwall points will vary depending on the total amount of paved surface for an

Typical Watershed Run-off Coefficients	
Watershed Area	**Run-off Coefficient**
Downtown Business District	0.70–0.95
Residential Developments	0.30–0.75
Industrial Parks	0.50–0.90
Roadways, Parking Lots	0.70–0.95
Unimproved Areas	0.10–0.30
Lawns, Parks, & Playgrounds	0.05–0.35

Figure 29.3 Typical Watershed Run-off Coefficients

airfield, including runways, taxiways, parking aprons, ramps, roads, and other impervious surfaces. Also, the number of headwalls will vary depending on the configuration of these surfaces. For airfields where the runways, taxiways, and aprons are in close proximity to each other, fewer headwalls may be needed. For airfields where these surfaces are widely distributed, more headwalls will be needed. If the number of headwalls is not known, a rule of thumb is one headwall for each runway, each major taxiway, and each major parking apron or ramp area, plus one additional headwall for other miscellaneous paved structures. This will provide a conservative estimate.

Detailed Estimates for Mine Drainage Systems
The following items should be considered when preparing detailed estimates for mine drainage passive water systems.

Settling Pond
A settling pond can be used downstream of an ALD and upstream of a wetland to remove metal precipitate sludge and sediment, which may interfere with natural wetland processes and/or cause turbidity problems downstream. In addition, the residence time in a pond generates oxygenation of the water to assist natural microbial processes downstream. Figure 29.4 provides a rule of thumb to help determine when settling ponds are appropriate for passive water systems.

Wetland Sizing Criteria
The wetland area is based on sizing criteria designed for either treatment of an abandoned mine lands (AML) site or to meet compliance requirements for effluent discharge. These criteria take into account how much mass of metal can be removed per unit area of the wetland over a given time period. Manganese is more difficult to remove than iron, and therefore requires more wetland area than iron for an equivalent influent metal concentration. AML criteria are used to cost-effectively reduce metal concentrations, but may not consistently meet effluent limits. Using compliance criteria results in a more conservative design that is better able to consistently meet effluent limits. In addition, a settling pond will be sized with increased retention time if compliance-sizing criteria are used.

Type of System vs. Settling Pond	
Type of System	**Appropriate for Settling Pond**
Storm Water Filter	N/A
Detention Pond	N/A
Airport Drainage	N/A
ALD without Compost	Yes
ALD with Compost	Yes
Anaerobic without ALD	No
Anaerobic with ALD	Yes
Aerobic without ALD	Yes
Aerobic with ALD	Yes

Figure 29.4 Use of Settling Ponds in Passive Water Systems

Liner

The accumulated metal sludge will not be considered an RCRA hazardous waste for most treatment applications. In that case, a liner is not generally required for a constructed wetland. This implies that the compacted soil at the base of the constructed area does not have a high infiltration rate, and that it can support a permanent level of water. If it is necessary to protect groundwater from hazardous leachate infiltration (i.e., high levels of acidity and heavy metals), a liner can be constructed from a 12" layer of compacted clay overlaid by geotextile fabric or a 40-mil layer of high-density polyethylene (HDPE) overlaid by geotextile fabric.

Vegetation

Cattails or other emergent vegetation are initially planted in a portion of the shallower areas, spaced at 36". Typically, anaerobic wetlands are less densely planted than aerobic wetlands. The usual method of estimating the extent and cost of vegetation is to determine the percentage of the total wetland area that will be planted. If specific criteria are not available, the percentage of the wetland area that is planted can be assumed as 33% for anaerobic wetlands and 50% for aerobic wetlands.

Related Costs

Passive water treatment technology implementation may include other costs not directly estimated as part of the passive water treatment system, such as:

Land Acquisition: If adequate land is not available to construct a passive water system on site, then acquisition of adjacent property may be required.

Airport Storm Drainage Piping: The passive water systems described in this section presume that storm water drainage piping is in place, and the storm water has been collected to the point of a headwall. In some cases, the stormwater piping may not be in place or included in estimates for a new or improved airfield. If so, then the cost for collection and distribution piping and associated inlets, manholes, lift stations and other system elements needs to be included in the estimate.

Backup Treatment: Backup treatment systems may be needed to either treat or store water that has not been adequately treated by the passive systems, particularly if systems are not designed to handle higher-capacity storm events. Backup treatment may also be a regulatory requirement.

Sludge Removal: Periodic sludge removal may be required for some systems to keep the wetland operating properly or to prevent filling in of retention ponds. In some cases, this sludge could be contaminated or even classified as hazardous waste. Costs for removal of sludge and secondary treatment or disposal should be considered and included in estimates of construction and operating cost.

Sludge Hauling and Disposal: If sludge removal is required, then costs for sludge hauling and disposal should also be included as appropriate.

Treatment of Compost: Compost is used in some types of passive water systems as a filtration media. For open-top systems, this compost must be removed and replaced periodically, approximately every 4 years. In some cases, depending on the nature of contaminants being treated, the compost must be treated as a contaminated or possibly hazardous waste prior to disposal or re-use.

Groundwater Monitoring: Groundwater monitoring may be required for some classes of passive water systems, particularly wetlands. Monitoring ensures that the passive water treatment is not contaminating an underlying aquifer. If monitoring is required, groundwater-monitoring wells may be needed. (See Chapters 56 and 57 for these cost elements.)

Surface Water/Sludge Monitoring: This type of monitoring is commonly required to ensure that waste streams are within permitted limits. (See Chapter 57 for estimating monitoring costs.)

Site Work and Utilities

If site work and utilities apply, they must also be accounted for in the estimate. Site work and utilities applicable for dewatering may include:

- Security fencing and signage
- Access roads
- Electric power (to supply monitoring wells, if required)

Conclusion

Passive water systems are designed to operate with minimal maintenance and upkeep. These systems are efficient from an operating cost perspective because no utilities are required, there is generally no residual hazardous waste to be treated or disposed of, and because the systems use a "natural approach" to remediation. (In the case of storm run-off, the systems meet requirements imposed by most state governments that stormwater be retained and treated on-site rather than discharged to a municipal collection system requiring waste water treatment.) Because of these attributes, passive water systems are an attractive and generally cost-effective option. However, these systems do require relatively large parcels of land in many cases, which may be expensive and perhaps impossible in urban areas. The benefits and challenges must be weighed against active treatment systems that are generally more expensive to operate, but more compact.

Chapter 30

Phytoremediation

Phytoremediation is the name given to a set of technologies that use plants to clean contaminated sites. Phytoremediation uses living plants for in situ and ex situ remediation of contaminated soil, sludges, sediments, and groundwater through contaminant removal, degradation, or containment. Phytoremediation has been used to treat the following types of contaminants: metals, pesticides, solvents, explosives, and polycyclic aromatic hydrocarbons. Phytoremediation has been used for point and non-point source hazardous waste control.

Applications and Limitations

Applications

Phytoremediation applications are shown in Figure 30.1. Applications are classified based on contaminant fate, degradation, extraction, contaminant, or a combination of these.

In practice only a few of these compounds have been proven to be feasibly treatable in pilot scale field treatments. Most have been proven feasible in laboratory pilots. A few are extrapolated as being feasible from studies of similar compounds.

Limitations

There are a number of limitations to phytoremediation.

- It is limited to shallow soils, streams, and groundwater. Sites where contamination is relatively deep and those with pools of nonaqueous phase liquids (NAPL) would not be good applications.
- High concentrations of hazardous materials can be toxic to plants, and phytoremediation may fail in these instances.
- Climatic or seasonal conditions may interfere or inhibit plant growth, slow remediation efforts, or increase the length of the treatment period. Winter operations may pose problems for phytoremediation when deciduous vegetation loses its leaves, transformation and uptake cease, and soil water is no longer transpired.
- Contamination may be transferred across media, e.g., from soil to air.

Type of Phytoremediation	Process Involved	Contaminant Treated*
Phytoextraction, phytoaccumulation, or hyperaccumulation	Metals and organic chemicals taken up by the plant with water, or by cation pumps, sorption, and other mechanisms.	Nickel, zinc, lead, chromium, cadmium, other heavy metals, selenium, radionuclides, BTEX (benzene, toluene, ethylbenzene, and xylenes), pentachlorophenol, short-chained aliphatic compounds, and other organic compounds
Rhizofiltration or contaminant uptake	Compounds taken up or sorbed by roots (or sorbed to algae and bacteria)	Heavy metals, radionuclides, and hydrophobic organic chemicals
Phytostabilization	Plants control pH, soil gases and redox conditions in soil and mine tailing ponds that change speciation. Humification of some organic compounds is expected.	Proven for heavy metals in mine tailing ponds and expected for phenols, chlorinated solvents (tetrachloromethane and trichloromethane) and hydrophobic organics
Rhizosphere Bioremediation, rhizodegradation, phytostimulation, or plant-assisted bioremediation	Plant exudates, root necrosis, and other processes provide organic carbon and nutrients to spur soil bacteria growth by two or more orders of magnitude in number. Exudates stimulate enzyme induction and cometabolic degradation by mycorrhizal fungi and microbes. Roots provide diverse habitat and retard chemical movement. Live roots can pump oxygen to aerobes and dead roots may support anaerobes.	Polyaromatic hydrocarbons, BTEX, and other petroleum hydrocarbons, perchlorate, atrazine, alachlor, polychlorinated biphenyl (PCB), and other organic compounds
Phytotransformation or phytodegradation	Aquatic and terrestrial plants take up, store, and biochemically degrade organic compounds to harmless byproducts, products used to create new plant biomass, or byproducts that are further broken down by microbes and other processes to less harmful products. Growth and senescence enzymes, sometimes in series, are used by certain plants in metabolism or detoxification of compounds. Reductive and oxidative enzymes may be used in series in different parts of the plant.	Munitions (TNT, DNT, HMX, nitrobenzene, picric acid, nitrotoluene), atrizine, chlorinated solvents (trichloromethane, hexachloroethane, carbon tetrachloride), methyl bromide, tetrabromoethane, tetrachloroethane, dichloroethane, DDT and other chlorine and phosphorous based pesticides, polychlorinated biphenols, and phenols and nitrites.

Figure 30.1 Types of Phytoremediation

- Phytoremediation is not effective for strongly sorbed (e.g., PCBs) and weakly sorbed contaminants.
- Degradation of organics may be limited by mass transfer capacity. This is because the desorption and mass transport of chemicals from soil particles to the aqueous phase, which is how the contaminants move from the soil into the vegetation, is limited and may become the rate-determining step.
- Phytoremediation will likely require a large surface area of land.
- Phytoremediation is unfamiliar to regulators. It is still being tested and has not been completely proven as a remediation technique.

Typical System Design Elements

The Ground-Water Remediation Technologies Analysis Center defines and provides applications for five types of phytoremediation.

- Phytotransformation
- Rhizosphere Bioremediation
- Phytostabilization
- Phytoextraction
- Rhizofiltration

Phytotransformation

Phytotransformation refers to the uptake of organic and nutrient contaminants from soil and groundwater and the subsequent transformation by plants. Phytotransformation depends on the direct uptake of contaminants from soil, water, and the accumulation of metabolites in plant tissue. For environmental application, it is important that the metabolites which accumulate in vegetation be non-toxic or at least significantly less toxic than the parent compound.

Potential applications include phytotransformation of petrochemical sites and storage areas, ammunition wastes, fuel spills, chlorinated solvents, landfill leachates, and agricultural chemicals (pesticides and fertilizers). Many times, phytoremediation is not the sole treatment option, but rather it is used in conjunction with other approaches, such as removal actions, ex situ treatment of highly contaminated wastes, or as a polishing treatment.

Oxygen, water, and carbon transport mechanisms can vary among plant species. Plants supply oxygen to the soil rhizosphere, but roots also demand oxygen for respiration. Root turnover is a key mechanism that adds organic carbon to the soil profile. Seedlings in the laboratory can transport considerable quantities of oxygen to roots in the rhizosphere (0.5 mol^2 per m^2 of soil surface per day).[1] Plants are able to take up contaminants directly from the soil water or release exudates that help to degrade organic pollutants via co-metabolism in the rhizosphere. *(See "Rhizosphere Bioremediation" in the next section of this chapter.)*

Another form of phytotransformation is *phytovolatilization*, whereby volatile chemicals or their metabolic products are released to the atmosphere through plant transpiration. The transfer of contaminants from the soil or groundwater to the atmosphere is not as desirable as in situ degradation, but it may be preferable to prolonged exposure in the soil environment and the risk of groundwater contamination.

Rhizosphere Bioremediation

Phytoremediation of the rhizosphere increases soil organic carbon, bacteria, and mycorrhizal fungi, all factors that encourage degradation of organic chemicals in soil. Rhizosphere bioremediation is also known as *phytostimulation* or *plant-assisted bioremediation.* J.L. Jordahl, L.A. Licht, and J.L. Schnoor in *Riparian Poplar Tree Buffer Impact on Agricultural Non-Point Source Pollution,* showed that the numbers of beneficial bacteria increased in the root zone of hybrid poplar trees relative to an unplanted reference site.[2] Denitrifiers, *Pseudonomad* spp., BTEX degrading organisms, and general heterotrophs were enhanced. Also, plants may release exudates to the soil environment that help to stimulate the degradation of organic chemicals by inducing enzyme systems of existing bacterial populations, stimulating growth of new species that are able to degrade the wastes, and/or increasing soluble substrate concentrations for all microorganisms. Researchers have characterized the molecular weight distribution of organic exudates from root systems of hybrid poplar trees. Exudates include short chain organic acids, phenolics, and small concentrations of high molecular weight compounds (enzymes and proteins).

Phytostabilization

Phytostabilization primarily refers to immobilizing toxic contaminants in soils. Establishment of rooted vegetation may also prevent windblown dust, an important pathway for human exposure at hazardous waste sites. Phytostabilization is especially applicable for metal contaminants at waste sites where the best alternative is often to hold contaminants in place. Metals do not ultimately degrade, so capturing them *in situ* is sometimes the best alternative at sites with low contamination levels (below risk thresholds) or in vast, contaminated areas where a large-scale removal action or other *in situ* remediation is not feasible. Plants cannot die or be removed during the phytostabilization design period. Low-level radionuclide contaminants can also be held in place by phytostabilization, and this alternative can result in significant risk reduction if their half-lives are relatively short. Cadmium is readily translocated to leaves in many plants, which represents a risk to the food chain, and this pathway may be the limiting consideration in applying phytostabilization at some metals-contaminated sites.

Phytoextraction

Phytoextraction refers to the use of metal-accumulating plants that translocate and concentrate metals from the soil in roots and above ground shoots or leaves. Phytoextraction may offer cost advantages over alternative schemes of soil excavation and treatment or disposal. An important issue in phytoextraction is whether the metals can be economically recovered from the plant tissue or whether disposal of the waste is required. Design considerations include the accumulation factor (ratio of metal in the plant tissue to that in the soil) and the plant productivity (kg of dry matter that is harvestable each season). In order to have a practicable treatment alternative, one needs a vigorously growing plant (>3 tons dry matter/hectares per year) that is easily harvested and which accumulates large concentrations of metal in the harvestable portion (>1,000 mg/kg metal).

As a general rule, readily bioavailable metals for plant uptake include cadmium, nickel, zinc, arsenic, selenium, and copper. Moderately bioavailable metals are cobalt, manganese, and iron; while lead, chromium, and uranium are not very bioavailable. Lead can be made significantly more bioavailable by the addition of EDTA to soils. Lead, chromium, and uranium can be removed by binding to soils and root mass via rhizofiltration.

Rhizofiltration/Constructed Wetlands

Rhizofiltration refers to the use of plant roots to sorb, concentrate, and precipitate metal contaminants from the surface or groundwater. Roots of plants are capable of sorbing large quantities of lead and chromium from soil water or from water that is passed through the root zone of densely growing vegetation. The potential for treatment of radionuclide contaminants has received a great deal of attention in the press. Rhizofiltration has been employed by Phytotech® using sunflowers at a U.S. Department of Energy (DOE) pilot project with uranium wastes at Ashtabula, Ohio, and on water from a pond near the Chernobyl nuclear plant in the Ukraine.

Constructed wetlands have been engineered and maintained to support plants and microbial consortia. Groundwater or waste water is pumped through the system for the removal of contaminants by microorganisms and rhizofiltration.

Phytoremediation Design

Design of a phytoremediation system varies according to the contaminants, the conditions at the site, the level of clean-up required, and the plants used (Phytoremediation Technology Evaluation, Schnoor). A thorough site characterization will provide the needed data to design any type of remediation system. Clearly, phytoextraction has different design requirements than phytostabilization or rhizodegradation. Nevertheless, it is possible to specify a few design considerations that are a part of most phytoremediation efforts. Site characterization data will provide the information required for the designer to develop a properly functioning system. The design considerations include:

- Plant selection
- Literature review
- Treatability study
- Irrigation, agronomic inputs, and maintenance
- Groundwater capture zone and transpiration rate
- Contaminant uptake rate and clean-up time required

Design Elements
Plant Selection

Plants are selected according to the application and the contaminants of concern. For phytotransformation of organics, the design requirements are that vegetation is fast growing and hardy, easy to plant and maintain, and transforms the contaminant concern to non-toxic or less toxic products. In temperate climates, phreatophytes (e.g., hybrid poplar, willow, cottonwood, aspen) are often selected because of fast growth, a deep rooting ability down to the surface of groundwater, large transpiration rates, and the fact that they are native throughout most of the country. A screening test or knowledge from the literature of plant attributes will aid the design engineer in the selection of plants.

Plants used in phytoextraction include sunflowers and Indian mustard for lead; *Thaspi caerulescens* for zinc, cadmium, and nickel; and sunflowers and certain aquatic plants for radionuclides. Two categories of aquatic plants are used in constructed wetlands applications: emergent and submerged species.[3] Emergent vegetation transpires water and is easier to harvest if required. Submerged species do not transpire water, but provide more biomass for the uptake and sorption of contaminants.

Plant Density and Pattern

Planting density depends on the application. Louis Licht of Ecolotree, Inc. has pioneered the use of hybrid poplar trees as riparian zone buffer strips, landfill caps, and at hazardous waste sites. For hybrid poplar trees, 1,000–2,000 trees per acre are typically planted with a conventional tree planter at 12–18" depth or in trenched rows 1–6' deep. Poplars have the ability to root along the entire buried depth. If a row configuration is used, the trees may be spaced with 2' between them and 10' between rows. The poplars are planted simply as "sticks," long cuttings that will root and grow rapidly in the first season. Several phreatophytes in the Salix family, such as willow and cottonwood, can be planted in a similar manner. Hardwood trees and evergreens may require a lower planting density initially. A high planting density can result in an increased rate of evaportranspiration.

Option for Utilizing Wax Tubes and Perforated Polyethylene Piping

One option for promoting accelerated root growth to the depth of contaminated groundwater includes the use of wax tubes and perforated polyethylene piping. Trees are sometimes planted in wax tubes which extend from the ground surface to approximately one-third of the depth to groundwater. These wax tubes promote downward growth of the tree roots. In addition, a perforated polyethylene pipe is placed with each tree within the wax tube. The perforated polyethylene pipe extends from about one foot above the ground surface all the way down to the capillary fringe of the groundwater surface. This piping allows atmospheric air to the subsurface that promotes continued root growth to the groundwater (see Figure 30.2).

Cost assemblies are available in the *ECHOS Environmental Remediation Cost Books* to estimate the cost for this option. In general, the quantity (in feet) required for the wax tubes would be:

(number of trees) × (depth to groundwater) × .33

The quantity (in feet) required for perforated polyethylene pipe would be:

(number of trees) × (depth to groundwater + 1)

Additional Groundwater Decision Tree Information

The information listed below will assist you in determining whether the contaminated site's groundwater is a candidate for phytoremediation.

- Site characterization is needed to determine whether the groundwater and contaminants are within root-depth range of the plants or trees to be used.
- If the groundwater is to be pumped to the surface and then applied to the plants (some form of irrigation), state regulations must be reviewed. There may be restrictions on the use of contaminated water for irrigation.
- Greenhouse studies of selected plants may be required to determine the ability of candidate plant species to survive in the

contaminated environment. Determining which plant reacts best is based on a number of different requirements.

- The accumulation of waste in the plants may present a problem with contaminants entering the food chain. Relative concentrations of contaminants in the plant tissue must be determined. Proper harvest and disposal methods must be developed and approved by regulatory agencies.

- Transpiration of heavy metals, such as mercury, or organic contaminants (TCE) must be evaluated to determine if the process creates a hazard to human health or the environment.

- The octanol-water partition coefficient (log K_{ow}) of the organic contaminant should be between 1–3.5 (moderately hydrophobic organic chemicals) to be susceptible to uptake by plants. Hydrophobic chemicals (log K_{ow} > 3.5) are bound too strongly to roots and soil to be translocated within the plants. Water-soluble chemicals (log K_{ow} < 1.0) are not sufficiently sorbed to roots nor actively transported through plant membranes.

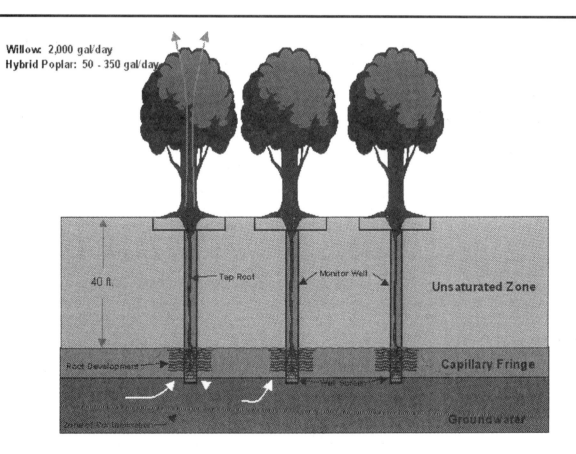

Figure 30.2 Phytoremediation for Deep Water Table Conditions

- Hydraulic control is a form of containment. Groundwater contaminant plume control may be achieved through water consumption in plants that increase evaporation and transpiration from a site. Trees and other plants can be used as inexpensive solar pumps that use the energy of the sun to raise contaminated water to the surface.
- Phytoremediation takes a very long time to reach final cleanup levels. If the cleanup is time-critical, phytoremediation may not be a suitable option.

Additional Soil Decision Tree Information

The information listed below will help to determine whether the contaminated site's soil is a candidate for phytoremediation.

- A thorough site characterization will determine if the contaminant or contaminants are within the range of the plants, typically 1–2' below ground surface.
- Experiments are underway using deep rooting plants (up to 5'), such as Prairie Grass. Rhizodegradation of organics at these depths is under investigation.
- Plants can remove metals, radionuclides, and certain organic compounds (petroleum hydrocarbons) from soil by direct uptake.
- Greenhouse studies of selected plants may be required to determine the ability of the candidate plant species to survive in the contaminated environment. The greenhouse studies will identify the best candidate plant species for the site.
- "Hot spots" may exist on the site which include high concentration areas of contamination. These hot spots may be toxic to plants and would reduce or even eliminate the use of phytoremediation. In these instances, it must be determined if they can be economically treated or removed. Removal of the phytotoxic hot spots will make phytoremediation an option to "polish" the site and remove the remaining contamination.
- The accumulation of waste in the plants may present a problem with contaminants entering the food chain or cause the plants to become a secondary waste disposal issue. The relative concentrations of contaminants in the plant tissue must be determined, and proper disposal methods established and approved by regulatory personnel.
- Plants that transpire heavy metals, such as mercury or organic contaminants (TCE), may create a hazard to human health or the environment. The transpiration products will need to be evaluated to determine if they are a hazard.
- Phytoremediation may take longer than traditional methods to reach final cleanup levels. Site characterization data should allow the phytoremediation designer to estimate the cleanup time.

Additional Sediment Decision Tree Information

The information listed below must be considered when using the decision tree for phytoremediation of sediments.

- Dredging activities and dredged sediments (also known as dredge spoils) are regulated by the U.S. Army Corps of Engineers and will have regulatory requirements beyond those for groundwater and soil.
- Normally, dredge spoils are held in holding ponds behind 50' high

dikes. It can take up to 20 years for the spoil material to dry sufficiently for final disposal. Innovative use of thinner "lifts" of dredge spoil and lower dikes allows the material to settle out faster.

- Dredge spoils normally lack organic matter, which is washed out by the process that creates the spoils.
- Dredge spoils normally pick up salt from seawater and become highly acidic when removed from the water and exposed to the air.
- If the contaminants are to be treated in-place or in a constructed wetland, state regulations must be reviewed. Different regulatory agencies may be involved in constructed wetlands as in-place treatment.
- There may be public opposition to treating dredge spoil as a soil or creating a wetland with the spoil material. There has been a great deal of public opposition to having dredge spoil used for other projects. The normal course of events is to have the dredge spoil dumped at sea or land-filled. There are restrictions on these activities also as the contaminants are not treated, they are just moved away from contact with people
- An example of creating a large wetland using dredge spoil is the Sonoma Baylands project. This project in the San Francisco Bay used 2.7 million tons of dredged material to restore 348 acres of tidal wetlands.

Seeding Mixture

Selection of a seed mixture and planting protocol needs to be site-specific. There is no substitute for understanding the local environmental conditions, soil properties, and contaminant characteristics at a site. In addition, there is usually a wealth of local knowledge of what grows well in an area from local sources including, but not limited to, county agricultural extension office, state universities, state agricultural agencies, local USDA and soil conservation service offices, and local seed suppliers.

For phytoremediation, an important consideration is contaminant composition and concentration. At lower contamination levels, many species grow quite well. At high TPH levels, however, phytotoxicity may limit seed germination and plant growth. This problem can be addressed by selecting species that are more petroleum hydrocarbon-tolerant, and by increasing seeding rates. Depending on the site, it may be useful to run germination trials prior to seeding a site to determine if plants will establish, and if seeding rates should be increased to accommodate an expected low rate of germination.

Time of Planting

Time of planting should be determined by local conditions, the availability of moisture for seed germination, and plant species characteristics. Warm-season species will often need to be established in the spring. Cool-season species are often established best in late summer or fall, though some of these can be spring-seeded. Again, site specific considerations are important. Seed germination requires good seed-soil contact under moist conditions and the appropriate temperature for a given species.

Seeding Rates

In general, planting conditions at contaminated sites will be more stressful than most agricultural fields and landscaping situations. Accordingly, seeding rates should usually be higher than recommended for other purposes, perhaps doubling the seeding rates recommended for lawn establishment in the area when seeding tall fescue. If contamination levels affect germination and seedling growth, then seeding rates may need to be even higher. Another important influence on seeding rate is water availability. Under irrigation and higher rainfall conditions, plant populations can be denser than under drier conditions. This suggests higher seeding rates for wetter conditions because more plants can be supported under these conditions, thus accelerating the phytoremediation process.

Following is a sample seeding mixture (and rates) composed of tall fescue, annual rye grass, and legume:

- 8 lbs/1,000 S.F. tall fescue
- 2 lbs/1,000 S.F. annual rye grass
- 1 lb/1,000 S.F. legume (such as white clover, yellow sweet clover, or birdsfoot trefoil)

This example is a rather high seeding rate, similar to a mixture used under natural rainfall conditions with average annual natural rainfall rates of about 40–50" per year. Local conditions need to be considered.

Mixtures involving native plants or trees will require site-specific considerations. Seeding rates for native mixtures will often be much lower than the example given above.

Basic Information Needed for Estimating

It is possible to create a reasonable cost estimate using a few required parameters. More detailed information can provide for a more precise and site-specific estimate using a secondary set of parameters. To estimate the cost of phytoremediation systems, the following information must be known.

Contaminated Media

These parameters consist of the media of concern including **soil**, **ground water**, and **surface water**. Any one or combination of these can be the driver for the system definition.

Fencing

Fencing is commonly used in phytoremediation systems. Because phytoremediation sites are generally large, fencing can be a major cost item. Typical choices for fencing, if required, include 6' galvanized chain-link fence, barbed-wire, or wood privacy fencing.

Site Distance

This is the average distance to the site that the contractor's crew has to travel. The site distance drives worker productivity and mobilization costs.

Safety Level

Level E is the appropriate default value for most sites where phytoremediation is appropriate. Worker safety is affected by the contaminant(s) at the site. Safety level refers to the 4 levels required by OSHA in 29 CFR Part 1910: A, B, C, and D; where "A" is the most protective, and "D" is the least protective. A safety level of E is also included to simulate normal construction, "no hazard" conditions as prescribed by the EPA.

The following sections provide specific information needed to prepare estimates depending on the contaminated media.

Required Information: Surface Water
The following information is needed if the system is used to treat surface water.

Flow Rate to Area Conversion Factor
The Flow Rate to Area Conversion Factor is used to determine the area of the constructed wetland. The flow rate, measured in gallons per minute (GPM) is multiplied by the Flow Rate to Area Conversion Factor to arrive at the area of the constructed wetland, measured in acres. If field demonstrations have not been performed, a default value of 0.025 GPM/acre can generally be used for estimating purposes. The typical valid range for the Flow Rate to Area Conversion Factor is 0.0004–0.100 GPM/acre. Figure 30.3 shows conversions for the Flow Rate to Area Conversion Factor in terms of GPM per acre.

Type of Contaminant
Possible contaminants include:

- Acids/Caustics
- Fuels
- Low-Level Radioactive
- Metals
- Ordnance (Not Residual)
- Ordnance (Residual)
- PCBs
- Pesticides
- Semi-Organic Volatile Organic Compounds (SVOCs)
- Volatile Organic Compounds (VOCs)
- Other

The **Type of Contaminant** can be "none."

Required Information: Groundwater
System Approach
There are two types of approaches available in application of phytoremediation to groundwater: in situ and ex situ.

In Situ. The in situ option assumes that the phytoremediation project will be performed in situ (in place) by planting trees. In situ systems

---

Figure 30.3 Flow Rate to Area Conversion Factors

0.100	= 10 GPM/acre
0.025	= 40 GPM/acre (default)
0.004	= 250 GPM/acre

can be used where the depth to groundwater is 3–19', and the depth to the base of contamination is 3–20'. The tree options are as follows:

- 3' Whip—(assume 1,500 whips per acre)
- 5' Tree—(assume 150–5' trees per acre)
- 15' Tree—(assume 50–15' trees per acre)

The tree size options allow selection of the type of vegetation that will be used at the site. The 3' whip will be the least expensive approach, but will take longer for the roots to grow to be effective. The 15' tree is more expensive, but will take a shorter period of time for the roots to be effective in their uptake of contaminants. This is an important point to consider for depth of contamination as well. If the contamination depth is deeper than a few feet, consider using either 5' or 15' trees so that the roots will be able to reach the contamination.

Wax tubes and plastic pipes can be used to enhance root growth. The wax tube forces the roots to grow down towards the contamination for its moisture. The plastic pipe is used to aid in the aerating of the tree roots and bioremediation process.

Ex Situ. The ex situ option assumes that the contaminated groundwater will be pumped up to the surface, with a wetland area constructed to remediate the groundwater. If an ex situ approach is selected, the project will usually involve a constructed wetland area. The depth to groundwater valid range is 3–600', and the depth to base of contamination valid range is 3–750'.

Area of Remediation
The Area of Remediation is the area that will be remediated with trees, not the overall site area. Choices include:

- **Full Coverage** assumes that there will be trees placed throughout the area of remediation.
- **Hydraulic Control** assumes that there will be trees placed on only approximately 25% of the remediation area.

Groundwater Contamination
Depth of Groundwater: valid range is 3–600'.

Depth to Base of Contamination: valid range is 3–750'.

Contaminant Type
Possible contaminants are the same as listed for Surface Water Contamination in the previous section. Again, the type of contaminant may be listed as "none."

Required Information: Soil
Depth to Contamination
The typical valid range is 0–2'. For soils, the types of plants that are most effective at phytoremediation have a maximum root penetration of 2'. Therefore this is the limiting depth. If deeper contamination exists beyond possible root penetration, then excavation of the soils and placement in some type of phytoremediation treatment cell should be considered.

Area of Contamination
The area is the basis for determining how many plants are required and the irrigation requirements.

Type of Contamination

This item documents the basis for type of plants and sampling requirements. The list of possible contaminants is the same as listed in the "Groundwater" section earlier in this chapter. As with groundwater and surface water contaminants, the type of contaminant can be listed as "none."

Irrigation

Irrigation options include:

Existing Service Connection: This option assumes that there is an existing connection available for irrigation at the site. The following items would be included in the soil costs:

- Full Circle Sprinkler Head, 30' Diameter
- 1,000 Gallon Nalgene Horizontal XLPE Tank without legs
- Portable Water Pump, 2", 10,000 GPH, Gas-Powered, with wheels
- Utilities Hook-up Fee
- 2" Polyethylene, flexible piping, SDR15, 125 psi

Extraction Well: This option assumes that extraction wells will need to be installed to obtain water for irrigating the plants. The number of extraction wells should be based on the following criteria (and similarly up to 180 acres):

- 0 to $\leq$ 5 Acres = 1 Well
- >5 to $\leq$ 10 Acres = 2 Wells
- >10 to $\leq$ 15 Acres = 3 Wells

None: This option assumes that irrigation is not required for the plants in the phytoremediation project and adds no additional costs to the soil cost.

Required Information: Constructed Wetlands

The following items are required information for estimating if a wetland area is proposed to remediate the contaminated surface water.

Constructed Wetland Area

The overall area of the wetland, which drives excavation and construction costs.

Flow Rate

The typical valid range is 1–500 GPM. The flow rate represents the flow of water through the wetland, which will either increase or decrease the size of the wetland area.

Additional Area Required for Operation Under Cold-Temperature Conditions

The required area of the constructed wetland is based on the flow-rate of water requiring treatment. A rule of thumb is 1 acre per 40 GPM. Specific area is defined as the area of land required for the constructed wetland to treat a specified flow rate of water. The rule of thumb value assumes that the constructed wetlands system will operate at near optimum temperature (i.e., a constant temperature of about 20 °C).

Biodegradation is one of the primary removal mechanisms for organic contaminants in constructed wetlands systems. However, biodegradation rates are temperature-dependent. Over a temperature range from about 5–25 °C, biodegradation rates decrease by about 50%

for each 10 °C decrease in temperature. The default specific area value mentioned above (1 acre per 40 GPM) assumes a water temperature of about 20 °C (68°F). However, if temperatures decrease during winter, a greater area will be required to achieve the same amount of treatment at the design flow rate. For example, a system operating at a water temperature of 10 °C (50°F) will require about twice the area of that required at 20 °C (68°F). Figure 30.4 provides recommended additional area requirements for operation of constructed wetlands systems under reduced temperature conditions.

Removal of contaminants in constructed wetlands may occur through both biotic and abiotic mechanisms. For contaminants that are removed primarily via abiotic processes, the removal rates are usually less strongly dependent on temperature. Thus for some types of contaminants (e.g., some metals), additional area may not be required for operation of constructed wetlands systems under reduced-temperature conditions. Technical staff should always be consulted during preparation of cost estimates that involve the design of constructed wetlands systems.

Loading Rate Conversion Factor

The Loading Rate to Area Conversion Factor is used to determine the area of the constructed wetland. The flow rate, measured in gallons per minute (GPM) is multiplied by Loading Rate to Area Conversion Factor to arrive at the area of the constructed wetland, measured in acres. If field demonstrations have not been performed, a default value of 0.025 GPM/acre can generally be used for estimating purposes. The typical valid range for the Flow Rate to Area Conversion Factor is 0.0004–0.100 GPM/acre. Figure 30.3 shows conversions for the Flow Rate to Area Conversion Factor in terms of GPM per acre.

It must be emphasized that design of constructed wetlands for the types of contaminants encountered on most environmental remediation projects is empirical. Although there are design equations for parameters, such as biochemical oxygen demand (BOD) and ammonia, design for other contaminants almost always requires laboratory and pilot studies. Typically, the specific area value for the constructed wetland will increase as the concentration of the contaminant of concern increases, and as the regulatory discharge level decreases. It should also be noted that there are some types of contaminants that are not amenable to treatment using constructed wetlands systems.

Winter Water Temperature	Additional Area Recommended
20 °C	0%
15 °C	50%
10 °C	100%
5 °C	150%
1 °C	200%

Figure 30.4 Temperature Adjustments to Wetland Size

Gravel Volume

The volume of gravel in 6" lifts, used to construct the wetland, is based on an assumption that 2' of gravel would be placed across the entire bottom of the wetland. This should be enough volume to account for potential gravel costs and allow for flexibility in the design, such as possible submerged flow areas in a portion of the wetland. If it is known that the system is expected to be completely submerged flow, then the volume of gravel can be doubled to account for gravel costs.

Other Related Costs

Capital costs for a phytoremediation system include design, excavation, soil placement, planting, irrigation systems, and associated control systems. Other items that may be required include extraction wells for irrigation water supply and replacement of trees if damaged or diseased during the remediation period, or if erosion occurs. Operating costs also include utility purchase if extraction wells and pumps are used for irrigation. Sampling and analysis testing will generally be required on a regular schedule—usually monthly for the first year, and quarterly for the duration of the treatment.

Site Work and Utilities

Site work and utilities that may apply to neutralization include:

- Access roads
- Overhead electrical distribution (if extraction wells are required)
- Fencing and signage

These must also be included in the estimate.

Conclusion

Phytoremediation is relatively inexpensive, partly because it uses the same equipment and supplies used in agriculture. Conventional engineering-based technologies for soil remediation are generally more expensive. Engineering-based approaches (e.g., soil removal, soil washing) are designed for relatively small areas with high levels of pollution. Phytoremediation, on the other hand, is ideally suited for sites where large areas of surface soil are contaminated. An important aspect of phytoremediation is that establishing vegetation on a site reduces soil erosion by wind and water, which helps prevent the spread of contaminants to other sites. Grasses appear to be ideal for phytoremediation of surface soils because their fibrous root systems form a continuous dense rhizosphere.

Chapter 31

Soil Flushing

The use of soil flushing to remove soil contaminants involves flushing organic and/or inorganic constituents from in situ soils for recovery and treatment. The site or treatment area is flooded with an appropriate flushing solution, and the contaminated flushing solution is collected in a series of shallow wellpoints or subsurface drains. The flushing solution is then treated and/or recycled back into the site. The treatment area is flushed until it is completely saturated, a process that is known as a pore volume flush. Effective soil flushing may require numerous (5–50) pore volume flushes.

Applications and Limitations

Applications

- Works best in soils with high permeability, such as gravel or sand.
- May significantly increase the transport of NAPLs and the need for their subsequent removal.
- Potentially applicable to all types of soil contaminants.

Limitations

- Soil with permeabilities less than 1×10^{-3} cm/sec (1.969×10^{-3} ft/sec) are not feasible for soil flushing due to the slow infiltration rates and long cycle times.
- Underground structures or utilities may preclude the use of soil flushing.
- Soils with high levels of fracturing or preferential pathways, or soils with underground debris may preclude soil flushing.
- Groundwater quality may be adversely affected by addition of co-solvents or surfactants.
- Generally a long-term technology.

Soil Flushing Process Configurations and Treatment Train Considerations

- Soil flushing is enhanced by the use of a surfactant or a co-solvent. Surfactants promote wetting, solubilization, or emulsification of contaminants. Co-solvents enhance the solubility of some organic compounds.
- Co-solvent concentrations must be greater than 20% to cause contaminant mobilization. Surfactants operate effectively at much lower concentrations.

- The treatment area is flushed until it is completely saturated. This is known as a pore volume flush. To effectively perform soil flushing, numerous pore volume flushes (5–50) may be required.
- Flushing fluid is introduced through spraying, injection wells, infiltration galleries, or a percolation network.
- After treatment, it may be necessary to control infiltration into the treated area to prevent uncontrolled contaminant mobilization.
- Injection well permits may be required.
- Soil flushing is usually part of a treatment train involving the application of soil flushing solutions, extraction wells, water treatment, and/or biodegradation.
- Sites with a combination of contaminants with divergent properties will require complicated soil flushing process design to ensure capture of all contaminant groups.
- Pre-testing is required to determine the site-specific interaction potential of the chosen surfactants.

Typical System Design Elements

Soil flushing is not a stand-alone technology—it is a part of a treatment train involving the application of soil flushing solutions, extraction wells, water treatment, and/or biodegradation. Figure 31.1 provides an illustration of the soil flushing system discussed in this chapter.

During the flushing process, contaminants are mobilized into the flushing solution via solubilization, formation of emulsions, or chemical reaction with the flushing solution. The flushing solution must be collected to prevent uncontrolled contaminant migration through uncontaminated soil and into receiver systems, including ground and surface waters. The flushing solution may be handled in one of three ways:

- It can be recycled back through the soil for treatment by degradation, using appropriate additives and application rates for controlled biodegradation.
- It can be treated and recycled back to the soil system.
- It can be treated and discharged to a publicly owned treatment works or surface water stream.

Flushing solutions may include water, acidic aqueous solutions (sulfuric, hydrochloric, nitric, phosphoric, and carbonic acid), basic solutions (e.g., sodium hydroxide), and surfactants (e.g., alkylbenzene sulfonate). Water alone can be used to extract water-soluble or water-mobile constituents. Acidic solutions are used for metals mobilization and ultimate recovery and for basic organic constituents (including amines, ethers, and anilines). Basic solutions are used for metals (including zinc, tin, and lead), phenols, and complexing and chelating agents. Surfactants are used for neutral organics. Both inorganic and organic contaminants are suitable for soil flushing if they are sufficiently soluble in water or other cost-effective solvents.

The addition of any flushing solution to the system must be based on an understanding of the chemical reaction(s) between the solvent and solute, and the solvent and the site/soil system. Treatability testing is required to determine the interactions between the contamination, flushing solution, and soil systems. Soil flushing is applicable on soils with permeabilities of 1×10^{-3} cm/sec (2.84'/day) or greater.

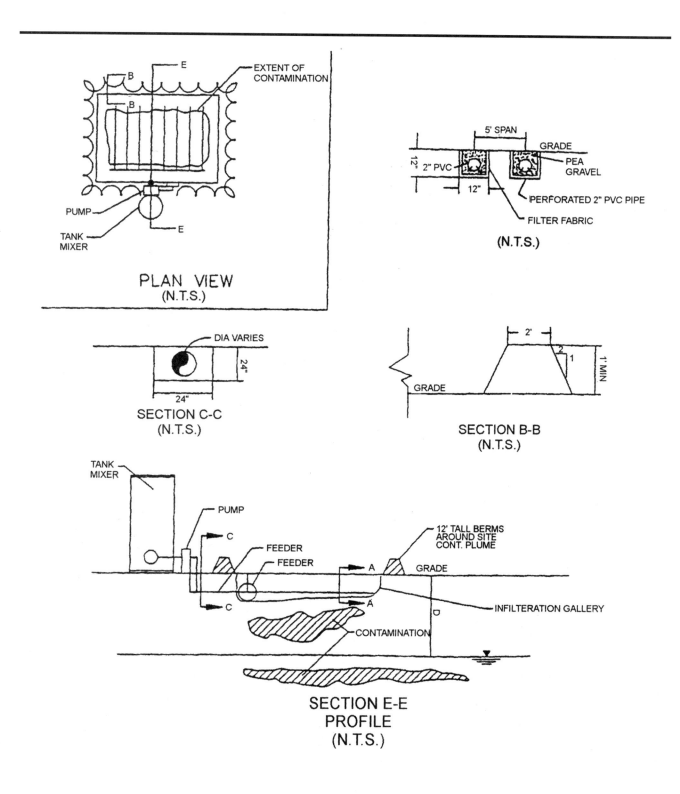

Figure 31.1 Soil Flushing Process Defaults

The soil flushing operation can be operated in temperatures below freezing if the application of the flushing solutions is below the frost line.

Process options for soil flushing involve the methods of applying the flushing solutions to the soils. Options include an infiltration gallery, spray irrigation system, injection wells, or simply flooding the surface. For distributing flushing solutions evenly over large areas, an infiltration gallery is used. The infiltration gallery consists of 2" perforated PVC pipe on 5' centers placed either on the land surface, beneath deposits of lower permeability, or beneath the frost line.

Basic Information Needed for Estimating

It is possible to create a reasonable cost estimate using a few required parameters. If more detailed information is known, one can create a more precise and site-specific estimate using a secondary set of parameters.

To estimate the cost of the soil flushing system, certain information must be known. This information is discussed in the following paragraphs.

Area of Contaminated Soil

The area of contaminated soil affects the cost by determining the required volume of flushing solution and quantity of PVC piping.

Depth to Groundwater/Confining Unit

Soil contamination is removed by flushing the contaminants, in solution, to the groundwater table/confining unit, where groundwater extraction wells collect the contaminated groundwater and pump it to the treatment system. The depth of contamination is not a major cost driver because the limiting factor is the groundwater interface or a confining unit, whichever is shallower. The depth to groundwater/confining unit affects the cost based on the volume of flushing solution required to completely saturate the treatment area and the time required for the flushing solution to cycle through the treatment area.

Soil Permeability

The vertical permeability of the soils in a treatment area affects remediation costs based on the amount of time required for flushing solutions to cycle through the treatment area. Soil with permeabilities of 1×10^{-3} cm/sec (2.84'/day) could accept water and surfactant flushing solutions at a rate of 3" per day. Soil with higher permeabilities—1×10^{-2} cm/sec (28.4'/day) or 1×10^{-1} cm/sec (284'/day)—would have higher infiltration and application rates, thus decreasing the time to complete the soil flushing cycles. Soil permeabilities less than 1×10^{-3} cm/sec (1.969×10^{-3} ft/min) are not feasible because of slow infiltration rates and long cycle times. The permeabilities and application rates for soil flushing are:

Permeability: 1×10^{-1} cm/sec (284'/day)

   Application Rate: 12"/day

   Typical Soil Types: Coarse sand and gravel

Permeability: 1×10^{-2} cm/sec (28.4'/day)

   Application Rate: 6"/day

   Typical Soil Types: Coarse to fine sand

Permeability: 1×10^{-3} cm/sec (2.84'/day)

Application Rate: 3"/day

Typical Soil Types: Fine to silty sand

The duration of the treatment technology varies with the soil permeability, depth of contamination, number of pore volume flushes, area of contaminated site, and porosity of the soil. A safety factor of two times the theoretical duration should be applied, assuming vertical permeability as the driving variable.

Worker Safety Level

Worker safety is affected by the contaminant(s) at the site. Safety level refers to the levels required by OSHA in 29 CFR Part 1910. The 4 levels are designated as A, B, C, and D; where "A" is the most protective, and "D" is the least protective. A safety level of E is also included to simulate normal construction, "no hazard" conditions as prescribed by the EPA.

Design Information Needed for Detailed Estimates

Following are descriptions of the types of detailed information that, when available, can add detail and accuracy to estimates. Also included are design criteria and estimating rules of thumb that the estimator typically uses to determine values that are not known, or to check information provided by others.

Flushing Solutions

The flushing solution depends on the type and concentration of the contaminant as well as the partitioning coefficient. Flushing solutions for dilute acidic solutions are assumed to have a pH of 3, whereas dilute basic solutions are assumed to be introduced into the subsurface at a pH of 10. Packed column soil tests can determine site-specific flushing solutions and associated pH. Options for soil flushing solutions are listed below:

- Water
- Surfactants and water
- Alkylbenzene sulfonate, bulk
- Acidic aqueous solutions
- Sulfuric acid solution, 220 lbs drummed liquid
- Basic aqueous solutions
- Sodium hydroxide solution, 100 lbs container

The most common flushing solution is water. Surfactant can be added to water at 0.05% by weight (0.004169 lbs/gal) to act as a soil penetrant. Surfactants for soil flushing must be approved for agricultural use. To make up the dilute acidic and basic aqueous solutions, sulfuric acid and sodium hydroxide are added to water at the rates of 4.1 lbs/1,000 gal and 1.5 lbs/1,000 gal, respectively. The appropriate chemical additive(s) is added to the water via a chemical metering/mixing system.

The cost of water is site-specific. Possible locations for process water are an upgradient well, downgradient well after water has been treated, river, lake, potable water source, etc. Where possible, a recirculating system is used in which water is extracted downgradient of the affected site and is treated through a waste water treatment system and piped back to the infiltration gallery to be flushed through the soil.

The extraction well(s) and waste water treatment system are considered separate treatment technologies and are discussed in other chapters of this book.

Number of Pore Volume Flushes

The effectiveness of soil flushing depends on the solubility of the contaminants, the concentrations of the contaminants, and the number of pore volume flushes. The number of pore volume flushes is directly related to the original contaminant concentration and the cleanup goal concentration. The greater the difference between the original contaminant concentration and the cleanup goal, the greater the number of pore volume flushes. The volume of flushing solution required for one pore volume flush is greater than the porosity volume alone because of the specific retention capacity of the soil. Specific retention capacity is the quantity of water held by molecular attraction and capillary forces to the soil particles and is expressed as a percentage of the total soil volume.

Once the specific retention capacity of the soil is reached, the remainder of the flushing solution volume will equal the porosity of the soil. The typical range of pore volume flushes is 1–20. If the number is unknown, a reasonable estimate can be based on 10 pore volume flushes. For cost estimating purposes, the soil may be assumed to have a total porosity of 30%. Therefore, 1 C.F. of soil requires approximately 2.24 gallons per pore volume flush, once the specific retentive capacity of the soil has been met.

The following example illustrates a 100' × 100' treatment area with the groundwater table/confining unit 10' below ground surface. Water and surfactants are distributed evenly over the 10,000 S.F. treatment area at an application of 3" per flushing episode (18,700 gallons). Infiltration rates of the flushing solution from the surface to the groundwater (10'), at permeabilities of 1×10^{-3} cm/sec (2.84'/day), require approximately 4 days (theoretically) to reach the ground water/ confining unit after the specific retentive capacity of the soil is met. The porosity of a soil that has a permeability of 1×10^{-3} cm/sec is approximately 30%. Thirty percent of the total volume (100,000 C.F.) multiplied by gal/C.F. (7.48 gal/C.F.) yields the total volume of flushing solution (224,400 gallons) to flush one pore volume.

Other Related Costs

Capital costs for soil flushing vary according to the area to be treated. The capital costs are the PVC piping, pumping system, and mixing tank. Operational costs include electrical costs to operate the system, costs for periodic sampling of the waste water, and surfactant costs. All costs for sampling and analysis are addressed in Chapter 57, "Monitoring." Sampling and system maintenance, with the associated labor costs, are assumed to occur once a week for the first four weeks, and once a month thereafter to gauge the system efficiency and compliance.

Other miscellaneous costs include an earth berm around the site to avoid overflow from the flushing solution as the water and surfactants are added to the infiltration gallery. In addition, demolition and disposal of the piping system are required for removing the system at the end of the project.

Site Work and Utilities

Site work and utilities that may need to be included in the estimate are:

- Water distribution
- Overhead electrical distribution
- Fencing and signage

Conclusion

Soil washing can be an effective and inexpensive method of treating contaminated soils. Cost drivers include the volume of the area to be treated, soil permeability, the cost of the flushing solution, and installation and operating costs for the extraction wells and treatment systems. The estimator can help the design team optimize the system by developing and comparing different design solutions.

Chapter 32

Soil Vapor Extraction

Soil vapor extraction (SVE) removes volatile organic compounds (VOCs) from a soil matrix. The SVE system is comprised of a series of vapor extraction wells, commonly called *vapor extraction points* (VEPs), monitoring wells, and air blowers that draw air through the soil and into the VEPs. The SVE system also includes piping to collect the extracted air and mechanisms to remove contaminants from the extracted air. SVE is well suited for treating soil under structures where soil excavation is impractical.

Soil vapor extraction (SVE) is an in situ process for the removal of volatile organic compounds (VOCs) from vadose (unsaturated) zone soils. The system consists of a series of vapor extraction wells, commonly called vapor extraction points (VEPs), monitoring wells (MWs), and air blowers to draw air through the soil and into the VEPs. It also includes piping to collect the extracted air, and systems to remove contaminants from the extracted air. SVE is well suited to the treatment of soil located under structures where soil excavation would be impractical. Dewatering is not commonly used in the construction of the SVE system unless the site has a perched water table, and contamination extends below the layer on which the groundwater is perched.

Applications and Limitations

Applications

- Removes Volatile Organic Compounds (VOCs) like TCE, benzene, and toluene, and some fuels from contaminated soils in the vadose zone.
- Generally applies only to volatile compounds with a dimensionless Henry's Law (H) constant greater than 10 atm/mole fraction or a vapor pressure greater than 0.02"-Hg.
- Vertical extraction wells are typically used at contaminated zone depths ranging from 5–300'.
- Horizontal SVE wells may be applicable for extraction of vapors under buildings or structures.
- Can remove volatile contaminants near or under structures.
- Often induces in situ biodegradation of low-volatility organic compounds.

- Can be used to treat large areas with minimal site disturbance.
- Can be used for saturated soils if dewatering is practical.

Limitations

- Effectiveness limited in heterogeneous soils where the airflow may not contact all target soil zones.
- Process hindered in soils with high clay or moisture content (low air permeability).
- Not commonly used in consolidated soils.
- Effectiveness limited in soils with high organic content or extremely dry soil. (Both conditions cause high sorption capacity of VOCs.)
- Low soil temperatures reduce a contaminant's tendency to volatilize, thereby reducing the effectiveness of SVE.
- Will not remove heavy oils, metals, PCBs, or dioxins.

Extraction Process Configurations and Treatment Train Considerations

SVE applications are affected by contaminant, soil, and climatic issues. Some key considerations that affect design and operation of SVE systems include:

- Following a SVE treatment phase, many SVE systems can be operated at reduced flow rates to achieve additional contaminant reductions by biodegradation.
- Treatment requirements (and discharge permits and requirements) for extracted vapor depend on location-specific regulations. In some locations, direct discharge may be allowed for low daily organics loading (e.g., < 1 lb/day) or for low vapor concentrations (e.g., < 0.1 ppm total organics).
- For organic vapor concentrations lower than 200 ppm, vapor phase carbon adsorption may be cost-effective for treating SVE off-gas.
- For organic vapor concentrations exceeding 200 ppm, thermal oxidation or catalytic oxidation may be cost-effective for treating SVE off-gas.
- For organic vapor concentrations exceeding 10,000 ppm, internal combustion engines (ICE) may be cost-effective for treating SVE off-gas.
- Surface capping or sealing may be needed for shallow SVE systems where air can be drawn from the surface, causing "short circuiting" and reduced effectiveness from collection of subsurface vapors.
- Condensate from SVE may be a significant stream for treatment and/or waste management depending on the moisture content of site soils.
- Short-circuiting and preferential pathways can develop due to soil heterogeneity.
- SVE may be combined with groundwater pumping and treatment where contamination has reached an aquifer.

Typical System Design Elements

The physical basis for the successful application of SVE for VOC remediation is contaminant volatility, which can be expressed through *Henry's Law Constant*. According to Henry's Law, when a dilute liquid solution is in equilibrium with air, the concentration of the compound (contaminant) in the air is directly proportional to the concentration in water. This proportionality constant is Henry's Constant—a function of the compound's vapor pressure, molecular weight, and solubility. Henry's Constant represents the ratio of the concentration in air to the concentration in water at equilibrium. Thus the higher the Henry's Constant, the more easily a compound can be removed by contact with clean air. Henry's Law Constant makes air stripping and SVE viable cleanup technologies. Most vapor in the subsurface soil matrix is adsorbed to soil particles by being "attached" with water.

Factors such as soil permeability and moisture content affect the performance of SVE applications. Permeability must be sufficient to permit adequate air flow through the contaminated soil. The contaminant removal efficiency decreases as the moisture content increases. As the moisture content approaches 100% of the pore space, purging may be necessary prior to SVE.

After the extent of soil contamination is determined, a series of VEPs and associated piping for collecting the extracted vapor are installed and connected to a vacuum blower. When a vacuum is applied on the VEPs, a subsurface vacuum develops with the strongest vacuum adjacent to the VEP extraction point and decreasing vacuum as the distance from the vacuum point increases. The array of VEPs is designed to create an acceptable vacuum across the entire area of contamination. Stagnant air is forced to move toward the point of vacuum application, promoting contact with adsorbed product. Laden air (contaminated vapor) is extracted from the soil. If the soil contains excessive moisture, an air/water separator may need to be added to the system. Contaminated water removed from the air stream is either processed on site through an air stripper or disposed off site at a properly permitted treatment facility. Exhaust air may need to be treated when state or local regulations limit or prohibit the release of contaminant-laden air.

A series of monitoring wells is sometimes installed to provide soil gas samples to verify the effectiveness of the SVE process over time. Existing site monitoring wells are generally used to monitor remediation progress when groundwater is near the surface. The monitoring well and VEP screen intervals depend on the depth of contamination and depth to the water table. VEPs are installed inside the contaminated soil area, and monitoring wells are installed at strategic locations. VEPs are very similar in construction and installation to groundwater monitoring wells except that the VEP heads are sealed and connected to a vacuum system (see Figure 32.1). VEP screens are usually set above the water table and within the contaminated vadose zone; monitoring wells may be set within or outside of the contaminated zone. Throughout the remediation process, extracted vapors at each VEP are analyzed using field detection devices. At the end of remediation, soil samples are obtained and analyzed to confirm whether the soil cleanup target level has been reached.

Two types of VEP installations are widely used: vertical and horizontal. Vertical installation is most common, and is generally considered most effective at depths greater than 5'. Vertical systems are based on VEP spacing in a configuration that promotes constant airflow in the site at all affected depths. For sites over 5' deep, this approach can be very effective. Spacing is based on soil conditions.

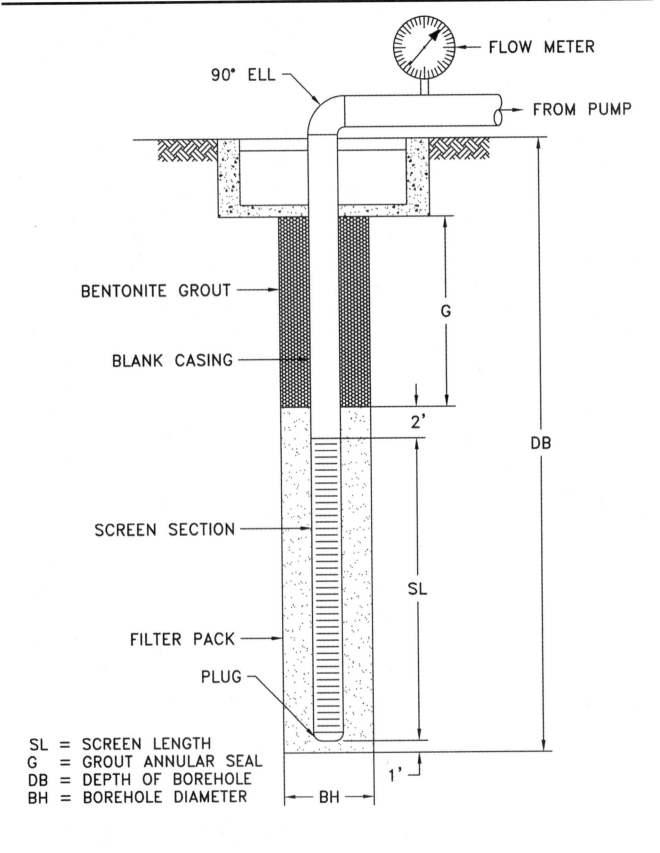

Figure 32.1 Schematic of Vertical VEP

Horizontal installation has a horizontal screened interval and is limited in depth (see Figure 32.2). Horizontal installation is often used for SVE systems situated in shallow water tables, and is most commonly used when an impervious surface layer, such as concrete or asphalt, covers the extraction point. This installation promotes horizontal airflow and limits short circuiting from air entering the subsurface directly above the extraction point. Typically, horizontal VEPs are limited to a maximum depth of 30'. Generally, the horizontal points should be located at an average depth of contamination so that soil can be treated above and below the VEPs.

Soil properties are determined during the remedial investigation stage. On the basis of contaminant characteristics and physical properties of the soil, pilot scale studies are generally designed and conducted using a limited number of VEPs to obtain vacuum and flow rate readings at the monitoring well locations. SVE pilot tests should be performed at the site because most subsurface soil matrices are non-homogeneous. Soil physical properties limit the maximum amount of air that can move through the subsurface matrix. The design goal is to determine the optimal number of VEPs per unit area and the optimal vacuum pressures. Insufficient VEP density will result in incomplete contaminant removal, and excessive VEP density will result in higher costs.

Figure 32.3 illustrates a conceptual approach to SVE. Systems are typically designed assuming a pressure gradient in a homogeneous subsurface matrix. Because it is nearly impossible to determine a precise definition of the extent of contaminated soil, SVE systems are typically over-designed so that the impacted soil is completely enveloped by the system. Subsurface soil gas surveys performed during monitoring well installation in the Remedial Investigation/Feasibility Study phase, along with pilot tests during the Remedial Design phase, provide the data necessary to best design the operational SVE system.

Basic Information Needed for Estimating

It is possible to create a reasonable cost estimate using a few required parameters. If more detailed information is known, one can create a more precise and site-specific estimate using a secondary set of parameters.

To estimate the cost of the SVE system, certain information must be known. This information is discussed in the following paragraphs.

Type of Installation
The type of installation is either vertical or horizontal VEP installation.

Area of Contaminated Soil
The area of contaminated soil is the approximate area measured in square feet of the contamination to be remediated.

Soil Type
The soil properties greatly affect the design of the SVE system. The primary controlling parameter is soil permeability, which should be sufficient to permit adequate flow of air through the contaminated matrix. The radius of influence of applied vacuum at the VEP extends over a greater distance in soils with higher permeability.

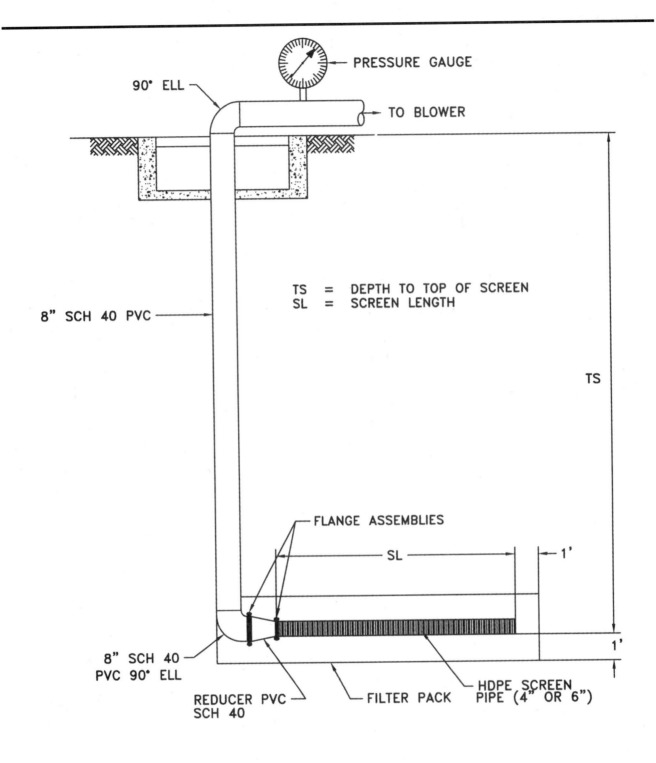

Figure 32.2 Schematic of Horizontal VEP

286

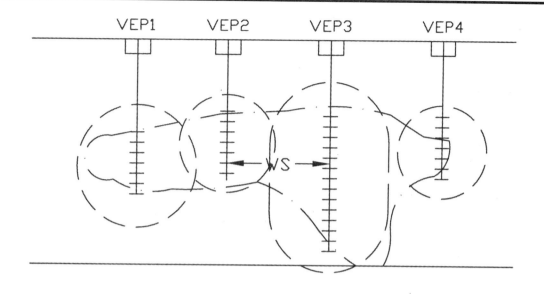

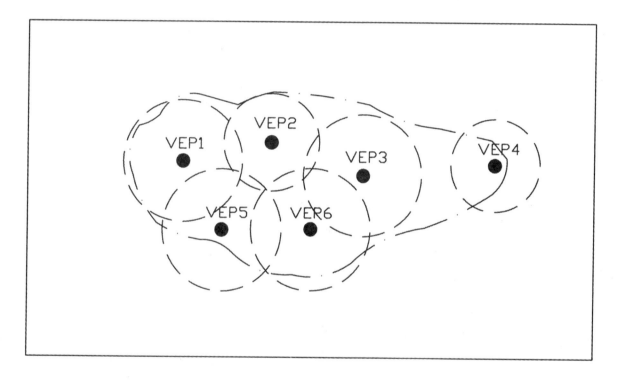

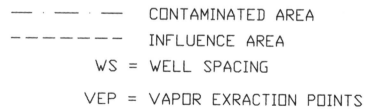

CONTAMINATED AREA

INFLUENCE AREA

WS = WELL SPACING

VEP = VAPOR EXRACTION POINTS

Figure 32.3 SVE Conceptual Approach

Soil permeability is directly related to soil particle size. Figure 32.4 shows the range of soil permeability for four soil types, which are categorized based on particle size.

Average Depth to the Top of Screen/Trench Depth
In vertical installation, the average depth to the top of screen is used to estimate the cost of drilling and construction materials. In horizontal installation, trench depth is used to estimate the cost of trenching and construction materials.

Screen Length
In the vertical SVE system, the screen length is designed to span the vertical extent of soil contamination. The total depth of the vertical SVE wells is the sum of the depth to the top of the screen plus the screen length.

In horizontal installation, the screen length is designed to effectively remediate the entire site. The screen length is based on the radius of influence of the vapor extraction well and the area of contaminated soil.

Treatment Period
The total treatment duration is divided into startup and operations and maintenance (O&M). The costs associated with the startup period (e.g., equipment acquisition, installation, optimization) are considered capital costs. The O&M costs are identified separately.

Worker Safety Level
Worker safety is affected by the contaminant(s) at the site. Safety level refers to the levels required by OSHA in 29 CFR Part 1910. The 4 levels are designated as A, B, C, and D; where "A" is the most protective and "D" is the least protective. A safety level of E is also included to simulate normal construction, "no hazard" conditions as prescribed by the EPA.

Design Information Needed for Detailed Estimates

Following are descriptions of the types of detailed information that, when available, can add detail and accuracy to estimates. Also included are design criteria and estimating rules of thumb that the estimator typically uses to determine values that are not known, or to check information provided by others.

VEP Design
The following parameters are used to design the VEP system.

Soil Permeability	
Soil Type	**Range of Soil Permeability (cm/Sec.)**
Silty Clay, Clay	1.0×10^{-6} to 1.0×10^{-3}
Mixed Sandy, Silty, Clayey Soils	1.0×10^{-4} to 1.0×10^{-1}
Primarily Sand	1.0×10^{-2} to 1.0
Sand and Gravel	1.10×10^{-1} to 10

Figure 32.4 Soil Permeability

VEP Spacing

VEP design depends primarily on the soil type. The radius of influence depends on the soil type; therefore, the VEP spacing, number of VEPs, gas flow rate, and blower specifications also depend on the soil type. Figure 32.5 shows typical values for VEP spacing and gas flow rate.

Number of VEPs

The number of VEPs (N) is calculated based on well spacing using the following equations:

For Vertical Installation:

$$N = \frac{A}{(p \times L^2/4)} \quad \text{Round up to the next whole number}$$

For Horizontal Installation:

$$N = \frac{A}{(L \times SL)} \quad \begin{array}{l} \text{Round up if the remainder is} > 0.5 \\ \text{Round down if the remainder is} < 0.5 \end{array}$$

Where:

A = Surface area of contaminated soil (S.F.)
L = Well spacing (ft)
SL = Screen length (ft)

Gas Flow Rate

The quantity of blowers is determined from the total flow rate (Q). Q is calculated from the following equation:

$$Q = SL \times (GFR) \times N$$

Where:

SL = Screen length (ft)
GFR = Gas flow rate (valid range: 0.01–99.99 CFM/L.F.)
N = Number of VEPs

Blower Specifications

Four blower sizes are listed below. These blowers represent the range of sizes that are typically used for SVE remediation projects.

- 98 SCFM, 1 H.P.
- 127 SCFM, 1.5 H.P.
- 160 SCFM, 2 H.P.
- 280 SCFM, 5 H.P.

Figure 32.5 Soil Vapor Extraction System Design Parameters

Soil Vapor Extraction System Design Parameters		
Soil Type	VEP Spacing (ft)	Gas Flow Rate (CFM/L.F.)*
Silty Clay, Clay	15	0.6
Mixed Sandy, Silty, Clayey Soils	35	1.5
Primarily Sand	50	3.55
Sand and Gravel	100	15.5

*CFM/L.F. = Cubic feet per minute/linear feet

Figure 32.6 provides guidelines on the selection and quantity of blower types.

Vertical VEP Installation

Following are descriptions of parameters for the design of vertical VEPs.

Diameter

Two-inch diameter vertical VEPs are most commonly used. Four-inch diameter vertical VEPs are also available. The VEP diameter affects the diameter of the bore hole and the costs of construction materials and drill cutting containment (drumming).

Drilling Method

Vertical VEPs can be installed using three different common vertical drilling techniques, depending on site hydrogeology and the desired depth of the bore hole. The three vertical drilling techniques included in this section are:

- Hollow stem auger
- Water/mud rotary
- Air rotary

The hollow stem auger method is used for vertical VEP installation when the depth is less than 150' below ground surface (bgs). The water/mud rotary method is used for drilling depths greater than 150' bgs. Air rotary drilling is also available as an option, but is not used in most cases. If the subsurface is consolidated, then the user should use water/mud rotary or air rotary rather than hollow stem augers, even for depths less than 150' bgs.

Professional labor hours for a staff hydrogeologist includes field supervision of drillers and installation of the SVE points. The drilling supervision includes Organic Vapor Analyzer (OVA) screening, decontaminating bailers, and collecting split spoon samples. The estimator can use the following guidelines to determine staff hydrogeologist hours for installing SVE points:

- If soil sample collection is required, then supervision for the drilling and construction of the SVE points will be at a rate of 20' per hour plus 2 hours per point for SVE completion.

Blower Specification		
Flow Rate (Q) SCFM	Type of Blower	Quantity Of Blowers
$Q \leq 98$	98 SCFM, 1 H.P.	1
$98 < Q \leq 127$	127 SCFM, 1.5 H.P.	1
$127 < Q \leq 160$	160 SCFM, 2 H.P.	1
$Q > 160$	280 SCFM, 5 H.P.	Q/280*

*Round to the next whole number

Figure 32.6 Blower Specifications

- If soil sample collection is not required, then supervision for the drilling and construction of the SVE points will be at a rate of 40' per hour plus 2 hours per point for SVE completion.

Figure 32.7 lists bore hole diameters for different drilling methods, along with construction materials and drilling methods.

Construction Materials

Vertical VEPs are typically constructed of either PVC (Schedule 40 or Schedule 80) or stainless steel screen and casing. Primary selection considerations are cost and material compatibility with the contaminant.

Schedule 40 PVC is generally used for the construction of all vertical VEPs that are less than 85' deep. When the vertical VEP is deeper than 85', Schedule 80 PVC material is used.

Connection piping is generally installed above ground. If buried piping is required, then costs for trenching, pipe installation, backfill, and surface restoration should be included in the estimate. The amount of connection piping can be estimated as the radius of influence times the number of VEPs. The amount of manifold piping can be estimated at half the length of the connection piping, and is the same material as the connection pipe. A pressure gauge and other piping appurtenances will also be required. Connection and manifold pipe size criteria for vertical VEPs are presented in Figure 32.8.

Containment of Drill Cuttings

The drill cuttings are generally placed in 55-gallon drums and stored until disposal options have been evaluated.

The VEP screen, riser, caps, and drilling tools (e.g., hollow stem augers) are decontaminated prior to and between each bore hole/well installation. Decontamination procedures consist of steam-cleaning with a high-pressure steam-generating pressure washer and detergent.

Decontamination procedures for split spoon samplers, bailers, and hand augers are as follows:

- Clean with tap water and detergent using a brush.
- Rinse thoroughly with tap water.

Figure 32.7 Drilling Methods and Construction Materials for VEP Installation

Formation Type	Average Well Depth	Drilling Method	Casing Diameter	Bore Hole Diameter	Well Material
Consolidated	0–100	Air Rotary	2	6	PVC SCH 40
Consolidated	101–300	Air Rotary	4	8	PVC SCH 80
Consolidated	301–500	Air Rotary	4	8	SS
Consolidated	>500	Air Rotary	4	8	SS
Unconsolidated	0–100	Hollow Stem Auger	2	8	PVC SCH40
Unconsolidated	101–300	Air Rotary	4	8	SS
Unconsolidated	301–500	Air Rotary	4	8	SS
Unconsolidated	>500	Air Rotary	4	8	SS

- Rinse with deionized water.
- Rinse twice with pesticide-grade isopropanol.
- Rinse with organic-free deionized water.
- Allow to air dry.

Soil Sample Collection Option

Sample collection during bore hole advancement characterizes the geology beneath the site and defines the magnitude and extent of contaminants in the vadose zone. Soil samples should be collected every 5' or at each change in lithology, whichever is less for lithologic description. Drill cuttings can be collected as the bore hole is advanced for general geologic information. Discrete samples are collected in unconsolidated sediment using a variety of methods, including split spoon, shelby tubes, and California brass ring.

Soil samples are generally collected using the split spoon sampler with a standard penetration test at 5' intervals during bore hole advancement. Samples are screened with an OVA for volatile organics; the geologist supervising drilling describes the samples for the lithologic log.

Horizontal VEP Installation

Following are descriptions of parameters for the design of horizontal VEPs.

Diameter

Two-inch diameter horizontal VEPs are most common for installation depths less than or equal to 10'. Four-inch diameter horizontal VEPs are more common for depths of 10'–20'.

When the installation depth is greater than 20', installation of horizontal VEPs by the Horizontal Dewatering Systems, Inc. (HDSI) proprietary method is most cost-effective. This construction method uses either 4" or 6" diameter screened-high-density polyethylene (HDPE) horizontal pipe.

Trenching Method

Horizontal installation involves excavating a narrow trench and installing a screened or perforated pipe at a common elevation. The horizontal installation method used depends on the depth of installation. Chain trenchers are used when the depth is less than or

Figure 32.8 Piping Specification Defaults for Vertical VEPs

Piping Specification Defaults For Vertical VEPs		
VEP Specifications	**Connection Piping**	**Manifold Piping**
2″ Vertical PVC	2″ Sch. 40 PVC	4″ Sch. 40 PVC
2″ Vertical Stainless Steel	2″ Sch. 40 S.S.	4″ Sch. 40 S.S.
4″ Vertical PVC	4″ Sch. 40 PVC	4″ Sch. 40 PVC
4″ Vertical Stainless Steel	4″ Sch. 40 S.S.	4″ Sch. 40 S.S.

equal to 4'. A crawler-mounted, hydraulic excavator is the most common method when the depth is greater than 4' but less than 20'. Cave-in protection may be required for SVE systems in trenches deeper than 10'. Additional controls such as a trench box, well points, sheeting, or side sloping may be required for certain soil conditions.

The HDSI proprietary method is commonly used for horizontal VEP installation between 21' and 30'. The HDSI method uses specialized equipment to drill a 14" diameter hole in which to set a vertical PVC blank pipe. After drilling, the machine digs in either a forward or backward direction to create a horizontal VEP. As it digs, an HDPE screen pipe is laid horizontally. The pipe is simultaneously covered with a filter pack and connected to the vertical PVC pipe.

These trenching methods do not permit discrete soil samples to be collected for laboratory analysis. Therefore, the soil sample collection is not provided for horizontal VEP installation.

Required Parameters for Estimating SVE

Trenching

Length

The total length of horizontal trenching required. The trench length must be greater than the horizontal screen length value.

Width

The width of piping trench as measured at the bottom of the excavation. When determining the dimensions of the trench, consider the diameter of the largest pipe to be buried and enter a width great enough to allow for any desired clearance.

Depth

The average depth from grade to the bottom of the trench.

Percent of Excavated Material to Be Used as Backfill

The percentage of excavated material to be used as backfill. If the excavated material is contaminated, portions or all of it may not be suitable for reuse as backfill. Generally, the estimator may assume that any excavated material that will not be used as backfill will be stockpiled for subsequent removal/treatment. The cost for this removal and/or treatment should be included in the estimate. Since most SVE installations will be performed in areas of the site that are contaminated, it is likely that the excavated material cannot be used as backfill.

Source of Additional Fill

If portions or all of the material removed during trenching are not suitable for reuse as backfill, then borrow material must be used to bring the excavation back to grade. The estimator should identify the source and cost of the borrow material.

Dewatering Required

If the depth of excavation is greater than the depth to groundwater, or if reduction in the moisture content of saturated soil is required, dewatering efforts should be employed. Well points can be used to reduce the moisture content of saturated soil. Dewatering is not commonly used in the construction of SVE systems, unless a perched water table exists.

293

Soil Type

Refers to the existing soils underlying the site. It should be noted that the terms used to describe soils have been generalized for the purpose of estimating costs. Generally, soils can be grouped into one or more of the following categories for estimating purposes:

- Gravel/Gravel Sand Mixture
- Sand/Gravelly Sand Mixture
- Sand-Silt/Sand-Clay Mixture
- Silt/Silty Clay Mixture

Existing Cover

The type of existing surface cover that will be demolished (usually by power equipment) prior to excavation efforts. Costs for transportation and disposal of demolished cover material should be included. Note that if the existing cover is soil/gravel, then no demolition costs are included. The types of existing cover that are generally encountered include:

- Asphalt
- Soil/Gravel
- < 6" Concrete, Mesh-Reinforced
- < 6" Concrete, Rod-Reinforced
- < 6" Concrete, Non-Reinforced
- 7–24" Concrete, Rod-Reinforced

Replacement Cover

The material that will be used in the installation of a replacement cover over the excavated area. Aesthetics and erosion problems, as well as site usage, often make it desirable to replace the cover over the excavated area. Options generally include:

- Asphalt
- Soil/Gravel
- < 6" Concrete, Mesh-Reinforced
- < 6" Concrete, Rod-Reinforced
- < 6" Concrete, Non-Reinforced
- 12" Structural Slab on Grade
- Polyethylene Vapor Barrier
- 6" Soil Bentonite Liner

Horizontal Drilling

In some cases, drilling is required underneath structures (such as a roadway or a building). A continuous well bore is drilled by boring a pilot hole from entrance to exit, then enlarging the hole by back-reaming from the exit to entrance while pulling the piping material into the bore hole. Since the drill string remains in the bore hole until the completion materials are in place, the likelihood of bore hole collapse is reduced. This is especially important in unconsolidated formations.

Construction Materials

Connection piping is generally installed above ground. If buried piping is required, the cost for excavation, pipe installation, backfill and surface restoration should be included in the estimate. The amount of connection piping can be estimated as the radius of influence times the number of VEPs. The amount of manifold piping can be estimated at half the length of the connection piping and is the same material as the connection pipe. A pressure gauge and other piping appurtenances will be required.

Typically, 2" diameter schedule 40 PVC connection piping and 4" schedule 40 PVC manifold pipe are used when a 2" diameter screen pipe is specified. Four inch connection and 4″ manifold pipe are used when a 4" diameter screen pipe is specified. Six inch connection and 8" manifold pipe are used when a 6″ diameter screen pipe is specified.

Containment of Trench Cuttings

Trench cuttings can be placed in 55-gallon drums and stored until disposal options have been evaluated. The waste soil is usually backfilled into the trench to be treated along with the in situ contaminated soil.

Decontamination procedures for the VEP screen, riser, and caps, as well as decontamination of trenching tools, will be conducted prior to and between each VEP installation. Procedures consist of steam cleaning with a high-pressure steam-generating pressure washer and detergent.

Other Related Costs

Maintenance of the soil vapor extraction system includes adjusting the blower flow rate and valves, general maintenance, and collecting samples. For estimating purposes, assume a sample crew to be on site once a week for the first month, and once a month thereafter to perform sampling tasks. An air blower effluent air sample will be collected at each sampling event and analyzed for volatile organics. An organic vapor analyzer will be rented for each sampling event. Refer to Chapter 57, "Monitoring," for further details.

One 55-gallon drum per blower will be used to collect condensate that accumulates within the piping.

Site Work and Utilities

Site work and utilities that may be included in the estimate are as follows:

- Overhead electrical distribution
- Fencing and signage
- Monitoring wells
- Clear and grub
- Demolition of pavements
- Parking lots
- Load and haul

Conclusion

Soil vapor extraction is a proven method of remediating contaminated soils. In situ soil vapor extraction can be very cost-effective on sites ranging from a few thousand square feet to 25 acres or more. The primary cost drivers for a soil vapor extraction system are the size of the field, the depth of VEP installation, and the operating period. For sites larger than 5 acres, it can be more cost-effective to divide the site into cells and remediate each cell separately. This reduces the amount of connection and manifold piping required and reduces the size of the blower unit. If the cells can be remediated in phases, the overall cost of SVE equipment can be reduced, since the blowers can be used repetitively. The cost engineer should work with the design team to develop alternative approaches that can be compared to determine the most cost-effective solution.

Chapter 33

Soil Washing

Soil washing is an ex situ, water-based process for mechanically scrubbing and leaching waste constituents from contaminated soil for recovery and treatment. The process removes contaminants from soils by dissolving or suspending them in the wash solution or by concentrating them into a smaller volume of soil through simple, particle-size separation techniques. Soil-washing units should be arranged in series. The soil is first screened to remove rocks and debris. Then it enters a soil-scrubbing unit where it is sprayed with washing fluid and rinsed. Next, the fluid and soil are separated, with the soil being separated further into fines and coarse grains. The fines are then processed to remove contamination.

Applications and Limitations

Applications

- Removes volatile organic compounds (VOCs) like TCE, benzene, and toluene, and some fuels from contaminated soils. Empirical data indicates that volatiles can be removed with 90–99% efficiency.
- Semivolatile organics may be removed with 40–90% efficiency.
- Typically applicable only to volatile compounds with a dimensionless Henry's Law Constant greater than 0.01 or a vapor pressure greater than 0.02"-Hg.

Limitations

- Metals and pesticides, which are more insoluble in water, often require acids or chelating agents for removal.
- Soil washing does not eliminate contaminants, it reduces the volume of contamination into finer fractions for collection and treatment.
- Soils with greater than 50% clay and silt content may not be amenable to soil washing due to difficulties in removing contaminants from fine particles.
- Generally not used on soils with high explosive potential.
- Complex mixtures of contaminants may be difficult to remove.

Typical Process Design Elements

Most organic and inorganic contaminants have a tendency to bind, either chemically or physically, to fine-grained soils (silt and clay). The silt and clay particles are, in turn, attached to sand and gravel particles by compaction and adhesion. Washing processes separate the fine clay and silt particles from the coarser sand and gravel particles, concentrating the contamination into a smaller volume of soil for further treatment or disposal. The remaining coarser soil fraction can often be returned to the site for reuse. Most soil washing systems are based on this physical process.

Soil washing is effective on a wide variety of chemical contaminants. Removal efficiencies depend both on the type of contaminant and the physical characteristics of the soil. Soil washing is fairly effective on volatile organic contaminants, but is less effective on semi-volatiles unless a washing agent is used to enhance contaminant removal. Soil washing can also remove metals and radionuclides. However, the process residuals that result from treating radionuclide-contaminated soil must be disposed of in an approved low-level waste disposal facility. Although soil washing is an appropriate volume reduction technology for radionuclide-contaminated soils, regulatory constraints regarding the decontamination and the demobilization of the treatment may render the process cost-prohibitive.

Successful application of soil washing requires that the feed soil be free of rocks, metal scraps, and other debris. Before the feed soil enters the process unit, it is screened to remove particles larger than approximately 2–4". Often, these larger particles can be rendered non-hazardous by spray washing. After the feed soil has been screened, it is mixed with washwater, and possibly washing agents, then subjected to intense scrubbing, which disintegrates soil clumps, freeing contaminated fine particles from the sand and gravel fraction. The finer clay and silt particles become suspended in the washwater. In addition, surficial contamination is removed from the coarse sand and gravel by the abrasive scouring action of the particles themselves.

In many cases, water alone can remove contaminants. To improve the efficiency of the process, washing solutions such as surfactants, detergents, acids, or bases may be used to scrub surface contaminants from larger particles. Chelating agents may also be used to leach contaminants from finer particles. The selection of a washing solution depends on the types of contaminants as well as their initial and target concentrations. Hydrophobic contaminants may require the use of surfactants. Metals and pesticides, which are less soluble in water, often require chelating agents or acids for successful washing.

After the initial washing cycle, the washwater containing suspended fine clay and silt particles is decanted, leaving behind the coarser particles. The coarse soil fraction is then washed with clean water and removed from the process. Contamination in the coarse sand and gravel fraction is normally only superficial; in most cases, this material is suitable for reuse after the initial washing cycle. The finer soil particles are recovered from the spent washwater as sludge and further dewatered in a belt filter press. This is accomplished by gravity separation or by flocculation.

Soil washing does not reduce the toxicity of a contaminant. Instead, it reduces the contaminant volume by concentrating the contamination in the finer fraction of the feed soil, which is generally defined as the fraction smaller than 63–74 microns. The feed soil should contain no more than 25–35% fines by weight, since the fines will contain considerably higher levels of contamination than the original feed soil and will, therefore, require further treatment. Consequently, clays and silts, which are primarily fines, are generally poor candidates for soil washing.

The contaminated fines are relatively uniform in size. This provides an efficient feedstock for downstream destruction or immobilization processes. The contaminated fines can be treated by a variety of technologies including solidification/stabilization, incineration, low-temperature thermal desorption, chemical dechlorination, or biodegradation. Spent washwater is treated by biological or physical means. After treatment, the washwater is normally recovered and reused in the washing process to reduce overall water consumption. Although the process requires a continuous supply of make-up water, only a small quantity of water accumulates in the system. This water requires treatment and disposal once the project is completed.

A typical soil washing plant contains a vibrating grizzly, feed unit, wet vibrating screen, cyclone(s), sand dewatering unit, sludge thickening unit, filter press, and all associated feed hoppers and conveyors. Depending on the types of contaminants being treated, various components may be deleted or added, including trommels, wet scrubbers, jigs, spirals, and dissolved air flotation. For example, petroleum-contaminated soils require an oil/water separation module to recover free petroleum from the washwater. For heavy metal contamination, the oil/water separator would be replaced by a dissolved air flotation module to remove dissolved heavy metal hydroxide fractions from the washwater. However, substitution of one component for the other has little impact on overall costs.

Soil washing is not an "off the shelf" technology. The system design and operating parameters must be evaluated for each individual case. Factors such as contaminant type and concentration, cleanup criteria, soil mineralogy, particle size distribution, and moisture content all affect system performance and are normally evaluated during treatability studies.

This chapter discusses the labor and equipment costs for operating a transportable soil washing process unit. The process begins with contaminated soil entering the soil washing system. Feed soil is assumed to be coarse, screened of all debris larger than 4" in diameter before entering the system. At the end of the process, the clean, coarse soil is stockpiled for reuse, and the contaminated fines are stockpiled to await ultimate treatment and disposal (see Figure 33.1).

Chapter 41, "Excavation," can be used for estimating costs for excavating contaminated soil from its original location. Costs for transporting contaminated soil to the process unit and for transporting clean soil to its final destination should also be added to the estimate. A disposal or destruction technology would normally be used for final disposal of the contaminated fines. The cost of purchasing process water should also be included. Washwater is treated and recycled within the soil washing system and is normally disposed of when the project is completed. Soil washing vendors typically hire a subcontractor to transport the washwater off site for treatment and disposal.

Basic Information Needed for Estimating

It is possible to create a reasonable cost estimate using a few required parameters. If more detailed information is known, one can create a more precise and site-specific estimate using a secondary set of parameters.

To estimate the cost of the soil washing system, certain information must be known. This information is discussed in the following paragraphs.

Volume of Contaminated Material

The weight of contaminated material is the primary cost driver for the soil washing process. Ex situ soil quantities are normally expressed as volume in loose cubic yards (L.C.Y.). However, soil washing process equipment is sized in units of tons per hour; therefore, the cost

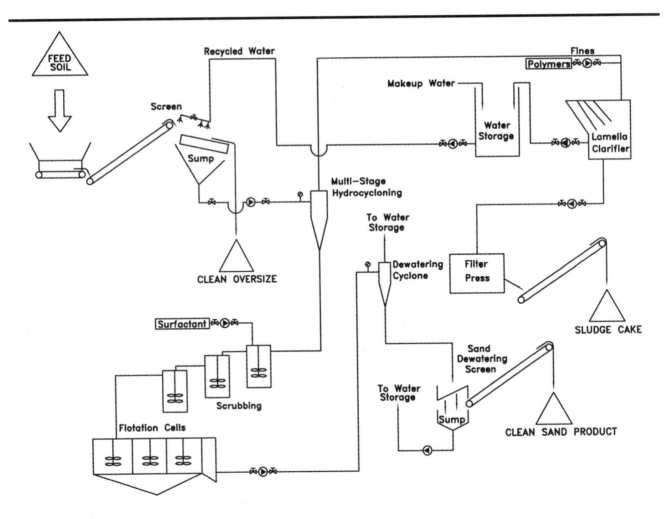

Figure 33.1 Flow Diagram of Soil Washing Process
Courtesy Alternative Remedial Technologies, Inc.

engineer will need to convert the volume of contaminated material to weight by multiplying by an assumed density (see next paragraph).

Density of Contaminated Material
The weight of the contaminated material is measured in loose cubic yards (L.C.Y.). If the soil density is unknown, a rule of thumb is 2,600 lbs per L.C.Y. (1.3 tons per L.C.Y.).

Weight of Contaminated Material
As stated previously, the weight of contaminated material is the primary cost driver for the soil washing process. The tonnage of contaminated material, if known, can be used directly. Otherwise, calculate the tonnage based on the volume and density of contaminated material.

Soil Washing Plant Size
Typical soil washing plants range in capacity from 25–100 tons of feed soil per hour. Selection of a larger unit increases equipment costs, but also reduces treatment time and, in many cases, per-ton treatment costs. Soil washing plants include the following components:

- Vibrating grizzly/screen
- Rotary feeder module
- Feed conveyor assembly
- Trommel washer/de-agglomeration unit
- Cyclone(s)
- Attrition scrubber unit
- Dense media separation column
- Dewatering unit
- Clarifier
- Filter press
- Product discharge conveyor
- Plant air compressor

All modules are skid-mounted, pre-piped, and pre-wired. The actual design of a soil washing plant is site specific, and various components of the basic plant may be added and deleted based on the types of contaminants and the physical components of the soil. However, adding and deleting components has little impact on the project cost.

Mobilization Distance
The mobilization distance is the one-way travel distance from the point of origin of the soil washing plant to the site. Mobilization/demobilization charges for soil washing plants are based on the number of trailers required to transport the system and a loaded mile transportation charge. Assembly, startup, disassembly, and decontamination are each addressed as separate items.

Worker Safety Level
Worker safety is affected by the contaminants at the site. Safety level refers to the levels required by OSHA in 29 CFR Part 1910. The 4 levels are designated as A, B, C, and D; where "A" is the most protective and "D" is the least protective. A safety level of E is also included to simulate normal construction, "no hazard" conditions as prescribed by the EPA.

Design Information Needed for Detailed Estimates

Following are descriptions of the types of detailed information that, when available, can add detail and accuracy to estimates. Also included are design criteria and estimating rules of thumb that the estimator typically uses to determine values that are not known, or to check information provided by others. The process design information is divided into two groups: operations parameters and additives parameters.

Operations Parameters

The operations parameters address the operating time of the system and the design of the working surface or operations pad that houses the soil washing system. The operations parameters are as follows.

Hours of Operation per Day

The hours of operation per day affect the required treatment duration. This parameter, in conjunction with the quantity of contaminated material and the plant size, affects the labor cost for operating the system. Typically, the most economical operation is 16 hours of operation per day, or two 8-hour shifts. However, this operating period must be coordinated with the excavation and post-treatment processes to ensure that the total throughput of soil is efficient.

Hours of Down-time per Day

A certain amount of down-time will be required during the work day to allow for routine maintenance. The hours of operation per day, minus the hours of down-time per day, equals the actual hours of feed per day. Typically, approximately one hour of down-time is required per 8-hour shift.

Days of Operation per Week

Most soil washing projects operate on a 5-day work week. However, when time constraints require an accelerated cleanup schedule, a 7-day work week may be used.

Weeks of Operation per Year

The duration of a soil washing project is typically calculated based on the assumption that the process plant will not be available for a full 52 weeks a year. Severe weather or equipment repairs often result in temporary suspension of soil washing operations. To account for this, most soil washing vendors include an on line" or "availability" factor in their project duration calculations. The most frequently used factor is 80%, or 42 weeks of operation per year.

Additives Parameters

The additives parameters address the selection and dosages of wash additives as well as the temperature of the washwater. The additives parameters are as follows.

Surfactant Additive Rate

The washing agent used depends on the type and concentration of the contaminant as well as its partitioning coefficient. Surfactants are frequently used to solubilize contaminants and mobilize the highly contaminated fines material. Typically, surfactant is added at a rate of 4 lbs. of surfactant per ton of raw feed material. If surfactant addition is not required, this parameter should be zero. The valid range is 0–50 lbs. per ton.

Soil Type

Particle size distribution is a factor in the effectiveness of the soil washing process. Figure 33.2 provides guidelines for particle size distributions based on soil type. Soil washing concentrates the majority of the contamination into the finer fraction of the feed soil, thereby reducing the quantity of material requiring further treatment. Therefore, feed soils containing more than 35% fines by weight are generally poor candidates for soil washing.

Supply Water Temperature

The supply water temperature refers to the process make-up water at its source. Water entering the soil washing plant should be at least 55°F (12.8 °C). Lower water temperatures tend to diminish the effectiveness of the washing process. Boilers may be used for heating process make-up water. If boilers are required, they are sized based on the make-up water flow rate and the difference in supply and process water temperatures. If the supply and process water temperatures are the same, the process make-up water will not be heated.

Process Water Temperature

The process water temperature refers to the process make-up water as it enters the soil washing plant. Process water should be at least 55°F, as lower temperatures may reduce the effectiveness of the washing process. In colder climates, heating the process water facilitates year-round operation of the soil washing plant. Heating process water may also increase the effectiveness of surfactant washing processes, depending on the types and concentrations of contaminants present. Process water temperatures in excess of 120°F significantly increase utilities costs while offering little improvement in performance of the process.

Make-up Water Flow Rate

Soil washing processes generally require 1,000–2,000 gallons of water per ton of soil treated. However, the actual quantity of fresh water that must be purchased is about 50–100 gallons per ton of soil, as most of the washwater can be treated and recycled within the soil washing plant. A small percentage of the washwater exits the process as moisture in the clean solids or the filter cake and must be replaced by make-up water. The filter cake comprised of the contaminated fines typically exits the process at a dry solids content of only 40–55% by weight and is thus responsible for the greatest water loss from the system. The dry solids contents of the entering and exiting soil streams,

Figure 33.2 Percent Fines as a Function of Soil Types

Percent Fines As A Function Of Soil Type	
Soil Type	Percent Fines
Mixed Sandy, Silty Clayey Soil	13
Primarily Sand	10
Sand and Gravel	4

as well as the fines content of the feed soil, will impact make-up water requirements. The make-up water flow rate depends on the plant size and is used in sizing boilers for washwater heating. Figure 33.3 provides guidelines for make-up water requirements.

Boiler Capacity Required
If the process water temperature specified is greater than the supply water temperature, the process water will be heated, typically using a gas-fired boiler and a heat exchanger. The required boiler capacity is calculated based on the make-up water flow rate and the difference between the supply and process water temperatures.

Other Related Costs

Other related costs associated with this technology include the following.

Material Handling
Typically, a 2 C.Y. wheel loader will be used to transfer soil from the stockpile to the feed hopper. While the soil washing plant is operating, the wheel loader will be billed at the full hourly rate. A standby rate will be charged for down-time between shifts. Washed soil and contaminated fines are assumed to be stockpiled to await final disposal. Costs for excavating contaminated soil from its original location and transporting it to the process plant must also be added (see Chapter 41, "Excavation").

System Maintenance and Spare Parts
An allowance for maintenance and spare parts expressed as a cost per ton of soil treated is standard procedure for most soil washing vendors.

Support/Utilities
The working surface or foundation pad that houses the soil washing plant must be able to support the weight of the equipment and control surface run-off. A typical foundation pad consists of a 6" rod-reinforced concrete slab surrounded by a 12" tall concrete berm. Also included are two concrete sumps, two 15-GPM sump pumps, and holding tanks for containing accumulated run-off or process spillage. In addition to a foundation pad, the soil washing process requires four-phase electrical service and a source of process make-up water. The process also requires natural gas if the process make-up water must be heated.

Treatment/Disposal of Process Residuals
The soil washing process generates three residual streams: clean solids, contaminated fines, and process water. The clean solids consist

Make-Up Water Requirements	
Soil Washing Plant Size (Tons/Hr.)	Make-up Water Flow Rate (GPM)
25	25
50	50
100	100

Figure 33.3 Make-Up Water Requirements

mainly of the soil particles larger than 200 mesh. This material is often suitable for use as backfill after the initial washing cycle. The estimate should include costs for transporting clean material to its final destination. The majority of the contamination is concentrated in the fines, which typically range from 5–35% by weight of the original feed soil. The fines are accumulated in a dewatered filter cake whose volume swells approximately 30% from the inclusion of water. This material requires additional treatment and disposal. Treatment options for the contaminated fines include, but are not limited to, landfilling, incineration, low-temperature thermal desorption, and solidification/stabilization.

Most of the fresh water entering the soil washing process exits as moisture in the clean solids or the filter cake. However, the soil washing process typically accumulates one to three gallons of water per ton of soil treated—this accumulated water must be treated and disposed of once the process is complete. Typical washwater treatment options include ion exchange and chemical precipitation. In some cases, washwater treatment systems are added to the soil washing process, but it is typically more cost-effective to subcontract the washwater treatment and disposal.

Sampling and Analysis

The sampling and analytical requirements for soil washing projects depend largely on the types and concentrations of contaminants present and are thus highly site-specific. Chapter 57, "Monitoring," contains a wide variety of sampling techniques and analytical methods and may be used to estimate any sampling and analytical costs.

Site Work and Utilities

Site work and utilities that may need to be included in the estimate are:

- Clearing and grubbing
- Overhead electrical distribution
- Natural gas distribution
- Access roads
- Fencing

Conclusion

Soil washing can be a very effective method of reducing the volume of contaminated soils that must be treated to remediate hazardous waste. The most significant cost driver is the quantity of contaminated material to be treated. The quantity impacts the sizing of the soil washing equipment; the project duration; and the quantity of electricity, water, and washing agents consumed. Because there is a fixed cost for equipment and setup, soil washing is not cost-effective for sites with less than 5,000 tons of material to be treated.

The costs for fines treatment after soil washing depend on the treatment technology chosen and can vary significantly from one site to another. In many cases, the "throughput" rate of the soil in the treatment train will determine the size of the equipment needed, the area of storage required for contaminated fines before final treatment, and other factors. The estimator and the design team should consider the entire treatment train for soil remediation, including soil washing and the post-washing fines remediation, when designing the project. These combined technologies can be optimized to manage the overall cost of soil remediation.

Chapter 34

Solvent Extraction

Solvent extraction is an ex situ process in which contaminated sediment, soil, or sludge is mixed with a solvent to separate the contaminant from its existing matrix. This process was developed as a low-energy alternative to distillation. When solvent extraction is used for site remediation, it concentrates the contaminants, thus reducing the quantity of hazardous waste. The resultant waste stream may be suitable for either recycling or reuse, or it may require additional treatment/disposal.

Applications and Limitations

Applications

- Applicable contaminants include petroleum hydrocarbons, polychlorinated biphenyls (PCBs), organic pesticides, polycyclic aromatic hydrocarbons (PAHs), volatile organic compounds (VOCs), pentachlorophenols (PCPs), and dioxins.

Limitations

- Generally not used for inorganics and metals. Organically bound metals may be co-extracted with other organic compounds, but this process may generate residuals that require special handling.
- Least effective on highly hydrophilic and/or high molecular weight organic compounds.

Process Configurations and Treatment Train Considerations

- The resultant waste stream may be suitable for either recycle or reuse, or it may require additional treatment/disposal.
- Some form of physical or chemical pretreatment is typically required to prepare the influent for the solvent extraction process.
- High concentrations of metals in the treated waste stream may restrict disposal options.
- Some waste streams may require moisture control measures to either reduce or increase moisture content for processing.
- pH adjustment may be required to ensure solvent stability in the process or to reduce corrosive effects on equipment.
- The presence of detergents or emulsifiers in the incoming stream may create foam, which reduces the process efficiency.

- Contaminants that may be removed using solvent extraction include petroleum hydrocarbons, polychlorinated biphenyls (PCBs), organic pesticides, polycyclic aromatic hydrocarbons (PAHs), volatile organic compounds (VOCs), pentachlorophenols (PCPs), and dioxins. Figure 34.1 shows the effectiveness of solvent extraction on general contaminant groups, and Figure 34.2 identifies the solvent extraction waste types and their associated EPA Hazardous Waste Numbers.

Because specific solvents are used for specific distinctive waste streams, it is important that the waste stream be well defined before beginning remediation. It is just as important to evaluate the media matrix, since it must be insoluble in the solvent.

Applicability Of Solvent Extraction To General Contaminant Groups			
	Applicability		
Treatability Group	Soil	Sludge	Sediment
Halogenated Volatiles	+	+	+
Halogenated Semivolatiles	×	+	×
Nonhalogenated Volatiles	×	×	×
Nonhalogenated Semivolatiles	×	×	×
PCBs	×	×	×
Pesticides	×	+	+
Dioxins/Furans	×	+	×
Organic Cyanides	+	+	+
Organic Corrosives	+	+	+

+ Indicates potential applicability based on expert opinion.
× Indicates demonstrated applicability based on treatability studies.
Note: Based on expert opinion, solvent exraction is not applicable for treating inorganics or oxidizers.

Figure 34.1 Applicability of Solvent

EPA Hazardous Waste Codes For Solvent Extraction	
Waste Type	Code
Wood Treating Wastes	K001
Water Treatment Sludges	K044
Dissolved Air Flotation (DAF) Float	K048
Slop Oil Emulsion Solids	K049
Heat Exchanger Bundles Cleaning Sludge	K050
American Petroleum Institute (API) Separator Sludge	K051
Tank Bottoms (leaded)	K052
Ammonia Still Sludge	K060
Pharmaceutical Sludge	K084
Decanter Tar Sludge	K089
Distillation Residues	K101

Figure 34.2 EPA Hazardous Waste Codes

Typical System Design Elements

Two primary processes are used in solvent extraction: solvent liquid extraction and supercritical fluid extraction. *Solvent liquid extraction* is a continuous process. The typical liquid solvents used are triethylamine, kerosene, or other hydrocarbon solvents. Large mixing devices are used as contact chambers for the solvent and the waste stream. Once the solvent and waste stream have been mixed, the contents are allowed to settle. The solvent is then decanted and processed through the solvent recovery system.

The *supercritical fluid extraction* process differs primarily in solvent selection. The solvent must be a near-critical and/or supercritical fluid; that is, the solvent must be near its thermodynamic critical temperature and pressure in the operating environment. Carbon dioxide is typically used as the solvent in these systems. The advantages of using this type of solvent is that it is very easy to separate from the solid fraction, contaminant, and water, and it has extremely high solubilities. Supercritical fluid extraction systems are not widely used because of the extraction vessel's pressure and temperature requirements. However, these systems are now using less expensive solvents and operating at lower pressures and temperatures to produce similar removal efficiencies, thus making the process more economical.

Figure 34.3 illustrates a basic solvent extraction process. In this process, the influent is screened to ensure that the feed material is small enough

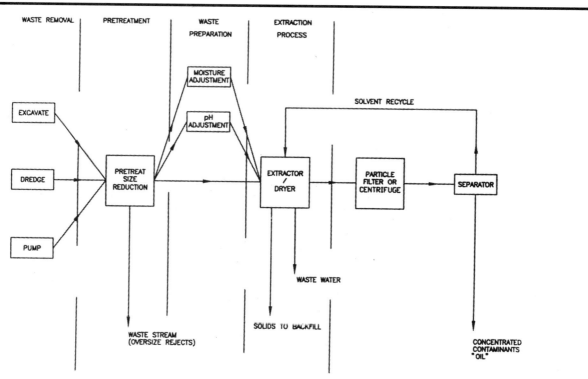

Figure 34.3 Solvent Recovery

to result in an effective solvent/solid particle contact. Once the solvent is added to the waste stream, it is mixed and allowed to separate by gravity. After the two phases have separated, the solvent is removed from the extractor, and the process is repeated until the cleanup objective is achieved. The number of cycles is typically determined from pilot tests before system start-up. Once extracted, the contaminant-laden solvent is processed through a filter or centrifuge to separate any remaining solids fraction. The solvent is then recovered through temperature or pressure adjustments and recycled through the system. The concentrated contaminant is then stored until a significant amount has accumulated.

The concentrated contaminant fraction may be disposed of in a variety of ways, including incineration, reuse, recycling, solidification, and landfill disposal. The water fraction may be either used during soil washing or stored prior to disposal. Depending on the solvent extraction system, additional water may be required for the solid washing step. After washing, which removes any residual solvent, the solid material may be suitable for on-site backfill or other applications. If the soil has significant levels of insoluble contaminants or heavy metals, additional treatment or disposal may be required. It is important to remember that solvent extraction is a separation technique, not a destruction technology.

Solvent extraction systems are designed to operate on a continuous basis (i.e., 24 hours/day, 365 days/year). Typically, three shifts operate the system, and supervisors and maintenance personnel work only one shift. Each crew consists of a supervisor, a maintenance person, and 2–4 system operators. Depending on the system, down-time ranges from 10–40%.

The solvent extraction process equipment is typically assembled on site. Certain site characteristics are required before a commercial-scale solvent extraction system can be deployed. The physical requirements include a leveled, cleared, and graded area of 0.5–1.5 acres. This area contains not only the process facility, but also staging areas for the influent, pretreatment equipment, and effluents. The foundation is between 1,800–12,000 S.F. and must be capable of supporting 250–400 lbs/S.F. Since the units are usually prefabricated, there should be a suitable access road to the site. Skid-mounted and trailer-mounted units are available; however, their application is limited because of their low feed rates.

The solvent extraction process discussed in this chapter begins when the waste stream enters the pretreatment equipment. At the end of the process, the concentrated contaminant and water are in storage tanks and the solid is stockpiled. Since the quantity of material is a significant cost driver, it is critical that a minimum volume (5,000 C.Y. or 1 million gallons) of waste be available at the site. Because of the large capital costs of setting up the system, the process becomes economically unattractive below these minimum volumes. The entire treatment train for solvent extraction typically includes excavation of waste for feed stream preparation (see Chapter 41, "Excavation"). The system generates three waste streams (solid, liquid, and sludge) that require disposal. Options for disposal include discharge to POTW, incineration, or landfill disposal. Chapters 27, 45, and 48 of this book discuss these technologies.

It is possible to create a reasonable cost estimate using a few required parameters. If more detailed information is known, one can create a more precise and site-specific estimate using a secondary set of parameters. To estimate the cost of the solvent extraction system, certain information must be known. This information is discussed in the following paragraphs.

Type of Material

The type of material, especially the water content, can affect the performance of the solvent extraction systems. Therefore, the type of material is based on liquid content. Material may be grouped into three types. Performance characteristics for each type are shown below.

Material	Liquid Content %	Physical Characteristic
Soil	0–30	Not pumpable
Sludge	31– 70	May or may not be pumpable
Liquid	71–100	Pumpable

Although solvent extraction processes can handle waste streams of up to 100% liquid, the majority of the applications have been on soil.

Process System

Three sizes of process systems are discussed in this chapter. Size is indicated by the system's throughput rate. The smallest system is 1,500 C.Y. per month. The middle unit processes a maximum of 6,000 C.Y. per month, and the largest unit processes up to 18,000 C.Y. per month. Depending on the quantity of waste to be treated and the time requirements, different units will provide the best economic alternative. The estimator should investigate different alternatives to determine the duration and cost of remediation for each of the units. Figure 34.4 defines the appropriate feed rates for the respective process units.

Quantity of Material

The quantity of soil, sludge, or liquid is the main cost driver for the solvent extraction process. Generally, a solvent extraction system is not cost effective for sites with less than 5,000 C.Y. of soil or 1,000,000 gallons of liquid. A combination of factors such as treatment duration, quantity of material, down-time, and treatment difficulty is used to calculate the system feed rate.

System Selection	
Feed Rate	**Process Unit**
≤ 1,500 C.Y./MO.	1,500 C.Y./MO.
1,501-6,000 C.Y./MO.	6,000 C.Y./MO.
>6,000 C.Y./MO.	18,000 C.Y./MO.

Figure 34.4 System Selection

C.Y./MO. = cubic yards per month

Worker Safety Level

Worker safety is affected by the contaminant(s) at the site. Safety level refers to the levels required by OSHA in 29 CFR Part 1910. The 4 levels are designated as A, B, C, and D; where "A" is the most protective, and "D" is the least protective. A safety level of E is also included to simulate normal construction, "no hazard" conditions as prescribed by the EPA.

Design Information Needed for Detailed Estimates

Following are descriptions of the types of detailed information that, when available, can add detail and accuracy to estimates. Also included are design criteria and estimating rules of thumb that the estimator typically uses to determine values that are not known, or to check information provided by others.

Pretreatment Requirements

The material in the feed stream must be reduced to less than 1" in size, and for some systems should be less than 1/2". This is accomplished through several different methods. The most common is to use some type of screening technique. Larger material and wet material may require other techniques to reduce the size of the influent. When pretreatment is required, a common solution is to include an infeed hopper followed by a conveyor, which transports waste into a crusher. As the material exits the bottom of the crusher, it is screened and conveyed to the staging area.

Down-time

Down-time represents the amount of time the process equipment is unused as a result of maintenance, breakdown, and any process modification or interruptions. Down-time is typically measured as a percentage of operating time, averaging from 10–40%. A typical system operating for more than one year will experience approximately 15% down-time.

Treatment Difficulty

The type of material, contaminant, and water content all directly affect the ability of solvent extraction to treat the contaminated media. The treatment difficulty affects process equipment requirements—as projects become more difficult, solvent consumption and/or the number of extraction cycles will increase. Difficulty is measured as the percentage of the material that is difficult to treat. Vendors use a percent contingency based on the quantity of material. The range is 0–100%, where the lower end represents a perfect situation and the upper end represents a situation where the material requires extensive additional treatment by the solvent extraction process. Many vendors use 20% as a value for a typical site.

Treatment Duration

The treatment duration, typically measured in months, defines the time required or allocated to complete the remediation activity. The duration is determined from the throughput of the selected process system and the quantity of material. The treatment duration will decrease with increasing process unit throughput. The duration is also affected by the amount of down-time and treatment difficulty.

Other Related Costs

Following are the other related costs for solvent extraction.

Effluent Handling

Waste water and oil are handled by storing quantities in on-site tanks or tankers. Once sufficient quantities have accumulated, they will be transported off site for treatment. Transportation and treatment or disposal costs need to be added to the estimate. Upon exiting the extraction system, the soil effluent is stockpiled. It may be required to stay in the stockpile while samples are being analyzed. The soil is then disposed of by landfilling.

Sampling and Analysis

Monitoring programs are site- and contaminant-specific. The typical sampling and analysis includes PCB, Total Petroleum Hydrocarbons, Volatile Organic, and PAH analyses. The number of samples taken is based on two random samples from the effluent soil every 24-hour period. Oversized material and the waste water may require sampling and analysis prior to disposal.

Site Work and Utilities

Site work and utilities that may apply include:

- Access roads
- Clearing and grubbing
- Excavation, cut and fill
- Gas distribution
- Load and haul
- Underground electrical distribution
- Water distribution

These must also be included in the estimate.

Conclusion

Solvent extraction is an innovative technology that can be used effectively for waste volume reduction prior to follow-on treatment and disposal. As such, it can be a cost-effective way of reducing the overall cost of remediating a large volume of contaminated soil or water. However, as an innovative technology, there is a higher degree of uncertainty than there would be for other technologies with a longer-proven track record. The estimator should consider this uncertainty when preparing an estimate for a solvent extraction system, and should work with the design team and/or system vendors to identify uncertainty in the system so that appropriate steps can be taken to estimate and manage contingencies.

Chapter 35

Thermal and Catalytic Oxidation

Vapor emission oxidation is used to treat contaminated gas streams that result from other remedial technologies. Environmental remediation processes, such as soil vapor extraction or air stripping, generate gas waste streams that contain volatile organic compounds (VOCs). These gas streams are characterized by high humidity levels and high initial concentrations of VOCs, which decay rapidly to lower values. In the oxidation process, oxygen and organics react under high temperatures to produce carbon dioxide, water vapor, and sometimes acidic gases (such as hydrochloric acid). Oxidation systems are relatively simple devices that can achieve destruction efficiencies for VOCs of 98% or greater.

Oxidation equipment used for emission control can be divided into three categories: flares, thermal oxidation, and catalytic oxidation. Flares are typically used for waste streams that have large volumes and high organic concentrations. Since remediation organics concentrations are relatively dilute, flaring is not an applicable technology and is not addressed in this section. This section covers thermal and catalytic oxidation systems. In *thermal oxidation*, the gas stream is heated to a sufficiently high temperature with adequate residence time to oxidize the hydrocarbons to carbon dioxide and water. In *catalytic oxidation*, a catalytic mechanism alters the oxidation reaction rate and causes it to proceed faster and/or at lower temperatures than with direct thermal oxidation.

The concentration of VOCs in the waste stream determines whether oxidation is economically feasible and, if so, which oxidation method is the most economically attractive option. Typical environmental remediation waste streams contain high initial hydrocarbon concentrations—5,000 parts per million per volume (ppm/vol.)—which decay rapidly to concentrations of less than 100 ppm/vol. Auxiliary fuel costs often make use of oxidizers that are unattractive at the lower concentrations.

Applications and Limitations

Applications

- Used to treat contaminated gas streams that result from other remedial technologies (e.g., SVE and air stripping).
- Suitable treatment for volatile and semi-volatile organic compounds (VOCs and SVOCs), as well as petroleum and fuel hydrocarbons.
- Base metal catalysts have been developed which can effectively treat halogenated and chlorinated hydrocarbons, such as TCE, TCA, methylene chloride, and 1,1-DCA.
- Catalytic oxidation is typically applied to low-VOC content streams, since high-VOC concentrations can generate high combustion temperatures that may deactivate the catalyst.
- Catalytic oxidation operates at lower temperatures than thermal oxidation, which reduces fuel and operating costs.

Limitations

- Incomplete products of oxidation may lead to formation of aldehydes and organic acids.
- Pollutants (sulfur dioxide, nitrogen oxide, hydrochloric acid, and hydrofluoric acid) may result from treatment of organic compounds where sulfur and halogens are present. Pollutants must be treated by use of a flue gas scrubber, which is costly.
- Damage to catalyst may result from high-particulate loadings or from the presence of sulfur, halogenated compounds, lead, arsenic, sulfur, silicone, phosphorous, bismuth, antimony, mercury, iron oxide, tin, or zinc in the emissions stream. This may lead to replacement or cleaning of the expensive catalyst.
- Gas concentrations fed into the process must be less than 25% of the lower explosive limit for catalytic and thermal oxidation.

Process Configurations and Treatment Train Considerations

There are several key issues that affect both the selection of thermal and catalytic oxidation as a treatment approach and, if selected, specific considerations regarding the design. Key issues include:

- Flame arrestors are always installed between the incoming gas source and the thermal oxidizer unit.
- Thermal oxidation usually becomes cost-effective when the organic content of the incoming stream is greater than 200 ppm.
- Heat exchangers are commonly used to achieve energy recovery at rates of 40–60%.
- Supplemental combustion air may be required to maintain the oxygen content of the incoming stream at greater than 16%.
- Performance of the catalyst is affected by aging, poisoning, and masking. Aging causes sintering; poisoning occurs when contaminants chemically react with catalyst sites; and masking is the physical covering of catalytic sites with char.
- Thermal oxidizer units can generally be converted to catalytic operation after influent concentrations decrease to less than 1,000–5,000 ppm/V.

Typical System Design Elements

Oxidation equipment size is based on the influent gas flow rate. The influent flow rate is the sum of the waste gas from the remediation system, supplemental dilution air, supplemental combustion air (to maintain an oxygen content greater than 16%), and supplemental fuel (to provide heat content for combustion). Heat exchangers are almost always installed on thermal and catalytic oxidizers to recover energy, maximizing fuel efficiency. Heat exchangers commonly have energy recovery rates of 40–60%, with a maximum of approximately 80%. Construction for emission controls may include manifold piping, flowmeters, a knock-out drum, flame arrestors, vacuum blowers, exhaust stacks, and a heated gas injection line.

Oxidation processes do have some drawbacks. Incomplete products of oxidation can result in the formation of aldehydes and organic acids. Oxidizing organic compounds that contain sulfur or halogens produce unwanted pollutants such as sulfur dioxide, nitrogen oxides, hydrochloric acid, hydrofluoric acid, and possibly phosgene. These contaminants typically can be removed with a scrubber. Scrubbers, which are required to address post-oxidation acid gas, generally render oxidation economically impractical for remediation projects, forcing the use of an alternative technology such as carbon adsorption. Scrubbers are not included in this chapter.

Figure 35.1 is a diagram of a thermal/catalytic incineration system.

Thermal Oxidation

There are four basic forms of thermal oxidation: simple, recuperative, regenerative, and flameless. Recuperative, regenerative, and flameless methods are variations on the simple thermal oxidation process. Each form is discussed in the following paragraphs.

Simple Thermal Oxidation

In simple thermal oxidation, the combustible waste gases pass over or around a burner flame into a residence chamber, where oxidation of the waste gases is completed. A simple thermal oxidation unit typically operates at a temperature of 1,400–2,200°F for most combustible

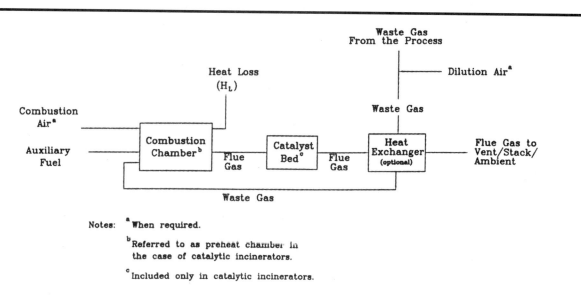

Figure 35.1 Diagram of a Thermal/Catalytic Incineration System

pollutants. Residence times range from 0.2–2 seconds. The simplicity and high final destruction efficiency of volatile organics may be offset by the high energy requirements for this process.

Each of the following thermal oxidation methods are variations of this process.

Recuperative Thermal Oxidation. Recuperative heat recovery is provided by a heat exchanger that can recover 35–80% of the heat. Capital costs are higher when the heat exchanged is added, but operating fuel costs are lower than for simple thermal oxidation.

Regenerative Thermal Oxidation. In regenerative oxidation, inlet gases pass through a packed bed of ceramic or stone to collect heat, then through a combustion chamber where supplemental fuel is added. The oxidized effluent then passes through another packed bed, where heat is recovered at efficiencies of 80–98%. One disadvantage of this system is that its continuous destruction efficiency of VOCs is seldom greater than 95%. System economics are optimized when the flow rates are high (e.g., greater than 10,000 SCFM), and the organic contaminant concentration is low (e.g., less than 800 ppm/vol.). The overall weight of the system (because of the multiple packed beds) may be a constraining factor.

Flameless Thermal Oxidation. Flameless thermal oxidation uses a ceramic matrix that is preheated to 1600°F–1800°F. A portion of the heat released from the oxidation reaction is absorbed by the ceramic bed to maintain the reaction zone temperature. The oxidizer is preheated, either electrically or by natural gas. The residence time is short, usually less than or equal to 0.20 seconds.

Catalytic Oxidation

In a catalytic oxidation system, typical temperatures range from 600–1,000°F, and residence times range from 0.03–0.1 seconds. Catalytic oxidation is also used to force more complete oxidation than can be achieved without a catalyst, regardless of time or temperature. The advantage of catalytic systems is reduced fuel consumption, thus lower operating costs. The disadvantages include catalyst fouling, poisoning, and splintering, which can result in maintenance down time and costly repairs or replacement.

The catalyst is deposited on a metal or ceramic structural support in a configuration that minimizes pressure drop. Catalytic beds must provide the maximum catalytic surface area per SCFM of waste gas, maintain uniform density at elevated temperatures to prevent channeling or bypassing, provide for a moderately low pressure drop, and demonstrate structural integrity and durability. Catalytic oxidizers may include recuperative heat recovery to decrease the fuel requirements. The catalyst bed may be either fixed or fluidized. Fixed beds are more common.

Fixed Bed Catalysts

Fixed beds typically use a finely divided noble metal, such as palladium or platinum, on metal or ceramic supports. Potential problems include deactivation of the catalysts resulting from halogens, sulfur dioxide, or nitrogen dioxide, and fouling by dust.

Fluidized Bed Catalysts

Fluidized bed oxidizers use non-precious metals that are less susceptible to fouling and poisoning and more applicable in contaminant streams containing sulfur or chlorinated organics. Typically, the bed is packed with 1/8" diameter pellets. Fluidized units provide an even temperature distribution across the catalyst, which prevents thermal damage to the catalyst and allows more concentrated contaminant streams. Abrasive forces on the catalyst surface require catalyst replacement over time.

Basic Information Needed for Estimating

It is possible to create a reasonable cost estimate using a few required parameters. If more detailed information is known, one can create a more precise and site-specific estimate using a secondary set of parameters.

To estimate the cost of the thermal or catalytic oxidation system, certain information must be known. This information is discussed in the following paragraphs.

Oxidation Method

Oxidation method options are listed below. Oxidation units include (as appropriate) a mist eliminator; waste air filter; dilution air filter; oxidation chamber; burner or electric heater; extraction blower; flame arrestor; flow sensor; explosion-proof controls package, including a control panel; snub stack; heat exchanger; and initial catalyst.

Thermal Oxidation Options

- Simple thermal oxidation
- Recuperative thermal oxidation
- Regenerative thermal oxidation
- Flameless thermal oxidation
- Recuperative flameless thermal oxidation

Catalytic Oxidation Options

- Fixed bed catalysts
- Recuperative fixed bed catalysts

Figure 35.2 lists the oxidizers that are generally available. An oxidizer is selected based on the oxidation method and influent flow rate. As illustrated in Figure 35.2, units are not available for every situation.

Table Of Available Oxidizers											
Influent Flow Rate (SCFM)	**5**	**100**	**150**	**250**	**500**	**1000**	**2000**	**2500**	**3000**	**4000**	**5000**
Simple Thermal			×	×	×	×					×
Recuperative Thermal			×	×	×	×					×
Regenerative Thermal								×			×
Flameless Thermal	×	×				×					×
Recuperative Flameless Thermal						×					×
Fixed Catalytic		×	×	×	×	×					×
Recuperative Fixed Catalytic		×	×	×	×	×	×		×	×	×

Figure 35.2 Table of Available Oxidizers

Waste Gas Flow Rate

Typical waste gas flow rates for remediation-related emissions are between 50–2,000 SCFM.

Treatment Period

The total treatment period is divided into startup and operations and maintenance (O&M). The costs associated with the startup period are equipment acquisition, installation, and optimization. O&M costs are for operating and maintaining the system throughout the project life.

Worker Safety Level

Worker safety is affected by the contaminants at the site. Safety level refers to the levels required by OSHA in 29 CFR Part 1910. The 4 levels are designated as A, B, C, and D; where "A" is the most protective, and "D" is the least protective. A safety level of E is also included to simulate normal construction, "no hazard" conditions as prescribed by the U.S. Environmental Protection Agency (U.S. EPA).

Design Information Needed for Detailed Estimates

Auxiliary fuel supplies the heat needed to support combustion and is added as a gas to the process stream. The auxiliary fuel requirement has two components: the type of fuel and the fuel addition rate.

Type of Fuel

The heat that is needed to initiate the oxidation reaction is supplied from propane or natural gas. Natural gas is generally cheaper if a ready supply is available at the site. If not, propane is used.

Fuel Addition Rate

The fuel addition rate may vary over the course of the remediation, based on the waste stream organic concentration and whether the process is in startup or operation mode.

If the fuel addition rate is unknown, the estimator can calculate a rate based on the oxidation method and fuel type. The waste gas flow rate will be multiplied by one of the values in Figure 35.3 to determine a fuel addition rate. The values in this figure were calculated based on a waste gas heat content of zero. Zero provides for a conservative cost estimate and is representative of the majority of the remediation period, since typically remediation streams have a low waste gas heat content after initial startup.

The values in Figure 35.3 are based on engineering evaluations of different waste streams. These represent "typical values" and were calculated using the following formula:

$$\frac{SF}{WF} = \frac{1.1 \, HCL \, (CT - FIT) - HCE \, (WIT - FIT) - WHC}{FHV - 1.1 \, HCL \, (CT - FIT)}$$

Where:

SF = Supplemental fuel flow rate (SCFM)

WF = Waste gas flow rate (SCFM) (required parameter)

CT = Combustion chamber temperature (°F) (See Figure 35.4.)

HCL = Heat capacity leaving combustion chamber (BTU/(SCF) measured in °F)

FIT = Fuel inlet temperature (°F)

HCE = Heat capacity entering combustion chamber (BTU/(SCF) measured in °F)

WIT = Waste gas inlet temperature (°F)

WHC = Waste gas heat content = 0 (BTU/SCF)

FHV = Fuel net heating value (BTU/SCF) (See Figure 35.6.)

Assume that no combustion or dilution air is needed.

The factors used in the calculations are illustrated in Figures 35.4 through 35.6.

Auxiliary Fuel Ratios To Waste Gas Stream		
	Auxiliary Fuel Ratio	
Oxidation Method	Natural Gas SCF/SCF of Waste Gas	Propane SCF/SCF of Waste Gas
Simple Thermal Oxidation	0.0345	0.0120
Recuperative Thermal Oxidation	0.0192	0.0067
Regenerative Thermal Oxidation	0.0058	0.0020
Flameless Thermal Oxidation	0.0429	0.0149
Recuperative Flameless Thermal	0.0185	0.0064
Catalytic Oxidation	0.0121	0.0043
Recuperative Catalytic Oxidation	0.0067	0.0024

Figure 35.3 Auxiliary Fuel Rations to Waste Gas Stream

Auxiliary Fuel Equation Assumptions		
Oxidation Method	Combustion Temp. (°F)	Exchanger Efficiency (%)
Simple Thermal	1500°	
Recuperative Thermal	1500°	50
Regenerative Thermal	1800°	95
Flameless Thermal	1800°	
Recuperative Flameless Thermal	1800°	65
Catalytic	600°	
Recuperative Catalytic	600°	50

Figure 35.4 Auxiliary Fuel Equation Assumptions

Simple Thermal Example

The following example can be used to illustrate how the data in Figures 35.3 through 35.6 are used. The following assumptions are the basis of this example.

CT = Combustion chamber temperature = 1,500°F (Figure 55.4)

HCL = Heat capacity leaving combustion chamber = 0.0193 (BTU/(SCF) measured in °F) (Figure 35.5)

The combustion chamber outlet temperature is assumed to be equal to the combustion temperature (CT), since the waste gas heat content is assumed to be zero.

FIT = Fuel inlet temperature = 70°F

HCE = Heat capacity entering combustion chamber = (BTU/(SCF) measured in °F)

WIT = Waste gas inlet temperature = 70°F

WHC = Waste gas heat content = 0 BTU/SCF

FHV = Fuel net heating value (Figure 35.6)

Figure 35.5 Heat Capacity of Air

Heat Capacity Of Air	
Temperature (°F)	Mean Heat Capacity of Air (Btu/SCF Measured in °F)
70°	0.0179
300°	0.0182
600°	0.0186
1200°	0.0190
1500°	0.0193
1700°	0.0195
1800°	0.0196

The heat capacity for air is used since air comprises over 90% of the waste gas, before and after combustion.

Figure 35.6 Heating Values for Fuels

Heating Values For Fuels	
Fuel	Net Heating Value
Natural Gas	900 Btu/SCF
Propane	2,522 Btu/SCF or 91,500 Btu/gal.

If the fuel is natural gas, the following computation is used:

$$\frac{SF}{WF} = \frac{1.1 \times 0.0193\,(1500 - 70) - 0.0179\,(70 - 70) - 0}{900 - 1.1 \times 0.0193\,(1500 - 70)} = \frac{30 - 0}{900 - 30} = 0.0345$$

If the fuel is propane, the following computation is used:

$$\text{Propane} = \frac{30 - 0}{2522 - 30} = 0.0120$$

Recuperative Thermal Example

Waste gas inlet temperature = Waste gas inlet temperature before heat exchanger + heat exchanger efficiency (combustion chamber temperature – waste gas inlet temperature before heat exchanger).

$$\text{WIT} = 70 + 50\%\,(1{,}500^\circ - 70^\circ) = 785^\circ$$

The maximum waste gas inlet temperature is 1,100°F, above which temperature preignition could occur.

Regenerative Thermal Example

Waste gas inlet temperature = Waste gas inlet temperature before heat exchanger + heat exchanger efficiency (combustion chamber temperature – waste gas inlet temperature before heat exchanger).

$$\text{WIT} = 70 + 95\%\,(1{,}800^\circ - 70^\circ) = 1{,}714^\circ$$

Flameless Example

Flameless oxidation uses the same formula as simple thermal oxidation.

Recuperative Flameless Example

Waste gas inlet temperature = Waste gas inlet temperature before heat exchanger + heat exchanger efficiency (combustion chamber temperature – waste gas inlet temperature before heat exchanger).

$$\text{WIT} = 70^\circ + 65\%\,(1{,}800^\circ - 70^\circ) = 1{,}194.5^\circ$$

Fixed Bed Catalytic Example

Fixed bed catalytic oxidation uses the same formula as simple thermal oxidation.

Recuperative Fixed Bed Catalytic Example

Waste gas inlet temperature = Waste gas inlet temperature before heat exchanger + heat exchanger efficiency (combustion chamber temperature – waste gas inlet temperature before heat exchanger).

$$\text{WIT} = 70^\circ + 50\%\,(600^\circ - 70^\circ) = 335^\circ$$

Other Related Costs Other costs associated with thermal and catalytic oxidation include maintenance labor, foundation slab construction, interconnecting ductwork, and sampling and analysis of the effluent stream. In addition, electricity is consumed by the system fan.

Monthly maintenance includes cleaning the particulate filter, checking sheaves and belts, and cleaning dirt from the motor and grease bearings in the extraction blower. Bimonthly tasks include changing the oil in the extraction blower and cleaning the flame sensor lenses.

The foundation support for the system is an 8" concrete slab. The area of the slab is based on unit size. Oxidation units capable of treating a range of flow rates from 1–5,000 SCFM range in size from 50–300 S.F.

Four-inch PVC piping is provided for interconnecting ductwork.

Sampling and analysis consist of oxidation unit influent and effluent samples. If influent sampling is included in the preceding treatment process (i.e., air stripping or soil vapor extraction), the quantities should be reduced for this technology to avoid double counting. Influent and effluent air are sampled weekly during the startup period and monthly during the O&M period. Samples are collected for Organic Vapor Analyzer (OVA) screening and for total VOCs by U.S. EPA method 25A.

No fuel storage tanks are included in the estimate. Natural gas is assumed to be supplied through utility line connection. Given the large fuel requirements, propane fuel tanks are typically provided at no cost by the propane supplier.

A cost related only to catalytic oxidation is the catalyst. The catalyst cost is based on the type of catalyst and the flue gas flow rate. Precious metal catalysts are used in fixed bed oxidation. The lifespan of the catalyst may be assumed to be three years for replacement. For estimating purposes, assume 2 SCF of precious metal per 1,000 SCFM flow rate for replacement.

Site Work and Utilities

Site work and utilities that may apply to thermal and catalytic oxidation include the following:

- Overhead electrical distribution
- Underground electrical distribution
- Access roads
- Gas distribution

Conclusion

These would also be included in the estimate.

Thermal and catalytic oxidation are proven approaches to treating air that is contaminated with VOCs. The primary cost drivers for this technology are the system flow rate, the makeup fuel requirements, and the operating period. These parameters are dictated to a large extent by the quantity of air being generated by "upstream" treatment processes (e.g., soil vapor extraction or air stripping). The estimator should consider the entire treatment train when preparing an estimate for an oxidation system and consider alternatives that might increase the efficiency of the process and/or reduce cost.

Part III

Cost Estimating for Remediation —Containment Technologies

Chapter 36

Capping

Capping refers to a layered system of vegetative cover, natural soils, rock, synthetics, pavement, and/or polymeric liners that are used to control hydrogeologic processes. Capping is used primarily to contain and immobilize hazardous waste in soil and keep it from infiltrating into groundwater. Capping a hazardous waste site is one of the most common passive remediation technologies. The objectives of capping include:

- Control stormwater run-off
- Reduce infiltration
- Control erosion
- Contain landfill gases
- Support vegetation

The advantages to using capping include low maintenance and low life-cycle costs. Through different design options, capping can be implemented for a wide variety of sites.

A Resource Conservation and Recovery Act (RCRA) multi-layered cap may be appropriate for low-level radioactive waste sites, with additional considerations for the type of radioactive material. RCRA multi-layer caps have been used for mixed radioactive and chemical waste. Caps using designs similar to RCRA requirements have also been used at waste sites containing uranium mill tailings. Additional considerations for cap design at radioactive waste sites include depth of the waste (or thickness of cap) for radiation shielding and radon gas retention purposes, and expected life of the cap (because of the long half-lives of some radionuclides). State regulatory agencies should be consulted before installing an RCRA cap over a radioactive site.

Applications and Limitations

Applications
- Typically used to close a site where remediation activities have been completed.
- Used to contain and immobilize contaminants in soil.
- Objectives of capping include: minimize contaminant migration, control storm water run-off, reduce infiltration, control erosion, contain volatile off-gases, and support vegetation.

- Minimize contaminants leaching into the groundwater.
- Eliminate contaminant contact with receptors.

Limitations

- Gas vents with passive or active collection systems may be necessary to remove gases that may build up under the cap.
- Site factors, such as terrain and floodplain location, can complicate or eliminate cap implementation.
- This technology does not reduce contaminant concentrations.

Process Configurations and Treatment Train Considerations

- State regulatory agencies and/or the EPA should be consulted prior to installing an RCRA cap.
- Surface water collection and diversion may be needed to control run-off.
- Cap design is site-specific and should be driven by the type of closure and site conditions.
- Passive venting is the most common technique for removing gases. Active venting using mechanical suction may be required when large volumes of gas are present.
- Cap maintenance may include vegetation control and repairs due to cover erosion, settlement, and subsidence.
- Covers can range from one layer of vegetated soil to multiple layers of soils and geosynthetic liners.
- Soil barrier layers are usually compacted clays with a hydraulic conductivity no greater than 1×10^{-7} cm/sec.
- Geosynthetic barrier layers include geomembranes and geosynthetic clay liners.

A cap's hydraulic conductivity is influenced by the method of compaction, moisture content during compaction, compactive energy, clod size, and degree of bonding between lifts.

Typical System Design Elements

Cap design is driven primarily by the type of closure and the nature of the site. There are 2 general types of closure for hazardous waste sites: clean closure and contingent closure. The choice between the 2 depends on post-remediation or closure contaminant levels present at the site as defined by RCRA.

Contingent closure is applicable if the subject site cannot be remediated to meet local, state, and federal target levels because of exorbitant cost, risk to health and safety, or other defensible arguments. Using a contingent closure requires certain environmental controls to be implemented, based on regulatory requirements and guidelines. Environmental monitoring may include evaluation and quality analyses of air, soil, groundwater, and surface water matrices. A post-closure monitoring plan may require an extensive program over several years. A contingent closure is typically considerably more expensive than a clean closure.

Clean closure is applicable if the site has been remediated to target levels defined by local, state, and federal regulatory requirements. No post-closure environmental monitoring is required.

Basic Information Needed for Estimating

It is possible to create a reasonable cost estimate for capping using a few required parameters. If more detailed information is known, one can create a more precise and site-specific estimate using a secondary set of parameters.

To estimate the cost of a capping system, certain information must be known, it is discussed in the following paragraphs.

Scope

The scope of the project is the acreage of a site to be capped. Generally, the cap will cover the entire waste area plus a slight overlap.

Types of Caps

Three types of cap designs are available:

- Standard cover (see Figure 36.1)
- Geosynthetic/composite cover (see Figure 36.2)
- Asphalt cover (see Figure 36.3)

These are the most common types of caps used at contaminated sites. The selection depends on site conditions, waste characteristics, and other site-specific conditions. Various regulatory agencies may require more stringent or variations on the cap designs included in this system. Requirements for soil liner thickness and/or flexible membrane liner (FML) thickness, as well as other capping construction specifications, may vary by state and/or regulatory requirements. In some cases, a vent layer may be added to any of these caps.

Gas Vent System Requirements

Gas vent systems are used to remove methane and other gas buildup from landfills. The most common design is a passive gas venting system, which vents to the atmosphere without using a mechanical vacuum. Generally, the gas venting system is implemented within the perimeter boundaries of the landfill cap. In some cases, however, perimeter venting may be preferred at the sites. Then the user may need to incorporate additional vent system piping. Gas venting is a common practice at landfills that accept sanitary refuse, since methane or other gaseous byproducts are produced in the breakdown of the materials stored there. Gas venting may also be needed if either jet fuel or gasoline was disposed of in construction debris or sanitary landfill.

Generally, areas that are capped do not require active gas venting. Active venting is the process of mechanically inducing suction over a piping system set out over a grid, either within the capped area or at its extremities. Active venting is required when off-gas volumes are extremely high or when required by state regulations. Sanitary landfills are classified as Solid Waste Management Units (SWMUs) and are currently administered through the RCRA subtitle "D" regulations. Active landfill collection and treatment generally includes the installation of pumps, blowers, flares, and collection piping associated with active gas withdrawal.

Post-Closure Monitoring Period

The post-closure monitoring period starts when a section of the cap closes and ends when the specified time period expires. RCRA guidelines recommend a 30-year post-closure period. The post-closure period will determine maintenance costs.

Final Daily Cover

The final daily cover is the layer of fill placed over garbage, contaminated material, or other landfilled or disposed material, before a cap is placed over the affected area. Generally, this cover is not required for an inactive site, but is almost always required for an active landfill site where wastes are still being deposited.

Location Conditions

Geographic location can influence cap design. Locations in arid regions generally use a top cover of rock or other non-vegetative material, while other areas generally use a vegetative cover or paved top layer to manage erosion.

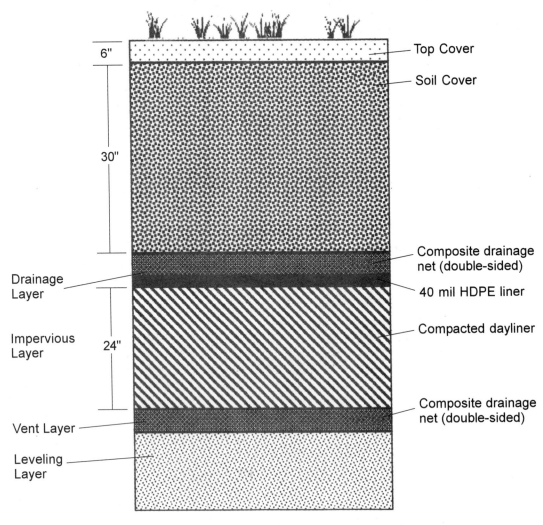

Figure 36.1 Standard Cover

Design Information Needed for Detailed Estimates

The following discussion provides the detailed information that, when available, can result in more accurate capping estimates. Also included are design criteria and estimating rules of thumb that the estimator typically uses to determine values that are not known, or to check information provided by others.

Cap Geometry

General cap geometry parameters are:

- Side slopes of cap (ratio; e.g., 3:1 [33%])
- Length of side slopes
- Top slopes of cap (33:1 [3%] to 20:1 [5%])
- Length of top slopes

These parameters are defined in the following paragraphs.

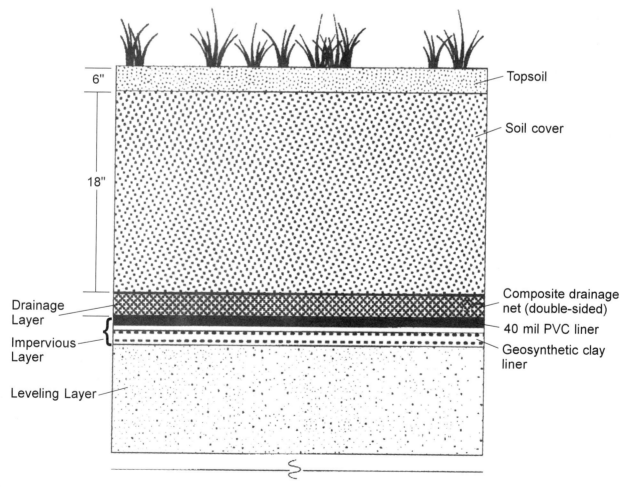

Figure 36.2 Geosynthetic/Composite Cover

Side Slopes of Cap

The side slopes ratio depends on regulatory requirements and guidelines. Regulations and guidelines on allowable side slopes vary from state to state. An example of side slopes is a ratio of 5:1 (20%), where five is the horizontal run and one is the vertical rise.

Generally, the maximum side slopes in the field are 3:1 (33%). Steeper slopes may cause the underlying layers of sand, gravel, or geotextiles to slide or fail along the contact interface. Also, steeper slopes increase maintenance and the potential for erosion and soil loss. Slopes may need to be benched at steeper grades to control potential erosion and promote stability in the cap. Regulatory requirements and guidelines will dictate whether or not benching is required.

Slope affects cost proportionally: as the slope increases, the quantity of materials (liners, soil layers, etc.) also increases. Increased quantities will, in turn, yield a higher overall cost. A maximum 3:1 (33%) slope would have the net effect of a cost increase of 5% greater than a flat surface. Thus the effect of slope on the overall cost can be significant.

Length of Side Slopes

The length of side slopes is the length from the outer edge of the cap to the location where the side slope and top slope meet. For example, the slope may change from 5:1 (20%) to 33:1 (3%).

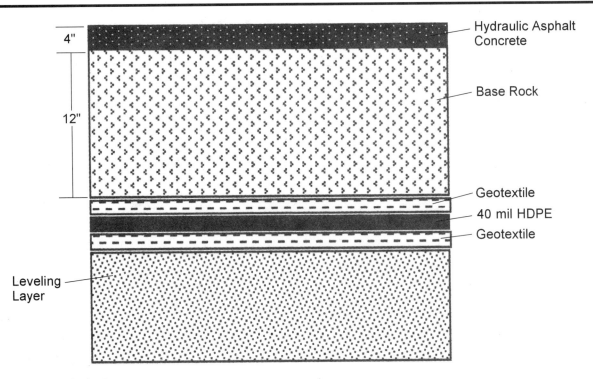

Figure 36.3 Asphalt Cover

Top Slopes of Cap

Regulations and guidelines on the maximum allowable top slopes vary from state to state. EPA guidelines require top slopes to be within a range of 33:1 (3%) to 20:1 (5%). This slope requirement reduces the amount of erosion that could occur if a steeper top slope were used.

Length of Top Slopes

The length of the top slopes is the horizontal length from the top of the cap down to where the top slope meets the side slope.

Cap Layer Details

The cap layer details describe the layers that make up the capping technology. Each cap type is made up of different layers that perform different functions. Figures 36.1, 36.2, and 36.3 provide default values for different layers for the standard cover, the geosynthetic/composite cover, and the asphalt cover. The following sections describe both the default layers and options for different construction methods for each type of cap.

Standard Cover

Standard cover design alternatives include:

- Topsoil
- Soil cover
- Impervious layer
- Leveling layer

In 1989, the EPA issued a revised guidance document concerning closure and final cover for hazardous waste facilities. The defaults for each layer are based on these guidelines.

Topsoil

The topsoil layer serves as the final (top) layer of the cap. The topsoil is used in conjunction with vegetation to reduce erosion and infiltration of rainwater and to protect the underlying layers of cap from water, wind erosion, and dehydration.

Topsoil is the most common type of top cover used to protect the underlying layers of a cap. It can be used at most sites, provided maintenance is included. The estimator should consider the source of topsoil and the cost to purchase it, if any, along with transportation to the site.

The default topsoil for the standard cover includes a 6" soil layer and a vegetative (seed) layer. The topsoil depth, the top cover material, and vegetative cover type can vary depending on site conditions and will affect the soil volume and cost.

Soil Cover

This layer provides root support for the topsoil/vegetative layer. It must be of sufficient thickness to protect the underlying liners from vegetative root disturbance and to act as a cushion between vehicles and underlying liners, which could be stressed and torn by vehicles working on the surface. The soil cover will also provide the necessary protection from frost. The soil cover parameters are listed and described in detail below.

Depth of Soil Cover: The standard cap has 24" of soil cover (unclassified fill). It is not critical that the impervious layer (flexible membrane layer and the compacted soil components) be below the average depth of frost penetration. The depth of the soil cover can be adjusted to allow the FML to lie below the frost line, if required.

Source of Fill: The soil cover can be composed of unclassified fill material, either from on-site or off-site. The estimator should consider the source of fill material, the cost of purchase, if any, and the cost to haul the material to the project site.

Impervious Layer

The impervious layer reduces the amount of water percolating down through the soil, which would otherwise come in contact with the underlying waste layer. The barrier formed by the impervious layer protects the subsurface groundwater from becoming contaminated with water-bearing waste (leachate). This layer of the cap consists of a flexible membrane liner (FML) and/or a compacted clay layer comprised of a geosynthetic clay liner (GCL) or a standard compacted clay (SCC).

Flexible Membrane Liner: The flexible membrane liner is a low hydraulic conductivity layer used to bridge areas of settling and in friction areas (side slopes) between the geomembrane and the compacted soil layer. Other membrane selections can be added to the estimate as required. The typical options for the FML are:

- 40 mil HDPE (default)
- 60 mil HDPE
- 80 mil HDPE
- 30 mil PVC
- 40 mil PVC

Compacted Clay Layer

The compacted clay layer is an important design component to ensure low hydraulic conductivity of the overall cover. For the standard cover, standard compacted clay is used for the compacted clay layer. If a compacted clay layer is used, the estimate should also address the depth of the clay and the source and cost of the clay material.

Leveling Layer

This layer, comprised of unclassified fill, is used to level the area to be covered by the cap prior to installing the actual components of the cover. The estimator should consider the source of fill material, the cost of purchase, if any, and the cost to haul the material to the project site. The standard depth for the leveling layer is 6", but the actual layer can be up to 18", depending on site conditions.

Geosynthetic/Composite Cover

The geosynthetic/composite cover design alternatives are the same as for the standard cover, and include:

- Topsoil
- Soil cover
- Impervious layer
- Leveling layer

This topsoil, soil cover, impervious, and leveling layers are identical to those of the standard cover, described above. As with the standard cover, the soil cover can be made of unclassified fill material, either from on-site or off-site. The flexible membrane liner is also the same.

Compacted Clay Layer

Two options are typically available for the clay layer:

- Geosynthetic clay liner
- Standard compacted clay

Geosynthetic Clay Liner: These liners, which can replace compacted clay for certain site conditions, consist of bentonite clay — either sandwiched between two geotextile layers or bonded to a geomembrane to provide an effective hydraulic barrier ($1 \times 10E^{-9}$ m^3/sec/m^2 flux rate).

Standard Compacted Clay: If a compacted clay layer is used, the estimate should also address the depth of the clay and the source and cost of the clay material. The standard depth for the leveling layer is 6" of unclassified fill, but the actual layer can be up to 18", depending on site conditions.

Asphalt Cover

Asphalt cover design alternatives include:

- Top cover
- Base rock
- Impervious layer
- Leveling layer

The impervious layer, flexible membrane liner, compacted clay layer, and leveling layer for the asphalt cover are the same as for the standard cover, detailed above.

Top Cover

Hydraulic Asphalt Concrete Depth: The top cover material for the asphalt cover is comprised of hydraulic asphalt concrete, which is used as a hydraulic barrier. In some cases, the asphaltic layer can be used for vehicle traffic, but consideration for this design is important. Covers used for vehicle traffic will generally be designed as a structural system with a thicker top layer and base rock layer. The default thickness is typically 4". The valid range for top cover depth is 4–8".

Base Rock

The base rock layer is used to separate the asphalt layer of the cover from the impervious layer. The typical design approach uses a 12" layer of crushed base rock that will be spread over the entire cap area. The valid range for base rock is 12–24".

Passive Gas Vent

The gas vent layer is used primarily at landfill sites. Passive gas venting releases gases to the atmosphere by the path of least resistance without using mechanical means. The gas vent layer is composed of geocomposite, sand, or gravel. Both interior and perimeter gas venting may be required.

If a double-sided geocomposite is to be used, no additional geotextiles are required. A separation geotextile will be required if a sand or gravel gas vent is being estimated.

The passive gas vent design parameters include:

- Geotextile
- Type of material
- Material depth
- Source of material
- Gas collection piping

Geotextile

The amount of geotextile fabric is assumed to be equal to the area of the cap. Options include:

- Filter fabric
- Drainage fabric
- Liner protection fabric
- Composite drainage netting (default)
- Geogrid

Material Options

- Sand
- Gravel

Material Depth

The typical depth of material is 12", which meets the minimum EPA requirements for gas vent layer thickness. Vent layers can range from 6–24".

Source of Material

The estimator should consider the source of fill material, the cost of purchase, if any, and the cost to haul the material to the project site.

Gas Collection Piping

The gas collection piping system rule of thumb is a 6" PVC pipe with vertical vents spaced at 200", with each vertical vent being 10'. For estimating purposes, a reasonable estimate is a total of 200' of vent per acre (horizontal and vertical pipe). Collection pipes are slotted, whereas vertical piping and connections above the impervious layer are not.

Maintenance

A 30-year maintenance period for capping is recommended by RCRA regulations. There are a number of items that may be classified as maintenance costs for capping, depending on the design of the system.

Maintenance for Vegetative Covers

If the cap is a vegetative cover, maintenance normally includes the following:

- Grass mowing, as needed, once the vegetative cover (or grass) has been established. An estimating rule of thumb is 1 mowing per month, year round for the duration of the closure and post-closure monitoring period.
- Re-fertilization of the total area of the cap (in acres) approximately once a year.
- Re-seeding/re-mulching periodically to maintain the vegetative cover. An estimating rule of thumb is to re-seed/re-mulch 1/15 of the surface area per year, over the life of the post-closure maintenance period.

Maintenance for Rock Covers

If the cap is rock, refill/grade washed out rock may be required. The type of rock, either rip-rap or gravel, will depend on the type chosen in the original system. A typical quantity for refill/grade rock is 1/30 of the cap surface area multiplied by the rock depth per year. This number is then multiplied by the post-closure monitoring period to determine the total amount of rock to replace over the life of the facility. The range is 0–5,000,000 C.Y.

For pavement covers, maintenance normally includes replacing washed out or cracked pavement. The type of pavement to be replaced, either concrete or asphalt, will depend on the type chosen. With nominal inspections and maintenance reviews, the pavement is assumed to last 30 years.

Maintenance for Polymeric Covers

If the cap has a polymeric cover, maintenance normally includes the following:

- Replacing washed out or cracked polymeric liner covers. The type of polymeric to be replaced will depend on the type chosen in the original design. When installed above ground, polymerics generally lose their permeability characteristics from degradation by UV light emitted by the sun. The useful life of the polymeric may be a maximum of 10 years, depending on the manufacturer's recommendations.
- Replacing aboveground gas vents because of degradation of PVC or HDPE piping from UV light or alternatively from damage by moving equipment. Since permeability is not a factor with the vents, they can be left in place longer than an aboveground polymeric liner.

Site Work and Utilities

Any applicable site work and utilities must be included in the estimate. Site work and utilities for capping may include:

- Cleanup and landscaping
- Fencing and signage
- Clear and grub
- Monitoring wells
- Decontamination facilities
- Storm sewer
- Retaining wall, C.I.P. concrete

Conclusion

Caps are a common application for remedial site closure, and they are likely to be used for some time. The primary cost drivers for a cap are its size, the type and number of layers, and the source and cost of the clay or bentonite. The cost engineer should carefully review these items and make cost comparisons between different design alternatives to help the engineer design the most appropriate solution.

Chapter 37

Permeable Barriers

Permeable barriers are a passive groundwater remediation technique in which contaminants are treated/removed as groundwater flows through an in situ treatment bed of permeable material. When combined with cut-off walls, such as sheet piling or slurry walls, the design is termed a **funnel and gate system**. In this arrangement, a low permeability cut-off wall diverts and funnels groundwater through a higher permeability gate (treatment bed).

Applications and Limitations

Applications

- Best suited for shallow aquifers (< 100') that are bounded below by a low hydraulic-conductivity layer, such as clay or bedrock.
- Used on sites where surface development, construction, or other use is desired.
- Capable of treating a wide range of contaminants due to the variety of treatment media available.

Limitations

- Passive treatment walls may lose their reactive capacity, requiring replacement of the reactive medium.
- Limited to a subsurface lithology that has a continuous aquitard at a depth that is within the vertical limits of trenching equipment.
- Biological activity or chemical precipitation may limit the permeability of the passive treatment wall.
- Location of walls may be limited by factors such as property boundaries, subsurface obstructions (utilities, boulders, etc.), or surface obstructions (buildings, landscape features, etc.). Any combination of these factors may require that the wall be installed within the contaminated area.

Process Configurations and Treatment Train Considerations

- Removable media cassettes may be used for sites where the media must be replaced or varied during the treatment period.
- Cut-off walls for funnel and gate systems can be constructed from sheet piling or slurry walls.
- Treatment and cut-off walls that are not keyed into an underlying layer of low permeability are termed hanging and are susceptible to untreated groundwater passing underneath.

- The presence of large rocks and cobble in the underlying soil matrix may increase costs or prohibit the use of techniques such as sheet piling.
- Monitoring wells should be installed upgradient and downgradient of the wall to determine effectiveness.
- Since most permeable barriers can be capped upon completion, surface development and vehicular activity can occur.
- Zero-valent metals are used to degrade chlorinated organics into non-toxic dehalogenated compounds.
- Limestone aggregate can be used to neutralize acidic mine drainage.

Basic Information Needed for Estimating

It is possible to create a reasonable cost estimate using a few required parameters. If more detailed information is known, one can create a more precise and site-specific estimate using a secondary set of parameters.

To estimate the cost of a permeable barrier system, the following information must be known.

General

Values must be provided for all required parameters, which include:

- Permeable Barrier Type
- Gate Dimensions
- Sheet Piling Dimensions
- Slurry Wall Dimensions
- Safety Level

Permeable Barrier Type

A permeable barrier may be used alone or in conjunction with a cut-off wall to form a funnel and gate system. If a cut-off wall is not used, the design will incorporate a stand-alone permeable wall to treat the portion of a contaminant plume that flows through the treatment media. If a cut-off wall is used as a funnel to route the groundwater through the treatment media, the funnel section can be constructed from either sheet piling or a slurry wall. Three design options are typically considered:

- Treatment Wall Only
- Gate with Sheet Piling
- Gate with Slurry Wall

Gate Dimensions

A trench will be excavated to emplace the treatment media. This permeable section will serve as either a stand-alone treatment wall or gate, if a funnel section is included. Sheet piling will be installed around the sides of this trench as shoring to prevent cave-in of the soil during excavation. Generally, the treatment trench is installed in uncontaminated soil at a distance downgradient to the plume, so the excavated material is suitable for backfilling. The trench is typically excavated so that it is wider than the treatment bed in order to accommodate bracing and excavation equipment. The excavation should continue through clay or bedrock (aquitard) a distance of 2' below the trench depth, in order to key-in the wall.

Sheet Piling Dimensions

This parameter applies only to cases in which sheet piling is used to form a cut-off wall. Driving sheet piling may not be practical in soil types containing a high percentage of large rocks and cobble. Characterization of the soil lithology should be performed before deciding to install sheet piling. Length refers to the total length of cut-off wall constructed with sheet piling to form the funnel portion.

Slurry Wall Dimensions

This parameter applies only in cases in which a slurry wall is used to form the cut-off wall. A slurry wall estimate, which allows you to adjust additional parameters pertinent to slurry wall construction, can be made using the guidelines in Chapter 38, "Slurry Walls."

Treatment Media

These parameters include:

- Primary Treatment Media
- Other Treatment Media
- Gate Volume

An estimate of the height in the trench from the bottom of the fill to the water table must be prepared in order to determine the treatment media volume. The bottom of the fill is 2' below the trench depth to allow for a keyed-in wall.

An extra layer of treatment media can be added above the average water table height at the site in order to account for seasonal variations in the water table height. An effective treatment bed thickness must also be determined. Figure 37.1 shows different treatment media and contaminants treated by each.

Treatment Media	Contaminant(s) Treated
Iron Fillings	Chlorinated Organics
Activated Carbon, Coal Derived	Organics and Heavy Metals
Crushed Limestone	Acid Neutralization and Heavy Metals
Clinoptilolite	Radionuclides
Montmorillonite Clay	Cationic Metal and Organic Species
Glauconitic Greensands	Heavy Metals and Radionuclides
Fuller's (Diatomaceous) Earth	Pesticides, Herbicides, Oils, and Grease
Peat Moss	Organics and Heavy Metals
Proprietary Metal Oxidizing Powder	Organics
Proprietary Iron-Foam Aggregate	Chlorinated Organics
Proprietary Humic-Acid Adsorbent	Organics, Heavy Metals, and Radionuclides
Pea Gravel	None (Functions as Filter Pack)
User Supplied (Other)	Dependent on Media

Figure 37.1 Treatment Media and Contaminants Treated

Safety Level

The contaminant(s) at the site determine its safety level. Four safety levels defined by OSHA in 29 CFR Part 1910 include A, B, C, and D, where level "A" is the most protective, and "D" is the least protective. A safety level of E (Modified Level D) is also included to simulate normal construction (no hazard) conditions as prescribed by the EPA.

Design Information Needed for Detailed Estimates

Following are descriptions of the types of detailed information that, when available, can add accuracy to estimates. Also included are design criteria and estimating rules of thumb that the estimator typically uses to determine values that are not known, or to check information provided by others.

Soil/Backfill

The Soil/Backfill secondary design parameters include:

- Soil Type
- Borrow Material (on-site and off-site)
- Cap Type

Soil Type

Excavating the trench and slurry wall requires additional effort if large rocks, cobble, and boulders are present in the soil. An extra volume of soil will be removed as well in order to excavate around boulders and large rocks. The presence of boulders may also hamper pile driving, or even prohibit its application if a low permeability cut-off wall is desired. The estimate should incorporate the soil type, if known, and make adjustments for soil conditions that will either inhibit or prohibit construction of a permeable barrier.

Backfill: Volume of trench backfill is a significant cost driver. It is expressed in cubic yards of the treatment wall (including the key-in portion), less the combined volume of all treatment media added. The backfill volume requirement increases if the soil type changes from Normal to Cobble, to account for extra excavation in the trench to remove boulders and large rocks.

Borrow Material

Borrow material from an on-site or off-site source may be required for use as backfill. The excavated material from the treatment wall will be reused as backfill, if possible, once the media has been placed. If the excavated material is contaminated and cannot be used as backfill material, then borrow material will be used. The estimator should consider the source of fill material, the cost of purchase, if any, and the cost to haul the material to the project site.

Cap Type

The treatment wall (gate) can be capped to reduce erosion and infiltration of rainwater or to act as a barrier layer, depending on the design option chosen. Upon completion of the backfilling operation, a slurry wall is normally covered with a cap to protect the surface from drying and cracking. A soil/vegetative cap is most common. Suitable topsoil material is required for this application. The estimator should consider the source of fill material, the cost of purchase, if any, and the cost to haul the material to the project site. The cap will be installed over both the trench and slurry wall areas of the site, if a slurry wall is used. When vehicular traffic must travel over a treatment or slurry wall, a cap of either asphalt or aggregate would normally be used. Cap options include:

- Vegetative with Off-site Topsoil
- Vegetative with On-site Topsoil
- Rip-rap with Separation Fabric
- Gravel with Separation Fabric
- Asphalt
- None

Wells

Secondary design parameters for wells include:

- Process Monitoring Wells
- Well Spacing Distance
- Screen Length
- Well Construction Material
- Well Diameter
- Media Replacement Frequency

Process Monitoring Wells

Process monitoring wells may be installed in the treatment wall and are constructed by installing vertical pipes in the excavation before the media is placed. The process monitoring wells span the depth of the trench. The placement of media and/or packing pea gravel around the pipes secures the pipes in place. The treatment/removal efficiency of the media is monitored by sampling these wells. If a specific monitoring plan is not available, assume that a first sample is obtained at the front of the treatment bed, a second is obtained mid-way through the treatment bed, and a third sample is obtained at the back of the treatment bed. Thus, groundwater is sampled at 3 collinear points as it flows perpendicularly through the treatment wall.

Well Spacing Distance

This is the spacing distance between process monitoring wells along the length of the treatment wall. At each sampling location there will be three collinear well points: one at the front of the media, the second mid-way within the media, and the third at the back end of the media. Well spacing distance will generally be about 10' if either *Gate with Slurry Wall* or *Gate with Sheet Piling* are the selected barrier types. If *Treatment Wall Only* is the selected barrier type, then the default well spacing can be assumed to be 50'. This implies that a treatment wall 20' in length would have two sampling locations, each 10' apart along the length of the wall (totaling 6 individual wells, $2 \times 3 = 6$), for this example. Different spacing distances may be used if site conditions so dictate.

Screen Length

The length of the intake screen for the process monitoring well is measured in feet. The typical screen length is 5', but can vary from 1–10'.

Well Construction Material

The material used for the process monitoring well (standpipe material) is usually PVC, but if corrosive substances are present, stainless steel may be specified.

Well Diameter

This is the inner diameter of the process monitoring well measured in inches. The default for this technology is a 4" well, but 2" or 6" wells may also be used.

Media Replacement Frequency

A major variable for permeable barriers is the site-specific useful life of the treatment media. The site hydrology and groundwater contaminants could lead to premature exhaustion of the treatment media, prior to the contaminant plume being fully remediated. In such cases, the spent media would need to be excavated and replaced with fresh media.

The specific media replacement frequency for a particular treatment media is best determined through a combination of pilot/full-scale testing and manufacturer recommendations. A rule of thumb is once every 10 years, but treatment media can last up to 30 years. Typically, if media replacement is required more often than once every 3 years, an alternate treatment system would be used.

Related Costs

The most significant related cost for permeable barriers is the installation of slurry walls, if required. Slurry walls are used with permeable barriers to create a gate and funnel system to direct groundwater through the barrier. See Chapter 38, "Slurry Walls," for estimating guidance.

The project may also require supplementary soil for backfill if the excavated soil is contaminated. If this is the case, the contaminated excavated soil would require treatment. Surface restoration may be required after construction of the permeable barrier and could include landscaping, paving, or other restoration.

Site Work and Utilities

If site work and utilities apply, they must also be accounted for in the estimate. This category may include an access road, fencing, and signage.

Conclusion

Permeable barriers are a groundwater treatment method that can be quite effective in reducing overall treatment costs for hazardous wastes by using natural groundwater flows and biological processes to treat water without requiring pumping or other mechanical processes. The primary cost drivers are the size of the system, the design options chosen, the duration of the operating period and associated monitoring, and replenishment of media if required. The cost engineer should be able to determine these items from the design team early in the design process, and should work with the designer to optimize the system design.

Chapter 38

Slurry Wall

A *slurry wall* is a vertical subsurface barrier used to contain, capture, or redirect groundwater flow in the vicinity of a contaminated site. The slurry wall is excavated under a slurry and backfilled with a material that forms a low-permeability barrier. The slurry, which is usually a mixture of bentonite and water, hydraulically shores the trench to prevent collapse. The slurry also forms a filter cake on the trench walls to prevent high fluid losses into the surrounding ground.

Slurry walls are typically categorized by the materials used to backfill the trench. The soil-bentonite slurry wall, which consists of a backfill mixture of bentonite slurry and soil, is the most common. Another type is the cement-bentonite slurry wall, is constructed by excavating the trench under a slurry of Portland cement, bentonite, and water, which is left to harden in place. This chapter addresses soil-bentonite slurry walls.

Applications and Limitations

Applications

- To contain contaminated groundwater, divert contaminated groundwater from drinking water sources, divert uncontaminated groundwater, and/or provide a barrier for a groundwater treatment system.
- Applicable to sites where the extent of contamination precludes treatment.
- Used to contain all contaminant types.
- Typically placed at depths from 20–80', generally 2–4' thick.

Limitations

- Most implementations involve large amounts of heavy construction.
- Future remediation efforts may be necessary, as the contaminant is only contained by use of slurry wall, and not removed.
- The wall may degrade or deteriorate over time. Soil-bentonite backfills are subject to degradation by naturally occurring acids, bases, salt solutions, and other organic chemicals.
- Cost of backfill materials (e.g., bentonite) may be quite high.

Process Configurations and Treatment Train Considerations

- Soil-bentonite and cement-bentonite slurry walls are the most common types of wall construction.
- Slurry walls are commonly used in conjunction with pump-and-treat and capping.
- Because the slurry wall will, in most cases, be in contact with the contaminants, chemical compatibility is an issue.
- Proper extension and sealing of the wall to an aquitard is required to prevent under-wall seepage.
- Wet/dry cycles may result in desiccation and damage to slurry walls, thereby increasing their porosity.

Typical System Design Elements

Slurry walls can be installed in a wide variety of configurations, including upgradient or downgradient of the contaminated zone, or in a circumferential configuration that completely encompasses the contaminated zone. The circumferential installation is the most common and offers several advantages:

- Greatly reduces the amount of uncontaminated groundwater entering the site from upgradient, thereby reducing the amount of leachate generated.
- Reduces the amount of leachate that escapes on the downgradient side.
- When used in conjunction with an infiltration barrier and a leachate collection system, maintains the hydraulic gradient in an inward direction and prevents leachate escape.

An upgradient placement diverts clean groundwater around a contaminated zone in high-gradient situations. An upgradient wall will not stop the generation of leachate, but may slow its generation by stagnating groundwater behind the wall. A downgradient placement captures floating contaminants, but configuration often proves ineffective or inappropriate because it requires direct contact between the wall and the leachate.

Regardless of the configuration, a positive cutoff of groundwater flow is essential for proper containment of the contaminant. This cutoff is normally accomplished by keying the wall into the underlying confining layer, which is usually a clay deposit or bedrock layer. The confining layer must be sufficiently low in permeability to retard downward migration of the contaminant and must be thick enough to allow excavation of an adequate key-in. A key-in depth of 2–3' is typical.

In some cases, slurry walls are constructed by terminating the excavation a few feet below the groundwater table without keying the trench into the underlying confining layer. This is referred to as a "hanging" slurry wall. Although a hanging wall can be used to trap floating contaminants, the hanging design requires the wall to be in direct contact with the contaminant, which can drastically reduce the effectiveness of the wall. The use of hanging slurry walls in contaminated zones is rare and usually ineffective.

The contaminant must be compatible with the wall, especially when the wall must be in direct contact with the contaminant. Certain chemical contaminants can actually increase the permeability of a slurry wall. The contaminant's compatibility with the proposed backfill should be verified early in the design phase through permeability testing of the proposed backfill material with actual leachate or groundwater. The results of such testing can be used to determine the most appropriate wall configuration and backfill composition, and to select any additional measures necessary to enhance the performance of the wall.

The permeability of a slurry wall installed to control contaminated groundwater depends largely on the backfill material and is generally 1×10^{-7} cm/sec to 1×10^{-6} cm/sec. Soil used in backfill must have a sufficient fines content 30% finer than a number 200 sieve to ensure low permeability of the wall. Backfill usually contains between 6–12% bentonite. Excavated soil is normally used for backfill, provided it is free of contamination and can be treated to ensure sufficient fines content. Borrow soil is used when the excavated soil is contaminated or contains insufficient fines.

Site topography can be a limiting factor in the use of a soil-bentonite slurry wall, which are best suited to level terrain, since both the slurry and backfill will flow under stress. Cement-bentonite slurry walls are more appropriate for steeply sloping terrain. The amount of clear working space around the trench excavation may also affect the feasibility of slurry wall installation. If there is not enough clear working space beside the trench for slurry and backfill mixing these operations will have to be located off-site, and the slurry and backfill will have to be transported to the trench.

Construction of a soil-bentonite slurry wall is a relatively straightforward process. The type of equipment used depends largely on the depth of the wall. For depths of up to 25', no special equipment is required. Hydraulic excavators with extension booms are required for depths from 25–75'. Deeper excavations require the use of a clamshell or dragline. Depths greater than 120' typically require special equipment for both trench excavation and backfill placement, and are beyond the scope of this chapter. Although slurry wall trenches can be excavated to limited depths in rock, such installations are not feasible and are beyond the scope of this chapter.

Regardless of the excavation equipment chosen, the slurry is introduced immediately after the trench is opened and before the water table is reached. As excavation continues, more slurry is added so that slurry is in the trench at all times. Backfilling normally begins once a sufficient length of trench has been excavated. Backfill is carefully mixed to the proper consistency and then placed in the trench using a bulldozer. The completed slurry wall is typically covered with a compacted soil cap, but an asphalt or gravel cap may be used when vehicular traffic must cross the wall.

As a passive measure, a slurry wall itself requires very little maintenance, other than the maintenance of the cap atop the wall. However, maintenance of leachate collection systems and infiltration barriers used in conjunction with the slurry wall is important to the wall as part of the entire remedy. Groundwater levels are normally monitored inside and outside the wall to ensure that design head levels are not exceeded.

This chapter covers construction of a slurry wall to depths of 120'. If adequate clear space is not available in the vicinity of the trench for slurry and backfill mixing, transportation from off-site mixing facilities is required. The discussion in this chapter assumes that all slurry wall construction will take place outside of the contaminated zone. When a slurry wall penetrates through a contaminated zone, the excavated material will require treatment or disposal. Treatment and disposal of contaminated soil is not discussed in this chapter, but can be estimated using information in other chapters of this book, depending on the treatment and disposal option required.

Basic Information Needed for Estimating

It is possible to create a reasonable cost estimate using a few required parameters, described in the following paragraphs. If more detailed information is known, one can create a more precise and site-specific estimate using a secondary set of parameters.

Length of Wall

The total length of the slurry wall is measured in feet. For circular or curved installations, this parameter would represent the perimeter of the wall.

Depth of Wall

The depth of wall is measured, in feet, from the working surface to the bottom of the excavation. The depth determines the type of equipment used to excavate the trench. For depths to 25', a hydraulic excavator is typically used to excavate the trench. For depths between 25–75', a hydraulic excavator with an extension boom is used, and for depths between 75–120', a dragline is used. Depths greater than 120' typically require special equipment for both trench excavation and backfill placement.

Soil Type

The type of soil being excavated has an impact on the productivity of the excavation equipment. Typical soil types are as follows:

- Normal (clay)
- Clay/sand with boulders

Bedrock Key-In

Slurry walls are normally keyed into an underlying confining layer to create a hydraulic barrier at the base of the wall. If this is required, the key-in depth is normally 2–3'.

Worker Safety Level

Worker safety is affected by the contaminant(s) at the site. Safety level refers to the levels required by OSHA in 29 CFR Part 1910. The 4 levels are designated as A, B, C, and D, where "A" is the most protective, and "D" is the least protective. A safety level of E is also included to simulate normal construction, "no hazard" conditions as prescribed by the EPA.

Design Information Needed for Detailed Estimates

Following are descriptions of the types of detailed information that, when available, can add detail and accuracy to estimates. Also included are design criteria and estimating rules of thumb that estimators use to determine values that are not known, or to check information provided by others.

Width of Wall

The width of the slurry wall trench is determined in part by the width of the bucket used to excavate the trench. The width of the wall is measured in feet. Widths of 2–4' are typical for depths up to 70', and widths of 3–4' are typical for depths greater than 70'.

Percent Bentonite by Weight for Slurry

The unit weight of bentonite is 150 lb/C.F., and 62.4 lb/C.F. of that weight is water. A typical percentage range for bentonite for slurry is 5–15%.

Percent Bentonite by Volume for Backfill

The percent by volume of bentonite in the soil-bentonite backfill typically ranges from 5–25%; lower values in the 5–10% range are most common.

Percent Slurry Loss Due to Seepage

The approximate percentage of slurry that will be lost due to seepage is used to estimate the volume of slurry required. A seepage loss of approximately 30% is typical.

Percent of Soil with Insufficient Fines Content

Excavated material must have a fines content of at least 30% to be suitable for use as backfill. In other words, at least 30% of the soil must be finer than a No. 200 sieve. Typically, approximately 20–40% of any excavated material will have insufficient fines content and will be replaced by borrow material.

Percent of Contaminated Soil

The excavated material that is assumed to be contaminated cannot be used for backfill. The percent of contaminated material is used to determine the quantity of borrow material required for backfill mixing. The estimator can determine costs for transportation and disposal of contaminated material using one of the disposal technologies discussed elsewhere in this book.

Width of Working Surface

A sufficient working surface must be available on both sides of the trench for slurry and backfill mixing and storage. This parameter refers to the total width of the working surface. The length of the working surface is assumed to be equal to the length of the slurry wall trench. Typically, the working surface will be graded level and compacted. For most slurry wall installations, a working surface width of 75' is sufficient. When site conditions limit the size of the working surface, slurry and backfill mixing operations may have to be located off site.

Type of Cap

Once the backfilling operation is complete, the slurry wall is normally covered with a soil cap to protect it from drying and cracking. Typically, a soil/vegetative cap is required, and suitable topsoil material is available on site. When vehicular traffic must cross a wall, traffic caps of either asphalt or aggregate with geotextiles are normally used. Options for cap construction are as follows:

- Vegetative with on-site topsoil
- Vegetative with off-site topsoil

- Rip-rap with separation fabric
- Gravel with separation fabric
- Asphalt

Width of Cap

The width of the cap over the slurry wall is measured in feet. Typically, the cap extends across the entire width of the wall and 5' on either side.

Thickness of Cap

The thickness of the cap is measured in inches and applies only to vegetative, rock, and gravel caps. For vegetative caps, the typical thickness is 6", and for rock and gravel caps, 12" is common. Asphalt caps typically consist of a 10" subgrade, an 8" base, and a 1-½" topping.

Containment Berm Type

Depending on job–site conditions, it may be desirable to use inflatable containment berms as slurry or backfill mixing basins. Inflatable containment berms may also be used for temporary storage of contaminated materials. Containment berms are available in a variety of sizes, as listed below.

10' × 10' × 17"	750 Gallon
13' × 13' × 17"	1,800 Gallon
18' × 18' × 17"	3,400 Gallon
24' × 24' × 17"	6,100 Gallon
32' × 32' × 17"	10,800 Gallon
32' × 32' × 34"	21,600 Gallon
74' × 34' × 34"	53,400 Gallon
45' × 15' × 17"	7,600 Gallon
65' × 16' × 17"	11,000 Gallon
50' × 22' × 17"	11,600 Gallon

Containment Berm Quantity

This is the number of containment berms required including the size. This would be determined based on the quantity of material to be stored and the size of the storage area(s) available at the site.

Other Related Costs

Depending on the soil type and the presence of contamination, it may be necessary to either supplement or replace the excavated material with borrow material for use as backfill. The quantity of borrow material is a function of the percent of contaminated soil and the percent of soil with insufficient fines content. Also, any contaminated material excavated will have to be treated and disposed of properly. Treatment and disposal of contaminated material are addressed in other chapters of this book depending on the methods used.

Site Work and Utilities

Site work and utilities that may need to be addressed in the estimate are:

- Clearing and grubbing
- Overhead electrical distribution
- Access roads
- Fencing

Conclusion   Slurry walls can be an effective passive treatment methodology to contain contaminants. The cost drivers are the length, depth, and width of the wall; the amount of bentonite required; the quality and usability of the existing soil as backfill; and the availability of on-site mixing. The estimator should work closely with the design team to develop and compare alternative design approaches to minimize costs while meeting the project's technical objectives.

Chapter 39

Underground Storage Tank Closure

Underground storage tanks are one of the primary sources of groundwater contamination in the United States. An *underground storage tank* (UST), as defined by Subtitle I of RCRA, is a tank system (including piping) that has at least 10% of its volume underground. Most leaking UST systems are at least 15–20 years old, are constructed of carbon steel, and are prone to corrosion.

This chapter covers the costs associated with closure of UST sites. UST closure is not a stand-alone treatment technology. Once the underground storage tanks have been either disposed in place or removed, the surrounding soil and groundwater may require remediation, depending on the results of the closure assessment. Closure of leaking tanks is often followed by remediation processes, such as soil vapor extraction to treat contaminated soil, or air stripping to treat contaminated groundwater. Thus UST closure is actually part of a treatment train. Only tank closure is addressed in this chapter. Other remediation methods (soil vapor extraction, air stripping, excavation of buried waste, etc.) are discussed elsewhere in this book.

Applications and Limitations

Applications

- Closure of a UST through either disposal in place or removal.
- Typical UST materials include carbon steel, fiberglass, or 6" thick mesh-reinforced concrete.
- In-place disposal may be appropriate when physical barriers, site conditions, or safety constraints make removal impractical.

Limitations

- Closure assessments may be necessary to determine the nature and extent of contamination caused by the tank or system of tanks.
- Surrounding soils and groundwater may require remediation.
- Removed tanks are usually decontaminated by steam-cleaning or sand-blasting. Residue from decontamination may require treatment and disposal.

Typical System Design Elements

Permanent closure of a UST system can be accomplished either through disposal in place or removal from the ground. Tank removal is the preferred method because it physically removes the contaminant source. In-place disposal is appropriate when tank removal may damage or undermine adjacent structures or when the presence of underground utilities, such as water and sewer lines or electrical cables, renders removal impractical.

This chapter covers cost estimating associated with closure of a UST site by either in-place disposal or removal. The USTs addressed in this chapter may be constructed of either carbon steel, fiberglass, or 6" thick mesh-reinforced concrete. UST removal, as defined in this chapter, involves completely excavating the site and removing all of the tanks as well as all feed lines. Options are also discussed for in-place disposal of feed lines.

Removing USTs involves several steps: demolishing surface structures or pavement over the tank; draining the tank; purging the tank vapors; excavating the tank cover; removing the tank; backfilling; and restoring the surface.

Dry ice is typically used to purge all tanks of vapors prior to removal. Projects generally include decontamination of tanks by either steam-cleaning or sandblasting. The method of decontamination used depends on the construction of the tanks. Carbon steel and fiberglass tanks are typically removed from the ground intact and decontaminated by steam-cleaning, whereas concrete tanks and containment vaults are sandblasted and demolished.

Once the tanks are removed, the excavation is backfilled. If no tanks in the excavation have leaked, all excavated material may be safely backfilled. However, if any tanks in the excavation have leaked, the excavated soil is assumed to be contaminated, and the excavation is filled with borrow material. Treatment or transportation and disposal of excavated soil is not included in this chapter, but is discussed in other chapters of this book, depending on the remediation approach to be used.

As stated previously, in-place disposal may be appropriate when physical barriers and constraints at a site make tank removal impractical. In-place disposal is normally accomplished by excavating to the tops of the tanks, pumping out remaining liquid, purging all tanks of vapors, and then filling the tanks with an inert substance, such as sand, concrete, or foam. Sand is the most common material used for filling tanks.

Regardless of the closure method chosen, closure assessments are normally required to determine the nature and extent of contamination caused by the storage tank system and to determine whether additional site investigation is necessary.

This chapter covers estimating methods that are appropriate for UST sites ranging from small service stations with only a few tanks to large tank farms with multiple clusters of underground tanks. For estimating purposes, this chapter uses a 3-level hierarchy to define UST sites. This hierarchy makes it possible to cost sites with multiple tank sizes in the same excavation. Following are definitions of each of the 3 levels referred to throughout this chapter. Figure 39.1 illustrates this hierarchy.

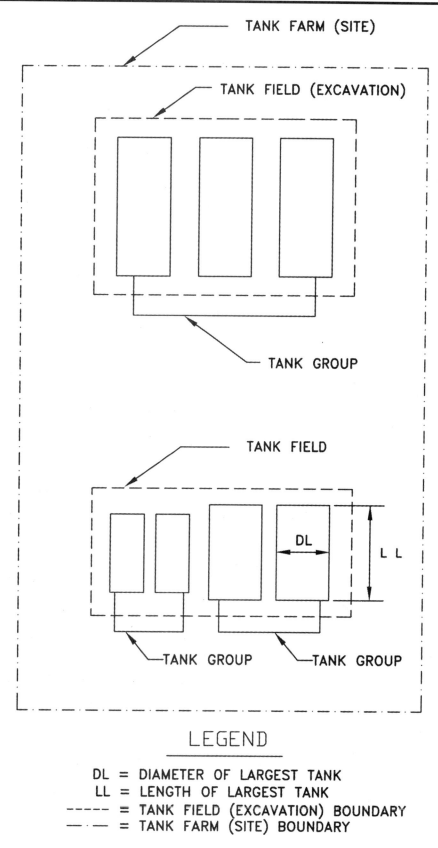

Figure 39.1 Underground Storage Tank Closure

Tank Farm: One contiguous site that may contain multiple tank fields.

Tank Field: One contiguous excavation or cluster of tanks, which may have multiple tank groups.

Tank Group: Within each tank field or excavation, different tank groups may be defined to categorize similar tanks (i.e., all tanks of the same size) together.

Certain states and principalities have jurisdiction over hazardous substance sites. Occasionally, state or local regulatory agencies have more stringent regulatory requirements than the federal regulatory agency. This chapter discusses UST closures based on federal regulatory requirements. The estimator should evaluate local requirements applicable to the site to determine if any additional requirements are likely to increase project costs.

Basic Information Needed for Estimating

It is possible to create a reasonable cost estimate using a few required parameters described in the following paragraph and illustrated in Figures 39.2-39.4. If more detailed information is known, one can create a more precise and site-specific estimate using a secondary set of parameters.

Figure 39.2 shows a plan and schematic view of a single tank closure. Figure 39.3 shows a multiple tank application for tanks in a single field. Figure 39.4 shows a multiple tank application with the tanks located inside a vault.

Tank Field Data

The site-specific parameters that drive the costs associated with tank fields include the following.

Type of Closure

Closure of UST systems may be accomplished either by removal or by disposal in-place. Removal is the most commonly accepted method. However, in-place disposal may be appropriate when barriers such as adjacent structures or underground utilities render tank removal impractical. Tank removal involves complete excavation of the tank field. All tanks are purged of vapors, decontaminated, and completely removed from the excavation. In-place disposal, on the other hand, involves only enough excavation to gain access to the tops of tanks. The tank contents are removed; the inner tank air is thus rendered non-explosive through purging of ambient vapors. The tanks are then filled with sand.

Existing Cover

The existing cover is the cover above the tanks, which will be demolished to gain access to the tanks. Existing cover options typically include the following:

- Asphalt
- Soil/gravel
- < 6" concrete, mesh reinforced
- < 6" concrete, rod reinforced
- < 6" concrete, non-reinforced
- 7–24" concrete, rod reinforced Normally, the cover over the tanks is demolished regardless of the closure option chosen. If soil/gravel is chosen as the existing cover, then no demolition costs are normally included.

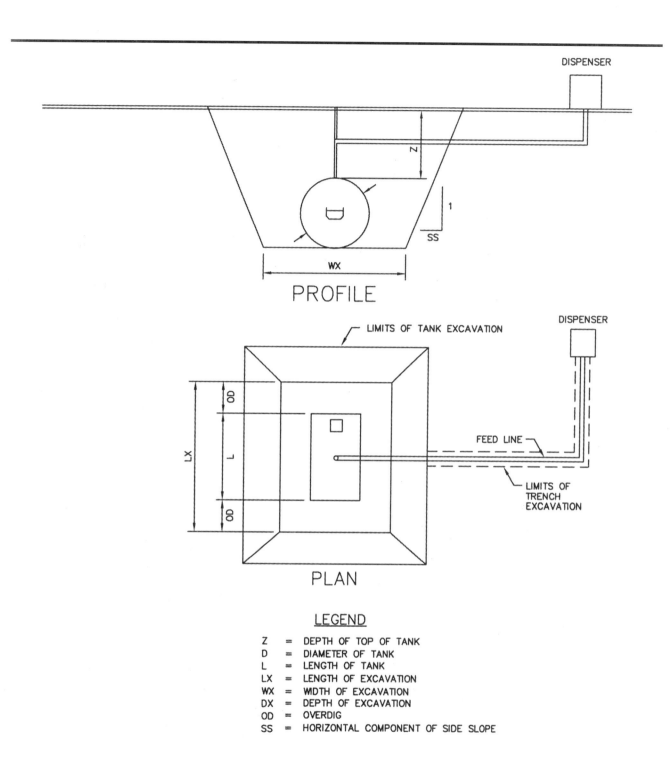

DISPENSER

Z

1

SS

WX

PROFILE

DISPENSER

LIMITS OF TANK EXCAVATION

OD

LX

L

OD

FEED LINE

LIMITS OF
TRENCH
EXCAVATION

PLAN

LEGEND

Z   =   DEPTH OF TOP OF TANK
D   =   DIAMETER OF TANK
L   =   LENGTH OF TANK
LX =   LENGTH OF EXCAVATION
WX =   WIDTH OF EXCAVATION
DX =   DEPTH OF EXCAVATION
OD =   OVERDIG
SS =   HORIZONTAL COMPONENT OF SIDE SLOPE

Figure 39.2 Plan/Schematic View for Single UST Closure

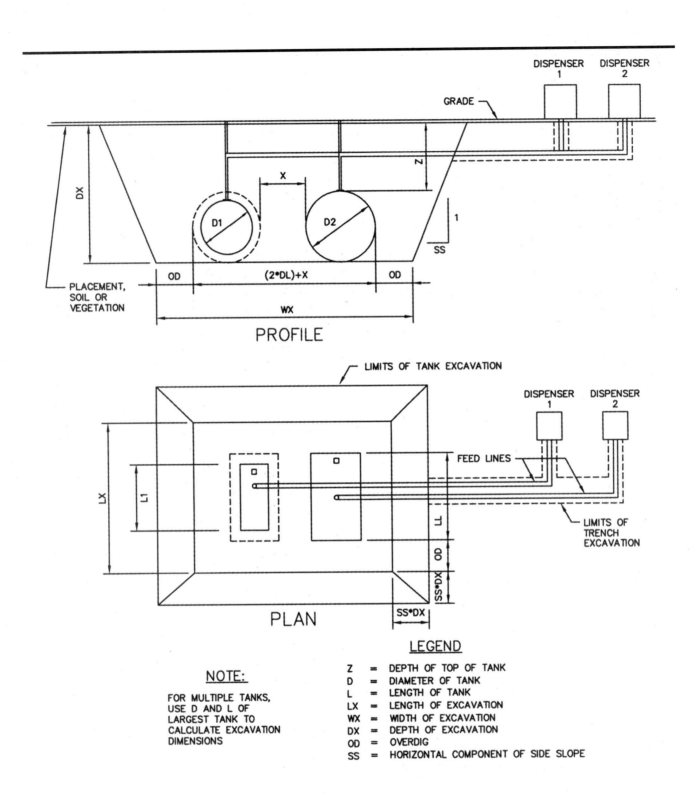

PROFILE

PLAN

NOTE:

FOR MULTIPLE TANKS,
USE D AND L OF
LARGEST TANK TO
CALCULATE EXCAVATION
DIMENSIONS

LEGEND

Z	=	DEPTH OF TOP OF TANK
D	=	DIAMETER OF TANK
L	=	LENGTH OF TANK
LX	=	LENGTH OF EXCAVATION
WX	=	WIDTH OF EXCAVATION
DX	=	DEPTH OF EXCAVATION
OD	=	OVERDIG
SS	=	HORIZONTAL COMPONENT OF SIDE SLOPE

Figure 39.3 UST Closure, Multiple Tanks in Single Field

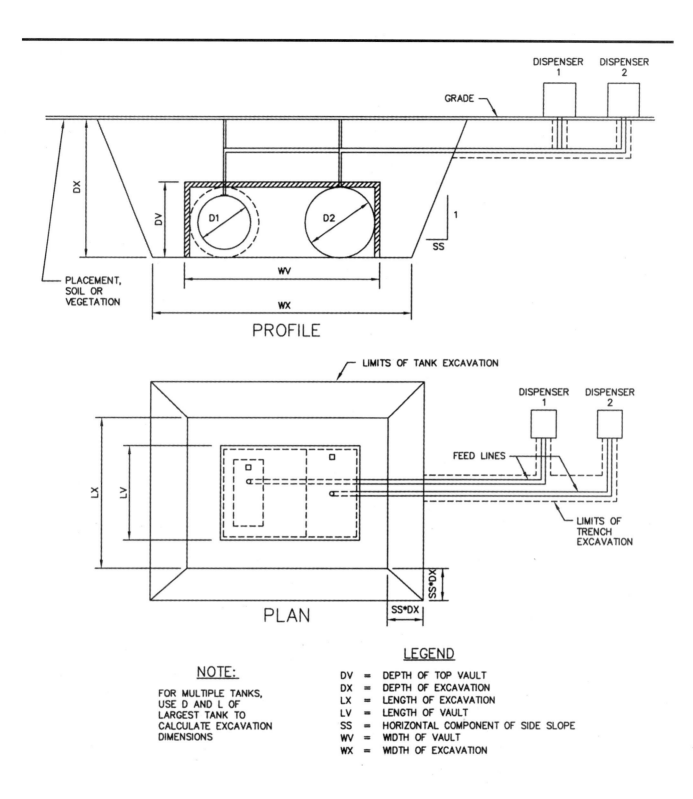

Figure 39.4 UST Closure, Multiple Tanks in Vault

Side Wall Protection

Current OSHA regulations require excavations deeper than 5' to be protected against cave-in. This is normally accomplished either by installing sheeting or by sloping the excavation walls. If the side slope method is used, the estimator must define the side slope ratio in terms of horizontal (run) to vertical rise.

Depth to Groundwater

The depth to groundwater, measured in feet, determines the depth of soil borings. The depth to groundwater also drives assumptions regarding the installation of groundwater monitoring wells.

Backfill

When USTs are removed in conjunction with new tank installation, the cost of backfilling the excavation after the new tanks are installed is typically addressed in the storage tank installation portion of the estimate and should, therefore, be excluded from the UST closure portion of the estimate. Placement of these costs in a specific part of the estimate is not critical, as long as they're included and not double counted.

Tanks in Containment Vault

USTs are sometimes enclosed in secondary containment systems such as concrete vaults. Normally, the vaults are demolished when the tanks are removed. If tanks enclosed in concrete vaults are to be disposed in-place, then the vault as well as the tanks are filled with sand. Decontamination costs for the demolished concrete vaults should be included. The estimate may also need to address transportation and disposal of the resulting concrete rubble.

Worker Safety Level

Worker safety is affected by the contaminant(s) at the site. Safety level refers to the levels required by OSHA in 29 CFR Part 1910. The 4 levels are designated as A, B, C, and D, where "A" is the most protective, and "D" is the least protective. A safety level of E is also included to simulate normal construction, "no hazard" conditions as prescribed by the EPA.

Tank Group Data

Within a tank field or excavation, tanks are defined in groups of similar tanks. The following parameters are assumed to be the same for all tanks within a group.

If all of the parameters are the same for all tanks within a field, then only one tank group needs to be defined for that field. The tank group definition makes it possible to define the parameters for similar tanks in one step rather than defining the parameters for every individual tank.

Tank Group Identification Number

This is an assigned number that the estimator can use to track data and costs.

Number of Tanks in Group

This parameter refers to the number of similar tanks (same volume, same construction, etc.) that will be defined in the same group.

Volume of Tanks

The volume of each tank in the group is normally in the range of 500–150,000 gallons. The volume also drives the tank diameter and length assumptions. For estimating purposes, a conservative approach would be to use the largest diameter tank when multiple tanks are removed. If a site under consideration contains USTs larger than 50,000 gallons, a qualified tank removal contractor should be contacted for details regarding equipment and methods used in the tank removal process.

Age of Tanks

The age of the tank, in years, drives assumptions regarding the operational integrity of the tank. Tanks that were installed prior to 1985 are generally constructed of carbon steel and are susceptible to corrosion. One can usually assume that a single-wall, carbon steel tank older than 15 years is leaking.

Leaking

This parameter refers to the operational integrity of the tanks in the field and drives assumptions for sampling and analysis, borrow quantity, and other assessment requirements. The options for this parameter are simply yes or no.

Tank Construction

Tanks are generally constructed from one of three materials:

- Carbon steel
- Fiberglass reinforced plastic (FRP)
- Concrete

Tank construction drives assumptions regarding tank removal. Carbon steel or fiberglass tanks are removed from the ground intact, whereas concrete tanks are demolished and then removed. Carbon steel is the most common type of tank for sites over 15 years old and can be assumed if site information is not available.

Depth to Top of Tanks

The depth to the top of the tank, in feet, drives the excavated soil volume costs. Excavations deeper than 5' will require either steel sheeting or a side slope to prevent cave-in.

Liquid Remaining

The liquid remaining in the tank drives the cost of evacuating the contents prior to closure. Typically, tank liquids are recycled or re-used to avoid costs for handling evacuated liquids. For estimating purposes, there are 5 tank volume levels:

- Near empty (only sludges remaining)
- 1/4 full
- 1/2 full
- 3/4 full
- Full

Number of Feed Lines

The number of feed lines connected to each tank in a group drives the cost of purging and removing the lines. Typically, there is 1 feed line per tank, but up to 4 lines may be used for larger tanks.

General Parameters

The general parameters address other items associated with tank closure projects. Unlike the tank group parameters that apply only to tank groups, the general parameters apply to the entire tank field. The general parameters include the following.

Replacement Cover

The replacement cover is the type of cover installed after the tank closure operation is complete. Options for the replacement cover include:

- Asphalt
- Soil/gravel
- 6" concrete, mesh-reinforced
- 6" concrete, rod-reinforced
- 6" concrete, non-reinforced
- 12" structural slab on grade

Tank Decontamination

This parameter is used to specify whether or not tanks in a field will be decontaminated, typically, tanks that will be disposed in-place are not decontaminated; tanks that are removed are decontaminated. If decontamination is required, carbon steel and fiberglass tanks are normally steam-cleaned, and concrete tanks and vaults are decontaminated via sandblasting. The steam-cleaning and pressure-washing processes generate residue at a rate of approximately 4 gal/S.F. The sandblasting process generates residue at a rate of 2 lbs/S.F. The estimate should include treatment and disposal of decontamination residue.

Remove Feed Lines

This parameter specifies whether or not the feed lines will be removed. Feed lines are usually removed regardless of the tank closure option chosen.

Number of Feed Line Trenches in Tank Field

For purposes of estimating excavation quantities, the size of the feed line trenches is based on the total number of feed lines in the tank field and the total number of feed line trenches.

Length of Each Feed Line in Tank Field

The total length of each feed line in the tank field is measured in feet. Different feed lines may be of different lengths, but to simplify the estimate, all feed lines may be assumed at an average length.

Overdig

Overdig, measured in feet, represents the horizontal dimension between the excavation wall and the outside diameter of the tank. Figure 39.2 shows a tank excavation with overdig. Typically, 2' of overdig is appropriate, not counting any side slope requirements for worker safety.

Percent of Borrow Material Available On Site

When tanks are removed, borrow material must be used to fill in the volume previously occupied by the tanks. This parameter is used to calculate the volume of borrow material that must be purchased or hauled from an off-site source.

Number of Monitoring Wells

This parameter refers to the number of monitoring wells to be installed on the site. Normally, monitoring wells will be required at 1 upgradient and 3 downgradient locations when the depth to groundwater is 50' or less. If the depth to groundwater is deeper than 50', then groundwater monitoring is generally not required. The estimator should determine whether any existing monitoring wells on the site can be used. Typically, monitoring wells used for UST projects are 2" PVC wells. Different sizes and types of wells are available.

Sampling and Analysis

Most UST closure operations include a closure assessment, which is normally required regardless of the tank closure method chosen. Closure assessments determine the nature and extent of contamination in the tank field whether additional site investigation is necessary. The results of closure assessments are also often used to evaluate remediation options for contaminated soil and groundwater. Closure assessments normally include soil and groundwater sampling.

For in-place disposal of tanks, assume that a minimum of 4 soil borings will be placed around the tank field, with a maximum distance of 20' between borings. Borings extend either to the groundwater table or to 10' below the base of the excavation, whichever is less. Each boring in the tank field is sampled at 5' vertical intervals, and OVA screening of each sampled interval is assumed. Typically, a hollow stem auger drill rig with a split spoon sampler is used for acquiring soil samples.

For removal of tanks, assume that a minimum of 4 soil samples will be obtained from each side of the excavation. For large excavations, a maximum distance of 20' between sample locations is assumed. In addition, one sample will be taken from the base of each tank.

In addition to tank field soil samples, assume that 1 sample will be required for every 20' of feed line trench. When feed lines are to be left in place, assume that the feed line cover is not demolished, and samples are obtained by hand augering through the feed line cover to a depth of 3'. Include costs for disposable materials and decontamination materials associated with obtaining soil samples. Laboratory analyses for soil samples include Total Petroleum Hydrocarbons (EPA Method 8015) and Metals Screen (EPA Method 6010). The metals screen is used primarily to distinguish lead contamination, which may be apparent in underlying strata near older USTs that stored leaded gasoline. Other analyses are discussed in Chapter 57.

Groundwater monitoring is also required on many sites. Current RCRA regulations require monitoring upgradient and downgradient from the contaminant source. Installation costs for monitoring wells should be included in the estimate if the wells are not already in place. The number of monitoring wells will also be used to determine the number of groundwater samples and analyses required. Laboratory analyses for groundwater include Volatile Organics (EPA Method 624) and Polynuclear Aromatic Hydrocarbons (EPA Method 610).

Sampling and analysis are also required to verify that all tanks have been completely decontaminated. The tank decontamination sampling protocol involves taking 2 grab samples after clean water is poured over a decontaminated area of the tank. The samples are then analyzed for chlorides, phenols, sulfur, and metals. These indicator parameters provide positive or negative results based on the effectiveness of the tank decontamination process. If the sample tests are positive, the tank must be decontaminated again.

Other Related Costs

Once a tank has been removed from the ground, it must be disposed of in an appropriate manner. The disposal option depends largely on the construction of the tank as well as its condition upon removal. Federal, state, and local regulations may also impact the choice of disposal options. Transportation and disposal of removed or demolished tanks and vaults should be included in the estimate. The estimate should address such factors as distance to disposal facility, number and type of trucks, and dump charges.

Treatment or disposal of excavated soil must also be included as part of the treatment process if the tanks are leaking. Options include landfill disposal, land farming, and ex situ soil vapor extraction, discussed in other chapters of this book.

Site Work and Utilities

Site work and utilities that may apply to UST closure include the following:

- Fencing
- Clear and grub

These would also have to be included in the estimate.

Conclusion

UST closure is the most common type of remediation performed in the United States. Hundreds of thousands of leaking USTs have been remediated to avoid groundwater and soil contamination. The approach to remediation discussed in this chapter is well understood by the practitioners in the industry. The primary cost drivers for a UST closure are the removal method; the number, size, and depth of the tanks; and the extent of contamination in adjacent soil and groundwater. All of these factors are generally known once the project begins, except for the extent of adjacent contamination. However, the remediation of adjacent contamination can be the largest portion of the total project cost if the contamination is extensive, or if off-site groundwater contamination has occurred through migration of the groundwater plume. The estimator should work with the design and site characterization team to define these issues and to incorporate both known factors and uncertainty into the estimate.

Part IV

Cost Estimating for Remediation —Removal Technologies

Chapter 40

Drum Staging

Leaking drums can be a primary source of surface and subsurface contamination at hazardous waste sites. Removing drums from contaminated sites reduces the risk of fire, explosion, or contaminant release and is, therefore, frequently necessary before other remedial actions can be safely implemented.

Applications and Limitations

Applications

- Removal of buried or surface drums containing any wastes.
- A systematic approach for testing and combining wastes for further treatment or disposal.

Limitations

- In some cases, personnel may be required to attach lifting devices to drums.
- Severely degraded drums may require manual removal.

Typical Process Design Elements

This chapter describes the process for estimating the costs associated with removing drums from a hazardous waste site, including:

- Transferring the drums to a staging area
- Sampling and analyzing drum contents
- Overpacking leaking drums
- Consolidating compatible wastes

The following paragraphs describe typical design options for each of these steps, not including excavation, site access roads, transportation, treatment, or disposal. These processes may be part of the overall drum removal process, and are described in other chapters of this book.

Transferring Drums to a Staging Area

Drum removal normally requires a temporary staging area, which protects the site from contaminated run-off from the staging operation and provides a means for containing accidental spills. Options such as spill pallets and drum storage vaults are also available for inflatable containment berms and secondary containment systems. The temporary staging area consists of an excavation approximately one foot deep with an HDPE liner. The staging area is assumed to be sloped enough that any accumulated liquids will drain to one end of the excavation.

The temporary staging area described here is a generic design appropriate for most short-term operations. However, staging area and containment system design is often dictated by federal, state, and local regulations, as well as job-site conditions. This discussion assumes that all drums will be transported off site within 90 days of staging. Sites on which drums are stored for longer than 90 days are classified by 40 CFR as storage facilities and are thus subject to the treatment, storage, and disposal facility requirements of 40 CFR Parts 264 and 265, as well as the permitting requirements of 40 CFR Part 270. These requirements include waste analysis, record keeping, personnel training, security, contingency and emergency plans, and special spill collection and containment systems, which are beyond the scope of this chapter.

Equipment appropriate for removing drums includes horizontal drum-grabs attached to forklifts, vertical drum-grabs or slings attached to backhoes, and drum grapplers. Equipment choice depends on the type of contaminants, the condition of the drums, and geographical barriers present at the site. A *drum grappler* is normally used when leaking or shock-sensitive drums need to be removed. A drum grappler is a remote handling device that can lift drums, including those that are damaged or dented, in a number of orientations. Most other drum-lifting equipment requires that personnel be in close proximity to the drums to affix lifting devices and ensure that the drums retain their original shape.

Sampling and Analyzing Drum Contents

Uncontrolled hazardous waste sites often contain drums that are either incorrectly labeled or completely unmarked. In such cases, the drum contents must be sampled to assess the risk involved in the removal process and evaluate possible transportation and disposal options.

Preliminary screening is often accomplished by analyzing drum head spaces using oxygen meters, explosimeters, or organic vapor analyzers. This simple screening process can determine if drums should be segregated or can identify drums requiring more extensive testing. Normally, all drums are subjected to a preliminary head-space screening using an organic vapor analyzer.

Liquid-filled drums often contain more than one phase and thus require more extensive testing. In such cases, each phase is sampled individually. Drum "thieves" are typically used to obtain discreet samples from each liquid phase within a drum. (Drum thieves are sampling devices that can be inserted through the fill opening in a drum to take discreet samples of the various types and states of liquid contents of a drum without disturbing the structural integrity of the drum.) To avoid chemical reactions, each drum is sampled individually, and samples are not combined into composites.

Analyses of waste characteristics are generally required for any drums containing unknown substances. Waste characteristics analyses generally include pH, ignitability, corrosivity, and reactivity. In addition to identifying drum contents and evaluating transportation and disposal options, waste characteristics analyses also verify that drum contents can be safely consolidated. The normal sampling protocol provides for a field technician to obtain one sample per drum using a disposable drum thief. One sample per drum is sufficient for drums containing homogeneous substances, but drums containing several different liquid phases may require more extensive sampling.

Overpacking Leaking Drums

Leaking or damaged drums are normally either overpacked or emptied into new containers in the field prior to staging. Drums that are known to be free of explosive or shock-sensitive materials can be opened using manual tools, such as bung removers or drum cutters. Drums that contain explosive or shock-sensitive materials, or appear overpressurized, are usually barricaded and covered and then opened or de-pressurized by remote means such as a non-sparking spike mounted on a drum grappler. These drums are normally placed a safe distance from each other to reduce the risk of one explosion leading to a chain reaction. Blast shields or temporary walls are used to protect personnel from splashing, massive releases of vapor, reactions of drum contents with air or water, or explosions.

Consolidating Compatible Wastes

Depending on the type of contaminants and the disposal method, it is often cost effective to consolidate compatible wastes for transport to the disposal facility. When handling drums containing unknown materials, the contents should be consolidated only after analysis of the drum contents has verified that the consolidation process will not result in adverse reactions or render the wastes unsuitable for off-site disposal. Consolidation is usually performed by combining compatible wastes in a mix tank and then transferring the resulting mixture to a tank truck for transport to the disposal facility. Solid wastes are usually loaded directly into box trailers or dumpsters. Once the contents of the drums are consolidated, the empty drums are decontaminated and then either crushed, shredded, or recycled.

Basic Information Needed for Estimating

It is possible to create a reasonable cost estimate using a few required parameters. If more detailed information is known, one can create a more precise and site-specific estimate using a secondary set of parameters.

To estimate the cost of drum removal, certain information must be known. This information is discussed in the following paragraphs.

Total Number of Drums to be Removed

The total number of drums to be removed from the site includes leaking or damaged drums, which will be overpacked and then staged, and drums whose contents will be consolidated. Also included are undamaged drums, which will be transferred to the staging area and then transported off-site. Staging, as defined in this chapter, does not include loading the drums on the disposal truck. When determining the number of drums requiring staging, the estimator should exclude any drums that have already been staged and are ready for loading and transport. A drum grappler attached to a backhoe normally picks up the drums and transports them to an adjacent staging area at a rate of 5 drums per hour.

Number of Overpacks Required

Drums that are leaking or damaged cannot be safely moved. Normally, leaking or damaged drums are overpacked and then staged. If there are

no leaking or damaged drums on a site, then no overpacks
are required.

Number of Drums to be Consolidated

Consolidation generally occurs after the drums have been staged.
Empty drums resulting from the consolidation process are usually
triple-rinsed for decontamination. For estimating purposes, drums are
normally collected by a recycler at no cost to the generator.

Type of Waste to be Consolidated

If wastes are to be consolidated, the estimator should determine
whether the waste is solid, liquid, or sludge. The type of waste
determines the consolidation method. Normally, solid and liquid
wastes are not combined. If the site under consideration contains both,
then the consolidation of each waste type should be estimated
separately. Normally, liquid wastes are pumped into a storage tank at a
rate of 4 55-gallon drums per hour, and solid wastes are manually
emptied directly into box trailers at a rate of about 1 drum per hour.

Average Percent Full per Drum

Generally, drums will not be entirely full, nor will all drums on a site
necessarily contain the same amount of material. Drums often lose a
percentage of their contents over time, usually because of leakage. This
parameter is used to represent an average percent full for drums to be
consolidated and is necessary to determine the actual volume of waste
to be consolidated.

Number of Drums to be Sampled

A number of drums will require a waste characteristics analysis to
determine the type of waste present.

Temporary Staging Area Size (S.F.)

The purpose of the temporary staging area is to protect the site from
contaminated runoff from the staging operation and to provide a
means for containing accidental spills. If a suitable staging area already
exists on site, then staging area construction may not be required. Trash
pumps may be used to remove accumulated liquids from the staging
area. Inflatable containment berms and spill pallets may be used either
in conjunction with or in lieu of a temporary staging area, depending
on job conditions.

The size of the staging area (in S.F.) depends on the number of drums
and whether or not the drums will be stacked. The estimator should
allow approximately 4 S.F. per drum. If drums are to be stacked, the
size of the staging area may decrease accordingly.

Worker Safety Level

Worker safety is affected by the contaminant(s) at the site. Safety level
refers to the levels required by OSHA in 29 CFR Part 1910. The 4 levels
are designated as A, B, C, and D, "A" is the most protective, and "D" is
the least protective. A safety level of E is also included to simulate
normal construction, "no hazard" conditions as prescribed by the EPA.

Design Information Needed for Detailed Estimates

Following are descriptions of the types of detailed information that, when available, can add detail and accuracy to estimates. Also included are design criteria and estimating rules of thumb that estimators use to determine values that are not known, or to check information provided by others.

Samples per Drum

Normally, only one sample per drum is required. Sometimes, however, liquid-filled drums contain more than 1 liquid phase. In such cases, each liquid phase should be sampled individually. The number of samples per drum should be increased if the site under consideration has drums containing more than one liquid phase.

Overpack Type

Options for overpacks include 85-gallon, 16-gauge steel salvage drums and 85-gallon composite overpacks.

Drum Storage Type

Depending on the type of contaminants being stored and the condition of the drums, the drums may need to be staged on spill pallets or in portable storage vaults. The most common drum storage system is a polyethylene spill pallet with an 85-gallon sump and a capacity of 4 55-gallon drums. Other options that are typically available include:

- Poly Spill Pallet, 4 Drum Cap
- Poly Drum Storage System, 2 Drum Cap
- Steel Drum Storage System, 4 Drum Cap
- Poly Drum Storage System, 1 Drum Cap

Containment Berm Type

Depending on job-site conditions, a containment berm may be used as a staging pad. Inflatable containment berms may also be used to store bulk liquids or contain decontamination fluids. Typical berm sizes are listed below.

- 10' × 10' × 17", 750 Gallon
- 13' × 13' × 17", 1,800 Gallon
- 18' × 18' × 17", 3,400 Gallon
- 24' × 24' × 17", 6,100 Gallon
- 32' × 32' × 17", 10,800 Gallon
- 32' × 32' × 34", 21,600 Gallon
- 74' × 34' × 34", 53,400 Gallon
- 45' × 15' × 17", 7,600 Gallon
- 65' × 16' × 17", 11,000 Gallon
- 50' × 22' × 17", 11,600 Gallon

Polymeric Liner

Polymeric liners are generally required for the temporary staging area. The size of the liner depends on the size of the temporary staging area. The most common liner type is 60 mil HDPE. Other types of liners include:

- 20 mil Polymeric Liner, VLDPE
- 30 mil Polymeric Liner, VLDPE
- 40 mil Polymeric Liner, VLDPE
- 60 mil Polymeric Liner, VLDPE
- 80 mil Polymeric Liner, VLDPE

- 100 mil Polymeric Liner, VLDPE
- 36 mil Polymeric Liner, CSPE
- 45 mil Polymeric Liner, CSPE
- 20 mil Polymeric Liner, PVC
- 30 mil Polymeric Liner, PVC
- 40 mil Polymeric Liner, PVC
- 60 mil Polymeric Liner, PVC
- 80 mil Polymeric Liner, PVC
- 100 mil Polymeric Liner, PVC
- 40 mil Polymeric Liner, HDPE
- 60 mil Polymeric Liner, HDPE
- 80 mil Polymeric Liner, HDPE

Related Costs

All equipment used in the drum removal process is normally decontaminated upon completion of the drum removal project. The unit costs for staging, overpacking, and consolidating drums include costs for equipment decontamination.

All empty drums must be triple-rinsed after the consolidation process. For estimating purposes, assume that drums can be triple rinsed at a rate of 10 drums per hour. The triple-rinsing process will generate approximately 10 gallons of decontamination fluid per drum.

In most cases, drum removal projects are fewer than 90 days in duration, and design requirements and restrictions related to site conditions will prohibit decontamination fluids from running back onto the site. However, the estimator should determine whether the project requires systems for containing or disposing of decontamination fluids and treating or disposing of contaminated run-off pumped out of the staging area.

Site Work and Utilities

Site work and utilities that may be applicable for drum removal are:

- Clear and grub
- Access roads
- Fencing

These will also need to be accounted for in the estimate.

Conclusion

Drum removal is one of the more common site remedial action activities. The primary cost drivers are the number of drums, the handling requirements, and the disposal option selected. Generally, except for small projects, if wastes can be pre-treated on-site, with volume reduction, the overall costs will be lower than for hauling all wastes to an off-site disposal facility. However, the distance to the disposal facility, transportation costs, on-site handling costs, and other factors will impact this cost trade-off. The cost engineer should work closely with the design team to develop and explore different alternatives for drum handling and disposal.

Chapter 41

Excavation

Excavation is a method of removing contaminated surface and subsurface materials from hazardous waste sites. Excavation is often employed in cases where in situ remediation techniques are ineffective or inappropriate. Although excavation is most often used to remove contaminated soil, it can also be used to remove bulk waste, soil-like materials, or other materials that are located above the water table and can be excavated by conventional earthmoving equipment.

Excavation is not a stand-alone treatment technology. Contaminated material must be either treated or disposed. Depending on the nature of the material and the contaminants, excavated material may be treated by such methods as soil washing or thermal treatment, or it may be disposed by landfilling or incineration.

Applications and Limitations

Applications

- Applicable to all contaminant groups.
- Usually best for sites that are free of surface obstacles.
- Typically employed where prompt response to a spill is required.
- Usually best for small sites with concentrated areas of contamination.
- Typically used to remove contaminated soil, bulk waste, soil-like materials, or other materials above the water table.
- Employs conventional earthmoving equipment.
- Used in conjunction with other treatment or disposal technologies.

Limitations

- Potential generation of dangerous off-gas emissions during excavation.
- Surface structures and site conditions may preclude excavation.
- Potentially high costs dependent on: distance from contaminated site to nearest disposal facility, depth to buried waste, overlying media to be excavated, and type of waste.
- Double-handling (i.e., hand excavation) may be required for drum excavation.

Process Configurations and Treatment Train Considerations

- Depth to contamination will determine the need for sidewall protection. Side slope or sheeting should be used for excavations deeper than 5'.
- Excavation may require that the site be temporarily taken out of operation.
- Wastes from excavation can be treated or disposed.
- Pumps may be required to remove groundwater during excavation.
- Selective excavation may be necessary to ensure segregation of incompatible wastes.
- Fugitive dusts may require control by sprayed dust suppressants (usually water).
- Administrative controls may be required to minimize soil dispersion, spillage, and exposure to receptors.

Typical Process Design Elements

Excavation is a standard construction practice, and equipment and construction methods are readily available for the excavation and handling of contaminated materials. Typical excavation equipment includes bulldozers, scrapers, excavators, track loaders, and wheel loaders, all of which are available in a wide variety of sizes. The size and type of equipment chosen depends on such site-specific factors as site and material characteristics, excavation dimensions, desired project duration, degree of excavation accuracy required, and haul distance. Excavation is one of the most effective means of site remediation because it involves the physical removal of contaminated materials.

Excavations can vary in size from small trenches to large pits. Either side slope or sheeting is normally required for excavations deeper than 5'. Soil that is known to be uncontaminated, such as cover material, can be excavated in bulk. However, soil is normally excavated in lifts when intermediate sampling is required to confirm the depth of contamination. If there are buried drums on a site, the soil surrounding the drums is usually cleared away from the drums by hand and then removed from the pit by machine. This process of excavation is often referred to as *double handling*.

Contaminated material excavation can be extremely hazardous, especially at formerly uncontrolled waste sites where the nature and extent of contamination are unknown. Extensive monitoring plans and safety procedures may be necessary to ensure the protection of workers, the public, and the environment. Depending on what type of contaminants are present, fugitive dust and vapor transport may also be concerns. In such cases, a sprayed dust suppressant is normally applied over the entire excavation area. Also, selective removal of waste may be necessary to ensure the segregation of incompatible wastes or wastes requiring different treatment or disposal methods.

This chapter discusses the costs associated with excavating and backfilling a contaminated site, including either sheeting or side slope for excavations deeper than 5'. Contaminated material is assumed to be excavated to a stock pile and covered. Treatment or disposal of contaminated material is not addressed in this chapter. Options are discussed for either bulk excavating or excavating in lifts.

This chapter of the book also covers the excavation of soil around buried drums, but it does not account for removal of drums from the excavation. For purposes of discussion, buried drums are assumed to be 55-gallon drums, 3' tall and 23" in diameter.

Machine productivity, or the amount of material that a machine can excavate in a specified amount of time, is a major cost driver in excavation. Conditions such as soil type, hauling distance, operator skill, and on-site obstructions have a significant impact on productivity. This chapter employs machine productivity equations from the *Caterpillar Performance Handbook*, which contain modifying factors to account for these conditions. The defaults for productivity factors described below are a generalization of the way job site conditions affect machine productivity. The machine productivity charts and tables from the *Caterpillar Performance Handbook* can assist the estimator in tailoring estimates to match job site conditions. However, each excavation job is unique, and past experience and knowledge of the site are extremely important in creating accurate excavation estimates.

Two types of soil measurements are Bank Cubic Yards (B.C.Y.), which refers to soil resting in its natural, undisturbed state, and Loose Cubic Yards (L.C.Y.), which refers to soil excavated or disturbed from its natural state. Loose cubic yard measure accounts for the swell in the disturbed soil, which increases the volume.

Basic Information Needed for Estimating

It is possible to create a reasonable cost estimate using a few required parameters. If more detailed information is known, one can create a more precise and site-specific estimate using a secondary set of parameters.

To estimate the cost of the excavation system, certain information must be known. This information is discussed in the following paragraphs.

Length of Excavation
The length of the contaminated area is measured at the *bottom* of the excavation. When determining the dimensions of the excavation, the estimator should consider the number of buried drums, if any, and enter a length large enough to allow for any desired clearance around the drums.

Width of Excavation (ft)
The width of the contaminated area is also measured at the *bottom* of the excavation. When determining the dimensions of the excavation, the estimator should consider the number of buried drums, if any, and enter a width large enough to allow for any desired clearance around the drums.

Depth of Excavation (ft)
The depth of the contaminated area is measured downward from grade level, as shown in Figure 41.1. When determining the depth of excavation, the estimator should consider the depth of clean cover material, if any, and the depth at which drums are buried. The maximum practical depth of excavation depends on the method of side wall protection used. If sheeting is chosen, then the normal maximum allowable depth of excavation is 40'. If side slope is chosen, the depth may be up to 100' or more. However, the volume of excavation for side slope applications can be very large for deep excavations because of side slope stabilization requirements. The depth of excavation must be at least 3' if buried drums are present.

Number of Buried Drums
When buried drums are present on a site, soil surrounding the drums is

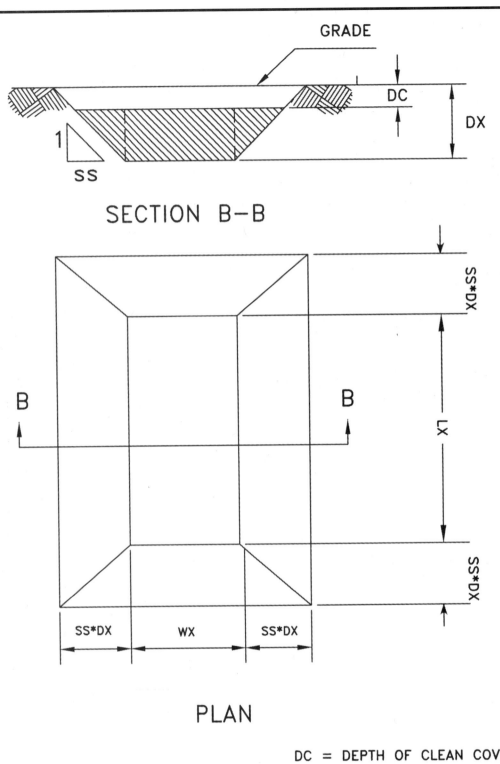

SECTION B-B

PLAN

= CONTAMINATED MATERIAL

= CLEAN MATERIAL

DC = DEPTH OF CLEAN COVER
DX = DEPTH OF EXCAVATION
SS = SIDE SLOPE
LX = LENGTH OF EXCAVATION
WX = WIDTH OF EXCAVATION

Figure 41.1 Excavation Size

often hand-excavated from around the drums and then removed from the excavation by machine. Figure 41.2 shows a schematic diagram of the method used to calculate excavation of buried drums.

Excavation Method

Excavation may be performed either in lifts or as continuous (bulk) excavation. Soil is normally excavated in lifts when intermediate sampling is necessary to determine the depth of contamination. Continuous excavation is appropriate when intermediate sampling is not required, although in such cases it may be necessary to conduct sampling upon completion of the excavation project to verify that contaminant concentrations in the remaining soil are below target levels. The excavation method chosen has a direct effect on the sampling frequency. Typical options for excavation method are:

- Continuous excavation
- 6" Lifts
- 12" Lifts
- 24" Lifts

Primary Equipment Type

The type of equipment that is used will affect production rates and costs. Different types of equipment are more or less efficient for different project conditions, such as soil type, total volume of soil to be excavated, moisture content of soil, and site access constraints.

The primary equipment will be used to excavate most or all of the material to be removed. Additional equipment, if desired, may be incorporated to meet special project requirements. The available equipment types are:

- Dozer
- Scraper
- Excavator
- Track loader
- Wheel loader

Side Wall Protection

Pursuant to current OSHA requirements, excavations deeper than 5' should be protected against cave-in. This protection is normally achieved either by installing sheeting or by sloping the excavation walls. If side slope is chosen, the estimator must determine the value for the horizontal component of the side slope. The allowable range for the horizontal component of side slope is 1 to 5. Figure 41.1 shows an excavation with sloped sides.

Rock Requiring Blasting

Blasting involves the use of explosives (ammonium nitrate) placed in bore holes to loosen and break up rock. Typically the boring diameter is 2-1/2" for bore holes to the depth of excavation. Blasted material will then be removed using excavation equipment. Rock blasting can cause other problems on contaminated waste sites, such as potential disbursement of contaminants or damage to remediation systems and equipment. Protection requirements should be considered and factored into the estimate as appropriate. A subsection on blasting is included later in this chapter.

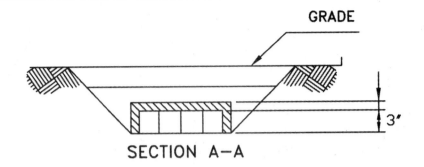

GRADE

SECTION A—A

3'

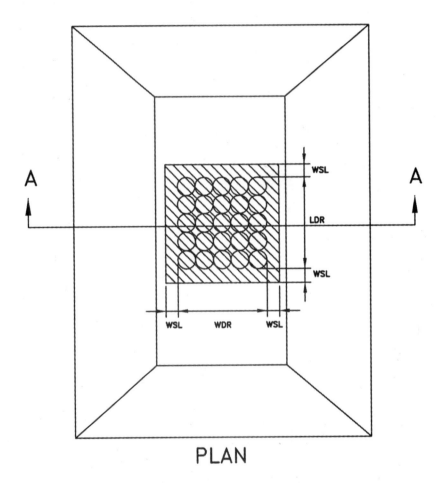

A   A

WSL

LDR

WSL

WSL   WDR   WSL

PLAN

LEGEND

WSL = WIDTH OF HAND—EXCAVATED
      SOIL LAYER AROUND DRUMS
DSL = DEPTH OF HAND—EXCAVATED
      SOIL LAYER ABOVE DRUMS
WDR = WIDTH OF DRUM MATRIX
LDR = LENGTH OF DRUM MATRIX
      = HAND—EXCAVATED SOIL LAYER

Figure 41.2 Buried Drum

Rock Requiring Ripping

Ripping is the process of using a high horsepower dozer with a plow-like shank that breaks rock to prepare for excavation. The dozer pulls the plow through rock or hard soil to break up and loosen the material to a state where it can be removed by excavation equipment. Generally, rippable rock is well-weathered, fractured, or fragmented, and includes most caliches and soft sedimentary rock (i.e., chalk and sand stone), glacial tills, and hard clays. Ripping is less expensive than blasting and should be used where possible.

If ripping is to be used, the estimator should determine the percent of the total excavation volume that requires ripping in order to determine ripping volume and equipment requirements.

Soil Type

It is important to identify the types of soils underlying the site, as it will impact the productivity of excavation equipment. There are thousands of different soil classifications and variables, but for estimating purposes, the following categories can be used:

- Gravel/Gravel Sand Mixture
- Sand/Gravelly Sand Mixture
- Sand-Silt/Sand-Clay Mixture
- Silt/Silty-Clay Mixture

Excavation Dewatering Required

If the excavation depth is greater than the depth to groundwater, excavation dewatering is required. Dewatering is accomplished by pumping water out of the excavation as work proceeds, using portable dewatering pumps. Discharge systems may also be required and, if the water is contaminated, follow-on treatment may be required prior to discharge. If excavation dewatering is required, indicate the dewatering duration in days.

Ground-Penetrating Radar

Ground penetrating radar is a non-destructive testing approach used to produce detailed maps of subsurface conditions of buried objects. Determining the size, location, and depth of buried drums, tanks, and waste pits is critical for establishing excavation requirements. If ground-penetrating radar is required, indicate the duration, in days, of the effort.

Project Duration

The project duration drives the number of dust suppressant applications as well as the professional labor and equipment stand-by hours. This chapter does not provide assumptions regarding the appropriate number of machines for a given excavation project. The hours calculated by the equations in this chapter are *total machine hours* per *each type* of excavation equipment. An hourly cost for equipment stand-by will be included based on the difference between the estimator-defined project duration and the total machine hours. For example, if an excavator is selected for a project of 1 week (40 hours) duration and the estimator has calculated 36 machine hours for the excavator, then the estimator should include 4 hours of stand-by time.

Worker Safety Level

Worker safety is affected by the contaminant(s) at the site. Safety level refers to the levels required by OSHA in 29 CFR Part 1910. The four levels are designated as A, B, C, and D; where "A" is the most protective and "D" is the least protective. A safety level of E is also included to simulate normal construction, "no hazard" conditions as prescribed by the EPA.

Design Information Needed for Detailed Estimates

Following are descriptions of the types of detailed information that, when available, can add detail and accuracy to estimates. Also included are design criteria and estimating rules of thumb that the estimator typically uses to determine values that are not known, or to check information provided by others.

General Parameters

The general parameters include such items as backfill, depth of clean cover, dust suppressant, and quantity of soil to be hand-excavated from around buried drums. The general parameters are defined in the following paragraphs.

Backfill

The backfill parameter specifies whether or not the excavated volume will be backfilled. Where possible, contaminated material will be stockpiled and covered for eventual treatment or disposal. Assuming the site must be restored, any clean material excavated is used as backfill; the remainder of the backfill is obtained off site. The volume of contaminated material is a function of the bottom area and the depth of the excavation and is not a function of side slope. The volume of excavation used for the side slope is generally considered to be clean soil. Figure 41.1 illustrates the assumptions regarding clean and contaminated material.

Existing Cover

It is necessary to identify the type of existing surface cover that will be demolished by power equipment prior to excavation efforts. Costs for transportation and disposal of demolished cover material should be included in the estimate. Chapter 44 of this reference provides guidance on estimating transportation and disposal costs. If the existing cover is soil/gravel, then no demolition costs are included. Typical options for existing cover include:

- Asphalt
- Soil/Gravel
- <6" Concrete, Mesh Reinforced
- <6" Concrete, Rod Reinforced
- <6" Concrete, Non-Reinforced
- 7–24" Concrete, Rod Reinforced

Replacement Cover

Aesthetics and erosion problems, as well as site usage, often make it desirable to replace the cover over the excavated area. Typical options for existing cover include:

- Asphalt
- Soil/Gravel
- 6" Unreinforced Concrete
- 6" Mesh Reinforced Concrete

- 6" Rod Reinforced Concrete
- 12" Structural Slab

Depth of Clean Cover

Clean cover material above the contaminated material is often used as backfill, thereby reducing the amount of borrow material required. The depth of cover is measured down from grade level, as shown in Figure 41.1.

Dust Suppressant Spraying Frequency (days)

During the project, the excavation area will be sprayed with dust suppressant a number of times. The most common dust suppressant is water, but chemical-based dust suppressants are also available.

Percent of Borrow Material Available on Site

A percent of the required borrow quantity will be available from an on-site or borrow pit. A material purchase price will normally be incurred only for off-site borrow material.

Depth of Hand-Excavated Soil Layer Above Buried Drums

To avoid unnecessary disturbances to buried drums, the soil immediately adjacent to and between the drums is excavated by hand. This parameter is used to determine the quantity of soil on top of the drum matrix that will be hand-excavated. Soil that is hand-excavated from above buried drums is assumed to be stockpiled within the excavation. This stockpile is then removed from the excavation by machine. This dimension is measured upward from the top of the drum matrix, as shown in Figure 41.2.

Width of Hand-Excavated Soil Layer Around Buried Drums (ft)

A quantity of soil around the drum matrix will be hand-excavated. Again, soil that is hand-excavated from around buried drums is assumed to be stockpiled within the excavation. This stockpile is then removed from the excavation by machine. This dimension is measured outward from the edge of the drum matrix, as shown in Figure 41.2.

Equipment Parameters

The equipment parameters may be used to select equipment desired in addition to the primary equipment described previously. The equipment parameters are as follows:

- Dozer quantity (B.C.Y.)
- Scraper quantity (B.C.Y.)
- Excavator quantity (B.C.Y.)
- Track loader quantity (B.C.Y.)
- Wheel loader quantity (B.C.Y.)

The sum of the quantities determined for all equipment types is generally the same as the total excavation required. However, in some cases the sum total for all equipment may exceed the total volume to be excavated to allow for handling material more than once or for using combinations of equipment.

Dozer Parameters: A dozer pushes dirt in front of a blade and can be considered a self-loading hauler. Dozers have excellent earth-moving and grading capabilities and are normally used to excavate, spread, and move materials. Dozers can be used in contaminated material excavation to remove fill or soil overburden. They are normally used in conjunction with other excavation equipment, such as hydraulic excavators, especially on sites containing buried drums.

Dozers can be either crawler-mounted or wheel-mounted. *Crawler-mounted dozers* are equipped with self-laying steel tracks that provide excellent ground contact, flotation, and traction capabilities. Crawler-mounted dozers are, therefore, well suited for excavating over rough, unstable surfaces. *Wheel-mounted dozers* have much greater mobility on level terrain than crawler-mounted dozers. Their maneuverability on rough, muddy terrain depends on the type of tires used. In such cases, tires with wide bases and low air pressure are used because they provide good flotation and traction.

Dozer hours are calculated by dividing the volume excavated by dozer, in loose cubic yards (L.C.Y.), by the maximum production rate, which is multiplied by the correction factors described below. The following guidelines can be used to generate a reasonable cost estimate. However, if more site-specific information is available, the estimator should modify the dozer parameters to reflect such information.

Dozer Type. Dozer trade names are based on Caterpillar equipment. If other brands of equipment are used, comparable information should be developed for that equipment. The optimum dozer selection is based on the following dozer quantities.

Dozer Type	Dozer Quantity
65 H.P. (D3) w/A Blade	1–1,000 B.C.Y.
80 H.P. (D4) w/A Blade	1,001–2,000 B.C.Y.
105 H.P. (D5) w/A Blade	2,001–3,500 B.C.Y.
140 H.P. (D6) w/A Blade	3,501–5,000 B.C.Y.
200 H.P. (D7) w/U Blade	5,001–6,500 B.C.Y.
335 H.P. (D8) w/U Blade	6,501–8,000 B.C.Y.
460 H.P. (D9) w/U Blade	8,001–10,000 B.C.Y.
700 H.P. (D10) w/U Blade	10,001–999,999 B.C.Y.

Dozer Quantity (B.C.Y.). The quantity of material to be excavated by dozer, in bank cubic yards (B.C.Y.), determines the dozer type.

Maximum Production Rate (L.C.Y/hr.). The maximum production rate is the maximum amount of material that a particular dozer can move over a given distance in one hour. The rate is different for each size and type of machine. The production rates listed below are based on a distance of 100'. The unit of measure is loose cubic yards per hour (L.C.Y./hr.).

Dozer Type	Production Rate
65 H.P. (D3) w/A Blade	100 L.C.Y./hr.
80 H.P. (D4) w/A Blade	200 L.C.Y./hr.
105 H.P. (D5) w/A Blade	300 L.C.Y./hr.
140 H.P. (D6) w/A Blade	360 L.C.Y./hr.
200 H.P. (D7) w/U Blade	700 L.C.Y./hr.
335 H.P. (D8) w/U Blade	960 L.C.Y./hr.
460 H.P. (D9) w/U Blade	1,200 L.C.Y./hr.
700 H.P. (D10) w/U Blade	1,700 L.C.Y./hr.

Loose Material Weight (lb/C.Y.). Loose material weight refers to the material to be excavated per cubic yard, measured in pounds per cubic yard (lb/C.Y.). Loose material weight ranges from 1,000 lb/C.Y. for ash or light coals to over 4,500 lbs/C.Y. for iron ores. The most common material is dry packed earth with a loose weight of 2,550 lbs/C.Y.

Work Minutes/Hour (min.). The number of minutes per hour that the dozer is actually excavating or working also accounts for down-time. Factors such as refueling, repairs, and operator break time contribute to down-time. The normal maximum production rate is 50 minutes, or an efficiency of 83% (50 minutes/60 minutes per hour), but project conditions and labor agreements often reduce efficiency to 50–75%.

Load Factor (%). Load factor converts bank density to loose density. One cubic yard of material in place does not equal one cubic yard of loose material, because swell and voids occur when the material is disturbed. The valid range for load factors is 0.50–1.00. For estimating purposes, most soil can be classified with a load factor of 0.75–0.80.

Blade Factor (%). Blade factor is used to adjust the production rate of the selected piece of equipment. The productivity of each machine depends on the type of blade used in the excavation. A straight or "S" blade has a factor of 1.0. A Universal or "U" blade has a factor of 1.2, since it can excavate and move a greater quantity of material. The factor for angling or "A" blades ranges from 0.5–0.75 because they average only 50–75% of straight blade production.

Grade Factor (%). The percent grade, or slope of the site to be excavated, affects machine productivity. The efficiency of the machine, relative to normal, would range from 1.6 × Normal for a 30% downhill grade to 0.3 × Normal for a 30% uphill grade. If the grade is not known, an appropriate grade for estimating purposes is 0%, which is a dozing factor of 1.00.

Visibility Factor (%). The visibility factor accounts for dust, rain, snow, fog, or darkness at the site. Any of these conditions would affect operator visibility and reduce production. For estimating purposes, if these factors are likely to be encountered, the productivity should be reduced to 0.80 × Normal.

Operator Efficiency Factor (%)

The skill of the operator is a major factor in the calculation of equipment productivity. An excellent or very skilled operator will excavate or move more material than a poorly skilled or new operator. The factors range from 0.50 for a poorly skilled operator to 1.00 for an excellent operator.

Material Correction Factor (%). The in situ state of the material to be excavated will affect the productivity of the dozer. More loose material can be excavated and moved than hard packed or hard to cut material. The material correction factor ranges from 1.2 × Normal for loose stockpiled material, to 0.60 for blasted rock material, to 0.80 for very sticky material. For estimating purposes, if the material is not known, one could assume dry packed earth—which is classified as "hard to drift" material. The material correction factor would be 0.80.

Scraper Parameters

Scrapers are normally used to remove and haul surface cover material. They can also be used to re-spread and compact cover soils. However, they are not appropriate for sites with drums buried near the surface. Scrapers are available as either self-loading, self-propelled vehicles or as models that are assisted by dozers. Self-loading scrapers are suitable for soft- to medium-density cover soils and fill, whereas push-pull scrapers are better suited for medium to hard rock and earth. All scrapers except for the 613 and 623 are assumed to be assisted by either 1 or 2 dozers, depending on the size of the scraper. The 613 and 623 do not require dozers.

Scraper hours are calculated by dividing the volume to be excavated, in bank cubic yards (B.C.Y.), by the efficiency factor times the maximum production rate. The following guidelines can be used to create a reasonable cost estimate. However, if more site-specific information is available, the estimator should modify the scraper parameters to reflect such information.

Scraper Type. The following is a list of common types and sizes of scrapers. Standard scrapers are the most common. The best scraper size for a particular job is based primarily on the total volume of excavation to be performed.

Scraper Type	Scraper Quantity
Standard, 15 C.Y. (621)	1–5,000 B.C.Y.
Standard, 22 C.Y. (631)	5,001–10,000 B.C.Y.
Standard, 34 C.Y. (651)	10,001–999,999 B.C.Y.
Elevating, 11 C.Y. (613)	
Elevating, 22 C.Y. (623)	
Tandem, 14 C.Y. (627)	
Tandem, 21 C.Y. (637)	
Tandem, 32 C.Y. (657)	

Scraper Quantity (B.C.Y.). The quantity of material to be excavated by scraper is measured in bank cubic yards (B.C.Y.). This parameter is used to determine the scraper type.

Maximum Production Rate (B.C.Y./hr.). The maximum production rate is the amount of material that a particular scraper can excavate in one hour, based on cycle time. This rate is different for each size and type of scraper. The production rate is found by using the calculated cycle time and the curve for the corresponding scraper. The values shown below have been calculated assuming a one-way haul distance of 2,000', level haul road, and no free water in the excavation.

Scraper Type	Production Rate
Standard, 15 C.Y. (621)	300 B.C.Y./hr.
Standard, 22 C.Y. (631)	500 B.C.Y./hr.
Standard, 34 C.Y. (651)	690 B.C.Y./hr.
Elevating, 11 C.Y. (613)	150 B.C.Y./hr.
Elevating, 22 C.Y. (623)	275 B.C.Y./hr.
Tandem, 14 C.Y. (627)	340 B.C.Y./hr.
Tandem, 21 C.Y. (637)	540 B.C.Y./hr.
Tandem, 32 C.Y. (657)	710 B.C.Y./hr.

Work Minutes/Hour (min.). The number of minutes per hour that the scraper is actually excavating or working also accounts for down-time. Factors such as refueling, repairs, and operator break time contribute to down-time. The normal maximum work minutes per hour is 50 minutes or an efficiency of 83% (50 minutes/60 minutes per hour).

Excavator Parameters

The hydraulic excavator is perhaps the most appropriate type of equipment for excavating contaminated materials, especially on sites that contain buried drums. Hydraulic excavators can excavate depths of 30' or more, depending on the size of the machine. Typical bucket capacity ratings range from 1/2–4 C.Y. Excavators are typically used when excavation is below grade level and can be done from a stable working surface such as a road or gravel pad.

Excavator hours are calculated by first dividing the volume to be excavated, in bank cubic yards (B.C.Y.), by the load factor, the bucket fill factor, and bucket capacity; then dividing that total by the number of cycles per hour. Each of these factors is described in the estimating guidelines that follow, which can be used to generate a reasonable estimate. However, if more site-specific information is available, the estimator should modify the excavator parameters to reflect such information.

Excavator Type. The excavator can be chosen from the following types. Selection depends on the required excavator quantity.

Excavator Type	Excavator Quantity
Hydraulic, 1 C.Y. (215)	1–2,000 B.C.Y.
Hydraulic, 1.25 C.Y. (225)	2,001–4,000 B.C.Y.
Hydraulic, 2 C.Y. (235)	4,001–6,000 B.C.Y.
Hydraulic, 3.125 C.Y. (245)	6,001–8,000 B.C.Y.
Hydraulic, 4 C.Y. (K1166)	8,001–10,000 B.C.Y.
Hydraulic, 5.5 C.Y. (K1266)	10,001–999,999 B.C.Y.

Excavator Quantity (B.C.Y.). The quantity of material to be excavated by hydraulic excavator, in bank cubic yards (B.C.Y.), is used to determine the excavator type.

Bucket Fill Factor. The bucket fill factor indicates the approximate amounts of material, as a percent of rated bucket capacity, that will actually be delivered per bucket per cycle. This factor depends on the type of material being excavated and the method of excavation being used. A wet or moist soil is cohesive and will stick together, giving a heaped bucket. A loose, dry material will not heap; thus the amount per bucket will be limited to a fraction of the size of the bucket. Also, when excavating in lifts or excavating around buried drums, it is unrealistic to expect a heaped bucket. For estimating purposes, reasonable assumptions for the bucket fill factor are 1.10 for continuous excavation and 0.60 for excavation in lifts.

Load Factor (%). The load factor converts bank density to loose density. One C.Y. of material in place does not equal 1 C.Y. of loose material, because swell and voids occur when the material is disturbed. Typically, the load factor ranges from 0.50–1.00. Normal soils generally fall in the range of 0.75–0.80.

Cycle Time (sec.). The digging cycle of the excavator has four segments: load bucket, swing loaded, dump bucket, and swing empty. Total excavator cycle time depends partly on machine size because small machines can cycle faster than large machines. Cycle time also depends on job conditions. Under normal job conditions, the excavator can cycle quickly. As job conditions become more severe (e.g., tougher digging, deeper excavation, more obstacles), the excavator will slow down. The average cycle time under normal conditions depends on the excavator chosen.

The following is a list of average cycle times for normal soils for different types of loaders.

Loader Type	Cycle Time
Hydraulic, 1 C.Y. (215)	18 seconds
Hydraulic, 1.25 C.Y. (225)	22 seconds
Hydraulic, 2 C.Y. (235)	25 seconds
Hydraulic, 3.125 C.Y. (245)	31 seconds
Hydraulic, 4 C.Y. (K1166)	40 seconds
Hydraulic, 5.5 C.Y. (K1266)	50 seconds

Work Minutes/Hour (min.). The number of minutes per hour that the excavator is actually excavating or working also accounts for down-time. Factors such as refueling, repairs, and operator break time contribute to down-time. The normal maximum work minutes per hour is 50 minutes, or an efficiency of 0.83.

Track Loader Parameters

Track loaders are crawler-mounted tractors equipped with buckets for digging, lifting, hauling, and dumping materials; self-laying steel tracks, which provide excellent ground contact, flotation, and traction. Track loaders are thus well suited to excavating over rough, unstable surfaces.

Track loaders are appropriate for shallow excavations that are free of buried drums. Deeper excavations or excavations containing buried drums are better suited to hydraulic excavators.

Machine hours are calculated by first dividing the volume to be excavated by track loader, in bank cubic yards (B.C.Y.), by the load factor, the bucket fill factor, and bucket capacity, and then dividing that total by the cycles per hour. These factors are explained in the estimating guidelines that follow, which can be used to create a reasonable estimate. However, if more site-specific information is available, the estimator should modify the track loader parameters to reflect such information.

Track Loader Type. The type of track loader can be chosen from the following options, depending on the track loader quantity required.

Track Loader Type	Track Loader Quantity
65 H.P., 1 C.Y. (931)	1–2,500 B.C.Y.
80 H.P., 1.5 C.Y. (943)	2,501–5,000 B.C.Y.
110 H.P., 2 C.Y. (953)	5,001–7,500 B.C.Y.
150 H.P., 2.5 C.Y. (963)	7,501–10,000 B.C.Y.
210 H.P., 3.75 C.Y. (973)	10,001–999,999 B.C.Y.

Track Loader Quantity (B.C.Y.). The quantity of material to be excavated by track loader, in bank cubic yards (B.C.Y.), determines the track loader type.

Load Factor (%). The load factor converts bank density to loose density. One cubic yard of material in place does not equal one cubic yard of loose material, because swell and voids occur when the material is disturbed. Typically, the load factor ranges from 0.50–1.00, with normal soils generally falling in the range of 0.75–0.80.

Bucket Fill Factor (%). The bucket fill factor indicates the approximate amounts of material as a percent of rated bucket capacity that will actually be delivered per bucket per cycle. This factor depends on the type of material being excavated. A wet or moist soil is cohesive and will stick together, giving a heaped bucket. A loose, dry material will not heap, and the amount per bucket will be limited to a fraction of the size of the bucket. For estimating purposes, dry, packed earth will normally achieve a fill factor of 0.90–1.10.

Load Time (Per Cycle) (min.). The time required for the track loader to excavate a full load or bucket depends on the type of material being excavated and the excavation method being used. The typical load time for dry packed earth ranges from 0.05–0.20 minutes.

Dump Time (Per Cycle) (min.). The dump time is dictated by the size and strength of the dump target and varies from 0.01–0.10 minutes. Typical dump times for highway trucks range from 0.04–0.07 minutes.

Travel Time (One Way) (min.). Travel time for a load and carry operation is comprised of haul and return times. The travel time depends on the distance and the machine selected. The following list shows travel times for different loaders based on an assumed one-way travel distance of 200'. Travel time is measured in minutes.

Loader Type	Travel Time
65 H.P., 1 C.Y. (931)	.60 min.
80 H.P., 1.5 C.Y. (943)	.40 min.
110 H.P., 2 C.Y. (953)	.35 min.
150 H.P., 2.5 C.Y. (963)	.35 min.
210 H.P., 3.75 C.Y. (973)	.35 min.

Maneuver Time (Per Cycle) (min.). The maneuver time includes basic travel, four changes of direction, and turning time, and will be about 0.22 minutes at full throttle for a competent operator.

Work Minutes/Hour (min.). The number of minutes per hour that the track loader is actually excavating or working also accounts for down-time. Factors such as refueling, repairs, and operator break time contribute to down-time. The normal maximum work minutes per hour is 50 minutes, or an efficiency of 83%.

Wheel Loader Parameters

Wheel loaders are tire-mounted tractors equipped with buckets for digging, lifting, hauling, and dumping materials. Wheel loaders are faster and have greater mobility than track loaders on level terrain. Their ability to maneuver on rough, muddy, or sloping terrain depends on the type of tires used. Wheel loaders are appropriate for shallow excavations. Deeper excavations are better suited to hydraulic excavators.

Wheel loader hours are calculated by first dividing the volume to be excavated by wheel loader, in bank cubic yards (B.C.Y.), by the load factor, bucket fill factor, and bucket capacity, and then dividing that total by the cycles per hour. These factors are explained in the following estimating guidelines, which can be used to produce a reasonable estimate. However, if more site-specific information is available, the estimator should modify the wheel loader parameters to reflect such information.

Wheel Loader Type. The type of wheel loader can be chosen from the following options. The selection is determined by the wheel loader quantity required.

Wheel Loader Type	Wheel Loader Quantity
65 H.P., 1.25 C.Y. (910)	1–1,500 B.C.Y.
80 H.P., 1.5 C.Y. (916)	1,501–3,000 B.C.Y.
100 H.P., 2 C.Y. (926)	3,001–4,500 B.C.Y.
155 H.P., 3 C.Y. (950)	4,501–6,000 B.C.Y.
200 H.P., 4 C.Y. (966)	6,001–7,500 B.C.Y.
270 H.P., 5.25 C.Y. (980)	7,501–9,000 B.C.Y.
375 H.P., 7 C.Y. (988)	9,001–10,500 B.C.Y.
690 H.P., 13.5 C.Y. (992)	10,501–999,999 B.C.Y.

Wheel Loader Quantity (B.C.Y.). The quantity of material to be excavated by wheel loader, in bank cubic yards (B.C.Y.), determines the wheel loader type.

Load Factor (%). The load factor converts bank density to loose density. One C.Y. of material in bank state does not equal 1 C.Y. of loose material, because swell and voids occur when the material is disturbed. Typically, the load factor ranges from 0.50–1.00, with normal soils generally falling in the range of 0.75–0.80.

Bucket Fill Factor (%). The bucket fill factor indicates the approximate amounts of material as a percent of rated bucket capacity that will actually be delivered per bucket per cycle. This factor depends on the type of material being excavated. A wet or moist soil is cohesive and will stick together, giving a heaped bucket. A loose, dry material will not heap, and the amount per bucket will be limited to a fraction of the size of the bucket. For estimating purposes, dry, packed earth will normally achieve a fill factor of 0.90–1.10.

Travel Time Empty (Per Cycle) (min.). The total travel time is comprised of haul or loaded travel time and the return or empty travel time. These times depend on the equipment chosen, percent grade at the site, and the distance traveled. The following list shows travel times for a level site and one-way travel distance of 200'.

Wheel Loader Type	Travel Time Empty
65 H.P., 1.25 C.Y. (910)	.28 min.
80 H.P., 1.5 C.Y. (916)	.32 min.
100 H.P., 2 C.Y. (926)	.34 min.
155 H.P., 3 C.Y. (950)	.16 min.
200 H.P., 4 C.Y. (966)	.18 min.
270 H.P., 5.25 C.Y. (980)	.17 min.
375 H.P., 7 C.Y. (988)	.18 min.
690 H.P., 13.5 C.Y. (992)	.21 min.

Travel Time Loaded (Per Cycle) (min.). The total travel time is comprised of haul or loaded travel time and the return or empty travel time. These times depend on the equipment chosen, percent grade at the site, and the distance traveled. The following list shows travel times for a level site and one-way travel distance of 200'.

Equipment Type	Travel Time Loaded
65 H.P., 1.25 C.Y. (910)	.28 min.
80 H.P., 1.5 C.Y. (916)	.32 min.
100 H.P., 2 C.Y. (926)	.34 min.
155 H.P., 3 C.Y. (950)	.18 min.
200 H.P., 4 C.Y. (966)	.19 min.
270 H.P., 5.25 C.Y. (980)	.18 min.
375 H.P., 7 C.Y. (988)	.20 min.
690 H.P., 13.5 C.Y. (992)	.22 min.

Load/Dump/Maneuver (Per Cycle) (min.). A basic cycle time (load, dump, maneuver) of 0.45–0.55 minutes is average for the loaders described in this chapter. However, variations can be expected in the field. The values for the different cycle time factors in the following list are based on normal operation.

Wheel Loader Type	Load/Dump/Maneuver Time
65 H.P., 1.25 C.Y. (910)	.45 min.
80 H.P., 1.5 C.Y. (916)	.45 min.
100 H.P., 2 C.Y. (926)	.50 min.
155 H.P., 3 C.Y. (950)	.50 min.
200 H.P., 4 C.Y. (966)	.50 min.
270 H.P., 5.25 C.Y. (980)	.55 min.
375 H.P., 7 C.Y. (988)	.58 min.
690 H.P., 13.5 C.Y. (992)	.70 min.

Work Minutes/Hour (min.). The number of minutes per hour that the track loader is actually excavating or working also accounts for down-time. Factors such as refueling, repairs, and operator break time contribute to down-time. The normal maximum work minutes per hour is 50 minutes or an efficiency of 83%.

Blasting: General Information Required

At a minimum, the following three items must be known in order to make a blasting estimate:

- Blasting Area
- Production Removal Required
- Production Blasting Area

Blasting Area

This is the portion of the excavation area that requires blasting. The blasting area cannot exceed the total excavation surface area.

Production Removal Required

When excavating rock for road cuts and quarries, clean-cut edges are required and can be accomplished by production removal blasting. This procedure is more expensive than general blasting and generally not required for bulk excavation. If production removal is required, then assume 5-1/2" diameter bore holes will be drilled with a track drill to the depth of the excavation.

Production Blasting Area

Indicates the area in square feet of cut wall that will be blasted.

Blasting — Detailed Information

More detailed information can be used to prepare a more detailed and accurate estimate. The following items can be used to further quantify the cost of blasting as part of an excavation project estimate.

- Depth of Borehole
- Area per Borehole
- Blasting Explosive Charge
- Production Blasting Explosive Charge

Depth of Borehole

This is the depth of each hole drilled for placement of explosive charges. The default value would be the excavation depth, but more precise depths can be provided if known. Typically excavation depths can range from 1–40'.

Area per Borehole

This is the square foot surface area per borehole. For example, if bore holes are 4' × 10' on center, the area per bore would be 40 S.F. The typical valid range is 10–200 S.F.

Blasting Explosive Charge

This item identifies the pounds of ammonia nitrate explosive required for each square foot of area blasted. A rule of thumb default value is 0.255 lbs/S.F. The valid range is 0.1–1.5 lbs/S.F.

Production Blasting Explosive Charge

The explosive charge is described in pounds of ammonium nitrate per square foot of blasted area. The default value is 147 lbs/168 S.F. of area, or 0.875 lbs/S.F. The valid range is 0.001–3.0 lbs/S.F.

Sampling and Analysis

Contaminated soils that are excavated for treatment or disposal are normally analyzed to determine the nature and extent of contamination. Sampling protocol for any given site is a function of both the type of contamination and the method of treatment chosen, and is thus highly site-specific. Excavation is commonly used to remove hydrocarbon contaminated soils. If this is the case, analysis of total petroleum hydrocarbons and purgeable aromatics will be required.

The sampling frequency is determined by the excavation method chosen and the volume of material to be excavated. If excavation in lifts is chosen, then soil samples for each lift will commonly occur on a 2,500 S.F. grid pattern with three composite samples per grid area. Three samples are assumed for areas smaller than 2,500 S.F. Composite samples are assumed to consist of grab samples taken from at least four separate locations and combined in one sample container for analysis. In addition, individual samples are normally collected from locations equally distributed throughout the surface area and from a depth of at least 6" below the surface.

For estimating and project control purposes, the typical contaminated area is divided into four quadrants. When excavation is performed in lifts, each lift is sampled one quadrant at a time. Thus the second quadrant is being excavated while the first quadrant is being sampled.

The analytical costs are generally based on an off-site conventional laboratory, assuming a 24-hour turnaround time. In this case, except for very small sites, the laboratory turnaround time does not affect machine productivity. However, for excavation sites smaller than 5,000 S.F., productivity down-time resulting from laboratory turnaround time becomes more significant.

For continuous excavation, sampling is typically necessary upon completion of the project to verify that contaminant concentrations in the remaining soil are below target levels. In this case, the number of samples is based on sampling 1 lift. The volume of contaminated material is a function of the bottom area and the depth of excavation and is not a function of side slope (see Figure 41.1). The number of samples will, therefore, be the same for an excavation with vertical sides as it would be for one with sloped sides.

Related Costs

Upon completion of the excavation project, all equipment is normally decontaminated. The estimator should determine the actual number of machines chosen for the site and size the decontamination facilities accordingly. Sheeting should be decontaminated upon removal from the excavation, whether it is disposed or salvaged. Typically, sheeting is decontaminated by steam cleaning.

Site Work and Utilities

If site work and utilities apply to the excavation, they must be covered in the estimate as well. Site work and utilities that may be applicable are:

- Access roads
- Fencing
- Clear and grub

Conclusion

Excavation is one of the most common activities performed on remediation projects. The cost drivers for excavation are the volume of excavation, the type of excavation method to be used, the distance to the dump point, the soil characteristics, and the toxicity of the soil. The design of an excavation project is really a logistics process design. Decisions on equipment selection, requirements, and other related factors can have significant cost implications, particularly for large projects. The cost engineer should work closely with the design team and the construction team to develop and compare alternative excavation approaches.

Chapter 42

Free Product Removal (French Drain)

A *free product removal* system is used to remove or contain non-aqueous phase liquid (NAPL) or free-phase product that has accumulated on or below the water table. NAPLs are characterized as either "light" NAPLs (LNAPLs) or "dense" NAPLs (DNAPLs). LNAPLs are also known as *floaters* because they are less dense than water and tend to float on the surface. LNAPLs include gasoline fuels, aviation fuels, and diesel. DNAPLs are also known as *sinkers* because they are more dense than water, and include creosote mixtures and most chlorinated solvents. DNAPLs will continue to sink until an impervious subsurface structure restricts or redirects movement. Free product removal is most appropriate for continuous large pools of NAPL (generally thicker than 1'). Without these conditions, it is unlikely that meaningful volumes of NAPL can be recovered through free product removal.

Using a French drain recovery system for LNAPL removal is much more common than for DNAPL removal; therefore, this chapter concentrates on LNAPL recovery. However, since the basic system components are similar, it is possible to create a reasonable cost estimate for a DNAPL system using the guidelines in this chapter. For effective DNAPL recovery by the French drain system, there must be a restrictive subsurface structure such as a shallow confining unit. Otherwise, the DNAPL will continue to flow downward to depths greater than would be economically feasible to use a French drain recovery system. For shallow contamination problems, drains can be more cost-effective than extraction wells, particularly in strata with low or variable hydraulic conductivity.

Applications and Limitations

Applications

- Removal of light non-aqueous phase liquids (LNAPLs), such as gasoline, diesel, and aviation fuels.
- Used primarily in cases where a fuel hydrocarbon lens more than 20 cm (8") thick is floating on the water table.
- Usually most effective for shallow pools of NAPL.

Limitations

- This process is generally not effective for DNAPLs (dense non-aqueous phase liquids).
- Residual saturation of contaminant in soil pores and any contaminant sorbed onto stationary soil media will not be removed.
- Handling and treatment of contaminated effluent is required after removal.
- The site geology and hydrogeology may limit the applicability and effectiveness of the process.

Typical System Design Elements

The basic design of the subsurface free product removal system closely resembles the design of a French drain system. The drain is comprised of a 6" perforated stainless steel collection pipe surrounded by a gravel pack. This system also incorporates a geotextile liner in the collection trenches to prevent the pipe from clogging and filling with silts and sands. Contaminated groundwater and free product enter the drain and flow by gravity to the sumps. Groundwater and product pumps in the sumps deliver the fluids via single-wall aboveground pipe to storage tanks for treatment and/or disposal.

The free product removal technology controls and collects liquid contamination and transports it via piping to on-site holding facilities. French drain installation includes the excavation of the trench as well as installation of the following: gravel pack, geotextile fabrics, drainage pipe, backfill, groundwater and product pumps, concrete sumps, single-wall aboveground piping and holding tanks.

The French drain system is designed to intercept the down-gradient flow of a contaminant or is placed throughout the plume as a collection system. When a French drain is placed within the plume area, physical constraints such as excavating in contaminated areas may risk the safety of workers, increase the volume of soil to dispose, and increase the likelihood of an explosion. These constraints increase the cost of such an installation. Figure 42.1 illustrates this technology.

French drain recovery systems may be passive or active. The passive system involves only the removal of product with no groundwater gradient control. French drain recovery systems typically depend on natural groundwater flows to collect NAPL. Groundwater pumps are included for the purpose of evacuating the sumps, rather than groundwater gradient control. This chapter is based on that typical case.

Normally, the French drain is installed outside the limits of the contaminant plume; thus no contaminated soil is excavated in the process. This chapter does not address costs for treatment or disposal of any excavated soils, recovered groundwater or product. If the specific project application indicates that these items are required, guidance is provided elsewhere in this book. Specifically, other technologies that may be considered as part of a treatment train in conjunction with a French drain system are slurry wall, air stripping, extraction wells, oil/water separation, air sparging, in situ bioventing, excavation—buried waste, load and haul, commercial disposal (incineration), landfill disposal, and decontamination facilities, all covered in this book.

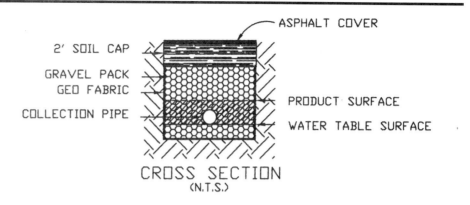

CROSS SECTION
(N.T.S.)

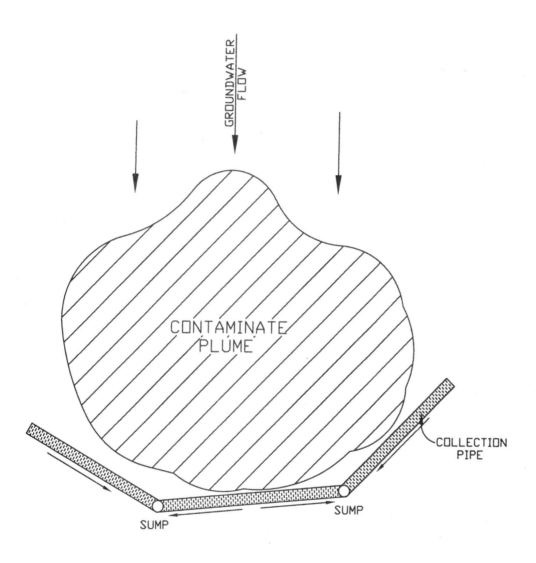

Figure 42.1 Down–gradient Free Product French Drain

Basic Information Needed for Estimating

It is possible to create a reasonable cost estimate using a few required parameters. If more detailed information is known, one can create a more precise and site-specific estimate using a secondary set of parameters.

To estimate the cost of the free product removal system, certain information must be known. This information is discussed in the following paragraphs.

Depth to Product

The depth to product is the distance from the ground surface to the top of the product layer. The thickness of product is added to the depth to groundwater to calculate the thickness of the gravel pack in the trench.

Depth to Groundwater

The depth to groundwater is the distance from the ground surface to the top of the water table. This parameter determines the total depth of the trench, which is typically equal to the depth to groundwater plus 2'. The thickness of product is added to the depth to groundwater to determine the thickness of the gravel pack in the trench.

Length of Trench

The total length of the trench includes laterals (if any) as well as the main collection pipe. The design of the collection pipe and trench should be based on the size and dimensions of the free product plume.

Soil Type

The soil types shown below have been generalized for the purpose of estimating the costs of excavation and backfill. The soil type will also affect the number of sumps. A generalized soil hydraulic conductivity will be assigned to each soil type.

Soil type options are:

Soil	Approximate Hydraulic Conductivity
Clay	0.000142 in/hr
Clay/sand	0.014200 in/hr
Clay/sand w/boulders	1.420000 in/hr
Sand	14.200000 in/hr

The soil type affects the excavation and backfill quantities as different soils have different shrink/swell factors. A quantity of stone backfill will be brought on site and used to backfill the trench from the bottom of the trench to 4' above the product level. The remaining portion of the excavation will normally be backfilled with excavated material; and remaining excavated material (e.g., equal to the volume of stone backfill and drainage piping) will be loaded and hauled off-site. If the assumed 4' thickness of the gravel pack exceeds the total depth of the trench, then the value of the gravel pack will equal the thickness of the trench with no soil cap.

Figure 42.2 provides ranges of hydraulic conductivities (permeabilities) for various soil types.

Manual Product Removal

Free product recovery can be manual, automated, or both. Manual product removal by hand-bailing can be cost-effective, particularly in remote sites where electric power is not readily available. If manual product removal is used, a two-person crew usually travels to the site on a weekly basis for the duration of the operations and maintenance (O&M) period.

Treatment Period

The total treatment period is divided into startup and O&M. The costs associated with the startup period (e.g., equipment acquisition, installation, and optimization) are considered capital costs, and the O&M costs are identified separately.

Worker Safety Level

Worker safety is affected by the contaminant(s) at the site. Safety level refers to the levels required by OSHA in 29 CFR Part 1910. The 4 levels are designated as A, B, C, and D; where "A" is the most protective and "D" is the least protective. A safety level of "E" is also included to simulate normal construction, "no hazard" conditions as prescribed by the EPA.

Typical Ranges Of Hydaulic Conductivity (Permeabilities)	
Soil Type	Ranges Of Permeabilities (In./Hr.)
CLAY:	
Clay	1.42×10^{-7} – 1.42×10^{-4}
Sandy Clay	1.42×10^{-4} – 1.42×10^{-3}
SAND:	
Clayey Sand	1.42×10^{-3} – 1.42×10^{-1}
Silty Sand	1.42×10^{-2} – 1.42×10^{1}
Very Fine Sand	1.42×10^{-1} – 1.42×10^{1}
Fine Sand	1.42×10^{1} – 1.42×10^{1}
Coarse Sand	1.42×10^{1} – 1.42×10^{3}
Sand w/Gravel	1.42×10^{2} – 1.42×10^{3}
ROCK:	
Gravel	1.42×10^{3} – 1.42×10^{5}
Well Cemented Sandstone	1.42×10^{-5} – 1.42×10^{-3}
Friable Sandstone	1.42×10^{-3} – 1.42×10^{1}
Unjointed Crystalline Limestone	1.42×10^{-5} – 1.42×10^{-1}
Karst Limestone	1.42×10^{-1} – 1.42×10^{3}
Unfractured Igneous Rock	1.42×10^{-9} – 1.42×10^{-4}
Fractured Igneous Rock	1.42×10^{-3} – 1.42×10^{1}
OTHERS:	
Peat	1.42×10^{-4} – 1.42×10^{-2}
Silt	1.42×10^{-5} – 1.42×10^{-2}
Sandy Silt & Till	1.42×10^{-3} – 1.42×10^{-1}
Glacial Till	1.42×10^{-7} – 1.42×10^{1}

Figure 42.2 Typical Ranges of Hydraulic Conductivity

Note: To convert inches/hr. to cm/sec, multiply In./Hr. by 7.056×10^{-4}

Design Information Needed for Detailed Estimates

Following are descriptions of the types of detailed information that, when available, can add detail and accuracy to estimates. Also included are design criteria and estimating rules of thumb that the estimator typically uses to determine values that are not known, or to check information provided by others.

Trench Details

A 6" stainless steel screen is typically used as the collection pipe within the trench, but other pipe diameters are available depending on project conditions. Other trench details include the following.

Trench Depth

The typical value for trench depth is the depth to groundwater plus 2'.

Trench Width

The typical value for trench width is 3', but trenches may be up to 10' wide.

Side Wall Protection

Pursuant to current OSHA requirements, side walls of excavations greater than 5' deep should be protected against cave-in. This is normally accomplished by installing sheeting or trench boxes, or by sloping the excavation walls. If the trench is less than 5' deep, no side wall protection is normally required.

If side wall protection is needed, trench boxes or sheeting are the best options. Side sloping for deeper trenches creates a larger area in which free product may spread and contaminate previously uncontaminated areas.

Dewatering

Normally, dewatering is required for trenching applications because the default trench depth extends 2' into the water table. However, dewatering may not be necessary for extremely firm soils or low yielding formations. Wellpoints will be used to remove groundwater from the saturated soils during excavation and construction of the trench. If the trench is less than 10' deep, then a reasonable estimating assumption would be one-month's rental of 600' of header pipe with wellpoints at 5' on center for each 4,400 L.F. of trench. If the depth of trench is greater than 10', assume 225' of header pipe with well points 5' on center for each 1,650 L.F. of trench.

Treatment may be required for the groundwater extracted from the wellpoints. The groundwater that is recovered during the dewatering process, if contaminated, must be either stored, hauled off site, treated, or disposed. Since the trench will be installed outside the contaminated area, this treatment is not normally required. If treatment is needed, these costs may be accounted for by selecting other remedial technologies discussed in this book.

Soil Hydraulic Conductivity

The hydraulic conductivity, sometimes referred to as the permeability, is based on the soil type. This is the velocity at which the water flows through the aquifer. The default soil hydraulic conductivity is based on the soil type. Refer to Figure 42.2 for the hydraulic conductivity of various soils.

Hydraulic Gradient

The hydraulic gradient is the slope of the hydraulic grade line. This is the slope of the aquifer; in shallow aquifers it generally follows the slope of the surrounding terrain. If the hydraulic gradient is not known, a reasonable rule of thumb is 0.01 ft/ft. See the discussion under the next parameter, "Number of Sumps," for further examples.

Number of Sumps

The number of sumps is based on the following equation:

$$TNS = L_X/L_S \text{ \{Round up to next whole number\}}$$
$$L_S = [(k_g/12) \, (I_t) \, (W_x)] \, / \, [(k_s/12) \, (I_s)] \text{ \{Round up to the next whole number\}}$$

Where:

TNS = Total number of sumps
L_X = Length of French drain (ft)
L_S = Sump spacing (ft)
k_g = Hydraulic conductivity of the gravel in the French drain (in/hr)
I_t = Hydraulic gradient of the French drain trench (ft/ft)
W_x = Width of the French drain trench (ft)
k_s = Hydraulic conductivity of the aquifer (in/hr)
I_s = Hydraulic gradient of the aquifer (ft/ft)

L_{Smin} = 250' where $k_s < 0.142$
= 500' where $k_s > 0.142$
L_{Smax} = 3,000'

Pump Options

The parameters for pump options are as follows.

Product Pump

The product pump selection is based on the calculated flow rate into each sump. Assume that the sump has a maximum wet well capacity of 105 gallons. This is 2 vertical feet of sump length. Options include various product pumps, total fluids pump, and a solvent (DNAPL) pump.

Quantity of Product Pump(s)

The typical value for quantity of product pump(s) is one product pump per sump.

Groundwater Pump

Normally, groundwater pumps are not required because the product pumps are dual-phase pumps, which can handle both liquid and product. Groundwater pumps, if installed, are intended to keep the sump free of contaminated groundwater and to allow product to easily flow into the sump, rather than to control the groundwater gradient.

Quantity of Groundwater Pump(s)

If groundwater pumps are required, this parameter is used to specify the quantity of groundwater pumps. (See "Groundwater Pump" parameter above.)

Holding Tanks

The recovered product and groundwater are transferred to individual storage tanks via aboveground piping. The size and type of recovered groundwater and product tanks should be determined. Some of the factors to consider when selecting tank size are:

- The amount of NAPL at the site
- The porosity and permeability of the soils
- The number of pumps
- The percent of time the pumps will be operational
- How often the holding tanks will be pumped out

The holding tank parameters are as follows.

Groundwater Holding Tank

This parameter refers to the size of the recovered groundwater holding tank. The dual-phase product pump will pump groundwater into the groundwater tank and product into the product tank. Groundwater infiltration into the sump should be minimal.

Quantity of Groundwater Holding Tank(s)

This parameter refers to the number of groundwater holding tanks. (See "Groundwater Holding Tank" parameter above.)

Product Holding Tank

Assumptions for the product holding tank include a 90% tank fill capacity factor and 24 hours per day, 7 days per week operation. Clay soils have very low hydraulic conductivity rates, and will therefore require pump out less than once a week. Other soil types with higher hydraulic conductivity will require pump out on a weekly or even daily basis. The typical range in product holding tank sizes is 550 gallons to 30,000 gallons. The cost of pumping the tanks should be included in the estimate.

Quantity of Product Holding Tank(s)

This parameter refers to the number of product holding tanks. The number of tanks required is based on the information in Figure 42.3.

Secondary containment is used to include all tanks in one containment berm. The secondary containment is designed to hold 110% of the largest tank volume.

Pipe/Surface Cover

This discussion covers the pipe used to transfer the groundwater and product from the sump to the holding tanks, and the type of existing surface cover that will be demolished prior to excavation of the trench. The parameters for pipe/cover are as follows.

Type of Pipe

The most convenient type of pipe is 4" single-wall carbon steel. The type of pipe is generally based on local or state regulatory standards. Double-wall piping may be required in some cases. Options for pipe include:

- Class 200 PVC
- Polyethylene
- Carbon steel
- Stainless steel
- Double-wall PVC
- Double-wall carbon steel
- Double-wall stainless steel

Length of Pipe

If the pipe run from each sump to the holding tanks is not known, a rule of thumb is 200' per sump. Additional piping may be needed, depending on the design configuration.

Existing Cover

Types of existing cover construction above the French drain include asphalt, soil/gravel, and concrete. Normally, power equipment will be used to demolish the cover. Costs for transportation and disposal of demolished cover material should be considered. If soil/gravel is the existing or replacement surface cover, then no demolition or replacement costs are added because the trench will be completed with a soil or gravel backfill. Options for existing cover construction are:

- Asphalt
- Soil/gravel
- 6" unreinforced slab on grade
- 6" mesh reinforced slab on grade
- 6" structural slab on grade
- 12" structural slab on grade

Product Holding Tanks		
Quantity Of Tanks	**Tank Size In Gallons**	**Max. Flow (GPH)**
1	550	0.00–2.95
1	1,000	2.96–5.36
1	2,000	5.37–10.71
1	3,000	10.72–16.07
1	5,000	16.08–26.79
1	8,000	26.80–42.86
1	10,000	42.87–107.00
1	12,000	107.01–142.86
1	15,000	142.87–160.50
1	20,000	160.51–750.00
1	30,000	750.01–1,250.00
Tank$_p$ 30,000	>1,250*	

If Max. Flow >1,250 GPH, then Tank$_p$ = [MAXQ(24)/30,000] + 1 [Round Up]
MAXQ = PRODTHICK *LX*k$_s$/12 *7.48* GRAD/0.001
Where:
    MAXQ = Model design limitation (maximum flow condition)
    PRODTHICK = Product thickness (ft.)
    LX = Total trench length (ft.)
    k$_s$ = Soil hydraulic conductivity (in./hr.)
    7.48 = Gallons per cubic foot conversion (gal./C.F.)
    GRAD = Aquifer hydraulic gradient (ft./ft.)
    0.001 = Trench hydraulic gradient (ft./ft.)

Figure 42.3 Product Holding Tanks

Replacement Cover

The options for replacement cover are the same as those listed above for existing cover. Typically, demolished cover will be replaced with the same type of cover.

Manual Product Removal

Some sites with automated product recovery systems may still require some manual product removal. This is performed by establishing a hand-bailing schedule. The hand-bailing schedule parameters include the following.

Number of Crew Members

The crew members will be field technician-type personnel. The crew can consist of 1–5 field technicians. Typically, 2 field technicians are needed per site visit.

Distance to Site

The distance to the site is the distance the contractor will have to travel to get to the site. The costs include truck or van mileage, and a mobilization fee based on mileage. If the site is more than 100 miles away, then a per diem charge will normally be added per field technician per visit.

Frequency

The frequency of monitoring determines how often hand-bailing will occur at the site. Typically, the monitoring will be performed weekly. Each weekly visit is generally eight hours per field technician.

Duration

Duration is the length of total time the hand-bailing will take place. This will be the entire operations and maintenance (O&M) period unless project conditions are unusual.

Related Costs

O&M costs include electrical costs for running the product pumps, groundwater pumps, and any required compressors. Pump control and maintenance costs are also included in the O&M cost. Analysis is not usually conducted on free product; therefore, there are no free product samples. However, samples may need to be taken from the recovered groundwater in the storage tank before hauling and disposal. These costs are usually associated with disposal fees, and should be included with the hauling and disposal charges.

Site Work and Utilities

Site work and utilities that may be applicable for free product removal are:

- Clear and grub
- Fencing
- Load and haul (for any demolished concrete or asphalt)

These must also be included in the estimate.

Conclusion

French drain systems are common in remediation and spill recovery applications. The primary cost drivers are the size and depth of the system, the sump recovery system, the soil and groundwater characteristics, and the operating period. To a large extent, these items are dictated by the volume of contaminant to be recovered and the site geology and hydrogeology. The cost engineer should work closely with the designer and the site geotechnical scientists to determine these items as a basis for the estimate.

Chapter 43

Groundwater Extraction Wells

Extraction wells are installed to access, then remove, groundwater and/or soil vapor. Extraction wells enhance free product recovery, contain the dissolved contaminant plume, and reduce the mass of contamination in the aquifer.

Groundwater extraction, "pump and treat," and soil vapor extraction (SVE) treatments are widely applied remedial technologies. Pump and treat is ineffective primarily because the sources of groundwater contamination remain. These sources consist of contaminated soils and immobilized contaminants in the vadose zone. To restore aquifers to health-based levels, pump and treat is commonly applied in conjunction with other technologies, such as SVE, air sparging, and bioventing. Groundwater extraction wells are intended to be part of a treatment train that would include, at a minimum, water treatment and disposal.

Applications and Limitations

Applications

- Enhances free product recovery.
- Helps to contain a dissolved contaminant plume.
- Helps to recover dissolved contamination and reduces the mass of contaminant in aquifer.

Limitations

- Site hydrogeology and contaminant characteristics/distribution may inhibit groundwater flow and contaminant recovery.
- Contaminants may be difficult to desorb from the aquifer soils.
- Extracted contaminated groundwater may require treatment.
- Extraction alone may be insufficient to meet remedial targets, since contaminants are likely to remain sorbed onto soil particles and immobilized in vadose zone.
- Biofouling and/or inorganic fouling may increase operating costs.
- DNAPLs (Denser than water Non-Aqueous Phase Liquids) pool at the bottom of aquifers and are extremely difficult to recover.

Typical System Design Elements

This chapter describes estimating methods for drilling and installing vertical, slant, or horizontal wells. The process of collecting soil samples via vertical soil boring is also discussed. This chapter does not include estimating guidance for technology-specific components such as pumps, vacuum extraction blowers, or bailers. The only materials discussed are well completion materials. Technology-specific components are addressed in the appropriate chapters for other remedial action technologies: SVE, air stripping, etc.

Groundwater extraction wells used in aquifer remediation are typically located near the area of highest contaminant concentrations or near the leading edge of the plume. If placed in the area of highest contamination, the groundwater withdrawal typically intercepts the downgradient extent of the contamination plume.

Extraction wells are installed in both unconfined and confined aquifers. Most impacted aquifers are unconfined, since the confining unit overlaying a confined aquifer would also inhibit downward migration of contaminants into the confined aquifer. Water table or unconfined aquifers receive recharge from downward seepage through the unsaturated zone. Removing water from the aquifer through an extraction well results in a decline in the position of the water table near the well as time progresses. In confined aquifers, recharge occurs through a recharge area when the aquifer crops out, or through slow downward leakage through a leaky confining unit. Removing water from a confined aquifer through an extraction well does not affect aquifer thickness. The hydraulic behavior of confined and unconfined aquifers is not identical; extraction well design must reflect the differences.

Vertical Wells

Subsurface remediation has historically been accomplished with vertical wells. Generally, vertical wells are cased inside the bore hole with a non-corrosive material down to the level of the groundwater, and then a screen material continues to the base of the well. Although vertical wells are installed in both confined and unconfined aquifers, contamination in confined acquifers is uncommon. The aquifer type determines the well construction specifications and flow rate calculations.

The primary cost drivers for installing vertical wells are the depth to the groundwater, depth to the base of contamination, soil type, and diameter of the well. These factors combine to determine the depth of the well and the drilling method that will be used to drill the bore hole.

The annular space is the area between the well casing and the outside diameter of the bore hole. For an extraction well, the filter pack is backfilled into the annular space to a height 2' above the top of the screened interval. A 6" bentonite seal is placed on top of the filter pack. The remainder of the annular space is filled with cement grout.

Confined or multiple aquifer extraction well design includes double casing to the confining unit. The typical drilling sequence is to advance a bore hole 3–5" in diameter larger than the outer casing to a depth within the confining unit. The outside casing is placed in the hole, and the annular space is grouted and allowed to dry. A bore hole is then advanced inside the casing, usually by rotary drilling. The construction material, well diameter, and well depth are assumed to be the same as in an unconfined aquifer. The outside casing interval will equal the depth to the top of the confining unit plus 2'. The inside casing extends to the base of the confining unit, and the screen interval is equal to the depth of the well minus the cased interval. As with unconfined well construction, the filter pack is backfilled into the annular space to a height 2' above the top of the screened interval. A 6" bentonite seal is placed on top of the filter pack. The remainder of the annular space is filled with cement grout.

There are three drilling methods for installing wells for environmental monitoring and remediation:

- Hollow stem auger
- Water/mud rotary
- Air rotary

The *hollow stem auger* method uses an auger bit that is attached to the leading auger flight and cuts a hole for the flights to follow. The cuttings are brought to the top of the hole by the flights, which act as a screw conveyer. Auger sections are added until the desired depth is reached. The hollow stem auger method is the most widely used method for extraction wells in unconsolidated materials in North America. The USEPA (1986) generally recognizes 150' as the maximum drilling depth and 4" as the maximum well diameter of hollow stem augers in unconsolidated materials. Hollow stem augers are preferred for environmental drilling for three reasons: they create minimal disturbance to the surrounding soil, the flights act as a temporary casing to prevent caving, and the method allows accurate sample collection.

Water/mud rotary drilling techniques use a rotating bit to advance the bore hole. Cuttings are removed by continuous circulation of a drilling fluid as the bit penetrates the formation. In direct rotary drilling, drilling fluid is pumped down through the drill pipe and upward in the annular space, carrying the cuttings in suspension to the surface. At the surface, the fluid is channeled to a settling pit, where the cuttings settle out and the fluid is recirculated to the drill pipe. In reverse circulation, the drilling fluid gravity flows into the annular space and is pumped back to the surface through the drill stem. The disadvantages to this method are:

- Drilling fluid could spread contamination vertically and horizontally or introduce contaminants.
- It is difficult to distinguish the groundwater table elevation.
- Circulation is lost in highly fractured or permeable formations.
- Well hydraulics are altered.

In spite of these disadvantages, the water/mud rotary method is the most common method for drilling extraction wells, since the typical diameter for an extraction well is 6" or more. A 6" extraction well contains adequate space for pumps and hoses for most extraction systems.

Air rotary drilling uses compressed air as a drilling fluid. It is used in hard rock formations and formations that contain cobbles and small boulders.

Figure 43.1 illustrates a typical extraction well in an unconfined aquifer. Well design is based on the type of contaminants expected, the depth of the water table, well utilization, and aquifer characteristics. Construction aspects common to most wells are a screened interval, a cased interval, annular space with filter material and seal, and wellhead protection.

Sample collection during bore hole advancement allows characterization of the geology beneath the site and definition of the magnitude and extent of contaminants in the vadose zone. Typically, soil samples will be collected every 5' or at each change in lithology, whichever is less, for lithologic description. Soils that will be analyzed for volatile constituents are taken with a California ring or equivalent sampler. Drilling cuttings can be collected as the bore hole is advanced for general geologic information. Discrete samples are collected in rock by coring, and in unconsolidated sediment using a variety of methods, including split spoon, Shelby tubes, and the California brass ring. Samples are screened with an organic vapor analyzer (OVA) for volatile organics and described for the lithologic log by the geologist supervising drilling.

Slant Drilling

Surface obstructions may render the installation of vertical wells impractical or impossible. In such cases, slant or directional wells may be viable alternatives.

Slant bore holes are drilled by tilting or slanting the mast of the drill rig at a predetermined angle. Most slant drill rigs are capable of drilling at angles as great as 45° off vertical, although sample collection during drilling is very difficult, if not impossible, at angles greater than 30° off vertical. Slant bore holes are typically drilled using hollow stem auger or air rotary drilling techniques, and well completion materials (e.g., casing, screen, filter pack, and grout) are nearly identical to those used for vertical wells. In slant drilling, it is difficult to control the drill string and keep the bore hole straight. Consequently, well depths are typically limited to 100' or less, and well diameters are limited to 4". Target zones that are excessively deep, or large extraction areas may be more amenable to remediation using horizontal wells.

Directional Drilling

Directional drilling techniques used for environmental remediation are based on river crossing technology used to install utility conduits under rivers. Directional drill rigs remain stationary as they drill and are thus capable of drilling underneath structures. A bore hole drilled by a directional rig starts out at a predetermined angle and then deviates into a curved section. The curve transitions into the horizontal plane at the target depth. The bore hole may terminate in the horizontal plane, which is known as a *blind wellbore*; or it may extend through the horizontal plane, transitioning into a second curved section that returns to the surface, which is known as a *continuous* or *surface-to-surface wellbore*. Continuous wellbores are drilled by boring a pilot hole from entrance to exit and then enlarging the hole by back-reaming from exit to entrance while pulling the completion materials into the bore hole. Since the drill string remains in the bore hole until the completion

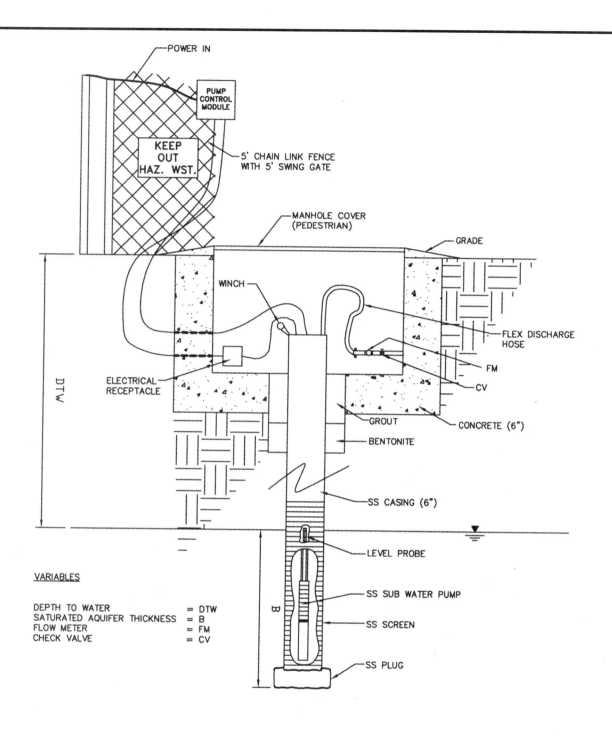

POWER IN

PUMP CONTROL MODULE

KEEP OUT HAZ. WST.

5' CHAIN LINK FENCE WITH 5' SWING GATE

MANHOLE COVER (PEDESTRIAN)

GRADE

WINCH

FLEX DISCHARGE HOSE

FM

CV

ELECTRICAL RECEPTACLE

DTW

GROUT

CONCRETE (6")

BENTONITE

SS CASING (6")

LEVEL PROBE

B

SS SUB WATER PUMP

SS SCREEN

SS PLUG

VARIABLES

DEPTH TO WATER	= DTW
SATURATED AQUIFER THICKNESS	= B
FLOW METER	= FM
CHECK VALVE	= CV

Figure 43.1 Typical Default Groundwater Extraction Well

407

materials are in place, the likelihood of bore hole collapse is reduced. This is especially important in unconsolidated formations. Continuous wellbore installation also subjects the completion materials to less stress during installation (see Figure 43.2).

Blind wellbores are drilled and cased to the end of the curved section, a pilot hole is drilled in the horizontal section, and the horizontal section is completed to the desired diameter with a hole opener. This is known as an *open hole completion*. Blind wellbores require less surface area than continuous wellbores, but installation of the completion materials is more difficult, and the chances of bore hole collapse or failure of the completion materials is considerably greater. Open hole completions are best suited to consolidated formations. Blind wellbores in unconsolidated formations are normally drilled using an overwash casing.

Regardless of the type of wellbore chosen, adequate surface area must be allowed for the drill rig and associated equipment. The location of the drill rig with respect to the target zone will be determined by the approach angle of the drill rig, the radius of curvature, and the step-off distance. *Approach angle* is a function of the drill rig and is generally not a limiting factor. The *radius of curvature* should be as long as possible to reduce stress on the completion materials and reduce the likelihood of the completion materials binding in the bore hole. As the radius of curvature decreases, the maximum allowable horizontal section length also decreases because of increased friction on the drill string. Generally, the radius of curvature, measured in feet, should be 100 times the diameter of the completion materials, measured in inches. *Step-off distance* is the horizontal distance between the entry hole and the beginning of the horizontal section of the wellbore; it is directly related to the radius of curvature. Unless space limitations at the site dictate otherwise, well design should be governed by radius of curvature rather than step-off distance.

Directional drilling costs are not always directly proportional to bore hole length or diameter. Increasing the radius of curvature will increase bore hole length, but may not necessarily increase costs, since the increased radius of curvature will facilitate easier installation of the well materials. Directional drilling costs are not readily expressed in terms of cost per linear foot. Contractors will adjust costs based on the expected degree of drilling difficulty as well as the anticipated risks of losing drill strings or completion materials down the hole. Consequently, directional drilling costs can vary significantly from one site to another.

Horizontal Drilling

Plume location and dimensions and soil properties are very important in evaluating the appropriateness of horizontal wells. Generally, plumes that are less than 25' thick and at least 100' long may be more effectively remediated by horizontal wells. This is especially true for groundwater pump and treat systems. Contaminant plumes are often restricted vertically and extended horizontally, and one horizontal well may provide a capture zone equivalent to a number of vertical wells. The relative effectiveness of horizontal wells with respect to vertical wells depends on the horizontal and vertical hydraulic conductivities. As vertical hydraulic conductivity increases with respect to horizontal conductivity, horizontal wells tend to become more effective.

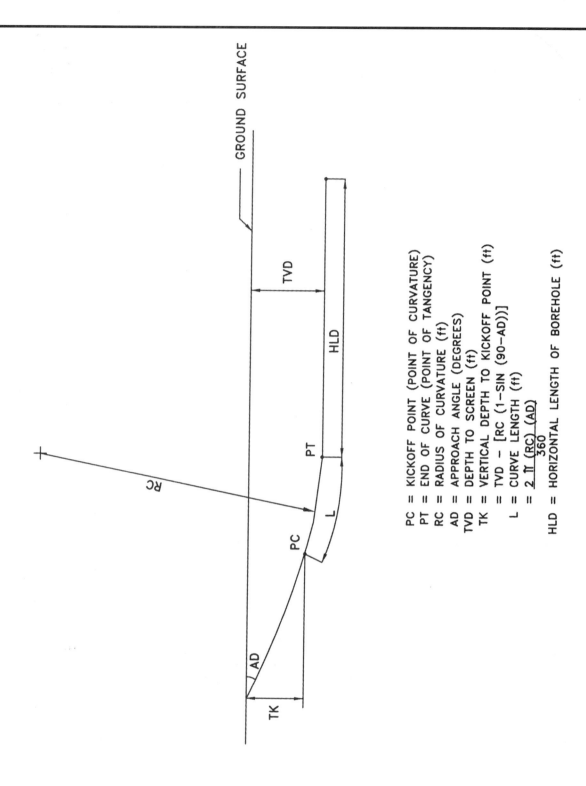

GROUND SURFACE

TVD

HLD

RC

PT

L

PC

TK

AD

PC = KICKOFF POINT (POINT OF CURVATURE)
PT = END OF CURVE (POINT OF TANGENCY)
RC = RADIUS OF CURVATURE (ft)
AD = APPROACH ANGLE (DEGREES)
TVD = DEPTH TO SCREEN (ft)
TK = VERTICAL DEPTH TO KICKOFF POINT (ft)
$$= TVD - [RC\ (1-SIN\ (90-AD))]$$
L = CURVE LENGTH (ft)
$$= \frac{2\ \pi\ (RC)\ (AD)}{360}$$
HLD = HORIZONTAL LENGTH OF BOREHOLE (ft)

Figure 43.2 Profile of Directional Bore Hole

409

There are 4 main horizontal well installation methods: chain trencher, backhoe, combination trencher/screen installer, and directional drill rig. The installation method depends on the dimensions of the target zone and the function of the wells. The *chain trencher* and *backhoe* are appropriate for downgradient capture wells or other applications that involve screen installation beyond the contaminated zone. Both of these methods generate large quantities of trench spoils and may require workers to enter the trenches. Trenching in sand, rock, or soil with boulders will affect trenching productivity. The maximum depths for the chain trencher and backhoe are 4' and 20', respectively.

A *combination trencher/screen installer* uses specialized trenching equipment to drill a 14" diameter hole and set a vertical PVC riser. After setting the riser, the machine digs in either a forward or backward direction to install a horizontal screen. As the machine digs, it fuses and installs a high density polyethylene (HDPE) screen and simultaneously covers it with filter pack. The machine automatically closes the trench behind it as it moves along. This installation option is patterned after a proprietary process developed by Horizontal Dewatering Systems, Inc. (HDSI). It is specifically designed to simultaneously fuse and install a HDPE screen and is not capable of installing other types of well materials. This process can install screens in both consolidated and unconsolidated formations up to 30' in depth. Depths greater than 30' require the use of directional drill rigs.

Basic Information Needed for Estimating

It is possible to create a reasonable cost estimate using a few required parameters. If more detailed information is known, one can create a more precise and site-specific estimate using a secondary set of parameters.

To estimate the cost of well drilling and installation, certain information must be known. This information is discussed in the following paragraphs.

General Parameters
The following general parameters apply to vertical, slant, and horizontal wells.

Number of Wells/Borings
The number of wells required on a site depends largely on the wells' purpose, the site hydrogeology, and the type of well being used.

Type of Well
The type of well refers to either vertical, slant, or horizontal well installation. While some sites may have more than one type of well, for simplicity this chapter deals with each type separately.

Formation Type
The formation type refers to the subsurface geology of the site. The formation may be either consolidated or unconsolidated. A *consolidated formation* refers to a soil stratum that may have been subjected to glacial or other consolidating loads in the geologic past. Consolidated formations are generally comprised of cemented sand (sandstone) or stiff clay deposits. An *unconsolidated formation* is a geologically recent deposit such as those found in deltas, alluvial plains, or marine deposits. Unconsolidated formations are comprised of loose to medium

silts, sands, and gravel. For vertical and horizontal wells, the default drilling method is generally determined based on the formation type. This parameter does not apply to slant wells.

Worker Safety Level

Worker safety is affected by the contaminants at the site. Safety level refers to the levels required by OSHA in 29 CFR Part 1910. The four levels are designated as A, B, C, and D; where "A" is the most protective and "D" is the least protective. A safety level of E is also included to simulate normal construction, "no hazard" conditions as prescribed by the EPA.

Vertical/Slant Well Parameters

These parameters are used to determine the properties of vertical and slant wells. Some of the parameters discussed here apply only to vertical wells.

Completion Type

The completion type refers to the number of casings, if any, to be installed in each bore hole. No casings are used for vertical soil borings for sample collection. Single cased wells are appropriate for drilling into a surficial or unconfined aquifer. When drilling through confining units and penetrating isolated or unconnected aquifers, multiple casings are required to prevent cross-contamination from one aquifer to another. Wells that penetrate a confining unit are typically double-cased from ground surface to the confining unit. The typical drilling sequence is as follows:

- Advance a bore hole into the confining unit.
- Place the outer casing in the hole.
- Grout the annular space and allow to dry.
- Advance an inner bore hole inside the outer casing, usually with a rotary drilling method.
- Complete the well as usual.

Wells that penetrate two confining units normally include triple casing. Multiple completion wells are not used for slant wells.

Depth to Bottom of Outer Casing

This parameter specifies the length of the outer casing for double- and triple-cased wells. To prevent contaminant migration from an overlying aquifer, the outer casing should terminate at a depth within the confining layer.

Depth to Bottom of Middle Casing

This parameter applies only to triple-cased wells. The depth to bottom of middle casing must be greater than the depth to bottom of outer casing.

Depth to Top of Screen

The depth to top of screen is measured from the ground surface. For multiple-cased wells, the screened interval should begin at or below the base of the confining layer. For slant wells, the depth to top of screen is measured along the axis of the drill rig, as shown in Figure 43.3. Typically, all well casings extend 3' above ground surface.

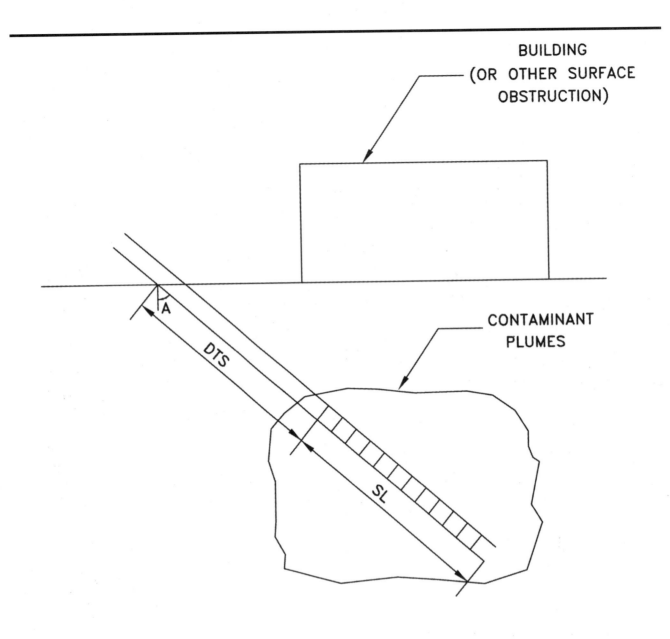

A = ANGLE OF DRILL RIG (MAX 45° OFF VERTICAL)
DTS = DEPTH TO TOP OF SCREEN
SL = SCREEN LENGTH

Figure 43.3 Slant Well

Screen Length

The screen length depends on the purpose of the wells. For example, vapor extraction wells are typically screened over the entire thickness of the contaminated zone, although in some cases the screens are set below the top of the contaminated zone. Monitoring wells, on the other hand, are screened over discrete intervals of the saturated zone. The total well depth is the sum of the depth to top of screen plus the screen length. For slant wells, the screen length is measured along the axis of the drill rig.

Depth of Boring

If the type of completion selected is boring only, this parameter is used to directly specify the depth of boring. For the other completion types, the depth of boring is calculated based on the depth to top of screen plus the screen length.

Horizontal Well Parameters

The following parameters are used to specify the properties of horizontal wells.

Depth to Screen

Depth to screen is measured from the ground surface to the centerline of the horizontal screen. The appropriate depth depends on the dimensions of the contaminant plume. Unless the specific design is known, a reasonable assumption is that all wells are installed to the same depth and that all screens extend 3' above ground surface. An "over/under" configuration, which consists of one horizontal well below the contaminant plume and one above it, is also commonly used.

Screen Length

Screen length is the horizontal distance over which the screen is installed.

Installation Method

As mentioned earlier, there are four horizontal well installation options. The chain trencher and backhoe have maximum depths to screen of 4' and 20', respectively. Both of these methods are for horizontal well installations outside the contaminated zone, such as downgradient capture wells. The chain trencher and backhoe both generate large trench spoil quantities and may require workers to enter the trenches. Thus these methods are not appropriate for well installation in contaminated soil. A proprietary trencher/screen installer moves along the surface, digs a trench, installs the HDPE well screen, and closes the trench as it moves. A directional drill rig can install wells to depths of 500'. Unlike the trencher/screen installer, the directional drill rig remains stationary as it drills, and is capable of installing horizontal wells beneath buildings and other surface obstructions. Following is a summary of these options:

- Chain trencher (maximum depth to screen = 4')
- Backhoe (maximum depth to screen = 20')
- Trencher/screen installer (maximum depth to screen = 30')
- Directional drill rig (maximum depth to screen = 500')

Design Information Needed for Detailed Estimates

Following are descriptions of the types of detailed information that, when available, can add detail and accuracy to estimates for well drilling and installation. Also included are design criteria and estimating rules of thumb that the estimator typically uses to determine values that are not known, or to check information provided by others. For well installation, this information is divided into two groups: vertical/slant wells and horizontal wells.

Vertical/Slant Wells

The following group of parameters applies to installation of vertical and slant wells.

Well Diameter

The appropriate well diameter depends on the purpose of the well. Vapor extraction wells or monitoring wells are typically no larger than 4" in diameter. Groundwater extraction wells are typically at least 6" in diameter. The only common well diameters available for slant wells are 2" and 4". Larger diameter slant wells are very difficult to install, and prices are normally quoted only on a site-specific basis. Well diameter options are summarized below.

- 2"
- 4"
- 6" (single-cased and double-cased wells)
- 8" (single-cased wells only)
- 10" (single-cased wells only)
- 12" (single-cased wells only)

Well Construction Material

The primary selection criteria for well construction material are cost and material compatibility with the contaminant. The most common material is PVC Schedule 40. If contaminants present at a site are not compatible with PVC well materials, stainless steel is generally used. Options for well construction material are:

- PVC Schedule 40
- PVC Schedule 80
- Stainless Steel

Drilling Method

The selection of a drilling method is a function of site-specific geologic conditions, well specifications, and the degree of subsurface disturbance. The drilling method depends on the well depth and formation type. The drilling methods listed below are applicable only for vertical wells.

- Hollow stem auger
- Air rotary
- Water/mud rotary

Figure 43.4 lists selection criteria for these drilling methods.

Hollow Stem Auger

An auger bit is attached to the leading auger flight and cuts a hole for the flights to follow. As mentioned earlier, the cuttings are brought to the top of the hole by the flights, which act as a screw conveyor. Auger sections are added until the desired depth is reached. Hollow stem augers create minimal disturbance to the surrounding soil, allow accurate sample collection, and the flights act as temporary casing to prevent caving. Hollow stem auger drilling is not available for single-cased wells larger than 8" in diameter or for multiple completion wells.

Air Rotary
Air rotary drilling uses compressed air as a drilling fluid. It can be used in hard rock formations and with double casing in unconsolidated formations. Air rotary drilling is not available for single-cased wells larger than 8" in diameter, or for multiple completion wells.

Water/Mud Rotary
Rotary drilling techniques use a rotating bit to advance the bore hole. Cuttings are removed by continuous circulation of a drilling fluid as the bit penetrates the formation. As mentioned earlier, there are disadvantages to this method, including the introduction of drilling fluid to the soils and the loss of circulation in highly fractured or permeable formations.

Sample Collection During Bore Hole Advancement
Sample collection during bore hole advancement allows for characterization of the geology beneath the site and definition of the magnitude and extent of contamination in the vadose zone. Sample collection is generally applicable only to vertical wells.

Sample collection is difficult, if not impossible, at angles greater than 30° to vertical.

Drum Drill Cuttings
During well installation, soil cuttings from the drill bit and subsequent hole are often drummed and stored until disposal options have been evaluated.

Well Development
Well development establishes hydraulic communication between the well and the aquifer and removes any fines from the well and filter

Figure 43.4 Extraction Well Drilling Methods

Extraction Well Drilling Methods			
Well Diameter (In.)	Well Depth (Ft.)	Formation Type Consolidated	Formation Type Unconsolidated
2	< 150	Water/mud rotary	Hollow stem auger
	> 150		Water/mud rotary
4	< 150	Water/mud rotary	Hollow stem auger
	> 150		Water/mud rotary
6–12		Water/mud rotary	Water/mud rotary

pack. Well development is conducted by surging and overpumping the well with a stainless steel submersible pump. Generally, extraction wells are developed, although wells that do not intercept the saturated zone may not require development.

Horizontal Wells

The following group of parameters applies to the installation of horizontal wells.

Type of Wellbore

As mentioned earlier, two types of wellbores are possible with directional drilling: a continuous wellbore and a blind wellbore. Since the drill string remains in the bore hole during the construction of continuous wellbore until the completion materials are in place, the likelihood of bore hole collapse is significantly reduced. The continuous wellbore provides access to both ends of the horizontal screen.

Blind wellbores have only an entrance hole and terminate at the target depth. Blind wellbores require shorter total bore hole lengths than continuous wellbores, but the probability of wellbore collapse is much greater, and installation of well completion materials is more difficult. Drilling blind wellbores in unconsolidated formations is extremely difficult. The blind wellbore option is only available for consolidated formations.

Horizontal Length of Bore Hole

In directional drilling applications, the horizontal segment of the bore hole may need to exceed the screen length. This is especially true in the case of continuous wellbores. The default horizontal length of bore hole is equal to the screen length plus 2'. Increasing the horizontal length of bore hole will increase the total bore hole length and the casing quantity. The horizontal length of bore hole may not be less than the user-specified screen length.

Angle of Approach

The angle of approach applies only to directional drilling. The angle of approach depends on the type of bore hole and the target depth. Approach angles for continuous wellbores are typically between 7–30° from horizontal. Approach angles for blind wellbores are steeper, ranging from 20–90°. The default depends on the depth to screen. The maximum allowable entry angle is the largest angle that will yield a non-negative value for the depth to the kick-off point.

Well Construction Material

Well construction material is normally chosen based on contaminant compatibility and cost. The material depends on the installation method. If a filter pack is required, as in the case of groundwater extraction wells, a pre-packed well screen is commonly used. HDPE well materials are used for the trencher/screen installer. PVC construction materials are normally used for all other installation methods. Prepacks are available.

Thus the options for well construction material are:

- PVC
- Stainless steel
- HDPE (only for trencher/screen installer; not for chain trencher or backhoe)

- PVC prepack (only for directional drill rig)
- Stainless steel prepack (only for directional drill rig)
- HDPE prepack (only for directional drill rig)

Well Diameter

Well diameter refers to the nominal outer diameter of the well screen. Prepack filter material typically adds at least an inch to the diameter of the well. Thus a 6" diameter prepack screen would actually measure 7" or more in diameter. Consequently, prepack screens require larger bore holes. The range of well diameters available for horizontal well installation is typically limited by the equipment used to install the wells. Well diameter also depends on the purpose of the well.

Well diameter options are as follows:

- 2" (not for trencher/screen installer)
- 4"
- 6"
- 8" (only for directional drill rig; prepacks not available in 8" diameter)

Sidewall Protection

Sidewall protection applies only to the backhoe installation method. Trenches deeper than 5' deep typically require side wall protection to avoid cave-in. This is accomplished by installing trench boxes or by sloping the sides of the excavation. In some instances, steel sheeting may be used to support the trench walls.

Sidewall protection options, then, are as follows:

- Side slope
- Trench box
- Sheeting
- None (not an option if depth to screen > 5')

Drum Drill Cuttings

Drum drill cuttings apply only to the trencher/screen installer and directional drill rig. During well installation, soil cuttings from the drill bit and subsequent hole are often drummed and stored until disposal options have been evaluated. Although the trencher/screen installer does not actually drill a bore hole, it still generates a quantity of spoil material that is displaced by the screen and filter pack. This spoil material is normally drummed for secure disposal. To estimate the quantity of spoil material, assume that the trencher/screen installer displaces a "core" of material 14" in diameter extending the full length of the trench. To estimate the quantity of drill cuttings generated by the directional drill rig, assume that the bore hole diameter is 1.5 times the diameter of the well.

Well Development

Well development establishes hydraulic communication between the well and the aquifer and removes any fines from the well and filter pack. Well development is conducted by surging and overpumping the well with a stainless steel submersible pump. Most wells will be developed, although wells that do not intercept the saturated zone may not require development. If the installation method is a chain trench or backhoe, well development is not applicable.

Related Costs

Other costs associated with well drilling and installation include rig decontamination and drilling supervision. Professional field labor for drilling installation is addressed in Chapter 58 of this book. This chapter does not include costs for technology-specific remediation equipment such as pumps or vacuum extraction blowers. These components are discussed with the specific technology applications that form the treatment train.

Site Work and Utilities

Site work and utilities that may apply to well drilling and installation are:

- Access roads
- Clear and grub
- Fencing

These must also be included in the estimate.

Conclusion

Extraction wells are used for all types of ex situ groundwater and soil gas remediation. The cost drivers for extraction wells include the capacity of the well, the well depth, soil characteristics, and drilling method (vertical, horizontal, slant). There is often more than one option for the design of extraction wells, and the cost engineer should work with the design team to determine the most cost-effective approach.

Chapter 44

Transportation

For the purposes of this discussion, transportation means moving hazardous waste from a generator to a treatment, storage, or disposal (TSD) facility. The waste may need to be prepared for loading, or it may already be loaded on the transport unit. Once loaded, the material is transported to its destination.

Applications and Limitations

Applications

- For transportation of all contaminant groups, hazardous and non–hazardous wastes.

Limitations

- The generator is ultimately responsible for safe collection, transportation, disposal, and elimination of waste. Selection of the landfill operator is therefore a critical decision.
- Manifest requirements by generators, storage facilities, transporters, and disposers of wastes can be a significant cost item.
- Characterization of hazardous wastes to be transported can also be a substantial expense.
- The distance from the site to the treatment or disposal facility will directly affect cost.
- The transportation methods and associated cost described in this chapter apply to hazardous and toxic waste. This chapter is not applicable to miscellaneous residual waste (demolished cover, clean fill).
- Costs for treatment and/or disposal are not addressed in this chapter.

Process Configurations and Treatment Train Considerations

- The condition and characteristics of the waste will determine the size, number, and types of transportation units.
- Bulk solids (moisture content to 30%) can be loaded with a wheel loader.
- Bulk liquids (moisture content greater than 70%) is pumpable.
- Bulk sludge (moisture 30–70%) may be pumped, dredged, or excavated.
- Bulk solids and sludge are measured in C.Y., and liquids in gallons.
- Containerized (drummed) wastes are charged per number of containers.

Overpack containers may be used to package smaller drums that are in poor condition, or to containerize bulk wastes.

Typical Process Design Elements

Off-site transportation of material, whether hazardous or non-hazardous, is regulated by the U.S. Department of Transportation (DOT). Hazardous waste transportation is also regulated by both the Hazardous Materials Transportation Act (HMTA) and the Resource Conservation and Recovery Act (RCRA) Subtitle C. Under Chapter 3003 of the RCRA, the U.S. Environmental Protection Agency (EPA) was directed to establish standards, in coordination with the DOT, for the transportation of hazardous waste. The resolution between these 2 agencies resulted in the EPA's adoption of DOT regulations pertaining to labeling, placarding, and spill reporting. The EPA further developed the manifest system that is used to track the waste "from cradle to grave. The regulations pertaining to the manifest system are found in 40 Code of Federal Regulations (CFR) Parts 262 and 263.

The DOT organizations that are responsible for tracking hazardous wastes are:

- United States Coast Guard
- Federal Aviation Administration
- Federal Highway Administration
- Bureau of Motor Carrier Safety
- Federal Railroad Administration
- Research and Special Programs Administration, Office of Hazardous Materials Transportation

Outside of the DOT, regulations, ordinances, and codes pertaining to waste transportation may be administered through the EPA and state and local governments. Most of the applicable DOT hazardous waste regulations are included in 49 CFR Parts 100–199. It is important to understand that DOT considers hazardous waste a hazardous material.

The type of waste being transported can have a significant impact on its shipping cost. Transportation of hazardous waste is more expensive than non-hazardous waste because of cargo liability, regulatory restraints, and equipment requirements. This chapter covers multiple types of waste that are transported by truck and rail. A detailed waste analysis is generally required prior to waste transportation and acceptance by a TSD facility. Therefore, the chemical characteristics of the material to be transported must be well defined.

With the existing regulatory system, the potentially responsible party (PRP) can be anyone involved in the cradle-to-grave process. In 49 CFR, the PRP is defined as the person offering goods for shipment in commerce. This person is responsible for properly preparing the manifest; packing, marking, and labeling the goods to be transported; and supplying the shipper with the correct and applicable placards. The manifesting system, detailed in 40 CFR Parts 262 and 263, aids in the accountability process; however, it is not a release of liability. Some waste generators have gone out of business as the result of irresponsible actions taken on the part of the transporter or TSD facility. Criteria that should be considered when selecting a hazardous waste carrier are, in order of importance:

- Regulatory integrity
- Credibility

- Cost
- Financial strength
- Experience
- Unique capability

These factors are important in determining the environmental risk associated with the transportation of hazardous materials.

Packaging of hazardous material is regulated by the Research and Special Programs Administration (RSPA). This branch of the DOT regulates all hazardous material containers except containers for bulk marine and high-level radioactive waste material, which are regulated by the Coast Guard and the Nuclear Regulatory Commission, respectively. RSPA outlines the transportation requirements and limitations for hazardous materials in 49 CFR Part 172. Table 172.101 of this part specifies requirements and limitations for highway, rail, air, and vessel transportation of hazardous materials. References within this table point to specific sub-parts of 49 CFR Part 173, which detail packaging requirements. Although the minimum packaging requirements are detailed in Part 173, the generator may want to evaluate the mode of transportation and storage facilities at the TSD before making a final decision on waste packaging.

When transporting containerized waste, the generator should evaluate the mode of transportation and the TSD facility requirements. The requirements for the mode of transportation may range from exposure of the waste to the elements to equipment capacities. TSD facility requirements may include BTU content, storage facility requirements, and storage duration (e.g., 90-day maximum storage). Many container vendors will aid generators in the selection of containers by asking the following questions:

What chemicals are in the waste?

- Where is the waste going for disposal?
- Who is transporting the waste?
- What are the package size requirements?
- What is the hazard classification?
- How many containers are needed?
- How will the containers be stored at the TSD facility?

Pretreatment of materials may be a requirement for either transportation or disposal. Pretreatment may occur at the TSD facility or at the generator's site, depending on the composition of the material. The type of pretreatment can range from acid-based neutralization to metal precipitation/solidification. Other common pretreatments are hypochlorite oxidation of cyanide and sulfide, flash point reduction, and removal of free liquid by adding solids, lime, fly ash, polymers, or other materials. If pretreatment is required before the material can be transported, it may increase or decrease the amount of waste; thus potentially increasing or decreasing the transportation cost.

Paperwork is another cost associated with the transportation of hazardous waste. For hazardous materials, certain registrations, fees, and notifications are likely to be required before and during the transportation process. These fees are specific to the state and local agency to which the material is being transported and may be more stringent than corresponding federal laws. Although the fees are typically annual, some are per load of hazardous waste. State and local laws may require additional fees and special routing. Routing requirements may result in increased transportation distances, thus increasing transportation costs.

Clearly, transportation costs have many different components. The first and most significant is the actual cost of the equipment, fuel, and operator. In most cases, this cost includes fees, registrations, and other annual expenses. Other cost considerations are containers, material loading, pretreatment costs, and other incidentals.

Basic Information Needed for Estimating

It is possible to create a reasonable cost estimate using a few required parameters. If more detailed information is known, one can create a more precise and site-specific estimate using a secondary set of parameters.

To estimate the cost of transportation, certain information must be known. This information is discussed in the following paragraphs.

Condition of Waste Prior to Transportation

The condition of the waste, along with the type of waste, determines the size, number, and type of transportation units needed. If the waste will be containerized prior to transportation, the most common container is a DOT 55-gallon steel drum (with a closed head for liquid waste and an open head for solid and sludge waste). One advantage of containerized waste is that it does not require that the contents be compatible, as long as each container is appropriately labeled. Options for waste condition include:

- Bulk to remain as bulk
- Bulk to be transferred to containers
- Containers to be transferred to bulk
- Containers to remain as containers

Waste Type

The waste material should be classified as either *hazardous* or *non-hazardous*, depending on their waste characteristics. The EPA has developed two ways of determining if a material is a hazardous waste. The first is based on the four characteristics of the solid waste (as per RCRA definition—40 CFR Part 261):

- Ignitability
- Corrosivity
- Reactivity
- Toxicity

There are three types of listed hazardous waste:

- Specific source (40 CFR Part 261.31)
- Specific Source (40 CFR Part 261.32)
- Commercial Chemical Products (40 CFR Part 261.33)

Non-hazardous waste is waste material that is contaminated, but does not exhibit the aforementioned hazardous definition. Miscellaneous residual waste (demolished cover, clean fill) are in this category. Costs for hauling non-hazardous/non-contaminated waste are much lower than for contaminated and hazardous waste and loads should not be mixed, as the cost for the entire load is priced at the highest hazard level. Figure 44.1 provides a listing of common hazardous waste classifications.

Waste Form

For the purposes of this technology, there are two waste forms: solid and liquid (sludge). Bulk solid is assumed to be loaded by a wheel loader and have a moisture content of less than 30%. Bulk liquid is assumed to be pumpable material that has a moisture content of greater than 70%. Bulk sludge is any material with a moisture content between 30–70%. This material is assumed to be pumped and carried via tanker trucks.

Volume of Waste

The volume of waste to be transported determines the number of transport units, which directly affects costs. Bulk solids and sludge are measured in cubic yards, and bulk liquids are measured in gallons. Containerized waste is measured by the number of containers.

Travel Distance

Travel distance is the most important parameter for estimating the costs for transporting any material. The distance is based on the number of miles traveled. Generally, transporters base their rates on either a

DOT Hazardous Materials Classifications			
Class No.	Division Number	Class/Division Name	49 CFR Ref.
None		Forbidden Materials	173.21
None		Forbidden explosives	173.53
1	1.1	Explosives (with a mass explosion hazard)	173.50
1	1.2	Explosives (with a projection hazard)	173.50
1	1.3	Explosives (w/predominately a fire hazard)	173.50
1	1.4	Explosives (with no significant blast hazard)	173.50
1	1.5	Very insensitive explosives; blasting agents	173.50
1	1.6	Extremely insensitive detonating substances	173.50
2	2.1	Flammable gas	173.115
2	2.2	Non-flammable compressed gas	173.115
2	2.3	Poisonous gas	173.115
3		Flammable and combustible liquid	173.120
4	4.1	Flammable solid	173.124
4	4.2	Spontaneously combustible material	173.124
4	4.3	Dangerous when wet material	173.124
5	5.1	Oxidizer	173.127
5	5.2	Organic peroxide	173.128
6	6.1	Poisonous materials	173.132
6	6.2	Infectious substance (Etiologic agent)	173.134
7		Radioactive material	173.403
8		Corrosive material	173.136
9		Miscellaneous hazardous material	173.140
None		Other regulated material: ORM-D	173.144

Figure 44.1 DOT Hazardous Materials

Reference: 49 CFR Part 173.2

running mile or a loaded mile. A *running mile rate* includes all of the miles traveled by the transporter. The charges begin when the truck leaves the terminal and end when the truck is back at the terminal. The *loaded mile rate* is a charge associated only with the number of miles between the generator and the ultimate disposal location.

The loaded mile rate is the most common method of calculating transportation costs. For short hauling distances, the costs will be based on either a loaded mile or a minimum charge, depending on the type of material. For example, the distance from Miami, Florida, to Fairbanks, Alaska, is approximately 5,000 miles. The calculated number of trips necessary is based on the volume of waste divided by the mode of transportation capacity.

Worker Safety Level

Worker safety depends on the potential human interaction with the contaminants in the loading and en-route to the disposal facility. Safety level refers to the levels required by OSHA 29 CFR Part 1910. The 4 levels are designated as A, B, C, and D; where "A" is the most protective and "D" is the least protective. A safety level of E is also included to simulate normal construction, "no hazard" conditions as prescribed by the EPA.

The safety level is a reflection of the level of productivity and affects all labor categories. Safety level will not affect the productivity of the driver during transportation, since this would violate DOT and EPA regulations.

Design Information Needed for Detailed Estimates

Following are descriptions of the types of detailed information that, when available, can add detail and accuracy to estimates. Also included are design criteria and estimating rules of thumb that the estimator typically uses to determine values that are not known, or to check information provided by others.

Transportation Mode

The selection of a specific mode of transportation is based on the condition, type, and volume of waste. For bulk material, a transport unit may be assumed to be filled to 85% of its total volume capacity. A liner is included to reduce the risk of a spill. Figure 44.2 lists readily available options.

Container Type

The container type is based on the condition of waste, type of waste, and hazardous waste type. The container selection may affect both the material cost for the containers and the required number of transportation units. Figure 44.3 lists the options for non-radioactive waste containers. The most common container for non-radioactive waste is a DOT steel, 55-gallon, closed-head drum.

Radioactive container systems are generally custom–built to meet DOT and EPA requirements for a specific radioactive material. The specific regulations for the packaging of radioactive materials are in 49 CFR Part 173 Subpart I. There are 2 general classifications of radioactive material: Type A and Type B. (For additional information on the classifications, Type A and Type B, refer to 49 CFR Parts 173.403 through 173.478).

Figure 44.4 shows typical options for radioactive waste containers. The containers listed in Figure 44.4 represent only a fraction of the number of containers available for transporting radioactive waste. The estimator should evaluate the container requirements for radioactive material since it can become a significant cost driver. For budget estimating purposes, if the container type is unknown, a fuel cask container can be used for liquid, sludge, or solid radioactive waste.

Fill Capacity Factor

This factor is the average percent to which drums are filled. This parameter applies to either non-leaking drums that will remain drummed or for bulk to be drummed. The Fill Capacity Factor is used to determine the actual volume of waste and/or the number of drums required. Because drums are generally not entirely full, a rule of thumb of 90% full is commonly used. The valid range is 60–100%.

Overpack Container Type

Overpack containers may be used to package waste from bulk condition to a containerized condition or as a secondary containment system for waste that is already in a container. Typically, overpacks are used when there are leaking drums or drums that are in poor condition. Overpack container options include:

Transportation Mode				
Transport Unit	**Bulk Solid**	**Bulk Liquid**	**Bulk Sludge**	**Containerized**
Van Trailer (105 C.Y.)	a			x
Dump Trailer (20 C.Y.)	x		a	
Dump Trailer (26 C.Y.)	a		a	
Dump Trailer (32 C.Y.)	a		a	
Dump Trailer (36 C.Y.)	a		a	
Tanker Trailer (5,000 gal.)		a		
Tanker Trailer (6,500 gal.)		x		
Tanker Trailer (7,700 gal.)		a		
Vacuum Trailer (5,000 gal.)		a	x	
Rail Box Car (180 C.Y.)				a
Rail Box Car (280 C.Y. lt. wt.)				a
Rail Box Car (280 C.Y. med. wt.)				a
Rail Box Car (370 C.Y.)				a
Rail Gondola (15 C.Y.)	a		a	
Rail Gondola (64 C.Y.)	a		a	
Rail Gondola (83 C.Y.)	a		a	
Rail Gondola (97 C.Y.)	a		a	
Rail Gondola (119 C.Y.)	a		a	
Rail Gondola (131 C.Y.)	a		a	
Rail Gondola (262 C.Y.)	a		a	
Rail Tanker (22,000 gal.)		a		

x = typical application
a = available application

Figure 44.2 Transportation Mode

425

- 110-gallon, open-head steel drum
- 95-gallon, DOT E9618 polyethylene with twist lid
- 85-gallon, open-head steel drum
- 85-gallon, DOT E9775 polyethylene with clamp ring lid
- 83-gallon, open-head steel drum

Number of Transport Units

The number of transport units is based on the volume of waste, weight, volume capacity, and fill capacity of each mode of transportation. For very dense materials, the fill capacity may not be a critical factor because of payload weight limitations.

Non–Radioactive Waste Container Options	
55 gallon 17C Steel Drum closed head	
55 gallon 17C Steel Drum open head	
55 gallon 17H Steel Drum closed head	
55 gallon 17H Steel Drum open head	
30 gallon 17C Steel Drum open head	
30 gallon 17H Steel Drum open head	
30 gallon 17E Steel Drum open head	
20 gallon 17C Steel Drum open head	
20 gallon 17E Steel Drum open head	
15 gallon 17C Steel Drum open head	
55 gallon 5C S.S. open head	
55 gallon 5C S.S. seamless open head	
55 gallon 5C S.S. closed head	
55 gallon 5C S.S. seamless closed head	
55 gallon 17E S.S. closed head	
30 gallon 5C S.S. closed head	
55 gallon Polyethylene open head	
35 gallon Polyethylene open head	
30 gallon Polyethylene open head	
20 gallon Polyethylene open head	
15 gallon Polyethylene open head	
55 gallon Polyethylene closed head	
35 gallon Polyethylene closed head	
30 gallon Polyethylene closed head	
20 gallon Polyethylene closed head	
15 gallon Polyethylene closed head	
10 gallon 20″ diameter DOT 21C-250 Polyethylene/Polyester lined	
20 gallon 20″ diameter DOT 21C-250 Polyethylene/Polyester lined	
20 gallon 23″ diameter DOT 21C-250 Polyethylene/Polyester lined	
55 gallon 21C Fiber open head	
30 gallon 21C Fiber open head	
HazMax 1 C.Y. box w/12 mil liner including pallet	
250 gallon Plastic Tote with metal cage	
350 gallon Plastic Tote with metal cage	
110 gallon Steel Drum open head	(overpack
85 gallon Steel Drum open head	(overpack)
83 gallon Steel Drum open head	(overpack
95 gallon DOT E9618 Polyethylene twist lid	(overpack)
85 gallon DOT E9775 Polyethylene clamp ring lid	(overpack)

Figure 44.3 Non-Radioactive Waste Container Options

426

Waste Material Density

The density of the waste material is determined to ensure that the loaded equipment does not exceed payload or gross vehicle weight (GVW) limits. The first step in this determination is to calculate the waste volume per transport unit. That quantity of waste is then multiplied by the appropriate density to determine the weight of the load. Once the weight of the load is computed, it is compared to the GVW and/or the equipment payload. This identifies whether the load is volume- or weight-limited. If the load is weight-limited, the estimator should calculate the maximum volume per transfer unit based on weight. Once this volume is determined, the number of transport units is recalculated based on maximum weight instead of maximum volume. Typical values for material loads for highway trucks range from 38,000–44,000 lbs.

For budget estimating purposes, if the exact density of the waste is unknown the estimator can assume that the density for solid waste is 2,500 lbs./C.Y., with a range of 1,000–4,000 lbs./C.Y. Sludge waste can be estimated at 1,900 lbs./C.Y. (9.40 lbs./gal.), with a valid range of 1,000–4,000 lbs./C.Y. Liquid waste can be estimated at 8.3 lbs./gal., with a valid range of 0.6–113 lbs./gal. Figures 44.5 and 44.6 provide a reference for the relative densities of different liquid and solid materials.

Waste Loading

The selection of a loader is based on the condition and type of waste. For bulk solid waste, a 1.25 cubic yard wheel loader is typical. Bulk liquid waste is pumped, typically with on-board tanker pumping equipment. This equipment is assumed to be able to fill the tanker truck trailer in a maximum of 2 hours. Bulk sludge loading is typically performed by the vacuum tanker on-board equipment. Again, this equipment is assumed to be able to fill the tanker in a maximum of 2 hours. Containerized wastes are assumed to be on pallets in a staging area, ready to be loaded with a fork truck. Other loading options, based on the waste form, are listed in Figure 44.7.

Rail Tariff Rate

The railroad industry requires project-specific information before calculating tariff rates for hazardous waste. Figure 44.8 lists Class I railroads and telephone numbers. The estimator should call the company in the appropriate district for a quote. The cost of rail transportation depends on a number of different factors, including the exact locations to ship from and to, the date, and the quantity and type of waste.

Other Related Costs   The primary cost driver for transportation is the mileage charge, which is based on travel distance and the loaded mile rate. The loaded mileage charge for highway truck transport typically includes two hours for loading and unloading. It also takes into account the equipment and operator rates and consumables. Other cost factors that are typically not included in the loaded mileage charge include:

- Truck wash-out
- Manifest discrepancies
- Hourly, overnight, and maximum 24-hour demurrage time

- Additional stops
- Daily and monthly trailer drops

If these costs will be incurred, they should be included in the estimate as an additional cost item. Some states also charge a "per trip" charge for hazardous wastes. Depending on the route selected, these charges can vary from $10.00–$550.00 per load, per state.

A final cost is a waste stream analysis. Typically, a waste stream evaluation will be performed as part of other technology applications prior to the transportation process. However, in some cases the waste streams may need to be evaluated prior to transport.

Radioactive Waste Container Options
Type A:
Tall 55 gallon drum for 250 lb. UO2
5,020 lb., 30" Cylinder enriched UF6 req. overpack
27,560 lb., Cylinder UF6
55 gallon drum for 2, 5 gallon pails UO2
5", 55 lb., UF6 Cylinder overpack
8", 250 lb., UF6 Cylinder overpack
12", 430 lb., UF6 Cylinder overpack
30", 2.5 ton, UF6 Cylinder overpack
48", 10 ton, UF6 Cylinder overpack
48", 14 ton, UF6 Cylinder overpack
Type B:
14 - 55 gallon drum cask rental up to 20R/hr. (daily)
14 - 55 gallon drum cask rental up to 20Rhr. (monthly)

Figure 44.4 Radioactive Waste Container Options

Liquid Material Densities (At Atmospheric Pressure and 68°F)	
Material	Density Lb./Gal.
Benzene	7.47
Carbon Tetrachloride	13.22
Crude Oil	7.13
Gasoline	5.67
Glycerin	10.48
Hydrogen (-430°F)	0.61
Kerosene	6.74
Mercury	112.89
Oxygen (-320°F)	10.05
SAE 10 Oil	7.64
SAE 30 Oil	7.64
Water	8.31

Figure 44.5 Liquid Materials Densities

Site Work and Utilities

Site work and utilities that may be required to meet site requirements include:

- Access roads
- Railroad tracks and crossings
- Load and haul

Conclusion

Transportation of hazardous materials is an integral part of many remediation projects when waste will be hauled to a landfill or

Bulk Solid Density		
Type of Solid Materials	Loose Lb./C.Y.	Loose Lb./gal.
Cinders	950	4.71
Clay		
Natural Bed	2,900	14.36
Dry	2,500	12.38
Wet	2,800	13.87
Clay and Gravel		
Dry	2,400	11.89
Wet	2,600	12.88
Decomposed Rock		
75% Rock, 25% Earth	3,300	16.35
50% Rock, 50% Earth	2,650	14.36
25% Rock, 75% Earth	2,650	13.13
Earth		
Dry Packed	2,550	12.63
Wet Excavated	2,700	13.37
Loam	2,100	10.40
Granite–Broken	2,800	13.87
Gravel		
Pitrun	3,250	16.10
Dry	2,550	12.63
Dry 6-50 mm (1/4"-2")	2,850	14.12
Wet 6-50 mm (1/4"-2")	3,400	16.84
Limestone-Broken or Crushed	2,600	12.88
Sand		
Dry, Loose	2,400	11.89
Damp	2,850	14.12
Wet	3,100	15.36
Sand and Clay		
Loose	2,700	13.37
Compacted	4,050	20.10
Sand & Gravel		
Dry	2,900	14.36
Wet	3,400	16.84
Sandstone	2,550	12.63
Shale	2,100	10.40
Slag–Broken	2,950	14.61
Stone–Crushed	2,700	13.37
Top Soil	1,600	7.93

Figure 44.6 Bulk Solid Density

treatment location. In many instances, the transportation cost of waste can be a very significant part of the overall cost of the project. The primary cost drivers for hazardous waste transportation are the total weight or volume of the waste to be hauled and the distance. Other significant cost drivers include the cost of loading and unloading, pre-packaging of the material before loading, permits, and decontamination of the transportation equipment. The estimator should work with the project management team to consider different alternatives to determine the most advantageous transportation approach.

Waste Loading Equipment	
Bulk Solid Waste: Wheel Loaders	Average Output (CY/hr.)
1.25 C.Y.	46
1.5 C.Y.	51
2 C.Y.	67
4 C.Y.	174
7 C.Y.	275
13.5 C.Y.	452
Bulk Sludge Waste: Dredging Equipment Vacuum Trailer Equipment	1,200 GPM or 60 C.Y./hr. 50-60 GPM
Bulk Liquid Waste: Pump Size 1.5 H.P. 3.0 H.P. 10.0 H.P. Tanker Pumping Equipment	75 GPM 150 GPM 300 GPM 50-60 GPM
Containerized Waste: Fork Lift Truck	40 containers/hr.

Figure 44.7 Waste Loading Equipment

Class I Railroads	
Railroad	**Phone Number***
Eastern District: Consolidated Rail Corp. CSX Transportation, Inc. Illinois Central Norfolk Southern Railway	215-209-7281 904-359-3100 312-755-7500 757-446-5435
Western District: Atchison, Topeka & Santa Fe Burlington Northern Chicago & North Western Denver & Rio Grande Western Kansas City Southern Missouri Pacific St. Louis Southwestern Soo Line Southern Pacific Union Pacific	913-357-2000 612-298-2121 312-559-7000 303-629-5533 816-556-0303 402-271-5000 415-541-1000 612-347-8000 713-223-6000 402-271-5000

Figure 44.8 Class I Railroads   * Telephone numbers are subject to change

Part V

Cost Estimating for Remediation —Discharge Technologies

Chapter 45

Discharge to POTW

A publicly-owned treatment works (POTW) system is used in the storage, treatment, recycling, and reclamation of liquid municipal sewage or industrial wastes. The sewer system may be part of the POTW. Typically, hazardous wastes *cannot* be discharged directly to a POTW. In this chapter, we assume that all sewage is non-hazardous, or that pre-treatment has brought the sewage to a non-hazardous level.

Applications and Limitations

Applications

- Disposal of untreated or pretreated, non-hazardous wastes.
- Aqueous solutions with low to medium concentrations of pollutants.
- Wastes typically discharged to a POTW (publicly-owned treatment work) include contaminated groundwater, leachate, and surface run-off.
- Typical ranges for sewer systems are 50–100 GPM.
- POTWs are designed to reduce the organic and metals content of influent.

Limitations

- Hazardous wastes *cannot* be discharged directly to a POTW.
- Truck transportation of waste is economically feasible for low flow rates only.
- Some municipalities have high to extremely high industrial sewer connections fees.

Process Configurations and Treatment Train Considerations

Several key issues should be considered as part of the decision to use discharge to POTW in lieu of other treatment approaches and, if selected, there are considerations that impact decision and operation. Key issues include:

- POTW influent standards must be known and accounted for in the design of discharge systems.
- Gravity lines or pump stations and force mains are used to transport waste liquids to the POTW.
- Sewer design is based on sufficient scope and pipe diameter to enable gravity flow.

- Manholes are typically installed every 300–500'.
- Influent temperatures above 40 °C may inhibit POTW biological activity, thereby reducing capacity.

Typical System Design Elements

Untreated or pretreated wastes are typically discharged to a POTW for treatment and disposal. The types of aqueous wastes commonly discharged to a POTW include, but are not limited to: contaminated groundwater, leachate, and surface runoff. When considering discharge to a POTW as a disposal alternative, major technical considerations include:

- Treatment technologies used by the POTW
- Treatment capacity
- Distance of conveyance
- Contaminant characteristics of the influent
- Expected flow rates
- Duration of discharge

A high flow rate over an extended period of time may require a capital expenditure to enlarge the treatment works. This can be a complex, time-consuming, and expensive process and is beyond the scope of this book. This discussion assumes that the aqueous wastes to be discharged have been analyzed and approved (or can be approved) by the proper POTW officials, and that all pertinent permits have been obtained. However, what follows is a brief description of the methodology involved in attempting to evaluate the compatibility of a POTW with a specific set of contaminants and their concentrations.

Most POTWs reduce the concentrations of organics and metals. The removal efficiency depends on the type of contaminants in the influent and their associated concentrations. Removals are primarily attributed to stripping in aeration basins, adsorption onto biological floc, and biological degradation. The need for treatability testing or waste stream pretreatment is based on the probable effect of the contaminants on the POTW. Treatment processes at POTWs may include:

- **Aerobic processes:** Rotating biological contractors, oxidation ditches, activated sludge reactors, and trickling filters.
- **Anaerobic processes:** Anaerobic contact reactors, anaerobic filters, fluidized bed systems, and various fixed-film systems.
- **Physical/chemical processes:** Dissolved gas flotation, chemical coagulation, sedimentation, and filtration.

POTW influent characteristics such as 5-day biological oxygen demand (BOD), total suspended solids, and pH need to be determined to ensure that the POTW's treatment capacity is not exceeded and there is no interference with the treatment process. In addition, pollutants that raise the temperature at the POTW above 40 °C and inhibit biological activity must be restricted.

Discharges to POTWs are regulated by the Clean Water Act (CWA), which implements National Pretreatment Standards (40 CFR 403) to control pollutants that pass through or interfere with treatment processes at POTWs or that contaminate sewage sludge. In addition to the CWA, two USEPA policies affect discharges to POTWs: U.S. EPA's Procedures for Planning and Implementing Off-site Response Actions (40 CFR 300.400), and U.S. EPA's policy memorandum, "Discharge of Waste water from CERCLA Sites into POTWs."

Several steps can be taken to determine the feasibility of discharge to POTW. These steps include:

- Identify and characterize waste water discharge
- Identify local POTWs
- Involve POTW in the evaluation process; screen POTWs
- Evaluate pretreatment requirements
- Identify and screen pretreatment alternatives
- Analyze the POTW discharge alternative

Administrative considerations include:

- Obtaining or changing permits
- Anticipating and dealing with delays associated with the permitting process
- Acknowledging restrictions imposed by local ordinances
- Determining whether a POTW will accept the discharge in light of potential liabilities

If the POTW has not developed local limits for all compounds detected in the discharge (which is usually the case), then it will have to develop new limits. The amount of time to develop new local limits or to revise existing ones must be considered. If site cleanup does not have a high priority, this process could take several months.

The main costs involved with discharging by sewer to a POTW include disposal fees, if applicable, and installation of the sewer line during the remedial action. Cost estimates may include direct costs of sewer installation, lift stations, waste water storage tanks, and tank trucking. Capital costs include direct costs (e.g., construction, equipment, labor, materials) and indirect costs (e.g., engineering expenses, startup costs, legal fees, license/permit costs, health and safety costs, contingency allowances). Operations and maintenance (O&M) costs are covered later in this chapter (see "Related Costs").

Basic Information Needed for Estimating

It is possible to create a reasonable cost estimate using a few required parameters. If more detailed information is known, one can create a more precise and site-specific estimate using a secondary set of parameters.

To estimate the cost of a discharge to a POTW system, certain information must be known. This information is discussed in the following paragraphs.

Flow Rate

If the discharge water moves to the POTW via sewer, the discharge flow rate is used to size the pumps and piping. Typical ranges for sewer systems range from 50 GPM to over 1,000 GPM. For smaller quantities, short time frames, or extremely long distances from the source to the POTW, it may be more feasible to use tanker trucks. If the mode of transportation to the POTW is tanker truck, the flow rate determines the size of necessary holding tanks. The typical flow range for discharge to POTW via tanker truck is 1–50 GPM.

Mode of Transportation

The mode of transportation is either sewer or truck. Typically, truck transportation is not feasible for flow rates that exceed 50 GPM.

Distance to Nearest Sewer Connection/Distance to POTW

If the discharge water moves to the POTW via sewer, the distance to the nearest sewer connection, in feet, will affect the quantities for discharge piping and trenching. In some instances, the cost of property acquisition or permitting associated with off-site construction may be included.

If the mode of transportation is by tanker truck, the distance to the POTW, in miles, will affect the magnitude of the transportation costs associated with the estimate.

Connection Fee (Sewer Only)

This is the fee charged by the POTW to connect to their sewer collection and treatment system. The fees vary depending on the location and treatment facility. Typical connection fees range from $1,000–$100,000.

Waste Water Disposal Fee

This fee is charged by the POTW to treat the influent. The typical range is $0–$25 per 1,000 gallons.

Hours of Operation per Day

Hours of operation per day refers to the hours during which the POTW will receive discharge water from the site. If the mode of transportation is sewer, the typical operation is 24 hours of operation per day, which means that the POTW will receive discharge water at the specified flow rate of 24 hours per day. If the mode of transportation is tanker truck, the normal condition is 8 hours of operation per day. If extraction wells precede the remedial technology, 24-hour operation may be appropriate for plume containment, but on-site storage tanks can be used in lieu of 24-hour-a-day trucking.

Treatment Period

The total duration of discharge can be divided into startup and O&M. The costs associated with the startup period may be included with the capital costs. The O&M costs are identified separately.

Worker Safety Level

Worker safety is affected by the contaminant(s) at the site. Safety level refers to the levels defined by OSHA in 29 CFR Part 1910. The four levels are designated as A, B, C, and D, "A" is the most protective and "D" is the least protective. A safety level of "E" is also included to simulate normal construction, "no hazard" conditions as prescribed by the EPA.

Design Information Needed for Detailed Estimates

Following are descriptions of the types of detailed information that, when available, can add detail and accuracy to estimates. Also included are design criteria and estimating rules of thumb that the estimator typically uses to determine values that are not known, or to check information provided by others.

Sewer Parameters

If the selected mode of transportation is discharge by sewer, the following parameters apply.

Piping

The piping parameters are as follows.

Flow Mechanism. There are three options for the flow mechanism for the discharge water through the sewer transfer piping: gravity flow, pumping stations with force mains, or both gravity flow and pumping stations. The least expensive is gravity flow. However, gravity flow is limited by its capacity—if the sewage needs to go uphill, a force main and pumping system will be required.

Gravity Piping Length (ft). If the selected flow mechanism is gravity flow, the length of gravity piping would typically be equal to the distance to the nearest sewer connection. If the selected flow mechanism is both gravity and pumping stations with force mains, one can assume that the gravity piping distance is one-half the distance to the nearest sewer connection. If the selected flow mechanism is pumping stations with force mains, then no gravity piping is typically required.

The gravity piping length directly affects the quantity of gravity piping as well as the quantities associated with installing the gravity piping trench.

Force Main Piping Length (ft). If the selected flow mechanism is pumping stations with force mains, one can assume that the force main piping distance is equal to the distance to the nearest sewer connection. If the selected flow mechanism is both gravity and pumping stations with force mains, one can assume that the force main piping distance is one-half the distance to the nearest sewer connection. If the selected flow mechanism is gravity flow, then no force main piping is normally required.

The force main piping length directly affects the quantity of force main piping as well as the quantities associated with installing the force main piping trench.

Gravity Piping. Size and type options for gravity piping are shown in Figure 45.1. The default pipe diameter for gravity piping is based on sewer flow tables for circular sewers, with a maximum velocity of 2' per second (fps). This will maintain the slope required for self cleansing and keep excavation costs to a minimum. Design default values for gravity piping are shown in Figure 45.2.

Force Main Piping. Size and type options for force main piping are shown in Figure 45.3. The default diameter for force mains is based on the Hazen Williams formula, with a maximum allowable pipe flow velocity of 10' per second (fps). Design defaults for force main piping are shown in Figure 45.4.

Gravity Trenching/Force Main Trenching
Many of the parameters associated with gravity trenching are the same as those for force main trenching. The parameters associated with gravity trenching and force main trenching follow. For simplicity, the two parameter sets are described simultaneously, and any differences are noted.

Piping Installation. Force main systems are typically installed below ground, but it is possible (and generally cheaper) to install these systems above ground. All gravity piping is assumed to be below ground. An illustration of underground pipe placement is shown in Figure 45.5.

Figure 45.1 Pipe Sizes/Types—Gravity Sewer

Pipe Sizes/Types–Gravity Sewer							
Inside Diameter Of Pipe (inches) a = Available x = Default							
Inches	RCPIII	RCPIV	RCPV	NRCP	CI	ESVCP	SPVC
4					a	a	a
6				a	a	a	x
8				a	a	a	x
10				a	a	a	x
12	a	a	a	a	a	a	x
15	a	a	a	a	a	a	x
18	x	a	a	a		a	
21		a	a	a			
24	x	a	a	a		a	

Figure 45.2 Gravity Flow Piping

Gravity Flow Piping	
Flow Rate	Default Piping
1–175 GPM	6″ PVC Sanitary Pipe
176–314 GPM	8″ PVC Sanitary Pipe
315–494 GPM	10″ PVC Sanitary Pipe
495–718 GPM	12″ PVC Sanitary Pipe
719–1,122 GPM	15″ PVC Sanitary Pipe
1,123–1,571 GPM	18″ Class 3 RCP
> 1,571 GPM	24″ Class 3 RCP

Figure 45.3 Pipe Sizes/Types—Forces Main

Pipe Sizes/Types–Force Main				
Inside Diameter Of Pipe (Inches) a = Available x = Default				
Inches	Class 200	Class 150 PVC	CS	SS
1	x		a	a
2	x		a	a
3	x		a	a
4	x		a	a
6	x		a	a
8		x	a	a
10		x	a	a
12		x	a	a

Figure 45.4 Force Main Piping

Force Main Piping	
Flow Rate	Default Piping
1-23 GPM	
24-95 GPM	
96-220 GPM	
221-375 GPM	
376-875 GPM	
876-1,550 GPM	
1,551-2,445 GPM	10″ Class 150 PVC
> 2,445 GPM	12″ Class 150 PVC

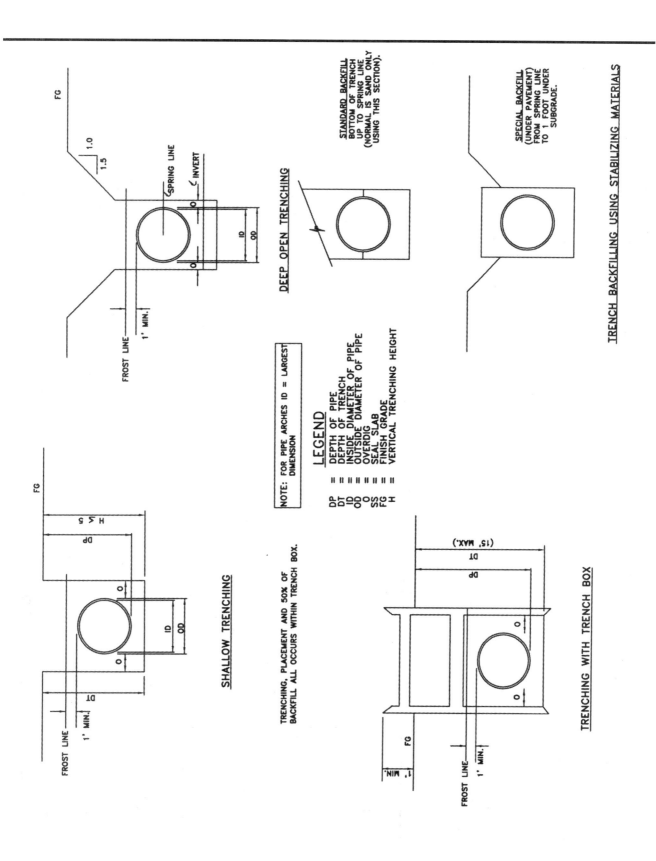

Figure 45.5 Sanitary Sewer Underground Pipe Placement

Soil Type The type of soil that will be excavated when installing the gravity or force main piping trenches can have a dramatic impact on excavation costs and should be investigated carefully. The typical choices are:

- Normal (clay)
- Clay/sand
- Clay/sand with boulders
- Sand
- Rock

Moisture Content The amount of moisture present in the excavated soil can have a significant impact on excavation costs, since wet soil is difficult to manage and is heavier than dry soils. For a given flow mechanism, the moisture content can be classified as one of the following:

- Dry
- Medium
- Saturated
- N/A (applies only to rock soil type.)

Average Piping Depth Average piping depth is the average depth from grade to the bottom of the inside of the pipe. For gravity pipe, the piping depth should be averaged over the length of run to account for the slope required to promote gravity flow. The force main pipe depth is generally a constant depth because the water is physically pumped instead of relying on gravity.

Gravity pipelines that carry fluids having high-suspended solids concentrations generally require a greater slope to maintain the flow velocity necessary to prevent settling of suspended solids. In such cases, deeper trenches are often required.

Seal Slab. A seal slab is a concrete slab placed along the bottom of the trench, 6" below the bottom of the pipe, that stabilizes the bedding material. Seal slabs are generally required for saturated soil types, but not for other soil types. The typical slab thickness is 6". The slab width is the pipe outside diameter plus two times the overdig width. If a seal slab is required, the following guidelines can be used to calculate the depth of trench:

If pipe material is carbon steel or stainless steel and:

- no seal slab is required, depth of trench = average pipe depth + 6"
- seal slab is required, depth of trench = average pipe depth + 12"

If pipe material is cast iron, PVC, or extra-strength vitrified clay and:

- no seal slab is required, depth of trench = average pipe depth + 12"
- seal slab is required, depth of trench = average pipe depth + 12"

If pipe material is RCP or high strength concrete and:

- no seal slab is required, depth of trench = average pipe depth + (inside pipe diameter/12) + 6"
- seal slab is required, depth of trench = average pipe depth (inside pipe diameter/12) + 12"

Trench Box. Using a prefabricated trench box during excavation prevents collapse of the trench walls. A trench box is normally used if the moisture content of the soil is saturated, or if the soil type is sand, and the depth of trench exceeds 6'. Figure 45.6 shows trench box design assumptions.

Vertical Trench Height (ft). The height of the vertical trench walls depends on the soil's angle of repose. If the overall depth of the trench is greater than the vertical trench height, the side walls of the trench are sloped above the vertical trench height at a 1.5:1 slope. Design assumptions are shown in Figure 45.7.

Backfill Method. Backfill method refers to the type of bedding and backfill materials as well as the configuration by which these materials will be placed in the trench. The backfill method may be different for the force main and gravity piping trenches. The six available methods are:

Excavated material: The excavated material is used for both bedding and backfill.

Normal: Sand is used for bedding material, and excavated material is used for backfill.

Standard: Cement-stabilized sand is used for bedding material, and excavated material is used for backfill.

Special: This is used under pavements or heavy loads. Cement-stabilized sand is used for bedding material and for backfill (to 1' under subgrade).

Rock: Sand is used for bedding material, and borrowed soil is used for backfill. (This is the only available method if the soil type is rock and is not applicable to any other soil types.)

Figure 45.6 Trench Box Design Parameters

Trench Box Design Parameters		
Type Of Soil	**Moisture Content**	**Trench Box Default**
Normal (Clay)	Dry	No
	Medium	No
	Saturated	Yes
Sand	Dry	*
	Medium	*
	Saturated	Yes
Clay/Sand	Dry	No
	Medium	No
	Saturated	Yes
Clay/Sand w/Boulders	Dry	No
	Medium	No
	Saturated	Yes
Rock	N/A	No

*No–if depth of trench is less than or equal to 6.0 feet
Yes–if depth of trench is greater then 6.0 feet

Trench box: Sand is used for bedding material, and excavated material is used for backfill.

Overdig (ft). Overdig represents the horizontal dimension between the vertical trench wall and the outside diameter of the pipe. The typical value is 1' for both gravity and force main trenching. The overdig value ranges from 0–10'.

Dewatering Pump. Dewatering pumps may be required to remove rainwater or seepage of groundwater from the trench. Pumps are normally required only for saturated soil conditions. If pumps are required, an estimating rule of thumb is to assume a one-day rental for each 500' of trench.

Vertical Trench Height Values			
Type Of Soil	**Moisture Content**	**Trench Box**	**Default Vertical Trench Height (Ft.)**
Normal	Dry	No	5
Normal	Dry	Yes	Depth of Trench
Normal	Medium	No	3
Normal	Medium	Yes	Depth of Trench
Normal	Saturated	Yes	Depth of Trench
Normal	Saturated	No	0
Sand	Dry	No	0
Sand	Dry	Yes	Depth of Trench
Sand	Medium	No	0
Sand	Medium	Yes	Depth of Trench
Sand	Saturated	Yes	Depth of Trench
Sand	Saturated	No	0
Clay/Sand	Dry	No	4
Clay/Sand	Dry	Yes	Depth of Trench
Clay/Sand	Medium	No	2
Clay/Sand	Medium	Yes	Depth of Trench
Clay/Sand	Saturated	Yes	Depth of Trench
Clay/Sand	Saturated	No	0
Clay/Sand w/Boulders	Dry	No	4
Clay/Sand w/Boulders	Dry	Yes	Depth of Trench
Clay/Sand w/Boulders	Medium	No	2
Clay/Sand w/Boulders	Medium	Yes	Depth of Trench
Clay/Sand w/Boulders	Saturated	Yes	Depth of Trench
Clay/Sand w/Boulders	Saturated	No	0
Rock	None	No	Depth of Trench

Figure 45.7 Vertical Trench Height Values

Wellpoints. Wellpoints reduce the moisture content of saturated soil, and are not normally required for unsaturated soils. If wellpoints are required, the following guidelines can be used for estimating purposes:

- If the depth of trench is less than or equal to 10', assume one month's rental of 600' of header pipe with wellpoints at 5' on center for each 4,400 L.F. of trench.
- If the depth of trench is greater than 10', assume 225' of header pipe with wellpoints at 5' on center for each 1,650 L.F. of trench.

Number of Manholes. Manholes are typically required for a run of gravity piping, but are not usually used for force main trenching. An estimating rule of thumb is one manhole per 300' of pipe. Manhole size depends on the depth of the trench.

Number of Lift Stations. Lift stations are required for a run of force main piping (and do not apply to gravity piping). Wet wells are normally used for lift stations. Packaged lift stations are generally used for this application. Packaged systems are generally available up to approximately 800,000 GPD (555 GPM) capacity. For flow rates greater than 555 GPM, multiple package systems are generally used in series or in parallel application. For example, if there are three points along the run of transfer piping at which lift stations will be required, and the flow rate is 1,000 GPM, then the actual quantity of packaged lift stations will be 6 because 2 of the largest available units will be required for each lift station point.

Existing Cover

Generally, the existing cover overlying the trenching area may be vegetative, asphalt, or concrete. Demolition of vegetative cover actually refers to clearing and grubbing. The cover demolition quantities can be any combination of the three cover types. The parameters associated with each existing cover type are as follows:

Existing Vegetative Cover: Type of vegetative cover can have a significant cost impact. The available options are: Heavy Brush with Light Trees, Medium Brush with Medium Trees, and Light Brush with Heavy Trees. Determine the type and area of existing cover that must be removed or demolished.

Existing Concrete Cover: *Type of reinforcement* options are: Unreinforced, Rod Reinforced, Mesh Reinforced.

Determine *thickness of existing concrete:*, measured in inches and the area of demolition.

Existing Asphalt Cover: Determine *thickness of existing asphalt (in)*, not including base and subgrade, and the area of *asphalt cover demolition (ft)*.

Replacement Cover

A replacement cover is installed over the trenched area. Aesthetics and erosion problems, as well as site usage, often make it necessary to replace the cover over the trenched area. There are three common replacement cover options: vegetative, asphalt, and concrete. The parameters associated with each type are as follows:

Replacement Vegetative Cover

- *Type of vegetative cover* options include sodding and seeding for grass. Trees and large bushes are generally discouraged because roots can interfere with the piping.
- *Length of vegetative cover replacement (ft)*

Replacement Concrete Cover

- *Type of reinforcement* options include: Unreinforced, Rod Reinforced, and Mesh Reinforced.
- *Thickness of replacement concrete (in)* is normally 4", but the range is 4–12".
- *Length of concrete cover replacement (ft)*.

Replacement Asphalt Cover

- *Thickness of replacement asphalt (in)* does not include base and subgrade. The normal case is 2.5".
- *Thickness of replacement asphalt base (in)* does not include asphalt or subgrade.
- Length of asphalt cover replacement (ft).

Tank Truck Parameters

If tank trucks are used, the flow rate is generally required to be less than or equal to 50 GPM. This cut-off rate is based on the rationale that one day of waste water storage capacity (72,000 gallons) is generally required for safety/regulatory reasons. A flow rate of 50 GPM would require twelve 6,000-gallon tanker truck loads for every 24-hour period of operation. However, if the hours of operation are 8 hours per day, 3 days will be required to discharge a volume of water equivalent to what would be discharged in 24 hours of continuous operation.

The major parameters associated with a tank truck operation are as follows.

Number of Holding Tanks

The number of holding tanks required depends on the size of tank and discharge flow rate, and is based on the capacity required for a 24-hour period. This number can be determined as follows:

Number of Tanks = (Flow Rate × 60 mins/hr × 24 hrs) / tank capacity (in gallons)

Size of Holding Tanks

Four sizes of holding tanks are commonly available:

- 550 Gallon
- 4,000 Gallon
- 6,000 Gallon
- 21,000 Gallon

Generally, the 21,000 gallon tank is the most cost-effective alternative. The estimator should conduct a cost analysis comparing rental and purchase costs to determine which acquisition method is most cost effective.

Related Costs

The total costs for remedial action include long-term power and equipment requirements, including electrical charges for equipment, equipment maintenance and rework, and sampling and analytical costs.

The following items may be categorized under Other Related Costs for discharge to a POTW.

- **Electricity** is required for pumping stations and transfer pumps, which will be included in the estimate if the mode of transportation is sewer, and the flow mechanism is force main. Electrical costs will not apply for any other conditions (e.g., gravity flow mechanism, or transportation via tanker truck).
- **Equipment maintenance and rework** will be a consideration if pumping stations and transfer pumps are included in the estimate, and if the discharge to the POTW will exceed 18 months. The motor and pumps should be inspected and reworked, if necessary, after 18 months of operation. This includes checking and replacing the bearings, shaft, and gasket.
- **Sampling and analysis** include obtaining one sample per month and analyzing for BOD, COD, cyanide, pH, dissolved solids, suspended solids, and 13 metals.

Site Work and Utilities

Site work and utilities that may apply to discharge to a POTW are:

- Electrical distribution (if a force main and/or pumping station are used.)
- Fencing

If applicable, these must be included in the estimate.

Conclusion

Discharge systems to a POTW are used in many remediation projects. The cost drivers for this application include the type of transfer mechanism (sewer line or truck), the capacity of the system, and the distance from the site to the discharge or connection point. In some instances, these factors represent trade-offs with other remedial technologies. For example, by relocating a carbon adsorber to a different location on site, the sewer distance may be reduced, or a gravity system may be used instead of a force main system. This relocation may create a need for more piping for the carbon adsorption system. The cost engineer should work with the design team to help optimize these situations.

Chapter 46

Infiltration Gallery

An infiltration gallery is a system for discharging water that has already been treated in a groundwater treatment system. Infiltration galleries function much like the drainage fields associated with conventional household septic tanks in that perforated subsurface drainage piping, surrounded by crushed stone or gravel, is used to discharge water into the vadose (unsaturated) zone. Here it infiltrates downward and ultimately enters the water table (surficial aquifer).

Applications and Limitations

Applications

To discharge previously treated groundwater back into a groundwater system.

- Typically used in conjunction with a pump and treat system.
- Can be used to provide nutrients and moisture to the vadose zone.

Limitations

May require demolition of existing land cover (e.g., concrete and asphalt).

- A minimum infiltration rate of 0.1"/hr is required for adequate infiltration.
- Can transport contaminants from the vadose zone to the groundwater under certain conditions.
- Hydrogeology of site may limit rate at which released water will infiltrate the vadose zone and recharge the groundwater system.

Typical System Design Components

Figures 46.1 and 46.2 are plan and section views of an infiltration gallery. Installation of the gallery includes, but is not limited to, the following tasks:

- Demolition of the existing land cover (vegetation, asphalt, concrete) over the area where the gallery will be located; this is site-specific and may not be required if the existing land cover is soil or grass.
- Excavation of a pit or gallery with a predetermined length, width, depth, and side slope.

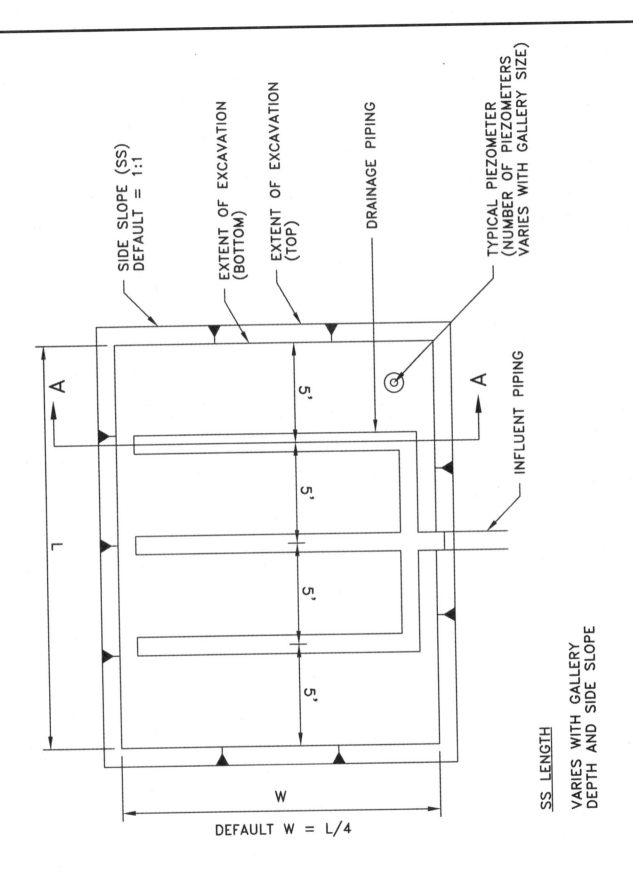

Figure 46.1 Infiltration Gallery, Plan View

448

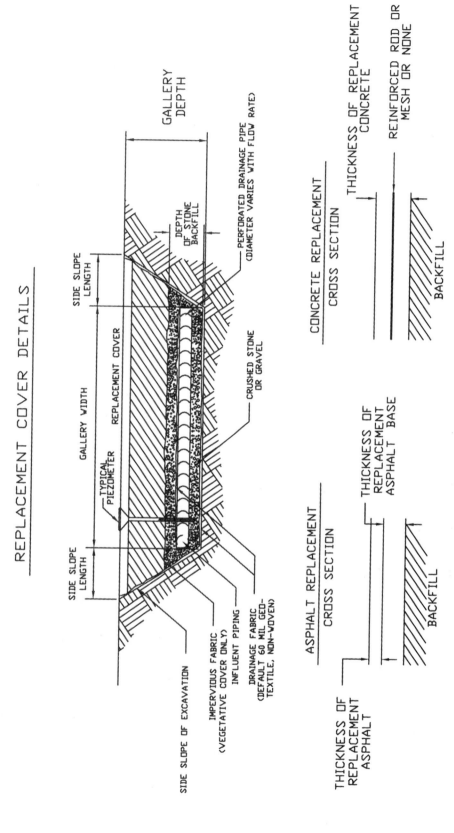

Figure 46.2 Infiltration Gallery, Cross Section

449

- Installation of a drainage fabric (liner) along the bottom and sides of the gallery to prevent the intrusion of soil into the porous backfill material.
- Placement of porous backfill material (crushed stone or gravel) on top of the drainage fabric to a depth of approximately 6".
- Installation of perforated drainage piping on top of the stone backfill. Typically, several parallel runs of drainage piping distribute the treated discharge water over the entire area of the gallery.
- Placement of additional stone backfill around and over the drainage piping to a predetermined depth.
- Installation of additional drainage fabric over the top of the stone backfill to prevent intrusion of the soil backfill. If the replacement land cover is vegetative, an impervious fabric is also installed over the top of the stone backfill to prevent the intrusion of rainfall into the gallery; this impervious fabric is not required if the replacement land cover is asphalt or concrete.
- Placement of clean soil backfill into the remaining portion of the excavation.
- Compaction of the soil backfill.
- Installation of a replacement cover over the excavated areas (vegetation, asphalt, concrete); this is site-specific, as a replacement cover may not always be required.

Piezometers, equipped with level sensors, may be needed to monitor the water level in the gallery. This process is briefly described in "Gallery Details" later in this chapter.

When infiltration galleries are used in conjunction with groundwater recovery and treatment systems, it is often possible, through proper analysis, to predict the impact of mounding and drawdown on the hydrogeology of the site. This information can be used to design and implement a closed, in situ cycle of extraction, treatment, discharge, and recovery. The gallery must generally be located upgradient of the contaminated groundwater plume or recovery zone. Groundwater can then be pumped out of the area of contamination, treated in a groundwater treatment system, and discharged via an infiltration gallery back into the surficial aquifer. Here the drawdown from the extraction system and the natural hydraulic gradient will carry the treated water back toward the recovery zone. Once this in situ cycle has been established, it will increase the hydraulic gradient toward the extraction wells (forcing the plume to migrate to the wells, expediting recovery) and dilute the influent contaminant concentrations to the groundwater treatment system (reducing the treatment requirements of the system).

Regulatory agencies may not require the installation of a post-treatment system (such as carbon polishing) when an infiltration gallery is used, provided the primary treatment system is capable of meeting the discharge water quality standards. As a result, the infiltration gallery may be more cost-effective than other discharge alternatives. However, since this process is susceptible to distributing contamination as a result of treatment system failure, regulatory agencies can be very specific on design requirements, particularly the discharge water quality.

Physical site characteristics such as lack of adequate land area, shallow water table, and soils with low infiltration rates may eliminate the infiltration gallery as a disposal alternative. An infiltration rate of 0.1"/hr is typically the minimum design requirement, which corresponds to the permeability of a silty sand soil type. Projects with a large available land area may consider infiltration galleries viable in soils with lower permeability. Though infiltration galleries may not be the most suitable discharge method for all groundwater treatment systems, they serve as a viable alternative that should be evaluated on a site-specific basis.

Basic Information Needed for Estimating

It is possible to create a reasonable budget cost estimate using a few required parameters. If more detailed information is known, one can create a more precise and site-specific estimate using a secondary set of parameters.

To estimate the cost of the infiltration gallery system, certain information must be known. This information is discussed in the following paragraphs.

Flow Rate to Gallery

The flow rate to the gallery depends on the discharge flow rate from the groundwater treatment system. The flow rate is key to determining the required area of the gallery. The most common flow rates for infiltration galleries are between 1–100 GPM.

Required Gallery Area

The required area of an infiltration gallery depends on the flow rate to the gallery and the permeability of the underlying soil. In general, sandy or porous soils have higher permeabilities than soils composed of clay or silt and, therefore, require less infiltration area per unit flow. In fact, the use of infiltration galleries is often limited to sandy or porous soils (e.g., sand, limestone, fractured rock) because of the low permeabilities associated with soils composed of clay or silt.

Figure 46.3 lists permeability ranges for various soil types.

If the required gallery area is unknown, it can be estimated based on the flow rate to the gallery and the permeability of the soil using the following equation:

$$AG_{SF} = \frac{120.32 \times FR}{SP}$$

Where:

AG_{SF} = the area of the infiltration gallery (S.F.)

FR = the flow rate of the effluent (GPM)

SP = the soil permeability (in/hr)

Any approach to infiltration gallery design should include an analysis of the mounding of the groundwater table that will be encountered as the treated discharge water begins to saturate the soils below the gallery. The mounding analysis should verify that the mound will not rise above the bottom of the gallery. Mounding analyses are critical in areas where there is a shallow water table (i.e., less than 10' below land surface).

Gallery Length and Width

There is no standard for determining the dimensions of an infiltration gallery. However, rectangular configurations induce less mounding and are usually more efficient than square or round designs. The actual configuration is often one that conforms to the available land area. If the design is unknown, the estimator can assume that the gallery length will be 4 times the width.

The length and width define the "effective area of the gallery"—the actual area through which the treated discharge water will infiltrate the underlying soil. The effective area is equivalent to the bottom area of the gallery excavation and should not be less than the required area. The total excavated area at land surface may be considerably larger than the effective area, depending on the slope of the excavation—which is a function of the gallery depth—and the cohesive characteristics of the soil. For example, if the soil type is loose sand and the gallery depth is 10', a side slope of 3' per foot (run/drop) may be required to ensure that the sides of the excavation do not collapse. Any additional surface

Typical Ranges Of Permeabilities	
Soil Type	Range Of Permeabilities (In./Hr.)
Clay	
Clay	$1.42 \times 10^{-7} - 1.42 \times 10^{-4}$
Sandy Clay	$1.42 \times 10^{-4} - 1.42 \times 10^{-3}$
Sand	
Clayey Sand	$1.42 \times 10^{-3} - 1.42 \times 10^{-1}$
Silty Sand	$1.42 \times 10^{-2} - 1.42 \times 10^{1}$
Very Fine Sand	$1.42 \times 10^{-1} - 1.42 \times 10^{1}$
Fine Sand	$1.42 \times 10^{1} - 1.42 \times 10^{1}$
Coarse Sand	$1.42 \times 10^{1} - 1.42 \times 10^{3}$
Sand w/Gravel	$1.42 \times 10^{2} - 1.42 \times 10^{3}$
Rock	
Gravel	$1.42 \times 10^{3} - 1.42 \times 10^{5}$
Shale	$1.42 \times 10^{-9} - 1.42 \times 10^{-4}$
Well Cemented Sandstone	$1.42 \times 10^{-5} - 1.42 \times 10^{-3}$
Friable Sandstone	$1.42 \times 10^{-3} - 1.42 \times 10^{1}$
Unjointed Crystalline Limestone	$1.42 \times 10^{-5} - 1.42 \times 10^{-1}$
Karst Limestone	$1.42 \times 10^{-1} - 1.42 \times 10^{3}$
Unfractured Igneous Rock	$1.42 \times 10^{-9} - 1.42 \times 10^{-4}$
Fractured Igneous Rock	$1.42 \times 10^{-3} - 1.42 \times 10^{1}$
Others	
Peat	$1.42 \times 10^{-4} - 1.42 \times 10^{-2}$
Silt	$1.42 \times 10^{-3} - 1.42 \times 10^{-2}$
Sandy Silt & Till	$1.42 \times 10^{-3} - 1.42 \times 10^{-1}$
Glacial Till	$1.42 \times 10^{-7} - 1.42 \times 10^{1}$

Figure 46.3 Typical Ranges of Permeabilities

area generated along the sides of the excavation is not considered part of the effective area of the gallery.

Treatment Period

The total operational period of the gallery is divided into startup and operations and maintenance (O&M); these values should be related to the startup and O&M periods of the treatment system from which the gallery is receiving discharge water. The duration of discharge to the gallery could have a significant impact on cost of operation (e.g., sampling and analysis quantities, electrical cost for operating any pumps).

Worker Safety Level

Worker safety is affected by the contaminant(s) at the site. Safety level refers to the levels defined by OSHA in 29 CFR Part 1910. The 4 levels are designated as A, B, C, and D, where "A" is the most protective, and "D" is the least protective. A safety level of "E" is also included to simulate normal construction, "no hazard" conditions as prescribed by the EPA.

Design Information for Detailed Estimates

Following are descriptions of the types of detailed information that, when available, can add detail and accuracy to estimates. Also included are design criteria and estimating rules of thumb that the estimator typically uses to determine values that are not known, or to check information provided by others. The parameters are divided into 4 categories: gallery details; existing cover parameters; replacement cover parameters; and transfer piping parameters.

Gallery Details

The gallery details refer to the specifications of the infiltration gallery. The parameters associated with the gallery details are as follows.

Gallery Depth

The estimator should consider the depth to groundwater. For example, if the depth to groundwater is 5', the gallery depth should not exceed 4'. As previously stated, mounding analyses should be an integral part of any gallery design, particularly when there is a shallow water table. The typical range is 1–25'.

Depth of Stone Backfill

The stone backfill depth should be sufficient to provide at least 6" of stone above and below the drainage piping. Typically, a 2' depth is used unless larger pipes are used for discharge in very high permeability soil.

Soil Type

Soil type determines the production rates for excavation of the gallery. The soil type refers to the existing soils underlying the area where the gallery will be located. The terms used to describe soils for the purpose of conducting excavation and backfill operations do not apply to the hydrogeological characteristics of the soil. A vast range of infiltration rates may be encountered for any of the given generalized soil types (e.g., clay, clay/sand, clay/sand with boulders, and rock). For instance, unfractured igneous rock may have an infiltration rate as low as 1.42×10^{-9} in/hr, which is virtually impervious. On the other hand, Karst limestone rock may have an infiltration rate as high as 1.42×10^{3} in/hr, which is virtually unlimited.

The following soil types have been generalized for the purpose of estimating the costs of excavation and backfill, and do not in any way describe the infiltrative capacity of the soil.

- Normal (clay)
- Clay/sand
- Clay/sand with boulders
- Sand
- Rock

The soil type affects the excavation and backfill quantities. The following assumptions may be used to estimate production rates for excavation:

If the soil type is clay, clay/sand, clay/sand with boulders, or sand, the quantity of excavation will be equal to the volume of the gallery. A quantity of stone backfill, depending on the depth of stone, will be brought on site and used to backfill the bottom of the excavation. The remaining portion of the excavation will be backfilled with excavated material. Any additional excavated material (e.g., volume of stone backfill and drainage piping) will be loaded and hauled off site.

If the soil type is rock, the quantity of the excavation will be equal to the volume of the gallery. The entire volume of the excavated rock will be loaded and hauled off site. A quantity of stone backfill, depending on the depth of stone, will be brought on site and used to backfill the bottom of the excavation. A quantity of clean soil, equal to the volume of the gallery less the volume of stone backfill and drainage piping, will be brought on site and used to backfill the remaining portion of the excavation.

Side Slope of Excavation

The slope of excavation refers to the sides of the gallery excavation. The slope is 1 ft/ft if the soil type is clay, clay/sand, clay/sand with boulders or sand, and 0 ft/ft if the soil type is rock. The required area of the gallery should be equal to the area of the bottom of the gallery excavation (effective area); thus the slope impacts the quantities of excavation, backfill, and cover that will be generated in addition to the volume (L × W × D) of the gallery.

Number of Piezometers

The gallery will be equipped with piezometers, which will extend from slightly below land surface to the bottom of the gallery. The piezometers will be equipped with level sensors for detecting flooding and 12" × 7.5" manhole covers for protecting the surface. Gallery areas less than or equal to 200 S.F. normally need 1 piezometer. Gallery areas greater than 200 S.F. but less than 2,000 S.F. typically need 3 piezometers. If the gallery area is greater than 2,000 S.F., 1 piezometer is typically installed for every 30' of gallery length. Normally, the piezometers are placed into the open gallery excavation and backfilled; thus no drilling costs are associated with the installation of the piezometers.

Drainage Piping

Drainage piping size is based on flow rate. Common sizes of drainage piping are shown in Figure 46.4. Typically, parallel runs of drainage piping traverse the length of the gallery with a center-to-center spacing of 5'. Normally, the flow mechanism for the drainage piping in the gallery (not to be confused with the transfer piping from the treatment system to the gallery) is assumed to be gravity flow with a maximum pipe velocity of 2 FPS. If the influent flow rate exceeds 704 GPM, multiple runs of the largest available pipe diameter (e.g., 12" perforated PVC) should be used to maintain a maximum pipe velocity of 2 FPS. The number of parallel runs of drainage piping depends on the gallery width.

The recommended minimum gallery widths for flow rates greater than 704 GPM are given in Figure 46.5.

Drainage Fabric
A 60 mil geotextile, non-woven drainage fabric is usually used, but other options are available. The bottom and sides of the infiltration gallery, as well as the top of the stone backfill, are lined with drainage fabric to minimize the intrusion of soil into the crushed stone backfill.

Existing Cover Parameters
The existing cover over the area where the gallery will be located affects the type and quantity of demolition required before the gallery is excavated. There are 3 general options for the type of existing cover: vegetative, asphalt, and concrete.

Figure 46.4 Drainage Piping

Drainage Piping	
Flow Rate	**Piping Size**
1 - 77 GPM	4″ Perforated PVC
78 - 175 GPM	6″ Perforated PVC
176 - 314 GPM	8″ Perforated PVC
315 - 494 GPM	10″ Perforated PVC
495 - 2,800 GPM	12″ Perforated PVC

Figure 46.5 Minimum Gallery Widths

Minimum Gallery Widths For Flow Rates Greater Than 700 GPM		
Range of Flow Rates	**Minimum Number Of Pipe Runs Using 12″ Diameter Perforated PVC**	**Minimum Gallery Width**
700 - 1,400 GPM	2	10 Ft.
1,400 - 2,100 GPM	3	15 Ft.
2,100 - 2,800 GPM	4	20 Ft.

The cover demolition quantities can be any combination of the 3 cover types. The following discussion provides additional information that applies to each of the existing cover types.

Type of Vegetative Cover

Options for the vegetative cover over the gallery excavation include:

- Heavy brush with light trees
- Medium brush with medium trees
- Light brush with heavy trees

Estimated Thickness of Existing Asphalt

The estimated thickness of existing asphalt refers to the thickness of the asphalt only (i.e., it does not include base and subgrade).

Type of Existing Concrete

The options for the type of reinforcement in the existing concrete are:

- Unreinforced
- Rod-reinforced
- Mesh-reinforced

Estimated Thickness of Existing Concrete

The estimated thickness of existing concrete refers to the thickness of the concrete only (i.e., it does not include base and subgrade).

Replacement Cover Parameters

The replacement cover parameters refer to the type of replacement cover over the gallery excavation. There are 3 options for the type of replacement cover: vegetative, asphalt, and concrete. Vegetative cover is the most common but in some instances, the site may be paved (e.g., for a parking lot). The replacement cover quantities can be any combination of the 3 cover types. The parameters associated with each of the replacement cover types are as follows.

Vegetative Cover

Type of Vegetative Cover: This parameter refers to the type of replacement vegetative cover over the gallery excavation. Options include seeding and sod.

Area of Gallery Excavation Requiring Replacement of Vegetative Cover: Normally, this area refers to the entire area of the gallery excavation at land surface.

Asphalt Cover

Area of Gallery Excavation Requiring Asphalt Cover: This parameter refers to the area to be paved with asphalt, if any.

Estimated Thickness of Replacement Asphalt: The thickness of the replacement asphalt does not include base and subgrade. Typically, the thickness of the replacement asphalt is 2.5".

Estimated Thickness of Replacement Asphalt Base: The thickness of the replacement asphalt base does not include asphalt or subgrade.

Concrete Cover

Area of Gallery Excavation Requiring Replacement Concrete: This parameter refers to the area of concrete paving, if any.

Type of Replacement Concrete: Options for the type of reinforcement in the replacement concrete include unreinforced, rod-reinforced, and mesh-reinforced.

Thickness of Replacement Concrete: Typical options for thickness of replacement concrete are 4, 6, 8, or 12".

Transfer Piping Parameters

Transfer piping conveys the treated discharge water from the treatment system to the gallery. The transfer piping parameters include the following.

Distance from the Treatment System to the Gallery

The distance from the treatment system to the gallery directly affects the required length of transfer piping.

Flow Mechanism

The flow mechanism will be either gravity flow or force main flow. When the treatment system is near the gallery, gravity flow can usually be used. If the gallery input point is higher than the treatment system, then force main flow will be required. The flow mechanism and the influent flow rate to the gallery will determine the pipe diameter and material.

The pipe diameter for force main flow is based on the Hazen Williams formula, with a maximum allowable pipe flow velocity of 10 FPS. The pipe diameter for gravity flow is based on sewer flow tables for circular sewers, with a maximum velocity of 2 FPS. Selection criteria are shown in Figures 46.6 and 46.7. Other types of piping are also available.

Transfer Piping

Many types and sizes of transfer piping are available. In most cases, the transfer piping will be installed above ground for brief projects. This is the least expensive option. However, in some instances, it is desirable or even necessary to bury pipe below ground. For instance, if the selected flow mechanism is gravity and the flow rate is more than 700 GPM, then the typical pipe will be 15" in diameter or greater, Class 3 Reinforced Concrete Pipe (RCP). In such cases, below-ground piping is recommended.

Biofouling Prevention Chemical Feeders

In some areas, drainage fabric may clog as a result of biofouling; this can significantly reduce the infiltrative capacity of the gallery and create operational difficulties. Bypass chemical shot feeders can reduce or eliminate such operational difficulties.

Sump Tanks

Typically, the effluent from the treatment system is directed to a sump tank (holding/flow equalization tank) and then either pumped out or allowed to gravity-drain out of the sump into transfer piping, through which it is conveyed to the infiltration gallery.

Sump sizes are generally based on the flow rate from the treatment system to the gallery, as shown in Figure 46.8. However, it may be suitable to discharge directly from the treatment system to the transfer piping without using a sump. If the flow mechanism is force main and a sump is included, the estimator should include a sump pump based on the flow rate to the gallery. If the flow mechanism is force main and a sump is not included in the estimate, a centrifugal transfer pump should be included based on the flow rate to the gallery. Pumps are not normally included if the selected flow mechanism is gravity. Generally, any sumps included in the project will be equipped with high water level sensors to shut down all pumps (treatment system pumps included) in the event of a system malfunction.

Related Costs

The total costs for remedial action include electrical charges for equipment, equipment maintenance and rework, and sampling and analytical costs.

Electricity

Electricity is required for any pumps included in the estimate. If the flow mechanism for the treated discharge water from the treatment system to the gallery is force main, one or more transfer pumps are required based on the flow rate to the gallery. The electrical costs should be calculated based on the horsepower of each pump.

Gravity Transfer Piping	
Flow Rate	**Default Piping**
1 - 175 GPM	6″ PVC Sanitary Pipe
176 - 314 GPM	8″ PVC Sanitary Pipe
315 - 494 GPM	10″ PVC Sanitary Pipe
495 - 718 GPM	12″ PVC Sanitary Pipe
719 - 1,122 GPM	15″ PVC Sanitary Pipe
1,123 - 1,571 GPM	18″ Class 3 RCP
> 1,571 GPM	24″ Class 3 RCP

Figure 46.6 Gravity Transfer Piping

Force Main Transfer Piping	
Flow Rate	**Piping Type and Size**
1 - 23 GPM	1″ Class 200 PVC
24 - 95 GPM	2″ Class 200 PVC
96 - 220 GPM	3″ Class 200 PVC
221 - 375 GPM	4″ Class 200 PVC
376 - 875 GPM	6″ Class 200 PVC
876 - 1,550 GPM	8″ Class 150 PVC
1,551 - 2,445 GPM	10″ Class 150 PVC
>2,445 GPM	12″ Class 150 PVC

Figure 46.7 Force Main Transfer Piping

Equipment Maintenance and Rework

Equipment maintenance and rework will be a consideration if pumps are included in the estimate, and if the operational period of the gallery will exceed 18 months.

Generally no sampling and analysis are required since the discharge water is tested before discharge.

Site Work and Utilities

Site work and utilities that may be applicable in infiltration galleries are:

- RA piping
- Overhead electrical distribution (if force main is selected as the flow mechanism)
- Piping (if below-ground piping is desired)
- Fencing and signage

Conclusion

Infiltration galleries can be a cost-effective alternative for discharge of treated waste water. Assuming there is adequate space on site and conducive soil conditions, an infiltration gallery can be less expensive to operate than discharge to POTW or deep injection wells. The cost engineer should work with the design team to compare both the capital and O&M costs for these alternatives to select the most effective solution.

Sump Tanks	
Flow Rate	**Sump Size And Type**
1 - 5 GPM	550 - gal. Steel
6 - 10 GPM	1,000 - gal. Steel
11 - 15 GPM	1,500 - gal. Steel
16 - 20 GPM	2,000 - gal. Steel
21 - 50 GPM	5,000 - gal. Steel
51 - 60 GPM	6,000 - gal. Horz. Plastic
61 - 80 GPM	8,000 - gal. Horz. Plastic
81 - 100 GPM	10,000 - gal. Horz. Plastic
101 - 120 GPM	12,000 - gal. Horz. Plastic
121 - 150 GPM	15,000 - gal. Horz. Plastic
151 - 200 GPM	20,000 - gal. Horz. Plastic
201 - 250 GPM	25,000 - gal. Horz. Plastic
251 - 300 GPM	30,000 - gal. Horz.Plastic
301 - 400 GPM	40,000 - gal. Horz. Plastic
401 - 800 GPM	48,000 - gal. Horz. Plastic
801 - 2,800 GPM	2 - 48,000 - gal. Horz. Plastic

Figure 46.8 Sump Tanks

Chapter 47

Injection Wells

An injection well is used to inject water into a groundwater aquifer. Injection wells have a variety of purposes, including aquifer recharge; protection of water supplies; groundwater control; solution mining; waste disposal; and geothermal energy production. Appropriate well construction techniques vary according to the specific purpose of the well; but in all cases, construction must be undertaken carefully because injection wells are much more likely to fail than are typical water wells. This section deals primarily with aquifer recharge from sources such as a wastewater treatment plant, extraction well plume containment, and other environmental applications.

Applications and Limitations

Applications

- Re-introduction of treated groundwater to an aquifer.
- Aqueous waste disposal.
- Used in conjunction with pump and treat systems.

Limitations

- Large concentrations of suspended solids (greater than 2 ppm) can plug the injection well and obstruct the flow.
- May not be used in areas with a high likelihood of seismic activity.
- Metal or biological activity may foul injection system.
- Extensive site assessments are necessary to characterize site and obtain regulatory authority.
- Pretreatment of waste to be injected may be required to make it compatible with natural conditions at site and with mechanical components of the injection system.

Typical System Design Elements

The consequences of water-chemistry compatibility, air entrainment, thermal interference, and sand pumping are considerably more serious for injection wells than for extraction wells. For instance, pumping recharge water containing suspended solids (sand) at concentrations as low as 1 mg/l (or solids with diameters larger than the sand pack) can quickly congest injection wells. Air entrainment or water quality can contribute to injection pressure head buildup, which lowers well efficiency and ultimately inhibits mechanical reliability.

When water is discharged into an injection well, a cone of recharge that is hydraulically inverse to a cone of depression will surround the injection well. Theoretically, a properly designed injection well will recharge as much as the extraction capacity, but the effects associated with non-compatible water quality characteristics, high turbidity, and high water temperatures reduce the recharge over relatively short periods. In an ordinary water well, for example, some fine sediment will be filtered by the formation. In an injection well, there are no "natural" filtering mechanisms. Fine material will continuously collect in the well screen, filter pack, and formation around the bore hole. Over time, the discharge routes become congested, reducing the aquifer's capacity to receive water. Because this phenomenon is inevitable, most injection well designers specify that the injection well screen be much longer than for an extraction well of equal capacity, assuming that the aquifer is thick enough. This will decrease maintenance costs over the life of the injection well. Even dry sand or gravel zones above the aquifer may be screened if the well is used only for injection purposes.

Permits are usually required before an injection well is installed. Since permit costs vary from state to state, this chapter does not address them. Permit requirements also vary according to the particular implementing regulatory agency that has jurisdiction.

There are a number of other factors that can complicate the use of injection wells. Plugging of the formation around the screen can be caused not only by sand or incrustants, but also by air bubbles entrained in the injected water. When air is entrained with injection water, hydraulic conductivity is lost because air bubbles can effectively block the outward passage of water by filling available pore spaces within the aquifer.

Plugging by chemical precipitation is another common problem. Precipitates can either be carried with the injection water or formed by mixing waters of different quality. Injection water with a high mineral content can create incrustation.

Plugging by bacterial action also occurs occasionally. The change in temperature caused by injection can promote bacterial growth, especially when warmer water is added to a cool aquifer. Thus only treated- or bacteria-free-water should be injected.

Another problem associated with injection wells is fracturing of the formation caused by injection pressure. In weakly consolidated, stratified sediments, fracturing causes severe loss in hydraulic conductivity because the bedding planes are disturbed. On the other hand, formation fracturing may increase the rate of injection into massive consolidated rock. Pressures that cause fracturing range from a low of 0.5 psi/ft (11.3 kPa/m) for poorly consolidated coastal plain sediments to 1.2 psi/ft (27.1 kPa/m) for crystalline rock.

To ensure success in supplementing available groundwater, field conditions must provide for appropriate storage, movement, and use of recharge water. The California Department of Water Resources has listed the following physical requirements for recharging:

- Geology: The basin must be suitable for storage capacity and aquifer transmissivity.

- Water: Adequate recharge must be available.
- Infiltration: Recharge rates must be maintained at adequate levels.
- Drainage: When a water table is near ground surface, adequate storage capacity must be provided in the basin.
- Water quality: Recharge water must be chemically compatible with existing groundwater and have a suitable temperature.

When conditions allow, recharging the groundwater system can be effective in maintaining adequate water supplies at a reasonable cost. Figure 47.1 shows a schematic of a typical injection well.

Basic Information Needed for Estimating

It is possible to create a reasonable cost estimate using a few required parameters. If more detailed information is known, one can create a more precise and site-specific estimate using a secondary set of parameters.

To estimate the cost of injection wells, certain information must be known. This information is discussed in the following paragraphs.

Depth to Top of Aquifer

The depth to the top of the aquifer is the depth to the top of the groundwater layer that will receive the injection fluid. Typically, injection wells for environmental projects place water in the top aquifer, so double casing for well installation in multiple aquifers is not required.

The sum of the depth to the top of the aquifer plus the aquifer thickness is used to calculate the drilling depth. For multiple injection wells, this value may be considered to be an average drilling depth for all wells to be covered by a single estimate. Generally, drilling depths less than 500' are common for environmental restoration projects.

Aquifer Thickness

The aquifer thickness is the distance from the top of the aquifer to the bottom of the aquifer. This drives the secondary parameter of screen length, covered later in this chapter.

Injection Rate per Well

The injection rate drives the quantities and cost of the transfer piping and pumps. As mentioned in the introduction to this chapter, high injection pressures tend to fracture subsurface strata. The following equation can be used to determine the approximate injection rate per well:

Confined aquifer:

$$Q = \frac{Kb \times (h_w - H_o)}{528 Log_{10} \times (r_o/r_w)}$$

Unconfined aquifer:

$$Q_r = \frac{K \times (h_w^2 - H_o^2)}{1055 Log_{10} \times (r_o/r_w)}$$

Where:

Q_r − Rate of injection (GPM)
K = Hydraulic conductivity (GPD/S.F.)
h_w = Head above the bottom of aquifer while recharging (ft)

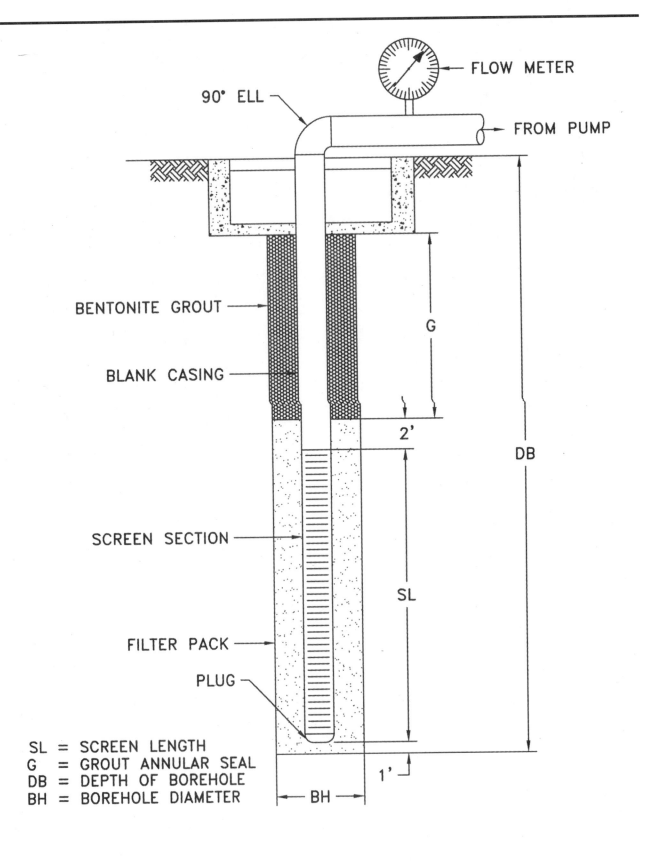

FLOW METER

90° ELL

FROM PUMP

BENTONITE GROUT

BLANK CASING

G

2'

DB

SCREEN SECTION

SL

FILTER PACK

PLUG

1'

SL = SCREEN LENGTH
G = GROUT ANNULAR SEAL
DB = DEPTH OF BOREHOLE
BH = BOREHOLE DIAMETER

BH

Figure 47.1 Schematic of Injection Well

H_o = Head above the bottom of aquifer when no pumping is taking place (ft)

r_o = Radius of influence (ft)

r_w = Radius of injection well (ft)

b = Aquifer thickness (ft)

Number of Wells

The total number of wells. This is determined by the total system flow rate.

Treatment Period

The total treatment duration is divided into startup and operations and maintenance (O&M). The costs associated with the startup period (e.g., equipment acquisition, installation, and optimization) are considered capital costs. The O&M costs are identified separately.

Analytical Soil Samples

Soil sample collection during bore hole advancement allows for definition of the magnitude and extent of contamination in the vadose zone. If the sampling plan has not been prepared or is not available, then a reasonable default includes the collection of 2 soil samples per well for chemical analysis.

Soil Analytical Template

The laboratory analysis methods to be performed on drummed drill cuttings and soil samples (collected during drilling) will drive the cost if analytical sampling is required. The number of analyses can be determined based on the number of samples required for each well and the total number of wells, plus any additional samples that might be required based on the analytical protocol. The cost of analysis can be determined based on catalog pricing or contacting the analytical laboratory providing services to the project.

Formation Type

The formation type refers to the subsurface geology of the site. The default drilling method, well diameter, and well construction material are determined based on the formation type. Refer to the equations above to see how formation impacts the flow rate default value. Options include:

- Consolidated Formation: A soil stratum that may have been subjected to glacial or other consolidating loads in the geological past. Consolidated formations are generally comprised of rock, cemented sand (sandstone), or stiff clay deposits. Mud drilling or air rotary drilling are recommended for consolidated formations.
- Unconsolidated Formation: A geologically recent deposit, such as those found in deltas, alluvial plains, or marine deposits. Unconsolidated formations are comprised of loose to medium silts, sands, and gravel.

Worker Safety Level

Worker safety is affected by the contaminant(s) at the site. Safety level refers to the levels required by OSHA in 29 CFR Part 1910. The 4 levels are designated as A, B, C, and D, where "A" is the most protective, and "D" is the least protective. A safety level of E is also included to simulate normal construction, "no hazard" conditions as prescribed by the EPA.

Design Information Needed for Detailed Estimates

Following are descriptions of the types of information that, when available, can add detail and accuracy to estimates. Also included are design criteria and estimating rules of thumb that the estimators use to determine values that are not known, or to check information provided by others.

Drilling Method

Normally, the hollow stem auger drilling method is used for injection well installation when the well depth is less than 150' below ground surface (bgs). The water/mud rotary method is typically used for drilling deeper than 150' bgs. Air rotary drilling is also an option. If the well will be drilled into an unconsolidated formation, the estimator should use water/mud rotary or air rotary rather than hollow stem augers, even for depths less than 150' bgs.

Well Material

Injection wells are typically constructed of either PVC (Schedule 40 or Schedule 80) or stainless steel screen and casing. Because PVC is cheaper, it is generally preferred when it is compatible with the injection water. If PVC is selected, the user should keep in mind that Schedule 40 PVC is not generally considered resilient enough for depths exceeding 85'.

Well Diameter

Wells are commonly sized at 2", 4", 6", or 8". Figure 47.2 shows sizing criteria for the well diameter.

Drum Drill Cuttings

The drill cuttings are generally placed in 55-gallon drums and stored until disposal options have been evaluated.

Soil Sample Collection

Sample collection during bore hole advancement allows characterization of the geology beneath the site and definition of the magnitude and extent of contaminants in the vadose zone. Typically, soil samples are collected every 5' or at each change in lithology, whichever is less for lithologic description. Drill cuttings can be collected as the bore hole is advanced for general geologic information.

Discrete samples are collected in unconsolidated sediment using the split spoon method. Samples are screened with an organic vapor analyzer (OVA) for volatile organics and described for the lithologic log by the geologist supervising drilling.

Screen Length

The screen length is assumed to be the saturated aquifer thickness. If the aquifer is confined, then screen length may vary with the pump head and aquifer pressure. However, it is generally assumed that the aquifer of concern is unconfined. Depending on the site conditions, the screen length may need to be modified.

Influent Pipe Material

The influent pipe material may be stainless steel, PVC class 150, or PVC class 200. The class designation refers to the rated pressure in pounds per square inch (psi). PVC is less expensive than stainless steel and should be used when it is compatible with the pipe material and influent.

Influent Pipe Length

Normally, all connection piping is installed above ground. If the design is unknown, the estimator may assume 100' of influent piping per well.

Type of Feed Tank

Feed tanks are used to temporarily store water before injection. These tanks help to level the flow rate when there are fluctuations in the treated water volume, or when the aquifer recharge rate is unable to handle a temporary increase in water pressure. Common feed tank options include:

- 4,000-gal. polyethylene holding tank
- 5,000-gal. steel holding tank
- 6,000-gal. polyethylene holding tank
- 10,000-gal. steel holding tank
- 20,000-gal. steel holding tank
- 35,000-gal. steel holding tank

Related Costs   Labor-hours related to well installation may be estimated using the following guidelines:

Wells are drilled at a rate of 20' per hour, plus 1 hour per 50' for well construction, and 2 hours per well for well completion. Total labor-hours are for drilling supervision by a staff hydrogeologist.

Decontamination procedures for the injection well screen, riser, caps, and drilling tools (e.g., hollow stem augers) are conducted prior to and between each bore hole/well installation. Procedures consist of steam-cleaning with a high-pressure steam-generating pressure washer and detergent.

Decontamination procedures for split spoon samplers and hand augers consist of:

- Clean with tap water and detergent using a brush.
- Rinse thoroughly with tap water.
- Rinse with deionized water.
- Rinse twice with pesticide-grade isopropanol.
- Rinse with organic-free deionized water.
- Allow to air dry.

Figure 47.2 Default Well Diameters

Default Well Diameters	
Injection Rate Range (GPM)	Well Diameter (In.)
$0.1 \leq Q < 50$	2
$50 \leq Q < 150$	4
$150 \leq Q < 300$	6
$300 \leq Q \leq 1,000$	8

Q = injection rate in gallons per minute

Maintenance of the injection well system includes adjusting the pumping rate and valves, general maintenance, and collecting injection water samples, if necessary. A conservative estimate can assume a maintenance crew of 2 field technicians to be on site once a week for the first month and once a month thereafter for system inspection and maintenance.

Site Work and Utilities

Site work and utilities that may be applicable to injection wells are:

- Overhead electric distribution
- Access roads
- Clearing and grubbing
- Fencing

If required, these should be added to the estimate.

Conclusion

Injection wells can be an effective tool for aquifer recharge in groundwater remediation. They can enhance the effectiveness of a groundwater treatment process by allowing an increased flow rate within the aquifer, thereby offsetting the cost of installing and operating the injection wells. The primary cost drivers are the depth of the wells, the number of wells, the operating period, and the geology. The cost engineer should work closely with the design team to understand these elements. Cost comparisons between different well spacing scenarios may be used to optimize the design. Contingencies should be considered for potential well failure and reduced efficiency over time, and costs should be adjusted accordingly.

Part VI

Cost Estimating for Remediation —Disposal Technologies

Chapter 48

Off-Site Transportation and Waste Disposal

Off-site transportation and waste disposal (landfill disposal) is a common element of many hazardous waste remediation treatment trains. In many instances, landfill disposal is preferred to on-site treatment or disposal because the landfill operator can deal with both the technical and administrative requirements associated with handling and storing the waste. Since the generator of the waste is ultimately responsible for its proper handling until it has been eliminated, selection of a landfill operator is a critical decision.

Applications and Limitations

Applications

- Removal of all hazardous wastes (hazardous waste landfill) and non-hazardous wastes (municipal landfill).
- Includes loading the waste from a containment berm or waste site, waste containerization, sampling of the waste stream, transporting waste from the site to a disposal facility, and the fee for accepting and ultimately disposing hazardous and non-hazardous wastes.

Limitations

- Dioxins and PCB wastes with concentrations greater then 500 parts per million (ppm) are banned from landfill disposal.
- RCRA manifest and recordkeeping requirements may increase administrative costs to the waste generators, storage facilities, transporters, and disposers.
- Characterization of hazardous wastes and identifying RCRA Secure Landfills may prove to be expensive.
- Pretreatment or stabilization of wastes may be required prior to off-site transport or to meet disposal facility requirements.

Process Configurations and Treatment Train Considerations

There are many considerations which can affect both the decision to transport waste off-site and, if this approach is chosen, the particular details. Key issues include:

- Bulking or consolidation of wastes is a cost-saving technique, but requires compatibility testing.
- Some transporters offer reduced rates to customers who are able to retain wastes until the transporter can arrange multiple pick-ups in a given area. Generators must be sure to abide by RCRA time limitations for waste storage.

- The transportation of hazardous wastes is regulated by the Department of Transportation (DOT), the Environmental Protection Agency (EPA), individual states, and in some cases, local ordinances and codes. Federal regulations apply to the transportation and disposal of highly toxic and hazardous material, such as PBCs and radioactive wastes.
- The type of waste transported can have a significant impact on the cost of shipment. Hazardous waste transportation is more expensive than non-hazardous transportation, generally due to the liability associated with the cargo.
- State taxes and other fees on hazardous wastes and substances can be significant cost drivers. These expenses are highly variable from state to state and are generically based on waste type (e.g., Non-RCRA, RCRA, Extremely Hazardous, mine tailings, etc.).

Typical Process Design Elements

To determine the feasibility of land disposal, one must be aware of RCRA regulations (40 CFR 260 to 268) and applicable state regulations. The land disposal restrictions contained in 40 CFR Part 268 identify hazardous wastes that are restricted from land disposal and define those limited circumstances under which exemptions are granted. A responsible party may be exempt from these restrictions, provided an approved petition shows that there will be no migration of hazardous constituents from the disposal zone; that an extension to an effective date was received; that the waste meets relevant treatment standards; or that the waste is placed in a surface impoundment and the requirements of 40 CFR 268.4 are met.

Land disposal restrictions in 40 CFR 268 also specify treatment standards and include storage prohibitions. Figure 48.1 is a map illustrating RCRA Secure Landfills. Each landfill has specific requirements regulating the type, condition, and source of waste that can be disposed there. Even if a specific waste is not characterized as hazardous by the EPA, an implementing state agency may (1) operate with more stringent definitions of hazardous wastes, and/or (2) define additional substances as hazardous wastes. The acceptance of a hazardous waste by a landfill is based on characterization of the waste at the site. Thus the total number of hazardous waste landfills is significantly higher than the number indicated in Figure 48.1. The user should characterize the waste prior to shipment and determine whether the disposal site can accept the waste.

Generators, storage facilities, transporters, and disposers of regulated quantities of hazardous waste must comply with manifest requirements when handling waste removed, or to be removed, from the site at which it was generated. These and other requirements for hazardous waste handlers are found in 40 CFR 262 through 265. In addition, the generator should ensure that the facility selected to receive the waste has an acceptable compliance history with federal, state, and local regulatory agencies. Permitted RCRA facilities must notify the generator in writing that they will accept specific wastes from the generator and that they are permitted to do so.

Preparation of Wastes

It is often most cost-effective to consolidate compatible wastes before disposal. Compatibility testing prior to bulking for off-site transport will ensure that consolidation will not result in the creation of toxic

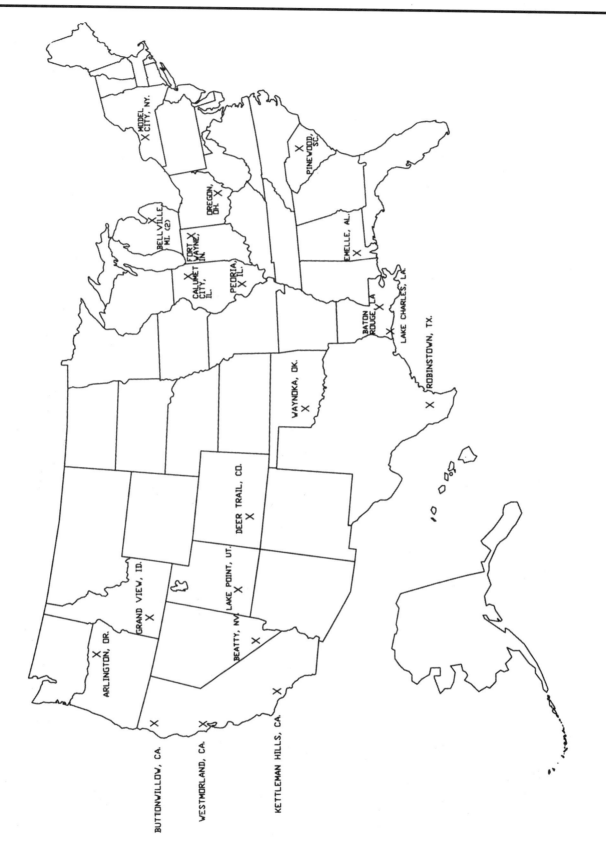

Figure 48.1 RCRA Secure Landfills

gases, vapors, or fumes, or large volumes of waste that are unacceptable for off-site disposal. Compatibility tests are simple, rapid, and cost-effective procedures that segregate wastes into broad categories. By identifying broad waste categories, compatible wastes can be safely bulked on site without additional risk of fire, explosion, or release of toxic gases. Disposal options can be determined without an exhaustive analysis of each waste type.

A detailed waste analysis is generally required before a waste is accepted by a treatment/disposal facility. Sampling and analysis requirements vary considerably depending on the facility permits, state regulations, physical state of the wastes, and the final disposal option selected.

Pretreatment or stabilization of wastes may be required prior to off-site transport or to meet disposal facility requirements. Stabilization can be accomplished by one of the following processes:

- Acid-base neutralization
- Metal precipitation/solidification
- Hypochlorite oxidation of cyanide and sulfide
- Flash point reduction
- Removal of free liquids by addition of soils, lime, fly ash, polymers, or other materials that remove free water

This chapter covers loading the waste from a containment berm or waste site, waste containerization, sampling the waste stream, transporting waste from the site to a disposal facility, and fees for accepting and ultimately disposing of the waste. Decontamination of bulk trucks is considered as part of the disposal fee.

Transportation

The transportation of hazardous wastes is regulated by the Department of Transportation (DOT), the Environmental Protection Agency (EPA), individual states, and, in some cases, local ordinances and codes. Federal regulations apply to the transportation and disposal of highly toxic and hazardous materials such as PCBs and radioactive wastes. Applicable DOT regulations include:

- Department of Transportation 49 CFR, Parts 172-179
- Department of Transportation 49 CFR, Part 1387 (46 CFR 30974, 47073)
- Department of Transportation DOT-E 8876

The U.S. EPA regulations under RCRA (40 CFR 262 and 263) adopt DOT regulations pertaining to labeling, placarding, packaging, and spill reporting. These regulations also impose administrative requirements for compliance with the hazardous waste manifest system.

Before a vehicle can leave the site, it should be rinsed or scrubbed to remove contaminants. Bulk liquid containers and box trailers should be checked for proper placarding, cleanliness, and excess waste levels. Bulk liquid containers should also be checked for proper venting, closed valve positions, and secured hatches. Box trailers should be checked to ensure correct liner installation, secured cover tarp, and locked lift gate.

The type of waste transported can have a significant impact on the cost of shipment. Generally, hazardous waste transportation is more expensive than non-hazardous transportation because of the liability associated with the cargo. This chapter addresses the transportation of hazardous wastes by truck. Additional modes of transportation, such as railroad and water, may be used, depending on user demand.

Taxes and Fees

State taxes and other fees on hazardous wastes and substances can be major cost drivers. The taxes and fees vary from state to state and are generally based on waste type (e.g., non-RCRA, RCRA, extremely hazardous, mine tailings). Landfill disposal sites often operate as treatment sites (incinerators) as well as storage areas.

The main fee categories include: post closure fee; Treatment, Storage, and Disposal Facility (TSDF) permit application fee; TSDF licensing fee; TSDF maintenance and inspection fee; generator fee; and disposal fee. A third party, such as a contractor or generator, is responsible for direct disposal fees. The National Solid Wastes Management Association publishes a detailed reference of disposal fees by state entitled "Guide to State Taxes and Fees for Hazardous Waste Generation and Management."

Basic Information Needed for Estimating

It is possible to create a reasonable cost estimate for landfill disposal using a few required parameters. If more detailed information is known, one can create a more precise and site-specific estimate using a secondary set of parameters.

To estimate the cost of the system, certain information must be known. This information is discussed in the following paragraphs.

Waste Type

Commercial waste disposal and transportation costs can vary greatly depending on the nature of the contaminant and the waste matrix. Waste material should be classified as either hazardous or non-hazardous, depending on its characteristics. The EPA has developed two ways of determining whether a material is a hazardous waste. The first is based on four characteristics of the solid waste (as per definition in RCRA in 40 CFR Part 261):

- Ignitability
- Corrosivity
- Reactivity
- Toxicity

There are three types of listed hazardous waste:

- Specific source (40 CFR Part 261.31)
- Specific Source (40 CFR Part 261.32)
- Commercial Chemical Products (40 CFR Part 261.33)

Non-hazardous waste is waste material that is contaminated, but is not listed or characterized as a hazardous waste. Miscellaneous residual waste (demolished cover, clean fill) is not applicable to this technology. Costs for hauling non-hazardous/non-contaminated waste are much lower than for contaminated and hazardous waste. Loads should not be mixed, as the cost for the entire load is priced at the highest hazard level.

Waste Form

There are two waste forms: solid and liquid/sludge. Bulk solid is assumed to be loaded by a wheel loader and to have a moisture content less than 30%. Bulk liquid is pumpable material with a moisture content greater than 70%. Bulk sludge is any material with a moisture content between 30–70%. This material is assumed to be pumped and transported via tanker trucks.

Condition of Waste

The condition of waste prior to disposal, either bulk or in drums, will affect preparation tasks such as container costs, transferring waste into drums, and loading waste into a truck. Typical options include:

- Bulk To Be Drummed
- Bulk To Remain as Bulk
- Non-Leaking Drums
- Leaking Drums

Leaking Drums or Non-Leaking Drums implies that the waste is already drummed and therefore, a cost is not added for purchasing drums or transferring waste into them. Leaking drums typically require overpacks. If the drums are already in overpacks, then overpacks should not be included in the estimate.

Quantity of Waste

The volume of waste is used to determine the number of transport units (vehicles/trips) and the number of drums required, if applicable. The quantity of waste directly affects the cost of transportation and disposal.

The quantity of waste should be determined both in terms of volume and weight. In some cases, volume will be the limiting factor for the number of transport units, but landfill fees are almost always calculated based on weight. Converting from volume to weight, or vice-versa, is based on density factors for different types of waste. Figure 48.2 provides the density of solid waste based on specific gravity for different types of material and void percentages.

The specific gravity of some common soils is as follows:

Sand	2.5–2.7
Clay	2.8–3.2
Silty sand	2.6–3.0
Sandy clay	2.5–2.9
Gravel	2.5–2.7

Sand generally has a low voids percent range from 20–30%, and clay is generally higher, at 45–55%

State Disposal Tax/Fee

The state charges for disposal of hazardous waste at a landfill in cost per cubic yard, gallon, or drum.

Distance to Off-Site Facility (One Way)

Travel distance is the most important parameter for estimating the costs for transporting any material. The cost is based on the number of miles traveled. Generally, transporters base their rates either on a running mile or loaded mile. A running mile rate includes all of the miles traveled by the transporter (i.e., the charges begin when the truck leaves the terminal and end when the truck is back at the terminal). The loaded mile rate is associated only with the number of miles between the generator and the ultimate disposal location. For short hauling distances, the costs will be based on either a loaded mile or a minimum charge, depending on the type of material. The number of trips calculated is based on the volume of waste divided by the mode of transportation capacity.

Worker Safety Level

Worker safety is affected by the potential interactions with the contaminant(s) at the site. Safety level refers to the levels required by OSHA in 29 CFR Part 1910. The four levels are designated as A, B, C, and D, where "A" is the most protective, and "D" is the least protective. A safety level of E is also included to simulate normal construction, "no hazard" conditions as prescribed by the EPA.

Design Information Needed for Detailed Estimates

Following are descriptions of the types of detailed information that, when available, can add detail and accuracy to landfill disposal estimates. Also included are design criteria and estimating rules of thumb that the estimator typically uses to determine values that are not known, or to check information provided by others.

Containment Berms

Once the contaminated soil/water/sludge has been removed, a containment berm may be required for temporary storage until the waste is transported to the disposal site.

Density Of Solid Waste (Lbs./C.Y.)									
Specific Gravity	Voids – (Percent)								
	15	20	25	30	35	40	45	50	55
2.0	2860	2700	2530	2360	2190	2020	1850	1680	1520
2.1	3010	2830	2650	2480	2300	2120	1950	1770	1590
2.2	3150	2970	2780	2590	2410	2220	2040	1850	1670
2.3	3290	3100	2910	2710	2520	2330	2130	1940	1740
2.4	3440	3240	3030	2830	2630	2430	2220	2020	1820
2.5	3580	3370	3160	2950	2740	2530	2320	2110	1900
2.6	3720	3500	3290	3070	2850	2630	2410	2190	1970
2.7	3870	3640	3410	3180	2960	2730	2500	2270	2050
2.8	4010	3770	3540	3300	3070	2830	2590	2360	2120
2.9	4150	3910	3660	3420	3180	2930	2690	2440	2200
3.0	4300	4040	3790	3540	3290	3030	2780	2530	2270
3.1	4440	4180	3920	3600	3400	3130	2870	2610	2350
3.2	4580	4310	4040	3770	3500	3230	2970	2700	2430

Figure 48.2 Density of Solid Waste (lbs/C.Y.)

Containment berms generally come in ten sizes:

- 10' × 10' × 17", 750 Gallon
- 13' × 13' × 17", 1,800 Gallon
- 18' × 18' × 17", 3,400 Gallon
- 24' × 24' × 17", 6,100 Gallon
- 32' × 32' × 17", 10,800 Gallon
- 32' × 32' × 34", 21,600 Gallon
- 74' × 34' × 34", 53,400 Gallon
- 45' × 15' × 17", 7,600 Gallon
- 65' × 16' × 17", 11,000 Gallon
- 50' × 22' × 17", 11,600 Gallon

Drums and Overpacks

If waste is either in leaking drums now, or needs to be drummed prior to shipment, the following parameters will apply.

- Type of Drum
- Fill Capacity Factor
- Quantity of Overpacks
- Type of Overpack

Type of Drum

Depending on the contaminants and the waste form, appropriate containers for waste transport may vary. Fifty-five-gallon steel, closed head drums are typically used. These containers are the most common for holding and transporting waste. Alternate container selection will affect the material cost for the containers. Common alternatives include:

- 55-gal, steel, closed-head drum
- 55-gal, steel, open-head drum
- 55-gal, polyethylene, closed-head drum
- 55-gal, polyethylene, open-head drum

Storage containers with capacities ranging from 10-350 gallons are available, but are less common.

Fill Capacity Factor

This is the average percent drums are filled and applies to either non-leaking drums that will remain drummed or bulk to be drummed. The fill capacity factor is used to determine the actual volume of waste and/or the number of drums required. Because drums are generally not entirely full, a rule of thumb of 90% full is commonly used. The valid range is 60-100%.

Quantity of Overpacks

The quantity of overpacks is assumed to be equal to the number of leaking drums. Additional overpacks may be required for project-specific purposes.

Type of Overpacks

The most common type of overpack is 85-gal steel. A materials compatibility test should be performed to certify that the contaminant is not incompatible with the steel drum material prior to selecting an option. The alternative is 85-gal polyethylene drums.

Related Costs

Waste samples must be analyzed before the waste can be accepted at a permitted landfill. Generally, analysis type and quantity are determined on a case by case basis, based on applicable regulations. The site-specific sampling and analysis plan dictate the type, frequency, and quantity of analyses. If the specific plan is unknown at the time of the estimate, assume that all wastes are "generically hazardous" and thus subject to TCLP (EPA Method 1311) analysis. The frequency of analysis is based on one sample per 1,000 C.Y. of bulk solid waste and one sample per 225,000 gallons of bulk liquid/sludge waste. (Note: These quantities correspond to approximately 1 sample per 50 truckloads of material, drummed or bulk.) Assume a rate of 4 samples per hour in a continuous operation. The estimator should be aware that this sampling frequency can be very costly for larger projects and that it is not uncommon for negotiations with regulators to reduce or increase the number of required samples.

Site Work and Utilities

No site work or utilities are required for commercial landfill disposal.

Conclusion

Landfill disposal is a reasonable alternative to on-site treatment and disposal for many hazardous waste sites. This is particularly true for sites that are closed or where alternative re-use is being considered. The cost of landfill disposal can be considerable, however, and should be compared to other alternatives. The primary cost drivers are the volume and type of waste. Volume reduction should be considered as a cost savings approach. The cost engineer should work closely with the design team to evaluate these alternatives.

Chapter 49

Residual Waste Management

Many technologies for investigating and remediating environmental contamination generate a variety of residual wastes. For example, when drilling groundwater monitoring wells or extraction wells, the drilling process normally generates soil cuttings that accumulate on the surface around the bore hole. Regulations and good management practices often dictate that the soil cuttings be placed in containers, sampled to determine whether contaminants are present, then transported off-site for disposal at a facility with the appropriate permits. Residual waste management provides rules of thumb for estimating the costs for transporting and disposing of residual wastes.

Applications and Limitations

Applications

- Residual waste management estimation techniques can be used to evaluate any costs derived from investigation or remedial action activities.

Limitations

The costs for managing residual wastes (such as spent activated carbon or dewatered sludge from a filter press generated through O&M of a remedial system) are usually calculated separately as part of O&M costs.

Residual waste management does not address the following types of waste:

- Excavation Technology—Fluids generated by dewatering the open excavation.
- Groundwater Extraction Wells Technology—Free product recovered from the subsurface.
- Trenching/Piping Technology—Fluids generated by dewatering the open trench.

The estimator should manually estimate the volume of these materials if they need to be included in the estimate based on estimated fluid volumes from dewatering and free product removal.

Process Configurations and Treatment Train Considerations

- Used at the completion of an investigation or a remedial action to manage residual wastes generated by these phases.
- May not cover all wastes generated by all construction activities, especially non-typical technology applications.

Basic Information Needed for Estimating

A reasonable cost estimate can be assembled if a few required parameters are available. If more detailed information is known, one can create a more precise and site-specific estimate using a secondary set of parameters.

Residual Wastes to be Included

Residual wastes should be listed and are typically derived from one of three sources:

- *Site Work*, such as wastes generated by clearing and grubbing
- *Technology-Specific*, such as drill cuttings generated by well drilling
- *Safety and Decontamination*, such as personnel protective equipment

Example residual wastes are listed in Figure 49.1.

Residual Wastes
Drill Cuttings
Drums Removed from Excavation
Development Water
Personnel Protection Equipment
Purge Water
Triple-Rinsed Drums
Decontamination Water
Water from Excavation Dewatering
Free Product
Product Pumped from USTs
Rinse Water
Sheet Piling Decontamination Water
Tank Decontamination Water
Water from Trench Dewatering
Concrete Material
Contaminated Soil
Clean/Treated Soil
Existing Cover
Excavated Material Not Used for Backfill
Filter Cake
Non-Backfilled Material
Soil Not Used for Backfill
Miscellaneous Range Scrap
Sand from Tank Decontamination
USTs Removed

Figure 49.1 Residual Wastes

Waste Characteristics

For each residual waste stream that appears in the list, the estimator should define the condition and quantity of the waste, and specify whether each residual waste stream is hazardous or non-hazardous.

Condition

The condition of a residual waste prior to disposal will affect preparation tasks, such as transferring waste into drums and loading waste into a truck, as well as container costs. There are typically five condition options:

- Bulk to remain as bulk
- Bulk to be drummed
- Non-leaking drums
- Leaking drums
- Tanks

If "leaking drums" is selected, the estimator should include the cost of placing the leaking drums into overpacks prior to transporting the drums off-site.

Typical condition options that are available for each unit of measure are summarized below:

U/M	Condition Options
Drum	Non-leaking drums (default)
	Leaking drums
C.Y.	Bulk to remain as bulk (default)
	Bulk to be drummed
	Non-leaking drums
	Leaking drums
Gal.	Bulk to remain as bulk (default)
	Bulk to be drummed
	Non-leaking drums
	Leaking drums
Tanks	Tanks

Quantity

This parameter defines the volume of residual waste to be transferred and disposed. This information is used to determine the number of transport units and drums required (if applicable). The quantity of waste directly affects the cost of transportation and disposal.

Waste Type

Commercial waste disposal and transportation costs can vary greatly depending on the nature of the contaminant and the waste matrix. The EPA has developed two methods that can be used by solid waste generators to determine whether a waste is classified as hazardous. The first based on the waste's characteristics per RCRA 40 CFR 261:

- Ignitability
- Corrosivity
- Reactivity
- Toxicity

The second method is to review lists of hazardous wastes:

- Specific Source (40 CFR 261.31)
- Specific Source (40 CFR 261.32)
- Commercial Chemical Products (40 CFR 261.33)

Typically, non-hazardous wastes are contaminated materials that do not exhibit one or more of the hazardous waste characteristics. The estimator should evaluate each residual waste to determine if it is hazardous or non-hazardous.

Disposal and Transportation

The following section provides guidance for specifying the transportation and disposal parameters for each residual waste stream.

Waste Type/Condition

There are typically ten different combinations of waste types/conditions. The management options depend on these categories and include:

- Non-Hazardous Drums
- Non-Hazardous Drums with Overpacks
- Non-Hazardous Bulk Solid
- Non-Hazardous Bulk Liquid
- Non-Hazardous Tanks
- Hazardous Drums
- Hazardous Drums with Overpacks
- Hazardous Bulk Solid
- Hazardous Bulk Liquid
- Hazardous Tanks

Unless the remediation scenario is extremely complicated with numerous technologies that generate numerous residual wastes, only a few of these options would be selected simultaneously. For example, if the only residual wastes for a phase are in drums, and they are specified as hazardous, the waste type/condition is Hazardous Drums.

The estimator should specify the Total Quantity, Distance to Disposal Facility, Waste Stabilization Required, Disposal Fees, and State Tax/Fees for each of the 10 Waste Type/Conditions.

Total Quantity

The total quantity is the sum of quantities for all residual waste streams with a given Waste Type/Condition. For example, if two different wastes were classified as Hazardous Bulk Solid, the number displayed would be the sum of the quantities for the two wastes. The quantities are summed up, within a given waste type/condition, in order to determine the total amount of each that will be transported for disposal or treatment.

Distance to Disposal Facility

Travel distance is the most important parameter for estimating the costs for transporting any waste. The cost is based on the number of miles traveled, with the rates based on a running mile or loaded mile. A running mile rate includes all of the miles traveled by the transporter (charges begin when the truck leaves the terminal and end when the truck is back at the terminal). A loaded mile rate is based on the number of miles between the generator and the ultimate disposal location.

For short hauling distances, the costs will be based on either a loaded mile or a minimum charge, depending on the type of material. Typical ranges for travel distance are 1–1,000 miles for non-hazardous wastes, and 1–5,000 miles for hazardous wastes. The number of trips calculated is based on the volume of waste divided by the capacity of the transport vehicle. Typical transport costs are presented in Figure 49.2.

Stabilization

Some hazardous wastes must be pretreated before they can be placed in a land disposal unit. Stabilization is one of the most common means of pretreating hazardous waste prior to disposal. Since it is conducted at the disposal facility, on-site pretreatment of the residual waste is not addressed in this chapter.

An example of waste that requires stabilization is sludge, which, as a bulk waste, is assumed to be in a liquid state. For each of the 10 hazardous waste types/conditions listed previously, the estimator should consider whether stabilization is required.

Disposal Fee

The cost to dispose of waste is another significant cost driver. Typical average disposal fees are presented in Figure 49.3.

Disposal costs for residual wastes can vary greatly depending on the nature of the contaminant and the waste matrix. The estimator should obtain actual cost quotes from the selected disposal facility prior to finalizing the estimate.

Description	Unit Cost
Transport 55-Gallon Drums of Hazardous Waste, Max 80 drums (per Mile)	$1.68
Transport Bulk Solid Hazardous Waste, Maximum 20 C.Y. (per Mile)	1.62
Transport Bulk Liquid/Sludge Hazardous Waste, Maximum 5,000-Gallon (per Mile)	1.68
Dump Truck Transportation Hazardous Waste Minimum Charge	740.52
Dump Truck Transportation Hazardous Waste 500 599 Miles (per Mile)	2.16
Dump Truck Transportation Hazardous Waste 1000+ Miles (per Mile)	1.99
Van Trailer Transportation Hazardous Waste Minimum Charge	756.51
Van Trailer Transportation Hazardous Waste 500-599 Miles (per Mile)	2.15
Van Trailer Transportation Hazardous Waste 1,000-1,099 Miles	1.97
Tanker Trailer Transport Hazardous Waste Minimum Charge	772.49
Tanker Trailer Transport Hazardous Waste 500-599 Miles (per Mile)	2.50
Tanker Trailer Transport Hazardous Waste 1,000+ Miles (per Mile)	2.24
Vacuum Trailer Transport Hazardous Waste Minimum Charge	852.40
Vacuum Trailer Transport Hazardous Waste 400-899 Miles (per Mile)	3.25
Rail Boxcar Transport, CWT	3.20
Rail Flatbed Transport, CWT	6.29

Source: ECHOS Assembly Cost Data, 2002.

Figure 49.2 Typical Transport Costs

State Tax/Fees

In every state, there is an applicable state tax or fee for disposal. Typical ranges are $0–1,000.00 per C.Y. of bulk waste, $0–100.00 per gallon of liquid waste, and $0–1,000.00 per drum for all drummed waste.

Safety Level

The safety level required for a particular activity is driven by the potential for human exposure to contaminants during loading, en route to the disposal facility, and during treatment and/or placement at disposal facility. These 4 levels are defined by OSHA in 29 CFR 1910 and are designated as A, B, C, and D; where "A" is the most protective, and "D" is the least protective. A safety level of E also is included to simulate normal construction "no hazard" conditions as prescribed by the EPA.

Description	Unit Cost
Landfill Hazardous Solid Waste, 55-Gallon Drum	$98.56
Landfill Non-Hazardous Solid Waste, 55-Gallon Drum	13.50
Landfill Drummed Solid Waste Requiring Stabilization, 55-Gallon Drum	268.51
Landfill Drummed Soil/ Sludge Requiring Stabilization, 55-Gallon Drum	378.25
Landfill Drummed Liquid Waste, 55-Gallon Drum	147.04
Landfill Drummed Liquid Waste Requiring Stabilization, 55-Gallon Drum	319.65
Landfill Drummed Inorganic/Organic Non-Hazardous Liquid/Sludge, 55-Gallon Drum	177.94
Landfill Mineral Acids, 0–40% Concentration, 55-Gallon Drum	548.73
Landfill Mineral Acids, 41–60% Concentration, 55-Gallon Drum	826.80
Landfill Mineral Acids, > 61% Concentration, 55-Gallon Drum	1,067.25
Landfill Fuel Substitutes, 0–10% Solids, 55-Gallon Drum	112.94
Landfill Fuel Substitutes, 10.1–25% Solids, 55-Gallon Drum	171.55
Landfill Fuel Substitutes, 25.1–50% Solids, 55-Gallon Drum	311.15
Landfill Fuel Substitutes, 50.1–75% Solids, 55-Gallon Drum	436.86
Landfill Fuel Substitutes, 75.1–100% Solids, 55-Gallon Drum	628.65
Landfill Packaged Lab Chemicals, > 45-Gallon Drum	384.69
Landfill Packaged Lab Chemicals Requiring Stabilization, > 45-Gallon Drum	1,032.66
Landfill Solid Palletized Waste	522.10
Landfill Liquid or Sludge Palletized Waste	506.21
Landfill Hazardous Solid Bulk Waste by Ton	170.45
Landfill Hazardous Solid Bulk Waste by C.Y.	149.17
Landfill Non-Hazardous Solid Bulk Waste by Ton	83.11
Landfill Non-Hazardous Solid Bulk Waste by C.Y.	94.30
Landfill Hazardous Liquid Bulk Waste (Gallon)	1.34
Landfill Non-Hazardous Liquid Bulk Waste (Gallon)	2.07
Landfill Hazard Liquid Bulk Waste Requiring Stabilization (Gallon)	2.62
Landfill Hazardous Nonfuel Liquid/Sludge	1.32
Landfill Non-Hazardous Nonfuel Liquid/Sludge (Gallon)	2.55

Source: ECHOS Assembly Cost Data, 2002.

Figure 49.3 Typical Average Disposal Fees

The safety level affects the level of productivity and all labor categories in defaulted or selected assemblies. Safety level will not affect the productivity of the driver during transportation, since this would violate DOT and U.S. EPA regulations. The default safety level for Residual Waste Management is D.

Site Work and Utilities
Applicable items include loading and hauling—movement of material around the site, or hauling of construction-related debris. If the site is remote, a temporary access road may also be required to collect and transport residual wastes for disposal.

Conclusion Residual waste management is a typical cost component at the end of the investigation or remediation cycle, yet it is often overlooked in the estimate. The main cost drivers are the quantity of waste, whether it is hazardous or non-hazardous, the distance it must be transported, and the disposal fee for each type of waste.

Part VII

Cost Estimating for Remediation —Ordnance Technologies

Chapter 50

Ordnance and Explosives Removal Action

Ordnance and Explosives (OE) Removal Action includes the costs of searching for, marking, and removing unexploded ordnance (UXO) from munitions-contaminated property. The definition of ordnance and explosive waste, for the purpose of this reference, is any chemical substance or physical item related to munitions that is designed to cause damage to personnel or material through explosive force, incendiary action, or toxic effects.

Applications and Limitations

Applications

- Locating and removing unexploded ordnance (UXO).
- Closed or transferring ranges.

Limitations

- Not applicable to underwater UXO operations that require diving or similar activities for detection and recovery.
- Removal, storage, transportation, and destruction of chemical warfare material (CWM) that is found in UXO or other containerized form only.
- Does not cover special handling methods for low-level radioactive ordnance, such as depleted uranium.
- Cleanup of buildings contaminated with explosive compounds is not included in this technology.
- Not designed for ranges still in operation. (For open ranges, use the "Active Target Clearance" technology.)

Process Configurations and Treatment Train Considerations

There are many factors that affect the approach and productivity for ordnance and explosives identification and removal. Key considerations include:

- Ex Situ Bioreactor or Incineration (off-site/on-site) should be used in the case of explosives compounds in soil.
- Advanced Oxidation Processes may be used to estimate costs for treating explosive-laden water.
- This technology is typically used in a treatment train that includes other remedial technologies to remove explosive compounds from water and soil. The contaminants are usually compounds such as trinitrotoluene (TNT), cyclotrimethylenetrinitramine (RDX),

cyclotetramethylene-tetranitramine (HMX), and tetryl. Related propellant and pyrotechnic chemicals generated from munitions production include nitrocellulose (NC), nitroglycerin (NG), nitroquanadine (NQ), ammonium perchlorate, dinitrotoluene (DNT), phosphorus, and others.

Basic Information Needed for Estimating

A reasonable cost estimate can be generated using a few required parameters. If more detailed information is known, one can create a more precise and site-specific estimate using a secondary set of parameters.

Determine Tasks to Include

Since there are several different types of tasks that can be performed during an OE Removal Action, the estimator should first determine which ones to include in the estimate prior to gathering information for estimating. Tasks include:

- Site Visit
- Surveying
- Vegetation Removal
- UXO Mapping
- UXO Removal
- Site Management
- Stakeholder Involvement

Characterize Removal Area

These parameters address the physical characteristics of the site and include:

- Removal Area
- Search Depth
- Topography
- Vegetation
- Range Type(s)
- Ordnance Characteristics

Removal Area

In the case of ordnance search operations, it may not be necessary to search the entire site, but only a portion of the site. The removal area should reflect the actual area over which the search and/or removal operation will be conducted. The valid range for removal area is 1–100,000 acres.

It is common to specify if there are multiple Areas of Concern within the project area. An "Area of Concern" (AOC) is an area that has unique attributes. There are several factors that can differentiate AOCs, such as the type of range, types of ordnance dropped, topography and/or vegetation, and land use. Breaking a site up into multiple AOCs allows the estimator to generate more accurate and precise estimates.

Search Depth

The search depth (also known as *depth of clearance*) is a factor used in calculating the project duration, number of personnel required for search and recovery operations, and equipment requirements. Ordnance, particularly on ranges, can be found to depths of 10' or more, depending on the soil type and the weapon or shell involved. Common search and clearance depths are up to 2' below ground surface, while some requirements are to remove anything that is detected with an ordnance locator. If the defined search depth is 2' or less, assume that there will be 1 backhoe per every 3 teams. If the search depth is between 2–10', assume that the total labor-hours required to remove anomalies will increase by 15% and will add 1 backhoe per team. The valid range for search depth is 0–10'.

Topography

Topography defines the condition of the terrain, which impacts the rate of search and thus the overall project duration. For example, mountainous terrain will take longer to survey, clear, and remove ordnance than will a flat terrain. "Flat" represents the mean productivity rate on which all others are based. The topography options include:

- Flat
- Gently Rolling
- Heavy Rolling
- Flat with Gorges or Gullies
- Rolling with Gorges or Gullies
- Mountainous

Vegetation

This item defines the amount of vegetation removal required to prepare the site for the various activities related to ordnance removal. More information is provided in the section entitled "Vegetation Removal." Typical choices for vegetation include:

- Barren or Low Grass
- Low Grass and Few Shrubs
- Heavy Grass with Numerous Shrubs
- Shrubs with Some Trees
- Heavy Shrubs with Trees

Range Type(s)

The type of range selected sets the default values for anomaly density. More information regarding densities of ordnance is provided below under "Anomaly Density." Typical range types include:

- Air-to-Air
- Air-to-Ground
- Artillery
- Bombing
- Burial Pits
- Guided Missiles
- Hand Grenade
- OB/OD
- Other
- Mortar
- Multiple/Combined Use
- Rifle Grenade, Anti-Tank Rocket
- Small Arms

Ordnance Characteristics

Ordnance characteristics are typically defined by 3 parameters:

- Ordnance Types
- Anomaly Density
- Scrap

Ordnance Type. Ordnance type refers to the types of munitions likely to be present within the defined "Removal Area." Figure 50.1 outlines the ordnance descriptions and their associated Department of Defense Munitions ID. Figure 50.2 provides more detailed information on specific munition types, characterized by Munition ID Code. Figure 50.3 is a photo of smaller-type ordnance found at a closed range.

Anomaly Density. Anomaly density refers to the actual number of UXO items (plus scrap) per acre. This number can vary widely depending on how the property was used and how often ordnance and scrap were picked up. False positive indications of ordnance (e.g., anomalies, rocks of high iron content) should be included in the anomaly density number, if known. The number of items per acre will impact the length of time it will take to clean an acre and thus the overall cost of remediation. Scrap metal from ordnance is often as insidious as the UXO itself because time is required to determine that the object is nothing more than inert scrap.

If it is known that the area was not screened for scrap on a regular basis and that there may be a high incidence of scrap in with the ordnance, the ordnance density number should be adjusted to account for this fact. The valid range for ordnance density is from 1–500 items per acre. Ordnance density affects the calculated value of project duration and the number of personnel. Default densities are shown in Figure 50.4.

Figure 50.1 Ordnance Descriptions and DODIC Munition IDs

DODIC/ MUNITION ID	Description
CTT01	Bombs, High Explosive
CTT02	Bombs, (WP, Incendiary, Photoflash)
CTT03	Bombs, Practice
CTT04	Demolition Materials (TNT, Dynamite, Black Powder, Detonators, Blasting Caps, Fuses, Cratering Charges, Bangalore Torpedoes, etc.)
CTT05	Hand Grenades, Live
CTT06	Hand Grenades, Practice
CTT07	Ground Rockets, Rifle Grenades, Live
CTT08	Ground Rockets, Rifle Grenades, Practice
CTT09	Land Mines
CTT10	Medium Caliber (20mm, 25mm, 30mm)
CTT11	Large Caliber (37mm and larger)
CTT12	Aerial Rockets (Live)
CTT13	Aerial Rockets (Practice)
CTT14	Guided Missiles
CTT15	Pyrotechnics (Smoke Grenades, Trip Flares, Signal Flares, Grenade & Artillery Simulators, etc.)
CTT16	Small Arms
CTT17	Other (Toxic Chemical Munitions, Sea Mines, Torpedoes, CADS, etc.)

CTT01 – Bombs, High Explosive

AN-M1A1 & AN M1A2, Cluster
AN-M30, General Purpose Bomb, 100 lbs
AN-M41, Frag Bomb, 20 lbs
AN-M56, Light Case Bomb, 4000 lbs
AN-M57 & AN-M57A1, GP, 250 lbs
AN-M58, Armor Piercing Bomb
AN-M59, Armor Piercing Bomb
AN-M64 & AN-M64A1, GP Bomb, 500 lbs
AN-M65 & AN-M65A1, GP Bomb, 1000 lbs
AN-M66 & AN-M66 A1 & A2, GP, 2000 lbs
AN-M88 & M81, Frag Bomb, 220 & 260 lbs
AN-Mk I, Armor Piercing Bomb
BL-755, British, Cluster Bomb
BLU-26B, 36B, 59B, 26T-1B, 36T-1B
BLU-61AB
BLU-63B, 63AB, 86B, 86AB, 63T-1B, 86T-1B
BLU-77, HEAT Frag Bomblet
BLU-82, Blast Cradled Bomb
BLU-97, 97B, 97AB
Bomb, General Purpose, Old Style
Dispenser, SUU-30
Fuze, Bomb, FMU-110
Fuze, Bomb, M904
Fuze, Bomb, M905
Fuze, Bomb, M906
Fuze, Bomb, AN-M110A1
Fuze, Bomb, FMU-54
Fuze, Bomb, FMU-7
Fuze, M907
GBU, Series 10
GBU, Series 12
GBU, Series 8
M104, M105, Bomb, Leaflet, 100 lbs & 500 lbs
M17, Adapter Cluster
M24, Adapter Cluster
M27, Cluster
M28 & M29, Frag Bomb, 90 lbs
M52, Armor Piercing Bomb
M61, Armor Piercing Bomb
M72, Frag Bomb, 23 lbs
M82, Frag Bomb, 90 lbs
M83, Frag Bomb, 4 lbs
Mk 1, British Cluster Bomb, 500 lbs
Mk 118, AT Bomb
Mk 20, Cluster, Rockeye
Mk 33, Armor Piercing Bomb
Mk 50, Depth Bomb, 100 lbs
Mk 81 Mk 82 Mk 83 Mk 84, GP
Mk 82, General Purpose Bomb, 500 lbs
Mk 83, General Purpose Bomb, 1000 lbs
Mk I & II, British Fragmentation Bomb, 8 lbs
Mk I & Mk II, British Med Capacity, 1000 lbs
Mk I - Mk IV, British GP Bomb, 1000 lbs

Figure 50.2 Bombs

CTT02 – Bombs (WP, Incendiary, Photoflash)	Mk I - Mk XII, British Med Capacity, 500 lbs
	Mk I Mk II & Mk III, British GP Bomb, 250 lbs
	Mk II Mk III & Mk V, British SAP, 500 lbs
	Mk II, Frag Bomb, 17 lbs
	Mk III, Frag Bomb, 25 lbs
	Mk IV Mk V & Mk VI, British GP, 250 lbs
	Mk IV, British GP Bomb, 500 lbs
	T12, General Purpose Bomb
	AN-M46, Photoflash Bomb, 100 lbs
	AN-M76, Incendiary Bomb, 500 lbs
	BLU 27, Fire Bomb
	BLU-73, Bomblet, FAE
	Dispenser, SUU-25
	Igniter, M23
	Instructional Incendiary Bomb
	LUU-2B, Flare, Parachute
	M122, Photoflash Bomb, 100 lbs
	M126, Incendiary Bomb, 4 lbs
	M19, M21, E48, E61, E67, Incen. Cluster, 500 lbs
	M19, M21, E61, E67, Incendiary Cluster Bomb
	M26, Flare, Parachute
	M35, Cluster Incendiary Bomb
	M36, Cluster Incendiary Bomb
	M47 series, Chemical Bomb, 100 lbs
	M50, Incendiary Bomb, 4 lbs
	M67 Incendiary Bomb, 10 lbs
	M74, Incendiary Bomb
	M74A1, Incendiary Bomb
	M89, M90, M91, M98, M100, Target ID, 250 lbs
	Mk 24, Flare, Parachute
	Mk 45, Flare, Parachute
	Mk 77, Fireye
	Mk I & Mk II, Incendiary Darts
	Mk I, Incendiary Bomb, 8 oz
	Mk I, British Incendiary Bomb, 30 lbs
	Mk III, Incendiary Bomb
	No 16 Mk II, British Cluster Bomb, 1000 lbs
	No 4 Mk I 500 lbs British Cluster Bomb
CTT03 – Bombs, Practice	AN-Mk 5, AN-Mk 23, AN-Mk 43, Prac
	BDU-12
	BDU-33
	BDU-35
	BDU-38
	BDU-42
	BDU-48, 10 lbs
	BDU-50
	Bomb, BDU-35
	Bomb, BDU-38
	Bomb, BDU-42
	Bomb, BDU-50
	Bomb, Practice, BDU-48
	Bomb, Practice, BDU 33
	Bomb, Practice, Signal, MK4
	Bomb, Practice, Signal, MK5

Figure 50.2 Bombs (cont.)

	Bomb, Practice, Signal, MK6
	Bomb, Practice, Signal, MK7
	M38A2, Practice Bomb, 100 lbs
	M85, Practice Bomb, 100 lbs
	Mk 106, Practice Bomb, 5 lbs
	Mk 15 Mod 3, Practice Bomb, 100 lbs
	Mk 15 series, Practice Bomb, 100 lbs
	Mk 5, Mk 15, Mk 21, Prac., 250 lbs
	Mk 5, Mk 15, Mk 21, Prac., 500 lbs
	Mk 65, Practice Bomb, 500 lbs
	Mk 76, Practice Bomb
	Mk 86, Mk 87, Mk 88, Prac., 250-1000 lbs
	Mk 86, Practice Bomb, 250 lbs
	Mk 89, Practice Bomb, 56 lbs
	Mk I, Practice Bomb, 100 lbs
	Mk II, Practice Bomb, 17 lbs
	Signal, Practice Bomb, Mk 4
	Signal, Practice Bomb, Mk 5
	Signal, Practice Bomb, Mk 6
	Signal, Practice Bomb, Mk 7
	Spotting Charge, CXU-1B, 2B, 3, 4B, 4AB
	Spotting Charge, CXU-3B, MK4, Mk5
	Spotting Charge, M1A1
	Spotting Charge, M39A1
CTT04 – Demolition Materials (TNT, Dynamite, Black Powder, Detonators, Blasting Caps, Fuses, Cratering Charges, Bangalore Torpedoes, etc.)	
	Blasting Caps, Elec & Non-elec., M6 & M7
	Blasting Caps, Electric, Commercial
	Blasting Caps
	CADS, PADS
	Explosive, Composition-4
	Explosives, Ammonium Nitrate
	Explosives, C-4 Blocks
	Explosives, Detonating Cord
	Explosives, Dynamite, Commercial
	Explosives, TNT
	Igniter, M23
	M60, Igniter
CTT05 – Hand Grenades, Live	Civil War, Hand Grenade, 6 Pound, Adams
	Civil War, Hand Grenade, Ketchum
	M26, Hand Grenade, Frag
	M33, Hand Grenade, Frag
	M67, Hand Grenade, Frag
	Mk II, Hand Grenade, Frag
CTT06 – Hand Grenades, Practice	Grenade, Practice, M69
	M21, Practice Hand Grenade
	M30, Practice Hand Grenade
	M62, Practice Hand Grenade
	M69, Practice Hand Grenade
	Mk 1A1, Practice Hand Grenade
	Mk 1A1, Training, Hand Grenade
	Grenade, Practice, M69

Figure 50.2 Bombs (cont.)

	M21, Practice Hand Grenade
	M30, Practice Hand Grenade
	M62, Practice Hand Grenade
	M69, Practice Hand Grenade
CTT07 – Ground Rockets, Rifle Grenades, Live	
	M17, Rifle Grenade, Fragmentation
	M28, Rocket, HEAT, 3.5"
	M30, Rocket, WP, 3.5"
	M31, Rifle Grenade, HEAT
	M6A1, Rocket, HEAT, 2.36"
	M6A3, Rocket, HEAT, 2.36"
	M72, Rocket, HEAT, 66mm
	M73, Rocket, Subcaliber, 35mm
	M9A1, Rifle Grenade, Anti-Tank~
	Mk I, VB Rifle Grenade, Live
	Rocket, SMAW, 83mm
CTT08 – Ground Rockets, Rifle Grenades, Practice	
	M11A2, Practice Rifle Grenade
	M29, Practice Rifle Grenade
	M29, Practice Rocket, 3.5"
	M7A1, Practice Rocket, 2.36"
	M7A3, Practice Rocket, 2.36"
	Mk I, VB, Practice Rifle Grenade
CTT09 – Landmines	M12, Mine, Practice Anti-Tank
	M16, Mine, Anti-Personnel
	M18A1, Mine, Anti-Personnel
	M1A1, Mine, Anti-Tank
	M2, Mine, Anti-Personnel
	M3, Mine, Anti-Personnel
	M4, Mine, Anti-Tank
	M5, Mine, Anti-Tank
	M68, Mine, Practice, Anti-Personnel
	M7A1, Mine, Anti-Tank
	M8, Mine, Practice, Anti-Personnel
	M81, Mine, Practice, Anti-Personnel
CTT10 – Medium Caliber (20mm, 25mm, 30mm)	
	20mm Cartridge Case
	20mm, Ball, M55A1
	20mm, Ball, MK1
	30mm TP, M788
	M183A1, Subcaliber, 14.5mm
CTT11 – Large Caliber (37mm and larger)	105mm, Fixed, HE & Prac, M38
	105mm, HE, M1
	105mm, HEAT-T, M622
	105mm, Illuminating, M314A3
	105mm, Smoke, M84 series
	105mm, Smoke, WP, M60
	105mm, TP-T, M67
	106mm, Recoilless Rifle, HEP-T, M346A1
	106mm, Recoilless Rifle, HEAT, M344
	12", AP, Mk 18
	12", AP, Mk 15
	12", HC, Mk 16
	12", TP, Mk 19

Figure 50.2 Bombs (cont.)

120mm, HE, M73
120mm, WP, XM929
155mm, Copperhead, M712
155mm, AP, M112
155mm, HE, M107
155mm, HE, MKI
155mm, Illumination, M118
155mm, Propelling Charge, M3
155mm, Propelling Charge, M4
155mm, Smoke, M116B1
155mm, Smoke, WP, M110
155mm, Smoke, WP, M825
16", AP, Mk 5
3" Subcaliber, M5
3", AP. M79
3", AP. M62
3", HE. M42 and M42A1
3", HE. MkIX
3", Mortar, HE, MK1
3", Practice. M42B2
3", Shrapnel. Mk I
3-Pounder, MK4
37mm, AP, M74
37mm, APC, M59
37mm, AP, M80
37mm, HE, M54
37mm, HE, MkII
37mm, Practice, M55A1
37mm, TP, M63
4.2", Mortar, HE, M3A1
4.2", Mortar, Illum, M335A2
4.2", Mortar, WP, M2A1
4.2", Mortar, WP, M328
4.5", Barrage Rocket, HE, M8
4.5", Barrage Rocket, HE
4.7", HE, M73
40mm, AP-T, M81
40mm, HE & HEI, Mk II
40mm, HE, M381
40mm, HE, M386
40mm, HE, M406
40mm, HEDP, M433
40mm, Parachute, Star, M583, M661, M662
40mm, Practice, M382
40mm, Practice, M385
40mm, Practice, M407
40mm, Practice, M781
57mm Recoilless, HE, M306A1
57mm Recoilless, HEAT, M307
57mm Recoilless, WP, M308A1
57mm, APC-T. M86
57mm, Recoilless Rifle, Canister, T25E5
57mm, Recoilless Rifle, HE, M306A1
57mm, Recoilless, HEAT, M307

Figure 50.2 Bombs (cont.)

6-Pounder
6", Mk 27
6", Mk 35
6", WP, Mk38 Mod 0
60mm, HE, M49
60mm, Illum, M83
60mm, Practice, M50A2
60mm, Sabot, M3
60mm, Smoke, WP, 302
60mm, Training, M69
7.2", Barrage Rocket, MkI
75mm Chemical, Smoke, M64
75mm Recoilless, WP, M311A1
75mm, AP, M72
75mm, Gun, HE, M48
75mm, How, HE, M41A1
75mm, Howitzer, HE, M48
75mm, Recoilless Rifle, HE, M309A1
75mm, Shrapnel, MKI
8", AP, Mk 21
8", Dummy, M14
8", HE, M106
81mm, Chemical, Smoke, M57
81mm, HE, M43
81mm, HE, M821
81mm, Illum, M301A2
81mm, Illum, M301A3
81mm, Illum, M853A1
81mm, Sabot, M1
81mm, Smoke, RP, M819
81mm, Smoke, WP, M370
81mm, TP, M43A1A1
81mm, Training, M68
84mm, AT-4, M136
90mm, AP. M77
90mm, APC-T. M82
90mm, HE. M71 and HE-T, M71A1
90mm, Practice Recoilless Rifle, M371
90mm, Practice. M58
90mm, Recoilless Rifle, HEAT, M371A1
Cartridge Case Specifications
Civil War, 10", Smoothbore Shot
Civil War, 100 Pound, Bolt
Civil War, 100 Pounder, Common
Civil War, 32 Pounder Common
Civil War, 32 Pounder, Bolt
Civil War, 32 Pounder, Dahlgren
Civil War, 42 Pounder, Common
Civil War, 42 Pounder, James
Civil War, 8" Grape Shot
Civil War, Fuzes
Civil War, Projectiles, General
Civil War, Projectiles, Smoothbore

Figure 50.2 Bombs (cont.)

CTT12 – Aerial Rockets (Live)	Civil War, Shell, Parrott
	Fuze, Point Detonating, M557
	Grenade, Duel Purpose, HE, M42
	11.75", Rocket, Tiny Tim
	2.75" Rocket Motor, Mk40
	2.75", Rockets General
	3.5", Rocket, Aircraft, MK4
	5", Rocket, HVAR
	5", Rocket, Zuni
	5", Rocket, Smoke, WP Mk 39
	Launcher, Rocket, LAU-3A
	Launcher, Rocket, LAU-68
	Rocket Launcher, LAU-3A
	Rocket Launcher, LAU-68
	Rocket, 11.75", Tiny Tim
CTT13 – Aerial Rockets (Practice)	115mm, Chemical Practice Rocket, M61
	2.25", Practice Rocket, MK6
	2.25", Practice Rocket, MK4
	2.25", Practice Rocket
	2.75", Practice Rocket, FFAR
	3.25", Target Rocket, M2
	3.25", Target Rocket, MK1
	5", Practice Rocket, Mk 8
	Rocket, 2.25", Practice, MK6
CTT14 – Guided Missiles	AGM-114, Missile, Hellfire
	AGM-45, Missile, Shrike
	AGM-62, Missile, Walleye
	AGM-65, Missile, Maverick
	AGM-88, Missile, HARM
	AIM-7E3, Missile
	AIM-9, Missile, Sidewinder
	BGM-71, Missile, TOW
	Dragon, Guided Missile
	E21, Warhead, Sergeant
CTT15 – Pyrotechnics (Smoke Grenades, Trip Flares, Signal Flares, Grenade & Artillery Simulators etc.)	
	AN-M14, Incendiary Grenade
	AN-M28 - 33, Signal, Double Star
	AN-M75, Signal, Illumination
	AN-M8, Smoke Grenade, HC
	AN-Mk4, 5, & 6, Signal, Drift
	M1, Smoke Pot, HC
	M110, Artillery Flash Simulator
	M115A2 Artillery Simulator
	M116A1, Grenade Simulator
	M117, M118, M119, Booby Trap Simulator
	M125A1, M158, M159, Signal, Illumination
	M126A1, M127A1, M195, Signal, Illumination
	M128A1, M194, M129A1, Signal, Smoke
	M15, Smoke Grenade, WP
	M16, Smoke Grenade
	M17A1, M19A1, M21A1, M51A1, Signal, Illumination,
	M18, Smoke Grenade

Figure 50.2 Bombs (cont.)

	M18A2, M20A1, M22A1, M52A1, Signal, Illumination
	M19, Rifle Grenade, WP
	M19A1, Rifle Grenade, Smoke, WP
	M22, Rifle Grenade, Smoke
	M49A1, Flare, Surface
	M4A2, Smoke Pot, HC
	M62, M64, M65, M66, Signal, Smoke
	Mk 13, Signal
	Mk 24, Flare, Parachute
	Mk 3, Ship Signal
	Simulator, Booby Trap, M117
	Simulator, Smokey Sam
CTT16 – Small Arms	Small Arms, General
CTT17 – Other	Any items not listed above

Figure 50.2 Bombs (cont.)

The default anomaly density is calculated using the following formula:

If removal acres are between 0 and 100 then:

$$\text{Density} = \text{ACRES} \times \text{ANOM}$$

If removal acres are between 101 and 10,000 then:

$$\text{Density} = (100 + [(\text{ACRES}-100)/5]) \times \text{ANOM}$$

If removal acres are between 10,001 and 50,000 then:

$$\text{Density} = (100 + [(10,000-100)/5] + [(\text{ACRES}-10,000)/25)]) \times \text{ANOM}$$

If removal acres are between 50,001 and 100,000 then:

$$\text{Density} = (100 + [(10,000-100)/5] \text{ s}+ [(50,000-10,000)/25)] + [(\text{ACRES}-50,000)/50]) \times \text{ANOM}$$

Where:

Density is in Total Anomalies for the given number of removal acres.

ANOM is in Anomalies per acre.
ACRES is the Removal Area, in acres.

Figure 50.3 Typical Small Ordnance

Default Ordnance Densities		
Type Of Range	**Default Density**	**Items per Acre**
Air-to-Air		50
Air-to-Ground		300
Artillery	200	
Bombing		50
Burial Pits		0
Guided Missiles	50	
Hand Grenade	50	
OB/OD	300	
Other		350
Mortar		250
Multiple/Combined Use	400	
Rifle Grenade, Anti-Tank Rocket	150	
Small Arms		250
Note: If multiple Range Types are selected, the default density is the highest individual density of the selected ranges.		

Figure 50.4 Ordnance Densities

It should be noted that these defaults assume that smaller acreages (up to 100) most likely represent a target area in which the density will be consistently high. As the acreage increases, it is assumed that the clearance area is covering more buffer and boundary areas in which the density per acre is significantly less. The valid range for total anomalies is 0–5,000,000 acres.

Scrap

This is the percentage of anomalies that are known or suspected to be scrap. For example, an anomaly density of 40 items per acre and a scrap percentage of 90% would actually mean that there are 36 scrap items per acre and 4 UXO. The scrap density will impact costs for on-site ordnance detonation by defining the amount of explosives required and the time required to destroy UXO. Scrap percentage does not have an effect on the amount of time required to "dig" anomalies due to the fact that an anomaly may be anything metallic (bomb, metallic rock, bottle cap, etc.). Therefore all anomalies take the same amount of time to dig and investigate. The valid range is 0–100%.

UXO Estimate Site Visit Task

This task includes costs related to conducting a sit visit. The objective of the site visit is for the cleanup team to gain familiarization with the site in general and to gather information required to assemble an acceptable and executable Work Plan. No UXO-related activities may be performed during the site visit. Prior to the site visit, an Abbreviated Site Safety and Health Plan (ASSHP) must be submitted to the contracting officer for review and approval. The site visit must be fully coordinated with the site project manager and any local points of contact, and must be in compliance with the ASSHP at all times. A daily safety briefing will be conducted prior to any site visits. Photographs and/or videotape will be required as part of the visit. Figure 50.5 displays typical default parameters.

Description	Quantity	UOM
UXO Supervisor (SUXO)	40	HRs
Project Manager	40	HRs
Staff Engineer	40	HRs
Airfare	3	EA
Per Diem	9	DAY
Car Rental	3	DAY
Other Direct Costs	1	LS

Note: These costs represent a 3 day site visit conducted by a UXO Supervisor, a Project Manager, and Staff Engineer.

Per diem has a quantity of 9 based on 3 people receiving per diem for 3 days (3 × 3 = 9). The daily per diem rate will be based on the location defined by the estimator.

Figure 50.5 Labor and Expenses for UXO Site Visit

Estimate Surveying Task

Determine Survey Area

Survey area defines the number of acres that need to be surveyed into 100' × 100' grids.

Grids serve to break up the removal area into multiple distinct (small) areas. Clearance will be conducted on a grid-by-grid basis. There is the possibility that some of the area in question may have been divided into grids during the study phase; in this case the estimator should reduce the number of acres to be surveyed correspondingly. Figure 50.6 shows productivity factors for different types of terrain. The number of grids is calculated by dividing the Survey Area by .230 (100' × 10' = 10,000 S.F., 43,560 S.F. in an acre, so 1 grid = 10,000/43,560 = .230 acre)

Identify Survey Method

Surveying is used for several different purposes when working ordnance sites. The first and most common is to positively identify and set property boundaries. The second purpose is to establish grids that will be used to subdivide the site into multiple small removal areas. The most important use of surveying in ordnance monitoring is to establish coordinates for magnetometer returns and found ordnance.

Surveying, as it is presented in this technology, can be conducted in one of 3 ways:

- Differential GPS Surveying with Automated Recording and Mapping System (potential accuracy to less than 1 meter).
- Hand-Held Global Positioning System (GPS) Units (50 meter accuracy)
- Conventional Surveying Methods

The default surveying method is differential GPS with mapping. All of the methods include a survey team, a UXO escort, and basic equipment. The different methods require specific equipment; selecting these methods will include the equipment required as follows:

- *Conventional Survey*—no additional equipment required.
- *Differential GPS Surveying with Automated Recording and Mapping System*—RACER will include a GPS base station (rental for task

Topography	PROD	Modifier	VPROD
Flat	2.00	100%	16
Gently rolling	1.90	95%	15.2
Heavy rolling	1.7	85%	13.6
Flat with gorges	1.6	80%	12.8
Rolling with gorges	1.4	70%	11.2
Mountainous	1	50%	8
PROD = ACRES/HOUR			
VPROD = ACRES/DAY			

Figure 50.6 Survey Productivity Table

duration) and a GPS system with automated recording and mapping features (rental for task duration).

- *Hand-Held Global Positioning System (GPS)*—Will add the purchase price of 3 hand-held GPS units (1 for each survey team member).

Estimate Survey Duration

The survey duration can be estimated using defaults in Figure 50.6. Survey productivity, and therefore duration, is affected by site topography, as shown in Figure 50.6

Where:

Survey Duration, Days = Total Acres/VPROD

Estimate Vegetation Removal Task

These parameters address vegetation removal within the site:

- Heavy Removal Acres
- Moderate Removal Acres
- Light Removal Acres
- No Removal Acres

The default value for the number of acres in each category is calculated by multiplying the total number of removal acres by the percentages in Figure 50.7. Different costs are associated with the amount of removal and the amount of vegetation. The estimator should evaluate these costs for each site, considering local market conditions.

Heavy Removal: Multiple trees and stumps and will be the most densely forested area within the given removal area. Note that a large number of heavy removal acres will result in very high vegetation removal costs.

Moderate Removal: Few trees and stumps, a medium amount of vegetation.

Light Removal: No trees and very few stumps, a light amount of vegetation.

| Vegetation Type | Removal Type* | | | |
	Heavy	Moderate	Low	None
Flat barren or low grass	0%	0%	25%	75%
Low grass and few shrubs	0%	0%	50%	50%
Heavy grass with numerous shrubs	0%	25%	50%	25%
Shrubs with some trees	25%	50%	25%	0%
Heavy shrubs with trees or forest	50%	25%	25%	0%
Productivity rate (acres/day)	1	2	5	N/A

*Example Calculation: If Total Acres = 100 and the vegetation type is "Shrubs with some trees," the default acres are: 25 acres—Heavy, 50 acres—Moderate, 25 acres—Light, and 0 acres—No removal.

Figure 50.7 Vegetation Removal Values

No Removal: No vegetation that will need to be removed and thus no removal costs. Examples might include meadows, desert, or beach areas.

It should be noted that the sum of the heavy, moderate, light and no removal areas must be equal to total removal area

Estimate UXO Mapping Task

The following parameters address UXO Mapping within the site:

- Geophysics
  - Acres
  - Towed Array
  - Navigational Tool
  - Number of Teams
  - Duration
- Mag and Flag
  - Acres
  - Number of Teams
  - Duration
  - Ordnance Locator
- Surface Clearance
  - Acres
  - Number of Teams
  - Duration

Geophysics

Acres

The total number of acres in which geophysics will be used to locate and map anomalies.

Towed Array

Use of a towed magnetometer array for use in monitoring (locating) ordnance and mapping the site. The towed array magnetometer will provide a magnetic anomaly map of the area in a shorter period of time than will manual mapping. Towed arrays work better on flat terrain with little brush or trees than on hilly property with dense shrubs. Any value from 0–100% of the total area for surveying with the towed magnetometer is appropriate. Selection of the towed magnetometer is independent of the hand-held magnetometers. The default value is based on topography as follows:

Flat	=	*85% Towed*
Gently Rolling	=	*75% Towed*
Heavy Rolling	=	*65% Towed*
Flat with Gullies and Gorges	=	*65% Towed*
Rolling with Gullies and Gorges	=	*40% Towed*
Mountainous	=	*0% Towed*

Towed array productivity information is presented in Figure 50.8.

Navigational Tool

This parameter refers to the type of navigation tool that will be used in conjunction with the EM-61 to map out anomalies. The following options are available.

Satellite: This is the default choice. Selecting this option would typically include the cost of a Differential GPS unit for the duration of the mapping phase. The unit includes a base station, repeater, and any other equipment required when using Differential GPS. Differential GPS requires that there are at least 5 satellites visible to the base station. Therefore, this option may not work well in heavily wooded areas or areas with many hills and valleys. This selection may add considerable cost to the mapping element, but it will result in far more accurate maps than the other options.

Manual: Selecting this option assumes that the maps are being generated manually based on the equipment operator entering data as they sweep the grid. This is the least accurate (and least expensive) of the options.

Number of Teams

This selection considers the number of mapping teams that will be used on the project for the geophysics task. Team makeup is 2 geophysicists and 1 UXO Technician III. The more teams, the shorter the duration of the mapping phase. The typical valid range for teams is 1–8.

Duration

This is the duration (in days) of the mapping element. Duration and number of teams are dynamically linked to each other. Extending the duration will lower the number of teams and vice versa. The default duration is calculated assuming that there are 3 teams working the site.

Mag and Flag

In a mag and flag operation, UXO technicians sweep the site with hand-held magnetometers. When anomalies are found, a flag is put into the ground to indicate the location of that anomaly. All of the flags will subsequently be removed and investigated.

Acres

This is the total number of acres in which mag and flag will be used to locate and map anomalies.

Number of Teams:

As discussed above, this selection considers the number of mapping teams that will be used on the project, specifically for the mag and flag

Topography	Rate, Grid/Team/Hour
Flat	10
Gently rolling	9.5
Heavy rolling	8.5
Flat with gorges	8.2
Rolling with gorges	7.5
Mountainous	6.0

Figure 50.8 Towed Array Productivity Rates

task. Team makeup is 2 Geophysicists and 1 UXO Technician III. The greater the number of teams, the shorter the duration of the mapping phase. The typical valid range for teams is 1–8.

Duration

This is the duration (in days) of the mapping element. Duration and number of teams are dynamically linked to each other. Extending the duration will lower the number of teams and vice versa.

Ordnance Locator

There are several locators available that cover most requirements. The default is the Schonstedt Technology GA-72CV, complete with all attachments. Other ordnance locators are:

- Geonics EM-61 Hand-Held Magnetometer
- Foerster M-26 Ordnance Locator
- Foerster Metex Locator
- Foerster Minex 2 FD
- Schonstedt Technology GA-72CV
- Geometrics Ordnance Locator Technology G-858 Magnetic Gradiometer

Selecting an ordnance locator does not affect any other parameter, but does have a cost implication due to rental/purchase costs of different units. It is important to note that different magnetometers are appropriate for different situations due to their different attributes. For example, the Schonstedt GA-72CV is not as sensitive as the Foerster M-26, but it is used extensively on jobs where the search depth requirement is 2' or less, and the ordnance items relatively large, like mortars or hand grenades. The GA-52CX does not have the sensitivity of the other locators and should only be used to find large, shallow items. The Foerster Minex 2 FD was developed for locating land mines. The Geometrics locator is basically equivalent to the M-26 locator, but it has an additional data-recording feature that plugs directly into mapping equipment. The G-858 is relatively new and not yet in widespread use by the military. For this reason, it is not the default unit.

Mag and flag productivity information is presented in Figure 50.9.

Surface Clearance

Acres

This is the total number of acres that will need to be surface-swept before anomaly identification begins. The default value is typically

Figure 50.9 Mag and Flag Productivity Rates

Topography	Rate, Grid/Team/Hour
Flat	1
Gently rolling	.95
Heavy rolling	.85
Flat with gorges	.82
Rolling with gorges	.75
Mountainous	.60

equal to the total removal acres. The number of acres to be surface-swept can be reduced depending on the history of the site. For example, if the site had been recently characterized (studied), it is likely that those areas have already been surface-swept. If there is no information available as to the history of the site, it should be assumed that the whole area will need to be swept before the mapping phase begins.

Number of Teams

As above, this selection refers to the number of sweep teams that will be used on the project for the surface clearance task. Team makeup is 2 UXO Technician II and 1 UXO Technician III. The greater the number of teams, the shorter the duration of the surface sweep phase. The typical valid range for teams is 1–8.

Duration

This is the duration (in days) of the surface sweep element. Duration and number of teams are dynamically linked; extending the duration will lower the number of teams and vice versa. The default duration is calculated assuming that there are three teams working the site.

Surface clearance productivity information is presented in Figure 50.10.

Estimate UXO Removal Task

These parameters address UXO Removal within the site:

- Ordnance Destruction
  - Percent and Amount of Ordnance Detonated by Electric Firing
  - Percent and Amount of Ordnance Detonated by Non-electric Firing
  - Percent and Amount of Ordnance Destroyed by Mass Detonation
- Operation Duration
- Number of Teams
- Number of Backhoes
- Explosives Requirements

Ordnance Destruction

Percent and Amount of Ordnance Detonated by Electric Firing

Ordnance that cannot be safely moved is often detonated in-place. This may be accomplished either electrically or mechanically. This parameter refers to the percentage of ordnance that will be detonated in place using electric methods. Electric detonation processes offer greater control and improved safety. The valid range is 0–100%. However, the

Topography	Rate, Grid/Team/Hour
Flat	8.0
Gently rolling	7.6
Heavy rolling	6.8
Flat with gorges	6.6
Rolling with gorges	6.0
Mountainous	4.8

Figure 50.10 Surface Clearance Productivity Rates

sum of the percentages detonated by electric firing, non-electric firing, and by mass detonation cannot exceed 100%. A typical default value is 30%. The amount of UXO to be destroyed by electric firing is calculated as follows:

Amount of Ordnance for Electric Firing (UXO Amount) = Total UXO amount (Anomalies—acres) × Electric Firing %

Percent of Ordnance Detonated by Non-electric Firing
This parameter refers to the percentage of ordnance that will be detonated in-place using non-electric or mechanical firing. Mechanical firing offers less control over the firing process than can be achieved by electric firing. The valid range is 0–100%. However, the sum of the percentages detonated by electric firing, non-electric firing, and mass detonation, cannot exceed 100%. A typical default value is 0%. The amount of UXO to be destroyed by non-electric firing is calculated as follows:

Amount of Ordnance for Non-electric Firing (UXO Amount) = Total UXO amount (Anomalies—acres) × Non-electric Firing %

Percent of Ordnance Destroyed by Mass Detonation (In-grid Consolidation)
Depending on the location and quantity of ordnance on a site, ordnance items may be moved to a central location and detonated en-masse. The valid range is 0–100%, but the sum of the percentages detonated in place by electric firing and non-electric firing, and the percent destroyed by mass detonation, cannot exceed 100%. A typical default value is 70%. The amount of UXO to be destroyed by mass detonation is calculated as follows:

Amount of Ordnance for Mass Detonation (UXO Amount) = Total UXO amount (Anomalies—acres) × Mass Detonation %

Operation Duration
The project duration for ordnance removal includes both setup and operational monitoring time. The duration for operations is calculated based on the difficulty of the terrain. The underlying driver is the amount of area 1 UXO team can cover per day. To estimate duration, the estimator needs to convert search rate to total duration for the job based on the number of UXO Technicians and the area to be swept.

To estimate duration, the estimator must consider productivity rates for the various phases of UXO Removal, as presented in Figure 50.11.

Durations can be estimated using the following equations.

Phase Duration: Reacquisition of anomalies (only applies to acreage in which geophysics was used)
Assume 2 teams are working on reacquisition as follows:

Team = (2 Geophysicists and 1 UXO Technician III) × 2

Phase Duration = Time to reacquire anomalies identified in the mapping phase (in team hours)

Geophysics Acres × Ordnance Density (Anomalies per acre)/ Reacquisition Rate (Anomalies per Team per Hour)

Phase Duration: Removal and Identification of anomalies

Assume 3 teams are working on removal as follows:

Team = 4 UXO Technician II and 1 UXO Technician III

Phase Duration = Time required to remove (dig) and identify anomalies (in team hours)

If depth < 2' then:

Phase Duration = Ordnance Density (Anomalies per Acre)/ Removal Rate (Anomalies per Team per Hour)

If depth > 2' then:

Phase Duration = Ordnance Density (Anomalies per Acre)/ Removal Rate (Anomalies per Team per Hour) × 1.15

Phase: Destroy (Render Safe) Anomalies Identified as UXO

Assume 2 teams are working on destruction as follows:

Team = (4 UXO Tech II and 2 UXO Tech III) × 2

Phase Duration = Time required to "Blow" (render safe) removed UXO (in team hours) = Unexploded Ordnance Density (Total UXO per Acre)/Destruction Rate (Anomalies per Team per Hour)

Number of Teams

Defaults are presented above for UXO (EOD) technician teams that perform removal and destruction. The default team makeup consists of 4 UXO Technician II and 1 UXO Technician III. In addition, the default is that 3 teams are available for removal activities, and 2 are used for destruction activities. The estimator should review these assumptions with the Site Supervisor; in particular, the number of teams. Changes to this default will affect the duration and cost of the removal action.

Number of Backhoes

The estimator should evaluate the number of teams to determine the number of backhoes that will be required to remove and identify anomalies. The default number is based on the search depth defined on the system definition screen. If search depth is equal to or less than 2', a reasonable assumption is 1 backhoe for every 3 teams. If the search

Removal Phase	Default Rate, Anomalies per Team per Hour	Description
Reaquire Anomalies	50	Time to reacquire anomalies identified in the mapping phase.
Remove and Identify Anomalies	10	Time required to remove (dig) and identify anomalies.
Destroy (Render Safe) Anomalies	10	Time required to "blow" (destroy) removed UXO.

Figure 50.11 UXO Removal Element Production Rates

depth is greater than 2', a good assumption is 1 backhoe for each team. The duration of the backhoe on site will be equal to the duration of the UXO removal effort.

Explosives Requirements

Explosives are required to render safe any anomalies that are determined to be a UXO (explosive hazard). Explosives requirements are calculated based on the total number of anomalies minus those anomalies considered scrap. For example, if the total number of anomalies is 100, and the scrap percentage is 90%, then 10 anomalies will be considered UXO and will require explosives. The default type of explosive is a 16-ounce TNT booster. C4 is also used as an explosive; however, C4 may be hard to obtain and requires approved storage facilities. The amount of explosives can be calculated as follows:

Amount of TNT, lbs (16 oz boosters; assume 1 lb per each detonation) = (Amount of Ordnance for Electric Firing × 1 lb TNT) + (Amount of Ordnance for Non-Electric Firing × 1 lb TNT) + (Amount of Ordnance for Mass Detonation × 1 lb TNT)

Amount of C4, blocks (assume 1 block per each detonation) = (Amount of Ordnance for Electric Firing × 1 block C4) + (Amount of Ordnance for Non-electric Firing × 1 block C4) + (Amount of Ordnance for Mass Detonation × 1 block C4)

The estimator should also include costs for detonation cord and initiators. Assume that the detonation cord is supplied in 1,000' rolls, and the minimum safe distance for each detonation between the detonator and the ordnance is 300'. Also, assume that 1 initiator is required for each detonation.

Design Information Needed for Detailed Estimates

The following types of detailed information, when available, can add detail and accuracy to estimates. Also included are design criteria and estimating rules of thumb that the estimator typically uses to determine values that are not known, or to check information provided by others.

Site Management

Site management includes days allowed for: Senior UXO Supervisor, Project Manager, UXO Supervisor, Quality Control Supervisor, and Safety Supervisor. Typically, the number of days is multiplied by 10 to calculate the total number of hours, since most OE Removal Action work is conducted in 10-hour days.

Senior UXO Supervisor Days

This is the number of days a Senior UXO Supervisor will be on the project site. The default value is equal to the entire project duration.

Project Manager Days

As with the Senior UXO Supervisor, the default value for the project manager is the entire project duration.

UXO Supervisor Days

This is the number of days that a UXO Supervisor (UXO Technician III) will be on the project site. The default value is 0 because a UXO Tech III is already included in many of the tasks. There may be certain situations in which a UXO Supervisor will need to be included for site management. In this case, the estimator should add the appropriate number of days that this person will be needed.

Quality Control Supervisor Days

The default value for the Quality Control Supervisor's time on the site is the entire project duration.

Safety Supervisor Days

The default value is equal to the entire project duration.

Reporting and Stakeholder Involvement

These parameters address Reporting and Stakeholder Involvement:

- Level of Detail Required in Reporting
- Level of Stakeholder Involvement: Number of Meetings
- Other Reports
  - UXO Removal Report
  - Work Plan
  - Explosives Safety Submission

Level of Detail Required in Removal Reporting

Several factors may contribute to this definition, such as the amount of public exposure associated with the site, the potential to cause damage (to the environment or to persons), the level of contamination, and the presence of special factors (endangered species, historical monuments on the site). The level of detail will determine the cost of the UXO Removal Report, the Work Plan, and the Explosives Safety Submission. Typical options include:

Low: Generally a small job (100 acres or less) with little public interest.

Moderate: Generally a medium size job (between 100–1,000 acres) with some public interest.

High: Generally a large project (1,000+ acres) with a high level of public interest. High should be selected if there are any endangered species, historically significant sites, or the potential for public exposure is high.

Level of Stakeholder Involvement: Number of Meetings

This is the anticipated number of meetings that will be attended by the site Project Manager (PM) and the Senior UXO Supervisor (UXOS). The total hours are calculated by multiplying the number of meetings by the hours associated with the level of detail specified, as indicated in Figure 50.12.

Reports

UXO Removal Report

The UXO Removal Report is the last step in an OE Removal Project. This report fully documents all activities performed during the project

Level of Detail	PM Hrs	SUXO Hours
Low	4	4
Moderate	6	6
High	8	8

Figure 50.12 Labor for Project Meetings

and includes quantities, costs, durations, and any other elements of the project. The cost for developing this report is based on the level of detail specified by the estimator. Figure 50.13 provides labor hours as a basis for the total report cost.

Work Plan:

Every UXO remediation project requires preparation and submittal of a site-specific Work Plan (WP) for approval prior to any field work other than the initial site visit. The WP describes the contractor's proposed method of accomplishing the required work in accordance the Basic Contract, this SOW, the current site-specific Explosive Safety Submission, and associated reference documents. Figure 50.14 provides labor-hours as a basis for the total cost of producing the report.

Level of Detail	Low	Moderate	High
Certified Industrial Hygienist	8	12	16
Drafter I	16	20	24
Project Manager	40	80	120
GIS Manager	16	24	32
Senior UXO Supervisor	40	60	80
Pro. Geophysicist	16	24	32
UXO QC	16	24	32
UXO SO	16	24	32
Word Processor	40	60	80
Staff Engineer	16	24	32
Senior Engineer	8	12	16
Site Project Manager	8	16	24

Figure 50.13 UXO Removal Report Hours Breakdown

Level of Detail	Low	Moderate	High
Certified Industrial Hygienist	12	16	20
Project Manager	20	40	60
GIS Manager	20	30	40
SUXOS	20	40	60
Geophysicist	20	24	28
UXO Quality Control	12	16	20
UXO Safety Officer	12	16	20
Program Manger	4	8	16
Word Processor	40	40	40
Staff Engineer	40	40	40
Senior Engineer	24	24	24
Contract Administrator	8	8	8

Figure 50.14 Work Plan Hours Breakdown

Explosives Safety Submission

An Explosives Safety Submission (ESS) describes the safety criteria to be employed during an Ordnance and Explosives (OE) Removal Operation. The ESS should be a separate document and should include the following items:

- *Reason for Presence of OE*: A brief description of why OE exists in the specific area(s) being covered by the submission.
- *Amount and Type of OE*: The expected amount(s) and type(s) of OE based on historical research or data generated during the study phase.
- *Most Probable Munition*: The most probable munition is the round with the greatest fragment distance that can be reasonably expected to exist in any particular OE area.
- *Start Date:* The date the removal operation will begin.
- *FrostLine:* The depth of the frost penetration for the given area.
- *Clearance Techniques:* Describe the techniques that will be used to locate, recover, and destroy OE.
- *Alternative Techniques:* If the on-site method to destroy UXO is other than detonation, the method should be described.
- *Off-site Destruction:* If OE cannot be destroyed on-site, explain why and how they will be destroyed.
- *Technical Support:* Summarize Explosives Ordnance Disposal (EOD), Technical Escort Unit (TEU), and/or contractor support for the project.
- *Land Use Restrictions:* Define and explain.
- *Public Involvement:* Describe the extent and the reason for it.
- *Maps:* Site maps, area maps, and any others that are of relevance to the project (including any geophysical maps, grid maps, etc.) should be provided.

Figure 50.15 provides labor-hours as a basis for the total report cost.

Level of Detail	Low	Moderate	High
Certified Industrial Hygienist	4	8	12
Project Manager	16	32	48
Senior UXO Supervisor	16	32	48
UXO Quality Control	4	4	4
Word Processor	40	40	40
Senior Engineer	4	8	12
Surveyor	16	32	48
Drafter I	12	24	36

Figure 50.15 Explosives Safety Submission Hours Breakdown

Safety Level

Safety level specifies the level of personal protection that is required to perform the ordnance survey and removal work. The normal protection level is Level "D" safety shoes, gloves, hardhat, eye protection and proper work clothing (coveralls). If chemical warfare material is expected, level "B" or level "A" clothing ensembles may be required. Unless you choose otherwise, the default safety level is Safety Level E. It should be noted that the productivity rates in this section are based on real project data. Therefore, estimating that work at any safety level other that E could produce artificially high cost estimates, due to the reduced productivity multipliers of other safety levels.

Related Costs

Costs for disposal of non-explosive materials as well as cleared vegetation should be considered in the estimate, if they are to be transported off-site. In addition, costs for security personnel may be appropriate to consider if they are necessary for high security or high-hazard areas prior to completion of the OE Removal Action.

Site Work and Utilities

Site work and utilities that may be applicable include:

- Fencing
- Signage
- Clear and Grub (non-explosive areas)

If the site is remote, a temporary access road may be required for use by the OE removal crews.

Conclusion

Ordnance and Explosives (OE) Removal Action includes the costs of searching for, marking, and removing unexploded ordnance (UXO) from munitions contaminated property. The primary cost drivers are the amount of acreage with UXO, the topography and vegetation, and the type of UXO. These, in turn, drive costs for labor, materials, and equipment rental. The cost engineer should work closely with a qualified UXO team to determine the various investigation, removal, and destruction approaches that are applicable for the site prior to developing the estimate.

Chapter 51

UXO Active Target Clearance

UXO Active Target Clearance is the process of clearing UXO (unexploded ordnance) from military active ranges. The major costs include labor and travel, explosive ordnance destruction materials, and other miscellaneous tasks required for Active Range Clearance. A *Military Active Range* is a range that is currently in military service. An *ordnance*, for the purpose of estimating, is any chemical substance or physical item related to munitions that is designed to cause damage to personnel or material through explosive force, incendiary action, or toxic effects. Information specific to six installations is included in this chapter. These are: Luke Air Force Base (AFB), AZ; Eielson AFB, AK; Warren Grove Air National Guard Base (ANGB), PA; Nellis AFB, NV; Hill AFB, UT; Eglin AFB, FL; and Avon Park AFB, FL. The algorithms used in this technology are based on data typical of these six installations. This section also includes the option to estimate for "large generic" and "small generic" bases, which use the same algorithms with fewer defaults.

The Active Target Clearance technology does not cover activities such as UXO response missions (off-range), environmental remediation efforts, range maintenance, target maintenance, VIP support, planning, or scrap removal. While all of these tasks are part of the overall UXO and Explosive Ordnance Disposal mission of the military, and all have an effect on the overall budget, they are outside the scope of this technology.

The information contained in this chapter is relevant only to the performance of UXO Active Target Clearance by contractor personnel. Military personnel often perform this task. However, the cost structure and target clearance activities for military personnel are different than those of commercial contractors. Thus, information and defaults contained herein are representative only of commercial contractor costs and clearance methods.

Applications and Limitations

Applications

Locating and removing unexploded ordnance (UXO) from Military Active Ranges.

- Covers operational ranges.
- Removal of ordnance items from the ground surface.

Limitations

- Not used for underwater UXO operations that require diving or similar activities for detection and recovery.
- Does not address removal, storage, transportation, and destruction of chemical warfare material (CWM) found in UXO or other containerized form.
- Does not cover special handling methods for low-level radioactive ordnance, such as depleted uranium.
- Does not address buried munitions sites.
- Does not include costs related to planning the operation or for scrap disposal.
- Does not include costs related to subsurface investigations. (See Chapter 50, "Ordnance and Explosives Removal Action Technology.")
- Information contained in this chapter does not include defaults or costs for military personnel. It is assumed that commercial contractor labor is used for active range clearance activities.

Process Configurations and Treatment Train Considerations

For reference purposes, the definition of ordnance includes the following: non-nuclear bombs and warheads; artillery, mortar and rocket ammunition; small arms ammunition; antipersonnel and antitank land mines; guided and ballistic missiles; demolition charges; pyrotechnics; grenades; and containerized and uncontainerized high explosives and propellants. Fuses, boosters, bursters and rocket motors are considered ordnance.

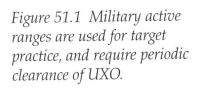

Figure 51.1 Military active ranges are used for target practice, and require periodic clearance of UXO.

The procedures for recovering CWM found in the field are well defined by and usually restricted to the military. If CWM is found with UXO, procedures are to secure the site and contact a military Technical Escort Unit (TEU) to perform recovery, removal and disposal. Therefore, the operations associated with CWM are not included in this chapter's technology.

Every member of an ordnance search and recovery team involved directly with searching for and handling ordnance must be a graduate of the Naval School, Explosive Ordnance Disposal Division and have at least 3 years operational experience. Qualified contractor personnel who meet the minimum requirements are known as UXO technicians. Throughout this text, the term *UXO Technician* is used to refer to contractor personnel. EOD technicians, on the other hand, can be military or contractor personnel.

Basic Information Needed for Estimating

It is possible to create a reasonable cost estimate using some basic, required parameters. With more detailed information, one can create a more precise, site-specific estimate using a secondary set of parameters. There are 5 main categories of basic parameters:

- Generic
- Operational
- Target
- Ordnance
- Travel

Generic Parameters
- Location
- Range Type
- Site Distance

Location
Figure 51.2 presents locations of specific U.S. Air Force Bases with active ranges and default assumptions for topography and vegetation. For other ranges, the estimator should determine the typical topography and vegetation characteristics.

Site Location	City/State	Topography	Vegetation
Luke AFB	Phoenix, AZ	Gently Rolling	Barren or Low Grass
Nellis AFB	Las Vegas, NV	Flat	Barren or Low Grass
Eglin AFB	Niceville, FL	Gently Rolling	Shrubs w/ Some Trees
Hill AFB	Salt Lake, UT	Heavy Rolling	Low Grass and Few Shrubs
Warren Grove ANG	Atlantic City, NJ	Gently Rolling	Heavy Shrubs w/ Trees
Avon Park AFB	Sebring, Fl	Flat	Shrubs w/ Some Trees
Eielson AFB	Fairbanks, AK	Rolling with Gorges	Heavy Grass

Figure 51.2 Major Air Force Weapons Ranges in the United States

Range Type

For this technology, the type of range selected affects whether or not there are default clearance areas. Point Targets have default clearance radii based on the clearance frequency. Area Targets require estimator knowledge of either the clearance radius or the total clearance area.

Point Target: A target with a definite, single aiming point that serves as the center of a distinct circular clearance pattern (e.g., a single target vehicle or a BDU-33 circle).

Area Target: A target with multiple aiming points 75' or greater across (length or width), which would create overlapping circular clearance patterns [e.g., a convoy of vehicles, an airfield complex, or a surface-to-air-missile (SAM) site].

Site Distance

Site distance refers to the one-way distance to the site, in miles, from the office of the personnel performing the clearance work. Having this information helps the estimator determine whether the crew will travel via car or van, or via airplane or other commercial transportation method. Travel and per diem costs should be included in the estimate and are discussed later in this chapter.

Operational Parameters

- Frequency
- Season
- Target Clearance Duration
- Distance of Access Roads

Frequency

The frequency selected affects the default clearance area (radius) if the scenario is designated as a "Point Target." The specific assumptions associated with the various frequencies are as follows.

Limited (quantity/use) Day Clearance Scenario
Periodic Range Residue Cleanup/Decontamination

The frequency for range residue cleanup is generally 3 months or 75 Use-Days. The targets used for missiles, rockets, and bomb testing/training of all UXO and inert residue are cleared to a total radius of 300'. The associated total default area for a Point Target is 6.5 acres. Evaluation of day clearance scenarios requires consideration of two separate areas that typically have different ordnance densities: an inner circle that is within 150' of the target, and an outer circle within the total bermed area that encompasses the 300' radius. Rules of thumb for estimating these two areas for a Point Target are displayed in Figure 51.3.

Annual Clearance Scenario

The areas around the targets used for missiles, rockets, and bomb testing/training of all UXO and inert residue are annually cleared to a radius of 1,000'. In addition, the access ways into the tactical targets, as well as the area 100' on either side of the access ways, are cleared annually. The associated default area is 72.1 acres.

Five-Year Clearance Scenario—Complete Clearance

A complete clearance on each existing range is performed every five years. The Complete Clearance includes inspection, removal, and disposal of munitions and unusable target debris and may be accomplished incrementally (e.g., 20% of the required area per year for five years). The criteria for complete clearance is a radius of approximately 3,000' (1 nautical mile) around each target, or an area that has a density factor of less-than-or-equal-to 5 whole ordnance items per acre, whichever is closer to the target. The associated default area is 775.5 acres.

Season

The season in which a clearance is being performed may have a significant effect on clearance operations. For this technology the only assumptions made are that the workday is 7 hours instead of 10 hours for bases in the southern states, and that clearance at Eielson AFB in the winter is illogical and therefore it is not an option. Rain and other factors should be considered when defining the clearance duration. However, there are no published rules of thumb about the effect of inclement weather (or other) conditions on target clearance productivity.

Target Clearance Duration

The duration of a clearance operation is very important because all activity on that target must be suspended during the clearance. Thus, the clearance must have a balance between timing, safety, and number of available technicians. The underlying driver is the amount of area one UXO team can cover per day. The clearance duration is used to calculate the default number of technicians required to perform the clearance. The typical maximum value for this parameter is 90 days.

Distance of Access Roads

This parameter is the distance along the access road from the front gate to the outside perimeter of the target that needs to be cleared. For the 5-year clearance scenario, this parameter affects the total clearance area by increasing it to include the access road area. The access road area is

Total Clearance Acreage	Inner Circle Clearance Acreage, Point Target	Outer Circle Clearance Acreage, Point Targer
0–1.6 acres	1.6 acres	0
1.7– 6.5 acres	1.6 acres	Total Acreage–1.6
6.6–72.1 acres*	1.6 acres	4.9 acres
> 72.1 acres*	1.6 acres	4.9 acres

*Note: For areas larger than 6.5 acres, the remaining acreage is typically cleared either during an annual or 5-year clearance event.

Figure 51.3 Rules of Thumb for Clearance Areas

calculated as the distance of the road (feet) multiplied by 200' (100' each direction from road center). A good assumption for a default density of UXO on access roads is 0.10 UXO/acre for the access road acreage. Typically, a maximum of 10 miles of access road distance is included.

Target Parameters

The required parameters under this category include:

- Topography
- Vegetation
- Is Range a Test Range?
- Clearance Area

Topography

Topography affects the rate of search and the search methodology, and thus the productivity rate of the clearance. Terrain can also have a major effect on the condition (wear and tear) on the vehicles being employed for the clearance. Figure 51.4 shows the impact of topography on clearance productivity.

Vegetation

The type of vegetation has an impact on the rate of ordnance recovery and safety. High vegetation densities tend to slow clearance operations by limiting the type of vehicles that can be used, as well as increasing the time required to locate and safely clear UXO. Figure 51.5 shows the impact of vegetation on clearance productivity.

Is Range a Test Range?

A Test Range significantly increases the duration and/or labor-hours required to perform the clearance. This is because a test range typically has a much greater area in which ordnance items have been dropped. This results in greatly reduced productivity rates that, in turn, affect overall project level of effort.

Figure 51.4 Topography and Clearance Productivity

Impact of Topography on Clearance Productivity	
Topography	Topography Productivity Rate
Flat	0
Gently rolling	5%
Heavy rolling	15%
Flat with gorges	15%
Rolling with gorges	25%
Mountainous	50%

Clearance Area

This is the area that the clearance scenario will cover. This value is typically expressed as either acres or as the distance to be cleared from target center in feet (radius). The 2 methods used to define area are dynamically linked; changing one will have a proportional effect on the other. Typically, to calculate "Total UXO" and project duration, the clearance area is added to the area calculated for the access roads.

Ordnance Parameters

The required parameters under this category include:

- Ordnance Type
- Total UXO

Ordnance Type

The type of ordnance will determine the amount of time it takes to recover each ordnance item. Each item has unique fuzing and safety characteristics. In addition, the larger the ordnance item, the greater the effort required to remove that item from the range. (Increased effort implies greater time to remove as well as increased dependence on machinery, such as backhoes.) These factors impact the cost of removal.

There is no typical default at a given range. Ordnance types should be selected from 1 of the 12 classes as they are recorded on the standard Department of Defense 3579 report for the given range. Figure 51.6 lists typical ordnance types. All that apply, as well as the associated total UXO count of each type, should be selected. If the type of ordnance known to exist does not have an exact match on the list, select the type that most closely resembles the expected ordnance. The type of ordnance will affect the explosive amounts, UXO density, and recovery rates.

Total UXO

Total UXO refers to the total actual number of ordnance items that need to be cleared. This number can vary widely depending on the type of range or target and the type of ordnance that was deployed on the selected target. Total UXO affects the project duration, the number of

Figure 51.5 Vegetation and Clearance Productivity

Impact of Vegetation on Clearance Productivity	
Vegetation Type	Vegetation Productivity Rate
Flat barren or low grass	0
Low grass and few shrubs	5%
Heavy grass with numerous shrubs	15%
Shrubs with some trees	15%
Heavy shrubs with trees or forest	25%

personnel required for the clearance, and the amount of explosives needed to complete the clearance. Default total UXO calculations assume that active clearance has been continually performed during the life of the target. The typical valid range for total UXO is 1–10,000 items.

UXO density over an area depends on the type of ordnance and the frequency of clearance. Figure 51.7 presents typical densities; the ordnance types are referenced in Figure 51.6.

To calculate Total UXO items that require clearance, the estimator must calculate the UXO items for each type of ordnance present and then add them together. The calculations are:

Day Clearance Scenario:

UXO Items (each type of ordnance, ORDA to ORDP) = Inner Target Acreage (ac) × Day Clearance Inner Target Density (UXO/Ac, from Figure 51.7) + Outer Target Acreage (ac) × Day Clearance Outer Target Density (UXO/Ac, from Figure 51.7)

Total UXO Items = SUM (UXO Items ORDA to ORDP)

Annual Clearance Scenario:

UXO Items (each type of ordnance, ORDA to ORDP) = Annual Clearance Acreage (ac) × Annual Clearance Target Density (UXO/Ac, from Figure 51.7)

Total UXO Items = SUM (UXO Items ORDA to ORDP)

Ordnance Types	Example Munitions
Sub-caliber Practice Bombs	BDU 33 / MK106
Practice Bombs	BDU 50 / BDU 56
Bombs	MK 82 / MK 84
Sub-munitions	BLU 97 / BLU 91
Unknown	Unknown
Dispersers	SUU 64 / MK 20
Grenades	GBS
Fuses	FMU 139 / M 904
Rockets	2.75" rockets / 5" rockets
Missiles	AGM 65 / AIM 9
Miscellaneous (CAD/PAD)	CXU 3 / M23A1 ignitors
Projectiles < 40 mm	N/A
Projectiles ≥ 40mm	N/A
Pyrotechnics	LUU-2 / MJU-7
Small Arms	7.62mm / .50 cal

Figure 51.6 Typical Ordnance Types

5-Year Clearance Scenario:

UXO Items (each type of ordnance, ORDA to ORDP) = [5-Year Clearance Acreage + Access Road Clearance Acreage (ac)] × 5-year Clearance Target Density (UXO/Ac, from Figure 51.7)

Total UXO Items = SUM (UXO Items ORDA to ORDP)

Travel Parameters

The required parameters under this category include:

- TDY Personnel
- Travel
- Per diem and hotels

TDY Personnel

This is the total number of personnel (typically UXO technicians) who will need to be mobilized from other locations to complete the clearance. It is reasonable to assume that any TDY personnel will require travel time and an additional 2 days of site-specific training, in addition to the time allotted for the clearance duration.

Travel

Airfare: The estimator should consider airfare costs for any personnel who need to travel to the site to perform the clearance activity.

Type of Ordnance/Code		Day Clearance Inner Target Density (UXO/Ac)	Day Clearance Outer Target Density (UXO/Ac)	Annual Clearance Target Density (UXO/Ac)	5-Year Clearance Target Density (UXO/Ac)
Subcaliber practice bombs	ORDA	753.125	185.102	8.110	0.179
Practice bombs	ORDB	101.875	25.102	0.747	0.014
Bombs	ORDC	3.750	1.020	0.061	0.003
Submunitions	ORDD	370.625	91.020	5.991	0.222
Unknown	ORDE	1.000	0.000	0.000	0.000
Dispersers	ORDF	1.250	0.408	0.015	0.000
Grenades	ORDG	0.625	0.204	0.015	0.000
Fuses	ORDH	5.625	1.429	0.030	0.000
Rockets	ORDI	2.500	0.612	0.046	0.000
Missiles	ORDJ	0.625	0.204	0.000	0.000
Misc. (CAD/PAD)	ORDK	8.125	2.041	0.030	0.001
Pyrotechnics	ORDL	8.175	2.245	0.091	0.003
Projectiles < 40mm	ORDM	388.800	94.490	10.780	0.007
Projectiles > 40mm	ORDN	5.625	1.429	0.107	0.004
Small arms	ORDP	63.125	15.150	1.189	0.001

Figure 51.7 Typical Ordnance Densities

Vehicle Usage: This is the number of miles that will be traveled each day using personal or rental vehicles. For personal vehicles, the cost is calculated by multiplying the total days by the number of miles each day by the appropriate rate per mile. For rental vehicles, the estimator should evaluate the project duration and apply appropriate rental rates. For government-supplied vehicles, the estimator should confirm that there are no additional charges that will be incurred by the contractor.

The typical vehicle is a standard 4 × 4 pickup truck ("6-Pack"). It is reasonable to assume that one truck will be added to the estimate for every team of UXO personnel, defined as 4 UXO Technicians and 1 UXO Supervisor. A dump truck and a front-end loader are also typically needed for the duration of the project.

Per Diem and Hotels

The estimator should calculate costs for per diem and hotels based on the duration of the project and the number of TDY personnel. Since the project will be performed for the Federal Government, the estimator should obtain the most recent Joint Federal Travel Regulations for the current per diem and hotel rates in various locations. Average default values are $42.00 per day for per diem, and $65.00 per day for hotel.

Estimating Labor-Hours

Labor-hours are estimated using the duration information provided by the estimator, and adjusting it for productivity factors, as demonstrated in the following calculation:

If range is not a training range:

Total Labor-Hours = Total UXO Items/SUM {[(Default Labor Productivity Rate × (100 - Topography Productivity Rate)]* (100 – Vegetation Productivity Rate)}$_N$

If range is a training range:

Total Labor-Hours = Total UXO Items/SUM {{[(Default Labor Productivity Rate × (100 - Topography Productivity Rate)]* (100 – Vegetation Productivity Rate)} /4}$_N$

Where:

Default Labor Productivity Rate is presented in Figure 51.8, expressed as UXO Item/Technician/Hour.

Topography Productivity Rate is presented in Figure 51.4, expressed as a percentage.

Vegetation Productivity Rate is presented in Figure 51.5, expressed as a percentage.

N(subscript) refers to the sum of the productivity rate calculations for each ordnance item selected.

To estimate the number of clearance personnel based on the total labor-hours required for the clearance, the following calculation can be used:

Total Number of Clearance Personnel = (Total Labor Hours / Duration, days) / Workday, hrs/day

Where:

Duration is in days, provided by the estimator

Workday is 7 hrs/day during the summer and 10 hrs/day during all other seasons.

As a rule of thumb, total technicians should not be less than 2 or more than 30 for safety reasons. If the calculation provides a number greater than 30, the team should consider either decreasing the number of UXO items for clearance or increasing the duration of the clearance activity.

The estimator can translate the total number of clearance personnel to labor categories using the rule of thumb that personnel work in teams. Each team is defined as a minimum of 2 and a maximum of 5 personnel, comprised of 4 UXO Technicians and 1 UXO Supervisor.

Estimating Explosives Costs

The amount and type of explosive materials used depends on the type of unexploded ordnance at the site. Figure 51.9 presents rules of thumb for estimating explosive materials needed for each ordnance code.

To determine the cost of each of the 3 explosives items (TNT, detonation cord, and igniters), the estimator should total the amount for the ordnance types/codes present at the site, add 5% to the total of each item, and multiply the quantity by the unit cost of each item.

Ordnance Code/Type (Figures 51.6, 51.7)	Default Labor Productivity Rate, UXO Item/Technician/Hour
ORDA	15
ORDB	1
ORDC	2
ORDD	15
ORDE	.01
ORDF	3
ORDG	3
ORDH	3
ORDI	2
ORDJ	4
ORDK	6
ORDL	6
ORDM	10
ORDN	3
ORDP	250

Figure 51.8 Labor Productivity by Ordnance Types

Design Information Needed for Detailed Estimates

Following are descriptions of the types of detailed information that, when available, can add detail and accuracy to estimates. There are 2 main categories of detailed information:

- Additional Labor Activities
- Special Safety Concerns

Additional Labor Activities

Additional costs could be incurred for the following labor activities, if they are necessary during the target clearance activity:

- Oversight Visit
- Escort

Oversight Visit

This item covers costs associated with senior level personnel visiting the site to conduct a project evaluation. If such a visit is required, it is normally performed by a Senior UXO Supervisor. The estimator should include the costs for travel and labor.

Escort

This accounts for costs related to escorting various personnel to the clearance area. If escort is required, it is reasonable to assume 10 hours of UXO technician time for each escort visit.

Ordnance Code/Type (Figures 51.6, 51.7)	Calculation of Amount of TNT Booster, 16 oz, Each	Calculation for Amount of Detonator Cord, Linear Feet	Calculation of Number of Igniters, Each
ORDA	UXO Items, ORDA × 0.15	0	(UXO Items, ORDA/100) × 2
ORDB	UXO Items, ORDB × 3	(UXO Items, ORDB × 3) + (UXO Items, ORDA/100) × 200	(UXO Items, ORDA/100) × 2
ORDC	UXO Items, ORDC × 1	0	UXO Items, ORDC × 2
ORDD	UXO Items, ORDD × 0.33	0	UXO Items, ORDD × 2
ORDE	UXO Items, ORDE × 2	0	UXO Items, ORDE × 2
ORDF	UXO Items, ORDF × 1	0	UXO Items, ORDF × 2
ORDG	UXO Items, ORDG × 0.33	0	UXO Items, ORDG × 1
ORDH	UXO Items, ORDH × 0.33	0	UXO Items, ORDH × 2
ORDI	UXO Items, ORDI × 1	0	UXO Items, ORDI × 2
ORDJ	UXO Items, ORDJ × 4	0	UXO Items, ORDJ × 2
ORDK	UXO Items, ORDK × 0.33	0	UXO Items, ORDK × 1
ORDL	UXO Items, ORDL × 0.33	0	UXO Items, ORDL × 1
ORDM	(UXO Items, ORDM/4) × 1	0	(UXO Items, ORDM/100) × 2
ORDN	UXO Items, ORDN × 1	0	UXO Items, ORDN × 2
ORDP	(UXO Items, ORDP/15) × 0.33	0	(UXO Items, ORDP/15) × 1

Figure 51.9 Booster and Detonation Guidelines

Special Safety Concerns

Additional costs could be incurred for the following special safety concerns, if they are relevant to the target clearance activity:

- Use of Encapsulation Suit
- Monitoring

Use of Encapsulation Suit

Should an encapsulation suit (Level "A") be required during any of the clearance activities, the estimator should work with the clearance team to determine the effect on productivity rates, and include the costs for the increased labor-hours as well as the cost for the actual suit itself.

Monitoring

Air monitoring and medical monitoring could be required under special circumstances dictated by the military. To account for these costs, the estimator should determine the number of days these activities are required, and assume that one individual performs the task continuously over each day for each type of monitoring. The requirements for medical monitoring differ with each site, and the estimator should be aware of applicable policies prior to developing the estimate for this activity.

Related Costs

- Environmental
- Archeological
- Endangered Species Survey

Environmental

There are many environmental issues associated with UXO. The EPA and DOD have varying opinions on the adverse environmental impacts caused by UXO. While environmental impacts are important, they are considered secondary to the acute, dangerous explosive hazard associated with UXO. If environmental concerns are noted, the estimator should work with the project team to determine how to estimate them. Following are some of the most common environmental concerns associated with UXO:

Small Arms Lead Contamination

Small arms firing ranges are essential to weapons training and the mission of the military. However, range use often produces soil contaminated with metals from spent bullets. This contamination can create environmental and occupational health problems during range operation and maintenance, as well as during redesign, reuse, and remediation of the range. Lead contamination in soils at firing range sites can be transported via the following mechanisms:

- *Airborne Particulate Lead:* Very small lead particles can become airborne if wind, foot traffic, or maintenance activities disturb contaminated soil. Airborne particles smaller than 10 microns can be inhaled, and fine particles smaller than 250 microns in diameter can be incidentally ingested. Soil particles smaller than 100–200 microns are likely to be ingested because fine particles adhere to skin, while larger particles are easily brushed off.
- *Storm Water Run-off and Erosion:* Storm water run-off has the potential to erode and transport contaminated soil and lead particles away from the normal confines of a firing range. Rainfall intensity, ground slope, soil type, and obstructions, such as

vegetation and fabricated structures, will influence the potential transport of lead away from the range. Once the contaminated soil is transported beyond the firing range's boundary, additional environmental impact (e.g., bioaccumulation or bioconcentration) and human exposure could occur.

- *Dissolved Lead in Groundwater/Surface Water*: At a neutral pH, lead is relatively insoluble. As water becomes more acidic (decreasing pH), lead solubility tends to increase. When storm water (normally slightly acidic) comes into contact with lead-contaminated soil, the lead can be dissolved into the water and transported to nearby groundwater or surface water. If sufficient lead is mobilized, environmental receptors can be affected, and risk to human health could occur if these sources are used for drinking water.

Refer to Chapters 18, "Ex Situ Solidification/Stabilization," and 33, "Soil Washing" for more information on estimating lead contamination remediation costs.

Explosive Soil Contamination

The impacts to the surrounding soil from UXO can vary widely. There are many parameters involved that make each situation different, including the type of UXO involved, its condition, the surrounding soil characteristics, and the local climate. It is likely that an environmental investigation would be required by personnel trained in UXO investigation procedures if the nature and extent of contamination were considered serious.

Archeological

In some cases, a systematic search and recording of any archeological sites or resources within the clearance area could be required. The estimator should consult archeological and cultural/resources specialists to determine the scope and level of effort of such an activity.

Endangered Species Survey

Endangered species surveys involve a search to locate all endangered/threatened species of concern within the clearance area. If there are endangered species issues related to the clearance, awareness training should also be provided to all personnel involved with the field investigation. Special important habitat information and indication of these species are typically recorded on site maps or other suitable maps. The estimator should consult specialists in this area to determine the scope and level of effort. Typical sub-tasks for an endangered species survey include:

- Field Survey for Flora: A systematic search and recording of the endangered/threatened flora species within the site boundaries.
- Field Survey of Fauna: A systematic search utilizing all necessary personnel and equipment to survey for fauna on the sample areas under investigation.

Site Work and Utilities

Due to the nature and constant use of active ranges, site work and utilities concerns are normally addressed by the military. The estimator should confirm that costs for activities such as fencing, signage, and other access control methods are being incurred by the military. If additional control is required, the estimator should include these costs in the estimate.

Conclusion

Active Target Clearance is the process of clearing UXO (unexploded ordnance) from military active ranges. The major costs include labor and travel, and explosive ordnance destruction materials. Due to the highly specialized nature of this technology, the estimator must work closely with personnel certified to perform these activities, and the associated military client, to evaluate the techniques, logistics, personnel, and equipment that will be used for the clearance activity.

Part VIII

Cost Estimating for Remediation —Radioactive Waste Technologies

Chapter 52

Dismantling Contaminated Building Materials

After a thorough decontamination of a nuclear facility has been completed, the next step in the decommissioning process is to perform segmenting and dismantling of contaminated building structures (e.g., floor slabs, walls, columns, and beams). Unlike construction demolition (e.g., bulldozer and wrecking ball) of non-contaminated structures, nuclear facility dismantlement requires a carefully executed plan of segmenting and removing contaminated materials prior to any mass-scale demolition. The reason for this approach is the need to control any further spread of contaminants and to segregate radiological from non-hazardous (e.g., construction rubble) materials. Dismantling techniques are often separated into non-thermal and thermal methods. The distinction between the two is that thermal methods utilize some type of combustion or heating source to cut concrete or metals.

Applications and Limitations

Applications

- Used for the dismantling and removal of radiologically contaminated building materials, such as neutron-activated concrete floors, walls, and support columns.
- Can be used strategically to minimize waste by disposing of only those radioactive materials that are contaminated beyond any point of cleaning or rehabilitation (e.g., neutron-activated concrete shielding blocks).

Limitations

- Not intended for segmentation and dismantling of internal process equipment, such as piping, pumps, glove boxes, and tanks.
- To apply this technology, the facility has to have already been deactivated and decontaminated so that the dismantled materials and equipment are stable for packaging, storage, and transport (e.g., non-leaking).

*Process
Configuration and
Treatment Train
Considerations*

*Basic Information
Needed for Estimating*

- It is assumed that the nuclear facility has already been deactivated such that any nuclear source materials (e.g., plutonium pits and fuel rods) have been removed.
- Prior to dismantlement, it may be necessary to undertake a thorough decontamination effort in order to remove as many surficial contaminants as possible.

It is possible to create a reasonable cost estimate using a few basic parameters. If more detailed information is known, one can create a more precise and site-specific estimate using a secondary set of parameters.

To estimate the cost of dismantling contaminated building materials, certain information must be known and falls into three main categories:

- Building Construction Parameters (Materials)
- Non-thermal Techniques for Dismantling
- Thermal Techniques for Dismantling

Building Construction Parameters
The estimate will be determined in part by the primary material used in construction of the building, such as steel, concrete, masonry, or wood.

Material Volume Factor
The volume of in-place building materials is based on intact building structures that have not been dismantled and segmented into separate waste fractions. Building materials that are contaminated in nuclear facilities include such items as concrete floors/walls, iron beams/girders, steel wall panels, wood studs, and bricks. The **Volume of Building Materials** is the amount of contaminated building material. This figure sets an upper limit for the valid range of several required parameters for non-thermal segmenting methods discussed in the next section. The valid range for material volume is 0.01–9.99 C.F. of building materials per C.F. of interior building space. The defaults are given below and are broken down by construction material:

- If the building is steel framed, for example, the Material Volume Factor = 0.61 C.F. of building materials per C.F. of interior space.
- If the building is concrete or masonry, the Material Volume Factor = 0.50 C.F. of building materials per C.F. of interior space.
- If the building is constructed of wood, the Material Volume Factor = 0.58 C.F. of building materials per C.F. of interior space.

Concrete Reinforcement
This parameter refers to the primary method of reinforcement used in concrete materials for this building, e.g., in the walls, floors, columns, stairs, and foundation of the structure. If no concrete materials whatsoever have been used in the construction of the building, then the last option for this parameter will apply, *No Concrete Used*. The options for this parameter are: *Mesh-reinforced, Bar-reinforced,* or *No Concrete Used*.

Building Floor Space Area

This is the total building floor space area in S.F., considering all floors. The typical range is 100–1,000,000 S.F.

Floor to Ceiling Height

The distance between the floor and ceiling of the typical story, or level, is usually in the range of 10–50', depending on building configuration.

Percent of Building Contaminated

This is the percentage of the interior building volume that is contaminated with radionuclides.

Volume of Contaminated Building Material

The volume of contaminated building material (C.F.) may be calculated as:

Volume = Building Floor Space Area × Floor to Ceiling Height × Material Volume Factor × (Percent of Building Contaminated/100)

Dismantling Using Non-Thermal Techniques

Conventional dismantling techniques can be separated into non-thermal and thermal methods. The distinction between the 2 is that thermal methods utilize some type of combustion or heating source to cut concrete or metals. Typical non-thermal segmenting and dismantling techniques, along with their valid ranges, are presented in Figure 52.1, and are described in more detail below.

| Technology | Non-Thermal Segmenting and Dismantling Techniques | | | |
	Applicable Materials	Upper Range Limit (Area in S.F. or Volume in C.F.)	Thickness of Cut (in.)	Length of Cuts (ft)
Drill & Spall	Concrete, Masonry	0 to Max. Area	N/A	N/A
Floor Sawing	Steel, Concrete, Masonry, Wood	N/A	0.1 to 36.0	0 to 99,999
Wall Sawing	Steel, Concrete, Masonry, Wood	N/A	0.1 to 36.0	0 to 99,999
Paving Breakers	Concrete, Masonry	0 to Max. Volume	N/A	N/A
Rock Splitters	Concrete, Masonry	0 to Max. Volume	N/A	N/A
Expansive Compounds	Concrete, Masonry	0 to Max. Volume	N/A	N/A
Controlled Blasting	Concrete, Masonry	0 to Max. Volume	N/A	N/A
Hydraulic Shears/ Concrete Cracker	Concrete, Masonry	0 to Max. Volume	N/A	N/A

Figure 52.1 Non-Thermal Segmenting and Dismantling Techniques

Drill and Spall

The drill and spall method is used to "flake" 2" thick layers of contaminated concrete off of a material surface. With this method, 1–1.5" diameter holes are drilled to depths of 3", spaced 1' on center. After a hole has been drilled, a hydraulically operated spalling tool bit is inserted into the hole, and its feathers are expanded under pressure. This expansion within the hole fractures a 2" thick layer of material from the working face. Drilling and spalling are used when the contamination penetration is at most 2" deep, sparing the underlying material from further costly removal. The method removes an additional 1/2" layer beyond that of scabbling and is also easier to work with on non-horizontal surfaces. The fully productive surface spalling rate is 20 S.F./hr of surface area per crew. Assume that the drill and spall will use 2 drilling and spalling tools.

Paving Breakers

Paving breakers remove sections of concrete by mechanical fracturing of the working face with a hardened steel bit powered by an air compressor, electric motor, or hydraulic source of pressure. Paving breakers can be worked in confined areas where larger equipment, such as a floor/wall saw cannot reach. Since this method generates dust as the tool bit impacts the surface, contamination can be controlled with the use of a portable ventilation enclosure aspirated by a HEPA-filtered exhaust fan unit. Vibration generation may be a concern as the bit is continuously impacting the working surface (25 impacts per minute). If reinforcing steel is present, it is cut with an oxyacetylene torch, increasing the removal costs. The fully productive paving breaker rates per crew are 40 C.Y./day for non-reinforced concrete, 32 CY/day for mesh-reinforced concrete, and 24 C.Y./day for reinforced concrete. For reinforced concrete scenarios, additional costs will be incurred due to the cutting of the reinforcing steel with oxyacetylene torches. Assume that the paving breaker crew will use 2 impact tools.

Rock Splitters

A rock splitter fractures off sections from a block of concrete or stone by hydraulically expanding a feathered wedge, which has been inserted into a drilled hole, approximately 1.5" wide by 1–2' deep. Pressures as high as 350 tons (700 kpsi) can be generated with a hydraulic pump and fluid, causing stress fractures within the matrix of the concrete or rock. Holes are spaced from 1–3' apart on center-line. An extremely thick block of concrete (e.g., biological shield) could be removed in this fashion by progressively removing 1–2' thick sections from the working face. The benefits of rock splitting are that vibration and dust generation are minimized, except when drilling the holes. (Concrete drills outfitted with HEPA-filtered dust collectors are available for this purpose.)

If reinforcing steel is present, it is cut with an oxyacetylene torch, increasing the removal costs. The fully productive rock splitting rates per crew are 60 C.Y./day for non-reinforced concrete, 50 C.Y./day for mesh-reinforced concrete, and 40 C.Y./day for bar-reinforced concrete. Assume that the rock splitting crew will use 2 splitting tools.

Expansive Compounds

These chemically expanding demolition compounds are poured into holes drilled into a block of concrete. The compounds are purchased in the form of a dry powder, which is then mixed with water when ready to use. As the material dries (typically within 10–20 hours), it expands and causes tensile fractures in the concrete. As sections of the concrete are split, the material can be removed manually, by bucket loader, or further broken down with a paving breaker. Extremely thick sections of concrete block may be removed as a 1–2' thick section from the working face during each drying and removal session. Dust and vibration generation are limited to the hole-drilling portion of the process. (A HEPA-filtered drill can be used.) If reinforcing steel is present, it is cut with an oxyacetylene torch, increasing the removal costs. The fully productive concrete removal rate per crew using expansive demolition compounds is 22 C.Y./day for non-reinforced concrete, 19 C.Y./day for mesh-reinforced concrete, and 16 C.Y./day for bar-reinforced concrete. Assume that the crew will use two drilling tools.

Controlled Blasting

Controlled blasting uses explosive compounds placed into drilled holes to radially fracture the material upon detonation. Although blasting creates noise, vibration, and smoke, the spread of contamination can be controlled with blasting mats (thick, reinforced rubber) and water fog sprays, in addition to a constructed contamination envelope. As percussion drills are available with drill bit lengths of up to 6', extremely thick sections of heavily reinforced concrete can be fractured and worked off with paving breakers or by a bucket loader. If reinforcing steel is present, it is cut with an oxyacetylene torch, increasing the removal costs. The fully productive concrete removal rate per crew using controlled blasting is 16 C.Y./day for non-reinforced concrete, 14 C.Y./day for mesh-reinforced concrete, and 12 C.Y./day for bar-reinforced concrete.

Hydraulic Shears/Concrete Cracker

This method is used to dismantle a concrete or masonry structure (e.g., a wall or column) up to 2' thick, provided a light-to-medium duty front-end loader is available, and there is ample working room. (Segmenting reinforcing steel within the concrete is limited to approximately 1.25" of metal thickness.) The hydraulic tool attachment on the wheel loader is used to crush and tear off pieces of concrete and reinforcing steel with its crusher jaws (pincers). Dust production can be controlled to an extent with ventilation or a water fog spray. This method of dismantlement is used in areas when vibration to surrounding structures must be minimized, thereby prohibiting the use of an alternative method such as controlled blasting. The fully productive demolition rates per crew (e.g., per one loader with tool attachment) are 20 C.Y./day for non-reinforced concrete, 16 C.Y./day for mesh-reinforced concrete, and 12 C.Y./day for reinforced concrete. Reinforcing steel thickness is limited to approximately 1.25" using this method.

Floor and Wall Sawing

Floor and wall saws can cut through a concrete floor up to 3' thick. Space limitations must be considered when using this equipment, however, as the diameter of the saw blade is typically 3 times the thickness of the cut. This method is not recommended for sawing through reinforced steel mesh or bars within the concrete, as the reinforcing steel wears excessively on the saw blades and can lead to blade kickback. The fully productive sawing rates per crew (1 saw) are 150 in²/min of cutting surface area for floors and 60 in²/min of cutting surface area for walls. Sawing through reinforced concrete, while not recommended, is feasible given that the blade would have to be replaced at a much greater rate than for a non-reinforced concrete application. Kickback hazards are another issue.

Dismantling—Thermal Techniques

Typical thermal segmenting and dismantling techniques, along with their valid ranges, are presented in Figure 52.2, and described in more detail below.

Oxyacetylene Torch

Standard oxyacetylene torches are generally unable to cut through stainless steel, aluminum, and other nonferrous metals because of the production of metallic oxides, which can have a melting point above that of the flame temperature. The ability to cut through thick metal plating is dependent on the skill of the cutter and the effectiveness of the oxidizing fuel mixture to clear away molten metal and oxides from the kerf. Generally, internal building structures with metallic components (e.g., handrails, I-beams, reinforcing steel) utilize ferrous metals such as carbon steel or cast iron, which usually can be segmented with an oxyacetylene torch. It is only when "exotic" metals (e.g., tungsten and stainless steel alloys) are used that a cutting method with a higher flame or arc temperature must be considered. The fully productive oxyacetylene cutting rate per torch for metals is 30 in²/min

Technology	Thermal Segmenting and Dismantling Techniques Applicable Materials	Thickness of Cut (in.)	Length of Cuts (ft)
Oxyacetylene Torch	Ferrous Metals	0.1 to 60.0	0 to 99,999
Oxy-Gasoline Torch	Metals	0.1 to 12.0	0 to 99,999
Thermite Reaction Lance	Metals	0.1 to 99.9	0 to 99,999
Metal Powder (Flame) Cutting	Metals, Concrete, Masonry	0.1 to 60.0	0 to 99,999
Arc Saw	Metals	0.1 to 12.0	0 to 99,999
Plasma Arc Saw	Metals	0.1 to 6.0	0 to 99,999

Figure 52.2 Thermal Segmenting and Dismantling Techniques

of cutting surface area. In addition, when the reinforcing steel in reinforced concrete is to be cut, the output per torch is estimated to be 6.0 C.Y./hr for mesh-reinforced, and 1.5 C.Y./hr for bar-reinforced concrete. Assume that the oxyacetylene crew will use 2 torches.

Oxy-Gasoline Torch

This cutting method generates a flame temperature that is several hundred degrees hotter (e.g., 1,500°F) than an oxyacetylene torch. The fuel source is 87-octane unleaded gasoline fed from a 2.5-gallon tank pressurized by a manual pump. Oxygen from a cylinder is used as the oxidizing gas. Since gasoline burns at a higher flame temperature and is cheaper on a heat content (e.g., $/BTU) basis than acetylene, this method is beginning to be considered in some decommissioning work because of reported savings in cutting time and fuel costs. The fully productive oxy-gasoline cutting rate per torch for metals is depth-dependent and is approximately: 45 in²/min of cutting surface area for cuts to 2" thick, 60 in²/min of cutting surface area for cuts 2–6" thick, 90 in²/min of cutting surface area for cuts 6–10" thick, and 100 in²/min of cutting surface area for cuts 10–12" thick. Assume that the oxy-gasoline crew will use 2 cutting torches.

Thermite Reaction Lance

Thermite reaction lances are hand-held iron pipes (e.g., 10.5' long) packed with oxidizable metal wires, such as aluminum, steel, or magnesium. Because all the metal components are consumed during the reaction, the lance stubs are discarded when they burn down to 2–3' in length. Compressed oxygen flowing through an annulus in the pipe sustains the reaction at 4,000–10,000°F. Since this is well above the melting point of most typical metal building components, it is effective in cutting most metals. The practical cutting depth is restricted only by the cutter's ability to keep the kerf free of molten metal and oxides. The fully productive cutting rate per thermite lance for metals is 12 in²/min of cutting surface area.

Metal Powder ("Flame") Cutting

Metal powder cutting, more commonly known as flame cutting, oxidizes a suspension of iron oxide and aluminum powder in a stream of oxygen gas to produce a thermite reaction with temperatures up to 16,000°F. At these temperatures, the flame tip literally disintegrates concrete or masonry materials into a powdered ash. Flame cutting torches can cut 2' deeper than wall/floor saws, and are not impeded by reinforcing steel. The cutting torch or lance is not consumed in this process and is thus reusable. The fully productive cutting rate per metal powder (flame cutting) torch is 144 in²/hr of cutting surface area.

Arc Saw

An arc saw uses a smooth, rotating circular blade to pass an electrical arc between the blade edge and a conductive material that comes into close contact with it. The separation distance between the cutting blade and the metal being cut is typically less than 1". As the material to be cut must be conductive, it is generally used only for metals. The rotation of the blade (e.g., 350–1,800 RPM) aids in removing molten metal and oxides from the kerf. Remote operation of these units is available. Blade wear during cutting is estimated at a few percent of the amount of metal that is removed from the kerf. Arc saws are not portable and require a cutting table. In addition, power requirements can be steep. (A 36" diameter blade used to cut up to 12" thick metals requires a power supply of 6,000 Amps.) The fully productive cutting rate per arc saw for metals varies somewhat according to the thickness and conductivity of the metal being cut. Generally, the thinner the metal, the faster the cutting rate. A reasonable assumption is an average cutting rate of 270 in^2/min of cutting surface area. This value represents cutting steel with an arc saw having a maximum cutting depth of 12".

Plasma Arc Saw

A plasma arc saw uses an inert gas, such as argon, flowing through a constricting orifice to intensify an arc between an electrode and any conductive material that comes into close contact with it. The separation distance between the electrode and the metal being cut is typically less than 1". Since the material to be cut must be conductive, this method is typically used only on metals. Remote operation of these units is common, and portable hand-held units are available. A plasma arc saw-cutting head may be mounted on motor-driven rollers and remotely driven over a section of the metal to be cut. The power supply requirements for plasma arc torches is somewhat less than arc saws, as a plasma arc torch with a 6" cutting capacity would require an electrical supply of 1,000 Amps. The fully productive cutting rate per plasma arc saw for metals varies somewhat according to the type of metal being cut. A good assumption for an average cutting rate is 18 in^2/min of cutting surface area. This value represents cutting carbon steel metals.

Design Information Needed for Detailed Estimates

Following are descriptions of the types of information that, when available, can add detail and accuracy to estimates. Also included are design criteria and estimating rules of thumb that the estimator typically uses to determine values that are not known, or to check information provided by others.

Demolition Factor

This parameter specifies the volume of waste per volume of in-place building material. A good default value is 1.5 C.F. of waste per C.F. of building material. The default demolition factor of 1.5 implies that for every 1.0 C.F. (in-place) of material removed, 1.5 C.F. of waste volume will be generated, due to material expansion upon removal. A reasonable range is 1–10 C.F. of waste per C.F. of building material.

Shipping/Disposal

Key cost elements of shipping and disposal of wastes generated from surface decontamination include the location of the disposal site, the distance to the disposal site, and the type of waste to be shipped.

Key locations for disposal of wastes contaminated with nuclear materials currently include:

- Barnwell, SC
- Hanford, WA
- Nevada Test Site, NV
- Envirocare, UT

The current rate charged for the disposal, and the distance to the disposal site, are cost drivers that should be evaluated. The disposal fees at each location vary as a function of variables such as the volume of waste, number of shipments, radionuclide composition, waste content activity (pCi/g), and repository location. The disposal fee includes costs such as off-loading the shipment at the disposal site, analytical tests performed by the repository, and long-term care and maintenance. The estimator should check with each repository option for the best estimate of the disposal fee at the time that the wastes will be shipped.

Shipments considerably less than 1,000,000 C.F. or small quantities of wastes generated by non-government facilities (e.g., power plants, research facilities, hospitals, etc.) may not qualify for these rates. It is the estimator's responsibility to obtain the applicable disposal fee at the time the estimate is being prepared.

In addition, the estimator should evaluate the type of wastes accepted at each site and the schedule for waste shipping. It is possible that a combination of shipping and disposal sites may be used to eliminate waste generated by surface decontamination activities, due to timing and disposal rate considerations.

It is common for the wastes to be packed into 55-gallon shipping drums and standard B-25 shipping boxes (4' × 4' × 6') prior to shipping. Drums and shipping containers are typically packed 90% full. At 90% material fill, each shipping box will hold 86.4 C.F. of scabbled concrete. Liners are not used because boxes generally contain only dry scabbled concrete. If a larger shipping box is needed, maritime containers with dimensions of 8' × 4' × 20' are available. In this case, assume 2 maritime containers per truck with a minimum bed length of 42'.

At 90% material fill, each drum will hold 6.6 C.F. of waste. Drums will be used to hold small trash items, such as used plastic sheeting, disposable coveralls, and discarded respirators. Assume that 1 C.F. of contaminated drummed wastes accumulates per every 100 S.F. of contaminated building floor space. Drum liners are used so that any trash wetted with liquids can be disposed.

Typically, trucks are used to ship all waste. Based on a 21-ton freight limit for a 105 CY van trailer, either 80 drums of paper and plastic wastes or 4 shipping boxes of concrete rubble may be loaded per trailer. Wastes will typically be removed from the drums and containers at the repository and placed into lifts. The repository will maintain possession of the containers.

Consumable Materials

Various consumable materials are used for contaminated building materials dismantling. These include:

- Splitting Tool Lubricant: Applied to the feathers and plug of the spalling and rock splitting tools at the rate of 1 can/day/tool.
- Saw Blades: Blade replacement costs are assessed per S.F. of cutting surface area.
- Drill & Tool Bits: Tungsten-carbide drill and impact bits are expected to have a maximum lifetime of 80 operating hours. They are also sharpened periodically between replacements, as they dull. This cost applies to all non-thermal processes except for sawing.

- Plasma/Arc Saw Replacement Parts: The operating life of the nozzle and electrode in plasma arc saws is 30 minutes and 3 hours, respectively. The cutting blade of the arc saw is replaced on a much less frequent basis. It is estimated that the cutting blade is worn down at less than 5% of the amount of metal removed from the cut.
- Expansive Demolition Compound Mix: The usage rate of compound mix, minus the weight of the added water, is estimated at 24 lbs/C.Y. of concrete.
- Explosive Demolition Supplies: Explosive demolition supplies include consumables such as the fuse, detonator wire, and the explosives used in breaking up the concrete.
- Acetylene Gas Usage: estimated at 0.2 C.F./in^2 of cut. In addition, when cutting steel in reinforced concrete, acetylene usage is estimated at 2.25 C.F./C.Y. of mesh-reinforced concrete and 9.0 C.F./C.Y. of bar-reinforced concrete. A small amount of combustible gas is used for the startup period of the flame-cutting torch and plasma arc saw. A reasonable assumption is that 5% of the cutting areas of the flame cutting torch and plasma arc saw will require acetylene startup gas.
- Oxygen Gas Usage: By stoichiometry, oxygen gas usage is 2.5 times the amount of all acetylene usage. In addition, the oxy-gasoline torch consumes oxygen at a rate of 0.5 C.F./in^2 of cut. When thermite reaction lances are used, oxygen usage (only gas consumed) is estimated at 0.83 C.F./in^2 of cut. When a flame-cutting torch is used, oxygen usage (only gas consumed) is estimated at 5.6 C.F./in^2 of cut.
- Argon Gas Usage: An inert gas, such as argon, is used in the plasma arc saw to intensify the current flow through an orifice resulting in an arc with a high current density. Argon gas usage is estimated at 0.075 C.F./in^2 of cut.
- Thermite Lance Holders and Lances: Thermite lance holders are replaced every 8 hour shift. A thermite lance will burn for 6 min. (72 in^2) from the time it is lit and used for cutting until it has burned down to a 2–3' long stub.
- Iron Oxide Powder: Consumed in the flame cutter at the rate of 14 lbs of iron/144 in^2 of cuts.
- Aluminum Powder: Aluminum powder is consumed in the flame cutter at the rate of 6 lbs of iron/144 in^2 of cuts.
- Plastic Sheeting/Bags: High-strength plastic sheeting (Herculite®) is used to erect temporary contamination envelopes around the work zone. The material is also used to wrap and secure pieces of removed material so that contamination is not spread from the work area. Plastic bags are used to dispose of any miscellaneous supplies, such as respirator cartridges. Plastic sheeting/bag usage is estimated at 5 S.F. of plastic per S.F. of contaminated building floor area.
- Miscellaneous Demolition Supplies: typically charged as a unit charge per S.F. of all surfaces cleaned. Includes items such as duct/packing tape, small bags, and labels.
- Unleaded Gasoline: Based on a heat content basis, 1 gallon of gasoline is equivalent to 100 C.F. of acetylene gas. Thus, the gasoline consumption rate is estimated at 0.002 gal/in^2 of cut when using an oxy-gasoline cutting torch.

Decontamination of Workers

This is a major cost item in surface decontamination technology, since the activity is labor-intensive and messy. A good assumption for decontamination crew size is as follows (full-shift personnel in each crew): drill and spall or hydraulic demolition – 5 crew members, floor or wall sawing – 3.25 crew members, paving breakers/rock splitters/expansive demolition compounds/controlled blasting – 6 crew members, oxyacetylene or oxy-gasoline torch cutting – 5 crew members, and thermite reaction lance/flame cutting/arc saw/plasma arc saw – 3.25 crew members. Decontamination crews are composed of personnel such as laborers, crew leaders (supervisors), skilled workers (equipment operators), and radiation monitors (health physics). A man week (mwk) is equivalent to 40 worker hours. Decontamination services include washing/cleaning all reusable protective/worker clothing items including uniforms, rubber gloves/boots, and protective outer clothing. Usage, heating, filtration, and disposal of water for showers are also included.

A reasonable assumption for personnel decontamination is 4 times/person/shift; thus, 4 changes of disposable clothing (e.g., coveralls, gloves, boot covers, etc.) are made/person/shift. Respirator cartridges are replaced on a daily basis (2/person/day). Typically, non-disposable safety equipment, such as full-face respirators, rubber boots/gloves, and washable coveralls are provided by the contractor as part of the overhead and thus are not charged as direct costs.

It is also reasonable to consider the cost of stocking a decontamination hygiene kit in the decontamination trailer. The kit includes 27 individual decontamination items including foam, hand soap, decontamination sprays, and hand towelettes. Use of this kit is estimated at 1/week for each demolition crew. (The 12 crews are drill and spall, floor sawing, wall sawing, paving breakers, rock splitting, expansive demolition, controlled blasting, hydraulic demolition, oxyacetylene cutting, oxy-gasoline cutting, thermite reaction lance, flame cutting, arc saw, and plasma arc saw).

Productivity

A weighted productivity loss factor is calculated using productivity losses from the combined effects of: height adjustments, protective clothing, Radiological Controls Program (RADCON) procedures, respiratory protection, and breaks. The unadjusted crew labor and equipment requirements are multiplied by the weighted productivity loss multiplier in order to estimate the adjusted crew labor and equipment requirements. Consumables such as wipes and cleaning solutions are not adjusted for productivity losses. Productivity loss considerations include:

- Height Adjustment: the productivity loss in percent due to working at elevated heights (e.g., ladders and scaffolding). A good default value is 15%.
- Protective Clothing: the productivity loss in percent due to working in protective clothing (e.g., coveralls, rubber boots, and gloves). This takes into account clothing changes during a shift and restricted movements to avoid heat stress. A reasonable default value is 20–25%.

- RADCON: the productivity loss in percent due to Radiation Control procedures. RADCON entails radiation control procedures involving safety and workplace training (e.g., mock-up training) to ensure that the worker is keeping his/her absorbed dose to a minimum. A good default value is 15%.
- Respiratory Protection: the productivity loss in percent due to wearing respiratory protection such as half-face and full-face respirators or SCBA (Self-Contained Breathing Apparatus) equipment. A reasonable default value is 35–40%.
- Breaks: the productivity loss in percent due to routine personnel breaks during a shift (e.g., bathroom, lunch, health). A good default value is 10%.

Related Costs

Costs for supply of water and power should be included in the estimate as follows.

Electric Power

All non-thermal demolition methods except for floor sawing and hydraulic demolition use an air compressor which peaks at approximately 75 H.P. and 2 HEPA air filtration systems of approximately 7.5 H.P./ea. In addition to the HEPA filters for sawing and hydraulic demolition, the floor or wall saw motor peaks at 35 H.P. Assume that these motors operate for 45% of the crew hours. To estimate electric power usage, a good conversion is 1 H.P. = 0.746 kW.

All thermal methods use a vapor collection system of approximately 7.5 H.P. motor capacity. Assume a 1/2 H.P. motor for the water fogger pump on the thermal demolition methods and a 1 H.P. motor for the water fogger pump for controlled blasting. The powdered metal dispenser for the flame cutting torch uses a compressed air supply estimated to require a compressor of about 25 H.P. Assume that these motors operate for 45% of the crew hours. To estimate electric power usage, a reasonable conversion is 1 H.P. = 0.746 kW.

For a plasma arc saw, the direct-current (e.g., 12 V) power supply of a saw with a 6" cut peaks at 1,000 A. Cutting speed is adjustable with power consumption, so assume a mid-point current draw of 500 A during cutting. This equates to an electrical consumption rate of 0.1 kWh/18 in^2 of cut.

For an arc saw, the direct-current (e.g., 35–50 V) power supply of a saw with a 12" cut peaks at 6,000 A. Cutting speed is adjustable with power consumption, so assume a mid-point current draw of 3,000 A at 42.5 V during cutting. This equates to an electrical consumption rate of 2.2 kWh/270 in^2 of cut.

Process Water

Thermal cutting processes generate high-temperature fumes that need to be cooled prior to HEPA filtration. Makeup water for the recirculated water fogger is estimated at 2 gallons/hour of cutting time, which is approximately 45% of the crew hours. A fog spray is also used around the controlled blast area to knock out any particulate that may have escaped HEPA filtration. Makeup water usage is estimated at 25 gallons/day of blasting. Typically, the process makeup water usage represents the volume of fog spray that is too contaminated for recycling because of its particulate and radionuclide content. Usually, this water will be hauled and treated off-site for a per-gallon fee that includes ultimate disposal and handling of the radionuclide content.

Conclusion Dismantling of contaminated building material is a process used in the nuclear decommissioning process to carefully segment and remove nuclear-contaminated materials prior to any mass-scale demolition. The primary cost driver is the volume of material to be dismantled, but costs can also vary widely depending on the technique used for the dismantling. The cost engineer should work closely with the construction operations team to compare the various dismantling approaches for applicability, cost, and efficiency.

Chapter 53

Decontamination and Decommissioning Sampling and Analysis

This chapter addresses the requirements and costs for sampling and analysis associated with building decontamination and decommissioning (D&D) projects. The technology can be used throughout the D&D process, from the initial characterization surveys through site close-out. Sampling and analysis costs include mobilization, sample acquisition, packaging, transportation, and analysis at a certified laboratory. The technology provides various analytical options, including on-site radiological scanning. Sampling and analysis defaults and algorithms are based on information obtained from the Multi-Agency Radiation Survey and Site Investigation Manual – MARSSIM (NUREG-1575), Department of Energy (DOE) Decontamination Handbook (DOE Order 5400.5), and from interviews with DOE employees and contractors.

Applications and Limitations

Applications

- The D&D sampling and analysis technology can be used during all phases of D&D activities at a site.
- The technology includes analyses for potentially radioactive materials and other contaminants including VOCs, fuels, pesticides, PCBs, metals, acids, and ordnance.

Limitations

- This technology does not include calculations or provisions for determining required sample sizes in conjunction with Data Quality Objectives.

Basic Information Needed for Estimating

A few required parameters can be used to create a reasonable cost estimate for this technology. A more precise, site-specific estimate will require more detailed information, involving a secondary set of parameters. There are 4 main categories of information needed for the basic estimate:

- Number and Type of Samples
- Sampling Crew and Rate
- Mobilization
- Laboratory Analyses

Number and Type of Samples

(It should be noted that special decontamination requirements may apply to equipment used for sampling of a radiologically contaminated site. In some cases, the equipment may become contaminated to the point that it must be left at the site to be disposed of as hazardous waste.)

Sampling Survey Grid Setup

Sampling survey grids are normally established prior to taking actual samples for buildings, soil, and surface water. A minimum setup time is usually 1 day. For a building, a good rule of thumb is that a 10' × 10' room (600 S.F., including walls, ceiling, and floor) can be fully gridded in one hour. For soil and surface water sampling, it is reasonable to assume that it takes 1 hour for setup for each 10,000 S.F. of area. This assumes that the water to be sampled is within the property boundary and immediate vicinity of the building, and does not have a separate grid. The number of hours to set up the grid can be calculated as:

Sampling Survey Grid Setup (hours) = (Soil sample survey area, S.F. + Water sample survey area, S.F.) / 10,000 + (Building sample survey area, S.F.) / 600

Number of Soil Samples and Survey Area

Soil samples are normally obtained for surface soil or sediment in the immediate proximity of the building being characterized. If subsurface samples are required, additional costs should be considered for processes such as using drill rigs and split spoon sampling, cone penetrometer testing (CPT), hand-augering, power-augering, and excavation equipment for open pit/trench excavations. Special decontamination requirements may apply to drill rigs and other equipment used for sampling of a radiologically contaminated site. In some cases, the equipment may become contaminated to the point that it must be handled as contaminated equipment/hazardous waste. The estimator needs to determine the total area to be sampled, and the number of samples within this area.

Number of Water Samples and Survey Area

If groundwater samples are required, additional costs should be allowed for performing hand bailing and/or pumping. The number of water samples should be estimated if required.

Number of Building Surface Samples and Survey Area

The most common types of samples obtained for building surfaces are swipe (smear) samples. These are sent to the laboratory and analyzed for specific particulate emissions or nuclides. If other types of sampling are required, including removal of paint and testing for lead, removal of suspected asbestos particles, analysis for asbestos containing materials (ACMs), and testing of ballast and other materials for PCBs, these additional costs should be considered.

Sampling Crew and Rate

Sampling Crew Size

The sampling crew size typically ranges from 1–5 people. If there is more than 1 person in the sampling crew, the technology assumes that the additional person is a health and safety officer, who monitors the ambient air and supervises the radiological technicians acquiring the samples. Following are typical configurations for sampling crews:

- 1 person crew: 1 Radiation Technician
- 2 person crew: 1 Radiation Technician & 1 Health and Safety Officer
- 3 person crew: 2 Radiation Technicians & 1 Health and Safety Officer
- 4 person crew: 3 Radiation Technicians & 1 Health and Safety Officer
- 5 person crew: 4 Radiation Technicians & 1 Health and Safety Officer

The crew size selected will affect both the mobilization and per diem cost. Larger crews may be able to take more samples per work hour and reduce costs by minimizing the amount of management and health and safety oversight time required at the project site. If the crew can work more efficiently with more people involved, considerations should be made for increasing the sampling rate for the entire crew as crew size increases. A typical crew for radiological survey work is 1 health and safety officer and 2 radiological technicians. However, a larger crew may be necessary depending upon the magnitude of the sampling effort.

Sampling Rate

The rate of sample acquisition is based on the crew productivity. The sampling rate includes the time for a crew to obtain swipe, soil, and/or water samples. It usually takes about 5–10 minutes to document and package each sample in normal conditions, including QA samples. Overall, a typical sampling rate is 12 samples/hour, or 96 samples per day (assuming an 8-hour day).

In addition to sampling, manual hand scanning can be performed for the purpose of conducting radiological scans. It is reasonable to assume that the same crew that is selected for sample acquisition will conduct the manual scans.

The time it takes to obtain samples is calculated as:

Sampling time, days = [(Number of Building (Swipe) Samples + Number of Soil Samples + Number of Water Samples) / Sampling Rate per Day + Number of Days for Manual Hand Scanning] × Weighted Productivity Loss Factor

Where: Weighted Productivity Loss Factor is assumed to be 1, but can be adjusted with more detailed estimating, as described below.

This time is multiplied by the number of personnel in the sampling crew and their rates to determine the labor cost of the sampling effort.

Mobilization and Per Diem

These costs will increase if crews must travel to the site instead of working locally.

Number of Mobilizations

The number of mobilizations determines the crew cost for travel and work preparation. Crews may travel several times throughout the lifetime of a project, including short distances from the home office to the site.

Mobilization Distance and Associated Costs

These factors will affect travel cost to and from the subject site. The sampling crew selection will have an effect on the mobilization and per diem costs. Crews who mobilize, but do not travel the required distance to collect per diem, will have a mobilization cost based on personal vehicle mileage allowances. Otherwise, the estimator should evaluate the costs for driving and/or airfare based on the distance.

Mobilization and per diem costs can be estimated as follows:

Mobilization Cost = Number of Mobilizations × Number of People in Sampling Crew × Cost per Mobilization

Per Diem Cost = Number of People in Sampling Crew × Sampling Time (days) × Per Diem Rate, Per Person per Day

Laboratory Analyses

Soil/Sediment Analyses

These types of analyses are typically conducted for radionucleides in surface soil and sediment samples.

Description	UM
Veg/Soil/Sed, Gross Beta—Total, Gas Flow Prop Count	EA
Veg/Soil/Sed, Gamma Isotopic, Gamma Spectroscopy	EA
Veg/Soil/Sed, Gross Alpha—Total, Gas Flow Prop.	EA

Water/Liquid Analyses

These types of samples are typically conducted for radionucleides in surface water bodies outside the building being surveyed.

Description	UM
Liquid, Gross Beta—Total, Gas Flow Proportional Count	EA
Liquid, Gamma Isotopic, Gamma Spectroscopy	EA
Liquid, Gross Alpha— Total, Gas Flow &/or Alpha Spec	EA

Smears/Wipes (Filter Paper)

These types of samples are typically obtained for radionucleide analyses of building surfaces via smear and wipe techniques. Other types of sampling and analyses that may be required would include: removal of paint and testing for lead, removal of suspected asbestos particles and analysis for asbestos containing materials (ACMs), and testing of ballast and other materials for PCBs. If these types of samples are required, the estimator should include the costs for these additional analyses in the estimate.

Description	UM
Veg/Soil/Sed, Gross Beta—Total, Gas Flow Prop Count	EA
Veg/Soil/Sed, Gamma Isotopic, Gamma Spectroscopy	EA
Veg/Soil/Sed, Gross Alpha—Total, Gas Flow Prop.	EA

Hazardous Waste Analyses

The following analyses are typical when hazardous waste sampling and analyses are conducted for any medium.

Description	UM
Purgeable Halocarbons (8010)	EA
Purgeable Aromatics (8020)	EA
Base Neutral and Acid Extractables (8270)	EA
BTEX/MTBE(Modified 8020)	EA
Pesticides/PCBs (8080)	EA
TAL Metals, Soil	EA
TAL Metals, Water	EA
Corrosivity (EPA 1110)	EA
pH (150.1)	EA
Ordnance Scan, EPA 8330	EA

Quality Assurance (QA) Samples

Soil/Sediment QA Blanks

QA Blanks include duplicates, trip blanks, or field blanks. The system default for QA Blanks is 15% of the number of soil/sediment samples. The total number of soil/sediment analyses is the sum of the soil/sediment samples plus the number of soil/sediment QA blanks.

Water/Liquid QA Blanks

QA Blanks include duplicates, trip blanks, or field blanks. The system default for QA Blanks is 15% of the number of water/liquid samples. The total number of water/liquid analyses is the sum of the water/liquid samples plus the number of water/liquid QA blanks.

Building QA Blanks

QA Blanks include duplicates, trip blanks, or field blanks. The system default for QA Blanks is 15% of the number of building surface samples. The total number of building surface analyses is the sum of the building surface samples plus the number of building surface QA blanks.

Design Information Needed for Detailed Estimates

Following are descriptions of the types of detailed information that, when available, can add accuracy to estimates. Also included are design criteria and estimating rules of thumb that the estimator typically uses to determine values that are not known, or to check information provided by others.

Analytical Factors

Turn-Around Time

The Turn-Around Time (TAT) is the amount of laboratory time required to process a sample. This period starts when a laboratory receives a sample and ends when the laboratory report is returned. Each selection for turn-around time has a corresponding cost mark-up. The TAT factors can be modified for each estimate. A reasonable default is 14 days.

The unit adjustment factor is used to calculate the adjusted extended cost. For example, 10 samples costing $100 at standard TAT rates would increase in cost to $200 if a 24 hour turn-around time were necessary.

These factors will vary from laboratory to laboratory and should be evaluated by the estimator prior to generating the final cost estimate.

Quality Control and Cost Adjustment Factors

The quality control (QC) or reporting level is the level of detailed documentation and analytical procedures required from the laboratory. Generally, 4 QC data package deliverables could be requested. A Level 1 QC data package is the least expensive and has a minimum amount of QC, whereas a Level 4 QC data package provides the most comprehensive quality control. The quality control required for each project varies depending on contract stipulations and negotiation with the particular EPA region involved, DOE regulations and any state or local regulations that may apply. DOE also refers to Levels 1 and 2 as *Screening* and Levels 3 and 4 as *Definitive*.

A standard default is Level 1. The selections for quality control level are as follows:

Quality Control QC LEVEL	Default Unit Adjustment Factor
Level 1 (Standard)	1.00 Screening
Level 2	1.10 Screening
Level 3	1.25 Definitive
Level 4 (CLP)	1.40 Definitive

The QC levels above refer to laboratory levels of documentation to meet differing project-specific QA/QC. A description of each level follows:

Level 1 (Screening): Includes analytical results as well as method detection limits, date of analysis, analyst information, and pertinent client and sample information. Generally, the laboratory's standard price schedule applies to this level of reporting, which corresponds to normally supplied deliverables. This package generally includes a method blank, and a water spike/spike duplicate. There is no surcharge for this level, since this is the lowest level available.

Level 2 (Screening): Includes analytical results and limited QC data summaries (blank results, spiked sample and spiked duplicate results, and surrogate recoveries). A 10% surcharge is common practice for this level of reporting.

Level 3 (Definitive): Provides QC and calibration data summaries for specific client- or project-related sample batches; i.e., the laboratory will schedule and analyze all QA samples by client or project delivery group rather than the total number of samples analyzed by the laboratory. Also includes chromatographs, but does not include raw data and spectra. Laboratories generally add a 25% surcharge for this level of documentation. Deliverables include blanks, matrix spikes/matrix spike duplicates, QC check samples, and calibration data.

Level 4 (Definitive): The Laboratory furnishes QC and calibration summaries along with hard-copy/raw data documentation for samples and QA samples. Scheduling and analysis are the same as in Level 3. All instrument hard copy and related documentation are provided in Level 4. The laboratory generally adds a 40% surcharge for Level 4 documentation. Full Contract Laboratory Program (CLP) methods and reportables are assumed to be priced by this markup.

An example application of the TAT & QC Factor follows:

Assume that contract requirements dictate a 14 day turn-around with a Level 4 (CLP) (Definitive) Quality Control Level. Assume a TAT Factor of 1.20 and Level 4 QC Factor of 1.40, which yields a combined factor of 1.6. This factor is applied to the sample quantity to account for TAT and QC level. Assume a sample's base cost is $100 and 10 samples are required. The adjusted cost is:

	Quantity	Material	Extended Cost
Original	10	$100	$1,000
Modified	16	$100	$1,600

Productivity

A weighted productivity loss factor is calculated using productivity losses from the combined effects of: height adjustments, protective clothing, Radiological Controls Program (RADCON) procedures, respiratory protection, and breaks. The unadjusted crew labor and equipment requirements are multiplied by the weighted productivity loss multiplier to estimate the adjusted crew labor and equipment requirements. Consumables such as wipes and cleaning solutions are not adjusted for productivity losses. Productivity loss considerations include:

- Height Adjustment: productivity loss in percent due to working at elevated heights (e.g., ladders and scaffolding). A reasonable default value is 15%. Height adjustments should be included when floor-to-ceiling heights exceed 10'.
- Protective Clothing: productivity loss in percent due to working in protective clothing (e.g., coveralls, rubber boots and gloves). This takes into account clothing changes during a shift and restricted movements to avoid heat stress. A good default value is 20–25%.
- RADCON: productivity loss in percent due to Radiation Control procedures. RADCON entails radiation control procedures involving safety and workplace training (e.g., mock-up training) to ensure that the worker is keeping his/her absorbed dose to a minimum. A good default value is 15%.
- Respiratory Protection: productivity loss in percent due to wearing respiratory protection such as half-face and full-face respirators or SCBA (Self-Contained Breathing Apparatus) equipment. A reasonable default value is 35–40%.
- Breaks: the productivity loss in percent due to routine personnel breaks during a shift (e.g., bathroom, lunch, health). A good default value is 10%.

Weighted Productivity Loss Multiplier

The 5 productivity loss parameters are used to determine a term called the Weighted Productivity Loss Multiplier, as referenced above, which can be calculated as:

Weighted Productivity Loss Multiplier = [1 + (Height Adjustment factor) + (Protective Clothing factor) + (RADCON factor)] × [1 + (Respirator factor)] × [1 + (Breaks factor)]

Consumable Materials

Various consumable materials are used for D&D Sampling and Analysis. These include:

- High-strength plastic sheeting (Herculite)—used to erect temporary barriers around the work zone. The material is also used in disposable plastic bags to contain trash, such as wipes, blotting papers, and spent decontamination materials. Plastic sheeting/bag usage is estimated at 1 S.F. per 1,000 S.F. of survey area.
- Miscellaneous decontamination supplies—are typically charged as unit charge per S.F. of all surfaces cleaned. These miscellaneous supplies include items such as duct/packing tape, small dust brushes, crevice tools (e.g., toothbrushes), small bags, tacks, labels, etc.

Shipping/Disposal of Waste Generated by Sampling

Locations for disposal of wastes contaminated with nuclear materials currently include:

- Barnwell, SC
- Hanford, WA
- Nevada Test Site, NV
- Envirocare, UT

The current rate charged for the disposal, and the distance to the disposal site, are cost drivers that should be evaluated. The disposal fees at each location will differ as a function of variables such as the volume of waste, number of shipments, radionuclide composition, waste content activity (pCi/g), and the repository location. The disposal fee includes costs such as off-loading the shipment at the disposal site, analytical tests performed by the repository, and long-term care and maintenance. The estimator should check with each repository option for the best estimate of the disposal fee at the time that the wastes will be shipped.

Shipments considerably less than 1,000,000 C.F. or small quantities of wastes generated by non-government facilities (e.g., power plants, research facilities, hospitals, etc.) may not qualify for these rates, so it is the responsibility of the estimator to get the most applicable disposal fee at the time that the estimate is being prepared. Disposal fees include costs such as off-loading the shipment at the disposal site, analytical tests performed by the repository, and long-term care and maintenance.

In addition, the estimator should evaluate the type of wastes accepted at each site and the schedule for waste shipping. It is possible that a combination of shipping and disposal sites may be used to eliminate waste generated by surface decontamination activities, due to timing and disposal rate considerations.

Wastes are commonly packed into 55-gallon shipping drums, typically 90% full. At 90% material fill, each drum will hold 6.6 ft^3 of waste. Drums will also be used to hold small trash items such as used wipes, used plastic sheeting, disposable coveralls, and discarded respirators. Assuming a demolition factor of 1.5 and a waste compaction ration of 2:1 for wastes such as crumpled wipes and sheeting, it is estimated that 1 C.F. of waste will result from 115 S.F. of plastic sheeting. The waste volume is increased by 20% to account for disposal of miscellaneous wastes. Drum liners are used so that any trash wetted with liquids can be disposed.

Trucks are normally used to ship all waste. Based on a 21-ton freight limit for a 105 C.Y. van trailer, 80 drums of paper and plastic wastes may be loaded per trailer. Typically wastes will be removed from the drums and containers at the repository and placed into lifts. The repository will maintain possession of the containers.

Related Costs

Costs for supply of water- and pressure-washing equipment should be included in the estimate. The pressure-washing unit consumes approximately 20 gallons per person per day for decontamination. Assuming 4 decontamination operations per day per person, this is 5 gallons per person per decontamination event. Other equipment that may require decontamination includes scaffolding or man-lifts, if needed for high building sampling. If these are required, assume 10 gallons per day per piece of equipment required for decontamination. It is reasonable to assume that a pressure-washing unit and the associated water will be used on a daily basis throughout the duration of the sampling.

For electric power, the compressor, vacuum, and filter motor ratings for the pressure-washing unit are estimated at 20 H.P. combined. The motors are typically operational for only 1 hour per day during the sampling duration, and thus the costs are negligible for sampling cost estimates.

If the filtered water discharged from the pressure-washing vacuum unit does not meet POTW discharge criteria, then costs for pretreatment prior to discharge to an existing sanitary sewer should also be included.

Conclusion

D&D Sampling and Analysis is used throughout the process of characterizing, decontaminating, and decommissioning nuclear facilities. The primary cost drivers are the number of samples to be taken (and their associated analyses), the size and rate of the sampling crew, and the crew mobilization costs. The cost engineer should work closely with the sampling team to evaluate the optimal approach, timing, and crew size of sampling efforts, including mobilization.

Chapter 54

In Situ Vitrification

In situ vitrification (ISV) is a technology that destroys and removes organic contaminants and immobilizes inorganic constituents, including many radionuclides, through in-place joule heating and melting of soil. The ISV process entails placing electrodes in the contaminated soil and passing a high-voltage electric current between the electrodes. Due to the low electrical conductivity (i.e., high electrical resistivity) of most soils, the electric current flowing between the electrodes generates significant amounts of heat, which causes the soil temperature to rise to levels well above its melting point.

Four electrodes are used in a typical ISV system. Since soil typically is a poor conductor of electricity, a mixture of graphite and glass frit is placed between the electrodes to provide a starter path. Once the graphite and glass frit melt, the heat generated by the passage of the electric current migrates outward from the starter path, raising the temperature of the surrounding soil. The melt typically advances at a rate of 1–2" per hour (i.e., approximately 3-6 tons of soil per hour). As the melt moves downward and outward from the starter path, a steep thermal gradient (150– 250 °C per inch) develops in front of the advancing melt.

As the thermal gradient advances, organic chemicals present in the soil vaporize and then pyrolyze (decompose in the absence of oxygen) into elemental components. Due to the high viscosity of the molten material, the gaseous pyrolysis products move slowly through the melt toward the upper melt surface. Some of these gases dissolve into the molten mass, while others move to the surface where they combust in the presence of air. The ISV system includes a hood that is placed over the area being treated to collect the gaseous products from the pyrolysis and combustion processes. The collected gases are treated on–site before being discharged into the atmosphere.

After the electrical current is terminated, the molten mass cools and solidifies. Solidification typically takes place over a period of several months to a year or more. During the melting process, the void spaces between the soil particles collapse, and the gases that were contained in the void spaces migrate toward the surface. The collapse of the void spaces causes the surface of the area being treated to subside. The volume reduction achieved by ISV depends on the characteristics of the soil being treated. Volume reductions of 20–40% are typical. At the completion of the process, the surface of the treated area is restored by placing clean backfill—and in some cases, an engineered cap—over the vitrified mass.

Applications and Limitations

Applications

This technology can be applied to soil contaminated with a wide variety of hazardous, radioactive, and mixed waste contaminants. In determining if ISV is applicable to a given site, factors such as the presence of rubble, void volumes, and other inclusions in the contaminated area need to be considered. Inclusions are defined as highly concentrated contaminant layers, void volumes, containers, metal scrap, general refuse, demolition debris, rock, or other non-homogeneous materials or conditions within the waste volume. Most inclusions, with the exception of very high–melting–point ceramics, are treated in the same manner as the hazardous organic and inorganic contaminants during ISV. It is necessary to evaluate the size, concentration, and chemical composition of such inclusions during applicability analyses.

Limitations

The maximum demonstrated melt depth for the ISV technology is 23'. For sites where there is a layer of clean soil overlying the contaminated material, and the contamination extends to depths below 23', it may be necessary to excavate the clean soil overlying the contaminated material. The costs for excavation of any clean overburden should be estimated separately.

The efficiency of ISV is reduced in situations where contamination extends near or below the groundwater table. This is because the presence of water greatly increases the electrical conductivity, which in turn decreases the amount of joule heating that occurs. In addition, significant amounts of heat will be expended in vaporizing the water. In such situations, it may be necessary to depress the groundwater table using a system of extraction wells (sometimes in conjunction with vertical subsurface barriers, such as sheet piling). When it is necessary to depress the groundwater table, it may also be necessary to treat the extracted groundwater. The costs for groundwater extraction, vertical barriers, and treatment systems should be estimated separately.

The ISV process should be performed at calculated safe distances from above ground and underground structures and utilities to prevent unintended damage to them. The primary concerns are thermal damage and subsidence due to soil densification. Pretreatment of all or a portion of the affected area may be required at sites where buried waste, tanks, drums, or sealed containers are present or may be present.

Process and Treatment Train Configurations

There are 4 distinct configurations for vitrifying contaminated soil:

- In Situ: In-place treatment of soils without excavation, staging, or other handling.
- Staged In Situ: Treatment of soils that have been consolidated and staged into a small area.

- Stationary Batch: Treatment of excavated soils in an engineered treatment cell.
- Continuous Ex Situ: Treatment of excavated soils in a stationary melter.

This chapter addresses only the in situ configuration. It is the most common and widely used method for containing radio nuclides.

The following technical factors affect the approach and ancillary systems for ISV. All should be considered when developing a cost estimate.

- Pretreatment of Affected Area
- Melting Methods
- Treatment of Off-gases
- Disposal of Process Residuals

Pretreatment of Affected Area

Pretreatment of all or a portion of the affected area may be required at sites where buried waste, tanks, drums, or sealed containers are or may be present. Sites with clay and weathered shale soils also may require pretreatment to promote gas-phase flow through the soils. The most common approach for pre-treating an area slated for ISV is to use a vibratory beam attached to a crane. When tanks, drums, or containers are present, the vibratory beam destroys the integrity of the containers, promoting controlled release of gases during subsequent ISV treatment. When clay and weathered shale soils are present, the vibratory beam disrupts the soil column, rendering the soil more permeable for gas-phase flow. Other methods are being developed for improving the permeability of soils prior to ISV treatment, but they are not yet proven.

Melting Methods

Two melting methods have been developed for ISV. The first, known as the horizontal or "top-down" method, is more conventional and more frequently applied. This is the preferred approach for sites with buried drums, sealed containers, and buried waste. The top-down method can be initiated at the surface or at depth. Surface-initiated vitrification progresses downward through the treatment zone, whereas subsurface-initiated vitrification progresses both downward and upward. Given its widespread use, this chapter addresses only the top-down method.

The *vertical* or *planar method* has been used on a small number of sites. In this method, separate melts originate along the vertical axis of the electrodes and progress outward and toward one another. This method is best suited to situations in which deeper or narrower melt configurations are required, and for sites where there is a potential for generating large amounts of gases. In the latter case, converging planar melts can treat materials such as buried waste, tanks, drums, or sealed containers with greater effectiveness and efficiency than can be achieved using the top-down method. However, the potential for generating large amounts of gases from buried drums, tanks, and containers is addressed most frequently by pre-treating the affected area using a vibratory beam (described above).

Treatment of Off-gases

The ISV system includes an off-gas treatment system, which consists of a wet quencher, wet scrubber, carbon filters, and particulate filters. In addition, for sites where organic constituents are present, a thermal oxidizer is added to the off-gas treatment train. The costs for off-gas treatment should be considered for any ISV estimate and included where appropriate.

Disposal of Process Residuals

Several residuals, most of which come from the off-gas treatment system, are generated during the ISV process. Typical residuals include scrubber liquor, spent carbon filters, spent particulate filters, and used protective equipment. All except for the scrubber liquor are disposed of by incorporating them into subsequent melts. After the last melt, these materials must be disposed at an appropriate location. Generally, the quantity of these materials remaining after the last melt is small. The scrubber liquor is often sent off-site for treatment; disposal costs should be estimated separately.

Basic Information Needed for Estimating

It is possible to create a reasonable cost estimate using a few required parameters. If more detailed information is known, one can create a more precise and site-specific estimate using a secondary set of parameters.

To estimate the cost of the in situ vitrification system, certain information must be known. This information is discussed below.

Contaminated Area

The scope of the project is the surface area of contamination. The size of the contaminated soil area will affect the amount of time and the number of setups required for the treatment. The typical minimum-to-maximum size range is 500–1,000,000 S.F. Smaller projects are generally economically infeasible for ISV. The largest projects require special consideration, and the ISV vendor should be consulted early.

Depth to Top of Contamination

The depth to the top of the contaminated soil layer will affect any decisions regarding subsurface excavation prior to placing the electrodes and the starter path. The typical range is 0-10'. If depths are greater, it may be necessary to remove the clean soil overburden as described previously.

Depth to Bottom of Contamination

The maximum demonstrated melt depth for the ISV technology is 23'. Accordingly, the typical valid range is 3–23". The minimum practical thickness of contaminated soil that can be treated using ISV is 3'. The value for this parameter must always be equal to or greater than the Depth to Top of Contamination plus 3'. The melt advance rate is typically 1–2" per hour, with a soil melting rate of 3–5 tons per hour. The ISV equipment is capable of processing a vitrified mass in the range of 800–1,000 tons of soil in a single setting. Larger volumes require disassembly and reconfiguration of the ISV equipment. The total time requirement is about 7–10 days per setting.

Depth to Groundwater

The presence of groundwater can greatly affect the efficiency and cost of ISV. Knowing the depth to groundwater, and more particularly, whether the groundwater depth is at or near the depth of the bottom of the melt, is critical to determining the cost of an ISV project.

Mobilization/Demobilization

Mobilization cost includes transporting the ISV system to the project site and setting it up. The rental cost for the three equipment trailers over the life of the project is included as part of the vitrification cost per ton. The mobilization cost is based on truck transportation of 3 equipment trailers from Richland, WA to the project site. Demobilization cost includes dismantling the ISV system and transporting it from the project site. The demobilization cost is based on transportation of 3 equipment trailers by truck from the project site to Richland, WA.

Design Information Needed for Detailed Estimates

Following are descriptions of the types of information that, when available, can add detail and accuracy to estimates. Also included are design criteria and estimating rules of thumb that the estimators use to determine values that are not known, or to check information provided by others.

Soil Properties

The items to consider include:

- Site Topography
- Soil Moisture Content
- Soil Density
- Volume Reduction Percentage

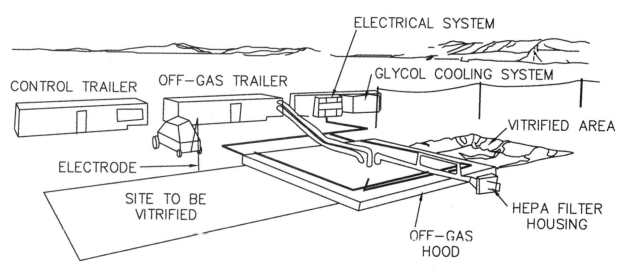

Figure 54.1 Typical Situ Vitrification Setup

Site Topography

The ISV process equipment can accommodate some variations in site topography without special preparation. A level area is required for placement of the equipment trailers. The off-gas collection hood has a flexible skirt at the ground-hood interface that is capable of accepting +/- 6" variations in the soil surface. The area supporting the hood should not slope more than 5%. With special equipment modification, the treatment area may be up to 6' above or below the level of the treatment trailers. In addition, rainwater or surface water should be prevented from flowing into the treatment area. The cost of preparing the surface to meet these criteria should be included in the estimate.

Soil Moisture Content

The ISV process is capable of treating saturated soils, but in doing so, can heat the material to 100 °C, at which temperature water is removed by vaporization. It takes about as much electric energy to remove one pound of water as it does to melt one pound of soil. Therefore, the treatment volume should be as dry as possible prior to ISV. Processing below the water table is generally economically feasible if soil permeability is less than 10^{-4} cm/sec. The vitrification cost is directly proportional to the moisture content of the soil. For every 1% change in soil moisture content, the cost will change by $2.00–$3.00 per ton. Typical ISV processes require the moisture content to be between 0–40% with 20% being a good rule of thumb for average soil if moisture content is not known or available to the estimator.

Soil Density

The density of the contaminated soil affects costs by converting the volume of soil (cubic feet) into a corresponding weight (tons). The typical range for soil density is 70–130 pounds per cubic foot (P.C.F.). The default value for soil density is 100 P.C.F.

Volume Reduction Percentage

The ISV system will result in a significant reduction in the volume of the material being treated. The typical range for this parameter is 20–40%, with 30% being an appropriate rule of thumb value if the project is not yet designed.

Operational Approach

Items to consider include:

- Melt Area
- Safety Level
- Backfill
- Re-vegetation
- Engineered Cap

Each of these parameters is described below:

Melt Area

A maximum melt area is about 900 S.F., with the width of the off-gas hood equal to 55'. The actual electrode spacing is typically 11–18', with the resulting width of the vitrified mass equal to 1.5–3.0 times the electrode spacing. Using a default melt area of 700 S.F. will produce a conservative estimate.

Safety Level

The contaminants present at the site are one of several factors that determine the appropriate worker safety level for the site work. Safety level refers to those levels for personnel protection as required by OSHA in 29 CFR Part 1910.120. The 4 levels are defined as A, B, C, and D, where level "A" is the most protective, and "D" the least protective. A safety level of E (Modified Level D) is also included to simulate normal construction (no hazard) conditions as prescribed by the EPA. The ISV model includes the levels of personnel protection specified in 29 CFR Part 1910.120.

Backfill

After the ISV process is complete, the vitrified mass has a volume of 20–40% less than the original soil volume. This volume reduction causes the surface of the treated area to subside. The depression is filled in with clean backfill, allowing for restoration of surface grades. The amount of backfill required is related to the volume reduction percentage, as well as the size of the treatment area. If backfilling is required, the following items must be specified and estimated:

Source of Backfill

- On-site: On-site fill costs include excavation from the borrow pit/ bank and transportation to the project site.
- Off-site: Off-site fill materials require excavation from the borrow pit/bank or purchase of fill material, transportation to the project site, and placement.

Type of Backfill

- Unclassified
- Sand
- Clay

Re-vegetation

After the treated area has been backfilled with clean soil, the site generally will be provided with a grass cover to prevent erosion of the soil. In some cases, an engineered cap may be placed over the treated area. If re-vegetation is required, the following options must be considered:

Source of Topsoil

- On-site Fill Materials: Includes excavation from the borrow pit/ bank and transportation to the project site.
- Off-site Fill materials: Requires excavation from the borrow pit/ bank or purchase of fill material, along with transportation to the project site and placement.
- None: No fill is required

Type of Cover

- Seeding
- Placement of Sod
- None Required

Engineered Cap

In some cases, an engineered cap may be required after the treated area has been backfilled. *See Chapter 36 of this book for discussion of capping.*

Power Supply

The ISV system requires 3-phase electric power at either 12,500 or 13,800 volts. The electric power may be supplied by the public utility or generated on-site by a portable diesel generator. The 3-phase power is supplied to a special multiple-tap transformer that converts the power to 2-phase and transforms it to the voltage levels needed throughout the processing. The equipment is controlled to draw around 3750 kW during operation. An on-site generator would be used only in remote sites since the leasing and operating costs are not generally competitive with public utilities.

Public Utility

The preferred power supply is a public utility, if available. Public utility power parameters will include the power line installation, the distance to power connections, and the cost to purchase the power to operate the system during the ISV operation. The options for each of these parameters are described below:

Installation Options:

- Overhead (This is the default for ISV)
- Underground: Direct Buried
- Underground: Duct Bank

Distance: The local electric utility company should be contacted to determine the location of the nearest 15 kV line. The appropriate appurtenances include poles, conduit, aluminum conductor/steel reinforced conductor, and terminal splicing.

Cost to Purchase Electricity: Rates will vary depending on the location of the project. The local electric utility company should be contacted to determine the applicable rates for industrial usage. The price of electrical power can impact costs by \$15.00–\$20.00/ton for each \$0.01/kwh change in purchased power rate.

On-Site Generator

The alternative to a public utility is an on-site diesel generator. The average cost of electric power for an on-site generator is \$0.10/kwh–\$0.15/kwh. This is based on a lease agreement for usage of the generator and diesel fuel.

Related Costs

The ISV operation costs included all direct costs of operations, including burdened labor, materials, electric power, off-gas treatment, movement between settings, and equipment maintenance.

Other costs that may be incurred included the following:

- Excavating and staging materials for processing (ex situ process option)
- Dewatering
- Breaking up concrete
- Site preparation activities other than grading
- Documentation/procedural requirements imposed by the client, its contractors, and/or regulators
- Permitting requirements
- Delays or stand-by costs not caused by the vendor
- Disposing of secondary waste

Site Work and Utilities

Site work and utilities that may apply to the ISV process are:

- Monitoring wells
- Access roads
- Fencing and signage
- Overhead electrical distribution

These must also be accounted for in the estimate.

Conclusion

ISV is a complex process that requires a high degree of planning. In general, ISV is only effective for sites with conducive soil conditions and where the immobilization of contaminants is acceptable. ISV is also an expensive process and is only cost–effective in situations (such as radioactive waste) where other processes will not work. The cost drivers for ISV include the volume of soil to be treated, moisture content, soil characteristics, electrical power cost, and mobilization distance. Each of these items is highly site–specific. The cost engineer should work closely with the design team and the ISV vendor to quantify these elements and adjust the estimate accordingly.

Chapter 55

Surface Decontamination

Surface decontamination in a nuclear facility refers to the removal of radionuclide contamination from surfaces such as floors, walls, ceilings, doors, handrails, and metal finishes (e.g., outer skin of a ventilation duct). Decontamination may be required prior to removal/dismantlement of contaminated buildings and equipment in order to minimize the spread of further contamination within the facility and to separate the contaminated from uncontaminated materials.

Applications and Limitations

Applications

- Suitable for surface removal of radionuclide contamination.
- Non-destructive techniques for surface decontamination include wiping, rubbing, surface polishing, flushing, low to moderate pressure blasting, vacuuming, and ultrasonic/vibratory finishing.
- Destructive techniques for surface decontamination include concrete spalling/scarification, abrasive impact blasting (e.g., steel shot or grit), grinding of metal surfaces, and high-pressure water cutting (e.g., 30–50 kpsi).

Limitations

- Generally, surface decontamination is unable to remove neutron activation products such as Co^{60} and Ni^{59} in steel and concrete.
- Surface structures and site conditions may preclude surface decontamination.
- Does not include segmenting and dismantling of contaminated building structures and the removal of neutron-activated piping and other equipment.
- High Level Waste (HLW) and Trans-Uranic (TRU) wastes require special disposal consideration, since repositories for such wastes may not be available. If repositories are not available, interim storage or disposal costs may be required. This model does not account for interim storage or disposal costs if required.

Process Configuration and Treatment Train Considerations

- The degree and extent of radioactive contamination in a building or piece of equipment must be thoroughly screened and characterized to develop a decommissioning work plan.
- Removal of nuclear source materials (e.g., plutonium pits and uranium fuel pellets) should occur prior to surface decontamination. This could include draining tanks and vessels, and flushing out pipes and other equipment to remove and collect loose surface contamination deposits (e.g., radioactive slimes, scales, and crusts).
- Surface decontamination usually is conducted prior to any sawing of concrete, cutting of pipes, and removal of process equipment.

Basic Information Needed for Estimating

It is possible to create a reasonable cost estimate using a few required parameters. If more detailed information is known, one can create a more precise and site-specific estimate using a secondary set of parameters.

Certain information, discussed in the following paragraphs, must be known in order to complete a basic estimate.

Number of Levels or Stories
Typically the number of contaminated levels will be between 1–20.

Floor-to-Ceiling Height
This distance between the floor and ceiling is generally between 10–50', depending on the building configuration.

Rooms per Floor
The average number of rooms (e.g., offices, laboratories, and separate enclosures) per floor is used to evaluate the number of surfaces requiring decontamination. Although each floor of the building is not likely to be the same in terms of layout and number of rooms, an average estimate of rooms will suffice for the purpose of determining surfaces. This value is typically in the range of one (for warehouse/storage facilities) to several hundred (for administrative facilities).

Room Dimensions
The typical room dimension (width and length, in feet) is used in conjunction with the number of rooms per floor to determine the amount of wall surface area per level. Estimating the typical room dimension based on the prevalent number of room types will yield a reasonable figure.

Length of Handrails
This parameter is the total length in feet of handrail barriers in the building to be decontaminated. A reasonable assumption for a typical handrail barrier construction is 2 parallel lengths of 2" O.D. steel tubing, separated by a spacing of 12". In addition, it is reasonable to assume that support posts 42" high are spaced at 4' intervals. The length of handrail barrier specified for this parameter consists of the length of the entire assembly and not of the individual components. Handrails are typically decontaminated manually using wiping cloths and a non-aqueous cleaning solution, instead of mechanical washing methods.

Total Building Surface Area

The total surface area in the building (square feet) may be calculated as:

Surface Area = [2 × (Room Width + Room Length) × Floor Heights × Number of Rooms × Number of Floors × (1.15)] + [(Room Width × Room Length × Number of Rooms) × 2 × Number of Floors × (1.15)] + Surface Area of Handrails

The first term in brackets denotes the surface area determined by walls, doors, and windows. This value is then added to the second set of terms in the bracket, which denotes the surface area due to floors and ceilings. This sum is then increased by 15% to account for additional surface area due to items such as window sills, ledges, desktops, benches, shelves, crevices, and cracks which must also be inspected and cleaned.

Design Information Needed for Detailed Estimates

The following types of detailed information, when available, can add detail and accuracy to estimates. Also included are design criteria and estimating rules of thumb that the estimator typically uses to determine values that are not known, or to check information provided by others.

Demolition Factor

This parameter specifies the volume of waste per the volume of in-place building material. A reasonable default value is 1.5 C.F. of waste per C.F. of building material. The default demolition factor of 1.5 implies that for every 1.0 C.F. (in-place) of material removed, 1.5 C.F. of waste volume will be generated due to material expansion upon removal. A reasonable range is 1–10 C.F. of waste per C.F. of building material.

Shipping/Disposal

Key cost elements of shipping and disposing of wastes generated from surface decontamination include the location of the disposal site, the distance to the disposal site, and the type of waste to be shipped.

Primary locations for disposal of wastes contaminated with nuclear materials currently include:

- Barnwell, SC
- Hanford, WA
- Nevada Test Site, NV
- Envirocare, UT

The current rate charged for the disposal, and the distance to the disposal site are cost factors to be evaluated. The disposal fees at each location vary based on volume of waste, number of shipments, radionuclide composition, waste content activity (pCi/g), and the repository location. The disposal fee includes costs such as off-loading the shipment at the disposal site, analytical tests performed by the repository, and long-term care and maintenance. The estimator should check with each repository option for the best estimate of the disposal fee at the time that the wastes will be shipped.

Shipments considerably less than 1,000,000 C.F. or small quantities of wastes generated by non-government facilities (e.g., power plants, research facilities, hospitals, etc.) may not qualify for these rates. The estimator must obtain applicable disposal fees at the time that the estimate is prepared. The estimator should also evaluate the type of wastes accepted at each site and the schedule for waste shipping. In some cases, a combination of shipping and disposal sites may be used to eliminate waste generated by surface decontamination activities.

Wastes are commonly packed into 55-gallon shipping drums and standard B-25 shipping boxes (4' × 4' × 6') prior to shipping. Drums and shipping containers are typically packed 90% full. At 90% material fill, each shipping box will hold 86.4 S.F. of scabbled concrete. Liners are not necessary because boxes generally contain only dry scabbled concrete.

At 90% material fill, each drum will hold 6.6 C.F. of waste. Drums are used to hold wastes such as wipes, used sheeting, and disposable coveralls. Assuming a demolition factor of 1.5 and a waste compaction ratio of 2:1 for wastes such as crumpled wipes and sheeting, it is estimated that 1 C.F. of waste will result from 115 S.F. of sheeting and blotting paper usage. The waste volume is increased by 20% to account for disposal of miscellaneous wastes including used HEPA and wet-vacuum filters, disposed coveralls, discarded respirators, and used tape rolls.

Typically trucks are used to ship all waste. Based on a 21-ton freight limit for a 105 C.Y. van trailer, either 80 drums of paper and plastic wastes or 4 shipping boxes of concrete rubble may be loaded per trailer. Typically, wastes will be removed from the drums and containers at the repository and placed into lifts. The repository will maintain possession of the containers.

Decontamination Process Considerations

Decontamination process/magnitude issues that affect costs include the *Surface Area to Be Decontaminated* and *Methods to be Used*. The Surface Area to be Decontaminated is Calculated as:

Surface Area to be Decontaminated = Total Surface Area
– Clean Surface Area

Where the Clean Surface Area is the interior surface area that is not contaminated by radionuclides (e.g., "clean"). A reasonable assumption for this area is 50–80% of the total surface area.

Various methods are used to clean surface areas. These include:

- Wiping: manual cleaning using non-aqueous cleaning solutions such as industrial strength 409® and Radiacwash®. A typical fully productive handrail wiping rate is 10.5 S.F./hr of tubing surface area per crew, which translates to a length of handrail barrier section of approximately 20'. A typical, fully productive surface wiping rate is approximately 60 S.F./hr of surface area per crew.
- Pressure washing: uses a stream of pressurized water (max. of 1,800 psi) to remove loose contamination for pickup by a suction nozzle. A wet-service vacuum unit with filter is used to separate collected particulate from the discharged effluent. A typical, fully productive cleansing rate for pressure washing is 150 S.F./hr per crew. The high-pressure water loosens and removes surface contaminants, but is adjusted so as to prevent excessive surface scouring and pitting.

- Scabbling: uses a machine to remove a top layer of contamination from hard surfaces such as concrete and has a practical working depth limit of 1.5". Scabbling a concrete surface will leave a rough and uneven finish. A typical default scabbling depth is 1/8". The fully productive scabbling rate is 50 S.F./hr per crew at a 1/4" depth or less. At depths greater than 1/4", the production rate decreases linearly by 9 S.F./hr for each 1/4" depth increase. Thus at the practical working limit of 1.5" depth, the production rate is only 5 S.F./hr. Scabbling is used to remove deeply penetrated contaminants that cannot be removed effectively by vacuuming, wiping, or pressure washing

Wiping is the most common method for decontaminating building surfaces. Reasonable rules of thumb, depending on the type of building and associated surfaces, are as follows:

Decontamination Method	Typical % of Total Surface Area Decontaminated
Wiping	5–20%
Pressure Washing	5–10%
Scabbling	5%

Consumable Materials

Various consumable materials are used for surface decontamination. They include:

- Wiping fluid: estimated at the rate of one gallon per 225 S.F. of surface area wiped. Since the wiping solution is non-aqueous based, the surface dries clean so that no further water removal or disposal is required.
- Wiping cloth: estimated at the rate of 260 S.F. of cloth per 100 S.F. of surface area wiped. Used cloths are disposed of as waste in 55-gallon drums.
- Blotting paper: estimated at 1.5 S.F. per each 1 S.F. of surface area pressure-washed. The blotting paper is used to remove any excess water and loosened contaminants that are not suctioned off the concrete surface.
- High-strength plastic sheeting (Herculite®): used to erect temporary barriers around the work zone. The material is also used in disposable plastic bags to contain trash such as wipes, blotting papers, and spent decontamination materials. Plastic sheeting/bag usage is estimated at 3 S.F. per S.F. of surface decontaminated.
- Miscellaneous decontamination supplies: typically charged as unit charge per S.F. of all surfaces cleaned. These miscellaneous supplies include items such as duct/packing tape, small dust brushes, crevice tools (e.g., toothbrushes), small bags, tacks, and labels.

Decontamination of Workers

This is a major cost item for the surface decontamination, which is labor intensive and messy. A reasonable assumption based on decontamination crew size is as follows (full-shift personnel in each crew): handrails–3.25, surface wiping–4.25, and pressure-washing or scabbling–3.75. Decontamination crews are composed of laborers, crew leaders (supervisors), skilled workers (equipment operators), and radiation monitors (health physics). A work week is equivalent to 40 labor hours. Decontamination services include washing/cleaning all reusable protective/worker clothing items including uniforms, rubber gloves/boots, and protective outer clothing. Usage, heating, filtration, and disposal of water for showers are also included.

Personnel decontamination typically takes place 4 times per person per shift; thus, 4 changes of disposable clothing (e.g., coveralls, gloves, boot covers, etc.) are made per person per shift. Respirator cartridges are replaced on a daily basis (2 per person per day). Non-disposable safety equipment such as full-face respirators, rubber boots/gloves, and washable coveralls are provided by the contractor as part of the overhead and thus are not charged as direct costs.

Provision of a decontamination hygiene kit (stocked in the decontamination trailer) is another cost to consider. The kit includes 27 individual decontamination items including foam, hand soap, decontamination sprays, and hand towelettes. The kit might be used once per week for each decontamination crew (the 4 crews being handrails, surface wiping, pressure washing, and concrete scabbling).

Productivity

A weighted productivity loss factor is calculated using productivity losses from the combined effects of: height adjustments, protective clothing, Radiological Controls Program (RADCON) procedures, respiratory protection, and breaks. The unadjusted crew labor and equipment requirements are multiplied by the weighted productivity loss multiplier to estimate the adjusted crew labor and equipment requirements. Consumables such as wipes and cleaning solutions are not adjusted for productivity losses. Productivity loss considerations include:

- Height Adjustment: the productivity loss in percent due to working at elevated heights (e.g., ladders and scaffolding). A good default value is 15%.
- Protective Clothing: the productivity loss in percent due to working in protective clothing (e.g., coveralls, rubber boots and gloves). This takes into account clothing changes during a shift and restricted movements to avoid heat stress. A reasonable value is 20–25%.
- RADCON: productivity loss in percent due to Radiation Control procedures. RADCON entails radiation control procedures involving safety and workplace training (e.g., mock-up training) to ensure that the worker is keeping his/her absorbed dose to a minimum. A reasonable default value is 15%.
- Respiratory Protection: productivity loss in percent due to wearing respiratory protection such as half-face and full-face respirators or SCBA (Self-Contained Breathing Apparatus) equipment. A reasonable value is 35–40%.
- Breaks: productivity loss in percent due to routine personnel breaks during a shift (e.g., bathroom, lunch, health). A good default value is 10%.

Related Costs Costs for supply of water and power should be included in the estimate. The pressure-washing unit consumes approximately 300 gallons per hour of water at 100% operation. For electric power, the compressor, vacuum, and filter motor ratings for the pressure-washing unit are estimated at 20 H.P. combined, and compressor and vacuum motor ratings for the mechanical scabbler are estimated at 17.5 H.P. combined. Assume that these motors are operational for 75% of the time that the crews are on the job. To estimate electric power usage, a good conversion is 1 H.P. = 0.746 kW.

If the filtered water discharged from the pressure washing vacuum unit does not meet POTW discharge criteria, then costs for pretreatment prior to discharge to an existing sanitary sewer should also be included.

Conclusion

Surface decontamination is used to remove radionuclide contamination from building surfaces, most often in a nuclear facility. The primary cost driver is the amount of surface area to be decontaminated. In very large decontamination efforts, where significant amounts of wipes, used sheeting, and disposable coveralls are generated as waste, costs are also incurred for handling, shipping, and disposal of these rad-contaminated materials to an approved landfill. The cost engineer should work closely with the construction operations team to compare the various decontamination approaches for applicability, cost, and efficiency.

Part IX

Cost Estimating for Remediation —Remediation Support

Chapter 56

Groundwater Monitoring Wells

The primary objectives of groundwater monitoring are to detect whether a site is discharging contaminants into the groundwater, determine whether the concentrations of contaminants are within prescribed limits, and measure the effectiveness of corrective measures taken at the site. This chapter is intended primarily for groundwater monitoring wells. However, through careful adjustment of casing and screen lengths, the guidance in this chapter may also be used to estimate the installation of vadose zone monitoring wells.

Applications and Limitations

Applications

- Monitoring wells are required under RCRA Subtitle C for hazardous waste sites, Subtitle D for landfills, and in some instances, Subtitle I for underground storage tank facilities.
- The particular design of a monitoring well depends largely on the hydrogeologic environment, the chemical nature of the contaminants, and whether the well bore will be used to conduct geophysical investigations. These factors will influence the well diameter, well construction materials, screen length, and the depth to top of screen.

Limitations

- This chapter does not address double- and triple-cased wells. If these are required, the estimator should work with local regulators to determine specifications.
- Well depth in this chapter is limited to 1,000'. It is rare that sampling would be required at a greater depth. (In such cases, the estimate should reflect drilling methods for deeper wells that are beyond the scope of this chapter.)

Typical System Design Elements

The design of a monitoring well depends largely on the hydrogeologic environment, the chemical nature of the contaminants, and whether the well bore will be used to conduct geophysical investigations. These factors will influence well diameter, well construction materials, screen length, and the depth to top of screen. Such factors also influence the number of different stratigraphic horizons at which samples must be taken.

Monitoring well samples are usually obtained from relatively thin zones in the aquifer. This is often accomplished by using multiple wells that have short screened intervals. A series of wells of different depths are often installed to obtain samples from several different depths within the aquifer. This method facilitates delineation of the vertical dimensions and contaminant strength of the plume. Multiple well depths may also be appropriate when a single well at each sampling location cannot adequately intercept and monitor the vertical extent of contaminant migration.

This chapter addresses well installation for up to 3 different aquifers (1 unconfined aquifer and 2 confined aquifers). For the first (unconfined) aquifer, up to 5 different well depths may be specified. Multiple well depths are appropriate when an aquifer must be monitored at different stratigraphic horizons. Cased wells would be used for the confined aquifers. Cased wells are required when confined (isolated or unconnected) aquifers are penetrated. The casing prevents contaminant migration from overlying aquifers. Normally, double-cased wells are used for the second aquifer, and triple-cased wells are used for the third aquifer.

Confined or multiple aquifer monitoring well design typically includes double casing to the confining unit. The typical drilling sequence is to advance a borehole 3–5" larger in diameter than the outer casing, to a depth within the confining unit. The casing is placed in the hole, and the annular space is grouted and allowed to dry. This process is repeated if triple casing is used. A borehole is advanced inside the casing, usually with a rotary drilling method, and the well is completed as usual.

This section addresses only the costs associated with monitoring well installation. Well drilling, screen, and casing costs are included, as are costs for professional field labor. Costs for sample collection during drilling are also included. However, no other sampling or analytical costs are included. These costs are discussed in Chapter 57, "Monitoring." Through adjustment of casing and screen lengths, the guidelines in this section may also be used to estimate the installation of vadose zone monitoring wells.

Basic Information Needed for Estimating

It is possible to create a reasonable cost estimate using a few required parameters. If more detailed information is known, one can create a more precise and site-specific estimate using a secondary set of parameters. To estimate the cost of groundwater monitoring wells, certain information must be known. This information is discussed in the following paragraphs.

Number of Aquifers
Monitoring wells for up to three separate aquifers may be used. Well parameters (e.g., depth, diameter, construction material) are determined separately for each aquifer.

Formation Type
The formation of subsurface geology of the site may be either consolidated or unconsolidated. *Consolidated formation* refers to a soil stratum that may have been subjected to glacial or other consolidating loads in the geological past. Consolidated formations are generally comprised of rock, cemented sand (sandstone), or stiff clay deposits.

An *unconsolidated formation* is a geologically recent deposit such as those found in deltas, alluvial plains, or marine deposits. Unconsolidated formations are comprised of loose to medium silts, sands, and gravel. The drilling method is based on the formation type.

Number of Well Depths in Each Aquifier

Multiple well depths may be necessary when a single well at each sampling location cannot adequately intercept and monitor the vertical extent of contaminant migration. The number of monitoring wells is defined and estimated separately for each aquifer.

Depth to Groundwater/Top of Groundwater Sampling Interval

For a single well depth, this parameter is used to specify the depth to the surface of the first aquifer, and the screened interval begins approximately 3' above the aquifer surface.

For multiple well depths, this parameter is used to specify the depth to the top of the groundwater sampling interval for each different depth group, and the screened interval begins at the depth to the top of the groundwater sampling interval.

A typical unconfined aquifer monitoring well is shown in Figure 56.1.

Depth to Top/Bottom of Confining Units

This parameter defines the depths and thicknesses of only the second and third aquifers. The depths and thicknesses of the confined aquifers, in turn, determine the typical casing and screen lengths for wells installed in the confined aquifers, where the screened interval is assumed to begin at the aquifer surface, which is located at the base of the overlying confining layer. The top of the underlying confining layer forms the base of the aquifer. Typically, double-cased and triple-cased wells are used for the second and third aquifers, respectively. A typical double-cased well is shown in Figure 56.2.

If the pressure within a confined aquifer is great enough, the hydrostatic head of the aquifer may exceed the ground surface elevation. In such instances, the well casing should be extended far enough above ground surface to prevent flow.

Guard Posts

Guard posts protect wells from damage by heavy equipment. Typically, guard posts are 5' tall, concrete-filled steel posts.

Worker Safety Level

Worker safety is affected by the contaminants at the site. Safety level refers to the levels required by OSHA in 29 CFR Part 1910. The 4 levels are designated as A, B, C, and D; where "A" is the most protective and "D" is the least protective. A safety level of E is also included to simulate normal construction, "no hazard" conditions as prescribed by the EPA.

Design Information Needed for Detailed Estimates

Following are descriptions of the types of detailed information that, when available, can add detail and accuracy to estimates. Also included are design criteria and estimating rules of thumb that the estimator typically uses to determine values that are not known, or to check information provided by others.

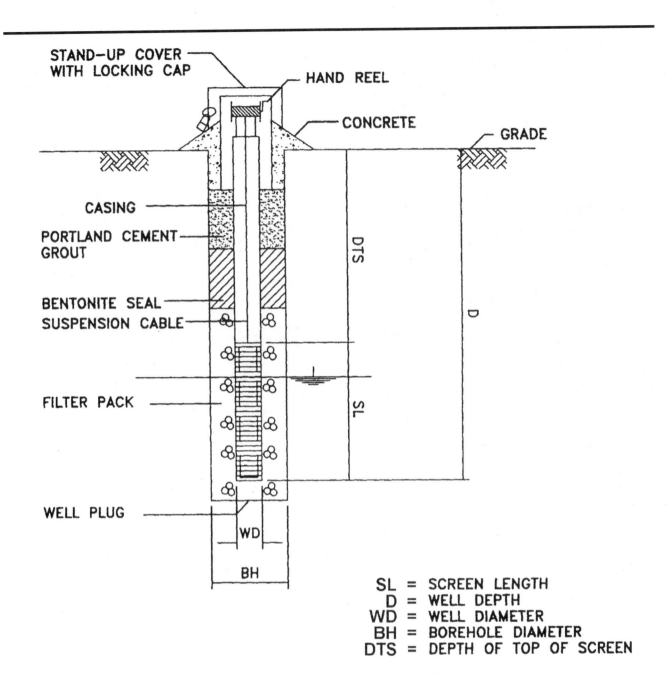

SL = SCREEN LENGTH
D = WELL DEPTH
WD = WELL DIAMETER
BH = BOREHOLE DIAMETER
DTS = DEPTH OF TOP OF SCREEN

Figure 56.1 Unconfined Aquifier Monitoring Wall

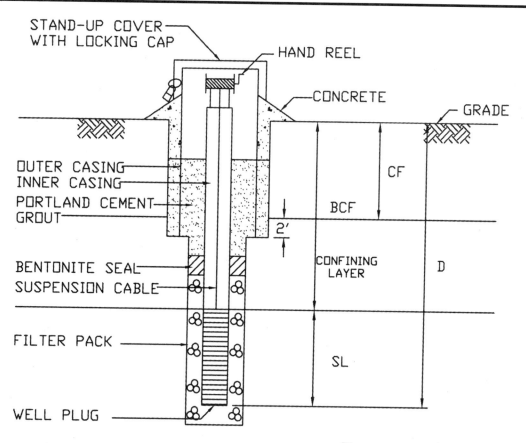

STAND-UP COVER WITH LOCKING CAP

HAND REEL

CONCRETE

GRADE

OUTER CASING
INNER CASING
PORTLAND CEMENT GROUT

CF

BCF

2'

BENTONITE SEAL
SUSPENSION CABLE

CONFINING LAYER

D

FILTER PACK

SL

WELL PLUG

SL = SCREEN LENGTH
D = WELL DEPTH
CF = DEPTH TO TOP OF CONFINING LAYER
BCF = DEPTH TO BOTTOM OF CONFINING LAYER

Figure 56.2 Confined Aquifer Monitoring Well

Well Construction Material

Well construction material is normally chosen based on contaminent compatibility and cost. The material depends on the installation method. If a filter pack is required, as in the case of groundwater extraction wells, a pre-packed well screen is commonly used. HDPE well materials are used for the trencher/screen installer. PVC construction materials are normally used for all other installation methods. Prepacks are available.

Thus, the options for well construction material are:

- PVC
- Stainless steel
- HDPE (only for trencher/screen installer; not for chain trencher or backhoe)
- PVC prepack (only for directional drill rig)
- Stainless steel prepack (only for directional drill rig)
- HDPE prepack (only for directional drill rig)

Well Diameter

Well diameter refers to the nominal outer diameter of the well screen. Prepack filter material typically adds at least an inch to the diameter of the well. Thus a 6" diameter prepack screen would actually measure 7" or more in diameter. Consequently, prepack screens require larger bore holes. The range of well diameters available for horizontal well installation is typically limited by the equipment used to install the wells. Well diameter also depends on the purpose of the well.

Well diameter options are as follows:

- 2" (not for trencher/screen installer)
- 4"
- 6"
- 8" (only for directional drill rig; prepacks not available in 8" diameter)

Sidewall Protection

Sidewall protection applies only to the backhoe installation method. Trenches deeper than 5' typically require side wall protection to avoid cave-in. This is accomplished by installing trench boxes or by sloping the sides of the excavation. In some instances, steel sheeting may be used to support the trench walls.

Sidewall protection options, then, are as follows:

- Side slope
- Trench box
- Sheeting
- None (not an option if depth to screen > 5')

Drum Drill Cuttings

Drum drill cuttings apply only to the trencher/screen installer and directional drill rig. During well installation, soil cuttings from the drill bit and subsequent hole are often drummed for follow-on analysis, treatment, or disposal.

The chosen well construction material should resist chemical and physical degradation and not interfere with the quality of groundwater samples. Well construction material can be either stainless steel or PVC.

Well Diameter

The typical well diameter is 2" for well depths less than 100' and 4" for well depths of 100' or more. For the first aquifer, 6" and 8" wells are available, but are not generally used for economic reasons.

Depth to Top of Screen

The typical depth for the first aquifer is either the depth to groundwater or the depth to the top of the sampling interval, depending on whether a single well depth or multiple well depths are chosen. For multiple well depths, the depth to top of screen is specified separately for each different well depth. For the second and third aquifers, the depth is typically equal to the depth to the base of the overlying confining layer.

Screen Length

Screen lengths often depend on location-specific groundwater level fluctuations. For the first and second aquifers, the typical screen length is either the aquifer thickness or 10', whichever is less. For the third aquifer, the typical screen length is 10'. The screen length is specified separately for each aquifer.

Average Well Depth

This measurement represents the average distance from the ground surface to the bottom of the completed well. This value, in conjunction with the Formation Type, determines the default values for drilling methodology, well diameter, and well construction material. The average well depth must be greater than the corresponding aquifer depth to groundwater and less than 1,000'. Figure 56.3 provides a summary of the most likely drilling methods based on depth and formation type.

Sample Collection During Drilling

Sample collection during borehole advancement characterizes the geology beneath the site and defines the magnitude and extent of contamination in the vadose zone. Samples will normally be collected during drilling using split spoon sample collection with standard penetration testing at 5' intervals during borehole advancement. Samples are normally screened with an Organic Vapor Analyzer (OVA) for volatile organics. Sampling requirements are specified separately for each aquifer.

Drilling Method

The selection of a drilling method is a function of site-specific geologic conditions, well specifications, and degree of subsurface disturbance. The typical drilling method depends on the well depth and formation type, as shown in Figure 56.3. Drilling methods are described as follows.

Hollow Stem Auger

An auger bit is attached to the leading auger flight and cuts a hole for the flights to follow. The cuttings are brought to the top of the hole by the flights, which act as a screw conveyor. Auger sections are added until the desired depth is reached. The hollow stem auger is the most widely used method of installing monitoring wells in unconsolidated materials in North America. Hollow stem augers are preferred for environmental drilling because they create minimal disturbance to the surrounding soil, allow accurate sample collection, and the flights act as temporary casing to prevent caving. The EPA (1986) generally recognizes 150' as the maximum drilling depth and 4" as the maximum well diameter for which hollow stem auger drilling is appropriate.

Air Rotary

Air rotary drilling uses compressed air as a drilling fluid. It is applicable in hard rock formations and with double casing in unconsolidated formations.

Water/Mud Rotary

Rotary drilling techniques use a rotating bit to advance the borehole. Cuttings are removed by continuous circulation of a drilling fluid as the bit penetrates the formation. The disadvantages of this method are introduction of drilling fluid to the soils/subsurface (which could spread contamination vertically and horizontally or introduce contaminants); difficulty in distinguishing the groundwater table elevation; loss of circulation in highly fractured or permeable formations; and alteration of well hydraulics. The water/mud rotary method is typically used for well depths greater than 150' in unconsolidated sediments. Water/mud rotary is also used for drilling in consolidated formations and is the only available drilling method for the second and third aquifers.

Drum Drill Cuttings

During well installation, soil cuttings from the drill bit and subsequent hole are often drummed and stored until disposal options have been evaluated. The conservative estimate would be that all drill cuttings will be drummed.

Drum Development Water

The number of drums required for development water is based on the assumption of purging four well volumes from each well. Typically, all development water is drummed until it is tested.

Formation Type	Average Well Depth	Drilling Method	Casing Diameter	Bore Hole Diameter	Well Material
Consolidated	0-100	Air Rotary	2	6	PVC SCH 40
Consolidated	101-300	Air Rotary	4	8	PVC SCH 80
Consolidated	301-500	Air Rotary	4	8	SS
Consolidated	>500	Air Rotary	4	8	SS
Unconsolidated	0-100	Hollow Stem Auger	2	8	PVC SCH 40
Unconsolidated	101-300	Air Rotary	4	8	PVC SCH 80
Unconsolidated	301-500	Air Rotary	4	8	SS
Unconsolidated	>500	Air Rotary	4	8	SS

Figure 56.3 Drilling Methods for Sampling Wells

Related Costs

Other costs associated with monitoring well installation include well covers, professional field labor, and equipment decontamination. Well covers can be locking steel stand-up covers or flush-mounted manholes. Both types are lockable. Professional field labor includes supervising drillers, OVA screening, well developing, and slug testing.

The following assumptions will provide a conservative estimate for labor hours related to well installation:

- For *unconfined/unconsolidated* conditions, labor hours are based on drilling at a rate of 25' per hour, plus 1 hour per 50' for well construction, and 2 hours per well for completion.
- For *unconfined/consolidated* conditions, labor hours are based on drilling at 15' per hour, plus 1 hour per 50' for well construction, and 2 hours per well for well completion.
- For *confined/consolidated* conditions, labor hours are based on drilling at 10' per hour, plus 1 hour per 50' for well construction, and 4 hours per well for installation of secondary casing and well completion.
- For *confined/unconsolidated* conditions, labor hours are based on drilling at 20' per hour, plus 1 hour per 50' for well construction, and 4 hours per well for installation of secondary casing and well completion.

Professional field labor costs are discussed in Chapter 58, "Remedial Action (RA) Professional Labor Management." Total labor hours listed above are for supervision of drilling and well installation by a staff hydrogeologist and are based on the assumption that only geotechnical sampling will be conducted during drilling. Chemical sampling during drilling will result in slower drilling rates. Drilling rates also depend on soil type. Staff hydrogeologist hours should be adjusted to reflect site-specific information.

The time required for well development depends on soil type and other site-specific conditions. Adjustments should be made if the site conditions will require more time for development. The following are assumptions regarding labor hours for well development:

- For wells less than 500': 2 hours of a field technician and 2 hours of a junior geologist per well.
- For wells 500' or deeper: 4 hours of a field technician and 4 hours of a junior geologist per well.

Decontamination procedures for the monitoring well screen, riser, casing, and drilling equipment will be conducted prior to and between each borehole/well installation. Decontamination procedures typically consist of steam cleaning with a high-pressure steam-generating pressure washer and detergent. Decontamination procedures for split spoon samplers, bailers, and hand augers are as follows:

- Clean with tap water and detergent using a brush
- Rinse thoroughly with tap water
- Rinse with deionized water
- Rinse twice with pesticide-grade isopropanol
- Rinse with organic-free deionized water
- Allow to air dry

Site Work and Utilities

Site work and utilities such as the following may apply. If so, they must be accounted for in the estimate.

- Access roads
- Clear and grub
- Fencing

Conclusion

Monitoring wells are used on virtually all sites requiring known or suspected groundwater remediation. The cost drivers are the number of wells, well depth, well diameter, a sample collection system, and the operating period. All of these items are within the designer's control, to some extent. The cost engineer should work with the design team to optimize well placement and installation methods, while meeting the technical project requirements.

Chapter 57

Monitoring

Environmental monitoring is the process of measuring the physical and/or chemical properties of an environmental medium such as air, soil, or water during the remediation process and after active remediation is completed. Monitoring technologies have numerous applications, most of which share the following objectives:

- Identify the presence or absence of a constituent(s) within a medium (or media).
- Determine the spatial distribution and concentration of the constituent(s) within the media.
- Characterize temporal variations of the constituent(s), such as expanding or diminishing distribution and increasing or decreasing concentration.

Applications and Limitations

Applications

- Useful for:
  - Early detection of releases to the environment.
  - Assessment of the nature and extent of contamination.
  - Evaluation of the progress of an ongoing remedial action.
  - Verification that a completed remedial action was successful.
  - Verification that cleanup standards have been reached.
  - Measurement of the effects of permitted discharges on neighboring ecosystems.
- Commonly implemented in projects that require sampling and analysis of multiple media, conducted on predetermined schedules.
- Typically used to evaluate natural attenuation, ongoing remediation, post-closure, and compliance.
- Can be performed periodically or continuously, depending on equipment used.

Limitations

- The results of monitoring serve as an indicator of contamination. They should be used concurrently with other investigation, engineering, and construction methods to definitively assess environmental contamination.

- Monitoring results for a given point in time do not represent the past or the future. Thus, continued monitoring over time is required to determine environmental contamination trends.
- Monitoring results are only representative of the locations monitored. While scientific methods exist to extrapolate monitoring data to predict the nature and extent of contamination, it should be noted that environmental anomalies often exist that hamper this process.

Process Configurations and Treatment Train Considerations

- General environmental monitoring can be performed at any time for any media.
- Monitoring for the purpose of evaluating remediation or technology effectiveness should be performed after the remediation is initiated.
- Environmental monitoring to determine treatment train effectiveness is generally performed on the affected medium (e.g., monitoring groundwater to determine the effectiveness of in situ biodegradation on groundwater treatment).
- Most remedial actions have a predetermined monitoring schedule to be implemented for each medium.
- Monitoring may produce "investigation-derived wastes" as a byproduct, such as drill cuttings, personal protective equipment, well development water, etc., that need to be evaluated for disposal or treatment.

Basic Information Needed for Estimating

Reasonable cost estimates for monitoring require a few parameters. With more detailed information, one can create a more precise and site-specific estimate using a secondary set of parameters. There are three main categories of basic information:

1. General Parameters
2. Media-Specific Parameters
3. Data Management Parameters

General Parameters

General parameters describe the overall work environment for the monitoring project and include the following.

Crew Size

The crew size represents the number and configuration of the monitoring crew. Typical crew sizes are composed of:

- 1 field technician
- 2 field technicians
- 1 field technician with 1 professional

Site Distance (one-way)

Site distance is the average distance to the site that the monitoring crew has to travel. This information helps the estimator determine whether the crew will travel via car or van, or via airplane or other commercial transportation method. Costs for travel and per diem should be included in the estimate.

Safety Level

Safety level refers to the four levels defined by OSHA in 29 CFR Part 1910 as A, B, C, and D; where level "A" is the most protective, and "D" is the least protective. A safety level of E (Modified Level D) can also be considered to simulate "no hazard" conditions as prescribed by the EPA. Typically, the Monitoring level is either Level E or Level D. However, there are times when Level C protection is required. The following factors are used when adjusting O&M labor costs for health and safety levels. These factors are multiplied by the "default" labor productivity at Level D.

- Level C – 1.48
- Level D – 1.0
- Level E – 0.82

Level A and B monitoring is very rare, and the overall project conditions need to be considered to determine productivity at that safety level. No default values are appropriate at those levels.

QA/QC Samples

QA/QC samples include duplicates, equipment blanks, trip blanks, field blanks, and miscellaneous spikes and blanks. If QA/QC samples are to be included, a default amount of 10% of the total number of samples is typically added to cover the cost.

Data Analysis and Reporting

Data analysis and reporting includes professional labor hours to evaluate laboratory results, plot them on a map and/or graph, and produce a simple letter report. Detailed data analysis and modeling are not included here. Such activities are site-specific and should be estimated separately. Following are typical professional labor defaults per sample:

- Project Scientist – 0.2 hours
- Field Technician – 0.2 hours
- Draftsman/CADD Operator – 0.1 hour
- Word Processing/Clerical – 0.2 hours

Media Parameters

Monitoring is estimated based on the types of media that are going to be monitored. These are usually broken down as follows:

- Groundwater
- Surface Soil
- Subsurface Soil
- Soil Gas
- Surface Water
- Sediment
- Air

The following parameters should be evaluated for any medium to be included in the Monitoring estimate:

- First Year Number of Events
- First Year Samples per Event
- Out-Years Number of Years
- Out-Years Events per Year
- Out-Years Samples per Event
- Average Sample Depth (does not apply to all media)
- Analyses to be Conducted

Monitoring during the first year and out-years are differentiated because first-year monitoring is usually conducted more frequently (more events per year) than is the case in the out-years. The costs for the various media sampled should consider the following components, in addition to those identified above:

- Labor to take the samples
- Equipment to take the samples (either rented or purchased)
- Cost for performing the laboratory analyses on the samples

First Year Number of Events

This is the number of sampling events that will occur for a particular medium for the first year of sampling. Scheduled monitoring frequencies should be converted to a number. For example, quarterly monitoring equals four sampling events a year. The typical valid range is 1–100 events for each medium to be monitored.

First Year Samples per Event

This is the number of samples that are to be taken for a given medium every time sampling occurs in the first year. For example, if there are 5 groundwater-monitoring wells, and 2 samples are required from each well every time samples are taken in the first year, then the "first year samples per event" for groundwater value is 10. The typical valid range is 1–500 samples per event for each medium to be monitored.

Out-Years Number of Years

This is the number of years that the medium is to be sampled after the first year. The typical valid range is 0–29 years per each medium to be monitored. This range, combined with the first year, provides the typical maximum monitoring duration of 30 years.

Out-Years Events per Year

This is the average number of sampling events that will occur for a particular medium in each out-year. If different sampling schedules are to be applied for different years, an average number should be developed. The typical valid range is 1–100 events per medium per out-year.

Out-Years Samples per Event

This is the average number of samples to be taken for a given medium every time sampling occurs in out-years. If different numbers of samples are to be taken in different years, an average number per event should be developed. The typical valid range is 1–500 samples per event per medium.

Average Sample Depth

Some media have Average Sample Depth parameters that should be considered, as follows:

- Groundwater: This is the average collection depth of groundwater samples. If different aquifers are to be sampled, the estimator should average the depths for a reasonable parametric estimate. For small monitoring projects, the estimator may choose to evaluate the individual costs for monitoring at various depths. The typical valid range is 1–500' below ground surface.
- Subsurface Soil: This is the average collection depth of subsurface soil samples. If different soil depths are to be sampled, the estimator should average the depths for a reasonable parametric estimate. Again, for small monitoring projects, the estimator may

evaluate the individual costs for monitoring at different depths. The typical valid range is 1–1,000'.

- Soil Gas: This is the average depth from which soil gas samples are to be taken. If different depths are to be sampled, the estimator should average the depths for a reasonable parametric estimate. As with groundwater and subsurface soil, small monitoring projects may call for evaluation of individual monitoring costs at various depths. The typical valid range is 1–100'.

Typical Sampling Level of Effort

The following rules of thumb apply to estimating the sampling level of effort.

Groundwater

The usual method for sampling groundwater is via bailers or pumps. Reasonable defaults for the level of effort vs. number of wells, based on crew size and depth to groundwater, are presented in Figure 57.1.

The assumptions for labor shown in Figure 57.1 also account for decontamination time between the wells, monitoring aquifer parameters (such as pH, turbidity, and electrical conductivity), and well development. Default sampling rates for other groundwater sampling methods are described later in this chapter in the "Detailed Estimates" section.

Subsurface Soil

Subsurface soil sampling is performed using a power auger. A good rule of thumb for sampling rate is 9' per hour. To determine the labor hours per sample, divide the total depth to be sampled at each location by this rate. Default sampling rates for other subsurface soil sampling methods are described in the "Detailed Estimates" section.

Surface Soil

The typical method of surface soil sampling is via a hand auger. A reasonable assumption of rate for this method is:

1–person crew = 15 minutes per surface soil sample location
2–person crew = 10 minutes per surface soil sample location

Depth to Groundwater	Number of Wells Sampled per Day with Bailers (crew of 2)	Number of Wells Sampled per Day with Bailers (crew of 1)	Number of Wells Sampled per Day with Pumps (crew of 2)	Number of Wells Sampled per Day with Pumps (crew of 1)
< 25'	8	7	10	9
25–50'	6	5	8	7
51–100'	4	3	6	5
> 100'	3	2	4	3

Figure 57.1 Groundwater Sampling Labor Hour Rates

Soil Gas

The typical method of soil gas sampling is via existing wells, by applying a vacuum. A reasonable assumption of rate for this method is:

1–person crew = 30 minutes per soil gas sample location
2–person crew = 20 minutes per soil gas sample location

Default sampling rates for other soil gas sampling methods are described below under the "Detailed Estimates" section.

Surface Water

Surface water sampling is usually done by wading, using glass sampling equipment. A reasonable assumption of rate for this method is:

1–person crew = 30 minutes per surface water sample location
2–person crew = 20 minutes per surface water sample location

Sediment

Stainless steel sludge samplers are used for sediment sampling. A reasonable assumption of rate for this method is:

1–person crew = 45 minutes per sediment sample location
2–person crew = 30 minutes per sediment sample location

Air

Air sampling is usually performed using portable air samplers. A reasonable assumption of rate for this method is:

1–person crew = 15 minutes per air sample location
2–person crew = 10 minutes per air sample location

Sampling Labor Calculation

To determine the labor effort for sampling, use the following calculations:

First Year Sampling Labor (for each crew member)

First Year Sampling Labor (hours per crew member) = sum for each Media of [First Year Number of Sampling Events × First Year Samples per Event × Sampling Rate (Hours per sample)]

First Year Sampling Labor Cost = sum for each crew member [crew member labor hours × hourly rate ($ per hour)]

Out-Years Sampling Labor (for each crew member)

Out-Year Sampling Labor (hours per crew member) = sum for each Media of [Out-Year Number of Years × Out-Year Number of Sampling Events per Year × Out-Year Samples per Event × Sampling Rate (hours per sample)]

Out-Year Sampling Labor Cost = sum for each crew member [Out-Year crew member sampling labor (hours) × hourly rate ($ per hour)]

If the estimate in the out-years is to reflect escalation, the estimator should determine the annual sampling cost for each out-year and apply the appropriate escalation factor prior to determining the total out-year sampling labor cost.

Analyses to be Conducted

Most monitoring is conducted in accordance with a monitoring plan and/or a regulatory agreement that specifies the laboratory analyses that should be conducted on the samples taken for each media. The estimator should refer to these documents to determine the costs of such analyses on a unit basis, in order to develop extended costs based on the number and type of samples to be collected for the monitoring activity.

To determine the analyses costs, the following calculations apply:

First Year Analyses Cost

First Year Analyses Cost = sum for each Media of [First Year Number of Sampling Events × First Year Samples per Event × Analysis Cost ($ per sample)]

Out-Years Analyses Costs

Out-Year Analyses Costs = sum for each Media of [Out-year Number of Years × Out-Year Number of Sampling Events per Year × Out-Year Samples per Event × Analysis Cost ($ per sample)]

If the estimate in the out-years is to reflect escalation, the estimator should determine the annual analyses cost for each out-year and apply the appropriate escalation factor prior to determining the total out-year analyses cost.

Data Management Parameters

There are generally four separate activities to be conducted for data management purposes:

- Develop Monitoring Plan
- Prepare Monitoring Reports
- Perform Data Evaluation
- Submit Analytical Data Electronically

Develop Monitoring Plan

This plan documents monitoring activities. Typically, there are two plan options: Abbreviated and Full. The Abbreviated Monitoring Plan is a letter report listing the sample locations, methods, and number of samples that will be collected. It includes brief sections on sampling methods, QA/QC and reporting. The default hours to develop an abbreviated monitoring plan are presented in Figure 57.2.

The Full Monitoring Plan is a more detailed document, and consists of the following sections:

- Introduction
- Site Description
- Monitoring Activities
- Field Sampling Methods
- Analytical Methods
- QA/QC
- Reporting

The full plan may also include a discussion of previous data, regulatory conditions, ARARs or other applicable standards, and health and safety considerations. The default hours to develop a full monitoring plan are based on the total number of samples to be collected in the first year, and are presented in Figure 57.3.

Prepare Monitoring Reports

These reports summarize monitoring results, again in either an abbreviated or full format. The Abbreviated Monitoring Report includes a hard copy of the data, summary data tables, and a brief presentation and interpretation of the data. It is assumed that the number of sampling locations is less than 50. The default hours to prepare an abbreviated monitoring report are as follows:

- Project Scientist = Number of Total Samples × 1 hour per sample
- Field Technician = Number of Total Samples × 0.5 hours per sample
- Draftsman = Number of Total Samples × 0.5 hours per sample
- Word Processing = Number of Total Samples × 0.5 hours per sample

The Full Monitoring Report is a more detailed document, and consists of the following sections:

- Introduction
- Site Description
- Monitoring Activities
- Field Data Results
- Analytical Results
- Conclusions/ Recommendations
- Appendices

Labor Category	Default Hours
Project Manager	4
QA/QC Officer	35
Project Engineer	30
Project Scientist	40
Staff Scientist	80
Draftsman/CADD	8
Word Processing/Clerical	12

Figure 57.2 Default Hours

Labor Category	0–49 Samples	50–149 Samples	> 150 Samples
Project Manager	8	20	28
QA/QC Officer	60	150	210
Project Engineer	40	100	140
Project Scientist	80	200	280
Staff Scientist	120	300	420
Draftsman/CADD	16	40	56
Word Processing/Clerical	32	80	112

Figure 57.3 Labor Requirements for Development of a Monitoring Plan

598

The default hours to develop a full monitoring report are based on the total number of samples to be collected in the first year, and are presented in Figure 57.4.

Perform Data Evaluation

This task involves data QA/QC and evaluation. Typically, there are two options: Data Evaluation Only, or Data Evaluation and Validation.

Data Evaluation Only: Includes comparison of sample results to QA/QC criteria, such as holding times, sample preservation, calibration, and matrix effects. A QA/QC report is prepared to document the evaluation. The default hours for data evaluation are:

Project Scientist = Number of Total Samples × 1.25 hours per sample

Data Evaluation and Validation: Includes all of the tasks described above under "Data Evaluation Only," as well as a comparison of values calculated from raw machine data to data reported by the laboratory. The default hours for data evaluation and validation are:

Project Scientist = Number of Total Samples × 2.5 hours per sample

Submit Analytical Data Electronically

This task involves electronic data submittal in a predetermined format to a client and/or regulatory agency. The effort includes ensuring that data are in the required database field, submission, and revisions to the initial submission. The default hours for analytical data electronic submission are:

Project Scientist = Number of Total Samples × 1 hour per sample

Design Information Needed for Detailed Estimates

Following are descriptions of the types of detailed information that, when available, can add detail and accuracy to estimates. Also included are design criteria and estimating rules of thumb that the estimator typically uses to determine values that are not known, or to check information provided by others.

Labor Category	≦ 15 Samples	16–50 Samples	≧ 50 Samples
Project Manager	8	16	24
QA/QC Officer	60	120	180
Project Engineer	40	80	120
Project Scientist	80	160	240
Staff Scientist	120	240	360
Draftsman/CADD	16	32	48
Word Processing/Clerical	32	64	96

Figure 57.4 Labor Requirements for Preparation of Monitoring Reports

The key information involves the methodology used to collect the samples of:

- Groundwater
- Subsurface soil
- Soil gas

Other Methodology parameters include:

- Turnaround Time
- Quality Control

Groundwater

Monitoring techniques for groundwater include existing wells and cone penetrometer testing equipment (using a hydropunch).

- **Existing Wells: Bailers** are the typical method. Assume that all groundwater-monitoring wells have already been installed and that the estimate includes only the costs associated with routine sampling and analysis. If monitoring wells need to be installed, they should be estimated separately (see Chapter 56). It is reasonable to assume that the monitoring wells are purged of approximately four well volumes of groundwater utilizing bailers.
- **Existing Wells: Pumps** may be substituted for bailers in deeper wells or when monitoring frequency is very high. Generally, use the same other assumptions as above for bailers regarding volumes and prior installation of wells. Generally, the pumps are rented.

The number of wells that can be sampled per day by a sampling crew for groundwater samples collected using either bailers or pumps depends on the depth to groundwater, recharge rate, crew size, specific yield, sampling methodology, and other hydrogeological characteristics of the site. A typical pump valid range is from 1–15 wells. Refer to Figure 57.1 for sampling rates for bailers and pumps.

- **Cone Penetrometer Test (CPT):** Rigs with a hydropunch attachment can be used to obtain groundwater samples. It is reasonable to assume that a rate of 300' per day is achieved using a 20-ton unit. The estimator should also include costs for grouting CPT test holes after hydropunching is completed.
- **Direct Push:** This method uses truck-mounted, non-hydraulic direct push rigs to obtain groundwater samples. As with CPT, it is reasonable to assume that test holes are grouted after direct pushing is completed. In addition, a rate in feet per day can be calculated based on the following equation:

  Feet per day direct push, groundwater = [262.9 – Sample Depth (ft)] / 2.29

- **Drum and Sample Development Water:** This approach considers the cost of drumming and sampling monitoring well development water. Development water is produced during the drilling and well equipment installation process. This water may be contaminated and is drummed for later disposal or treatment. Generally, this activity is performed for any monitoring well or extraction well installation. It is reasonable to assume that 1 drum is required per well per sampling event to store development water and that an additional sample will be collected and analyzed at each sampling event for development water characterization. If development water were not drummed, it would likely be discharged to the ground or surface water.

The estimator can determine the number of drums needed using the following calculation:

Number of Drums Required for Containment of Purge Water (per sampling event) = number of well volumes purged × number of wells × height of water in well (ft) × 3.14 × [well diameter (ft)/2]² × 7.48 gal/C.F. × 55 gal. drum

A reasonable assumption is that 4 well volumes are purged, wells are 4" in diameter, and the height of water in the well to purge is 10' (depth of well is 10' greater than the depth to groundwater). Also assume that each "sample" per event represents a well (exclusive of QA samples). If these assumptions are representative of the situation to be estimated, the equation is reduced to:

Number of Drums Required for Containment of Purge Water (per sampling event) = 0.475 × # of wells to be sampled

Subsurface Soil

Typical monitoring techniques for this media include hand auger, power auger, hollow stem boring, and cone penetrometer testing equipment.

- **Hand-Held Power Auger:** Power auger drilling is similar to hand auger drilling with the exception that the auger is gas, diesel, or electrically driven. This approach is preferable for shallow, subsurface sampling. This method is the normal assumed default for monitoring activities in subsurface soil. A typical rate is 9' per hour.
- **Hand Auger:** Manual hand auger drilling can be conducted at shallow depths, typically less than 20'. Hand auger bore holes are typically drilled in soft clay or silt. This type of drilling is more common in densely wooded, remote locations where electrical power is not available, and underbrush is too dense for maneuvering a drill rig, or if inexpensive shallow sampling is needed. A typical rate is 5' per hour.
- **Soil Sampling with Drill Rig (Hollow Stem Auger):** It is reasonable to assume that a hollow stem auger is used to advance the bore hole at each sampling location. The sampling device is then attached to the drilling rod and advanced to obtain a representative sample. Split spoon samples can be obtained in unconsolidated or consolidated subsurface conditions. Split spoon samples cannot be obtained in rock formations. Generally, the individual supervising the drilling describes the samples. A typical rate is 5' per hour.
- **CPT Punches:** Cone Penetrometer Test Rigs can be used to punch through soil to obtain soil samples at discrete depths. A sampling attachment is added to the end of the CPT rod, which is used to obtain a grab sample. The CPT is basically jacked or hammered into the ground by the weight of the truck. A reasonable assumption rate is a throughput of 300' per day (using a 20-ton unit). This method produces no drill cuttings to be drummed, and decontamination water is minimal due to the small diameter of the rod (1.5–2").

- **Direct Push Rigs:** These rigs can be used to punch through soil to obtain soil samples at discrete depths. This method produces no drill cuttings to be drummed, and decontamination water is minimal due to the small diameter of the rod. The rate in feet per day can be calculated based on the following equation:

    Feet per day direct push, soil =
    [102.9 – Sample Depth (ft)] / 0.29

Soil Gas

Typical soil gas monitoring techniques include existing wells, probes, and cone penetrometer testing equipment. Soil gas monitoring is conducted in the vadose (unsaturated) zone. Vadose-zone monitoring can provide an early warning to detect volatile organic compound releases before groundwater becomes contaminated.

- **Existing Wells:** Soil gas samples are collected from wells by applying a vacuum to remove stagnant air inside the well casing. The sample is collected at the end of the purge step by drawing off a portion of the flow from the well through a sample port into a canister. Gas sampling involves drawing a minimum of two well volumes from the wells or probes before the gas samples are collected for laboratory analysis. The samples are collected in a canister, previously evacuated to negative pressure, or in tight-sealed 10-liter tevlar sample bags maintained inside a vacuum bucket, at a rate of 1 liter per minute. This is the most common method for collecting soil gas samples. A typical rate is 20–30 minutes per sample.
- **Probes:** At each sample location, a 3/4" stainless steel probe (with a detachable perforated aluminum tip and polyethylene tubing) is driven to a depth of between 12–15'. The probe is removed, leaving the tip and tubing in the hole. The annulus of this hole is then backfilled with a fine-grained clean sand, such as #18 Monterey sand, to allow gas infiltration into the perforated tip. The top 2' of the annulus are backfilled with a bentonite grout, and a piece of 1" PVC casing with screw-top cap is installed at the surface. Sampling begins no sooner than 24 hours after probe installation. A typical rate is 45 minutes to 1 hour per sample.
- **CPT:** The use of CPT equipment for soil gas sampling is similar to that described above in subsurface sampling, with the addition of gas sampling equipment to the rig.
- **Direct Push:** Direct push equipment for soil gas sampling is also similar subsurface sampling, again with gas sampling equipment added to the rig.

Turnaround Time Factors

The turnaround time (TAT) is the amount of time required to process a sample in the laboratory for analysis. This period starts when a laboratory receives a sample and ends when the laboratory report is returned to the sampler. Each selection for turnaround time has a corresponding cost adjustment factor (markup). Typical turnaround time cost adjustment factors are shown in Figure 57.5.

The cost adjustment factor is used to calculate the adjusted cost. For example, a sample costing $100 in analysis fees ($ per sample) at standard turnaround time would cost $200 if a 1-day (24-hour) turnaround time were specified. These factors will vary from laboratory to laboratory and should be evaluated by the estimator prior to developing the cost estimate. A typical default is a standard turnaround time for all analyses.

Quality Control Factors

The quality control (QC), or reporting level, is the level of documentation and analytical procedures provided by the laboratory. Generally, there are four QC data package deliverables that could be requested. A Level 1 QC data package is the least expensive and correspondingly has a minimum amount of QC, whereas a Level 4 QC data package corresponds to the Contract Laboratory Program status and therefore provides the most comprehensive quality control.

The quality control required for each project varies depending on contract stipulations and negotiation with the particular regulator involved, and any state or local regulations that may apply. A typical default is a Level 1 (Standard) QC for all analyses. Cost adjustment factors for laboratory quality control level are shown in Figure 57.6, and are applied to each sample, as described in the Turnaround Time section.

The QC levels above refer to laboratory levels of documentation to meet differing project-specific QA/QC. These should not be confused with the EPA Data Quality Objective (DQO) levels.

Related Costs Costs for residual waste management of personnel protective equipment and sample spoils, such as drill cuttings (investigation-derived wastes), should be included as appropriate (see Chapter 49).

Turnaround Time	
Turnaround Time	**Default Cost Adjustment Factor**
Standard (2–3 Weeks)	1.00
14 Days	1.20
4–7 Days	1.50
24–72 Hours	2.00

Figure 57.5 Turnaround Time

Quality Control Level	
Quality Control	**Default Cost Adjustment Factor**
Level 1 (Standard)	1.00
Level 2	1.10
Level 3	1.25
Level 4	1.40

Figure 57.6 Quality Control Level

Site Work and Utilities

When applicable, site work and utilities must also be covered in the estimate. Site work and utilities may include:

- Fencing
- Signage
- Roads for access to monitoring locations

Conclusion

Monitoring is conducted at various times during the remediation process to evaluate the type and level of media contamination at a site. The primary cost drivers are the number of samples to be taken (and their associated analyses), the size and rate of the sampling crew, and the travel/per diem costs (if the monitoring crew is far away from the site and/or the monitoring is done over a long period of time). The cost engineer should work closely with the monitoring team to evaluate the optimal approach and crew size of monitoring efforts and the associated laboratory analyses.

Chapter 58

Remedial Action Professional Labor Management

This chapter focuses on professional labor costs incurred during the Remedial Action (RA) phase of a project. Professional labor includes activities that provide interpretation of the performance of remedial actions. The activities delineated in this technology generally incur costs during the construction, startup/shakedown (capital costs) and operation and maintenance (O&M) phases of the environmental remediation process.

Applications and Limitations

Applications

- Oversight of construction and operations and evaluation of data collected from operation of remediation systems.
- Oversight of site-specific construction activities, permit acquisition, and "as built" drawings.
- Evaluation of sampling and analysis data, comparison of results with project goals, coordination of field activities, and documentation and reporting of all efforts.

Limitations

- The amount of professional support labor is variable and highly project/site/contract-specific.
- Project estimates and bids often contain RA professional labor hours with the installation of technologies. To correctly use the system, these hours should be included in the RA Professional Labor technology specifically and not within each technology.
- RA Professional Labor does not include craft labor generally associated with construction and operations. It is important to understand the differences between professional and craft labor levels of effort for a project before developing the estimate.

Process Configurations and Treatment Train Considerations

- Because some RA professional support activities are project-oriented, and some are site-oriented, the estimator should coordinate the development of an estimate of professional labor costs with the selection of the Site Category (Project Activity or Actual Site) made during site identification.

Examples: An example of a project-oriented activity is the modification of a health and safety plan, which may be applicable to multiple sites.

Basic Information Needed for Estimating

An example of a site-oriented activity is the development of "as built" drawings, which are highly site-specific.

A reasonable cost estimate can be created with a few required parameters. A more precise estimate will require additional detail in the form of a secondary set of parameters.

Determine Method to Use

There are two different methods for calculating RA professional labor costs:

Percentage Method

The Percentage Method option assigns a default set of tasks and hours estimated for each task. The total RA construction cost determines the default hours allotted to each default task.

Manual Labor Hour Estimate by Task

This method is more typical. A pre-defined set of tasks and suggested list of labor categories provides a framework for making the estimate.

Evaluate Default Tasks for Applicability

The following suggested default tasks are common in estimating RA Professional Labor costs. The estimator should determine which of them should be included in the estimate. These tasks are used in both the percentage method and the manual labor hour estimating method. The default tasks include:

- **Project Management:** Hours associated with the professional oversight of construction and operations and maintenance efforts. May include contractor oversight, client and regulatory coordination, and contract administration.
- **Work Plan:** Generated to include proposed work tasks over the duration of the RA and/or O&M process. Work plans can be iterative and phased.
- **Construction Oversight:** Typically conducted to ensure compliance with Health and Safety requirements, record changes to the Remedial Design Plan, and to provide on-site guidance for craft labor.
- **As-Built Drawings:** After construction of RA technologies is completed and the system is operational, "as-built" or record drawings are typically produced to aid in maintenance or system upgrades. The as-built drawings will be modifications of the design plan that illustrate any modifications made due to construction nuances. As-built drawings are a site-specific activity.
- **Public Notice:** Includes notification of the nearby public of site-specific construction and operations activities and schedules. Also includes notification of temporary logistics issues (e.g., temporary changes in traffic patterns) and hazard potentials (e.g., emissions, open holes). For UST sites, notification typically occurs in the form of signage, print advertisements, and flyers. If a large community relations effort is required, estimate that effort separately.
- **Site Closure Activities:** Professional oversight of field activities required to complete the remedial action work and leave the site in its final closed state, and documentation of such activities for oversight agencies.

- **Permitting:** Permits typical and incidental to the remediation process, such as building/construction permits and occupancy permits. Does not include the effort required to obtain significant environmental permits, such as an NPDES discharge permit or an RCRA storage permit. Those types of permits should be estimated separately.
- **Responsible Party Costs:** Professional labor hours required to document costs incurred by a responsible party for cleanup of the site.
- **Reimbursement Claims Preparation:** Covers the professional labor hours necessary to prepare the documentation required to receive reimbursement from a state fund.
- **Other:** A general category to cover other costs not defined above. The default in this task is always zero.

Percentage Method Steps

Step 1. Select an RA Complexity

- *RA Complexity* gauges of the level of effort required by professional labor to perform the remedial action-post project activities. The complexities range from low to high, as defined in the following paragraphs. The multipliers associated with the complexities are presented in Figure 58.1.

Low: A low complexity would be assigned to a site that requires little amount of professional oversight (probably one professional, part-time).

Examples include:

- A site where there is one contractor who has already worked with and is familiar with the setting.
- A site involving simple remedial construction, such as small-scale excavation with off-site landfilling or installation of a groundwater extraction well with manual free product removal.
- A site involving a very short construction period (less than one month).

Moderate: A moderate complexity would be assigned to a site that requires one or two professionals for oversight of a series of conventional remedial technologies.

Examples include:

- A site involving the installation of a typical size air sparge/soil vapor extraction system.
- A site involving the installation of a groundwater extraction—carbon desorption—discharge treatment train.
- A site involving oversight of a contractor that has only one or two specialty subcontractors installing "package" systems or parts (e.g., catalytic oxidation).

High: A high complexity would be assigned to a site that requires several professionals for oversight of a series of unconventional technologies, several contractors, or an extremely large construction effort.

Examples include:

- A site involving a large excavation with several drums requiring special handling and treatment.
- A site involving a prime contractor overseeing several general subcontractors to install different technologies.
- A site involving a specialty or non-conventional technology, such as on-site low-temperature desorption.
- A site involving a series of technologies requiring significant equipment installation and construction, such as groundwater extraction, metals precipitation, sludge dewatering, discharge to POTW, and solidification.
- A site with a remediation scenario requiring professional discipline oversight, such as excavation and capping (geotechnical) combined with groundwater extraction (hydrogeological), advanced oxidation process (chemical), and discharge to POTW (civil).

Step 2. Calculate Total RA Costs

The total Remedial Action construction costs (including markups) for the cleanup scenario should be added to the first year Monitoring costs (see Chapter 57). This number calculation is used in the next step.

Step 3. Look up RA Professional Labor Percentages

The default percentages for each task are based on the total RA construction and first-year monitoring costs displayed in Figures 58.2a and b. The estimator should look up the percentage cost for each applicable RA Professional Labor Task—based on the Total RA Construction and First-Year Monitoring cost identified in the column headings.

Step 4. Calculate Raw RA Professional Labor Costs

Using the template in Figure 58.3, the estimator should calculate the Total Raw RA Professional Labor Costs (prior to applying the complexity factor).

RA Complexity Multipliers	
Complexity	**Multiplier**
Low	0.50
Moderately Low	0.75
Moderate	1.00
Moderately High	1.50
High	2.00

Figure 58.1 RA Complexity Multipliers

Step 5. Calculate Total RA Professional Labor Cost (Including Complexity)

The Total RA Professional Labor Cost is calculated as follows:

Total RA Professional Labor Cost ($) = Total Raw RA Professional Labor Cost $ (Figure 58.3) × RA Complexity Multiplier (Figure 58.1)

Manual Labor Hour Estimate by Task Method Steps

Step 1. Evaluate Tasks and Professional Labor Categories

The estimator should evaluate which of the tasks are to be included in the estimate, then determine which of the following suggested labor categories should be included for each task in the estimate, and finally, obtain loaded hourly rates for each applicable category:

Figure 58.2a RA Professional Labor Percentages, Based on Task and Total RA Construction and First Year Monitoring Cost

RAPL Task	<100K	100K–500K	500K–1M	1M–5M	5M–10M
Project Management (PM)	10.0%	7.5%	5.0%	4.0%	3.0%
Planning Documents (PL)	8%	7%	5%	4.0%	3.3%
Construction Oversight (CO)	6.5%	6.0%	5.5%	5.0%	4.5%
Reporting (RE)	1.5%	1.0%	.7%	.5%	.5%
As-Built Drawings (AB)	1.5%	1.0%	.7%	.5%	.5%
Public Notice (PN)	.50%	.30%	.15%	.07%	.05%
Site Closure Activities (SC)	0%	0%	0%	0%	0%
Permitting (PR)	10%	10%	10%	5%	2.5%
Responsible Party Costs (RP)	0%	0%	0%	0%	0%
Reimbursement Claims Preparation (RC)	0%	0%	0%	0%	0%
Other (OT)	0%	0%	0%	0%	0%

Figure 58.2b RA Professional Labor Percentages, Based on Task and Total RA Construction and First Year Monitoring Cost

RAPL Task	10M–15M	15M–30M	30M–50M	50M–75M	>75M
Project Management (PM)	2.5%	2.0%	1.5%	1.0%	1.0%
Planning Documents (PL)	2.4%	1.9%	1.6%	2.2%	0.8%
Construction Oversight (CO)	4.2%	4.0%	3.5%	3.0%	2.5%
Reporting (RE)	.5%	.5%	.5%	.5%	.5%
As-Built Drawings (AB)	.5%	.5%	.5%	.5%	.5%
Public Notice (PN)	.03%	.02%	.02%	.01%	.01%
Site Closure Activities (SC)	0%	0%	0%	0%	0%
Permitting (PR)	1.0%	1.0%	1.0%	1.0%	1.0%
Responsible Party Costs (RP)	0%	0%	0%	0%	0%
Reimbursement Claims Preparation (RC)	0%	0%	0%	0%	0%
Other (OT)	0%	0%	0%	0%	0%

- Sr. Project Manager
- Project Manager
- Sr. Staff Engineer
- Project Engineer
- Staff Engineer
- Sr. Scientist
- Project Scientist
- Staff Scientist
- QA/QC Specialist
- Certified Industrial Hygienist
- Field Technician
- Secretary/ Administrative Assistant
- Word Processor/Clerical
- Draftsman/CADD Technician
- UXO Disposal Technician
- UXO Supervisor
- Sr. UXO Supervisor
- Health & Safety Officer
- Computer Data Entry Technician

Step 2. Determine Labor Hours and Calculate Extended Costs per Task and Overall Cost

Figure 58.4 provides a template that can be used to fill in labor hours and calculate extended costs per task and the overall estimate. The estimator should use as many rows and columns as necessary to include all applicable tasks and labor categories.

Figure 58.3 Total RA Construction/First Year Monitoring Cost

Total RA Construction/ First Year Monitoring Cost: $ (fill in)		
Selected Tasks (List)	RA Professional Labor Percentage Default from Figure 58.2, based on Total RA Construction/ First Year Monitoring Cost	Extended Raw RA Professional Labor Cost per Task, $ (Column 2 × Total RA Construction/ First Year Monitoring Cost Above)
Task 1		
Task n		
Total Raw RA Professional Labor Costs, $	**(Sum this Column)**	

Conclusion

Estimating the Remedial Action (RA) Professional Labor management methodology involves assembling labor costs for activities that provide interpretation of the performance of remedial actions. The Percentage Method provides a reasonable estimate, while the Manual Labor Hour by Task Method provides a more precise estimate. The cost engineer should work closely with the Professional Team that will oversee the RA and O&M phases to determine the appropriate tasks and level of effort that will be required to oversee/interpret project performance.

Selected Tasks (Fill In)	Labor Category: (Fill In)		Labor Category:		Labor Category:		Extended Cost per Task, $ = SUM (Hours × Loaded Hr. Rate for Each Labor Category)
	Hours	Loaded Hr. Rate, $/hr	Hours	Loaded Hr. Rate, $/hr	Hours	Loaded Hr. Rate, $/hr	
Task 1							
Task n							
Total RA Professional Labor Cost, $							(Sum this Column)

Figure 58.4 Labor Category Table

Chapter 59

Remedial Design

The RD phase of the site restoration process begins after the optimum remedial action alternative has been selected and documented in the proper place, prior to the onset of remedial construction. There are two different methods for calculating remedial design costs: *the percentage method* and the *detailed labor-hour method.* The percentage method calculates the costs based on historic costs of remedial design as a percentage of the remedial construction cost. The detailed labor-hour method is used to build up an estimate of labor-hours required to develop the design from its inception to final plans and specifications.

Applications and Limitations

Applications

- Used to estimate the costs for the remedial design phase of cleanup.
- Includes professional labor-hours, other direct costs (mileage, reproduction, supplies, etc.), and any other treatability testing-related costs.

Limitations

- Does not include any field work-related costs (such as drilling bore holes, surveys, installation of wells, groundwater sampling) or any analytical costs. It is assumed that these costs will be incurred before the RD phase, presumably during the study phase.

Process Configuration and Treatment Train Considerations

Remedial design is the activity conducted following the feasibility study (CERCLA) or corrective measures study (RCRA) phase, and prior to the remedial construction (CERCLA) or corrective action construction (RCRA) phase of site cleanup. It is also conducted prior to the Interim Action phase when emergency or interim construction activities are undertaken.

Basic Information Needed for Estimating

Because of the nature of the remedial design process, the information presented in this chapter is the basic level needed to evaluate remedial design costs. The estimator must first decide which method is to be used to create the estimate: the percentage or the detailed labor-hour method. A description of both follows.

Percentage Method

The primary remediation approach applied to an Interim Action or Remedial Action phase determines the Remedial Design Percentage that calculates the Remedial Design costs. There are seven typical remediation categories for which remedial design costs can be estimated:

- In Situ Treatment: Treatment of contaminants and media in the ground, without removing them.
- In Situ Containment: Containment of contaminants and media in the ground.
- Ex Situ: Removal of contaminants followed by on-site, performance-based treatment or disposal. Since the contractor would be required to perform the remediation based on performance criteria, the design would be less detailed.
- Ex Situ: Removal of contaminants followed by on-site treatment or disposal. The contractor would perform the remediation based on a detailed design that had been developed.
- Ex Situ: Removal of contaminants followed by off-site treatment or disposal.
- Natural Attenuation: Site remediation through natural attenuation monitoring.
- Ordnance & Explosive Waste: Removal and/or in-place detonation of ordnance and explosive waste. The percentage is automatically adjusted so the total remedial design costs will equal $50,000, which is the pre-established cost by the U.S. Army Corps of Engineers.

A list of the default Remedial Design Percentage values follows. These percentages were developed based on remediation industry data and professional judgment by a work group consisting of professionals from private industry, engineering/construction firms, the U.S. Army Corps of Engineers, and the Air Force. To calculate the remedial design costs, find the cell in the table that corresponds to the appropriate RA approach and the estimated total construction cost. Multiply the percentage by the construction cost to determine the remedial design cost.

Remedial Action Construction Total Cost Range—Up to 250K

RA Approach	$0–10K	$10–25K	$25–50K	$50–100K	$100–250K
In Situ Treatment	15.0%	14.0%	13.0%	12.0%	11.0%
In Situ Containment	12.0%	11.0%	10.0%	8.5%	7.0%
Ex Situ Removal/ Performance Based On-site Treatment or Disposal	7.6%	7.0%	6.5%	6.0%	5.5%
Ex Situ Removal/ Detailed Design On-site Treatment or Disposal	15.0%	14.0%	13.0%	12.0%	11.0%
Ex Situ Removal/ Off-site Treatment or Disposal	5.0%	4.5%	4.5%	4.0%	3.5%
Natural Attenuation	7.5%	7.0%	6.5%	6.0%	5.5%

Remedial Action Construction Total Cost Range—250K to > $1M

RA Approach	$250 – 500K	$500K – 1M	$1M – 5M	$5 – 10M	> $1M
In Situ Treatment	10.0%	9.0%	8.0%	7.0%	6.0%
In Situ Containment	6.0%	5.5%	5.0%	4.5%	4.0%
Ex Situ Removal/ Performance Based On-site Treatment or Disposal	5.0%	4.5%	4.0%	3.5%	3.0%
Ex Situ Removal/ Detailed Design On-site Treatment or Disposal	10.0%	9.0%	8.0%	7.0%	6.0%
Ex Situ Removal/ Off-site Treatment or Disposal	3.5%	3.0%	2.5%	2.5%	2.5%
Natural Attenuation	5.0%	4.5%	4.0%	3.5%	3.0%

Detailed Labor-Hour Method

There are five project approaches listed below—the approach selected will determine the amount of level (hours) associated with each task:

- **In Situ 1:** In Situ Treatment: Treatment of contaminants and media in the ground.
- **In Situ 2:** In Situ Containment: Containment of contaminants and media in the ground.
- **Ex Situ 1:** Ex Situ Removal: Performance-based on-site treatment or disposal.
- **Ex Situ 2:** Ex Situ Removal: Detailed design of on-site treatment or disposal.
- **Ex Situ 3:** Ex Situ Removal: Off-site treatment or disposal.

Labor-hours required for remedial design can be affected by several factors. The two that affect the cost most are the site complexity and the level of design detail required by the client and/or regulator. The most effective way to take these factors into consideration is to evaluate the total hours required for the design, and to adjust these hours by multiplying by factors for site complexity and level of detail. The factors are summarized below.

Site Complexity

Site complexity is the overall rating of the site in terms of level of contamination, site characteristics, and cost. This factor is used to determine default professional labor-hours for model tasks. There are seven complexity levels starting with very low and going through very high. Moderate complexity applies a multiplier of one to all labor hours and associated costs. All other complexities use multipliers (stated in following definitions) that scale the RD costs to accurately reflect the given site.

Very Low Complexity

The least complex site. Generally there is only one contaminant, a small plume of contamination, few public safety issues, and a total cost of between $50,000–$200,000. Applies multiplier of .10 (10%).

Low Site Complexity

A site slightly more complex than very low in terms of contamination, site characteristics, site size, and site use. The cost should range between $200,000–$500,000. Applies multiplier of .40 (40%).

Moderately Low Complexity

A site slightly more complex than low in terms of contamination, site characteristics, site size, and site use. The cost should range between $500,000–$800,000. Applies multiplier of .60 (60%).

Moderate Site Complexity

A typical site in terms of contamination, site characteristics, and site use. This rating would normally be used for sites with costs between $800,000–$1,600,000. Applies multiplier of 1.0 (100%).

Moderately High Complexity

A slightly above-average site in terms of contamination, site characteristics, and site use. This rating would normally be used for sites with costs between $1,600,000–$5,000,000. Applies multiplier of 4.0 (400%).

High Site Complexity

A complex site in terms of contamination, site characteristics, and site use. This rating would normally be used for a site costing between $5,000,000–$8,000,000. Applies multiplier of 6.0 (600%).

Very High Complexity

The most complex site in terms of contamination, site characteristics, and site use. This rating would normally be used for a site costing more than $8,000,000. Applies multiplier of 10 (1000%).

Level of RD Detail

This is the overall amount of detail required for the project remedial design. Many factors may affect the amount of detail required in the RD. Following are some general guidelines to help determine the level of detail that best represents the subject site.

Low RD Detail

Multiply labor by factor of .85 (85%). Represents the least complex site in terms of contamination, site characteristics, and access. Example characteristics may include, but are not limited to, the following:

- Fuel storage facility with one or two isolated storage tanks.
- Single spill area less than 1/4 acre.
- Contaminated ditch less than 50 L.F.
- Contaminants consisting of only volatile organics or municipal garbage.
- Site is well-drained with no storm sewers, wetlands or significant surface water bodies nearby.
- Monogeneous lithologic strata and only one shallow aquifer.
- Surface characteristics represented by flat open field with good access, or in a rural area, or on an inactive facility.
- No endangered or threatened species; no cultural or historic landmarks; no hunting, fishing, or farming near the site.
- Low levels of dissolved constituents in site surface water and no sediment contamination.
- No or low soil contamination.

- Shallow water table with no or simple contamination (e.g., volatile organics).
- No or low air contamination; no modeling required.
- Only one or two stakeholders.
- Few or no public safety issues.

Moderate RD Detail

Multiply by a factor of 1.0 (100%). Represents an average site in terms of contamination, site characteristics, and access. Example characteristics may include, but are not limited to, the following:

- Fuel storage facility with less than 10 storage tanks
- Contaminated ditch between 50–250 L.F.
- Contaminants consisting of waste solvents, used oils.
- Aqueous contaminants with a specific gravity greater than 1.
- Potential for presence of endangered or threatened species; potential cultural or historic landmarks; potential for hunting and fishing near the site.
- Non-level, but not continuously varied site topography.
- Soil contamination with simple organics.
- One deep aquifer with simple, lithologic changes.
- Between two and five stakeholders.
- A few known public safety issues.

High RD Detail

Multiply by factor of 1.15 (115%). Represents the most complex site in terms of contamination, site characteristics, and access. Example characteristics may include, but are not limited to, the following:

- Fuel storage facility with more than 20 tanks or a hydrant system.
- Landfill greater than 20 acres with hazardous waste.
- Five or greater stakeholders.
- Disposal pit more than 2 acres containing buried drums.
- Many identified known public safety issues.
- Contaminated ditch greater than 250' or 2 acres.
- Contaminants consisting of PCBs, herbicides, pesticides, mercury, chlorinated solvents, low-level radioactive waste, munitions.
- Located in a floodplain with a pond or stream on-site.
- Complex lithologic changes and more than one aquifer.
- Located near a housing area or in an industrial area with buildings; on an operational facility.
- Known endangered or threatened species; cultural or historic landmarks; hunting, fishing, or farming; or critical or sensitive habitats on or near the site.
- Toxic metals or dioxin contamination in soil.
- Contaminated aquifer is a drinking water source, or multiple aquifers are affected by the contamination.
- Site is in a non-attainment zone, requiring on-site air data and significant modeling.

Labor-Hour Detail

There are 7 main tasks associated with remedial design when estimating using the detailed method:

- Project Planning
- Treatability or Other Studies

- Preliminary Design (30%)
- Intermediate Design (60%)
- Prefinal Design (90%)
- Final Design (100%)
- Bid Documents

In each task, there are several sub-tasks, with default hours based on the five approaches.

Project Planning
Includes four sub-tasks:

- Site Visit
- Remedial Design Work Plan
- Data Review
- Public Meetings

Site Visit. A visit to the site will be conducted to determine its specific RD requirements. A site visit report is also included in this sub-task. The report should document all personnel present at the visit and describe: decisions made during the visit, action items assigned, unusual occurrences, and any areas inaccessible at the time. Labor categories associated with the site visit include:

Task Hours Based on Moderate Complexity

Labor Category	In Situ-1	In Situ-2	Ex Situ-1	Ex Situ-2	Ex Situ-3
Project Manager	21	40	21	13	18
Office Manager	2	2	1	2	1
Project Engineer	4	3	1	3	1
Staff Engineer	10	17	10	13	8
Staff Scientist	40	74	2	40	1
QA/QC Officer	11	8	6	12	4
CH/HS	4	12	4	4	2
Field Technician	0	0	0	0	0
Secretarial/Admin	6	5	1	5	1
Word Processing	10	11	5	7	3
Draftsman	6	10	1	6	1

Remedial Design Work Plan. The RD work plan will state the existing and potential problems with the site and the objectives of the RD. This report will contain the following: site description, site history, summary of existing data, technical information for the various tasks to be performed, a detailed schedule for completion, and a project management plan. Labor categories associated with this task include:

Task Hours Based on Moderate Complexity

Labor Category	In Situ-1	In Situ-2	Ex Situ-1	Ex Situ-2	Ex Situ-3
Project Manager	9	12	5	12	3
Office Manager	3	4	1	3	1
Project Engineer	11	12	2	5	1
Staff Engineer	55	70	10	18	10
Staff Scientist	121	105	35	100	24
QA/QC Officer	21	28	10	10	7
CH/HS	0	5	0	0	0
Field Technician	0	0	0	0	0
Secretarial/Admin	12	20	4	8	2
Word Processing	28	35	14	15	9
Draftsman	13	25	5	10	3

Data Review. This phase includes hours related to reviewing, collecting, validating, and reporting on data needed for the Remedial Design. A Data Evaluation Summary Report will be generated in this phase to relate findings and recommendations based on the data reviewed. Labor categories associated with this task include:

Task Hours Based on Moderate Complexity

Labor Category	In Situ-1	In Situ-2	Ex Situ-1	Ex Situ-2	Ex Situ-3
Project Manager	38	8	7	25	7
Office Manager	18	4	5	20	3
Project Engineer	12	2	5	14	3
Staff Engineer	50	14	25	35	21
Staff Scientist	140	80	110	120	64
QA/QC Officer	38	6	40	25	28
CH/HS	32	0	0	20	0
Field Technician	50	75	30	30	15
Secretarial/Admin	9	0	10	12	7
Word Processing	36	0	26	21	21
Draftsman	16	0	0	5	0

Public Meetings. This phase includes tasks related to public awareness of the proposed project. Specific tasks completed include development of a Community Relations Plan (CRP) and an Explanation of Significant Differences (ESD) meeting to explain differences in the proposed design from alternatives proposed in the ROD/decision document. Labor categories associated with this task include:

Task Hours Based on Moderate Complexity

Labor Category	In Situ-1	In Situ-2	Ex Situ-1	Ex Situ-2	Ex Situ-3
Project Manager	12	12	12	12	12
Office Manager	0	0	0	0	0
Project Engineer	0	0	0	0	0
Staff Engineer	12	12	12	12	12
Staff Scientist	0	0	0	0	0
QA/QC Officer	0	0	0	0	0
CH/HS	0	0	0	0	0
Field Technician	0	0	0	0	0
Secretarial/Admin	0	0	0	0	0
Word Processing	4	4	4	4	4
Draftsman	0	0	0	0	0

Treatability or Other Studies

This task includes three sub-tasks:

- Treatability Study Work Plan
- Treatability Study Evaluation
- Procurement of Equipment/Vendor

Treatability Study Work Plan. The Treatability Study Work Plan (TSWP) describes the technologies to be tested, test objectives, test equipment or systems, treatability conditions to be tested, measurements of performance, analytical methods, data management and analysis, health and safety procedures, and residual waste management. The TSWP will also explain the pilot plant operation and maintenance procedures and operating conditions to be tested as well as any permitting requirements and the treatment process and performance standards (described in detail). The TSWP will also list all waste disposal/discharge requirements. Labor categories associated with this task include:

Task Hours Based on Moderate Complexity

Labor Category	In Situ-1	In Situ-2	Ex Situ-1	Ex Situ-2	Ex Situ-3
Project Manager	4	0	5	5	3
Office Manager	2	0	2	2	1
Project Engineer	14	0	20	20	14
Staff Engineer	51	0	75	35	35
Staff Scientist	36	0	68	30	40
QA/QC Officer	17	0	28	10	19
CH/HS	11	0	5	10	3
Field Technician	40	0	25	25	20
Secretarial/Admin	18	0	24	14	16
Word Processing	30	0	30	20	21
Draftsman	10	0	16	8	11

Treatability Study Evaluation. An evaluation is completed after the Treatability Study and describes the effectiveness, implementability, and cost of the technologies tested. Actual results will be evaluated and compared to the predicted results. The reports will also evaluate the full-scale application of the technology. Labor categories associated with this task include:

Task Hours Based on Moderate Complexity

Labor Category	In Situ-1	In Situ-2	Ex Situ-1	Ex Situ-2	Ex Situ-3
Project Manager	3	0	3	3	2
Office Manager	2	0	2	2	1
Project Engineer	16	0	22	22	15
Staff Engineer	32	0	29	45	20
Staff Scientist	35	0	64	50	44
QA/QC Officer	11	0	14	14	9
CH/HS	0	0	0	0	0
Field Technician	0	0	0	0	0
Secretarial/Admin	6	0	18	10	12
Word Processing	25	0	25	13	17
Draftsman	13	0	20	15	14

Procure Equipment/Vendor. The contractor shall address any necessary equipment, vendor, or facility needed to complete the study at this point. Labor categories associated with this task include:

Task Hours Based on Moderate Complexity

Labor Category	In Situ-1	In Situ-2	Ex Situ-1	Ex Situ-2	Ex Situ-3
Project Manager	1	0	1	1	1
Office Manager	1	0	1	1	1
Project Engineer	3	0	0	6	0
Staff Engineer	11	0	16	16	11
Staff Scientist	16	0	32	20	22
QA/QC Officer	0	0	0	0	0
CH/HS	5	0	8	2	5
Field Technician	0	0	0	0	0
Secretarial/Admin	1	0	1	3	1
Word Processing	3	0	3	1	2
Draftsman	0	0	0	0	0

Treatability (Bench) Tests. Bench treatability tests may or may not be needed to show the effectiveness of a proposed remedial action technology. The estimator generally includes a lump sum figure that incorporates all costs associated with the bench treatability tests. The valid range is $0–$100,000.

Bench scale treatability tests are tabletop laboratory tests conducted at an off-site laboratory on a sample (container) of soil, water, or air to determine the applicability (treatability) of several alternative Corrective Measure technologies. The RI/FS or CMS team proposes these alternative technologies as possible cleanup options. This process screens out ineffective alternatives. Alternatives that pass the bench scale treatability tests can then be pilot-tested at the site.

The EPA has documented numerous costs from bench scale treatability tests. The EPA data exhibits the following cost distribution:

Bench Scale Treatability Test with similar results to actual remediation but a cost of 0.5–2% of the remediation cost.

Preliminary Design (30%)
This task includes five sub-tasks:

- Design Criteria Memorandum
- Basis of Design Report
- Preliminary Plans and Specifications
- Value Engineering (VE) Screening Report
- Public Meetings

Design Criteria Memorandum. The Design Criteria Memorandum will include the preliminary design assumption and parameters, such as waste characterization, pretreatment requirements, volume and type of medium requiring treatment, treatment rates, waste stream qualities, performance standards, and long-term monitoring and operation and maintenance requirements. Labor categories associated with this task include:

Task Hours Based on Moderate Complexity

Labor Category	In Situ-1	In Situ-2	Ex Situ-1	Ex Situ-2	Ex Situ-3
Project Manager	3	4	3	3	2
Office Manager	2	2	2	2	1
Project Engineer	12	16	15	22	10
Staff Engineer	34	62	26	50	21
Staff Scientist	26	40	38	10	26
QA/QC Officer	8	8	7	14	4
CH/HS	0	0	0	0	0
Field Technician	0	0	0	0	0
Secretarial/Admin	5	10	3	8	2
Word Processing	15	20	14	18	10
Draftsman	0	0	0	0	0

Basis of Design Report. The Basis of Design Report (BDR) will provide a description of the evaluations conducted to select the treatment method. The supporting calculations, draft process flow diagram, detailed description on how the Applicable or Relevant and Appropriate Requirements (ARARs) will be met, a plan to minimize the environmental and public impacts, and heat and material balances will all be included. The report will also discuss permit requirements and deadlines, and procurement methods and availability concerns. The need for any land acquisitions/easement requirements for site access should be addressed in this document. Finally, the BDR will include a preliminary description of operation and maintenance activities along with a cost estimate projected on an annual basis. Labor categories associated with this task include:

Task Hours Based on Moderate Complexity

Labor Category	In Situ-1	In Situ-2	Ex Situ-1	Ex Situ-2	Ex Situ-3
Project Manager	21	40	21	13	18
Office Manager	2	2	1	2	1
Project Engineer	4	3	1	3	1
Staff Engineer	10	17	10	13	8
Staff Scientist	40	74	2	40	1
QA/QC Officer	11	8	6	12	4
CH/HS	4	12	4	4	2
Field Technician	0	0	0	0	0
Secretarial/Admin	6	5	1	5	1
Word Processing	10	11	5	7	3
Draftsman	6	10	1	6	1

Preliminary Plans and Specifications. An outline of general specifications, drawings, and schematics are all included in the preliminary plans and specifications, along with a preliminary RA schedule and cost estimate, and indications of any variances from the ROD. Labor categories associated with this task include:

Task Hours Based on Moderate Complexity

Labor Category	In Situ-1	In Situ-2	Ex Situ-1	Ex Situ-2	Ex Situ-3
Project Manager	5	4	5	7	4
Office Manager	1	2	1	1	1
Project Engineer	18	20	22	15	15
Staff Engineer	33	62	39	30	30
Staff Scientist	0	0	0	0	0
QA/QC Officer	8	6	10	10	7
CH/HS	0	0	0	0	0
Field Technician	0	0	0	0	0
Secretarial/Admin	6	3	2	8	2
Word Processing	8	9	18	15	13
Draftsman	23	24	21	33	14

Value Engineering (VE) Screening Report. The cost and function relationships are examined in the VE screening report, with a focus on high-cost areas. The results will determine if a full-scale VE study needs to be undertaken. Labor categories associated with this task include:

Task Hours Based on Moderate Complexity

Labor Category	In Situ-1	In Situ-2	Ex Situ-1	Ex Situ-2	Ex Situ-3
Project Manager	6	0	6	10	5
Office Manager	2	0	9	3	6
Project Engineer	13	0	14	10	9
Staff Engineer	24	0	22	30	16
Staff Scientist	0	0	0	0	0
QA/QC Officer	5	0	6	7	4
CH/HS	0	0	0	0	0
Field Technician	0	0	0	0	0
Secretarial/Admin	6	0	2	8	1
Word Processing	8	0	18	15	13
Draftsman	9	0	21	10	14

Public Meetings. This task includes meetings with regulators, public meetings, and review meetings with the customer and regulators. Labor categories associated with this task include:

Task Hours Based on Moderate Complexity

Labor Category	In Situ-1	In Situ-2	Ex Situ-1	Ex Situ-2	Ex Situ-3
Project Manager	12	12	12	12	12
Office Manager	0	0	0	0	0
Project Engineer	0	0	0	0	0
Staff Engineer	12	12	12	12	12
Staff Scientist	0	0	0	0	0
QA/QC Officer	0	0	0	0	0
CH/HS	0	0	0	0	0
Field Technician	0	0	0	0	0
Secretarial/Admin	0	0	0	0	0
Word Processing	4	4	4	4	4
Draftsman	0	0	0	0	0

Intermediate Design (60%)

This task includes three sub-tasks:

- Revised Basis of Design Report
- Intermediate Plans and Specifications
- Value Engineering Report

Revised Basis of Design Report. The revised BDR will update the information contained in the original report and include design calculations and assumptions, a revised process flow diagram, an evaluation of how the ARARs will be met, a plan to minimize environmental and community impacts, and heat and mass balances. The revised BDR will also include an updated permit plan, as well as a revision of the operating and maintenance requirements and cost estimate. The easement and access requirements will be identified and included as part of the intermediate design. Labor categories associated with this task include:

Task Hours Based on Moderate Complexity

Labor Category	In Situ-1	In Situ-2	Ex Situ-1	Ex Situ-2	Ex Situ-3
Project Manager	8	2	2	10	1
Office Manager	4	0	0	8	0
Project Engineer	23	2	4	30	2
Staff Engineer	75	12	24	50	16
Staff Scientist	70	2	0	60	0
QA/QC Officer	18	4	4	25	2
CH/HS	14	0	0	18	0
Field Technician	0	0	0	0	0
Secretarial/Admin	7	0	1	14	1
Word Processing	15	2	3	30	2
Draftsman	23	3	6	30	4

Intermediate Plans and Specifications

The preliminary plans and specifications, drawings and schematics will be expanded. The RA schedule and cost estimate will be updated and revised. As in the Preliminary Plans and Specifications, any variances from the ROD will be discussed along with any ARARs that cannot be met and a solution will be presented. Labor categories associated with this task include:

Task Hours Based on Moderate Complexity

Labor Category	In Situ-1	In Situ-2	Ex Situ-1	Ex Situ-2	Ex Situ-3
Project Manager	13	2	2	20	1
Office Manager	8	0	0	17	0
Project Engineer	36	4	4	40	2
Staff Engineer	70	15	20	100	14
Staff Scientist	95	0	0	115	0
QA/QC Officer	18	2	2	25	1
CH/HS	0	0	0	0	0
Field Technician	0	0	0	0	0
Secretarial/Admin	9	1	1	10	1
Word Processing	15	1	1	20	1
Draftsman	35	6	6	50	4

Value Engineering Report. This task is only performed if the VE Engineering study indicates that a full-blown study is needed. Labor categories associated with this task include:

Task Hours Based on Moderate Complexity

Labor Category	In Situ-1	In Situ-2	Ex Situ-1	Ex Situ-2	Ex Situ-3
Project Manager	3	0	0	6	0
Office Manager	1	0	0	2	0
Project Engineer	24	0	0	25	0
Staff Engineer	70	0	0	40	0
Staff Scientist	31	0	0	40	0
QA/QC Officer	14	0	0	20	0
CH/HS	0	0	0	0	0
Field Technician	0	0	0	0	0
Secretarial/Admin	8	0	0	16	0
Word Processing	15	0	0	30	0
Draftsman	2	0	0	0	0

Pre-final Design (90%)

This task includes two sub-tasks:

Pre-final Plans and Specifications
Construction QA Plan

- *Pre-final Plans and Specifications.* Any recommendations made as a result of the VE study will be implemented as part of the Pre-final Design Plans and specifications. A draft operations and maintenance manual will be prepared which will include a description of the normal operations of the equipment, potential operating problems, a quality assurance plan for operations and maintenance (including data collection and sampling requirements), procedures to prevent accidental releases, cleanup measures, safety plan, and records and reporting requirements. Labor categories associated with this task include:

Task Hours Based on Moderate Complexity

Labor Category	In Situ-1	In Situ-2	Ex Situ-1	Ex Situ-2	Ex Situ-3
Project Manager	17	8	4	15	2
Office Manager	10	4	16	10	11
Project Engineer	80	40	14	50	9
Staff Engineer	105	140	56	125	39
Staff Scientist	80	115	64	95	39
QA/QC Officer	39	60	7	50	4
CH/HS	39	45	18	20	12
Field Technician	0	0	0	0	0
Secretarial/Admin	22	35	5	20	3
Word Processing	50	80	38	40	26
Draftsman	70	115	8	70	5

- *Construction QA Plan.* A first draft of the construction QA plan will be prepared in this phase, with the final version completed in the 100% design phase. The first-draft plan includes a detailed synopsis of inspection activities to be implemented to monitor the construction and/or installation of the remedial action components. It also includes the scope and frequency of each type of inspection to be conducted, as well as compliance with environmental air quality and emissions records, waste disposal records, and any other concerns. Inspections will ensure compliance with health and safety procedures. This plan will outline sampling requirements specific to the site. Finally, the plan will describe reporting requirements including daily summary reports and inspection data sheets. Labor categories associated with this task include:

Task Hours Based on Moderate Complexity

Labor Category	In Situ-1	In Situ-2	Ex Situ-1	Ex Situ-2	Ex Situ-3
Project Manager	11	8	4	10	2
Office Manager	7	4	2	5	1
Project Engineer	47	20	0	25	0
Staff Engineer	80	105	15	100	10
Staff Scientist	85	55	36	100	25
QA/QC Officer	31	28	6	40	4
CH/HS	38	25	10	15	7
Field Technician	0	0	0	0	0
Secretarial/Admin	19	10	3	15	2
Word Processing	30	26	27	30	18
Draftsman	47	28	8	60	5

Final Design (100%)
This task includes 4 sub-tasks:

- Final Plans and Specifications
- Final Report
- Public Meetings
- Post-design Fact Sheet

Final Plans and Specifications. The specifications, drawings, and schematics, as well as the RA cost estimate and schedule are finalized during this phase. The BDR is updated and include design calculations and the status of the ARARs and necessary permits. Labor categories associated with this task include:

Task Hours Based on Moderate Complexity

Labor Category	In Situ-1	In Situ-2	Ex Situ-1	Ex Situ-2	Ex Situ-3
Project Manager	15	8	4	15	0
Office Manager	10	4	16	10	0
Project Engineer	78	40	14	50	0
Staff Engineer	100	146	46	125	0
Staff Scientist	79	110	54	95	0
QA/QC Officer	39	60	7	50	0
CH/HS	39	45	18	20	0
Field Technician	0	0	0	0	0
Secretarial/Admin	22	35	5	20	0
Word Processing	45	80	28	40	0
Draftsman	70	125	8	70	0

Final Report. All site-related documents shall be finalized in this phase including the construction QA plan and operations and maintenance plans. All resources and plans are gathered, bound, and submitted to the proper agencies and individuals. Labor categories associated with this task include:

Task Hours Based on Moderate Complexity

Labor Category	In Situ-1	In Situ-2	Ex Situ-1	Ex Situ-2	Ex Situ-3
Project Manager	11	8	4	15	0
Office Manager	7	4	2	10	0
Project Engineer	47	20	0	50	0
Staff Engineer	80	105	15	125	0
Staff Scientist	85	55	36	95	0
QA/QC Officer	31	28	6	50	0
CH/HS	38	25	10	20	0
Field Technician	0	0	0	0	0
Secretarial/Admin	19	10	3	20	0
Word Processing	28	26	25	40	0
Draftsman	47	28	8	70	0

Public Meetings. This task includes meetings with regulators, public meetings, and review meetings with the customer and regulators. Labor categories associated with this task include:

Task Hours Based on Moderate Complexity

Labor Category	In Situ-1	In Situ-2	Ex Situ-1	Ex Situ-2	Ex Situ-3
Project Manager	16	16	16	16	0
Office Manager	0	0	0	0	0
Project Engineer	0	0	0	0	0
Staff Engineer	16	16	16	16	0
Staff Scientist	0	0	0	0	0
QA/QC Officer	0	0	0	0	0
CH/HS	0	0	0	0	0
Field Technician	0	0	0	0	0
Secretarial/Admin	0	0	0	0	0
Word Processing	8	8	8	8	0
Draftsman	0	0	0	0	0

Post-design Fact Sheet. This task includes activities related to producing a fact sheet, or synopsis, of details related to the overall Remedial

Design of the project. Labor categories associated with this task include:

Task Hours Based on Moderate Complexity

Labor Category	In Situ-1	In Situ-2	Ex Situ-1	Ex Situ-2	Ex Situ-3
Project Manager	0	0	0	0	0
Office Manager	0	0	0	0	0
Project Engineer	0	0	0	0	0
Staff Engineer	0	0	0	0	0
Staff Scientist	10	10	10	10	0
QA/QC Officer	0	0	0	0	0
CH/HS	0	0	0	0	0
Field Technician	0	0	0	0	0
Secretarial/Admin	0	0	0	0	0
Word Processing	4	4	4	4	0
Draftsman	0	0	0	0	0

Bid Documents

This task includes three sub-tasks:

- Prepare Bid Documents
- Issue Invitations for Bids/ Request Proposals
- Contractor Bid Evaluation

Prepare Bid Documents. Information must be organized and packaged for contractors who are interested bidding on the project, for evaluation and bid preparation.

Task Hours Based on Moderate Complexity

Labor Category	In Situ-1	In Situ-2	Ex Situ-1	Ex Situ-2	Ex Situ-3
Project Manager	4	2	4	4	0
Office Manager	4	2	4	4	0
Project Engineer	3	1	3	3	0
Staff Engineer	3	1	3	3	0
Staff Scientist	0	0	0	0	0
QA/QC Officer	2	0	2	2	0
CH/HS	2	0	2	2	0
Field Technician	0	0	0	0	0
Secretarial/Admin	10	2	10	10	0
Word Processing	8	7	8	8	0
Draftsman	0	0	0	0	0

Issue Invitations for Bids/Request Proposals. Contractors interested in the job will be given the bid documents and invited to bid on the project. Proposals will be accepted and submitted for evaluation.

Task Hours Based on Moderate Complexity

Labor Category	In Situ-1	In Situ-2	Ex Situ-1	Ex Situ-2	Ex Situ-3
Project Manager	1	1	1	1	0
Office Manager	4	4	4	4	0
Project Engineer	0	0	0	0	0
Staff Engineer	0	0	0	0	0
Staff Scientist	0	0	0	0	0
QA/QC Officer	0	0	0	0	0
CH/HS	0	0	0	0	0
Field Technician	0	0	0	0	0
Secretarial/Admin	5	5	5	5	0
Word Processing	5	5	5	5	0
Draftsman	0	0	0	0	0

Contractor Bid Evaluation. All bids will be evaluated and discussed. The bid that most closely fits the needs of the project will then be selected.

Task Hours Based on Moderate Complexity

Labor Category	In Situ-1	In Situ-2	Ex Situ-1	Ex Situ-2	Ex Situ-3
Project Manager	2	1	2	2	0
Office Manager	3	2	3	3	0
Project Engineer	3	2	3	3	0
Staff Engineer	3	2	3	3	0
Staff Scientist	3	2	3	3	0
QA/QC Officer	3	2	3	3	0
CH/HS	0	0	0	0	0
Field Technician	0	0	0	0	0
Secretarial/Admin	3	1	3	3	0
Word Processing	3	1	3	3	0
Draftsman	0	0	0	0	0

Related Costs

Site Distance

Site distance refers to the one-way distance to the site, in miles, from the location of the people performing the site visit. The range is from 1–1,000 miles. The site distance is used to determine per diem rates and travel costs. Assume that 5 people will visit the site with 5 per diems and only one car. When site distance is less than 50 miles, only mileage is used (miles times $.31/mi). When mileage falls between 50–150 miles, the cost of 5 per diems is added to mileage costs. If mileage is greater than 150 miles, assume a rental car and 5 per diems.

Other Direct Costs

A way to estimate Other Direct Costs (ODCs) is based on the total estimated labor costs for each activity. ODCs include miscellaneous costs associated with the RD, such as telephone, regular and overnight mail, reproduction costs, and research materials. The ODCs are presented in lump sum dollars and may be adjusted as required for a specific sub-task. The default ODC amount is calculated as follows:

ODC = (total labor costs) × (percentage)

The default percentage for the entire RD is equal to 10% of the total estimated labor costs for the task. ODC percentages are broken down further by task as follows:

Project Planning = 2%
Treatability or other studies = 1.5%
Preliminary Design (30%) = 1%
Intermediate Design (60%) = 1%
Prefinal Design (90%) = 1.5%
Final Design (100%) = 1.5%
Bid Documents = 1.5%

Conclusion

Remedial design, occurring between the investigative and construction phases, is a significant phase of site cleanup. The primary cost driver for this part of the work is labor. There are two methods to develop an estimate of RD costs: the percentage method and the detailed labor-hour method. The percentage method is generally less accurate and requires an estimate of the total construction cost, but can be derived with much less effort. For the detailed labor-hour method, the estimator should evaluate which tasks are appropriate to include in the estimate, and should also evaluate the effect of complexity and level of detail modifiers on the total cost.

Part X

Cost Estimating for Remediation —Operations & Maintenance

Chapter 60

Cost Estimating for Remediation Operations & Maintenance

Many remedial systems include technologies and equipment that must be operated and maintained. Operational costs include operator labor, professional labor, energy, periodic replacement or regeneration of treatment media, treatment chemicals, consumables, system testing, and heating. Maintenance usually is conducted on a pre-scheduled, preventive basis. Maintenance costs include periodic servicing of pumps, blowers, and treatment vessels.

Operations & Maintenance (O&M) Cost Categories

The major cost categories to consider when estimating O&M costs include:

- **Operations Labor:** Includes routine remedial action systems operations, sampling, inspections, and record keeping.
- **Expendable Materials & Energy:** Includes granular activated carbon, acids, bases, flocculants, nutrients, oxidizing agents, natural gas, electricity, and fuel for system operations.
- **Analytical:** Includes routine lab testing to track the performance and operations of remedial action systems. Analytical labor and sampling are included in operations labor. Site sampling and analysis are included in the long-term monitoring phase.
- **Disposal of Wastes:** Transportation and disposal of spent treatment media, used disposable personnel protective equipment, and recovered free product.
- **Remedial Action Professional Services:** Outside engineering and scientific support to periodically assess and report remedial action progress and performance.
- **Contractor Travel:** Travel costs for site O&M activities.
- **Maintenance Materials and Labor:** Labor, parts, and other supplies and equipment to perform routine and minor unscheduled maintenance on process, mechanical, electrical, and instrumentation & control equipment.
- **Startup Costs:** Costs for the startup phase, prior to commencement of the full-scale remediation operation
- **O&M Markups:** General conditions, overhead, subcontractor markup, profit, risk (contingency), and owner costs.

Each section is discussed in greater detail below based on a step-by-step calculation approach.

Steps to Take Before Preparing an O&M Cost Estimate

The following 9 steps should be taken prior to preparing the O&M estimate. These steps result in a series of calculations and assumptions that are then used to estimate the costs for the listed categories.

Step 1: Evaluate Remediation Technologies Needing O&M

The estimator should determine the remediation scenario, and identify the technologies for which O&M costs need to be developed.

Step 2: Determine Startup and O&M Durations

Startup Duration

Determine a Startup Duration, which is usually expressed in weeks. The following list defines project sizes that will be referred to in the table below. These will be used in the table that follows, showing startup periods based on treatment train and project size.

Small: Has soil contamination only. Less than 0.25 acres.
Medium: Includes soil and groundwater contamination. Soil contamination is less than 0.25 acres. The groundwater contamination has a plume size less than 0.25 acres.
Large: Includes soil and groundwater contamination. The soil contamination is between 0.5–20 acres. The groundwater contamination plume size is 0.25–2 acres.
Very Large: Includes soil and groundwater contamination. The soil contamination area is greater than 20 acres. The groundwater contamination plume size is greater than 2 acres.

O&M Duration

Determine an O&M Duration, which usually ranges from several months to 30 years, depending on the nature and extent of contamination and the type of remediation scenarios. The following figures may help in determining the overall remediation complexity you should use when calculating the O&M duration. "Simple" complexities may reflect the ability to complete O&M within a few years; on the other end of the spectrum, "Very Complex" may reflect a cleanup time period, and hence an O&M period, of greater than 20 years.

Figure 60.1 defines the categories of relative in situ remediation complexity based on the site's hydrogeology and contaminant chemistry:

| Hydrogeology | Contaminant Chemistry | | | | | |
	Dissolved	Dissolved	Dissolved	Dissolved	Separate Phase LNAPL	Separate Phase DNAPL
Homogenous, Single Layer	Simple	Moderately Simple	Moderate	Moderate	Moderately Complex	Complex
Homogeneous, Multiple Layer	Simple	Moderately Simple	Moderate	Moderate	Moderately Complex	Complex
Heterogeneous, Single Layers	Moderate	Moderate	Complex	Complex	Complex	Very Complex
Heterogeneous, Multiple Layers	Moderate	Moderate	Complex	Complex	Complex	Very Complex
Fractured	Complex	Complex	Complex	Complex	Very Complex	Very Complex

Figure 60.1 In Situ Remediation Complexity Criteria

Technology	Project Size and Duration			
	Small	Medium	Large	Very Large
Air Stripping	1 week	2 weeks	4 weeks	6 weeks
Advanced Oxidation Processes	1 week	2 weeks	4 weeks	6 weeks
Air Sparging	1 week	2 weeks	4 weeks	6 weeks
Bioventing	1 week	2 weeks	4 weeks	6 weeks
Carbon Adsorption (Gas)	1 week	2 weeks	4 weeks	6 weeks
Carbon Adsorption (Liquid)	1 week	2 weeks	4 weeks	6 weeks
Capping	1 week	2 weeks	3 weeks	5 weeks
Coagulation/ Flocculation	1 week	2 weeks	4 weeks	6 weeks
Dewatering (Sludge)	1 week	2 weeks	4 weeks	6 weeks
Discharge to POTW	1 week	2 weeks	3 weeks	5 weeks
Ex Situ Bioreactors	2 weeks	3 weeks	5 weeks	8 weeks
Ex Situ Land Farming	1 week	2 weeks	3 weeks	5 weeks
Ex Situ Vapor Extraction	1 week	2 weeks	4 weeks	6 weeks
French Drain	1 week	2 weeks	3 weeks	5 weeks
Groundwater Extraction Wells	1 week	2 weeks	4 weeks	6 weeks
Heat Enhanced Vapor Extraction	2 weeks	3 weeks	5 weeks	8 weeks
Injection Wells	1 week	2 weeks	4 weeks	6 weeks
In Situ Land Farming	1 week	2 weeks	3 weeks	5 weeks
In Situ Biodegradation (Sat Zone)	2 weeks	3 weeks	5 weeks	8 weeks
Media Filtration	1 week	2 weeks	4 weeks	6 weeks
Metals Precipitation	2 weeks	3 weeks	5 weeks	8 weeks
Neutralization	1 weeks	2 weeks	3 weeks	6 weeks
Oil/Water Separation	1 week	2 weeks	4 weeks	6 weeks
Permeable Barriers	1 week	2 weeks	3 weeks	5 weeks
Slurry Walls	1 week	2 weeks	3 weeks	5 weeks
Soil Vapor Extraction	1 week	2 weeks	4 weeks	6 weeks
Thermal and Catalytic Oxidation	1 week	2 weeks	4 weeks	6 weeks

Figure 60.2 defines the categories of relative ex situ remediation complexity based on the site's waste characteristics and contaminant chemistry.

Step 3: Evaluate O&M Durations for Each Technology

It is possible that some technologies will be "turned off" early, or "started late" over the overall O&M duration. For example, a secondary filter for treated groundwater might not be needed for the entire O&M duration if the groundwater quality improves such that the groundwater can be discharged with only primary treatment. Or an off-gas treatment system might be started later than the primary groundwater treatment system if there is no immediate off-gas generated that needs to be treated. The estimator should evaluate the anticipated remediation scenario with the engineering/construction team to determine the estimated duration of individual technologies within the overall O&M duration.

Step 4: Determine O&M Labor and Safety Levels

Level of O&M Labor

The level of O&M labor is a significant cost driver for many sites. Calculation methods and defaults are provided later in this chapter for the following O&M Labor Levels:

- **None:** No O&M labor needed.
- **Minimal:** Typically on the order of 75–150 hours per year for a field technician, and 15–30 hours per year for a field engineer. The low number is typical for a wet treatment process, such as air stripping, and the high number is typical for a gas phase process, such as bioventing.
- **Moderately Low:** Typically on the order of 150–250 hours per year for a field technician, and 30–50 hours per year for a field engineer.

Waste		Mobile Light Contaminant → Strongly Sorbed Heavy Contaminant					
Uniform	Easy To Handle	Simple	Moderately Simple	Moderate	Moderate	Moderately Complex	Complex
⇓	⇓	Simple	Moderately Simple	Moderately	Moderately	Moderately Complex	Complex
⇓	⇓	Moderately	Moderately	Complex	Complex	Complex	Very Complex
⇓	⇓	Moderately	Moderately	Complex	Complex	Complex	Very Complex
Non-Uniform	Difficult To Handle	Complex	Complex	Complex	Complex	Very Complex	Very Complex

Figure 60.2 Ex Situ Remediation Complexity Criteria

The low number is likely for a 200 GPM air stripping technology, and the high number for a 100 SCFM bioventing technology.

- **Moderate:** Typically on the order of 200–350 hours per year for a field technician, and 40–70 hours per year for a field engineer. The low number is normal for a 200 GPM air stripping technology, and the high number for a 100 SCFM bioventing technology.
- **High:** Typically about 25% higher than the "moderate" category for field technician and field engineer labor.
- **Very High:** Generally about 50% higher than the "moderate" category for field technical and field engineer labor.

If the estimator has more detailed O&M labor information, such as Labor Crew Size and estimated annual labor expenditures, this information should be used.

Level of Professional Labor

Professional labor expense is often incurred during the O&M phase as treatment and/or construction professionals monitor the operation for achievement of remediation goals. Defaults are provided later in this chapter for the following Professional Labor Levels:

- **None:** No professional labor needed.
- **Minimal:** A minimum level of professional labor support is expected. This level of effort is estimated based on 10% of the operations labor at the site.
- **Moderate:** A moderate level of professional labor support is anticipated. This level of effort is estimated based on 20% if the operations labor at the site.
- **High:** A high level of professional labor is expected. This level of effort is estimated based on 30% of the operations labor at the site.

O&M Health and Safety Level

As with investigation and construction activities, the level of health and safety measures provided during O&M affects labor productivity and costs. Safety levels A, B, C, and D are based on the Occupational Safety and Health Administration (OSHA) regulations in 29 CFR Part 1910. Safety Level E (Modified level D) corresponds to the EPA "No Hazard" designation. The O&M level is usually Level E or D, although there are times when Level C protection is required. The following factors are used when adjusting O&M labor costs for health & safety levels.

HSFACTOR Level C – 1.48

HSFACTOR Level D – 1.0

HSFACTOR Level E – 0.82

Step 5: Evaluate Overall System Maintenance Levels

The estimator can determine the year-by-year annual allowances for maintenance material costs for the entire treatment train by evaluating the systems maintenance level. This level can vary substantially, depending on many factors, including:

- **Operators:** The degree of operating expertise and level of adherence to operating and preventive maintenance (PM) procedures have an impact on the Systems Maintenance Level. A high level of expertise and adherence to PM procedures results in an overall lower requirement and cost for systems maintenance. A lower level of operating expertise and adherence to preventive maintenance results in an overall higher requirement and cost for systems maintenance.

- **Systems Reliability and Durability:** The quality of the equipment, appropriate systems integration design, proper installation, and systems automation are variables in systems reliability and durability. Combinations of relatively high-quality equipment, proper design and installation, and automation for alarms and system shutoffs result in overall lower systems maintenance levels. Combinations of relatively low-quality equipment, inappropriate design and installation, and lack of automation for alarms and system shut-offs result in overall higher systems maintenance levels.
- **Operating Requirements:** Systems operating requirements include system cycling frequency (on/off), operation level relative to design limits, and operating period duration (e.g., continuous every day, a few hours per week, etc). A low frequency of system cycling, operating well within system design limits, and relatively low continuous operating period requirements result in overall lower requirements for systems maintenance. Frequent system cycling, operating near or above the system design limits, and a high continuous operating period create a need for overall higher levels of systems maintenance.
- **Systems Environment:** The systems environment includes weather exposure and conditions, and exposure to corrosive chemicals. Good protection from, or low risk of exposure to, weather and corrosive chemicals can result in overall lower levels of required maintenance. Relatively high risk of exposure to weather and corrosive chemicals can lead to overall higher levels of maintenance.

Calculations are provided later in this chapter for the following Systems Maintenance Levels. Typically these levels are used to select multipliers that are applied to the overall treatment train capital cost to estimate annual materials costs for O&M. The estimator should work with technology and O&M specialists to select a category.

- **Exclude from Estimate:** Excludes maintenance materials and labor costs from the treatment train operations and maintenance.
- **Low:** Operator, systems reliability and durability, operating requirements, and systems environment factors all indicate lower systems maintenance levels.
- **Moderate:** Most operator, systems reliability and durability, operating requirements, and systems environment factors indicate lower systems maintenance levels, and some indicate somewhat higher maintenance levels—generally 2 times higher than "low."
- **High:** Most operator, systems reliability and durability, operating requirements, and systems environment factors indicate higher systems maintenance levels, and some indicate somewhat lower maintenance levels—generally 5 times higher than "low."
- **Very High:** All operator, systems reliability and durability, operating requirements, and systems environment factors indicate higher systems maintenance levels—generally 10 times higher than "low."

Step 6: Evaluate Analytical Costs

In this step, the estimator calculates the cost for collecting and analyzing samples to verify that the treatment train is operating properly. These costs apply only to the O&M of the remedial technologies; the cost for collecting and analyzing samples to evaluate contaminant concentrations in soil or groundwater should be estimated using the monitoring technology described in Chapter 57.

Frequency

Typically, 1 of 7 options is selected:

Exclude from Estimate: Excludes sampling and frequency costs from the treatment train operations and maintenance estimate.

- Semi-annual
- Quarterly
- Monthly
- Bi-weekly
- Weekly
- Daily
- Custom

Number of Samples

Figure 60.3 provides a rule of thumb for estimating number of samples taken at each sampling event.

Technology	Samples Per Event Per Matrix	Matrix		
		Water	Air	Soil
Advanced Oxidation Processes	1	1	0	0
Air Stripping	1	1	1	0
Air Sparging	# Wells/ 10	0	1	0
Carbon Adsoprtion, Gas	1	0	1	0
Carbon Adsorption, Liquid	1	1	0	0
Coagulation/ Flocculation	1	1	0	0
Dewatering (Sludge)	1	1	0	1
Discharge to POTW	1	1	0	0
Ex Situ Bioreactors	1	1	1	0
Free Product Removal	# Wells/ 10	1	0	0
Groundwater Extraction Wells	# Wells/ 10	1	0	0
Injection Wells	# Wells/ 10	1	0	0
In Situ Biodegradation	# Wells/ 10	1	0	0
Media Filtration	1	1	0	0
Metals Precipitation	1	1	0	0
Neutralization	1	1	0	0
Oil/ Water Separation	1	1	0	0
Passive Water Treatment	1	1	0	0
Phytoremediation	1	0	0	1
Soil Vapor Extraction	# Wells/ 10	0	1	0
Thermal/Catalytic Oxidation	1	0	1	0

Figure 60.3 Rule of Thumb Estimates for Number of Samples

Step 7: Determine Travel Costs

If operators and professional staff are not located near the site (>50 miles), travel costs should be considered for O&M activities. Generally these costs are estimated on an annual basis for each person traveling by considering the following:

- Number of trips per year
- Reimbursable travel hours (labor) per trip
- Travel costs per trip (airfare, automobile mileage)
- Average duration per trip, in days
- Per diem cost

Travel costs can be calculated as follows:

Travel costs per person = Number of trips per year × {[Reimbursable travel hours per trip × hourly rate] + [Travel costs per trip] + [Average duration per trip × per diem cost]}

Step 8: Determine Heating Requirements

In cold climates, the electricity costs to heat process streams and buildings can be a considerable O&M expense. These can be estimated as follows:

Estimate Process Stream Heating Requirements

These usually include both air and wet-flow streams and apply 3 factors:

- **Flow:** the flow of air in the stream in C.F.M., or the water stream in GPM.
- **Temperature Difference:** how many degrees the air or water stream will need to be heated.
- **Percent of Run Time:** percentage of the total annual time when the system is running that the air or water stream will require heating.

The annual process stream heating requirements are calculated as follows:

Electrical usage (kwh), Air Stream = [(Flow in C.F.M.) × (0.24 BTU/lb/°F) × (temperature difference, °F) × (% run time/100) × (0.08 lbs P.C.F.) × (525,600 minutes/year)] / [(0.8 efficiency) × (3,414 BTU/kwh)]

Electrical usage (kwh), Water Stream = [(Flow in GPM) × (1 BTU/lb/°F) × (temperature difference, °F) × (% run time/100) × (8.34 lbs/gallon) × (525,600 minutes/year)]/[(0.8 efficiency) × (3,414 BTU/kwh)]

Estimate Facility Heating Requirements

This calculation considers 4 factors:

- **Area:** floor area of the facility in S.F.
- **Height:** height, in feet, of the facility to be heated.
- **Temperature Difference:** how many degrees the air in the facility will need to be heated.
- **Months per Year:** number of months in the year that the facility will require heating.

The annual facility heating requirements are estimated as follows:

Electrical usage (kwh) = {(0.14 thermal conductivity in BTU/(S.F. × hr × °F)) × [(Area, S.F.) + (4 × Height, ft) × ((Area, S.F.) ^0.5)) × (temperature difference, °F) × (months/year) × 730 hrs/month)}/ 3,415 BTU/kwh

Step 9: Evaluate Technology-Specific O&M Run Time Percentages

Various technologies and unit processes are taken off-line at various times during the year for maintenance activities or because the process is not needed to run full-time concurrent with the rest of the treatment train. The average default run time percentage is 97%. The estimator should evaluate the run time percentage for each technology in particular the following, which may have different run time percentages:

- Air Stripping
- Advanced Oxidation Processes
- Air Sparging
- Bioventing
- Carbon Adsorption (Gas)
- Carbon Adsorption (Liquid)
- Coagulation/Flocculation
- Dewatering (Sludge)
- Discharge to POTW
- Ex Situ Bioreactors
- Groundwater Extraction Wells
- Injection Wells
- In Situ Biodegradation (Saturated Zone)
- Media Filtration
- Metals Precipitation
- Neutralization
- Oil/Water Separation
- Soil Vapor Extraction
- Thermal & Catalytic Oxidation

The run time percentage is multiplied times annual O&M costs specific to the technology.

Steps for Preparing an O&M Cost Estimate

Step 1: Estimate Operations Labor

O&M labor tends to be performed primarily by field technicians, with occasional support from a field engineer. Figure 60.4 presents calculations for this labor based on the level of O&M labor previously described. These calculations should be conducted for each technology in the remediation scenario that requires O&M labor. The resultant sum of labor hours is the total annual operations labor for the remediation scenario.

Where:

LABORMIN, LABORLOW, TECHMIN, and Y are identified in Figure 60.5.

HSFACTOR is the Health & Safety Factor previously identified.

TECHACTUAL is the technology-specific value of the technology size, in the same units as TECHMIN in Figure 60.5. For example, TECHACTUAL for a 300 GPM air stripper is equal to 300.

Figure 60.5 shows values for TECHMIN and Y for various technologies.

Level of O&M Labor	Calculation For Annual Field Technician Hours For Each Technology Requiring O&M	Calculation For Annual Field Engineer Hours For Each Technology Requiring O&M
None	0	0
Minimal	Field Tech Labor Minimal = LABORMIN × HSFACTOR	Field Engineer Labor Minimal = Field Tech Labor Minimal × 0.2
Moderately Low	Field Tech Labor Moderately Low = Field Tech Labor Moderate × 0.75	Field Engineer Labor Moderately Low = Field Tech Labor Moderately Low × 0.2
Moderate	Field Tech Labor Moderate = [(TECHACTUAL/TECHMIN) ^Y]/ LABOR LOW	Field Engineer Labor Moderate = Field Tech Labor Moderate × 0.2
High	Field Tech Labor High = Field Tech Labor Moderate × 1.5	Field Engineer Labor High = Field Tech Labor High × 0.2

Figure 60.4 Field Labor Hours

Technology	LBRMIN Hrs/Year	LBRLOW Hrs/Year	MINPARM (Technology Specific)	Y (exponent)
Advanced Oxidation Process	150	300	50 GPM	0.4
Air Stripping	75	150	50 GPM	0.235866
Air Sparging	75	150	50 SCFM	0.231378
Bioventing	150	300	50 SCFM	0.231378
Capping	8	1	0.5 acres	0.462756
Coagulation/Flocculation	125	250	50 GPM	0.4
Dewatering	See note	See note	See note	See note
Discharge to POTW (Pumped)	60	120	50 GPM	0.119061
Discharge to POTW (Gravity)	12	24	50 GPM	0.119061
Ex Situ Bioreactors	300	600	50 GPM	0.6
Free Product Removal (Manual Removal from Wells)	55	110	3 wells	0.638086
French Drain	8	16	100 L.F.	0.5
GAC Adsorption (gas)	80	160	200 SCFM	0.397274
GAC Adsorption (liq)	80	160	50 GPM	0.397274
GW Extraction Wells	55	110	3 wells	0.5
In Situ Biodegredation (Saturated Zone)	110	220	3 wells	0.4
Infiltration Gallery	8	16	100 L.F.	0.5
Injection Wells	55	110	3 Wells	0.5
Media Filtration	80	160	50 GPM	0.4
Metals Precipitation	250	500	50 GPM	0.4
Neutralization	175	350	50 GPM	0.4
Permeable Barriers	4	8	100 S.F.	0.5
Oil/Water Separation	40	80	50 GPM	0.4
Slurry Walls	4	8	100 L.F.	0.5
Soil Vapor Extraction	150	300	250 SCFM	0.231378
Thermal/Catalytic Oxidation	150	300	500 SCFM	0.499948

Note: Field Technician Labor Moderate (Dewatering) = [(24 hrs/day) × (0.5 hr/cycle) × (365 days/yr) × (0.97 operations factor)] / (2 × dewatering cycle time, hours)

Field Technician Labor Moderate (Dewatering) = 2,100/ Dewatering Cycle Time, hours

Figure 60.5 Labor Factors for Common Remediation Technologies

For the Dewatering technology, the calculation of annual hours for Field Technician Labor Moderate is:

Field Technician Labor Moderate (Dewatering) = [(24 hrs/day) × (0.5 hr/cycle) × (365 days/yr) × (0.97 operations factor)] / (2 × dewatering cycle time, hours)

Field Technician Labor Moderate (Dewatering) = 2,100/dewatering cycle time, hours

Example Calculation:

An air sparging unit is sized at 500 SCFM flow rate. What is the annual labor estimate for the field technician and the field engineer for a moderate level of O&M labor?

Field Tech Labor Moderate = [(TECHACTUAL/TECHMIN) ^Y]/ LABOR LOW

TECHACTUAL = 500 SCFM (given)

TECHMIN = 50 SCFM (from Figure 60.5)

Y = 0.231378 (from Figure 60.5)

LABORLOW = 150 hours per year (from Figure 60.5)

Field Tech Labor Moderate = [(500/50)^0.231378] / 150 = 255 hours per year

Field Engr Labor Moderate = Field Tech Labor Moderate × 0.2 = 255 × 0.2 = 51 hours per year

Step 2: Estimate Expendable Materials and Energy
This cost can be estimated using information from Figure 60.6.

Step 3: Estimate Analytical Costs
The process for estimating analytical costs is largely summarized under Step 6 of "Steps to Take Before Preparing an O&M Cost Estimate" in the previous section of this chapter. One additional item the estimator should determine is the type of laboratory analyses that are to be conducted on each sample and the cost for each.

Analytical Costs are calculated as follows:

Analytical Costs per year = Frequency (Events /yr) × Number of Samples per Event (Figure 60.3) × Analytical Cost per Sample

Step 4: Estimate Waste Disposal Costs
To determine waste disposal costs for wastes generated by the O&M process, the estimator should refer to Chapter 48, "Off-Site Transportation and Waste Disposal" and Chapter 49, "Residual Waste Management." Example types and quantities of wastes are summarized in Figure 60.7.

Step 5: Estimate Professional Labor Costs
Professional labor support levels are discussed previously in Step 4 of "Steps to Preparing an O&M Cost Estimate." Hours can be calculated using the rules of thumb in Figure 60.8. These hours are based on the calculations in Figure 60.4, and are to be estimated for each technology that might require professional labor oversight and review.

Category	Technology	Equation to determine quantity of materials
Electricity	General	Kwh/yr = Flow rate, GPM × 0.0256 kw/GPM × 8,760 hr/yr
	Groundwater Extraction Wells	Kwh/yr = Flow rate, GPM × (30 + Depth to Water table, feet) × 0.00031 kwh/GPM × 8,760 hr/yr
	Air Stripping, Air Sparging, Bioventing, Carbon Adsorption Gas, Soil Vapor Extraction	Kwh/yr = Flow rate, CFM × 0.005 hw/SC.F.M × 8,760 hr/yr
	Advanced Oxidation	Kwh/yr = Flow rate, GPM × 0.06 kw/GPM × 8,760 hr/yr
	Coagulation/ Flocculation	Kwh/yr = Flow rate, GPM × .009 kw/GPM × 8,760 hr/yr
	Ex Situ Bioreactors, Metals Precipitation	Kwh/yr = Flow rate, GPM × 0.058 kw/GPM × 8,760 hr/yr
	Neutralization	Kwh/yr = Flow rate, GPM × 0.049 kw/GPM × 8,760 hr/yr
	Dewatering	Kwh/yr = Flow rate, lb/hr × 2,400
Expendables, Carbon	Carbon Adsorption, Liquid	If Chlorinated Organics Concentration ≥ 0.5 ppm:Carbon, lb/yr= [0.083 × (Total Organic Carbon, ppm) + 0.63 log (Chlorinated Organics, ppm) + 0.565] × flow rate, GPM × 526 lb/yr
		If Chlorinated Organics Concentration < 0.5 ppm:Carbon, lb/yr = [0.083 × (Total Organic Carbon, ppm) + 0.375] × flow rate, GPM × 12 lb/yr
	Carbon Adsorption, Gas	Carbon, lb/yr ={ [(Total Organic Carbon, ppm) × flow rate, CFM × 0.526 × 0.0808 lb/C.F.] / [5 × (log (Total Organic carbon, ppm)) + 5]} × 100
Expendables, Natural Gas	Thermal Oxidation	If Waste Gas Flow < 1001 SCFM,Gas, C.F./yr = (0.0345 × Waste Gas Flow, SCFM × 525,600 min/yr) / 1000 C.F.
		If Waste Gas Flow > 1001 SCFM,Gas, C.F./yr = (0.0432 × Waste Gas Flow, SCFM × 525,600 min/yr) / 1000 C.F.
	Catalytic Oxidation	If Waste Gas Flow < 1001 SCFM,Gas, C.F./yr = (0.0432 × Waste Gas Flow, SCFM × 525,600 min/yr) / 1000 C.F.
		If Waste Gas Flow > 1001 SCFM,Gas, C.F./yr = (0.0068 × Waste Gas Flow, SCFM × 525,600 min/yr) / 1000 C.F.
Expendables, Personal Protective Equipment	General	Days of PPE per year = (SUM of Field Technician Hours for All Technologies/yr + SUM of Field Engineer Hours for All Technologies/yr) / PPE Duration of 8 hrs/day
Expendables, Seeding, etc.	Capping	Fertilizer, Acres = Cap Size, acres × 2 passes fertilizer/yr
		Mowing, Acres = Cap Size, acres × 6 cuts/yr
		Seeding, Acres = Cap Size, acres × 0.1 reseed factor
Expendables, Ozone System	Advanced Oxidation	Expendables per year = [(Flow rate, GPM/20 GPM) round up] × 52 wks/yr
Chemicals, Hydrogen Peroxide	Advanced Oxidation	H_2O_2, drums per year = Flow rate, GPM × 0.5 drums/GPM
	In Situ Biodegradation	H_2O_2, drums per year = Flow rate, GPM × 5.3 drums/GPM
Chemicals, Polymer	Coagulation/ Flocculation	Polymer, lb/yr = Flow rate, GPM × 17.5 lb/yr per GPM
	Dewatering, Sludge	Polymer, lb/yr = Flow rate, GPM × 0.42 lb/yr per GPM
Chemicals, Lime	Ex Situ Bioreactors	Lime, ton/yr = Flow rate, GPM × 0.79 ton/yr per GPM
	Neutralization	If Effluent pH > Influent pH:Lime, ton/yr = Flow rate, GPM × [10^ (- influent pH) – 10^ (- effluent pH)] × 790 If Effluent pH ≤ Influent pH:Lime, ton/yr = Flow rate, GPM × 0.071 ton/yr per GPM

Figure 60.6 Expendable Materials and Energy

	Metals Precipitation	If Effluent pH > Influent pH:Lime, ton/yr = {Flow rate, GPM × [10^ (- influent pH) – 10^ (- effluent pH)] × 790} + Flow rate, GPM × Metals Concentration, ppm × 5,100 If Effluent pH ≤ Influent pH:Lime, ton/yr = Flow rate, GPM × 0.079 ton/yr per GPM
Chemicals, Sulfuric Acid	Ex Situ Bioreactors	Sulfuric Acid, 750 lb drum/yr = flow rate, GPM × 2.5 drum/yr per GPM
	Metals Precipitation, Neutralizationma	If Effluent pH < Influent pH:Sulfuric Acid, 750 lb drum/yr = Flow rate, GPM × [10^ (influent pH-14) – 10^ (effluent pH-14)] × 278If Effluent pH ≥ Influent pH:Sulfuric Acid, 750 lb drum/yr = Flow rate, GPM × 0.28 drum/yr per GPM
Microbes	In Situ Biodegradation	Microbes, lb/yr = Number of Wells × lb/well
Bionutrients	In Situ Biodegradation	Bionutrients, 50 lb bag/yr = flow rate, GPM × (1 bag/wk/50 GPM)

Figure 60.6 Expendable Materials and Energy (cont.)

Type of Waste	Equation to Estimate Quantity
Personnel Protective Equipment	Drums of PPE per year = [(SUM of Field Technician Hours for All Technologies/yr + SUM of Field Engineer Hours for All Technologies/yr) / PPE Duration of 8 hrs/day] / 20 drums per day
POTW Discharge	Discharge, Kgal = (Flow, GPM × Hrs operation per day × 60 min/hr × 365 days/yr) / 1,000 gal/Kgal
Bulk Waste, Sludge from Dewatering	Bulk Waste, ton/yr = Dry Solids Flow Rate, lb/hr × 8.5 ton/yr/lb/hr

Figure 60.7 Example Types and Quantity of Waste

Level of Professional Labor	Hours for Staff Engineer	Hours for Sr. Staff Engineer
None	0	0
Minimal	Staff Engineer Minimal = Field Tech Labor Minimal Hours × 0.1	Sr. Staff Engineer Minimal = Staff Engineer Minimal × 0.1
Moderately Low	Staff Engineer Moderately Low = Field Tech Labor Moderately Low Hours × 0.15	Sr. Staff Engineer Moderately Low = Staff Engineer Moderately Low × 0.1
Moderate	Staff Engineer Moderate = Field Tech Labor Moderate × 0.2	Sr. Staff Engineer Moderate = Staff Engineer Moderate × 0.1
High	Staff Engineer High = Field Tech Labor High × 0.3	Sr. Staff Engineer High = Staff Engineer High × 0.1

Figure 60.8 Professional Labor

Step 6: Estimate Contractor Travel Costs

Contractor travel costs should be estimated using the method presented under Step 7 of "Steps to Take Before Preparing an O&M Cost Estimate," earlier in this chapter.

Step 7: Estimate Maintenance Materials and Labor Costs

Maintenance materials and labor are typically calculated for the entire treatment train, based on capital costs for installing each technology in the treatment train, and the duration in each year that the technologies will operate. The maintenance materials and labor per year for the entire treatment train are calculated as:

Annual maintenance materials and labor, $ per year = Sum (Capital costs for Treatment Train Technologies) × (Year-Specific %, Figure 60.9) × (Complexity Factor, Figure 60.10)

Figure 60.9 presents Maintenance Materials and Labor costs percentage factors for each year of the treatment train O&M.

O&M Year	Factor
1	0.01
2	0.02
3	0.01
4	0.02
5	0.05
6	0.01
7	0.02
8	0.01
9	0.02
10	0.1
11	0.01
12	0.02
13	0.01
14	0.02
15	0.05
16	0.01
17	0.02
18	0.01
19	0.02
20	0.1
21	0.01
22	0.02
23	0.01
24	0.02
25	0.05
26	0.01
27	0.02
28	0.01
29	0.02
30	0.1

Figure 60.9 O&M Adjustment Factor by Year

Figure 60.10 presents complexity factors based on Maintenance Complexity, as described previously under Step 5 of "Steps to Take Before Preparing an O&M Cost Estimate," earlier in this chapter.

Step 8: Estimate Markups

O&M Markups include general conditions, overhead, subcontractor markup, profit, risk (contingency), and owner costs. The estimator should refer to Chapters 62, 63 and 64 for information on estimating markups.

Step 9: Estimate Annual O&M Costs for the Remediation Scenario/Treatment Train

Annual O&M costs are estimated in summary fashion as follows:

Total Annual O&M Costs for Treatment Train = Sum (Annual Operations Labor Costs + Annual Expendable Materials and Energy Costs + Annual Analytical Costs + Annual Waste Disposal Costs + Contractor Travel Costs + Annual Maintenance Materials and Labor Costs) × Markups

Step 10: Estimate Startup Costs

Startup costs are typically estimated on a one-time basis and include costs to test the system prior to commencing full-scale operation. Rules of thumb for estimating startup durations are summarized under Step 5 of "Steps to Preparing an O&M Cost Estimate," earlier in this chapter. Startup costs are estimated as follows:

If Startup Duration < 4 weeks:

Startup Costs = [(Startup Duration, weeks)/13] × [1st Year Annual O&M Costs for Treatment Train]

If Startup Duration > 4 weeks:

Startup Costs = [0.31 + (Startup Duration, weeks - 4)/26] × [1st Year Annual O&M Costs for Treatment Train]

Related Costs

Equipment Replacement

System components may need to be replaced, and the costs may be incurred in the O&M portion of the project, depending on: purchased system or rented/leased system, level of corrosive conditions or adverse weather conditions for equipment, continuous vs. intermittent operation, equipment preventive maintenance programs, and equipment quality.

Treatment Train System Maintenance Complexity	Complexity Factor
Exclude from Estimate	0
Low	1
Moderate	2
High	5
Very High	10

Figure 60.10 O&M Complexity Factor

Other

Other costs that may need to be considered include technology license fees, permit renewals, salvage value of used system, system tax or energy credits, system cleanup/demobilization costs, site closure costs (these are often accrued in a separate site close-out phase), and miscellaneous outside professional services (e.g., surveying, system safety training, etc).

Site Work and Utilities

Site work and utilities that may be applicable include:

- Overhead electrical distribution
- Fencing
- Signage
- Access Roads
- Sanitary Sewer
- Sprinkler System
- Storm Sewer
- Water Storage Tanks
- Load and Haul
- Cleanup and Landscaping

If the site is remote, all of these items may be required to operate the remediation system and/or to access the site during the O&M period. When applicable, site work and utilities must also be covered in the estimate.

Conclusion

Estimating annual operations and maintenance costs involves knowledge of the remediation scenario/treatment train and all of the technologies that will be included. The technologies are most often selected and designed—and capital costs estimated—before a detailed O&M estimate is created. Parametric estimates can be developed using methods detailed in this chapter, as long as basic technology information is known. Annual O&M costs are estimated using a 9-step process. Startup costs are estimated based on equations that take into account the startup duration and the first year annual O&M costs for the entire treatment train. The cost engineer should work closely with the engineering team and operations specialists to understand the technical components of the treatment train technologies and the likely operational conditions.

Part XI

Remediation Work Breakdown Structures

Chapter 61

Remediation Work Breakdown Structures

Two main work breakdown structures are used for remediation projects. These are:

- The Hazardous, Toxic, and Radiological Waste (HTRW) Work Breakdown Structure (WBS), dated February 1996, developed by the Federal Government and used primarily by DOD. This report contains 3 major sections: HTRW RA WBS, HTRW RD WBS, and HTRW O&M WBS.
- The Federal Government Environmental Cost Element Structure (ECES) WBS, dated September 1999, developed by the Federal Government's environmental cost engineering committee and used primarily by the DOE and the EPA.

Work breakdown structures are used to organize the estimate and to evaluate costs in logical groupings. The work breakdown structures are summarized in Figures 61.1, 61.2, and 61.3.

WBS	HTRW Description	Example Technology Options	Unit of Measure
32	**HTRW STUDIES ACTIVITIES**		
321	HTRW STUDIES		
321.20.91	Other	Archives Search Report	
321.20.91	Other	Corrective Measures Study	
321.20.91	Other	Engineering Evaluation/Cost Analysis (EE/CA)	
321.20.91	Other	Feasibility Study	
321.20.91	Other	Preliminary Assessment	
321.20.91	Other	RCRA Facility Investigation	
321.20.91	Other	Remedial Investigation	
321.20.91	Other	Site Inspection	
321.20.91	Other	Petroleum UST Site Assessment	
33	**HTRW CONSTRUCTION ACTIVITIES**		
331	**HTRW REMEDIAL ACTION (CONSTRUCTION)**		
331.01	**MOBILIZATION AND PREPARATORY WORK**		
331.01.04	Setup/Construct Temporary Facilities	Decontamination Facilities	EA
331.02	**MONITORING, SAMPLING, TESTING, AND ANALYSIS**		
331.02.04	Monitoring Wells	Groundwater Monitoring Well	EA
331.02.91	Other	Monitoring	
331.03	**SITEWORK**		
331.03.01	Demolition	Demolition, Buildings	SY
331.03.01	Demolition	Demolition, Curbs	SY
331.03.01	Demolition	Demolition, Fencing	SY
331.03.01	Demolition	Demolition, Pipes	SY
331.03.01	Demolition	Demolition, Catch Basins/Manholes	SY
331.03.01	Demolition	Demolition, Pavements	SY
331.03.01	Demolition	Demolition, Sidewalks	SY
331.03.02	Clearing & Grubbing	Clear & Grub	ACR
331.03.04	Roads/Parking/Curbs/Walks	Access Roads	SY
331.03.04	Roads/Parking/Curbs/Walks	Cleanup & Landscaping	SY
331.03.04	Roads/Parking/Curbs/Walks	Parking Lots	SY
331.03.04	Roads/Parking/Curbs/Walks	Resurfacing Roadways/Parking Lots	SY
331.03.05	Fencing	Fencing	L.F.
331.03.06	Electrical Distribution	Overhead Electrical Distribution	L.F.
331.03.08	Water/Sewer/Gas Distribution	Sanitary Sewer	L.F.
331.03.08	Water/Sewer/Gas Distribution	Water Storage Tanks	L.F.
331.03.11	Storm Drainage/Subdrainage	Storm Sewer	L.F.
331.03.14	Fuel Storage Tanks (New)	Storage Tank Installation	EA
331.03.91	Other	Bulk Material Storage	
331.03.92	Other	Miscellaneous Field Installation	
331.03.92	Other	Sprinkler System	
331.03.93	Other	Trenching/Piping	
331.04	**ORDNANCE AND EXPLOSIVE - CHEMICAL WARFARE MATERIAL (OE-CWM) REMOVAL & DESTRUCTION**		
331.04.01	Ordnance Removal & Destruction	Ordnance & Explosives Removal Action	ACR
331.04.91	Other	Ordnance & Explosive Waste Monitoring	

Figure 61.1 HTRW Remedial Action Work Breakdown Structure

WBS	HTRW Description	Example Technology Options	Unit of Measure
331.06	**GROUNDWATER COLLECTION & CONTROL**		
331.06.01	Extraction & Injection Wells	Groundwater Extraction Wells	EA
331.06.01	Extraction and Injection Wells	Special Well Drilling & Installation	EA
331.06.03	Slurry Walls	Slurry Walls	S.F.
331.06.91	Other	Injection Wells	
331.08	**SOLIDS COLLECTION & CONTAINMENT**		
331.08.01	Contaminated Soil Collection	Excavation	C.Y.
331.08.05	Capping of Contaminated Area/Waste Pile (Soil/Asphalt Cap)	Capping	ACR
331.10	**DRUMS/TANKS/STRUCTURES/MISCELLANEOUS DEMOLITION & REMOVAL**		
331.10.01	Drum Removal	Drum Removal	EA
331.10.04	Asbestos Abatement	Asbestos Removal	S.F.
331.10.91	Other	UST Closure	
331.11	**BIOLOGICAL TREATMENT**		
331.11.03	Land Treatment/Farming (Solid Phase Biodegradation)	Ex Situ Land Farming	C.Y.
331.11.03	Land Treatment/Farming (Solid Phase Biodegradation)	In Situ Land Farming	C.Y.
331.11.04	In Situ Biodegradation/Bioreclamation	In Situ Biodegradation (Saturated Zone)	C.Y.
331.11.12	Bioventing	Bioventing	S.F.
331.11.91	Other	Ex Situ Bioreactors	
331.11.91	Other	Natural Attenuation	
331.12	**CHEMICAL TREATMENT**		
331.12.02	Solvent Extraction	Solvent Extraction	MGA
331.12.06	Neutralization	Neutralization	MGA
331.12.08	Ultraviolet Photolysis	Advanced Oxidation Processes	MGA
331.12.91	Other	Permeable Barriers	
331.13	**PHYSICAL TREATMENT**		
331.13.01	Filtration/Ultrafiltration	Media Filtration	MGA
331.13.04	Coagulation/Flocculation/Precipitation	Coagulation/Flocculation	MGA
331.13.04	Coagulation/Flocculation/Precipitation	Metals Precipitation	MGA
331.13.07	Air Stripping	Air Stripping	MGA
331.13.09	Soil Washing (Surfactant/Solvent)	Soil Washing	C.Y.
331.13.10	Soil Flushing (Surfactant/Solvent)	Soil Flushing	C.Y.
331.13.11	Solids Dewatering	Dewatering (Sludge)	C.Y.
331.13.12	Oil/Water Separation	Oil/Water Separation	MGA
331.13.19	Carbon Adsorption - Gases	Carbon Adsorption (Gas)	C.F.
":331.13.20	Carbon Adsorption - Liquids	Carbon Adsorption (Liquid)	MGA
331.13.23	Soil Vapor Extraction	Soil Vapor Extraction	C.Y.
331.13.32	Air Sparging	Air Sparging	MGA
331.13.91	Other	Air Sparged Hydrocyclone	
331.13.91	Other	Ex Situ Vapor Extraction	
331.13.91	Other	Free Product Removal	
331.13.92	Other	French Drain	
331.13.93	Other	Heat Enhanced Vapor Extraction	
331.13.94	Other	Low Level Rad Soil Treatment	
331.13.95	Other	Passive Water Treatment	

Figure 61.1 HTRW Remedial Action Work Breakdown Structure (cont.)

WBS	HTRW Description	Example Technology Options	Unit of Measure
331.14	**THERMAL TREATMENT**	On-site Incineration	C.Y.
331.14.01	Incineration	On-site Low-temp. Thermal Desorption	C.Y.
331.14.02	Low Temperature Thermal Desorption	Thermal & Catalytic Oxidation	
331.14.91	Other	In Situ Vitrification	C.Y.
331.15	**STABILIZATION/FIXATION/ENCAPSULATION**		
331.15.02	In Situ Vitrification	In Situ Solidification	C.Y.
331.15.03	In Situ Pozzolan Process		
	(Lime/Portland Cement)	Ex Situ Solidification/Stabilization	C.Y.
331.15.07	Sludge Stabilization (Aggregate/Rock/Slag)	Contaminated Building Materials	S.F.
331.17	**DECONTAMINATION AND DECOMMISSIONING (D&D)**		
331.17.04	Dismantling Activities	Surface Decontamination	S.F.
331.17.04	Dismantling Activities	Infiltration Gallery	
331.18	**DISPOSAL (OTHER THAN COMMERCIAL)**		
331.18.91	Other	Load & Haul	TON
331.19	**DISPOSAL (COMMERCIAL)**		
331.19.21	Transportation to Storage/Disposal Facility	Transportation	TON
331.19.21	Transportation to Storage/Disposal Facility	Discharge to POTW	TON
331.19.22	Disposal Fees & Taxes	Off-site Transportation	
		and Landfill Disposal	TON
331.19.22	Disposal Fees & Taxes	Off-site Transportation	
		& Thermal Treatment	TON
331.19.22	Disposal Fees & Taxes	Professional Labor - RA	MO
331.22	**GENERAL REQUIREMENTS (Optional Breakout)**		
331.22.03	Warehouse, Materials Handling, &		
	Purchasing	Institutional Controls (OEM)	
331.22.90	Other		

Figure 61.1 HTRW Remedial Action Work Breakdown Structure (cont.)

WBS	HTRW Description	Example Technology Options	UM
342.06	**GROUNDWATER COLLECTION AND CONTROL**		
342.06.01	Extraction & Injection Wells	Groundwater Extraction Wells	EA/YR
342.06.03	Slurry Walls	Slurry Walls	S.F./YR
342.06.91	Other	Injection Wells	
342.08	**SOLIDS COLLECTION AND CONTAINMENT**		
342.08.05	Capping of Contaminated Area/ Waste Pile (Soil/Asphalt Cap)	Capping	ACR/YR
342.11	**BIOLOGICAL TREATMENT**		
342.11.04	In Situ Biodegradation/ Bioreclamation	In Situ Biodegradation (Saturated Zone)	C.Y.
342.11.12	Bioventing	Bioventing	S.F.
342.11.91	Other	Ex Situ Bioreactors	
342.12	**CHEMICAL TREATMENT**		
342.12.06	Neutralization	Neutralization	MGA
342.12.08	Ultraviolet Photolysis (UV Oxidation)	Advanced Oxidation Processes	MGA
342.12.91	Other	Permeable Barriers	
342.13	**PHYSICAL TREATMENT**		
342.13.01	Filtration/Ultrafiltration	Media Filtration	MGA
342.13.04	Coagulation/Flocculation/ Precipitation	Coagulation/Flocculation	MGA
342.13.04	Coagulation/Flocculation/ Precipitation	Metals Precipitation	MGA
342.13.07	Air Stripping	Air Stripping	MGA
342.13.11	Solids Dewatering	Dewatering (Sludge)	C.Y.
342.13.12	Oil/Water Separation	Oil/Water Separation	MGA
342.13.19	Carbon Adsorption—Gases	Carbon Adsorption (Gas)	C.F.
342.13.20	Carbon Adsorption—Liquids	Carbon Adsorption (Liquid)	MGA
342.13.23	Soil Vapor Extraction	Soil Vapor Extraction	C.Y.
342.13.32	Air Sparging	Air Sparging	MGA
342.13.91	Other	Free Product Removal	
342.13.92	Other	French Drain	
342.13.95	Other	Passive Water Treatment	
342.14	**THERMAL TREATMENT**		
342.14.91	Other	Thermal & Catalytic Oxidation	
342.18	**DISPOSAL (OTHER THAN COMMERCIAL)**		
342.18.91	Other	Infiltration Gallery	
342.22	**GENERAL REQUIREMENTS (Optional Breakout)**		
342.22.91	Other	Operations and Maintenance	
342.91	**OTHER**		
342.91.91	Other	Discharge to POTW	

Figure 61.2 HTRW O&M Work Breakdown Structure

Category	WBS	ECES Description	Example Technology Options
1. ASSESSMENT			
1.02		**PROJECT MANAGEMENT & SUPPORT**	
		(Operable Unit/Solid Waste Management Unit, Project Specific)	
	1.02.01	Project Management/Support/ Administration	Operations & Maintenance
	1.02.01	Project Management/Support/ Administration	Professional Labor Management
	1.02.01	Project Management/Support/ Administration	Site Inspection
	1.02.03	Regulatory Interaction	Permitting
	1.02.04	Institutional Controls	Ordnance & Explosive Institutional Controls
1.04		**STUDIES/DESIGN & DOCUMENTATION**	
	1.04.01	Hazardous, Toxic, or Radioactivity Ranking System	Ordnance & Explosives Removal Action
	1.04.04	Risk Assessment Documentation	Archives Search Report
	1.04.04	Risk Assessment Documentation	Archives Search Report
	1.04.05	Remedial Investigation Report	Remedial Investigation
1.05		**SITE WORK**	
	1.05.02	Cleanup/Landscaping/Revegetation	Cleanup & Landscaping
	1.05.03	Clear & Grub	Clear & Grub
	1.05.04	Demolition	Demolition, Pipes
	1.05.04	Demolition	Demolition, Buildings
	1.05.04	Demolition	Demolition, Catch Basins/Manholes
	1.05.04	Demolition	Demolition, Fencing
	1.05.04	Demolition	Demolition, Curbs
	1.05.04	Demolition	Demolition, Sidewalks
	1.05.04	Demolition	Demolition, Pavements
	1.05.05	Excavation & Earthwork	Trenching
	1.05.05	Excavation & Earthwork	Excavation, Buried Waste
	1.05.08	Access Roads	Access Roads
	1.05.14	Fencing	Fencing
	1.05.15	Parking Lots	Parking Lots
	1.05.18	Sprinkler System	Sprinkler System
	1.05.22	Fuel Storage Tanks	Storage Tank Installation
	1.05.27	Water Storage Tanks	Water Storage Tanks
	1.05.28	Storm Sewer	Storm Sewer
	1.05.31	Overhead Electrical Distribution	Overhead Electrical Distribution
	1.05.31	Overhead Electrical Distribution	Sitework & Utilities
	1.05.33	Sanitary Sewer	Sanitary Sewer
1.07		**INVESTIGATIONS & MONITORING/SAMPLE COLLECTION**	
	1.07.01	Site Reconnaisance	Preliminary Assessment
	1.07.01	Site Reconnaissance	Site Inspection
	1.07.01	Site Reconnaissance	Preliminary Assessment
	1.07.03	Site Contaminant Surveys/ Radiation Monitoring	Site Characterization Survey
	1.07.15	Monitoring Well	Groundwater Monitoring Well
1.33		**DISPOSAL - COMMERCIAL**	
	1.33.02	Transport Waste to Commercial Disposal Facility	Transportation
	1.33.02	Transport Waste to Commercial Disposal Facility	Load & Haul

Figure 61.3 ECES Work Breakdown Structure

Category	WBS	ECES Description	Example Technology Options
	1.33.03	Tipping Charges & Taxes	Off-site Transportation & Landfill Disposal
	1.33.03	Tipping Charges & Taxes	Discharge to POTW
	1.33.03	Tipping Charges & Taxes	Off-site Transportation & Thermal Treatment
1.91	**OTHER (Use Numbers 90-99)**		
	1.91.91	Other	O&M Startup Costs
2. STUDIES			
2.02	**PROJECT MANAGEMENT & SUPPORT** **(Operable Unit/Solid Waste Management Unit, Project Specific)**		
	2.02.01	Project Management/Support/ Administration	Operations & Maintenance
	2.02.01	Project Management/Support/ Administration	Professional Labor Management
	2.02.01	Project Management/Support/ Administration	Site Inspection
	2.02.03	Regulatory Interaction	Permitting
	2.02.04	Institutional Controls	Ordnance & Explosive Institutional Controls
2.04	**STUDIES/DESIGN & DOCUMENTATION**		
	2.04.01	Hazardous, Toxic, or Radioactivity Ranking System	Ordnance & Explosive Waste Remediation
	2.04.04	Risk Assessment Documentation	RCRA Facility Investigation
	2.04.04	Risk Assessment Documentation	RCRA Facility Investigation
	2.04.05	Remedial Investigation Report	Remedial Investigation
	2.04.07	Screen Environmental Alternatives	Corrective Measures Study
	2.04.10	Document FS (CMS)	Feasibility Study
	2.04.16	Engineering Evaluation/Cost Analysis	EE/CA
	2.04.16	Engineering Evaluation/Cost Analysis	OE Engineering Evaluation/Cost Analysis
2.05	**SITE WORK**		
	2.05.01	Mobilization	Decontamination Facilities
	2.05.01	Mobilization	Miscellaneous Field Installation
	2.05.02	Cleanup/Landscaping/Revegetation	Cleanup & Landscaping
	2.05.03	Clear & Grub	Clear & Grub
	2.05.04	Demolition	Demolition, Pipes
	2.05.04	Demolition	Demolition, Buildings
	2.05.04	Demolition	Demolition, Catch Basins/Manholes
	2.05.04	Demolition	Demolition, Fencing
	2.05.04	Demolition	Demolition, Curbs
	2.05.04	Demolition	Demolition, Sidewalks
	2.05.04	Demolition	Demolition, Pavements
	2.05.05	Excavation & Earthwork	Trenching
	2.05.05	Excavation & Earthwork	Excavation, Buried Waste
	2.05.08	Access Roads	Access Roads
	2.05.14	Fencing	Fencing
	2.05.15	Parking Lots	Parking Lots
	2.05.18	Sprinkler System	Sprinkler System
	2.05.22	Fuel Storage Tanks	Storage Tank Installation
	2.05.27	Water Storage Tanks	Water Storage Tanks
	2.05.28	Storm Sewer	Storm Sewer
	2.05.31	Overhead Electrical Distribution	Overhead Electrical Distribution

Figure 61.3 ECES Work Breakdown Structure (cont.)

Category	WBS	ECES Description	Example Technology Options
	2.05.31	Overhead Electrical Distribution	Sitework & Utilities
	2.05.33	Sanitary Sewer	Sanitary Sewer
2.07		**INVESTIGATIONS & MONITORING/SAMPLE COLLECTION**	
	2.07.01	Site Reconnaissance	Preliminary Assessment
	2.07.01	Site Reconnaissance	Site Inspection
	2.07.01	Site Reconnaissance	Preliminary Assessment
	2.07.03	Site Contaminant Surveys/ Radiation Monitoring	Site Characterization Survey
	2.07.15	Monitoring Well	Groundwater Monitoring Well
2.33		**DISPOSAL - COMMERCIAL**	
	2.33.02	Transport Waste to Commercial Disposal Facility	Transportation
	2.33.02	Transport Waste to Commercial Disposal Facility	Load and Haul
	2.33.03	Tipping Charges & Taxes	Off-site Transportation & Landfill Disposal
	2.33.03	Tipping Charges & Taxes	Discharge to POTW
	2.33.03	Tipping Charges & Taxes	Off-site Transportation & Thermal Treatment
2.91		**OTHER (Use Numbers 90-99)**	
	2.91.91	Other	O&M Startup Costs
3. DESIGN			
3.02		**PROJECT MANAGEMENT & SUPPORT (Operable Unit/Solid Waste Management Unit, Project Specific)**	
	3.02.01	Project Management/Support/ Administration	Operations & Maintenance
	3.02.01	Project Management/Support/ Administration	Professional Labor Management
	3.02.01	Project Management/Support/ Administration	Site Inspection
	3.02.03	Regulatory Interaction	Permitting
	3.02.04	Institutional Controls	Ordnance & Explosive Institutional Controls
3.04		**STUDIES/DESIGN & DOCUMENTATION**	
	3.04.11	Environmental Management Project Design	Remedial Design
	3.04.12	Decontamination/Dismantlement Project Design	Remedial Design
	3.04.16	Engineering Evaluation/Cost Analysis	EE/CA
	3.04.16	Engineering Evaluation/Cost Analysis	OE Engineering Evaluation/Cost Analysis
3.05		**SITE WORK**	
	3.05.01	Mobilization	Decontamination Facilities
	3.05.01	Mobilization	Miscellaneous Field Installation
	3.05.02	Cleanup/Landscaping/Revegetation	Cleanup & Landscaping
	3.05.03	Clear & Grub	Clear & Grub
	3.05.04	Demolition	Demolition, Pipes
	3.05.04	Demolition	Demolition, Buildings
	3.05.04	Demolition	Demolition, Catch Basins/Manholes
	3.05.04	Demolition	Demolition, Fencing
	3.05.04	Demolition	Demolition, Curbs
	3.05.04	Demolition	Demolition, Sidewalks
	3.05.04	Demolition	Demolition, Pavements

Figure 61.3 ECES Work Breakdown Structure (cont.)

Category	WBS	ECES Description	Example Technology Options
	3.05.05	Excavation & Earthwork	Trenching
	3.05.05	Excavation & Earthwork	Excavation, Buried Waste
	3.05.08	Access Roads	Access Roads
	3.05.14	Fencing	Fencing
	3.05.15	Parking Lots	Parking Lots
	3.05.18	Sprinkler System	Sprinkler System
	3.05.22	Fuel Storage Tanks	Storage Tank Installation
	3.05.27	Water Storage Tanks	Water Storage Tanks
	3.05.28	Storm Sewer	Storm Sewer
	3.05.31	Overhead Electrical Distribution	Overhead Electrical Distribution
	3.05.31	Overhead Electrical Distribution	Sitework & Utilities
	3.05.33	Sanitary Sewer	Sanitary Sewer
3.07	**INVESTIGATIONS & MONITORING/SAMPLE COLLECTION**		
	3.07.01	Site Reconnaissance	Preliminary Assessment
	3.07.01	Site Reconnaissance	Site Inspection
	3.07.01	Site Reconnaissance	Preliminary Assessment
	3.07.03	Site Contaminant Surveys/ Radiation Monitoring	Site Characterization Survey
	3.07.15	Monitoring Well	Groundwater Monitoring Well
3.33	**DISPOSAL – COMMERCIAL**		
	3.33.02	Transport Waste to Commercial Disposal Facility	Transportation
	3.33.02	Transport Waste to Commercial Disposal Facility	Load & Haul
	3.33.03	Tipping Charges & Taxes	Off-site Transportation & Landfill Disposal
	3.33.03	Tipping Charges & Taxes	Discharge to POTW
	3.33.03	Tipping Charges & Taxes	Off-site Transportation & Thermal Treatment
	3.91.91	Other	O&M Startup Costs
4. CAPITAL CONSTRUCTION			
4.02	**PROJECT MANAGEMENT & SUPPORT (Operable Unit/Solid Waste Management Unit, Project Specific)**		
	4.02.01	Project Management/Support/ Administration	Operations & Maintenance
	4.02.01	Project Management/Support/ Administration	Professional Labor Management
	4.02.01	Project Management/Support/ Administration	Site Inspection
	4.02.03	Regulatory Interaction	Permitting
	4.02.04	Institutional Controls	Ordnance & Explosive Institutional Controls
4.04	**STUDIES/DESIGN & DOCUMENTATION**		
	4.04.11	Environmental Management Project Design	Remedial Design
	4.04.12	Decontamination/Dismantlement Project Design	Remedial Design
4.05	**SITE WORK**		
	4.05.01	Mobilization	Decontamination Facilities
	4.05.01	Mobilization	Miscellaneous Field Installation
	4.05.02	Cleanup/Landscaping/Revegetation	Cleanup & Landscaping

Figure 61.3 ECES Work Breakdown Structure (cont.)

Category	WBS	ECES Description	Example Technology Options
	4.05.03	Clear & Grub	Clear & Grub
	4.05.04	Demolition	Demolition, Pipes
	4.05.04	Demolition	Demolition, Buildings
	4.05.04	Demolition	Demolition, Catch Basins/Manholes
	4.05.04	Demolition	Demolition, Fencing
	4.05.04	Demolition	Demolition, Curbs
	4.05.04	Demolition	Demolition, Sidewalks
	4.05.04	Demolition	Demolition, Pavements
	4.05.05	Excavation & Earthwork	Trenching
	4.05.05	Excavation & Earthwork	Excavation, Buried Waste
	4.05.08	Access Roads	Access Roads
	4.05.14	Fencing	Fencing
	4.05.15	Parking Lots	Parking Lots
	4.05.18	Sprinkler System	Sprinkler System
	4.05.22	Fuel Storage Tanks	Storage Tank Installation
	4.05.27	Water Storage Tanks	Water Storage Tanks
	4.05.28	Storm Sewer	Storm Sewer
	4.05.31	Overhead Electrical Distribution	Overhead Electrical Distribution
	4.05.31	Overhead Electrical Distribution	Sitework & Utilities
	4.05.33	Sanitary Sewer	Sanitary Sewer
4.07		**INVESTIGATIONS & MONITORING/SAMPLE COLLECTION**	
	4.07.03	Site Contaminant Surveys/ Radiation Monitoring	Site Characterization Survey
	4.07.15	Monitoring Well	Groundwater Monitoring Well
4.13		**DISPOSAL FACILITY/PROCESS**	
	4.13.12	Intermediate Depth Disposal (Burial Ground/Trenches/Pits)	Infiltration Gallery
4.15		**DRUMS/TANKS/STRUCTURES/MISC. & REMOVAL**	
	4.15.01	Drum Removal	Drum Removal
	4.15.02	Tank Removal	UST Closure
	4.15.04	Asbestos Abatement	Asbestos Removal
	4.15.05	Piping & Pipeline Removal	Excavation, Cut & Fill
	4.15.05	Piping & Pipeline Removal	Piping
	4.15.05	Piping & Pipeline Removal	Trenching/Piping
4.17		**SURFACE WATER/SEDIMENTS CONTAINMENT, COLLECTION, & CONTROL**	
	4.17.11	Pumping / Draining / Collection	Free Product Removal
4.18		**GROUNDWATER CONTAINMENT, COLLECTION, OR CONTROL**	
	4.18.01	Extraction Wells	Groundwater Extraction Wells
	4.18.02	Injection Wells	Injection Wells
	4.18.03	Subsurface Drainage / Collection/French Drain	French Drain
	4.18.04	Slurry Walls	Slurry Walls
4.19		**SOLIDS/SOILS CONTAINMENT (e.g., CAPPING/BARRIER) COLLECTION, OR CONTROL**	
	4.19.01	Contaminated Soil Collection	Excavation
4.21		**IN-SITU BIOLOGICAL TREATMENT**	
	4.21.03	Bioventing	Bioventing
	4.21.05	Constructed Wetlands	Passive Water Treatment
	4.21.06	Enhanced Bioremediation	In Situ Biodegradation (Saturated Zone)
	4.21.08	Natural attenuation	Natural Attenuation
	4.21.09	Phytoremediation	Phytoremediation
4.22		**EX-SITU BIOLOGICAL TREATMENT**	
	4.22.06	Land Farming	Ex Situ Land Farming

Figure 61.3 ECES Work Breakdown Structure (cont.)

Category	WBS	ECES Description	Example Technology Options
	4.22.12	Composting	Composting
4.23	**IN-SITU CHEMICAL TREATMENT**		
	4.23.03	Neutralization	Neutralization
	4.23.05	Soil Flushing (Surfactant / Solvent)	Soil Flushing
4.24	**EX-SITU CHEMICAL TREATMENT**		
	4.24.11	Solvent Extraction	Solvent Extraction
	4.24.13	Ultraviolet (UV) Photolysis	Advanced Oxidation Processes
	4.24.15	Coagulation / Flocculation / Precipitation	Coagulation/Flocculation
4.25	**IN-SITU PHYSICAL TREATMENT**		
	4.25.02	Air Sparging	Air Sparging
	4.25.09	Passive/Reactive Treatment Wall	Permeable Barriers
	4.25.11	Soil Flushing (Surfactant / Solvent)	Soil Flushing
	4.25.12	Solids Dewatering/Drying	Dewatering (Sludge)
	4.25.17	Soil Vapor Extraction	Soil Vapor Extraction
	4.25.17	Soil Vapor Extraction	Ex Situ Vapor Extraction
	4.25.21	Bioslurping	Carbon Adsorption (Gas)
4.26	**EX-SITU PHYSICAL TREATMENT**		
	4.26.04	Air Stripping	Air Stripping
	4.26.07	Compaction/Volume Reduction	Low Level Rad Soil Treatment
	4.26.18	Soil Vapor Extraction	Heat Enhanced Vapor Extraction
	4.26.18	Soil Vapor Extraction	Soil Vapor Extraction
	4.26.20	Media Filtration	Media Filtration
	4.26.23	Granular Activated Carbon Adsorption-Liquid	Capping
	4.26.30	Oil / Water Separation	Oil/Water Separation
	4.26.35	Soil Washing (Surfactant / Solvent)	Soil Washing
	4.26.36	Solids Dewatering/Drying	Dewatering (Sludge)
4.27	**IN SITU THERMAL TREATMENT**		
	4.27.07	Low Temperature Thermal Desorption	On-site Low Temp. Thermal Desorption
4.28	**EX SITU THERMAL TREATMENT**		
	4.28.02	Incineration	On-site Incineration
4.29	**IN SITU STABILIZATION/FIXATION/ENCAPSULATION**		
	4.29.03	Pozzolan Process	In Situ Solidification
	4.29.04	In-Situ Vitrification	In Situ Vitrification
4.30	**EX SITU STABILIZATION/FIXATION/ENCAPSULATION**		
	4.30.06	Sludge Stabilization (Aggregate Rock/Slag)	Ex Situ Solidification/Stabilization
4.31	**FACILITY DECOMMISSIONING & DISMANTLEMENT**		
	4.31.01	Nuclear Facility Shutdown & Inspection	Final Status Survey
	4.31.07	Radiological Inventory Categorization for D&D	D & D Sampling & Analysis
	4.31.08	Decontamination of Area & Equipment	Contaminated Building Materials
4.33	**DISPOSAL - COMMERCIAL**		
	4.33.02	Transport Waste to Commercial Disposal Facility	Transportation
	4.33.02	Transport Waste to Commercial Disposal Facility	Load & Haul
	4.33.03	Tipping Charges & Taxes	Off-site Transportation & Landfill Disposal

Figure 61.3 ECES Work Breakdown Structure (cont.)

Category	WBS	ECES Description	Example Technology Options
	4.33.03	Tipping Charges & Taxes	Discharge to POTW
	4.33.03	Tipping Charges & Taxes	Off-site Transportation & Thermal Treatment
4.34		**AIR EMISSION & OFF-GAS TREATMENT**	
	4.34.09	Internal Combustion Engine	Thermal & Catalytic Oxidation
	4.34.10	Granular Activated Carbon Adsorption Gas/Vapor	Carbon Adsorption (Liquid)
4.91		**OTHER (Use Numbers 90-99)**	
	4.91.91	Other	O&M Startup Costs
5. OPERATIONS & MAINTENANCE			
5.02		**PROJECT MANAGEMENT & SUPPORT (Operable Unit/Solid Waste Management Unit, Project Specific)**	
	5.02.01	Project Management/Support/ Administration	Operations & Maintenance
	5.02.01	Project Management/Support/ Administration	Professional Labor Management
	5.02.01	Project Management/Support/ Administration	Site Inspection
	5.02.03	Regulatory Interaction	Permitting
	5.02.04	Institutional Controls	Ordnance & Explosive Institutional Controls
5.05		**SITE WORK**	
	5.05.01	Mobilization	Decontamination Facilities
	5.05.01	Mobilization	Miscellaneous Field Installation
	5.05.02	Cleanup/Landscaping/Revegetation	Cleanup & Landscaping
	5.05.04	Demolition	Demolition, Pipes
	5.05.04	Demolition	Demolition, Buildings
	5.05.04	Demolition	Demolition, Catch Basins/Manholes
	5.05.04	Demolition	Demolition, Fencing
	5.05.04	Demolition	Demolition, Curbs
	5.05.04	Demolition	Demolition, Sidewalks
	5.05.04	Demolition	Demolition, Pavements
	5.05.08	Access Roads	Access Roads
	5.05.14	Fencing	Fencing
	5.05.15	Parking Lots	Parking Lots
	5.05.18	Sprinkler System	Sprinkler System
	5.05.22	Fuel Storage Tanks	Storage Tank Installation
	5.05.27	Water Storage Tanks	Water Storage Tanks
	5.05.28	Storm Sewer	Storm Sewer
	5.05.31	Overhead Electrical Distribution	Overhead Electrical Distribution
	5.05.31	Overhead Electrical Distribution	Sitework & Utilities
	5.05.33	Sanitary Sewer	Sanitary Sewer
5.07		**INVESTIGATIONS & MONITORING/SAMPLE COLLECTION**	
	5.07.03	Site Contaminant Surveys/ Radiation Monitoring	Site Characterization Survey
	5.07.15	Monitoring Well	Groundwater Monitoring Well
5.13		**DISPOSAL FACILITY/PROCESS**	
	5.13.12	Intermediate Depth Disposal (Burial Ground/Trenches/Pits)	Infiltration Gallery
5.17		**SURFACE WATER/SEDIMENTS CONTAINMENT, COLLECTION, & CONTROL**	
	5.17.11	Pumping / Draining / Collection	Free Product Removal

Figure 61.3 ECES Work Breakdown Structure (cont.)

Category	WBS	ECES Description	Example Technology Options
5.18		**GROUNDWATER CONTAINMENT, COLLECTION, OR CONTROL**	
	5.18.01	Extraction Wells	Groundwater Extraction Wells
	5.18.02	Injection Wells	Injection Wells
	5.18.03	Subsurface Drainage / Collection/French Drain	French Drain
	5.18.04	Slurry Walls	Slurry Walls
5.19		**SOLIDS/SOILS CONTAINMENT (e.g., CAPPING/BARRIER) COLLECTION, OR CONTROL**	
	5.19.01	Contaminated Soil Collection	Excavation
5.21		**IN SITU BIOLOGICAL TREATMENT**	
	5.21.03	Bioventing	Bioventing
	5.21.05	Constructed Wetlands	Passive Water Treatment
	5.21.06	Enhanced Bioremediation	In Situ Biodegradation (Saturated Zone)
	5.21.09	Phytoremediation	Phytoremediation
5.22		**EX SITU BIOLOGICAL TREATMENT**	
	5.22.06	Land Farming	Ex Situ Land Farming
	5.22.12	Composting	Composting
5.23		**IN SITU CHEMICAL TREATMENT**	
	5.23.03	Neutralization	Neutralization
5.24		**EX SITU CHEMICAL TREATMENT**	
	5.24.11	Solvent Extraction	Solvent Extraction
	5.24.13	Ultraviolet (UV) Photolysis	Advanced Oxidation Processes
	5.24.15	Coagulation/Flocculation/ Precipitation	Metals Precipitation
5.25		**IN SITU PHYSICAL TREATMENT**	
	5.25.02	Air Sparging	Air Sparged Hydrocyclone
	5.25.09	Passive/Reactive Treatment Wall	Permeable Barriers
	5.25.12	Solids Dewatering/Drying	Dewatering (Sludge)
	5.25.17	Soil Vapor Extraction	Ex Situ Vapor Extraction
	5.25.17	Soil Vapor Extraction	Heat Enhanced Vapor Extraction
	5.25.21	Bioslurping	Carbon Adsorption (Gas)
5.26		**EX SITU PHYSICAL TREATMENT**	
	5.26.04	Air Stripping	Air Stripping
	5.26.07	Compaction/Volume Reduction	Low Level Rad Soil Treatment
	5.26.18	Soil Vapor Extraction	Ex Situ Vapor Extraction
	5.26.18	Soil Vapor Extraction	Heat Enhanced Vapor Extraction
	5.26.20	Media Filtration	Media Filtration
	5.26.23	Granular Activated Carbon Adsorption- Liquid	Capping
	5.26.30	Oil/Water Separation	Oil/Water Separation
	5.26.35	Soil Washing (Surfactant/Solvent)	Soil Washing
	5.26.36	Solids Dewatering/Drying	Dewatering (Sludge)
5.27		**IN SITU THERMAL TREATMENT**	
	5.27.07	Low Temperature Thermal Desorption	On-site Low–temp. Thermal Desorption
5.28		**EX SITU THERMAL TREATMENT**	
	5.28.02	Incineration	On-site Incineration
5.29		**IN SITU STABILIZATION/FIXATION/ENCAPSULATION**	
	5.29.03	Pozzolan Process	In Situ Solidification
	5.29.04	In Situ Vitrification	In Situ Vitrification
5.30		**EX SITU STABILIZATION/FIXATION/ENCAPSULATION**	
	5.30.06	Sludge Stabilization (Aggregate/Rock/Slag)	Ex Situ Solidification/Stabilization

Figure 61.3 ECES Work Breakdown Structure (cont.)

Category	WBS	ECES Description	Example Technology Options
5.31		**FACILITY DECOMMISSIONING & DISMANTLEMENT**	
	5.31.01	Nuclear Facility Shutdown & Inspection	Final Status Survey
	5.31.07	Radiological Inventory Categorization for D&D	D & D Sampling & Analysis
	5.31.08	Decontamination of Area & Equipment	Surface Decontamination
5.33		**DISPOSAL - COMMERCIAL**	
	5.33.02	Transport Waste to Commercial Disposal Facility	Transportation
	5.33.02	Transport Waste to Commercial Disposal Facility	Load & Haul
	5.33.03	Tipping Charges & Taxes	Off-site Transportation & Landfill Disposal
	5.33.03	Tipping Charges & Taxes	Discharge to POTW
	5.33.03	Tipping Charges & Taxes	Off-site Transportation & Thermal Treatment
5.34		**AIR EMISSION & OFF-GAS TREATMENT**	
	5.34.09	Internal Combustion Engine	Thermal & Catalytic Oxidation
	5.34.10	Granular Activated Carbon Adsorption Gas/Vapor	Carbon Adsorption (Liquid)
5.91		**OTHER (Use Numbers 90-99)**	
	5.91.91	Other	O&M Startup Costs
6. SURVEILLANCE & LONG TERM MAINTENANCE			
6.02		**PROJECT MANAGEMENT & SUPPORT (Operable Unit/Solid Waste Management Unit, Project Specific)**	
	6.02.01	Project Management/Support/ Administration	Operations & Maintenance
	6.02.01	Project Management/Support/ Administration	Professional Labor Management
	6.02.01	Project Management/Support/ Administration	Site Inspection
	6.02.03	Regulatory Interaction	Permitting
	6.02.04	Institutional Controls	Ordnance & Explosive Institutional Controls
6.05		**SITE WORK**	
	6.05.01	Mobilization	Decontamination Facilities
	6.05.01	Mobilization	Miscellaneous Field Installation
	6.05.02	Cleanup/Landscaping/Revegetation	Cleanup & Landscaping
	6.05.08	Access Roads	Access Roads
	6.05.14	Fencing	Fencing
	6.05.15	Parking Lots	Parking Lots
	6.05.18	Sprinkler System	Sprinkler System
	6.05.22	Fuel Storage Tanks	Storage Tank Installation
	6.05.27	Water Storage Tanks	Water Storage Tanks
	6.05.28	Storm Sewer	Storm Sewer
	6.05.31	Overhead Electrical Distribution	Overhead Electrical Distribution
	6.05.31	Overhead Electrical Distribution	Sitework & Utilities
	6.05.33	Sanitary Sewer	Sanitary Sewer
6.07		**INVESTIGATIONS & MONITORING/SAMPLE COLLECTION**	
	6.07.03	Site Contaminant Surveys/ Radiation Monitoring	Site Characterization Survey

Figure 61.3 ECES Work Breakdown Structure (cont.)

Category	WBS	ECES Description	Example Technology Options
	6.07.15	Monitoring Well	Groundwater Monitoring Well
6.13	DISPOSAL FACILITY/PROCESS		
	6.13.12	Intermediate Depth Disposal (Burial Ground/Trenches/Pits)	Infiltration Gallery
6.18	GROUNDWATER CONTAINMENT, COLLECTION, OR CONTROL		
	6.18.01	Extraction Wells	Groundwater Extraction Wells
	6.18.02	Injection Wells	Injection Wells
	6.18.03	Subsurface Drainage/ Collection/French Drain	French Drain
	6.18.04	Slurry Walls	Slurry Walls
6.91	OTHER (Use Numbers 90-99)		
	6.91.91	Other	O&M Startup Costs
8. PROGRAM MANAGEMENT, SUPPORT & INFRASTRUCTURE			
8.02	PROJECT MANAGEMENT & SUPPORT (Operable Unit/Solid Waste Management Unit, Project Specific)		
	8.02.04	Institutional Controls	Ordnance & Explosive Institutional Controls
8.91	OTHER (Use Numbers 90-99)		
	8.91.91	Other	O&M Startup Costs

Figure 61.3 ECES Work Breakdown Structure (cont.)

Part XII

Determining Contractor Costs

Chapter 62

Contractor's General Conditions

General conditions are field-related tasks that are required to execute a contract, but are not specific to an environmental technology or restoration task. These items can include, but are not limited to, the following:

- Supervision
- Job trailers
- Storage trailers
- Portable toilets
- Temporary plants
- Personal protective equipment
- Travel
- Per diem
- Permits
- Taxes
- Insurance
- Bonds

For the purposes of this discussion, decontamination facilities are not considered a general conditions item. If required, they should be estimated as a direct cost. This chapter provides guidelines for estimating general conditions costs.

For purposes of this chapter, a "project" is defined as a continuous contract activity at a site or a group of sites with shared contractor management. For example, if a contractor is performing on-site remediation work and the contract is funded incrementally, but the funding is not interrupted and work is continuous, then the total funding at the site would be considered a single project. On the other hand, many government agencies and large private sector owners hire contractors for indefinite quantity contracts at multiple locations (e.g., the Army Corps of Engineer's Total Environmental Restoration Contracts, or TERC). These contracts are funded on a site-by-site basis; each site has separate general conditions requirements. Project size on these types of contracts is the funding for the individual site, not the total contract value.

The guidelines in this chapter are based on extensive review of contracts in the $100,000 to $25 million range. Methods for estimating general conditions costs on projects larger than $25 million are provided in this chapter, but the estimator is advised that there is only limited information available for these larger projects since, very few contracts for remediation projects in this size range have been completed.

Remedial action construction projects typically include some supervision and professional labor personnel, such as project managers, engineers, hydrogeologists, industrial hygienists, and health and safety engineers. These and other professional personnel are discussed in Chapter 58, "Remedial Action Professional Labor Management."

General conditions are applied at the total contract level of the estimate. Both prime and subcontractors will incur general conditions expenses, so the first step in estimating general conditions is to establish the distribution of work for a prime contractor and subcontractor. The costs discussed in previous chapters of this book are direct. There are no mark-ups applied to any direct cost for prime contractors or subcontractors. Therefore, a percentage of work that will be subcontracted must be established to apply both general conditions and overhead and profit. All subcontracted work will then have prime contractor mark-ups on subcontracted work, which will be less than the mark-ups on the prime contractor's own work. The distribution that is established in this chapter will also be used for contractor overhead and profit in Chapter 63.

It is possible to create a reasonable cost estimate using a few required parameters. If more detailed information is known, one can create a more precise and site-specific estimate using a secondary set of parameters.

To estimate the cost of general conditions, certain information must be known. This information is discussed in the following paragraphs.

Project Location

The project location affects general conditions items such as sales taxes, workers, compensation insurance, permits, and other items that are location- or state-specific.

Restoration Phase

The restoration phase will identify how the contracts are issued for the different phases of the restoration project. Options include:

- Single contract for studies through remedial action
- Studies contract
- Remedial action contract

Remediation Method/Treatment Train

This parameter provides an indication of the prime/subcontractor distributions based on technologies used for remediation of a project. Options are:

- Single technology
- Multiple technology

Basic Information Needed for Estimating

For the purpose of this discussion, a treatment train is defined as the single or multiple technologies (process) used to remediate a site. An example of a single technology treatment train is in situ biodegradation land treatment. Other examples include underground storage tank (UST) removal or in situ vitrification. A typical example of multiple technology treatment trains is pump and treat systems. This type of remediation process involves multiple technologies: well drilling, pumping, treating, and returning or disposing of treated material.

If a project site is remediated with a single technology treatment train, the prime contractor will probably be specialized in that type of remediation and thus will not require a great deal of subcontracted work. However, if the project is remediated with a multiple technology treatment train, there is a greater possibility that the prime contractor will not possess expertise in all of the types of remediation work and will subcontract a greater percentage of the work. The remediation method/treatment train parameter also applies to multiple-site projects in which a variety of contaminants may be present, and a variety of technologies may be used for remediation.

Construction Duration

Construction duration is the length of time the construction contract will last. This determines the length of time that the general conditions will be applied to the project cost.

Start of Construction Date

The start of construction date is the date on which the construction will begin. This date is generally after the contract has been awarded for construction, the contractor has mobilized on site, and actual field activity commences.

Worker Safety Level

Worker safety is affected by the contaminants at the site. Safety level refers to the levels required by OSHA in 29 CFR Part 1910. The four levels are designated as A, B, C, D, and E; where "A" is the most protective and "D" is the least protective. A safety level of E is also included to simulate normal construction, "no hazard" conditions as prescribed by the EPA. The safety level selected here will determine the type of personal protective equipment (PPE) required for the remediation work. The safety level chosen should be the most prevalent required at the project site, since some projects have different safety levels at different times and stages of the project. If different safety levels do exist, then the PPE requirements should be adjusted accordingly. The quantities of PPE cost items for the chosen safety level will be based on the number of field personnel and the project duration.

Design Information Needed for Detailed Estimates

Following are descriptions of the types of detailed information that, when available, can add detail and accuracy to estimates. Also included are design criteria and estimating rules of thumb that the estimator typically uses to determine values that are not known, or to check information provided by others.

Prime/Subcontractor Distribution

The prime contractor/subcontractor distribution determines the ratio of work performed by the prime contractor and subcontractors. If there are large subcontracts, the subcontractors will need supervision and on-site facilities such as office and storage trailers. The quantities of general conditions items required by subcontractors are based on the volume of subcontracted work and the project duration. This prime/sub work distribution is also used to determine values for prime and subcontractor overhead and profit. Figure 62.1 shows assumed values for prime and subcontractor work distribution based on different project conditions. These values can be used if the actual contracting strategy is unknown.

Field Expenses

This group of parameters establishes the values for the contractors' field professional staff and general construction expenses. Values are based on project direct costs and restoration phase. The field expenses parameters are as follows.

Site Project Manager

The site project manager is responsible for managing the job for the contractor. The site project manager is typically responsible for more than one project and, therefore, will not spend all of his or her time on a single project unless the project is very large. Figure 62.2 provides estimating values for remedial action contracts and turnkey studies through remedial action contracts. See Figure 62.3 for values for studies contracts.

Superintendent

The superintendent is the contractor's on-site representative who is responsible for job-site supervision. A superintendent may spend all of his or her time on the site if it is a large project, or the time may be divided among several smaller projects. Figure 62.2 provides estimating values for remedial action contracts and turnkey studies through remedial action contracts. See Figure 62.3 for values for studies contracts.

Figure 62.1 Default Prime/ Subcontractor Distribution

Default Prime/Subcontractor Distribution		
	Percent Of Work Performed By	
Type Of Contract	Prime	Subcontractor
Single Contract for Studies Through Remedial Action		
Single Technology	75	25
Multiple Technology	65	35
Studies Contract	35	65
Remedial Action Contract		
Single Technology	70	30
Multiple Technology	55	45

Clerks

The clerks on the job site are responsible for secretarial and clerical support to the project manager, superintendent, and other field professionals. Figure 62.2 provides estimating values for remedial action contracts and turnkey studies through remedial action contracts. See Figure 62.3 for values for studies contracts.

Vehicles

This parameter accounts for general purpose vehicles used at the project site for transporting supplies and personnel or running errands. The types of vehicles include vans and pick-up trucks. The total direct

Field Expenses Studies Through RA Contracts & RA Contracts (Value Based on Direct Cost Range)										
Direct Cost (Millions Of Dollars)										
Expense/Unit of Measure	<0.1	.1-.5	.5-1	1-5	5-10	10-15	15-30	30-50	50-75	>75
Site Proj. Mgr./FTE										
Prime	0.0	0.5	0.5	1.0	1.0	1.0	1.0	1.0	1.0	1.0
Sub	0.0	0.0	0.0	0.0	0.0	1.0	1.0	1.0	1.0	1.0
Superintendent/FTE										
Prime	0.0	1.0	1.0	1.0	1.0	1.0	2.0	2.0	3.0	3.0
Sub	0.0	0.0	0.0	0.0	0.0	1.0	1.0	1.0	2.0	2.0
Clerks/FTE										
Prime	0.0	1.0	1.0	1.0	1.0	1.0	2.0	2.0	3.0	3.0
Sub	0.0	0.0	0.0	0.0	0.0	1.0	1.0	1.0	2.0	2.0
Vehicles/PDE										
Prime	0.5	1.0	1.0	2.0	2.0	2.0	3.0	3.0	4.0	4.0
Sub	0.0	0.0	0.0	0.0	0.0	2.0	2.0	3.0	3.0	3.0
Photographs/Sets										
Prime	2	3	4	9	14	24	27	30	36	40
Sub	0	0	0	0	0	0	0	0	0	0
Videos/PDE										
Prime	0.0	0.5	1.0	1.0	2.0	3.0	4.0	6.0	8.0	10.0
Sub	0.0	0.0	0.0	0.0	0.0	0.0	0.0	0.0	0.0	0.0
Survey Crew/Days										
Prime	1	2	3	5	6	8	10	15	18	20
Sub	0	0	0	0	0	0	0	0	0	0
Security Personnel/Hr./Wk.										
Prime	0	0	0	0	0	0	0	0	0	0
Sub	0	0	0	0	0	0	0	0	0	0

FTE = Full Time Equivalent
PDE = Project Duration Equivalent

Figure 62.2 Field Expenses

cost is determined by multiplying the number of vehicles by the duration of the project in weeks and the number of work days in a work week. Figure 62.2 provides estimating values for remedial action contracts and turnkey studies through remedial action contracts. See Figure 62.3 for values for studies contracts.

Photographs

This parameter is the cost of supplying construction progress photographs. Figure 62.2 provides estimating values for remedial action contracts and turnkey studies through remedial action contracts. See Figure 62.3 for values for studies contracts.

Field Expenses Studies Contracts (Value Based on Direct Cost Range)										
Direct Cost (Millions Of Dollars)										
Expense/Unit of Measure	<0.1	.1-.5	.5-1	1-5	5-10	10-15	15-30	30-50	50-75	>75
Site Proj. Mgr/FTE										
Prime	0.0	0.0	0.0	0.0	0.0	0.0	0.0	0.0	0.0	0.0
Sub	0.0	0.0	0.0	0.0	0.5	1.0	1.25	1.5	2.0	2.0
Superintendent/FTE										
Prime	0.0	0.0	0.0	0.0	0.5	0.5	1.0	1.0	1.0	1.0
Sub	0.0	1.0	1.0	1.0	1.0	1.25	1.5	2.0	2.5	3.0
Clerks/FTE										
Prime	0.0	0.0	0.0	0.0	0.0	0.0	0.0	0.0	0.0	0.0
Sub	0.0	0.0	0.0	0.0	0.5	1.0	1.0	1.25	1.5	2.0
Vehicles/PDE										
Prime	0.0	0.0	0.0	0.0	0.5	1.0	1.0	2.0	2.0	2.0
Sub	0.0	1.0	1.0	1.0	1.0	1.5	2.0	2.0	2.5	3.0
Photographs/Sets										
Prime	2	3	4	9	14	24	27	30	36	40
Sub	0	0	0	0	0	0	0	0	0	0
Videos/PDE										
Prime	0.5	0.5	1.0	1.0	2.0	3.0	4.0	6.0	8.0	10.0
Sub	0.0	0.0	0.0	0.0	0.0	0.0	0.0	0.0	0.0	0.0
Survey Crew/Days										
Prime	1	2	3	5	6	8	10	15	18	20
Sub	0	0	0	0	0	0	0	0	0	0
Security Personnel/Hr./Wk.										
Prime	0	0	0	0	0	0	0	0	0	0
Sub	0	0	0	0	0	0	0	0	0	0

FTE = Full Time Equivalent
PDE = Project Duration Equivalent

Figure 62.3 Field Expenses

Video

This parameter is the cost of supplying construction progress videos. Figure 62.2 provides estimating values for remedial action contracts and turnkey studies through remedial action contracts. See Figure 62.3 for values for studies contracts.

Survey Crew

Survey crews are required by the contractor to lay out the construction site, perform site surveys, establish grades, or tie in to surrounding survey marks. The typical survey crew is comprised of 3 persons. The quantity is the number of days a crew is required for the project. Figure 62.2 provides estimating values for remedial action contracts and turnkey studies through remedial action contracts. See Figure 62.3 for values for studies contracts.

Security Personnel

Occasionally, security personnel are required at a site. There is no standard for security personnel; it is a site-specific cost.

Temporary Facilities

This parameter group includes facilities that are temporarily located on the job site. These facilities are removed at the end of the construction period. Assumed estimating values are based on the project direct cost. Both the prime contractor and subcontractors may require temporary facilities, depending on their roles and responsibilities on the project. The temporary facilities parameters are described in the following paragraphs.

Note: Temporary field labs and set-up are included in Chapter 57, "Monitoring."

Office Trailers

On-site office trailers are required for the field staff to conduct the business of running a project. Smaller projects and most subcontractors will not require an office trailer. For projects under $5 million in direct cost, the typical office trailer is a 32' × 8' mobile office trailer. If the direct cost is greater than $5 million, the office trailer is assumed to be a 50' × 10' mobile office facility. The total rental cost is the number of trailers per month multiplied by the duration of the project. Figure 62.4 provides estimating values for remedial action contracts and turnkey studies through remedial action contracts. See Figure 62.5 for values for studies contracts.

Storage Facilities

Storage facilities are often required for large projects, long duration projects, or remote sites. The typical storage facility is a 28' × 10' temporary storage trailer. The total rental cost is the number of trailers per month multiplied by the duration of the project. Figure 62.4 provides estimating values for remedial action contracts and turnkey studies through remedial action contracts. See Figure 62.5 for values for studies contracts.

Toilets

Temporary toilets are assumed to be rented to the prime contractor by a service contractor. The number of toilets depends on the project size and whether it is a single- or multiple-site project. See Figure 62.6 for the estimating values for the number of toilets per site.

Temporary Facilities Studies Contracts through RA Contracts (Value Based On Direct Cost Range)										
Direct Cost (Millions Of Dollars)										
Expense/Unit of Measure	<0.1	.1-.5	.5-1	1-5	5-10	10-15	15-30	30-50	50-75	>75
Office Trailers/#/Mo.										
Prime	0.0	1.0	1.0	1.0	1.0	2.0	2.0	2.0	2.0	2.0
Sub	0.0	0.0	0.0	0.0	0.0	0.0	0.0	0.0	0.0	0.0
Storage Facilities/#/Mo.										
Prime	0.0	0.0	0.0	1.0	1.0	1.0	1.0	1.0	1.0	1.0
Sub	0.0	0.0	0.0	1.0	1.0	2.0	2.0	2.0	3.0	3.0
Security Fencing/L.F.										
Prime	0	400	600	800	1,000	1,000	1,000	1,000	1,000	1,000
Sub	0	0	0	0	0	0	0	0	0	0
Construction Signs/S.F.										
Prime	25	25	30	40	60	100	150	200	250	300
Sub	0	0	0	0	0	0	0	0	0	0

Figure 62.4 Temporary Facilities

Temporary Facilities Studies Contracts (Value Based on Direct Cost Range)										
Direct Cost (Millions Of Dollars)										
Expense/Unit of Measure	<0.1	.1-.5	.5-1	1-5	5-10	10-15	15-30	30-50	50-75	>75
Office Trailers/#/Mo.										
Prime	0.0	0.0	0.0	0.0	0.0	1.0	1.0	1.0	1.0	1.0
Sub	0.0	1.0	1.0	1.0	1.0	2.0	2.0	2.0	2.0	2.0
Storage Facilities/#/Mo.										
Prime	0.0	0.0	0.0	0.0	0.0	0.0	1.0	1.0	1.0	1.0
Sub	0.0	0.0	0.0	1.0	1.0	2.0	2.0	2.0	3.0	3.0
Security Fencing/L.F.										
Prime	0	0	0	0	0	1,000	1,000	1,000	1,000	1,000
Sub	0	400	600	800	1,000	0	0	0	0	0
Construction Signs/S.F.										
Prime	0	25	30	40	60	100	150	200	250	300
Sub	0	0	0	0	0	0	0	0	0	0

Figure 62.5 Temporary Facilities

Temporary Toilets (Value Based On Direct Cost Range)										
Direct Cost (Millions Of Dollars)										
Expense/Unit of Measure	<0.1	.1-.5	.5-1	1-5	5-10	10-15	15-30	30-50	50-75	>75
Toilets Per Site/#/Mo.										
Prime	0	1	1	2	3	4	5	9	10	13
Sub	0	0	0	0	0	0	0	0	0	0

Figure 62.6 Temporary Toilets

Security Fencing

Security fencing is any fencing required to enclose the construction site and temporary facilities for the duration of the construction project. This does not include fencing specific to a long-term technology installed to remediate a site. The typical fence is a 6' high chain link fence. Figure 62.4 provides estimating values for remedial action contracts and turnkey studies through remedial action contracts. See Figure 62.5 for values for studies contracts.

Construction Signs

Construction signs are required by the contract specifications and supplied by the contractor. The signs describe the project, owner, contractor, and other pertinent public information. Figure 62.4 provides estimating values for remedial action contracts and turnkey studies through remedial action contracts. See Figure 62.5 for values for studies contracts.

Personal Protective Equipment

Personal protective equipment (PPE) includes all costs of outfitting personnel with clothing, breathing apparatuses, and personal monitoring devices required for protection during the project. The number and type of PPEs depend on the project size, duration, safety level, and percent of work performed by the prime contractor and subcontractors. This parameter group is used to determine a reasonable number of both disposable and non-disposable PPEs for the project. Different types of PPEs are required for each safety level. These assumptions are listed in Figure 62.7. The parameters for each contamination level are discussed in the following paragraphs.

Number of Work Days On-site

The number of work days on-site are the total working days personnel will be on the project site. This should be determined for each safety level: A, B, C, D, and E. Typically, if project-specific information is unavailable, the cost estimator may assume five working days per week of project duration. If the specific safety level for each work activity is unknown, the assumed safety level can be based on the predominant portion of the entire project work.

Number of Shifts Per Day

The number of shifts per day is the number of personnel shifts required per day for the project. For estimating purposes, a shift can be assumed to be eight hours.

Number of Persons Per Shift

The number of persons per shift is the total number of persons in the contaminated zone per shift per safety level. This parameter is available for four safety levels: A, B, C, and D. The number of persons per shift is equal to the number of personnel required for the project. The number of personnel required for the project may be approximated as follows:

$$\text{NPCP} = \frac{\text{(Total Direct Labor Cost—Prime)}}{\text{(Average Hourly Labor Cost)}} \div (\text{Duration [days]} \times 8 \text{ hr/day})$$

$$\text{NSCP} = \frac{\text{(Total Direct Labor Cost—Subcontractor)}}{\text{(Average Hourly Labor Cost)}} \div (\text{Duration[days]} \times 8 \text{ hr/day})$$

Where:

NPCP = Number of Prime Contractor Personnel

NSCP = Number of Subcontractor Personnel

For studies contracts, the equation should use only labor associated with field tasks. For remedial action contracts, use all remedial action labor. For turnkey studies through remedial action contracts, use the sum of the direct labor cost for field tasks from studies plus the direct labor cost for remedial action.

**Personnel Protection Equipment
Requirements By Safety Level**

Level A SCBA (1 per project)
    Basic Level "A" Suite (1 per project)
    Aluminized Outer Cover Suit (1 per project)
    Hard Hat (1 per project)
    Two-Way Radio (1 per project)
    Reusable Overboots (1 pair per project)
    Butyl Gloves (1 pair per project)
    Disposable Boot Covers (1 pair per decontamination)
    Disposable Gloves (1 pair per decontamination)
    Disposable Briefs (1 per decontamination)

Level B SCBA (1 per project)
    Basic Level "B" Suit (1 per project)
    Hard Hat (1 per project)
    Neoprene Boots (1 pair per project)
    Butyl Gloves (1 pair per project)
    Two-Way Radio (1 per project)
    Disposable Boot Covers (1 pair per decontamination)
    Disposable Gloves (1 pair per decontamination)
    Disposable Coveralls (1 per decontamination)

Level C Full Face Respirator (1 per project)
    Respirator Cartridges (2 per day)
    Hard Hat (1 per project)
    Two-Way Radio (1 per project)
    PVC/Nitrile Gloves (1 pair per project)
    Disposable Boot Covers (1 pair per decontamination)
    Disposable Gloves (1 pair per decontamination)
    Disposable Coveralls (1 per decontamination)

Level D Hard Hat (1 per project)
    PVC/Nitrile Gloves (1 pair per project)
    Escape Breathing Apparatus, 5 Minute (1 per project)
    Safety Glasses (1 pair per project)
    Disposable Coveralls (1 per decontamination)

Level E None

Figure 62.7 Personnel Protection Equipment

Number of Decontaminations Per Shift

The number of decontaminations per shift is the number of times per shift that crew personnel will stop to decontaminate their PPE. If the site health and safety plan is not available, estimating assumptions can be based on the following:

- Levels A and B: 4 times per shift
- Level C: 2 times per shift
- Level D: 1 time per shift

If specific requirements are unknown, assume that each person is outfitted as shown in Figure 62.7.

Mobilization

Mobilization costs include mobilizing and demobilizing contractor personnel and equipment to project site locations during initial project start-up and project close-out. This mobilization does not include specialized mobilization costs such as on-site incinerators, well rigs, or other special equipment. The equipment included in this parameter set are general use items for multiple tasks, such as tractors, earth-moving equipment, and other small pieces of equipment. The assumed costs of mobilization are based on the project direct cost. The values will be a percent of the direct cost and can be applied to the prime contractor and subcontractors. The mobilization parameters are as follows.

Personnel Mobilization

The cost of mobilizing a contractor's personnel to the project site includes moving in personnel, setting up the site, holding preconstruction meetings, and conducting orientation and training of personnel. See Figure 62.8 for remedial action contracts and estimating values for turnkey studies through remedial action contracts. See Figure 62.9 for studies contracts.

Mobilization Studies Through RA Contracts & RA Contracts (Value Based On Direct Cost Range)										
Direct Cost (Millions Of Dollars)										
Expense/Unit of Measure	<0.1	.1-.5	.5-1	1-5	5-10	10-15	15-30	30-50	50-75	>75
Personnel Mobilization/%										
Prime	1.00	0.50	0.50	0.25	0.20	0.10	0.10	0.07	0.05	0.05
Sub	0.00	0.00	0.00	0.00	0.00	0.00	0.00	0.00	0.00	0.00
Equip. Mobilization/%										
Prime	3.00	1.50	1.00	0.75	0.40	0.30	0.30	0.25	0.20	0.15
Sub	0.00	0.00	0.00	0.00	0.05	0.04	0.03	0.20	0.15	0.10
Demobilization/%										
Prime	3.00	1.50	1.00	0.75	0.40	0.30	0.30	0.25	0.20	0.15
Sub	0.00	0.00	0.00	0.00	0.05	0.04	0.03	0.20	0.15	0.10

Figure 62.8 Mobilization

Equipment Mobilization

The cost of mobilizing a contractor's equipment to the project site includes moving and setting up equipment used by a contractor for the duration of the project, such as cranes and earth-moving equipment. See Figure 62.8 for remedial action contracts and estimating values for turnkey studies through remedial action contracts. See Figure 62.9 for studies contracts.

Demobilization

Demobilization is the cost of breaking down and removing all temporary facilities and removing equipment from the project site. See Figure 62.8 for remedial action contracts and estimating values for turnkey studies through remedial action contracts. See Figure 62.9 for studies contracts.

Travel Expenses

Travel expenses are the costs of mileage and other travel costs to move personnel to and from the site. For estimating purposes, assume that 40% of the total on-site prime contractor personnel will require travel reimbursement. For subcontractors, assume 20% of the total subcontractor on-site personnel. Typically, only field-related task personnel for studies will receive travel expenses. If the travel distance is unknown, assume that personnel will travel 250 miles, each way, once during the project. Travel expenses for remedial action professional labor are not typically included as part of this parameter, but would be included with the RA professional labor support (see Chapter 58, "Remedial Action Professional Labor Management").

Mobilization **Studies Contracts (Value Based On Direct Cost Range)**										
Direct Cost (Millions Of Dollars)										
Expense/Unit of Measure	**<0.1**	**.1-.5**	**.5-1**	**1-5**	**5-10**	**10-15**	**15-30**	**30-50**	**50-75**	**>75**
Personnel Mobilization/%										
Prime	0.00	0.00	0.00	0.00	0.10	0.05	0.04	0.03	0.02	0.02
Sub	1.00	1.00	0.75	0.75	0.50	0.40	0.25	0.20	0.09	0.07
Equip. Mobilization/%										
Prime	0.00	0.00	0.00	0.00	0.10	0.10	0.07	0.05	0.05	0.05
Sub	1.00	1.00	0.75	0.75	0.50	0.50	0.30	0.20	0.10	0.10
Demobilization/%										
Prime	0.00	0.00	0.00	0.00	0.60	0.50	0.30	0.35	0.10	0.10
Sub	1.50	1.50	1.00	1.00	0.75	0.75	0.40	0.30	0.15	0.15

Figure 62.9 Mobilization

Per Diem

This parameter determines the cost of employee per diem expenses to the contractor for personnel who are working away from their home location. For estimating purposes, if the number is not known, assume that 40% of the prime contractor's on-site personnel will receive per diem. For subcontractors, assume 20% of total subcontractor on-site personnel.

Plants and Equipment

This parameter group establishes costs of temporary plants (such as batch plants), off-site camps, and their operational costs. Typically, these items are not required for U.S.-based projects unless the project site is very remote. However, in the event that these types of facilities are required, the plants and equipment parameters are discussed in the following paragraphs.

Off-Site Construction Camp

Off-site construction camps may be required to house construction personnel at remote project locations.

Off-Site Construction Camp Operational Expenses

This parameter refers to the operational expenses of an off-site construction camp, if required.

Construction Plant

Construction plants are temporary concrete or asphalt batch plants, aggregate crushers, and screeners. If one or more temporary plants are required for the construction of the project, costs would include rental/purchase of plant equipment, mobilization, and set-up costs.

Construction Plant Operational Expenses

This parameter refers to operational expenses of a construction plant or plants, if required.

Permits and Fees

Remediation projects often require the contractor to obtain building permits for construction of the remediation technology. These permits are in addition to environmental permits or hazardous waste and materials permits typically received during the studies and design phases of the restoration project. Normal environmental hazardous permits are included as part of site studies. A contractor may incur the cost of disposal fees or temporary discharge fees during the construction process. The cost of these fees can be applied to both prime contractors and subcontractors. The permits and fees parameters are as follows.

Building Permits

This parameter refers to the lump sum dollar amount of any building permits required for general construction of the remediation project.

Fees

Fees refer to the lump sum dollar amount of any discharge or disposal fees required for the construction of a remediation project that is not included elsewhere in the estimate.

State Permits

This parameter represents the lump sum dollar amount of any state permits required for the construction of a remediation project.

Federal Permits

This parameter represents the lump sum dollar amount of any federal permits required for the construction of a remediation project.

Taxes

Sales taxes are levied by local and state governments on materials purchased to construct a project. Sales taxes will be applied to material and equipment only. The taxes parameters are as follows.

State Sales Tax

State tax is the sales tax levied by the state in which the project is located. The tax percentage will be applied only to the total material and equipment cost.

Local Tax

Local taxes are any additional sales taxes levied by local government where the project is located.

Insurance and Performance Bonds

Insurance for restoration projects can be a significant cost to contractors. Errors and omissions insurance and liability insurance carried by professional services contractors are included in the office overhead cost previously discussed in this chapter. The insurance costs are typically based on the total project cost.

To protect the owner's interest, contractors are also frequently required to provide payment and performance bonds when executing remediation work. This is a surety bond, issued in behalf of the owner, that guarantees the contract work will be completed if the bonded contractor fails to meet all the required contract obligations. The cost of bonds will be a percentage of the total direct construction costs including general conditions.

Typical types of insurance and bonds used on remediation projects are as follows.

Builder's Risk Insurance

Insurance policies that cover physical damage to the construction project during construction are available in different scales of risk. The lower end of the scale is a builder's risk policy, which is generally a standard fire policy with some extended types of coverage, such as wind storms, explosion, or smoke. These policies can range from minimum risk coverage to all-inclusive policies that include theft, vandalism, and acts of God. The typical cost range for builder's risk insurance is 0.1–1% of the total direct construction costs including general conditions.

Contractor's Pollution Liability (CPL) Insurance

Insurance policies that cover any damage resulting from errant emissions or spills of toxic or hazardous materials during the remediation process are referred to as CPL policies. These policies are generally underwritten on a project by project basis, and coverage is limited to a specific remediation project. The typical cost range for this insurance is 1–5% of the total construction direct cost including general conditions.

General Liability Insurance

Liability insurance protects the contractor against liability resulting from the contractor's operations and against property damage liability to the general public. A public liability policy can be issued to cover a wide variety of circumstances; premium costs vary according to coverage. Costs for general liability insurance typically range from 1.5–5% of the total direct construction costs including general conditions.

Performance and Payment Bonds

Contractors may be required to provide performance and payment bonds for remedial restoration construction projects. A bond may be required by the owner. The typical cost of a performance and payment bond for a restoration project is 2.5–3% of the total direct construction cost including general conditions.

Conclusion

General conditions items are a significant part of the cost of a remedial action project. It is not uncommon for general conditions costs to exceed 15% of the project direct cost, or even 25% or more for projects with extensive health and safety requirements. General conditions costs are driven by the nature of the project, the project duration, the size of the field labor force, and the safety level of the work. Since these costs are based on an understanding of the total project, it is often difficult to prepare a valid estimate during the initial project planning stages. However, since these costs can be such a large part of the project, it is critical that the estimator work with experienced field management personnel to scope the project and look for ways that the project can be structured to minimize unnecessary general conditions items. Through proper planning and on-site management, the estimator and project manager can ensure that the project is set up efficiently.

Chapter 63

Contractor Overhead and Profit

To estimate the total contract cost for a project, contractor overhead and profit must be added to the direct cost. *Direct costs* are all costs that can be directly attributed to a particular item of work or activity, including material, labor, and equipment used to perform the actual contract task. The prime contractor's direct cost includes the subcontractor's total price for material, labor, and equipment, including subcontractor overhead and profit. Contractors' general conditions are also included in the direct cost base for purposes of computing overhead and profit. The final component in determining a complete estimate is the process of estimating indirect costs. *Indirect costs* are all costs other than direct costs that do not become a permanent part of the facilities nor contribute to the studies or design. For the purposes of definition, indirect costs include home office overhead and profit. All markups for operations and maintenance contracts are also included in this chapter.

Overhead and profit estimates are calculated after all other portions of the estimate are complete. Previously established project-specific information is used as a basis for estimating contractor overhead and profit. This information includes project direct cost, general conditions, project location, project duration, start of construction, prime/subcontractor distribution, and restoration phase.

A reasonable cost estimate can be created using only the required parameters listed above. However, if more detailed information is known, the estimator can create a more precise and site-specific estimate. Information that can be used to create a more precise estimate of overhead and profit includes the following topic areas:

- Professional services overhead
- Home office expenses
- Profit

Below are descriptions of these items and their impact on the estimate.

Professional Services Overhead

Professional services overhead is the overhead and general and administrative (G&A) expenses incurred by the professional services contractor performing the studies and RA professional services portion of an environmental restoration contract. Components of professional services overhead and home office expense are as follows.

Professional Labor Office Overhead

The costs of running a professional services office include insurance, office rent, office utilities, office supplies, depreciation, maintenance, job management, administrative labor, labor burdens, and other miscellaneous costs. Labor burdens include social security taxes, federal unemployment taxes, state unemployment taxes, Worker's Compensation, and fringe benefits. Professional labor office overhead rates typically range from 125–175% of direct professional labor salary, but may be as high as 250% or as low as 75%, depending on the size and duration of the project.

Professional Labor G&A

Professional labor G&A expenses include accounting costs, executive salaries, legal expenses, and job procurement and promotion. Typically, G&A rates range from 10–40% of the direct wage rate plus the professional labor office overhead.

Home Office Expense

Home office expense is the expense of field project support by the contractor's home office. These expenses include project managers, accounting, payroll, and clerical support, and are a percentage of the total direct cost for the project. The home office expense for a large project is a smaller percentage than the home office expense for a small project. The rate depends on the project size.

See Figure 63.1 for estimating values for remedial action contracts and studies through remedial action contracts. See Figure 63.2 for studies contracts.

Profit

The profit percentages are separated into three groups: prime contractor's profit on self-performed work, subcontractor's profit, and prime contractor's profit on subcontractor work. A profit percentage can be calculated for each group using a series of weighted factors based on factors such as degree of risk, difficulty of work, period of performance, and specialization of work.

Home Office Expenses Values Studies Through RA Contracts & RA Contracts (Value Per Direct Cost Range)									
Direct Cost (Millions Of Dollars									
Expense/Unit of Measure	<0.1	.1-.5	.5-1	1-5	5-10	10-15	15-30	30-50	50-75	>75
Home Office Expense/% Prime Sub	6.0 4.5	5.0 4.0	5.0 4.0	5.0 3.5	4.5 3.0	4.0 2.75	3.0 2.5	2.5 2.5	2.5 2.5	2.5 2.5

Figure 63.1 Home Office Expenses

Subcontractor Profit on Own Work

This parameter specifies the percentage of profit a subcontractor will charge on work completed by his or her own work force. A system of weighted factors can be used to determine a recommended percentage of profit. The subcontractor profit percentage is applied to the sum of direct and overhead costs for the subcontractor's portion of the work. Each factor determines a calculated weight. The calculated weight for the degree of risk through size of job factors is totaled to equal a profit percentage total. Figure 63.3 shows the profit factors, the relative weight of each factor, and the calculation method for subcontractor profit. The subcontractor profit factors are as follows.

Degree of Risk

If there are unknowns about the extent of the work and how the work will be executed, then the degree of risk will be high. If the project is well defined and there are minimal unknowns, then the degree of risk is low. The higher the degree of risk, the more profit the subcontractor will calculate based on unforeseen circumstances. The factor is determined by a sliding scale from 1–10, where 1 is a low degree of risk and 10 is a high degree of risk. The higher the scale value, the higher the calculated weight value. The degree of risk carries a weight of 20% of the total weight factors.

Home Office Expenses Values Studies Contracts (Value Per Direct Cost Range)										
Direct Cost (Millions Of Dollars)										
Expense/Unit of Measure	<0.1	.1-.5	.5-1	1-5	5-10	10-15	15-30	30-50	50-75	>75
Home Office Expense/% Prime Sub	 0.0 6.0	 0.0 5.0	 0.0 4.0	 0.0 3.5	 0.0 3.0	 0.0 2.75	 0.0 2.5	 0.0 2.5	 0.0 2.5	 0.0 2.5

Figure 63.2 Home Office Expenses

Subcontractor Profit Weight Factors			
Factor	Weight (%)	Rating (1-10 Scale)	Value
Degree of Risk	20	5	1.40
Relative Difficulty of Work	5	5	0.35
Location	5	5	0.35
Local Economic Conditions	30	5	2.10
Equipment Requirements	10	5	0.70
Size of Job	30	5	*(0.45-3.30)
Total Weight	100		

*Value varies based on project size.

Figure 63.3 Subcontractor Profit Weight Factors

Relative Difficulty of Work

As the difficulty of the work increases, the scale value should increase. The less difficult or complex the project, the lower the scale value should be. The scale ranges from 1–10, where 1 is the least difficult work and 10 is the most difficult work. The higher the scale value, the higher the calculated weight value. The relative difficulty of work carries a weight of 5% of the total weight factors.

Location

This factor specifies the location relative to the base operating area for the subcontractor. The scale ranges from 1–10. If the subcontractor is located within close proximity to the project, the scale value should be 1. The farther the project is located from subcontractors, the higher the value should be, or as the requirements for mobilization increase, the scale value should increase to a maximum of 10. The higher the scale value, the higher the calculated weight value. The location factor carries a weight of 5% of the total weight factors.

Local Economic Conditions

If economic conditions are poor, the scale value should be 1. As economic conditions improve, the scale value should increase, to a maximum of 10. The higher the scale value, the higher the calculated weight value. The local economic conditions factor carries a weight of 30% of the total weight factors.

Equipment Requirements

This factor specifies the requirement for subcontractor-owned equipment. When the work involves little or no subcontractor-owned equipment, the scale value should be 1. As the requirement for subcontractor-owned equipment increases, the scale value should increase, to a maximum scale value of 10. The higher the scale value, the higher the calculated weight value. The equipment requirements factor carries a weight of 10% of the total weight factors.

Size of Job

The calculated weight for size of job is based on the subcontractor's total project direct costs. Typically, as the scope of a project increases, a contractor will decrease his or her profit. The greater the project costs, the lower the calculated weight percentage. This value will range from 1.80 for projects with subcontractor's direct costs less than or equal to $500,000, to 0.45 for projects with subcontractor's direct costs in excess of $10,000,000. The size of job factor carries a weight of 15% of the total weight factors.

Profit Percentage Total

The total of the preceding calculated weight values is the total subcontractor's profit. This value is used to calculate the profit for the subcontractors.

Prime Profit on Own Work

This parameter is the percentage of profit a prime contractor will calculate on work completed by his or her own workforce. Weighted factors can be used to determine a recommended percentage of profit. The prime profit percentage is applied to the sum of direct and overhead costs for the prime contractor. Each factor will determine a calculated weight. The calculated weight for the degree of risk through size of job factors is totaled to equal a profit percentage subtotal. The profit percentage subtotal is then multiplied by the number of bidders factor to determine the profit percentage total. Figure 63.4 provides a breakdown of these factors and weights. The prime profit factors are as follows.

Degree of Risk

If there are unknowns about the extent of the work and how the work will be executed, then the degree of risk will be high. If the project is well defined and there are no unknowns, then the degree of risk is low. The higher the degree of risk, the more profit the contractor will calculate based on unforeseen circumstances. The factor is determined by a sliding scale from 1–10, where 1 is a low degree of risk and 10 is a high degree of risk. The higher the scale value, the higher the calculated weight value. The degree of risk factor carries a weight of 20% of the total weight factors.

Relative Difficulty of Work

As the difficulty of work increases, the scale value should increase. The less difficult or complex the project, the lower the scale value should be. The scale ranges from 1–10, where 1 is the least difficult work and 10 is the most difficult work. The higher the scale value, the higher the calculated weight value. The relative difficulty of work factor carries a weight of 15% of the total weight factors.

Contractor's Investment

If a project requires that a contractor will have to finance or invest his or her own resources during the project, then it is considered a contractor's investment. The scale ranges from 1–10, where a scale value of 1 signifies a small or below average investment. As the amount of investment increases, the scale value should increase to signify a large or above average investment. The higher the scale value, the higher the calculated weight value. The contractor's investment factor carries a weight of 5% of the total weight factors.

Prime Profit Weight Factors			
Factor	**Weight (%)**	**Rating (1-10 Scale)**	**Value**
Degree of Risk	20	5	1.00
Relative Difficulty of Work	15	5	0.75
Contractor's Investment	5	5	0.35
Assistance by Government	5	5	0.35
Percent Subcontracted	25	5	*(0.75-3.00)
Size of Job	30	5	*(0.45-1.80)
Total Weight	100		

*Computed Value

Figure 63.4 Prime Profit Weight Factors

691

Assistance by Owner

Use of owner facilities, equipment, etc., generates a reduction to the contractor's mark-up. The scale ranges from 1–10. A scale value of 1 should be used to reflect an above-average amount of government assistance. As the amount of assistance decreases, the scale value should be increased, to a maximum of 10 for little or no assistance. The higher the scale value, the higher the calculated weight value. The assistance by government factor carries a weight of 5% of the total weight factors.

Percent Subcontracted

When the amount of subcontracting is less than 80% of the total direct costs, the weight factor is calculated inversely proportional to the amount of subcontracting. In other words, the smaller the percentage of subcontracting, the higher the calculated weight value. Where 80% or more of the work is subcontracted, the calculated weight is set at 0.75. The percent subcontracted factor carries a weight of 25% of the total weight factors.

Size of Job

The weight value for size of job is based on the total project direct costs. Typically, as the scope of a project increases, a contractor will decrease his profit. The greater the project costs, the lower the calculated weight percentage. This value will range from 3.60 for projects with direct costs less than or equal to $500,000, to 0.90 for projects with direct costs in excess of $10,000,000. The size of job factor carries a weight of 30% of the total weight factors.

Profit Percentage Subtotal

The profit percentage subtotal is the total value of the preceding calculated weight values.

Number of Bidders

As the number of bidders on the project increases, the contractor mark-up decreases. The calculated weight for the number of bidders is multiplied by the profit percentage subtotal to determine the profit percentage total.

Profit Percentage Total

The total profit percentage that will be applied to the prime contractor's direct and overhead costs to calculate the total project cost is the prime contractor's profit. The default percent is the calculated weight of the number of bidders times the profit percentage subtotal.

Prime Profit on Subcontractor Work

The prime profit on subcontractor work represents the percentage of profit a prime contractor will make on work completed by subcontractors. A system of weighted factors is used to determine a recommended percentage of profit.

The prime profit on subcontractor's percentage is applied to the total subcontract project cost, including subcontractor's direct cost, overhead, and profit. Each factor will determine a calculated weight. The calculated weight for the degree of risk, based on the amount subcontracted, is totaled to equal a profit percentage total. The prime profit on subcontractor's factors are as follows.

Degree of Risk

If there are unknowns about the extent of the subcontract work and how the subcontract work will be executed, then the degree of risk will be high. If the project is well defined and there are no unknowns, then the degree of risk is low. The higher the degree of risk, the more profit the contractor will add to the subcontracted work. The factor is determined by a sliding scale from 1–10, where 1 is a low degree of risk and 10 is a high degree of risk. The higher the scale value, the higher the calculated weight value. The degree of risk factor carries a weight of 10% of the total weight factors. The default scale value is 5, as shown in Figure 63.5.

Market Conditions

The market conditions factor specifies the availability of subcontractor technical and support personnel required for special or unusual project requirements. The calculated weight is established using a sliding scale from 1–10. When the required resources are available, the scale value should be 1. As the availability decreases, the scale value should increase, up to a maximum of 10. The higher the scale value, the higher the calculated weight value. The market conditions factor carries a weight of 20% of the total weight factors.

Percent Subcontracted

When the amount of subcontracting is less than 80% of the total direct costs, the weight factor is calculated inversely proportional to the amount of subcontracting. In other words, the smaller the percentage of subcontracting, the higher the calculated weight value. When 80% or more of the work is subcontracted, the calculated weight is set at 0.25. The percent subcontracted factor carries a weight of 25% of the total weight factors.

Amount Subcontracted

The calculated weight for the amount subcontracted is based on the total project costs subcontracted. The greater the amount, the lower the calculated weight percentage. This value will range from 4.50 for projects with costs less than or equal to $500,000, to 0.45 for projects with costs in excess of $10,000,000. The amount subcontracted factor carries a weight of 45% of the total weight factors.

Prime Profit On Subcontractor Profit Weight Factors			
Factor	Weight (%)	Rating (1-10 Scale)	Value
Degree of Risk	10	5	0.50
Market Conditions	20	5	1.00
Percent Subcontracted	25	5	*(0.25-2.53)
Amount Subcontracted	45	5	*(0.45-4.50)
Total Weight	100		

*Calculated Value

Figure 63.5 Prime Profit on Subcontractor

Profit Percentage Total

The profit percentage total is the total of the preceding calculated weight values. This is the total prime contractor's profit on subcontractor's work, which is used to calculate the prime contractor's profit on the subcontractor's work.

Total Composite Prime Profit (Fee)

The composite profit is the percent fee the contractor will make on the total project. The total composite prime profit (fee) is the weighted average of the prime contractor's profit on his or her own work and the prime contractor's profit on subcontractor's work. The value is the prime contractor's profit percentage times the percent work done by the prime plus the prime profit percentage on subcontractor's work times the percent of work done by subcontractors.

Conclusion

Overhead and profit expenses are a function of the size of the project, the risk taken by the contractor, and the complexity of the job. Often, it is possible to structure contracts in such a way as to reduce overhead and profit expenses by reducing risk and optimizing project size. The cost engineer should work with the design team to package projects in a way that optimizes these elements to reduce overall cost.

Chapter 64

Determining Contractor Markups: Percentage Method

Chapters 62 and 63 of this book provide information to assist in preparing detailed cost estimates for Contractor General Conditions, Overhead, and Profit. This chapter offers an alternate approach using percentages to determine markup levels. This percentage method is most appropriate for planning-stage cost estimates when the specific contractors who will perform the work are not yet known, and when the project plan and detailed design are still being developed.

Markups must be added to the direct project cost in order to estimate the total contract cost. Direct project costs are all costs that can be directly attributed to a particular item of work or activity. The direct costs include material, labor, and equipment used to perform the actual contract task. The prime contractor's direct cost includes the total subcontractor's price for material, labor, and equipment, including subcontractor overhead and profit. Once all direct project costs are estimated, the final component in determining a complete estimate is the process of estimating markups, or indirect costs. Markups are all costs other than direct costs that do not become a permanent part of the facilities, nor contribute to the studies or design.

Markup templates can be used as a quick and effective method to estimate contractor markups. The templates contain factors that are used to calculate general conditions, overhead, risk, owner cost, and prime and subcontractor profit as a percentage of direct costs. Markup templates contain the percentages that can be applied to each project phase.

The markup values contained in this section were developed using remediation and general construction industry data. This data was obtained through review of approximately 40 remediation contracts and through interviews with 30 engineering and construction firms. A group consisting of representatives from the industry, Air Force, and Army Corps of Engineers reviewed the data and provided feedback.

Project Markups

Total Project Cost is the sum of *Total Contract Cost, Risk,* and *Owner Costs.* Markups are added to the direct costs calculated for the various remediation technologies to determine total project costs. The three major elements of Project Cost are listed below:

1. **Total Contract Cost** is the sum of direct costs, general conditions, overhead, and contractor profit.
2. **Risk,** sometimes called *contingency* or *management reserve,* is an allowance to account for the potential cost growth that may occur due to unknown or unforeseen conditions and uncertainty.
3. **Owner Cost** is an allowance to account for administrative and management costs incurred by the project owner for program management and oversight activities.

Markup Factors

These factors contribute to markup calculations. A markup template provides percentage values for each of the following areas. These percentages are guidelines only. The estimator should consider the unique conditions surrounding the project and adjust these factors up or down based on project-specific information.

Direct Costs

Direct costs include all of the costs that can be directly attributed to a particular item of work or activity required to accomplish the project. These items include the direct labor cost (which includes direct wage paid to employees who accomplish the work), the cost for purchasing materials used in the performance of the project, and the cost of construction equipment used in the performance of the work. The prime contractor's direct cost also includes the total subcontractor's price including overhead and profit.

General Conditions

General conditions costs are the field-related tasks that are required to execute a contract, but that are not specific to a technology or restoration task. For multiple-site projects, general conditions items are typically estimated for the overall project rather than for individual sites. Common general conditions cost components include:

- Supervision—Labor
- Temporary Facilities including:
  - Job trailers
  - Storage trailers
  - Portable toilets
- Temporary plants
- Personal protective equipment (PPE)
- Travel
- Permits, sales and labor taxes, insurance, bonds

Note: Decontamination facilities are not included in the general conditions percentages shown in this chapter. While these facilities might be considered a general conditions item for environmental remediation projects, it is generally preferable to estimate them as a direct cost, since the size and scope of decontamination facilities vary significantly based on the nature of contaminants and the remediation approach.

General conditions costs can be estimated on a percentage of the direct project cost basis. General conditions cost percentages tend to be higher for small projects, and smaller for large projects. However, every project is different, and the estimator should carefully consider the details in order to estimate these costs. Figure 64.1 provides guidelines for estimating general conditions cost.

Overhead

Overhead costs are the non-project specific costs required to support labor and general operations of the contractors' business. They include items such as:

- Fringe benefits for professional and craft labor, including paid vacation, medical insurance, holidays, retirement accounts, etc.
- Indirect labor time used for management, marketing, accounting, etc.
- Home office expenses, including rent, maintenance, utilities, supplies, depreciation, etc., as required to operate the contractor's offices.
- General and administrative (G&A) expenses, including corporate management, accounting, purchasing, legal, insurance, corporate level taxes, etc.

Typically these expenses are allocated to all contracts being performed by contractors as either a percentage of direct project costs, a percentage of direct labor expense on professional labor, or some other similar allocation method. Figure 64.2 shows overhead percentages that are calculated and allocated as a percentage of project Direct Costs for each of the four primary direct cost categories: Professional Labor, Craft Labor, Material, and Equipment.

Subcontractor Profit

This is the percentage of profit a subcontractor will charge on work completed by the subcontractor's own work force. The subcontractor

	General Conditions Percentage Markups on Direct Costs			
	Direct Project Cost Element			
Total Direct Cost Range	Professional Labor	Craft Labor	Material	Equipment
< $10,000	25%	25%	17%	40%
$10,000–$25,000	15%	20%	12%	30%
$25,000–$50,000	10%	17.5%	10%	20%
$50,000–$100,000	7.5%	15%	8%	15%
$100,000–$250,000	5%	12%	6.5%	10%
$250,000–$500,000	5%	10%	5%	8%
> $500,000	5%	8%	5%	6%

Figure 64.1 General Conditions as a Percentage of Direct Project Cost

profit percentage is applied to the sum of direct and overhead costs for the subcontractors. Profit can range from 0–20%, depending on market conditions. A rule of thumb is 8.5%.

Prime Markup on Sub

This markup is the percentage of profit a prime contractor will charge on top of work completed by subcontractors. Prime contractors apply profit to subcontractors' costs to cover the administrative, management, and financial costs of overseeing and approving subcontractor's work. The prime profit on subcontractors is applied to the total subcontract project cost, including subcontractor's direct costs, overhead, and profit. This value can range from 0–10% under normal market conditions. A rule of thumb is 3.5%.

Risk (Contingency)

Risk indicates the factor of relative risk of overall project cost growth. There are 2 issues associated with risk:

1. Does the project have cost growth risk?
2. Which party has the risk?

The risk assessment needs to consider both of these questions. First, regarding project cost growth risk: if there are unknowns about the extent of the work and how it will be executed, then the degree of risk will be high. If the project is well-defined, and there are no unknowns, then the degree of risk is low. Second, the question of "risk to whom?" needs to be considered. Risk may be born by the site owner or the potentially responsible person (PRP), or by the contractor, or may be shared by both parties. The way in which risk is distributed is largely driven by the type and scope of the contract. Cost-Plus and Time & Materials contracts generally leave all of the risk of scope/cost growth with the owner. If the project becomes more expensive than anticipated, then the owner pays the additional cost. Fixed price contracts transfer some or all of the risk from the owner to the contractor. If the costs for the project exceed the estimate, but are still within the scope of the original contract, then the risk of cost growth is carried by the contractor. However, if the requirements for the cleanup exceed the scope of the fixed price contract, then the contractor will generally have a valid claim against the owner for cost growth. In this case, the risk is shared between the owner and the contractor.

Figure 64.2 Overhead Percentages for Direct Cost Categories

| | Direct Cost Category | | | |
	Professional Labor	Craft Labor	Material	Equipment
Overhead Percentage Values	160%	30%	8%	8%

From the contractor's perspective, the higher the degree of risk, the more profit the contractor will charge based on unforeseen circumstances. The factor is often applied to performance-based contracts where a contractor must meet certain performance requirements regardless of the conditions encountered. The estimator needs to consider the overall project risk and the risk transfer mechanisms introduced by the contract and include risk/contingency as appropriate.

Prime Profit

This is the percentage of profit a prime contractor will make on work completed by the contractor's own work force. The system default percentage for prime profit is 8.5%.

Owner Costs

Owner cost is the last markup factor to be applied to the estimate. These costs are applied as a percentage and account for items such as the owner's work force costs to oversee the project, as well as other owner corporate costs. This value will vary considerably from one organization to another and may range from 0–20%. A rule of thumb is 5% for private owners, and 10% for public owners.

Markup Calculations

Following are the steps in the markup calculation process.

1. Determine the total Direct Costs in order to develop the General Conditions markup factors.
2. Multiply the General Conditions percentages by the Total Direct Costs to estimate General Conditions Costs.
3. Multiply the Overhead factor by the Total Direct Costs to estimate the Overhead Costs.
4. Add the General Conditions Costs and the Overhead Costs together to arrive at a Prime Contractor and a Subcontractor subtotal.
5. Calculate the Subcontractor Profit factor and then add it to the Subcontractor subtotal to estimate total Subcontractor Costs.
6. Multiply the prime contractor Markup on subcontractor by the Total subcontractor Costs to determine the amount of profit the prime contractor will charge for Subcontractor work.
7. Add this value to the Total Subcontractor Costs to create a Final Subcontractor Costs value.
8. Add the Final Subcontractor Costs to the Prime Contractor subtotal to create the Total Contract subtotal.
9. Calculate the Prime Contractor Profit and then add it to Total Contract subtotal to create a Total Contract Costs total.
10. Calculate the Risk Factor and add it to the Total Contract Cost to create the Subtotal.
11. Calculate the Overhead Factor and add it to the subtotal to create the Grand Total.

Conclusion The combined cost of contractor general conditions, overhead, and profit can be more than 30% of the total cost of a remediation project. The percentage method for computing contractor costs is simpler for the estimator than developing the more detailed estimates described in Chapters 62 and 63 of this book. This method produces reasonable results and is appropriate for use by owners and engineering consultants during the design stage of remediation projects. This approach is not sufficiently detailed for use as a *primary* estimating method for remediation contractors since it does not provide details on general conditions and overhead items required to support a remediation project. However, it can serve as a good check estimate against more detailed estimates of general conditions, overhead, and profit.

Glossary

ACSR Aluminum Conductor Steel Reinforced.

activated carbon adsorption A mass-transfer process of removing volatile organic compounds from a liquid or gaseous waste stream by transferring it to carbon.

activated sludge Bacteria and other microorganisms in a suspended floc that assist in bioremediation processes. (See *suspended growth systems*.)

AER Advanced Electric Reactor. A device that uses a new technology to rapidly heat materials to temperatures between 2000 °C and 3300 °C. It uses intense thermal radiation in the near-infrared region.

aerobic Any process that requires oxygen.

air entrainment A process of adding air bubbles to a liquid phase, generally to enhance volatilization processes.

air rotary drilling method A method of well installation that uses compressed air as a drilling fluid.

air sparging An in situ process in which air is bubbled through a contaminated aquifer to remove volatile contaminants from groundwater.

air stripping A process that removes volatile organic compounds from water.

ALD Anoxic Limestone Drains (passive water treatment).

AML Abandoned Mine Lands.

anaerobic Any process that occurs in the absence of oxygen.

annular space An area between a well casing and the outside diameter of a bore hole.

AOC Administrative Order on Consent.

AOP Advanced Oxidation Process.

aquifer Rocks and soil that allow groundwater to pass through the pores or fractures.

aquifer recharge A process of injecting water into an aquifer to restore its flow or to store water for future use.

aquitard A soil layer or synthetic layer that restricts or eliminates water flow.

ARAR Applicable or Relevant and Appropriate Requirements.

ASP Air Sparge Points.

ASTM American Society for Testing and Materials.

attached growth system An ex situ bioremediation system in which the contaminant must be brought to biofilm by the aqueous stream. The contaminant is degraded as it contacts the biomass.

backfill Soil or debris that is placed into a previously excavated area to fill the hole.

B.C.Y. Bank Cubic Yard.

bgs Below ground surface.

bioassay Tests used to determine the biological activity or potency of a substance.

bioaugmentation Nutrients added to existing organisms to aid in their growth to expedite bioremediation.

biofilm Bacteria aggregates adhering to a support media, such as a screen, used as a contact source in liquid bioremediation.

biofouling Biological compounds that deposit on a filter or other device, ultimately blocking the flow of liquids through the filter.

biological degradation The process of degrading a contaminant through a bioremediation process.

bioreactor (aerobic) A bioremediation process chamber where oxygen is present during the bioremediation process.

bioreactor (anaerobic) A bioremediation process chamber where oxygen is not present during the bioremediation process.

bioremediation The use of naturally occurring biological agents to degrade hazardous waste to a nonhazardous state.

biosolid A semisolid residual product of waste water treatment.

bioventing A process that intentionally stimulates in situ biodegradation; also called soil venting.

blind wellbore A bore hole that terminates in the horizontal plane.

BNA Bureau of National Affairs. A publisher of environmental regulations and related information.

BOD Biochemical Oxygen Demand. The quantity of oxygen used in the aerobic stabilization of waste water.

bore hole The hole created by a drilling rig when drilling a well.

boring log A log kept during the wellboring process that records drilling conditions, geologic data, and other parameters of the wellbore.

breakthrough A process in gas-phase or liquid adsorption whereby the adsorptive capacity of the carbon is exhausted and the contaminant concentration increases in the effluent.

bulk liquid A pumpable material that has a moisture content greater than 70%.

bulk sludge Material with a moisture content between 30% and 70%.

bulk solid Material with a moisture content less than 30%.

CA Cooperative Agreement.

CAG Community Advisory Group.

California brass ring A sampler used to collect soil samples during well installation. Used to collect samples for analysis of VOC content. (See *VOC*.)

cap A layered system of vegetative cover, natural soils, rock, synthetics, pavement, and/or polymeric liners that controls hydrogeologic processes.

cartridge filter A device that removes relatively small quantities of suspended solids from waste water, using one or more replaceable or renewable cartridges that contain the active element.

casing (well) The exterior lining of a well that is generally made of plastic or metal pipe material.

catalytic oxidation A process in which a catalytic mechanism alters the oxidation reaction rate and causes the process to move faster and/or at lower temperatures than with direct thermal oxidation.

cavitation The rapid formation and collapse of vapor pockets in a liquid in regions of very low pressure.

CBC Circulating Bed Incinerator.

CDE Consent Decree.

centrifugation A dewatering process that separates solids and liquids through the centrifugal force developed by rapid rotation of a cylindrical drum or bowl.

CERCLA Comprehensive Environmental Response Compensation and Liability Act. The law provides for a national emergency response program as well as for cleanup of sites that are not regulated under RCRA. Also known as the "Superfund Law," CERCLA was amended in 1986 by the Superfund Amendment Reauthorization Act (SARA).

CERCLIS Comprehensive Environmental Response, Compensation, and Liability Information System.

CIC Community Involvement Coordinator.

CIP Community Involvement Plan.

C.F. Cubic Foot.

CFM Cubic feet per minute.

CFR Code of Federal Regulations.

chain trencher A machine that uses a chain belt to excavate a trench.

chemical oxidation A chemical process that causes the loss of electrons from an element or ion.

chemical precipitation A process used to treat aqueous waste streams that have high concentrations of metals.

circulating bed incineration Incineration using a turbulent bed of inert granular material to improve the transfer of heat to the waste stream.

clarifier A tank or other device used to remove suspended solids from a liquid.

clean closure A land-cover cap used to cover a site where soil remediation has already occurred.

CLP Contract Laboratory Program.

CMI Corrective Measures Implementation.

CMP Corrugated Metal Pipe.

CMS Corrective Measures Study. The process of determining the remedy for hazardous waste remediation at a site regulated under RCRA.

coagulant A chemical added to a liquid to promote agglomeration of colloids.

coagulant aid A chemical added to waste stream to improve coagulation efficiency.

coagulation A process used to remove extremely fine particles and/or colloids from water and waste water.

COD Chemical Oxygen Demand: The oxygen equivalent of the organic matter susceptible to oxidation by a strong chemical oxidant.

colloid A homogeneous gelatinous substance in which a fine solid is dissolved in a liquid.

composting A process of natural degradation of plant materials.

cone of depression The area surrounding an extraction well in which the groundwater volume, flow, and pressure are impacted by the well.

cone of recharge The area surrounding an injection well in which the injected water volume, flow, and pressure are impacted by the well.

consolidated formation Soil strata that may have been subjected to glacial or other consolidating loads in the geologic past.

constituent An element or component of a unit or whole.

containment berm A physical barrier used to keep liquids from running outside of a protected area. It is generally made of soil, geomembranes, twister, or similar materials.

contingency An unknown or unforeseen condition that might increase costs during the execution of a project; used in an estimate to cover costs for these conditions.

contingent closure A land-cover cap used to cover a hazardous waste site prior to remediation of the soil.

continuous wellbore A horizontal well bore hole that extends through the horizontal plane, transitioning into a second, curved section that returns to the surface.

CPL Contractor's Pollution Liability (insurance).

CPT Cone Penetrometer.

CRZ Contamination Reduction Zone.

CWA Clean Water Act.

CWM Chemical Weapons Material.

C.Y. Cubic Yard.

DAF Dissolved Air Flotation. A process in which gas bubbles are produced when gas/air is dissolved in water at elevated pressures, and then released to atmospheric pressure.

decontamination A process of removing or neutralizing contaminants that have accumulated on personnel or equipment.

dewatering A physical unit operation that reduces the moisture content of slurries or sludges.

direct cost Any cost that can be directly attributed to a particular item of work or activity.

directional drill rig A drill rig that can drill wells in directions other than vertical; it can also drill a curved bore hole.

disposal Introduction of any constituent into the environment as the result of discharge, deposit, injection, dumping, spilling, leaking, or placing of any solid or hazardous waste into or on any land or water.

dissolved oil Oil measured from a filtered sample that passes a 0.45 micron filter by extraction with a low polarity solvent, such as methylene chloride.

DNAPL Dense Nonaqueous Phase Liquid. A liquid that is heavier than water and does not dissolve in water.

DNT Dinitrotoluene.

DOD Department of Defense.

DOE Department of Energy.

DOT Department of Transportation.

double handling Excavation process in which soil surrounding buried drums is cleared away by hand and then removed by machine.

downgradient The direction of groundwater flow in an aquifer.

down time Amount of time equipment is unused as a result of maintenance, breakdown, or process modification or interruptions.

DQO Data Quality Objective. The level of precision required for sampling and analysis activities.

DRE Destruction and Removal Efficiencies.

drum grappler Remote handling device that can lift drums in a variety of orientations.

drum shredder A device that shreds drums, separating the drum contents. Shredded drums are delivered in the form of plates, which can be recycled.

drying bed A dewatering method that uses gravity or vacuum-aided percolation through fine sand beds to dewater sludges.

drying lagoon A dewatering method that uses percolation and evaporation to remove water from a thickened waste stream.

DU Depleted Uranium. It is used by the U.S. military for armor-piercing shells, which contaminate the soil with low-level radionuclide uranium.

dual bed system A gas-phase or liquid adsorption treatment system with two carbon adsorbers, a pump, and associated piping, that can be configured in series or in parallel, depending on facility requirements.

DW Double-walled, as in a double wall well casing.

effluent The stream of liquid or gas that flows from a remediation process.

electron acceptor An element or ion that accepts free electrons during a chemical treatment process.

emulsified oil All oil, except free oil, including both dissolved and suspended oils.

ENR Engineering News Record. A technical trade reference.

environmental monitoring A process of measuring physical and/or chemical properties of an environmental medium, such as air, soil, or water.

environmental remediation The process of treatment, containment, or removal of hazardous or toxic wastes to protect human health and the environment.

EO Executive Order.

EOD Explosive Ordnance Disposal.

EPA (or U.S. EPA) The United States Environmental Protection Agency. The leading agency of the U.S. Government responsible for developing and enforcing environmental regulations and policy.

equipment blank A sample prepared from deionized water after cleaning the sampling equipment to determine the baseline for analyses performed on samples taken with a particular piece of equipment.

escalation Price adjustment, from the current date to the date on which work will be performed.

ESD Explanation of Significant Differences.

excavation A method of removing contaminated surface and subsurface materials from hazardous waste sites.

explosive waste Any chemical substance or physical item related to munitions that is designed to cause damage to personnel or material through explosive force, incendiary action, or toxic effects.

ex situ "Not in its original place." The term refers to remedial processes in which the contaminated media is removed prior to treatment, as in groundwater extraction or excavation.

FCOR Final Close Out Report.

feed tank A tank used to temporarily store water before injection.

field blank A sample prepared in the field using deionized water to establish a baseline for follow-on analysis performed on samples taken after the "blank" is prepared.

filter cake The residual solid or sludge left from a dewatering process.

floc Precipitated particles that result from a chemical process that creates larger particles from fine particles or colloids in a solution.

flocculation A process used to remove extremely fine particles and/or colloids from water and waste water.

flow rate The volume of liquid or gas that flows in a given time period, for example, gallons per minute or cubic feet per minute.

FML Flexible membrane liner, used to contain liquids or run-off in soil or on the soil surface.

FPS Feet per Second.

706

FR Federal Register.

free oil Oil that has particles or droplets large enough to float or sink within a few hours in a gravity or coalescing separation vessel.

free product Light nonaqueous phase liquids that are found in a free state, often floating on top of a groundwater aquifer or surface water impoundment.

free product removal Removing free product, typically by pumping the product into a storage container or into a treatment system.

french drain A passive device used to separate POL from surface water discharges.

FRP Fiberglass Reinforced Plastic.

G&A General and Administrative (expense).

GAC Granular Activated Carbon. This is the most commonly used adsorbent in gas-phase and liquid adsorption. It is a material used in several environmental processes to adsorb volatile organic compounds from water or gas.

gas-phase adsorption A natural process in which molecules of a gas are physically attracted to and held at the surface of a solid.

GM Geiger-Mueller. This is a type of detector commonly used to locate radioactive waste.

GPH Gallons per Hour.

GPM Gallons per Minute. A common measure used to define the flow rate of a liquid.

GPS Global Positioning System. It locates specific points or coordinates on the Earth.

granular media filter A device that removes suspended solids from waste water as the liquid is forced through a porous granular medium.

gravity sedimentation A process of settling particles from liquids; the particles settle from the liquid in a holding tank or other temporary storage device.

gravity separator A chamber in which oil rises and remains on the surface of waste water, until it is removed.

groundwater Water that is present in the saturated layer of soil, below the ground surface and typically in an aquifer.

GVW Gross Vehicle Weight.

half-life The period of time that the level of radioactivity for a substance decays by 50.

hand auger A nonmechanical device used to take soil samples.

HASP Health and Safety Plan.

hazardous waste Waste that has been determined to pose risks to human health or to the environment.

hazardous waste site A site at which hazardous waste is present.

Hazen Williams formula A formula based on flow rate that is used to determine pipe size.

HDPE High Density Polyethylene.

HDSI Horizontal Dewatering Systems, Inc.

heat-enhanced vapor extraction In situ process designed to remove volatile and semivolatile organic compounds from vadose zone soils.

Henry's Law Constant A measure of a compound's "strippability."

HMTA Hazardous Materials Transportation Act.

HMX Cyclotetramethylene-tetranitramine.

holding tank A storage tank that holds wash and rinse water from the decontamination pad.

hollow-stem auger drilling A method of well installation that uses an auger bit attached to the leading auger drill rod section (flight) and cuts a hole for the flights to follow.

hopper A funnel-shaped container that is used to temporarily store material, which is placed in the top and later discharged from the bottom.

H.P. Horsepower.

HRS Hazard Ranking System. It is used to score a hazardous or toxic waste site's risk to human health and the environment.

hydrogeologist A person who specializes in understanding groundwater.

hydraulic conductivity The rate at which a fluid flows through a porous substance, such as soil.

IAG Interagency Agreement.

IC Institutional Control.

ICAD A portable, air-monitoring device that is commonly used for UXO projects.

incineration An engineering process that employs thermal decomposition via thermal oxidation at high temperatures.

inclusions Highly concentrated contaminant layers, void volumes, containers, metal scrap, general refuse, demolition debris, rock, or other nonhomogeneous materials or conditions in the waste volume.

indirect cost Any cost other than a direct cost that does not become a permanent part of the facility or contribute to the studies or design.

indirect firing A thermal desorption process used when contaminant concentration is very high or when contaminants are less volatile in nature.

induced gas flotation A process by which a vacuum, created by rotary vanes, draws air into the bulk of the liquid through a gas intake pipe, thus generating and inducing gas bubbles that rise through the column of liquid.

infiltration gallery A system for discharging water that has already been treated in a groundwater treatment system.

inflatable containment berm A berm commonly used for temporary containment of water and other fluids at a hazardous waste site.

infrared furnace A furnace that uses an intense flux of near-infrared radiation to initiate and sustain pyrolysis of feed materials.

injection well A well used to inject water into a groundwater aquifer.

inorganic electrolytes Commonly used coagulants, such as aluminum sulfate (alum), lime, and various iron salts.

in situ "In its original place." Treatment processes that are used to treat hazardous waste in the media in which it exists, without removing the media.

in situ biodegradation A process used to degrade organic wastes through biological processes in the soil or groundwater.

influent A liquid stream that enters a process prior to treatment by that process.

ion exchange The process of either gaining or losing electrons from compounds in a chemical reaction.

IRIS Integrated Risk Information System.

IRP Installation Restoration Program. This is the U.S. Department of Defense (DOD) program that directs, funds, and manages cleanup of DOD hazardous waste sites.

ISV In Situ Vitrification. A process that electrically melts contaminated soil at temperatures well above the soil's initial melting range.

JP-4 Jet engine fuel.

land farming A process for treating contaminated soil that requires excavation and movement to a treatment cell.

landfill A site used to deposit solid waste.

leachate Liquid from rainfall, groundwater, or other sources that has percolated through a landfill mass and that contains biological and/or chemical wastes and dissolved or suspended materials. This waste is often hazardous and may need to be collected and treated to avoid groundwater contamination.

L.C.Y. Loose Cubic Yard. The volume of a soil after it has been excavated.

LDR Land Disposal Restrictions. Landfill disposal guidelines established by the U.S. Environmental Protection Agency. The regulations limit or prohibit the disposal of certain types of waste in landfills.

LII Liquid Injection Incinerator. A simple, refractory-lined cylinder equipped with one or more waste burners.

liquid adsorption A natural process in which molecules of a liquid are physically attracted to and held at the surface of a solid.

lithologic log A log of the structure and content of soils and rock; the log is typically recorded during drilling or excavation.

LLW Low-Level Waste. The term refers to radioactive waste with a low level of radioactivity.

LOAEL Lowest Observed Adverse Effective Level.

LNAPL Light Nonaqueous Phase Liquid. A liquid that does not dissolve in water and which has lower density than water.

loaded-mile rate A charge for only the number of miles between the generator and the ultimate disposal location.

LTO/LTM Long-term operations/long-term maintenance. The last phase of remediation that occurs after the remedial technology is put in place.

m Meter.

machine productivity The amount of material a machine can excavate in a specified amount of time.

magnetometer A tool for locating ordnance on the site. (See *ordnance*.)

make-up water Water added to a process to achieve a certain desired moisture content.

MCLs Maximum Contaminant Levels.

MBH One Thousand BTUs per hour. An expression of boiler capacity.

media filtration A physical process that removes suspended solids from an aqueous waste stream by forcing the fluid through a porous medium.

MINICAMS Miniaturized chemical agent monitoring system. Portable air-monitoring device commonly used for UXO (unexploded ordnance) projects.

MNA Monitored Natural Attenuation.

mobilization distance One-way travel distance from the point of origin of the soil-processing equipment to the site.

modular disposable system A gas-phase or liquid adsorption system with one adsorber that is disposed and replaced after the carbon is spent.

modular permanent system A gas-phase or liquid adsorption system with one adsorber that can be emptied and re-used on site.

MPH Miles per Hour.

MREM A unit of measure commonly used to monitor exposure to radiation.

mud rotary drilling method A drilling method that uses mud as the lubricant for the drill.

MW Monitoring Well. A well used to sample groundwater for follow-on analysis.

NAPL Nonaqueous Phase Liquid. A liquid that does not dissolve in water.

natural attenuation A remediation process that is based on allowing naturally occurring processes to decompose or degrade wastes.

NC Nitrocellulose.

NCP National Contingency Plan. It identifies circumstances under which removal or remedial actions are appropriate. The plan was developed by the U.S. EPA to implement the Comprehensive Environmental Response, Compensation, and Liability Act (CERCLA).

neutralization A process that renders acidic or alkaline waste noncorrosive by adjusting the pH.

NFPA National Fire Protection Agency.

NG Nitroglycerin.

NIOSH National Institute of Occupational Safety and Health.

"No Hazard" designation A designation indicating that a particular site or media poses no hazard to human health or to the environment.

NPL National Priorities List. The list of the nation's most hazardous waste sites, as determined by the U.S. EPA under the guidelines established in the National Contingency Plan (NCP).

NQ Nitroquanadine.

NRCP Nonreinforced concrete pipe.

NTIS National Technical Information Service.

O&M Operations and Maintenance. The process and activities required for operating and maintaining facilities, equipment, and other components of an environmental remediation project.

ODC Other Direct Cost.

OECA Office of Enforcement and Compliance Assurance

OH Overhead (costs).

oil-water separation The use of gravity or coalescing oil-water separators to divide free oil and water.

oil skimmers Special devices that remove or skim a floating oily layer from a bulk-liquid phase without disturbing the quiescent settling zone.

ordnance Any chemical substance or physical item related to munitions that is designed to cause damage to personnel or material through explosive force, incendiary action, or toxic effects.

organic polymers A commonly used coagulant.

OSHA Occupational Safety and Health Administration. The agency is responsible for regulating worker safety and health in the U.S.

OSSWER Office of Solid Waste and Emergency Response.

OU Operable Unit.

OVA Organic Vapor Analyzer. It is used to sample gasses for organic content.

overdig The amount of clean soil that is removed below or beyond the extent of contamination at a site to make sure all waste has been taken away.

PA Preliminary Assessment. The first phase of the remediation process under CERCLA; the preliminary assessment determines whether there is a reasonable probability that hazardous waste exists at a site.

PAH Polynuclear aromatic hydrocarbon.

packed tower air stripper A vertical air stripping tower; waste water enters from the top and air is blown into the bottom. Volatile compounds are "stripped" from the water as it percolates through the tower.

PCB Polychlorinated Biphenon Compound. A generic term that covers a highly toxic family of chlorinated isomers of biphenyl that are often found in sewage outfalls, industrial waste, and landfills.

P.C.F. Pounds per Cubic Foot.

PCOR Preliminary Close Out Report.

PCP Pentachlorophenol.

per diem A daily rate paid for certain items, including equipment rental and living costs for workers.

pH A measure of the relative acidity or alkalinity of a liquid. A pH factor between 0 and 6 is acidic, between 6 and 9 is neutral, and between 9 and 14 is alkaline.

piezometer An instrument for measuring changes in pressure and compressibility.

plume An area of containment floating on top of water.

pneumatic recovery pump An air-powered pump used to recover liquids.

POL Petroleum, oils, and lubricants.

polymeric liner A synthetic liner used to contain liquids inside a surface berm or an excavated area.

pore volume flush A soil-flushing process in which the treatment area is flushed until it is completely saturated.

POTW Publicly Owned Treatment Works. A publicly owned waste water treatment facility used to treat domestic and industrial waste water.

PPE Personal Protective Equipment. Gear worn by all field workers for protection from contamination or injury, as required by OSHA.

ppm Parts per million.

ppm/Vol. Parts per million per volume.

PRP Potentially Responsible Party. The term refers to a party who may have financial liability for hazardous waste site cleanup.

process water Water used in a process that renders the water potentially eligible for follow-on treatment to remove wastes generated by the process.

psi Pounds per square inch.

psig Pounds per square inch gauge.

pug mill A machine used in solidification/stabilization for mixing materials, such as clay and water, to the desired consistency.

PVC Polyvinyl chloride. A plastic commonly used to make pipe and other products.

pyrolyze To bring about a chemical change through the action of heat; it causes a decomposition in the absence of oxygen.

QA Quality Assurance.

QC Quality Control.

RA Remedial Action. The phase of the site remediation process in which remedial technologies are implemented, tested, and operated.

RADCON Radioactive Containment.

radiological screening A soil test that can determine approximate areas of local contamination.

radius of curvature A measure of the dimensions of a curve, as in the radius of curvature of a directional wall.

RAGS Risk Assessment Guidance for Superfund.

RAO Remedial Action Objective.

RCP Reinforced Concrete Pipe.

RCRA Resource Conservation and Recovery Act. The primary federal law that governs hazardous and toxic materials at operating facilities. It defines solid and hazardous waste, authorizes the EPA to set standards for facilities that generate or manage hazardous waste, and establishes a permit program for hazardous treatment, storage, and facilities.

RD Remedial Design. The phase of the site remediation process in which remedial technologies and processes are designed prior to installation.

RDX Cyclotrimethylenetrinitramine. An explosive commonly encountered in unexploded ordnance sites.

reactivated carbon Carbon that has been used for VOC adsorption, which is then treated for reuse.

reagent A substance used in analysis and synthesis of chemical reactions.

regulated unit The term for any surface impoundment, waste pile, land treatment unit, or landfill that received waste after July 26, 1982.

rem Rad equivalent man. These are units used to measure radiation as it affects humans.

remedial action A permanent remedy taken instead of, or in addition to, a removal action that is in response to a release or threatened release of hazardous substances.

removal action A short-term action in response to a release of hazardous substances that might present an imminent and substantial danger to human health or to the environment.

retention time The length of time a waste water is retained in a clarification tank for settling of suspended solids.

RFA RCRA Facility Assessment. A site investigation, regulated under RCRA, that is used to determine the nature and extent of contamination at a particular location.

RFI/CMS RCRA Facility Investigation/Corrective Measures Study. A combined project that includes both the RFI and CMS as a single integrated activity.

RH Relative Humidity.

RI Remedial Investigation. (See *RI/FS*.)

RI/FS Remedial Investigation/Feasibility Study. The phase of the site remediation process in which the nature of contaminants is determined and a remedial remedy is selected. It is a site investigation and cleanup selection process that includes activities such as project scoping, data collection, risk assessment, treatability studies, analysis of alternatives, and remedy selection.

RKI Rotary Kiln Incineration. Incineration using refractory-lined, rotating cylindrical shells mounted slightly inclined from horizontal

rock cover Top cover that is sometimes used to protect underlying layers in a cap when vegetative cover is not possible.

ROD Record of Decision. An agreement between the site owner(s) and other responsible parties and the regulators that stipulates the remedial action requirements, schedule, and cost sharing for cleanup.

rotary kiln A refractory-lined, rotating cylindrical shell incinerator used to treat hazardous waste through thermal destruction.

RSPA Research and Special Program Administration.

running mile rate A charge that includes all miles traveled by the transporter.

sampling point Any point at which a sample will be taken.

sand pumping The process of pumping sand by adding water to create a fluid.

SAP Sampling and Analysis Plan.

SARA Superfund Amendment Reauthorization Act. An amendment to CERCLA that funds government response actions, extends CERCLA, and adds new provisions.

SC Site Closeout. The final phase of remediation in which the site has been determined to pose no future significant health risk.

SCFM Standard Cubic Feet per Minute.

SCWO Supercritical Water Oxidation. A new technology used to treat water or soil as a dilute slurry.

seal slab A concrete slab placed along the bottom of a trench to stabilize bedding material.

Sedimentation A process of allowing sediments to settle out of a liquid.

S.F. Square Foot.

Shelby tube A sampling device used to collect soil samples during drilling.

SHSS Site Health and Safety Supervisor.

SI Site Investigation. The second phase of the preliminary assessment/site investigation process that includes a visual inspection of a site to determine whether there are visible signs of contamination.

SITE Superfund Innovative Technology Evaluation. A program managed by the U.S. EPA to demonstrate and evaluate innovative remedial technologies.

site characterization The process of determining, analyzing and defining the contaminants, media, and site characteristics to determine the nature and extent of contamination present.

sludge Solid byproducts of coagulation, flocculation, and sedimentation after water and waste water treatment.

slurry A suspension of a solid in a liquid.

slurry wall A vertical trench used to contain, capture, or redirect groundwater flow in the vicinity of a contaminated site.

SMOA Superfund Memorandum of Agreement

soil-bentonite slurry wall The most common type of slurry wall. It is made up of a backfill mixture of bentonite slurry and soil.

soil-bermed storage area A storage area designed to contain hazardous waste and to prevent accidental discharge from spills or storm-water drainage.

soil flushing A process that removes soil contaminants by flushing organic and/or inorganic constituents from in situ soils for recovery and treatment.

soil hydraulic conductivity A measure of the rate at which water will flow through a soil matrix.

soil permeability The property of soil, relating to the classification of soil particle size, that permits the flow of water.

soil venting (See *bioventing*.)

soil washing A volume-reduction process in which contaminants are concentrated in the finer fraction of the feed soil by an aqueous-based washing process.

solvent extraction An ex situ process in which contaminated sediment, soil, or sludge is mixed with a solvent to separate the contaminant from its existing matrix.

SPIM Superfund Program Implementation Manual.

split-spoon sampler A sampling device used to collect soil samples during well drilling.

S/S Solidification/Stabilization. A process in which chemical reagents are mixed with waste to produce complex chemical and physical reactions that improve physical properties and reduce contaminant solubility, toxicity, and/or mobility.

SSC Superfund State Contract.

start-up period The period after construction or installation of a remedial-action process during which the system is checked out prior to long-term operation.

steam injection The process of injecting steam into soil to aid in soil vapor extraction or groundwater extraction.

step-off distance The horizontal distance between the entry hole and the beginning of the horizontal section of the wellbore.

submersible differential pressure transducer A device used to measure groundwater depth in a monitoring well.

Supercritical fluid extraction A process of solvent extraction in which the solvent being used is at or near its thermodynamic critical state during the process.

Superfund Law Another name for CERCLA. (See *CERCLA*.)

surface-to-surface wellbore (See *continuous wellbore*.)

surfactant Chemicals that change the properties of surfaces with which they come into contact. In environmental remediation, a surfactant is used to solubilize contaminants and mobilize the highly contaminated fines material.

suspended oil An oil that cannot be caught on a 0.45 micron membrane filter. Includes finer oil that separates in advanced design separation vessels, such as induced gas flotation (IGF), dissolved air flotation (DAF), corrugated plate interceptors (CPI), or coalescing filters.

suspended growth system An ex situ bioremediation system in which active biological solids are mixed with waste water and held in suspension by aeration as the microbial bloc takes organic matter out of solution. Commonly called activated sludge system.

SVE Soil Vapor Extraction. A process that removes volatile organic compounds from a soil matrix through vacuum extraction of the air in the soil.

SWMA Solid Waste Management Unit. A waste management unit from which hazardous wastes or constituents may migrate.

synthetic polymer A commonly used coagulant.

TAG Technical Assistance Grant.

tank farm One contiguous site that may contain multiple tank fields, typically used for defining and classifying underground storage tanks and aboveground storage tanks.

tank field One contiguous cluster of tanks.

tank group One or more tanks within a tank field.

TAT Turnaround time. The amount of time required to process an analysis of a sample.

TBCs To be Considereds

TCE Trichloroethylene.

TCLP Toxicity Characteristic Leaching Procedure.

TEU Technical Escort Unit.

thermal desorption A process that removes organic contaminants (as vapors or condensed liquids) from soils, sludges, and other solid media, which may then be destroyed in a permitted incinerator or used as supplemental fuel.

thermal interference A naturally occurring process in which temperature differentials can interfere with the operation of injection wells.

thermal oxidation A process that heats a gas stream to a sufficiently high temperature with adequate residence time to oxidize the hydrocarbons to carbon dioxide and water.

TNT Trinitrotoluene.

TOC Total Organic Carbon.

TPH Total Petroleum Hydrocarbon.

treatment train A collection of independent remedial technologies that meet the requirements of particular contaminants affecting the site.

trench box A shoring device that prevents sidewall cave-in during trenching projects.

trip blank A sample prepared with deionized water and shipped with other samples taken at a site to establish a baseline for follow-on analysis.

TSCA Toxic Substance Control Act.

TSD Treatment, Storage, and Disposal.

TSDF Treatment, Storage, and Disposal Facility.

TSS Total Suspended Solids. A measure of the solid or particulate content of a liquid.

turbidity The clarity of water, measured by light transmission through a water sample.

UCS Unconfined Compressive Strength. A measure of soil bearing capacity.

unconsolidated formation A geologically recent deposit, such as those found in deltas, alluvial plains, or marine deposits.

upgradient The directional opposite of the flow of groundwater in an aquifer.

USCG United States Coast Guard.

SMOA Superfund Memorandum of Agreement.

UST Underground Storage Tank. A tank system that has at least 10% of its volume underground.

UU/UE Unlimited Use/Unrestricted Exposure.

UV Ultraviolet.

UV oxidation A destructive technology used on site to remediate and purify aqueous and gaseous waste streams.

UXO Unexploded ordnance. (See *ordnance.*)

UXO technician A contractor who (1) is trained as a military explosive ordnance disposal (EOD) technician and (2) meets minimum qualifying requirements.

vacuum filtration The most common method of dewatering for environmental applications in the U.S.

vadose zone The layer of unsaturated soil above the groundwater level.

vapor extraction system A system used with air sparging to remove the generated vapor phase contamination.

vapor extraction well A well used to extract soil vapor in a soil vapor extraction system. (See *VEP.*)

vegetative cover A common top cover that may be either seeding or sodding. It is used to protect underlying layers in a cap.

VEP Vapor extraction point. (See *vapor extraction well.*)

VI Vitrification. A process that transforms the chemical and physical characteristics of hazardous waste so that the treated residues contain hazardous material immobilized in a vitreous mass.

virgin carbon Carbon that has not been used previously for a carbon adsorption process.

VOC Volatile Organic Compound.

volatility The tendency of a substance to vaporize, or "escape," from the liquid phase or from the surface of a solid to the vapor phase.

WasteLan The regional datebase related to CERCLIS.

waste water Water that has been used in a process and that contains some contaminants.

water/mud rotary drilling A method of well installation that uses a rotating bit to advance the bore hole.

water table The level of water within the soil at which the water pressure is the same as the atmospheric pressure.

WBS Work Breakdown Structure.

wellpoint The point on the well at which water is extracted.

wet-air oxidation An oxidation process that takes place in a very high humidity environment.

wheel loader A tire-mounted tractor equipped with buckets for digging, lifting, hauling, and dumping materials.

References

Air Force Center for Environmental Excellence. 1997. *Long Term Monitoring Optimization Guide.*

Air Force Center for Environmental Excellence. 1995. *Technical Protocol for Implementing Intrinsic Remediation with Long-Term Monitoring for Natural Attenuation of Fuel Contamination Dissolved in Ground Water.*

Borns, D. J., Brady, M. V., & Brady, P. V. 1998. *Natural Attenuation: CERCLA, RBCA's and the Future of Environmental Remediation.* New York: Lewis Publishers.

Lebron, C. 1998. *NFESC Environmental Department: Intrinsic Bioremediation of Petroleum Hydrocarbons.*

Partnership of EPA, Air Force, Army Navy and Coast Guard. *Commonly Asked Questions Regarding the Use of Natural Attenuation for Petroleum Contaminated Sites at Federal Facilities.*

U.S. Environmental Protection Agency. 1997. *Remediation Technologies Screening Matrix and Reference Guide.* Federal Remediation Technologies Roundtable. **www.frtr.gov/matrix2/top_page.html**

U.S. Environmental Protection Agency. 1998. *Office of Underground Storage Tanks: Natural Attenuation.* **www.epa.gov/swerust1/cat/natatt.htm**

U.S. Environmental Protection Agency. 1997. Use of Monitored Natural Attenuation at Superfund, RCRA Corrective Action, and Underground Storage Tank Sites, OSWER Directive 9200.4-17. **www.epa.gov/swerust1/directiv/9200_417.htm**

Ground-Water Remediation Technologies Analysis Center. 1996. *Air Sparging. (Technology Overview Report TO-96-04).* Pittsburgh, PA: Miller, Ralinda.

Lim, C. H., Nolen, G., & Wong, J. 1997. *Design of Remediation Systems.* New York: Lewis Publishers.

Nyer, E. K. 1992. *Groundwater Treatment Technology, Second Edition.* New York: Van Nostrand-Reinhold.

Suthersan, S. S. 1997. *Remediation Engineering-Design Concepts.* New York: Lewis Publishers.

National Research Council. 1994. *Alternatives for Groundwater Cleanup.* Washington, D.C.: National Academy Press.

Anderson, W. C. (Ed.). 1995. *Innovative Site Remediation Technology: Bioremediation.* New York: Springer-Verlag/WASTECH.

Brunner, C. R. 1993. *Hazardous Waste Incineration, Second Edition.* New York: McGraw-Hill.

Conn, W. D., Geyer, L., Robinson, J. E., & Thompson, P. 1993. *Issues in Underground Storage Tank Management.* New York: Lewis Publishers.

Alphenaar, A.; De Witt, H.; Otten. A. & Pijls, C. 1998. *In Situ Soil Remediation.* Boston: Kluwer Academic Publishers.

Cookson, J. T., Jr. 1995. *Bioremediation Engineering.* New York: McGraw-Hill.

Cole, G. M. 1994. *Assessment and Remediation of Petroleum Contaminated Sites.* New York: Lewis Publishers.

Wentz, C. A. 1995. *Hazardous Waste Management, Second Edition.* New York: McGraw-Hill.

U.S. Environmental Protection Agency. 1991. *Engineering Bulletin: Chemical Oxidation Treatment.* (EPA Publication No. EPA/540/2-91/025). Washington, D.C.: U.S. EPA.

U.S. Environmental Protection Agency. 1997. *Remediation Technologies Screening Matrix and Reference Guide* Federal Remediation Technologies Roundtable. **www.frtr.gov/matrix2/top_page.html**

Jordan, T. Montana College of Mineral Science and Technology: Air sparged hydrocyclone. **www.clu-in.com**

Ground-Water Remediation Technologies Analysis Center. 1996. *Bioslurping (Technology Overview Report TO-96-05).* Pittsburgh, PA: Miller, Ralinda.

U.S. Environmental Protection Agency. 1998. *Office of Underground Storage Tanks: Bioventing.* **www.epa.gov/swerust1/cat/biovent.htm**

U.S. Environmental Protection Agency. 1995. *Bioventing Principles and Practice.* (EPA Publication No. EPA/540/R-95/534a). Washington, D.C.: Author.

U.S. Environmental Protection Agency. 1993. *Engineering Bulletin: Landfill Covers. (EPA Publication No. EPA/540/S93500).* Washington, D.C.: Author.

U.S. Environmental Protection Agency. 1991. *Engineering Bulletin: Granular Activated Carbon Treatment.* (EPA Publication No. EPA/540/2-91/024). Washington, D.C.: Author.

Wisconsin Department of Natural Resources, Emergency and Remedial Response Program. 1993. *Guidance for Design, Installation and Operation of Groundwater Extraction and Product Recovery Systems. (Publication No. PUBL-DW183-93).* Madison, Wisconsin: Author.

720

U.S. Environmental Protection Agency. 1994. *Engineering Bulletin: In Situ Biodegredation Treatment. (EPA Publication No. EPA/540/S-94/502).* Washington, D.C.: Author.

U.S. Environmental Protection Agency. 1997. *Recent Developments for In Situ Treatment of Metal Contaminated Soils. (EPA Publication No. EPA/542/R-97/004).* Washington, D.C.: Author.

U.S. Environmental Protection Agency, Clean-up information (CLU-IN) site. 1996. *Natural Attenuation.* **www.clu-in.com**

U.S. Environmental Protection Agency. 1998. *Office of Underground Storage Tanks: Natural Attenuation.* **http://www.epa.gov/swerust1/cat/natatt.htm**

Lebron, C. 1998. *NFESC Environmental Department: Intrinsic Bioremediation of Petroleum Hydrocarbons.* **www./nfesc.navy.mil/enviro/ps/projects/biorem1.htm**

U.S. Environmental Protection Agency. 1994. *Engineering Bulletin: Thermal Desorption Treatment. (EPA Publication No. EPA/540/S-94/501).* Washington, D.C.: Author.

U.S. Environmental Protection Agency. 1991. *Engineering Bulletin: Thermal Desorption Treatment. (EPA Publication No. EPA/540/S-91/008).* Washington, D.C.: Author.

Ground-Water Remediation Technologies Analysis Center. 1996. *Treatment Walls (Technology Evaluation Report TE-96-01).* Pittsburgh, PA: Vidic, Radisav & Pohland, Frederick.

U.S. Environmental Protection Agency. 1992. *Engineering Bulletin: Slurry Walls. (EPA Publication No. EPA/540/S-92/009).* Washington, D.C.: Author.

U.S. Environmental Protection Agency. 1991. *Engineering Bulletin: In Situ Soil Flushing. (EPA Publication No. EPA/540/2-91/021).* Washington, D.C.: Author.

U.S. Environmental Protection Agency, Clean-up information (CLU-IN) site. 1998. *Soil Flushing.* **www./clu-in.com/sflush.htm**

Ground-Water Remediation Technologies Analysis Center. 1997. *In Situ Flushing (Technology Overview Report TO-97-02).* Pittsburgh, PA: Roote, Diane.

U.S. Environmental Protection Agency. 1991. *Engineering Bulletin: In Situ Soil Vapor Extraction. (EPA Publication No. EPA/540/2-91/006).* Washington, D.C.: Author.

U.S. Environmental Protection Agency. 1990. *Engineering Bulletin: Soil Washing Treatment. (EPA Publication No. EPA/540/2-90/017).* Washington, D.C.: Author.

U.S. Environmental Protection Agency, Clean-up information (CLU-IN) site. 1998. *Soil Washing.* **http://clu-in.com/slwash.htm**

U.S. Environmental Protection Agency. 1993. *Engineering Bulletin: Solidification/Stabilization of Organics and Inorganics. (EPA Publication No. EPA/540/S-92/015).* Washington, D.C.: Author.

U.S. Environmental Protection Agency. 1994. *Engineering Bulletin: Solvent Extraction. (EPA Publication No. EPA/540/S-94/503).* Washington, D.C.: Author.

U.S. Environmental Protection Agency. 1990. *Engineering Bulletin: Solvent Extraction. (EPA Publication No. EPA/540/2-90/013).* Washington, D.C.: Author.

U.S. Environmental Protection Agency, Clean-up information (CLU-IN) site. 1998. Solvent extraction. **http://clu-in.com/slvtext.htm**

U.S. Environmental Protection Agency. 1994. *Engineering Bulletin: In situ Vitrification Treatment. (EPA Publication No. EPA/540/S-94/504).* Washington, D.C.: Author.

U.S. Environmental Protection Agency. 1997. *OSWER Directive: Use of Monitored Natural Attenuation at Superfund, RCRA Corrective Action, and Underground Storage Tank Sites. (OSWER Directive No. 9200.4-17).* Washington, D.C.: Author.

State of California, Department of Health Services. 1989. *Operations and Maintenance Cost Estimating Guidance Manual. (Revision No. 1).* Sacramento, California.: Author.

U.S. Army Corps of Engineers. 1997. *U.S. Air Force Presumptive Remedy Engineering Evaluation/Cost Analysis, Second Edition.* Washington, D.C.: Author.

U.S. Environmental Protection Agency. 1990. *Cost of Remedial Action Model: Users Manual. (Ver. 3). (EPA Publication No. OSWER-9375.5-06A/FS).* Washington, D.C.: Author.

Ground-Water Remediation Technologies Analysis Center. 1996. *Ultraviolet/Oxidation Treatment.* (Technology Overview Report TO-97-02). Pittsburgh, PA: Trach, Robert.

U.S. Environmental Protection Agency. 1998. *Ground Water Issue: Steam Injection for Soil and Aquifer Remediation. (EPA Publication No. EPA/540/S-97/505).* Washington, D.C.: Author.

U.S. Environmental Protection Agency. 1997. *Best Management Practices for Soil Treatment Technologies. (EPA Publication No. EPA/530/R-97/007).* Washington, D.C.: Author.

Doyle, Cliff. 1999. *Archives Search Report: A Safe Bet For BRAC.* St. Louis, Missouri. U.S. Army Technical Center for Explosives Safety.

U.S. Army Corps of Engineers. 1999. *Ordnance and Explosives Long Term Monitoring Report for Tierrasanta, Calif., and the Murphy Canyon Naval Housing Area, Draft Final.* Author.

Army Regulation 190-5. Chemical Agent Security Program.

U.S. Army Corps of Engineers. 1999. *ASR Assembly Level Detail Estimate.* Huntsville Engineering and Support Center. Author.

Bierschbach, M.C. 1996. *Pressurized Water Reactor Cost Estimating Computer Program.* Pacific Northwest National Laboratory.

Griest, W. H. A.J. Stewart, et. al. 1993. *Chemical and Toxicological Testing of Composted Explosives-Contaminated Soil, Oak Ridge National Laboratory.* Oak Ridge, TN.

Martin, Alan, and Harbison, Samuel A. 1986. *An Introduction to Radiation Protection, Third Edition.* Chapman and Hall.

Memorandum, Records Review of Ordnance and Explosives (OE) Response Projects from Patricia Rivers, Chief, Environmental Restoration Division, Directorate of Military Programs, CEMP-RF, 13 November 98.

Moghissi, A. Alan, Godbee, Herschel W., and Hobart, Sue A. 1992. *Radioactive Waste Technology.* The American Society of Mechanical Engineers.

Murray, Raymond L. 1994. *Understanding Radioactive Waste, Fourth Edition.* Battelle Press.

NES, Inc. 1996. *Basics of Decommissioning: Workshop Notes from New Orleans, LA Training Course.*

Noyes, Robert. 1995. *Nuclear Waste Cleanup Technology and Opportunities.* Noyes Publications.

Rast, Richard. Personal Communications with Personnel from U.S. Army Corps of Engineers, Huntsville Engineering and Support Center, July, August and September, 1999.

Presentation, "Practical Applications of Institutional Control Planning," U. S. Army Corps of Engineers, 27 May 98.

U.S. Army Corps of Engineers Safety and Health Requirements Manual, EM 385-1-1.

U.S. Army Corps of Engineers, Huntsville Engineering and Support Center, Draft Final Submission of EP 11100124, Establishing and Maintaining Institutional Controls for Ordnance and Explosives OE Project, 26 July 99.

U.S. Army Corps of Engineers, Huntsville Engineering and Support Center, Safety Concepts and Basic Considerations, Unexploded Explosive Ordnance, Rev 9, Sept. 92.

U.S. Department of Energy, Office of Environmental Restoration, Decommissioning Handbook, DOE/EM-0142P, March 1994.

Campbell, B., Hansen, J.E., and Timmerman, C. *In Situ Vitrification (ISV): An Evaluation of the Disposition of Contaminant Species During Thermal Processing.* Presented at 15th International Conference on Incineration and Thermal Treatment Technologies, Savannah, GA, May 1996.

Geosafe Corporation. 1989. *Application and Evaluation Considerations for In Situ Vitrification Technology: A Treatment Process for Destruction and/ or Immobilization of Hazardous Materials.*

Hansen, J., Timmerman, C., and Likala, S. *Status of In Situ Vitrification Technology: A Treatment Process for Destruction and/or Permanent Immobilization.* Geosafe Corporation, 1990.

Lowrey, P.S., and Trabalka, J.R. *Dynamic Compaction as a Pretreatment Option for Processing Buried Wastes During In Situ Vitrification— Engineering-Scales Tests, PNL-SA-2663.* Presented at the International Symposium on Environmental Technologies—Plasma Systems and Applications, Atlanta, GA October 8-11, 1996.

Shelly, S. "Turning Up the Heat on Hazardous Waste," *Chemical Engineering,* October 1990.

U.S. Environmental Protection Agency. Undated. *Cost and Performance Report, Parsons Chemical/ETM Enterprises Superfund Site.*

U.S. Environmental Protection Agency. *SITE Technology Capsule, Geosafe Corporation In Situ Vitrification Technology, EPA/540/R-94/520a, November 1994.*

U.S. Environmental Protection Agency. *Guide for Conducting Treatability Studies Under CERCLA, December 1989.*

U.S. Environmental Protection Agency. *The Superfund Innovative Technology Evaluation Program: Technology Profiles, EPA/540/5-88/033, November 1988.*

U.S. Environmental Protection Agency. *Technology Screening Guide for Treatment of CERCLA Soils and Sludges, EPA/540/2-88/004, September 1988.*

Phytoremediation Resource Guide, EPA 542-B-99-00. **www.epa.gov/tio**

A Citizens Guide to Phytoremediation, EPA 542-F-98-001. **http://clu-in.org/products/citguide/phyto2.htm**

Miller, R. *Phytoremediation.* Technology Overview Report from GWRTAC. **www.gwrtac.org**

Schnoor, J. *Phytoremediation.* Technology Evaluation Report from GWRTAC. **www.gwrtac.org**

U.S. Environmental Protection Agency. 1998. *Phytoremediation of TCE in Groundwater using Populus, EPA Status Report.* **www.gwrtac.org/html/tech_eval.html#PHYTO**

U.S. Environmental Protection Agency. 1996. *A Citizen's Guide to Bioremediation, Technology Fact Sheet, EPA NCEPI, EPA/542/F-96/007.*

U.S. Environmental Protection Agency. 1996. A Citizen's Guide to Phytoremediation, Technology Fact Sheet, EPA NCEPI, EPA/542/F-96/014.

Federal Remediation Technologies Roundtable. 1997. *Remediation Technologies Screening Matrix Reference Guide, Third Edition.*

USACE/SFIM-AEC-ET-CR-97053, NTIS PB98-108590

Watanabe, Myrna E. 1997. "Phytoremediation on the Brink of Commercialization." Volume 31, *Environmental Science & Technology/New.*

1999 Phytoremediation Work Group. *Phytoremediation Decision Tree.* Interstate Technology Regulatory Cooperation (ITRC).

Phytoremediation Plant Information:

Environmental Concern, Inc.
(410) 745-9620,
www.wetland.org

Aquatic and Wetland Company
(800) 886-9385
www.aquaticandwetland.com

Country Lane Wholesale Nursery
Franktown, CO

Lehle Seeds
www.arabidopsis.com

Environmental Technologies Group, Inc
1400 Taylor Ave.
P.O. Box 9840
Baltimore, MD 21284-9840

Foerster Instruments Incorporated
140 Industry Drive
RIDC Park West
Pittsburgh, PA 15275-1028
(412) 788-8976

Geometrics
395 Java Drive
Sunnyvale, CA 94089
(408) 734-4616
(G-858 Ordnance Locator)

Schonstedt Instrument Company
1775 Wiehle Ave.
Reston, VA 22090-1795
(703) 471-1795

Trimble Navigation Ltd.
645 North Mary Ave.
PO Box 3642
Sunnyvale, CA 94088-3642

Personal communication with:

Timmerman Craig
Geosafe Corporation
Kirkland, Washington
Schmitz, David Schmitz
D&D Environmental Consulting, Inc.

Index

Notes

Notes

Notes

Notes

Notes

Notes